USING
C-KERMIT

Josh Cockey
W4MHQ
1225 Woodstock Road
King George, VA 22485
[540]-663-3260

USING
C-KERMIT

COMMUNICATION SOFTWARE FOR
UNIX, VMS, OS/2, AOS/VS, OS-9, Amiga, Atari ST

Frank da Cruz and Christine M. Gianone

Digital Press
Boston Oxford Melbourne Singapore Toronto Munich New Delhi Tokyo

Copyright © 1993 by Butterworth–Heinemann

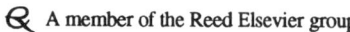 A member of the Reed Elsevier group

All rights reserved.

No part of this publication may be reproduced, stored in a retrieval system, or transmitted in any form or by any means, electronic, mechanical, photocopying, recording, or otherwise, without the prior written permission of the publisher.

 Recognizing the importance of preserving what has been written, Butterworth–Heinemann prints its books on acid-free paper whenever possible.

Trademarks and trademarked products mentioned in this book are listed on pages 497-500.

Cover design: Outside Designs
Production: Editorial Inc.
Typesetting: Frank da Cruz, using Scribe and PostScript output from Chiron, Inc.

C-Kermit software copyright © 1985, 1992, by the Trustees of Columbia University in the City of New York. Permission is granted to any individual or institution to use this software as long as it is not sold for profit and as long as this copyright notice is retained. C-Kermit software may not be included in commercial products or otherwise redistributed without written permission from Columbia University.

The C-Kermit software is a product of Kermit Development and Distribution, Columbia University Academic Information Systems, 612 West 115th Street, New York, NY 10025, USA. C-Kermit software is provided "as is"; no other warranty is provided, either express or implied, including, without limitations, any implied warranty of merchantability or implied warranty of fitness for a particular purpose.

Neither Columbia University nor any of the contributors to the C-Kermit development effort, including, but not limited to, AT&T, Digital Equipment Corporation, Data General Corporation, or International Business Machines Corporation, warrants C-Kermit software or documentation in any way. In addition, the following individuals and institutions do not acknowledge any liability resulting from program or documentation errors: the authors of any Kermit programs, publications, or documentation; Columbia University; any other contributing institutions or individuals.

Library of Congress Cataloging-in-Publication Data

da Cruz, Frank, 1944-
  Using C-Kermit: communication software for UNIX, VMS, OS/2, AOS/VS, OS-9, Amiga, Atari ST / Frank da Cruz and Christine M. Gianone.
    p.   cm.
  Includes index.
  ISBN 1-55558-108-0
  1. Communications software. 2. C-Kermit. I. Gianone, Christine M. II. Title.
  TK5105.9.D33   1993
  005.7'13--dc20   92-41716
                                                                   CIP

The publisher offers discounts on bulk orders of this book.
For information, please write:

Manager of Special Sales
Butterworth–Heinemann
313 Washington Street
Newton, MA 02158–1626

Order number: EY-J896E-DP

10 9 8 7 6 5 4 3

Printed in the United States of America

Contents

Preface *xv*

Chapter 1 Introduction 1
   Why Kermit? 1
   How Kermit Works 3
   Capabilities of C-Kermit 7
   Capabilities of Popular Kermit Programs 8
   Kermit Software Versions 9
   How to Get Kermit Software 9

Chapter 2 Running C-Kermit 15
   Starting C-Kermit 15
   Exiting from C-Kermit 17
   Entering Interactive Commands 17
   Command Files 23
   Describing Kermit's Commands 26
   Some Basic C-Kermit Commands 30
   The C-Kermit Initialization File 35

Chapter 3   Getting Connected   37
    Using C-Kermit in Local Mode   40
    A Test Drive   40
    Establishing a Serial Connection   42
    Direct Serial Connections   48
    Dialed Serial Connections   50
    Using Network Connections   67

Chapter 4   Terminal Connection   79
    The CONNECT Command   79
    Closing the Connection   82
    CONNECT-Mode Keyboard Escape Commands   82
    Terminal Emulation   88
    Key Mapping   91
    Logging and Debugging Your Terminal Session   92

Chapter 5   The Basics of File Transfer   95
    Basic File Transfer Commands   95
    Easy File Transfer Examples   98
    Local-Mode File Transfer   104
    Interrupting a File Transfer   109
    Transferring Text Files   112
    Transferring Binary Files   113
    File Names   114
    Filename Collisions   116
    Incomplete Transfers   117
    Keeping a Record of Your File Transfers   117
    Summary   118

Chapter 6   Solving File Transfer Problems   121
    Parity   122
    Speed and Flow Control in the Full Duplex Environment   124
    Half Duplex Communication   127
    Noise and Interference   128
    Timeouts   130
    Transparency Problems   132
    IBM Mainframe Linemode Communication   133
    IBM Mainframe Full-Screen Communication   135
    For X.25 Users Only   137
    Collecting the Evidence   138

Chapter 7 Using a Kermit Server   139
  Starting the Server   140
  Sending Commands to Kermit Servers   141
  Server Security   148
  Turning the Tables   150

Chapter 8 File Transfer Power Tools   151
  Overview of the Kermit Protocol   151
  Analyzing Kermit's Performance   153
  Improving File Transfer Performance   155
  File Attributes   165
  Displaying and Controlling File Transfer Options   168

Chapter 9 International Character Sets   169
  Proprietary Character Sets   170
  Standard Character Sets   171
  International Characters in Commands   174
  International Characters in Terminal Emulation   175
  Transferring International Text Files   180
  Translating without Transferring   194
  One-Sided Translation   196
  Labor-Saving Devices   197

Chapter 10 Transferring Files without the Kermit Protocol   199
  Downloading to C-Kermit   200
  Uploading from C-Kermit   202
  Encoding 8-Bit Data Files for Transmission   207

Chapter 11 Command Files, Macros, and Variables   209
  Command Files Revisited   210
  Command Macros   214
  Macro Arguments   219
  A Macro Sampler   222
  Variables   224

Chapter 12 Programming Commands   235
  The IF Command   235
  The STOP and END Commands   243
  The GOTO Command   246
  Structured Programming   249
  Built-in Functions   252
  Can We Talk?   261
  Special Effects   263

Contents   vii

User-Defined Functions   267
Reading and Writing Files and Commands   269

Chapter 13 Script Programming   273
Automated Connection Establishment   274
Synchronization Commands   276
Constructing a Login Script for VMS   283
A UNIX Login Script   289
An IBM Mainframe Linemode Login Script   291
An IBM Mainframe Fullscreen Login Script   292
Login Scripts for Commercial Data Services   294
A Directory of Services   297
Automated File Transfer   301
Passwords and Security versus Automation   303
The SCRIPT Command   307
Script Programming Ideas   309

Chapter 14 Command-Line Options   311
Option List   314
Command-Line Examples   321

Appendix I C-Kermit Command Reference   323
Command Summary   324

Appendix II A Condensed Guide to Serial Data Communications   359
Character Format and Parity   359
Modems   362
Cables and Connectors   370

Appendix III UNIX C-Kermit   375
Installation   375
Using UNIX C-Kermit   382

Appendix IV VMS C-Kermit   399
Preparing Your VMS Session for C-Kermit   399
Using VMS C-Kermit   401

Appendix V OS/2 C-Kermit   419
Installation   419
Using OS/2 C-Kermit   423
VT102 Escape Sequences   435

Appendix VI   AOS/VS C-Kermit   441
    Using C-Kermit in AOS/VS   442

Appendix VII   Other C-Kermit Versions   449
    Amiga C-Kermit   449
    Atari ST C-Kermit   452
    OS-9 C-Kermit   454

Appendix VIII   Character Set Tables   459
    The ASCII and ISO 646 IRV Character Set   461
    7-Bit Control Characters   462
    7-Bit Roman Character Sets   463
    West European Character Sets   464
    East European Character Sets   468
    Cyrillic Character Sets   470

Appendix IX   DOS/UNIX File Conversion Script   475

Appendix X   Hexification Programs   477

Appendix XI   Shift-In/Shift Out Filter   479

Acronyms and Abbreviations   481

Bibliography   491

Trademarks   497

Index   501

Illustrations

Figure 1-1	Remote and Local Computers 2
Figure 1-2	Connecting the Local and Remote Computers 3
Figure 1-3	Logging in to the Remote Computer 4
Figure 1-4	Transferring a File 5
Figure 3-1	C-Kermit in Remote Mode 38
Figure 3-2	C-Kermit in Local Mode 38
Figure 3-3	C-Kermit in the Middle 39
Figure 3-4	A Direct Connection 49
Figure 3-5	A Dialed Connection 50
Figure 3-6	Speed Matching 60
Figure 4-1	Terminal Connection 80
Figure 4-2	Command and Terminal Bytesize 89
Figure 5-1	Upload and Download 99
Figure 5-2	Uploading a File 99
Figure 5-3	Downloading a File 101
Figure 5-4	Kermit Text File Conversion 112
Figure 6-1	Character Formats 122
Figure 6-2	Hardware Flow Control 125
Figure 6-3	Terminal Server Connection 131
Figure 8-1	Kermit Packet Format 151
Figure 8-2	Stop-and-Wait Packet Exchange 152
Figure 8-3	Sliding Windows 159
Figure 9-1	Structure of an 8-Bit Latin Alphabet 173

Figure 9-2	Terminal Character Set Translation	178
Figure 9-3	International Text File Transfer	180
Figure 9-4	Linguini Transfer	184
Figure 12-1	Returning from Nested Command Files	244
Figure 13-1	Sample IBM 3270 Login Screen	293
Figure II-1	Character Formats	360
Figure II-2	Asynchronous Character Transmission Format	360
Figure II-3	Computers Connected by Modems	363
Figure II-4	Asynchronous Modem Cable Schematic	371
Figure II-5	Data Connectors	372
Figure II-6	Asynchronous Null Modem Schematics	372
Figure VIII-1	Structure of a Standard 8-Bit Character Set	460

Tables

Table 1-1	Kermit Software Features	8
Table 1-2	Kermit Software, Listed by Computer Type	10
Table 2-1	Special Characters in C-Kermit Commands	24
Table 2-2	Basic C-Kermit Commands	31
Table 2-3	C-Kermit Initialization File Name	36
Table 3-1	Sample Dialout Device Names	41
Table 3-2	Modem Types Known to C-Kermit	53
Table 4-1	C-Kermit CONNECT-Mode Escapes	83
Table 5-1	Special Characters in C-Kermit File Specifications	96
Table 5-2	Kermit Packet Types	108
Table 8-1	Kermit File Transfer Feature Summary	168
Table 9-1	Decimal Character Codes for Accented Capital Letter A	170
Table 9-2	ISO 646 National Character Sets, Differences from ASCII	172
Table 9-3	The ISO Latin Alphabets	173
Table 9-4	Right Half of Latin Alphabet 1	174
Table 9-5	DEC Multinational Character Set	174
Table 9-6	ANSI Escape Sequence Formats	177
Table 9-7	C-Kermit File Character Sets	181
Table 9-8	Language-Specific Transliteration Rules	192
Table 12-1	Comparison of IF and XIF Commands	249
Table 12-2	\Feval( ) Operators	258
Table 12-3	Selected VT100 Escape Sequences	264
Table 13-1	Notation for SCRIPT Command	308

Table	Title	Page
Table 14-1	C-Kermit Command-Line Option Summary	313
Table I-1	C-Kermit Return Codes	324
Table I-2	Summary of Backslash Codes	325
Table I-3	Summary of Built-in Variables	326
Table I-4	Summary of Built-in Functions	327
Table I-5	Summary of File Transfer Interruption Keys	328
Table I-6	C-Kermit CONNECT-Mode Escapes	329
Table II-1	RS-232-C Modem Signals and Pins	364
Table II-2	Selected Hayes Smartmodem 2400 Commands	366
Table II-3	Modem Modulation Techniques	368
Table II-4	Modem Error Correction and Compression Techniques	369
Table III-1	Setting Your Terminal Type in UNIX	383
Table III-2	UNIX Terminal Control Characters	385
Table IV-1	VMS Kermit SET FILE Commands	416
Table IV-2	MS-DOS – VMS File Transfer	417
Table V-1	Special PC Keys in CONNECT Mode	428
Table V-2	The Arrow Keys	429
Table V-3	The Numeric Keypad	430
Table V-4	Control Characters	435
Table V-5	VT102 Escape Sequences	436
Table V-6	VT102 Control Sequences	437
Table V-7	Set / Reset ANSI Mode Parameters	439
Table V-8	Set / Reset DEC Mode Parameters	439
Table V-9	Set Graphic Rendition Parameters	439
Table V-10	VT52 Escape Sequences	440
Table VI-1	AOS/VS Template Characters	446
Table VIII-1	Character Codes of ASCII and ISO 646 IRV	461
Table VIII-2	7-Bit C0 Control Characters	462
Table VIII-3	7-Bit National Character Sets, Differences from ASCII	463
Table VIII-4	West European Character Sets	464
Table VIII-5	East European Character Sets	468
Table VIII-6	Cyrillic Character Sets	470

Preface

"Who Is Kermit and Why Is He in My Computer?" asked a recent headline [52].[1] Kermit is not a "he" at all, but rather an inanimate, genderless, yet personable and friendly computer software package that lets just about any two computers in the world communicate effectively with each other, no matter how they may differ in size, appearance, location, power, architecture, manufacture, or nationality.

This book describes the Kermit program, *C-Kermit*, for UNIX computer systems, Digital Equipment Corporation VMS and OpenVMS systems, Data General AOS/VS systems, PCs with OS/2, the Commodore Amiga, the Atari ST, and computers with the OS-9 real-time operating system. The UNIX version of C-Kermit runs on most known modern implementations of UNIX (see page 13) and on computers ranging from PCs to large mainframes and supercomputers.

C-Kermit software gives you terminal connection, error-free file transfer and management, comprehensive support for national and international character sets, and a wide variety of communication methods including direct or dialed serial connections and (in some versions) TCP/IP or other kinds of network connections. You can use C-Kermit between two computers, or to access dialup information services like CompuServe or MCI Mail as well as subscriber-based public data networks like SprintNet and TYMNET, and even the worldwide TCP/IP Internet.

---

[1]Numbers in brackets refer to entries in the the bibliography on page 491.

With C-Kermit's powerful script programming language, you can have Kermit perform routine or time-consuming tasks for you automatically: let the computers handle the drudgery while you're attending to other matters.

C-Kermit transfers text and binary files efficiently and correctly. The Kermit file transfer protocol takes care of synchronization, error detection and correction, file format and character set conversion, and myriad details you should never have to worry about. The Kermit protocol was designed to work in hostile communication environments where other protocols fail.

The Kermit file transfer protocol was designed in 1981 at the Columbia University Center for Computing Activities (CUCCA), which has been "Kermit Headquarters" ever since. The Kermit protocol is simple, robust, adaptable to almost any style of communication and any computer architecture, and its specification is open and public [18]. Source code availability gives users confidence in this age of viruses and worms and it allows users to fix bugs, add features, and adapt the software to new computers or local conditions.

Kermit software is produced by dedicated volunteer programmers in all parts of the world, whose efforts are coordinated from Columbia, where a definitive collection of all Kermit software is maintained, supporting hundreds of different computers and operating systems. Kermit is the low-cost, high-quality alternative to commercial communication software.

Acknowledgments

C-Kermit was written by Frank da Cruz of Columbia University with contributions from hundreds of other developers and testers. The following are just a few of the contributors, all of whom have our deepest thanks (U = University, locations in the USA unless otherwise indicated):

Chris Adie (Edinburgh U, Scotland); Robert Adsett (U of Waterloo, Canada); Larry Afrin (Clemson U); Greg Andrews (Telebit Corp); Barry Archer (U of Missouri); Bengt Andersson (ABC-Klubben, Sweden); Robert Andersson (International Systems A/S, Oslo, Norway); Chris Armstrong (Brookhaven National Laboratory); William Bader (Software Consulting Services, Nazareth, PA); Fuat Baran (Columbia U); Stan Barber (Rice U); Jim Barbour (U of Colorado); Donn Baumgartner (Dell Computer Corp); Nelson Beebe (U of Utah); Karl Berry (UMB); Dean W Bettinger (State U of New York); Gary Bilkus; Marc Boucher (U of Montreal, Canada); Charles Brooks (EDN); Bob Brown; Mike Brown (Purdue U); Rodney Brown (COCAM, Australia); Jack Bryans (California State U at Long Beach); Mark Buda (DEC); Fernando Cabral (Padrão IX, Brasília, Brazil); Bjorn Carlsson (Stockholm U Computer Centre QZ, Sweden); Bill Catchings (formerly of Columbia U); Bob Cattani (formerly of Columbia U); Davide Cervone (Rochester U, NY); Seth Chaiklin (Denmark); John Chandler (Harvard U/Smithsonian Astronomical Observatory,

Cambridge, MA); John L Chmielewski (AT&T, Lisle, IL); Howard Chu (U of Michigan); Bill Coalson (McDonnell Douglas); Bertie Coopersmith (London, England); Chet Creider (U of Western Ontario, Canada); Alan Crosswell (Columbia U); Jeff Damens (formerly of Columbia U); Mark Davies (Bath U, England); S. Dezawa (Fujifilm, Japan); Joe R. Doupnik (Utah State U); Frank Dreano (US Navy); John Dunlap (U of Washington); Jean Dutertre (DEC France); David Dyck (John Fluke Mfg Co.); Stefaan Eeckels (Statistical Office of the European Community, CEC, Luxembourg); Paul Eggert (Twin Sun, Inc.); Bernie Eiben (DEC); Kristoffer Eriksson (Peridot Konsult AB, Oerebro, Sweden); John Evans (IRS, Kansas City); Glenn Everhart (RCA Labs); Charlie Finan (Cray Research, Darien, CT); Herm Fischer (Encino, CA); Carl Fongheiser (CWRU); Marcello Frutig (Catholic U, São Paulo, Brazil); Hirofumi Fujii (Japan National Laboratory for High Energy Physics, Tokyo); Chuck Fuller (Westinghouse); Andy Fyfe (Caltech); Hunter Goatley (Western Kentucky U); John Gilmore (UC Berkeley); German Goldszmidt (IBM); Alistair Gorman (New Zealand); Richard Gration (Australian Defence Force Academy); Chris Green (Essex U, England); Alan Grieg (Dundee Tech, Scotland); Yekta Gursel (MIT); Jim Guyton (Rand Corp); Vesa Gynther (Finland); Michael Haertel; Marion Hakanson; John Hamilton (Iowa State U); Steen Hammerum (U of København, Denmark); Simon Hania (Netherlands); Stan Hanks (Rice U); Ken Harrenstein (SRI); Eugenia Harris (Data General); David Harrison (Kingston Warren Corporation); James Harvey (Indiana/Purdue U); Rob Healey; Chuck Hedrick (Rutgers U); Ron Heiby (Motorola Computer Group); Steve Hemminger (Tektronix); Christian Hemsing (Rheinisch-Westfälisch Technische Hochschule, Aachen, Germany); Andrew Herbert (Monash U, Australia); Mike Hickey (ITI); R.E. Hill; Bill Homer (Cray Research); Randy Huntziger (US National Library of Medicine); Larry Jacobs (Transarc); Steve Jenkins (Lancaster U, England); Dave Johnson (Gradient Technologies); Mark Johnson (Apple Computer); Eric Jones (AT&T); Luke Jones (AT&T); Peter Jones (U of Quebec, Montreal, Canada); Phil Julian (SAS Institute); Peter Kabal (U of Quebec); Mic Kaczmarczik (U of Texas at Austin); Sergey Kartashoff (Institute of Precise Mechanics & Computer Equipment, Moscow); Howie Kaye (Columbia U); Rob Kedoin (Linotype Co, Hauppauge, NY); Mark Kennedy (IBM); Terry Kennedy (St Peter's College, Jersey City, NJ); Douglas Kingston; John Klensin (MIT); Tom Kloos (Sequent Computer Systems); Jim Knutson (U of Texas at Austin); John Kohl; David Kricker (Encore Computer); Thomas Krueger (U of Wisconsin at Milwaukee); Bo Kullmar (Central Bank of Sweden, Kista, and ABC-Klubben, Stockholm); R. Brad Kummer (AT&T Bell Labs, Atlanta, GA); John Kunze (UC Berkeley); Russell Lang (Monash U, Australia); Bob Larson (USC); Bert Laverman (Groningen U, Netherlands); Steve Layton; David Lawyer (UC Irvine); David LeVine (National Semiconductor Corp.); S.O. Lidie (Lehigh U); Tor Lillqvist (Helsinki U, Finland); Benny Löfgren (DIAB, Sweden); Dean Long; Kevin Lowey (U of Saskatchewan, Canada); Andy Lowry (Columbia U); David MacKenzie (Environmental Defense Fund, U of Maryland); John Mackin (U of Sidney, Australia); Martin Maclaren (Bath U, England); Chris Maio (formerly of Columbia U); Fulvio Marino (Olivetti, Ivrea, Italy); Peter Mauzey (AT&T); Tye McQueen (Utah State U); Ted Medin (NOSC); Ajay

Mehta (DEC); Hellmuth Michaelis (Hanseatischer Computerservice GmbH, Hamburg, Germany); Leslie Mikesell (American Farm Bureau); Gary Mills (U of Manitoba, Canada); Martin Minow (DEC); Pawan Misra (Bellcore); Ken Mizialko (IBM, Manassas, VA); Ray Moody (Purdue U); Bruce J Moore; Steve Morley (Convex); Peter Mossel (Columbia U); Tony Movshon (NYU); Lou Muccioli (Swanson Analysis Systems); Dan Murphy; Gary Mussar (Bell Northern Research); John Nall (Florida State U); Jack Nelson (U of Pittsburgh); Jim Noble (PRC, Inc.); Ian O'Brien (Bath U, England); John Owens; Michael Pins (Iowa Computer Aided Engineering Network); André Pirard (U of Liege, Belgium); Paul Placeway (Ohio State U); Piet Plomp (Groningen U, Netherlands); Ken Poulton (HP Labs); Manfred Prange (Oakland U); Christopher Pratt (APV Baker, UK); Frank Prindle (NADC); Tony Querubin (U of Hawaii); Phil Race (ICL, Manchester, England); Anton Rang; Scott Ribe; Alan Robiette (Oxford U, England); Michel Robitaille (U of Montreal, Canada); Kai Uwe Rommel (Technische Universität München, Germany); Larry Rosenman (Irving, TX); Jay Rouman (U of Michigan); Jack Rouse (SAS Institute); Stew Rubenstein (Harvard U); Bill Schilit (Columbia U); Michael Schmidt (U of Paderborn, Germany); Eric Schnoebelen (Convex); Benn Schreiber (DEC); Dan Schullman (DEC); John Schultz (3M); Steven Schultz (Contel); APPP Scorer (Leeds Polytechnic, England); Gordon Scott (Micro Focus, Newbury, England); Gisbert W. Selke (Wissenschaftliches Institut der Ortskrankenkassen, Bonn, Germany); David Sizeland (U of London Medical School, England); Fridrik Skulason (Iceland); Dave Slate; Bradley Smith (UCLA); Richard Smith (California State U); Ryan Stanisfer (UNT); Bertil Stenström (Stockholm U Computer Centre QZ, Sweden); James Sturdevant (CAP GEMENI AMERICA, Minneapolis, MN, and Medtronic, Inc., Fridley, MN); Peter Svanberg (Kungl. Tekniska Högskolan, Sweden); James Swenson (Accu-Weather, Inc., State College, PA); Chris Sylvain (U of Maryland); Andy Tanenbaum (Vrije U, Amsterdam, Netherlands); Tim Theisen (U of Wisconsin); Lee Tibbert (DEC); Markku Toijala (Helsinki U of Technology, Finland); Rick Troxel (US National Institutes of Health); Warren Tucker (Tridom Corp, Mountain Park, GA); Dave Tweten (NASA); G. Uddeborg (Sweden); Walter Underwood (Ford Aerospace); Pieter Van Der Linden (Centre Mondial, Paris, France); Ge van Geldorp (Netherlands); Fred van Kempen (MINIX User Group, Voorhout, Netherlands); Wayne Van Pelt (General Electric Corporate Research and Development); Mark Vasoll (Oklahoma State U); Konstantin Vinogradov (ICSTI, Moscow, Russia); Paul Vixie (DEC); Eduard Vopica (Prague School of Economics, Czechoslovakia); Dimitri Vulis (City U of New York); Roger Wallace (Raytheon); Stephen Walton (California State U at Northridge); Jamie Watson (Adasoft, Switzerland); Rick Watson (U of Texas); Robert Weiner (Programming Plus, New York City); Lauren Weinstein (Vortex Technology); David Wexelblat (AT&T Bell Labs); Bill Whitney (DEC); Joachim Wiesel (U of Karlsruhe, Germany); Lon Willett (U of Utah); Michael Williams (UCLA); Nate Williams (U of Montana); David Wilson; Patrick Wolfe (Kuck & Associates, Inc.); Gregg Wonderly (Oklahoma State U); Farrell Woods (Concurrent); Dave Woolley (CAP Communication Systems, London, England); Jack Woolley (SCT Corp); Frank Wortner; Ken Yap (formerly of U of Rochester, NY); John Zeeff (Ann Arbor, MI).

Of those listed above, special thanks are due to Bill Catchings for his work on the basic design of the Kermit protocol and for its first two software implementations; to Chris Maio and Bob Cattani for version 1 of UNIX Kermit (the predecessor of C-Kermit), circa 1983; to Bill Catchings and Jeff Damens for version 3 (1984, there was no version 2); and to Herm Fischer and Dan Schullman for large contributions to version 4, the first release of C-Kermit in its present interactive form (1985).

Version 5, too, was a cooperative effort. Kristoffer Eriksson, Bo Kullmar, Warren Tucker, and Peter Mauzey comprised the "modem committee," which worked long and hard to rationalize C-Kermit's treatment of modem signals in the many and varied UNIX environments. Kristoffer deserves a special Archaeology Achievement Award for a detailed study and unraveling of many years' accretion of incomprehensible magic in the infamous "ckutio" module (a collection of supposedly simple functions that gives the emphatic lie to all claims that UNIX is a "portable operating system").

Before we leave the special awards department, this year's Life Achievement Award goes to Terry Kennedy for endless and unenviable hours filling in the particulars for the infinitely complex VMS file system, and for helping out in numerous other ways. And thanks to the others who helped with VMS, especially Lee Tibbert, Mark Buda, William Bader, Alan Robiette, Hunter Goatley, and James Harvey.

Chris Adie adapted C-Kermit version 4 to OS/2 in 1988, and Kai Uwe Rommel adapted the OS/2 support to version 5A and to OS/2 2.00—no small task!—and contributed many other valuable ideas and insights.

The Data General AOS/VS support was originally done many years ago by Phil Julian at the SAS Institute for C-Kermit 4D. Special thanks to Data General Corporation for sponsoring the development of AOS/VS support in C-Kermit 5A as well as new developments in MS-DOS Kermit; to Eugenia Harris of Data General for doing the AOS/VS-specific programming as well as supplying lots of descriptive material, not to mention numerous good ideas; and to Mike Normile of DG, who supplied equipment, documentation, suggestions, and all-around support and encouragement.

Steve Walton took care of the Commodore Amiga (with help from Larry Rosenman), Bruce Moore is primarily responsible for Atari ST adaptation, and Christian Hemsing for OS-9 (with earlier work by Bob Larson).

Ken Yap contributed the first bit of TCP/IP sockets code for the Berkeley UNIX version. Marcello Frutig and Stefaan Eeckels supplied the X.25 support code. Chuck Hedrick found and fixed many bugs in the UNIX version and also gave lots of help along the way.

Thanks to the indefatigable and omniscient Professor Joe Doupnik (author of MS-DOS Kermit), who worked closely with the authors on the design of the sliding window algorithms, the script programming language, and the international character set support during the joint development effort for MS-DOS Kermit 3.0 and C-Kermit 5A (and in his spare time, Joe lent a hand with the AT&T 7300 UNIX PC and System V R4 versions of C-Kermit).

Our grateful acknowledgments to the specialists who contributed to the proposal for extending the Kermit protocol to accommodate international character sets: John Chandler (Harvard/Smithsonian Center for Astrophysics), Joe Doupnik (Utah State University), Hirofumi Fujii (Japan National Laboratory for High Energy Physics, Tokyo), John Klensin (Massachusetts Institute of Technology and chair of the ACM Standards Committee), Ken-ichiro Murakami (Nippon Telephone and Telegraph Research Labs, Tokyo), Vladimir Novikov (VNIIPAS, Moscow, Russia), André Pirard (University of Liege, Belgium), Gisbert W. Selke (Wissenschaftliches Institut der Ortskrankenkassen, Bonn, Germany), Fridrik Skulason (University of Iceland, Reykjavik), Johan van Wingen (Leiden, Netherlands, member of numerous ISO committees), and Konstantin Vinogradov (ICSTI, Moscow, Russia). And thanks to Valdemar Gunnarson for the Icelandic translation on page 196.

Thanks too to those who supplied specific information about the character sets used in the former Soviet Union today: Konstantin Vinogradov of ICSTI, Michael Yaroslavtsev and Sergey Kartashov of the Institute of Precise Mechanics and Computer Equipment of the (former) USSR Academy of Sciences, and Dimitri Vulis of D&M Consulting Services Inc. in New York City. And to Jay Sekora at Princeton University for the PostScript Cyrillic font used in this book.

Hirofumi Fujii supplied the algorithms and much of the code for conversion among the various Japanese Kanji character sets.

And thanks to the programmers who have been adding this protocol extension to other Kermit programs so C-Kermit can talk to them: John Chandler (Kermit-370), Joe Doupnik (MS-DOS Kermit), the "Kermit gang" at ICSTI, and Hirofumi Fujii (Kanji support in MS-DOS Kermit and C-Kermit).

Special thanks to Drs. Juri Gornostaev and A. Butrimenko of ICSTI for sponsoring the First International Kermit Conference in Moscow in May 1989, where the international character set extension was first discussed in public.

And thanks to the hundreds of others who tested C-Kermit 5A on countless hardware and software platforms and contributed bug reports, fixes, new features, and suggestions over its three-year development period.

Also thanks to the "Kermites" in the Kermit Factory, who do such a fine job at technical support, filling software orders, running our machines, and generally keeping the Kermit Distribution operation running smoothly: Max Evarts, Andy Newcomb, and the generations who came before, especially Bob Tschudi, Peter Howard, Lucy Lee, and Ken Suh.

Special thanks to those who reviewed the first draft manuscript of this book: Donn Baumgartner of Dell Computer, Max Evarts of Columbia University, Terry Kennedy of Saint Peters College, Kai Uwe Rommel of the Technical University of Munich, Benn Schreiber of Digital Equipment Corporation, Warren Tucker of Tridom Corporation, Bruce J. Moore, and particularly to Eugenia Harris of Data General Corporation and John Klensin of MIT for their detailed comments and suggestions.

Many thanks to our management and colleagues at Columbia University for their support, especially Vaçe Kundakçi, Deputy Vice President for Academic Information Systems, and Elaine Sloan, Vice President for Information Services and University Librarian; to Bruce Gilchrist and Howard Eskin, former directors of our organization; and to Lee Lidofsky, a Great Teacher, for an initial push in the right direction.

Finally, thanks to those who helped put this book together—the staff at Digital Press: John Osborn, Chase Duffy, Monica Broadnax, Will Buddenhagen, Beth French, Cindyrose Newfell, Jan Svendsen; and to Laura Fillmore and the staff of Editorial, Inc.: Steve Ackerman, the illustrator; Ann Hall, the copy editor; MaryEllen Oliver, the proofreader.

Frank da Cruz and Christine M. Gianone
New York City, December 1992

```
fdc@columbia.edu, cmg@columbia.edu
               KERMIT@CUVMA.BITNET
```

Chapter 1

Introduction

An ever-increasing amount of communication is electronic and digital: computers talking to computers—directly, over the telephone system, through networks. When you want two computers to communicate it is usually for one of two reasons: to interact directly with the remote computer or to transfer data between the two computers. Kermit software gives you both these capabilities, and more.

C-Kermit is a Kermit program written in the C language. It is portable among many different kinds of computers and operating systems, including UNIX, VMS and OpenVMS, AOS/VS, OS/2, OS-9, the Commodore Amiga, and the Atari ST, where C-Kermit's services include modem dialing, terminal connection, file transfer, file management, unattended automated operation, and in many cases, network capability too.

Why Kermit?

- Kermit software is universal. Kermit programs have been written for hundreds of different kinds of computers (see page 9). Chances are you'll find it already on any computer you use. If not, it is most likely available. And when your computer has Kermit software but the other computer does not, you can still use your own Kermit program for terminal emulation and "unguarded" file transfer.

- Kermit software communicates not only over dialup connections, but also over high-speed direct connections, local area networks, and wide area networks, so you can use the same software for most kinds of connections.

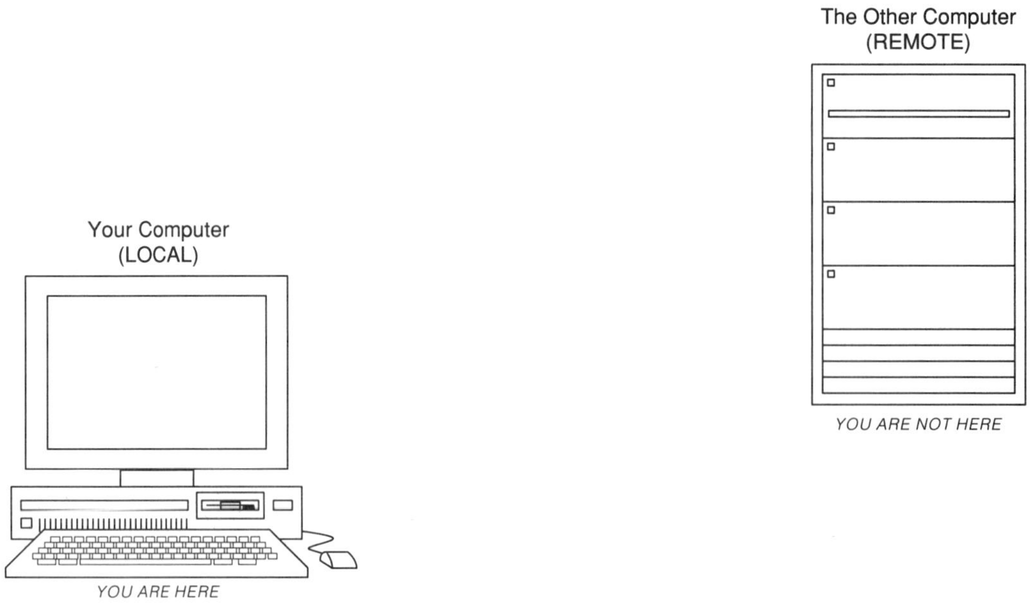

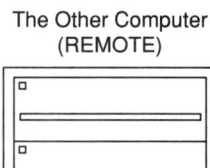
The Other Computer
(REMOTE)

YOU ARE NOT HERE

Your Computer
(LOCAL)

YOU ARE HERE

Figure 1-1 Remote and Local Computers

- Kermit software is flexible. It is adaptable to the styles and formats of the many computer manufacturers and communication service providers.

- Kermit software is easy to use. The commands are ordinary words, rather than cryptic codes. Menus are available upon demand.

- Kermit software is powerful. Procedures can be automated using a script programming language composed of ordinary Kermit commands.

- Kermit file transfer is rugged and efficient. It works in hostile or restrictive communication environments where other protocols fail.

- Kermit file transfer is international. It can transfer text in many languages and character sets without scrambling the special characters.

- Kermit software is accessible. Because it has a character-mode user interface, it is compatible with speech, Braille, and other enabling devices.

- Source code is available. You can make improvements, fix bugs, assure yourself that there is no virus infestation, and adapt the code to new platforms.

One software package for practically all your communication needs: no switching from package to package to communicate with different kinds of computers or services or to

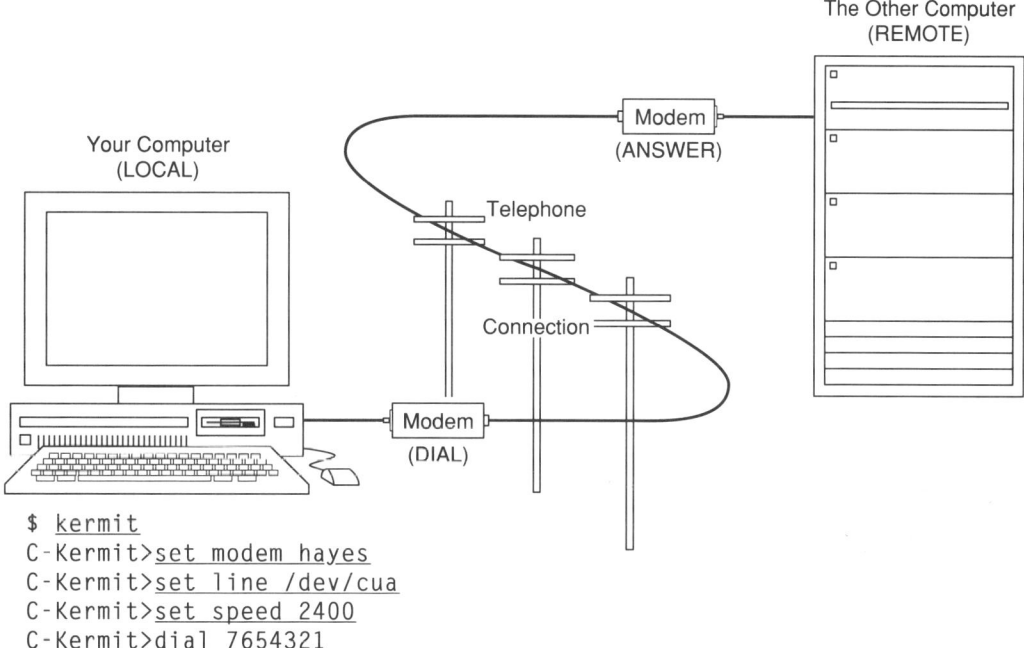

Figure 1-2 Connecting the Local and Remote Computers

use different communication methods; no need to support multiple packages. And as an added benefit, most Kermit software programs have the same basic set of commands and procedures—once you've learned one Kermit program, you've learned them all.

How Kermit Works

Picture two computers, like the ones in Figure 1-1. You are using one of them directly: it is a PC or workstation on your desk, or it is a timesharing system connected to a terminal (or terminal emulator) on your desk. Let's call this the *local* computer. You want to connect your local computer to a more distant, *remote* computer or service and transfer data.

> *IMPORTANT:* Remember the terms *local* and *remote*. They are used throughout this book. The local computer is the one you are making the connection *from*. The remote computer is the one you are making the connection *to*.

Let's say you are connecting the two computers by telephone. First be sure that both computers have a modem. Then you must know the name of the device that the modem is connected to on your local computer, a transmission speed that is common to both the local and remote modems, and the telephone number for the remote modem. Let's look at Figure 1-2. We start the local Kermit program simply by typing the word *kermit*.

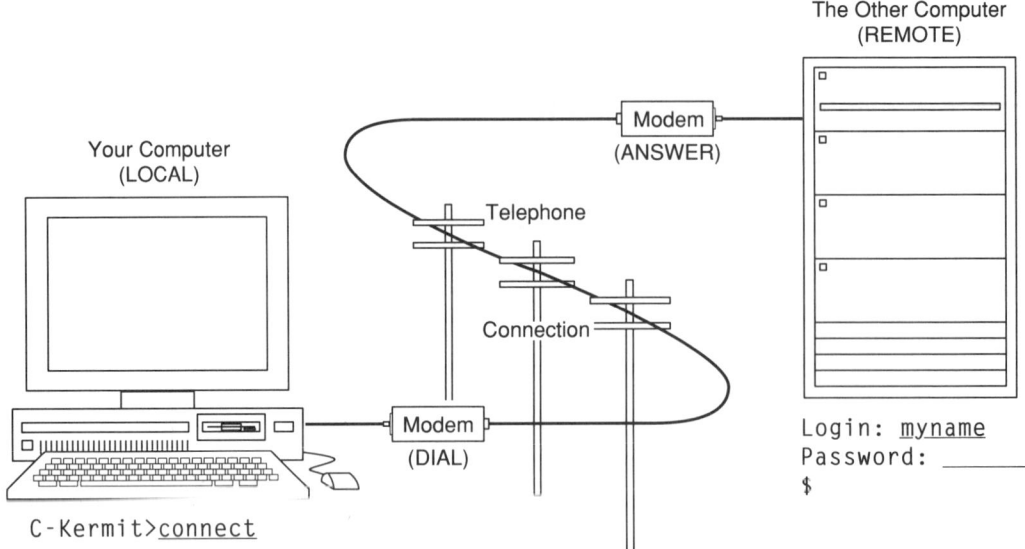

Figure 1-3 Logging in to the Remote Computer

IMPORTANT: In the figures, and in all examples used in this book, the text you type is underlined. When you are typing commands to your operating system or to a Kermit program, you must terminate them by pressing the Return or Enter key at the point where the underlining ends (unless otherwise indicated).

When the local Kermit's prompt appears, we give it commands to tell it the modem type and the communication device name and speed, and then we tell it to dial the other computer's phone number. When the other computer answers the phone, communication can begin. Give your local Kermit the CONNECT command and suddenly you are talking to the remote computer just as if you were using it directly. Identify yourself (log in) as shown in Figure 1-3 and carry on a dialog to conduct your business. Eventually you might decide that you want to move some data (a file) from one computer to the other.

To transfer a file, both computers must be running Kermit programs. Your local computer already is. Simply type "kermit" on the remote computer to start the remote Kermit program.[2] Now you must tell *each* Kermit program what to do: one of them must be told to send a file of a certain name and the other must be told to receive the file. The rule is: (1) Tell the remote computer what to do first (SEND or RECEIVE), then (2) get back to the local computer and tell it the opposite (RECEIVE or SEND), as shown in Figure 1-4.

---

[2] If there is no Kermit software on the remote computer, another file transfer method is also available. See Chapter 10.

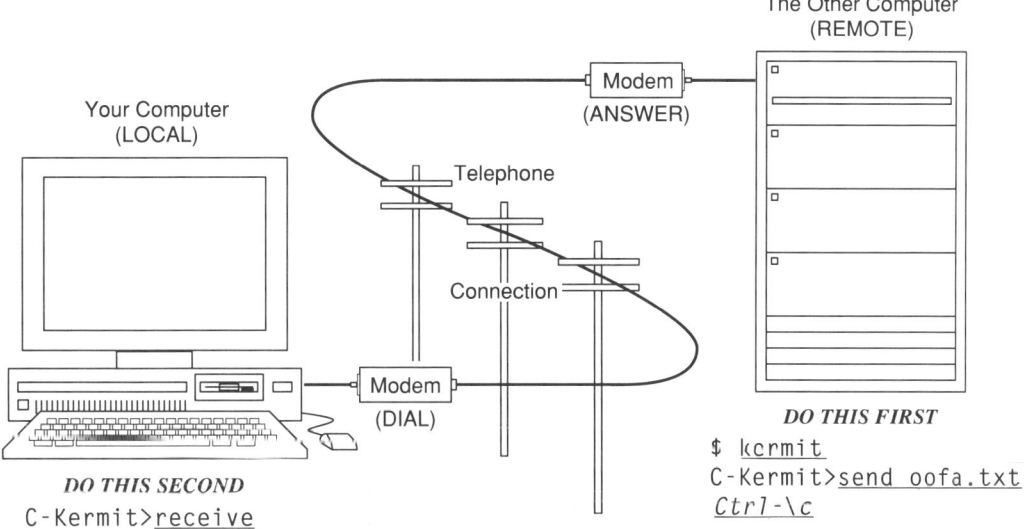

Figure 1-4 Transferring a File

How do you get back to the local computer? After you CONNECT to the remote computer, the local Kermit sends all the characters you type straight to the remote computer, without paying any attention to them itself. But one character is special during a CONNECT session. C-Kermit notices when you type this special character (usually a control character such as Ctrl-Backslash) and interprets the next character that you type as a command, for example the letter "C" to Come back to the prompt. This two-character sequence is shown in the figure as *Ctrl-\c*, and entering it is referred to as "escaping back."

Here is an example of the basic procedure, in which you are transferring the file OOFA.TXT from the remote computer to the local one, Your local computer is a UNIX workstation with C-Kermit and the remote computer is running OpenVMS, also with C-Kermit (both computers need not be running C-Kermit, but we assume that at least one of them is).

1. Start Kermit on your local computer:

   ```
   $ kermit
   C-Kermit 5A(188), 23 Nov 92, SunOS 4.1
   Type ? or HELP for help
   C-Kermit>
   ```

2. Tell it the modem type and the name and speed of the communication device:

   ```
   C-Kermit>set modem hayes
   C-Kermit>set line /dev/cua
   C-Kermit>set speed 2400
   ```

How Kermit Works 5

3. Have it dial the telephone number of the remote computer:

   ```
   C-Kermit>dial 7654321
   ```

4. Enter terminal mode:

   ```
   C-Kermit>connect
   ```

5. Log in to the remote computer and start Kermit there:

   ```
   Welcome to the Remote Computer
   Username: myname
   Password: _____
   $
   $ kermit
   C-Kermit 5A(188), 23 Nov 92, OpenVMS VAX
   Type ? or HELP for help
   C-Kermit>
   ```

6. Tell the remote Kermit program to send the file:

   ```
   C-Kermit>send oofa.txt
   Return to your local Kermit and give a RECEIVE command.
   ```

   ```
   KERMIT READY TO SEND...
   ```

7. Enter the key sequence to escape back from terminal mode to your local Kermit program and tell it to receive the file:

   ```
   Ctrl-\c
   C-Kermit>receive
   ```

Now the two Kermit programs begin talking to each other using specially formatted messages called packets, which contain not only data from your files, but also control information, such as "here is the file name," "here is the first piece of data from the file," "here is the second piece," "that was the last piece," "please send the second piece again," and so on. The data in each packet is encoded to contain only printable characters to ensure that it will pass through sensitive communication devices. All packets include error checking and sequencing information to prevent your data from being lost, duplicated, or damaged.

This is the basic scenario for file transfer. There are many variations: you can send files in the other direction (by exchanging the SEND and RECEIVE commands), you can transfer a group of files in a single operation, you can operate the remote Kermit as a fully protocol-driven file server, and you can automate the process to any desired degree using C-Kermit's script programming language. The details of the Kermit file transfer protocol are given in a separate book [18, Chapters 8–12].

Capabilities of C-Kermit

C-Kermit is among the most advanced and powerful of all the Kermit programs. Here is a brief list of some of its features. The terminology will be explained more fully as we go along.

- Support for nearly all known varieties of UNIX (see p. 13), for Digital Equipment Corporation VMS and OpenVMS, IBM OS/2, Data General Corporation AOS/VS, Microware OS-9, Commodore AmigaDOS, and Atari ST GEMDOS.

- Error-correcting, efficient file transfer using the Kermit protocol. Text or binary files may be transferred singly or in groups.

- Operation at a wide range of speeds using standard serial communication ports.

- Support for network connections including TCP/IP and X.25 on selected UNIX, VMS, OpenVMS, AOS/VS, and other configurations.

- Communication settings that can be matched to virtually any other computer.

- Automatic dialing with a wide variety of modems.

- Terminal connection to remote computers, including character set translation, key mapping, keyboard macros, and session logging capabilities.

- A simple, consistent, and intuitive command language with built-in help, in most ways compatible with MS-DOS Kermit.

- Command and initialization files.

- Command macros and a powerful script programming language.

- Logging, security, and debugging features.

- Kermit protocol capabilities including long packets, sliding windows, international text character-set conversion, checksum and CRC error correction, the ability to transfer 8-bit data through a 7-bit communications channel using both single and locking shifts, automatic parity detection, transmission of file attributes, server mode, run-length data compression, file management functions, file transfer interruption, and more. C-Kermit also has the ability to transmit and receive files without error checking when the other computer doesn't have a Kermit program.

Thus, C-Kermit combines all the features you need to communicate with other computers or services interactively (or automatically in your absence) and to transfer files with just about any other kind of computer.

Capabilities of Popular Kermit Programs

C-Kermit's capabilities are compared with other popular Kermit programs in Table 1-1. C-K is C-Kermit, MS-K is MS-DOS Kermit, Mac-K is Macintosh Kermit, K-370 is IBM Mainframe Kermit, K-11 is PDP-11 Kermit, K-80 is CP/M-80 Kermit, and K-65 is Apple II Kermit. This table represents the situation as of this writing, and naturally is not guaranteed to hold true forever.

Table 1-1 Kermit Software Features

Feature	C-K	MS-K	Mac-K	K-370	K-11	K-80	K-65
Local operation	Yes	Yes	Yes	No	Yes	Yes	Yes
Remote operation	Yes	Yes	No	Yes	Yes	No	No
Network support	Yes	Yes	No	No	No	No	No
Automatic feature negotiation	Yes	Yes	Yes	Yes	Yes	Yes	Yes
International text	Yes	Yes	Yes	Yes	No	No	No
File transfer interruption	Yes	Yes	Yes	Yes	Yes	Yes	Yes
Filename collision actions	Yes	Yes	Yes	Yes	Yes	Yes	Yes
Single shifts	Yes	Yes	Yes	Yes	Yes	Yes	Yes
Locking shifts	Yes	Yes	Yes	Yes	No	No	No
Run-length compression	Yes	Yes	Yes	Yes	Yes	No	No
Alternate block checks	Yes	Yes	Yes	Yes	Yes	Yes	No
Automatic parity detection	Yes	Yes	No	N/A	No	No	No
Dynamic packet length	Yes	No	Yes	Yes	No	No	No
Key mapping	Yes	Yes	Yes	N/A	No	No	No
Support for dialout modems	Yes	Yes	Yes	N/A	Yes	No	Yes
Act as server	Yes	Yes	Yes	Yes	Yes	No	No
Talk to server	Yes	Yes	Yes	Yes	Yes	Yes	Yes
Advanced server functions	Yes	Yes	Yes	Yes	Yes	Yes	Yes
Security for server	Yes	Yes	Yes	No	No	N/A	N/A
Local file management	Yes	Yes	Yes	Yes	Yes	Yes	Yes
Command/Init files	Yes	Yes	Yes	Yes	Yes	Yes	Yes
Long packets	Yes	Yes	Yes	Yes	Yes	No	No
Sliding windows	Yes	Yes	Yes	N/A	No	No	No
Attribute packets	Yes	Yes	Yes	Yes	Yes	No	No
Command macros	Yes	Yes	Yes	No	No	No	No
Script programming language	Yes	Yes	Yes	No	No	No	No
Raw file transmit and capture	Yes	Yes	Yes	N/A	Yes	Yes	Yes

Kermit Software Versions

C-Kermit is only one of many Kermit software programs. As you can see from Table 1-2, which begins on the next page, Kermit is available for almost any kind of computer you can think of. Kermit software is written in a wide variety of programming languages, and source code is always available.

The table does not show the hundreds of makes of computers and variations of operating systems for which C-Kermit, MS-DOS Kermit, and CP/M Kermit have been adapted. MS-DOS Kermit runs on countless IBM-compatible PCs and quite a few non-compatible models too. The CP/M versions have been adapted to about 70 different machines. The UNIX version of C-Kermit has been built successfully on at least 150 *different* platforms. Some of them are listed beginning on page 13, after Table 1-2.

How to Get Kermit Software

Kermit software can be ordered from Columbia University on 3.5-inch or 5.25-inch DOS-format diskettes, on 9-track magnetic tape in TAR, ANSI, or OS format, on quarter-inch tape cartridge in TAR format, on DEC TK50 tape cartridge in VMS BACKUP format, and possibly in other formats too. See the tear-out card in the back of this book.

For an up-to-date catalog and mail-order instructions, and to be placed on the subscriber list for the free journal, *Kermit News*, write to:

Kermit Distribution, Dept CI
Columbia University Center for Computing Activities
612 West 115th Street
New York, NY 10025, USA
Phone: (USA) (212) 854-3703

A modest distribution fee is charged for mail orders, depending on the materials, labor, and shipping costs involved. Various shipping and payment methods are available, and overseas orders are accepted.

If you have access to the TCP/IP Internet, you can also get Kermit software via anonymous FTP to IP host kermit.columbia.edu. Begin by getting and reading the file kermit/read.me. If you have access to the BITNET (CREN) or EARN network, send electronic mail to KERMSRV@CUVMA containing the text HELP for instructions. You can subscribe to the electronic Info-Kermit Digest by sending e-mail containing the text:

SUBSCRIBE I$KERMIT *your-name-here*

to LISTSERV@CUVMA.CC.COLUMBIA.EDU or to LISTSERV@CUVMA.BITNET, or you can read it in the COMP.PROTOCOLS.KERMIT newsgroup.

Table 1-2 Kermit Software Listed by Computer Type

Implementation	Computer	OS	Language
C-Kermit	many	UNIX	C
MS-DOS Kermit	many	MS-DOS	8088 Assembler
Kermit-80	many	CP/M-80	8080 Assembler
Kermit-86	many	CP/M-86	8088 Assembler
Kermit-TD	various	TurboDos	8080 Assembler
PICK-Kermit	various	PICK	DATA/BASIC
Kermit-UCSD	various	UCSD p-System	UCSD Pascal
BBC-Kermit	Acorn BBC	Acorn OS	6502 Assembler
Kermit-65	Apple II	DOS, PRODOS	6502 Assembler
Mac-Kermit	Apple Macintosh	Mac OS	C
Atari-Kermit	Atari 800	DOS	Action
C-Kermit	Atari ST	GEMDOS	C
Kermit-CT	Burroughs B20	BTOS	C
Kermit-B78	Burroughs A-Series	MCS/AS	Algol
Kermit-B68	Burroughs B6800	Burroughs	Algol
Kermit-B78	Burroughs B7800	Burroughs	Algol
Kermit-B79	Burroughs B7900	Burroughs	Algol
Kermit-CD3	CDC Cyber	NOS	Fortran-5
Kermit-CDC	CDC Cyber	NOS, NOS/BE	Fortran-77
Kermit-CYB	CDC Cyber	NOS 2.2	Compass
Kermit-NOS	CDC Cyber	NOS 2.4	Compass
CC-Kermit	Chinese PCs	CC-DOS	8088 Assembler
Kermit-C64	Commodore 64	DOS	6510A Assembler
Kermit-C64	Commodore 128	DOS	6510A Assembler
C-Kermit	Commodore Amiga	AmigaDOS	C
Kermit-CT	Convergent NGEN	CTOS	C
Cray Kermit	Cray-1	CTSS	Fortran-77
Cray Kermit	Cray-XMP	CTSS	Fortran-77
C-Kermit	DEC Alpha AXP	OpenVMS, OSF/1	C
Kermit-12	DEC PDP-8	OS/8	PAL-8 Assembler

Table 1-2 Kermit Software Listed by Computer Type (continued)

Implementation	Computer	OS	Language
Kermit-11	DEC PDP-11	IAX	Macro-11 Assembler
Kermit-11	DEC PDP-11	RSTS/E	Macro-11 Assembler
Kermit-11	DEC PDP-11	RSX-11	Macro-11 Assembler
Kermit-11	DEC PDP-11	RT-11	Macro-11 Assembler
Kermit-11	DEC PDP-11	TSX+	Macro-11 Assembler
MUMPS Kermit	DEC PDP-11	MUMPS	MUMPS-82
Kermit-12	DEC PDP-12	OS/12	PAL-8 Assembler
Kermit-11	DEC Pro-3xx	P/OS	Macro-11 Assembler
Kermit-11	DEC Pro-3xx	Pro/RT	Macro-11 Assembler
C-Kermit	DEC VAX	ULTRIX	C
C-Kermit	DEC VAX	VMS, OpenVMS	C
Kermit-12	DECmate I, II, III	OS/278	PAL-8 Assembler
C-Kermit	DECstation	ULTRIX, OSF/1	C
Kermit-10	DECsystem-10	TOPS-10	MACRO-10 Assembler
Kermit-20	DECSYSTEM-20	TOPS-20	MACRO-20 Assembler
C Kermit	Data General MV	AOS/VS	C
Kermit-RDOS	Data General Nova	RDOS	BASIC or Fortran-5
GEC-Kermit	GEC 4000	OS4000	MUM/SERC
Gould Kermit	Gould/SEL 32	MPX-32	Fortran-77+
HPM-Kermit	HP 1000	RTE	Fortran-77, Assembler
Rover-Kermit	HP 264x	ROM	8080 Assembler
HP3-Kermit	HP 3000	MPE	SPL
HPB-Kermit	HP 9xxx	HP BASIC	HP BASIC
HPP-Kermit	HP 9xxx	HP Pascal	HP Pascal
Aegis Kermit	HP/Apollo	Aegis	Pascal
HP8-Kermit	HP86, HP87	HP BASIC	HP BASIC
Kermit-H100	Harris 100	VOS	Fortran-77
Kermit-H800	Harris 800	VOS	Pascal, Assembler
MULTICS-Kermit	Honeywell	MULTICS	PL/I
HG-Kermit	Honeywell DPS6	GCOS	C

Table 1-2 Kermit Software Listed by Computer Type (continued)

Implementation	Computer	OS	Language
HB-Kermit	Honeywell DPS8	GCOS	B
HC-Kermit	Honeywell DPS8	CP-6	PL/6
CS9-Kermit	IBM CS9000	CSOS	Pascal
MS-DOS Kermit	IBM PC, PS/2	MS-DOS	C, 8088 Assembler
MS-DOS Kermit	IBM PC, PS/2	MS-Windows	C, 8088 Assembler
Windows Kermit	IBM PC, PS/2	MS-Windows	C
Kermit-370	IBM mainframe	CICS	370 Assembler
Kermit-370	IBM mainframe	MUSIC	370 Assembler
Kermit-370	IBM mainframe	MVS/ROSCOE	370 Assembler
Kermit-370	IBM mainframe	MVS/TSO	370 Assembler
Kermit-370	IBM mainframe	VM/CMS	370 Assembler
GUTS-Kermit	IBM mainframe	MVS/GUTS	370 Assembler
MTS-Kermit	IBM mainframe	MTS	PLUS, Pascal, Assembler
VME-Kermit	ICL 2900	VME	S3
Perq-Kermit	ICL/Perq	Perq OS	Pascal
Kermit-ISIS	Intel MDS	ISIS	PL/M
Kermit-MDS	Intel MDS	iRMX	8088 Assembler
Kermit-RMX	Intel MDS	RMX	PL/M
Kermit-LMI	LMI LISP Machine	LMI-LAMBDA	ZETALISP
Kermit-Lilith	Lilith Workstation	MEDOS	Modula-2
ABC-Kermit-80	Luxor ABC-80	ABC-DOS	Z80 Assembler
ABC-Kermit	Luxor ABC-800	ABC-DOS	ABC-BASIC-II
Kermit-B4	MAI Basic Four	BOSS/VS	BASIC BB86
Kermit-MODCOMP	MODCOMP Classic	MAX IV	Fortran, Assembler
Flex-Kermit	Motorola 6809	Flex	C or Assembler
C-Kermit	Motorola 680x0	OS-9	C
Kermit-9800	NCR 9800	VE	C
MS-DOS Kermit	NEC PC9801	MS-DOS	C, Assembler
Kermit-ND	Norsk Data	Intran III	ND-Pascal
C-Kermit	PC, PS/2	OS/2	C

Table 1-2 Kermit Software Listed by Computer Type (continued)

Implementation	Computer	OS	Language
Kermit-PE	Perkin-Elmer 3200	OS/32	Fortran
Kermit-PE7	Perkin-Elmer 7000	IDRIS	C
Prime-Kermit	Prime	PRIMOS	PL/P
Kermit-RML	RML 480Z	ROS	C
Kermit-QL	Sinclair QL	QDOS	C or BCPL
Kermit-1100	Sperry 1100	Exec	Assembler or Pascal
Kermit-VS9	Sperry 90/60	VS9	Assembler
Kermit-LMS	Symbolics 36xx	Symbolics	ZETALISP
Kermit-TI990	TI 990	DX10	Pascal
Kermit-TIX	TI Explorer	LISP	Common LISP
Kermit-CoCo	TRS-80 CoCo	DOS	EDTASM Assembler
Kermit-TRS80	TRS-80 I, II, III	TRSDOS	8080 Assembler
Kermit-M4	TRS-80 Model 4	TRSDOS	8080 Assembler
Tandem-Kermit	Tandem Nonstop	Guardian	TAL
Kermit-T100	Tandy 100	Tandy 100	BASIC

UNIX C-Kermit Versions

As of this writing, C-Kermit 5A(188) has been tested successfully on 16-bit, 32-bit, and 64-bit architectures under portable UNIX versions including 4.2 and 4.3BSD, 4.4BSD-Alpha, AT&T UNIX System III, AT&T UNIX System V Releases 2, 3, and 4, POSIX, OSF/1, and Solaris versions 1 and 2. This version of C-Kermit has also been built and tested successfully on the following specific platforms:

Altos ACS68000 with UNIX System III R2; Apollo workstations with DomainOS SR10.0 and 10.4; Amdahl mainframes with UTS UNIX 5.2.6b; Apple Macintosh II with A/UX; AT&T 3B2 and 3B20 systems with UNIX System V R2; AT&T 6300 PLUS with UNIX System V R2; AT&T 6386 WGS UNIX PC with UNIX System V/386 3.2; AT&T PC 7300 UNIXPC (3B1) System V R3.51m; Commodore Amiga with UNIX System V R4; Concurrent (Masscomp) computers with RTU 4.0 through 6.0; Concurrent (Perkin-Elmer) computers with Xelos System V R02; Convergent Technologies MiniFrame with CTIX System V R3; Convex C1 and C2 with Convex/OS 8.x and 9.x; Convex 3240, C220, and C240 with ConvexOS V10.x; Cray Y/MP with UNICOS 6.1 and 7.0; DEC Alpha AXP and DECstation with OSF/1; DEC PDP-11 with 2.11BSD; DEC VAX with 4.2BSD, 4.3BSD, 4.3BSD-Reno, 4.3BSD-Networking/2; DEC VAX with ULTRIX 1.0, 2.0, 3.0,

4.0, 4.2, and 4.3; DEC VAX with AT&T System V R3; DECstation with ULTRIX 4.2 and 4.3; Data General Aviion with DG/UX 5.4, 5.4.1, and 5.4.2; DIAB DS90 with DNIX 5.3; Dolphin Server Technology Triton 88/17 with Dolphin UNIX System V/88 R3.2; Encore Multimax with UMAX 4.3; Fortune 32:16 with For:Pro 2.1; Harris Night Hawk 68K and 88K with CX/UX; HP-9000 with HP-UX 5.21, 5.5, 7.0x, 8.0x; IBM 370-series mainframes with AIX/370 1.2; IBM PS/2 with AIX 1.2; IBM RS/6000 AIX 3.1 and 3.2; IBM RT PC with AIX 2.x and 4.3BSD-Reno; ICL DRS3000 and DRS6000 with DRS/NX UNIX System V R4; Integrated Solutions VS8 with ISI 4.2BSD; MIPS Computer Systems with RISC/OS UMIPS 4.52; Modcomp Realstar 1000 with REAL/IX D.1; Motorola VME Delta Series with System V/68 R3 and System V/88 R32 and R40; NCR Tower 32 with OS 2.01; NeXT workstations with Mach 1.0, 2.1, and 3.0; Nixdorf Targon/31 M15 with TOS 4.0.13; Norsk Data Uniline 88/17 with System V/88 R3.2; Olivetti CP 486 with UNIX System V R4; Olivetti LSX 3005 through 3045 with X/OS UNIX 2.3 through 3.0; Olivetti LSX 5020 with SCO UNIX 3.2.2; PCs with 386BSD (Jolix); PCs with AT&T UNIX System V R3.2; PCs with BSDI/386; PCs with Dell UNIX System V/386 R4.04 issue 2.2; PCs with ESIX System V R3 and R4; PCs with Interactive Systems Corporation System V/386 3.x; PCs with Linux/386; PCs with Mark Williams COHERENT/386 4.0; PCs with MINIX/386; PCs with Microport 3.0U3 and SVR4.0 V4.1; PCs with SCO ODT 1.1 and 2.0; PCs with SCO UNIX/386 3.2.x; PCs with SCO Xenix/286 2.3.3; PCs with SCO Xenix/386 2.2.x and 2.3.x; PCs with SunSoft Solaris 1.0; Pyramid MIS-T Series with OSx 5.1a; Sequent Symmetry with DYNIX 3.x and DYNIX/ptx 1.3 and 1.4; Silicon Graphics Iris with IRIX 3.3; Silicon Graphics Indigo with IRIX 4.0.x; Solbourne 5E/900 with OS/MP 4.1A; Sony NEWS with NEWS-OS 4.x; Stardent 1520 UNIX System V R3 2.2; Sun workstations, computers, and servers with SunOS 3.2 through 5.1; Tandy Model 6000 with XENIX 3.2; Tektronix 6130 with UTck OS; UNISYS S/4040 with CTIX SVR3.2; UNISYS U6000/65 MP with UNIX System V R4.

During its development, the UNIX version of C-Kermit 5A was also tested successfully on the following machines and operating systems:

Alliant FX/8 with Concentrix 4.1; Altos 486, 586, 986 with Xenix 3.0; Atari ST with MINIX ST 1.5.10.3; Bell Laboratories UNIX 7th Edition; Berkeley UNIX 4.1BSD; Charles River Data Systems Universe 680x0 with UNOS 9.2; Data General Aviion with DG/UX 4.30; FPS 500 with FPX 4.1; IBM RT PC with ACIS 4.2 and 4.3; Intel 302 with Bell Tech System V/386 R3.2; Luxor ABC-9000 with DNIX; NCR System 3000 with AT&T UNIX System V R4 2.0; NCR Tower 1632 and Minitower with System V R2; OkiStation 7300 Series; PCs with Consensys UNIX SV/386 R4V3; PCs with Mt Xinu Mach[386]; PFU Compact A Series with SX/A TISP V10/E50; Ridge 32 with ROS 3.2; Samsung MagicStation with System V R4; Sequent Balance 8000 and B8 with DYNIX 3.0; Tektronix XD88 series with UTekV OS; Tri Star Flash Cache with Esix SVR3.2; UNISYS 5000 with UTS V R5.2 and 5.3.

Chapter 2

Running C-Kermit

C-Kermit is a large program with many features, designed to be used on a wide variety of hardware and software platforms. If your computer does not have enough memory or does not offer certain capabilities, some of the C-Kermit features described in this book might not be available. C-Kermit's SHOW FEATURES command lists the features that are included and those that are missing. See the Appendix particular to your operating system, such as Appendix III for UNIX.

This book describes C-Kermit version 5A(188). If you are running an earlier version, you should get the latest release (see page 9). If you have a later version, consult the file CKCKER.UPD for notes about changes that were made since this book was published.

Starting C-Kermit

Remember, in the examples used throughout this book, the characters that you type are underlined. The characters that are not underlined are prompts or messages from the computer.

If the C-Kermit program is correctly installed on your computer, you should be able to run it simply by typing its name at the system prompt (which is shown as dollar sign in this example, but might be some other character or text):

```
$ kermit
```

In response, you should see a herald and a prompt looking something like this:[3]

```
C-Kermit 5A(188), 23 Nov 92, OpenVMS AXP
Type ? or HELP for help
C-Kermit>
```

What do the herald and prompt tell us? `C-Kermit` is the name of the program. `5A(188)` is the version number: the major release number is `5`, the minor release, or level, is `A`, the edit number is `188`, and the program release date is `23 Nov 92`. `OpenVMS AXP` is an identifier for the type of computer and operating system that C-Kermit was configured for.

The prompt, `C-Kermit>`, means that C-Kermit is ready for a command. The line above the prompt, `Type ? or HELP for help`, means just what it says. If you type a question mark at the prompt, you get a list, or menu, of commands that are available at that point. These are C-Kermit's *top-level* commands. If you type the word *help*, you get a brief introduction to Kermit's "user interface"—how to enter and edit commands and how to get more help.

C-Kermit's command style should be familiar to anyone who has used MS-DOS Kermit or other popular Kermit programs. A Kermit command is like an English sentence, usually consisting of a verb followed by objects. When the C-Kermit prompt appears, you can type a command. Commands are entered using ordinary letters, numbers, and punctuation, plus the special characters that are summarized in Table 2-1 on page 24. A command is executed only after you press the Return or Enter key. When the command has finished executing, the prompt appears again and you can type another command, and so on:

```
C-Kermit>version
C-Kermit 5A(188), 23 Nov 92, OpenVMS AXP
 Numeric: 501188
C-Kermit>echo Hello
Hello
C-Kermit>check character-sets
 Available
C-Kermit>
```

This style of operation is called *interactive command mode*, and it gives you full access to all of C-Kermit's features.

---

[3] If instead you see an error message such as "not found", "permission denied", or "unrecognized command verb", the program has not been installed or wasn't installed correctly. Or maybe it was installed with some other name, perhaps "ckermit" or "wermit." If you see a "Usage" message, beginning something like:

`Usage: kermit [-x arg [-x arg]...[-yyy]...]`

then you have either a very, very old version of C-Kermit, or else version 5A has been installed without an interactive command parser.

By the way, if you don't like C-Kermit's prompt, you can change it to suit your tastes:

```
C-Kermit>set prompt My Favorite Program>
My Favorite Program>
```

or, less frivolously:

```
C-Kermit>set prompt VAX-Kermit>
VAX-Kermit>
```

to remind you that you are using Kermit on a VAX. Later when you start to use Kermit to talk to two computers at once, this will help you keep track of which one you're talking to.

Exiting from C-Kermit

When you are finished using C-Kermit, type the command EXIT or QUIT and then press the Return or Enter key to return to the system prompt:

```
C-Kermit>exit
$
```

The system prompt varies with your operating system and other circumstances. When C-Kermit exits, it closes any files it might have had open, restores your command terminal to normal, and generally cleans up after itself. See page 331 for a complete description of the EXIT command.

Entering Interactive Commands

Kermit's interactive command language is easy for users of all levels. For novices, it is intuitive and nonthreatening. Commands are normal English words rather than cryptic codes. Help is available when you need it, but unlike a menu system, it does not force itself upon you when you don't want it. Later, when you become familiar with Kermit's commands, you will be able to enter them more quickly by using abbreviations, or even condensing multiple commands into short "macros," described in Chapter 11.

A command consists of one or more words separated by spaces, like a sentence. The words are called *fields*. In a Kermit command, a field can be a *keyword*, a *file name*, a *number*, or some other quantity. A keyword is a word chosen from a particular list; all words on that list are valid, other words are not.

Commands begin with a keyword, normally an English verb like SEND, RECEIVE, or SET. Keywords can be entered in uppercase or lowercase, or any combination. We show command keywords within running text in UPPERCASE for clarity (for example, the SEND command) but in lowercase in examples:

```
C-Kermit>send oofa.txt
```

because that is how people normally type them.

Getting Help within a Command

A question mark (?), typed at any point in a command, produces a message explaining what is possible or expected at that point. Depending on the context, the message can be a brief explanatory phrase, a menu of valid keywords, or a list of files. If you type a question mark at the prompt, you'll see a list of all C-Kermit's top-level commands. If you type a letter *s* at the prompt and then question mark, you'll see a list of the commands that start with *s*:

```
C-Kermit>s?
Command, one of the following:
 script           send             server           set
 show             space            statistics       stop
C-Kermit>s
```

After the help message is displayed, you can continue the command from where you left off. The *s* is still there, and now you can type a letter *e* and another question mark to see which commands start with *se*:

```
C-Kermit>se?
Command, one of the following:
 send             server           set
C-Kermit>set
```

You can continue this process to the next field of the command by typing a space and then another question mark:

```
C-Kermit>set ? Parameter, one of the following:
 attributes       background       block-check      buffers
 carrier          case             command          count
 delay            dial             duplex           escape
 file             flow-control     handshake        host
 input            key              language         line
 macro            modem-dialer     network          parity
 prompt           quiet            receive          retry
 many more are shown...
```

This tells you that Kermit wants you to type another keyword, the parameter that you want to SET. Kermit lists all the possibilities for you, such as SET FILE. Let's see how far we can go with the SET FILE command.

```
C-Kermit>set file ? File parameter, one of the following:
 bytesize         character-set    collision        display
 names            type
C-Kermit>set file type ? type of file, one of the following:
 binary           text
C-Kermit>set file type binary ?
 Type a carriage return to confirm the command
C-Kermit>set file type binary <CR>
C-Kermit>
```

At the end of the command, press the Return, Carriage Return, or Enter key (shown above, for emphasis, as <CR>) to have C-Kermit actually execute the command. Linefeed, Ctrl-J, Formfeed, and Ctrl-L also serve the same purpose.

We seem to have prepared C-Kermit for transferring binary files. Let's look at the command that actually sends the file:

```
C-Kermit>send ? File(s) to send
C-Kermit>send
```

At this point, you need to type the name of an existing file. Let's say you have forgotten its exact name, but you know it starts with the letter *O*. So you type an *O* and then a question mark to have Kermit list the files whose names start with *O*, you pick the right one, and then you enter the command:

```
C-Kermit>send o? File(s) to send, one of the following:
  oofa.bin     oofa.doc     oofa.hlp     oofa.txt
C-Kermit>send oofa.txt
Return to your local Kermit and give a RECEIVE command.

KERMIT READY TO SEND...
```

If your command doesn't make sense or it contains spelling or grammatical errors, Kermit gives you a brief error message and a new prompt:

```
C-Kermit>sned ?No keywords match: sned
C-Kermit>
```

No harm is done by spelling errors in keywords (unless your error corresponds to another valid keyword). An invalid command is not executed, and it has no side effects. But watch out for spelling errors in filenames or numbers, where Kermit usually has no way to tell the difference between what you typed and what you meant to type.

Abbreviating Keywords

You don't have to spell keywords out in full; you can abbreviate them as much as you want, as long as the result isn't ambiguous within its field. For example, the shortest way to enter the SET FILE TYPE BINARY command would be:

```
C-Kermit>set fi t b
```

If you abbreviate a keyword too much, Kermit complains that your command is "?Ambiguous." No harm is done, and the command is not executed:

```
C-Kermit>se ?Ambiguous - se
C-Kermit>se? Command, one of the following:
  send              server              set
C-Kermit>
```

Some command keywords are used so frequently that they have special one-letter abbreviations, even though more than one command begins with that letter. These include C for CONNECT, S for SEND, and R for RECEIVE. For example, the command:

```
C-Kermit>s oofa.doc
```

sends the file `oofa.doc`. Note that filenames can *not* be abbreviated.

Entering Interactive Commands **19**

Correcting Mistakes in Commands

If you make typographical errors or change your mind about a command before you enter it, you can alter or cancel it using the following special characters:

DEL   (The Delete, Rubout, or Backspace key, or Ctrl-H) Deletes the rightmost character from the command.

^W   (Ctrl-W) Erases the rightmost word from the command.

^U   (Ctrl-U) Erases the entire command.

^R   (Ctrl-R) Redisplays the current command.

The notation ^X or Ctrl-X means press the key marked X while holding down the key marked Ctrl or Control. X can be any letter A–Z, and also certain punctuation characters such as underscore (_), reverse slash (\), caret (^), or right bracket (]).[4] The Ctrl key is used like the Shift key. Characters entered in conjunction with the Ctrl key are called *control characters*. You can type the editing characters DEL and ^W repeatedly to delete all the way back to the prompt.

C-Kermit tries to keep your command line looking right: deleted characters, words, and lines "disappear" but the prompt stays where it was. But there are ways for the command line to become jumbled (for example, if someone sends you a message while you're in the middle of typing a command). That's what Ctrl-R is for; it redisplays the prompt and the current command, properly formatted:

```
C-Kermit>set fi
<BEEP>From olaf: What do you want on your pizza?
le type^R
C-Kermit>set file type
```

Keyword and Filename Completion

C-Kermit has a special reinforcement mechanism to help you make sure you have not abbreviated a keyword too much, or that the abbreviation you have used really stands for what you think it does, or to finish typing a filename for you.

This mechanism is called completion, and you invoke it by pressing the Esc (Escape) or Tab key, or Ctrl-I, whichever is more convenient for you. If the keyword or filename characters you have typed so far are sufficient, Kermit fills in the rest of the characters for you and positions you for the next field of the command:

```
C-Kermit>sen<ESC>d oofa.t<ESC>xt
```

---

[4]See Table VIII-1 on page 461 for a listing of all the control characters.

If not, Kermit beeps and waits for you to supply more characters:

`C-Kermit>`<u>`se`</u>`<ESC><BEEP>`<u>`n<ESC>`</u>`d oofa.<ESC><BEEP>`<u>`t<ESC>`</u>`xt`

In these examples, `<ESC>` signifies the Escape (Esc) key, and `<BEEP>` shows where you would hear a beep. If you are deaf, you can still tell when a beep occurs: whenever you press `<ESC>` and the cursor does not move.

When you use the completion feature in a filename, C-Kermit completes as much of the name as it can, and if more characters are required from you after that, C-Kermit beeps and waits for you to supply them. For example, suppose you have two files, `oofa.txt` and `oofa.new`, and they are the only two files whose names start with the letter *O*. If you type an *O* and then an Esc or Tab, Kermit supplies the characters "ofa." and then waits for you to finish the filename:

`C-Kermit>`<u>`send o<ESC>`</u>`ofa.<BEEP>`<u>`t<ESC>`</u>`xt`

The completion feature also can be used to fill in *default* values for fields that have them. If you press the Esc or Tab key at the beginning of a field, before typing any other characters, and if that field has a default value, Kermit fills it in:

`C-Kermit>`<u>`set block-check <ESC>`</u>` 1`

Here Kermit supplies the default block-check value, namely 1. If there is no default value for a field, Kermit beeps:

`C-Kermit>`<u>`send <ESC>`</u>`<BEEP>`

When the final field of a command has a default value, you can enter the command without specifying a value:

`C-Kermit>`<u>`set block-check`</u>

This sets the block-check parameter to its default value of 1.

Including Special Characters in Commands

Characters like question mark and Ctrl-U have special meanings within C-Kermit commands. What if you need to include them as part of the command itself without triggering their usual functions (help and erase)? You can enter such a character into a C-Kermit command literally by preceding it with the backslash character (\), for example:

`\?`

To enter a backslash literally, type two of them:

`\\`

Certain characters, however, such as Ctrl-C or Ctrl-Z (depending on your computer's operating system), cannot be quoted this way because they send a signal to the operating system to interrupt Kermit.

Entering Interactive Commands **21**

You can include problem characters in Kermit commands by using a backslash followed by the character's numeric ASCII code value; for example \3 for Ctrl-C, \26 for Ctrl-Z, \10 for linefeed, or \13 for carriage return (Table VIII-1 on page 461 lists these codes). Example:

```
C-Kermit>echo Hello!\13\10How are you\?
Hello!
How are you?
C-Kermit>
```

A common use for backslash is to include ? as a wildcard[5] in a file specification:

```
C-Kermit>send oofa.? File(s) to send, one of the following:
oofa.c    oofa.h    oofa.txt    oofa.hlp
C-Kermit>send oofa.\?
```

Without the backslash, the question mark gives you a list of filenames that match what you have typed so far. With the backslash, it is used to match any single character, so the SEND command in the example sends the files `oofa.c` and `oofa.h`.

In OS/2 and Atari GEMDOS the directory separator is backslash, the same as C-Kermit's quoting character. To include a backslash in a filename, use two of them:

```
C-Kermit>send c:\\dos\\autoexec.bat
```

This also applies when using C-Kermit to transfer files with MS-DOS Kermit. Fortunately, in OS/2, forward slash (/) is also recognized as a directory separator:

```
C-Kermit>get c:/dos/autoexec.bat
```

Interrupting a Command

After you have entered a C-Kermit command by pressing the Return or Enter key, the command begins to execute. You can interrupt most commands during their execution by typing Ctrl-C (hold down the Ctrl key and press the C key).[6]

This returns you to the C-Kermit prompt immediately, so you can enter another command. Example:

```
C-Kermit>type moon.doc
No celestial body has required as much labor for the study of its
motion as the moon. Since Clairault (1747), who indicated a way
of constructing a theory containing all the properties of ^C...
C-Kermit>
```

Note: ^C indicates a real Control-C character, not a circumflex followed by the letter C.

---

[5] A "wildcard" is a character used in a filename to indicate a group of files. Wildcard characters differ from system to system. See the Appendix for your system; for example, Appendix III for UNIX.

[6] The interrupt character might be something other than Ctrl-C; for example, in 4.3BSD UNIX it is your "intr" character.

Command Files

If you issue the same sequence of commands to Kermit every time you run it, that can add up to a lot of typing over the years. Better to enter the commands just once and let the computer remember them for you. Use your favorite text editor to record the commands in a *Kermit command file* and you won't ever have to type them again.

Kermit commands are lines composed of plain text characters. The text editor used to create or modify Kermit commands should be set up to handle these simple, unadorned lines of text. Editors like ED, EX, VI, and EMACS are appropriate for UNIX. EDT, EVE, and EMACS can be used in VMS or OpenVMS. SED or SPEED can be used in AOS/VS. Similar editors can be used in OS/2 and other operating systems. If you use a word processor or other utility that is concerned with fonts, boldface, italics, underscore, and similar frills, be sure to save your command file in plain-text (ASCII) format. To execute commands from a file, use the TAKE command:

TAKE *filename*
   Executes C-Kermit commands from the specified file. C-Kermit reads and executes the commands in order, from top to bottom, until the end of the file is encountered or until a command (such as EXIT) is executed that tells C-Kermit to stop. Example:

   `C-Kermit>take compuserve.tak`

Execution of a command file can be interrupted by typing Control-C (or whatever your system's interrupt character is[7]) at any time during its execution. If the TAKE command was given from the C-Kermit prompt, the interruption returns you directly to the prompt. The following sections describe features that are commonly used in command files, but you can also use them at the interactive program prompt.

Adding Comments to Commands

Kermit's commands can be annotated with comments. A full-line comment can begin with the word COMMENT or the single character semicolon (;) or number-sign (#):

```
COMMENT - This is a C-Kermit command file.
; I copied it from "Using C-Kermit".
# And I put lots of comments in it.
```

Commands can also have trailing comments. These are introduced by a semicolon or number-sign preceded by at least one space:

```
echo Hi there!      ; Print a friendly greeting.
space               ; Let's see how much disk space is free.
log transactions    ; I always want to keep a log of what I do.
```

---

[7] Ctrl-C is used in AT&T System V UNIX, even if your interrupt character is not Ctrl-C.

Table 2-1 Special Characters in C-Kermit Commands

Character	Function
<SPACE>	(the space bar) Separates fields.
?	(question mark) Requests a menu or help message for the current field.
-	(dash) At the end of a line only: this command is continued on the next line.
\	(backslash) At the end of a line only: continues this command on the next line. Elsewhere within the command: introduces a backslash code or quotes the following character. Backslash codes are listed in Table I-2.
;	(semicolon) At the beginning of a command, or within a command preceded by at least one space or tab: introduces a comment.
#	(number sign) Same as semicolon: introduces a comment.
<ESC>	(Esc or Escape key, or Ctrl-[) Attempt to complete the current field.
<TAB>	(or Ctrl-I) Within a field, same as <ESC>. Between fields, same as <SPACE> (but only in command files).
<DEL>	(or Backspace, or Rubout, or Ctrl-H) Deletes the rightmost character from the command.
Ctrl-H	Same as <DEL>.
Ctrl-I	Same as <TAB>.
Ctrl-W	Deletes the rightmost word.
Ctrl-U	Deletes the entire command, back to the prompt.
Ctrl-R	Redisplays the command.
Ctrl-C	Interrupts a command in execution, returns to the prompt. On some UNIX systems, this purpose is served by your interrupt character, which might be something other than Ctrl-C. Use **stty all** or **stty -a** to find out what your interrupt (intr) character is.
Ctrl-S	Stops screen output, if Xon/Xoff flow control is in effect.
Ctrl-Q	Resumes screen output, if Xon/Xoff flow control is in effect.
Ctrl-Z	Suspends Kermit so it can be continued later (UNIX only). On UNIX systems, this purpose is served by your suspend character, which might be defined as something other than Ctrl-Z. Use **stty all** or **stty -a** to find out what your suspend (susp) character is.
Ctrl-Y	In VMS or OpenVMS, Ctrl-Y either interrupts the current command and returns to the prompt, or else it interrupts C-Kermit and returns to the DCL prompt in such a way that C-Kermit can be CONTINUEd, depending on the context. In some UNIX systems, Ctrl-Y is a secondary suspend character.
<RETURN>	(Carriage Return, Return, Enter, Ctrl-M) Terminate and enter the command. Also written as <CR>.
<LINEFEED>	(Ctrl-J) Same as <RETURN>. Also written as <LF>.
<FORMFEED>	(Ctrl-L) Same as <RETURN>. Also written as <FF>.

Because ; and # are recognized as trailing comment indicators only when preceded by whitespace, you can also include these characters literally in commands by preceding them with printing characters:

```
get oofa.txt;3               ; Fetch file from VMS Kermit server.
remote host lpr -#4 oofa.txt # Print 4 copies of remote file.
```

In this example, `oofa.txt;3` is a VMS filename, and `lpr -#4` is the UNIX command to print four copies of a file.

If you need to include ; or # as part of a command and it must be preceded by a space, then quote it with backslash:

```
C-Kermit>echo Text ; with a comment
Text
C-Kermit>echo Text \; with a comment
Text ; with a comment
C-Kermit>
```

Continuing a Command

Kermit commands are by nature one line long. Some Kermit commands, however, can be quite lengthy—even wider than your screen. There is nothing to prevent you from typing past the end of your screen, and if your terminal emulator or console driver "wraps" your lines for you, you can even see what you're doing.

But the compulsive among us may wish to break long commands at nice places, so as to have a neat-looking screen or, perhaps more important, neat-looking command files.

C-Kermit commands can be continued by ending them with a dash (–) or a backslash (\) as the last character in the line:

```
C-Kermit>set -
file \
type -
binary
C-Kermit>
```

Note that the prompt doesn't come back until you (a) finish entering the command, (b) request a menu with ?, or (c) make a mistake. In command files only (not at the prompt), you may add trailing comments after the continuation character:

```
set -                         ; This is a SET command
file -                        ; related to files
type -                        ; in particular the file type
binary                        ; which is to be binary.
```

The command editing characters <DEL>, Ctrl-W, and Ctrl-U may be used with continued commands, but their effects are shown only on the current line. Use Ctrl-R to show the overall effect when you delete back into previous lines.

Describing Kermit's Commands

Before we can start explaining C-Kermit's commands, we need some notational conventions for describing their *syntax*, or form. We use special punctuation and typography to show what fields are required, what fields are optional, and what type of data goes into a field, as in this typical command syntax description:

Syntax: **SET** *{* **RECEIVE, SEND** *}* **END-OF-PACKET** *[number]*

This example illustrates the use of boldface to represent keywords literally, italic braces to enclose a list of alternatives, italic square brackets to show an optional field, and a word in italics to show a substitutable parameter. Here is a complete listing of the notation used in this book:

WORD

> An uppercase word in **BOLDFACE** means that the word should be typed literally. If it is a keyword (and it usually is), letters can be omitted from the end as long as what remains is enough to distinguish the word you have abbreviated from any other word that is valid in the same context. Letters may be typed in either lowercase or uppercase. For example, in:
>
> **SET FILE TYPE BINARY**
>
> all four words are keywords.

word

> A word in *italics* is a *parameter*, which is to be replaced by an actual value of your choice. The word in italics indicates what sort of quantity is expected: a *number*, a *filename*, a *directory-name*, a *variable-name*, and so forth. For example, in:
>
> **SET WINDOW** *number*
>
> the word *number* is to be replaced by an actual number, like 4 or 10.

[anything=value]

> Any word enclosed in italicized (slanted) square brackets is optional, meaning you don't have to include it in the command. If you see square brackets that are not italicized, they should be taken as literal brackets that you should type. The *=value* portion shows the value that is used if you don't specify one for this field, that is, the *default* value. Example:
>
> **SET BLOCK-CHECK** *[number=1]*

This means that the SET BLOCK-CHECK command takes an optional number. If you enter the command without specifying a number, then 1 is used:

```
C-Kermit>set block-check 2
C-Kermit>set block-check 1
C-Kermit>set block-check
```

{ something, something, something }
> Within italicized curly braces, a list of items separated by commas means that you should pick one of the items from the list. This notation is usually used for a list of keywords:
>
> **SET FILE TYPE** *[{* **TEXT, BINARY** *} =***TEXT** *]*
>
> This shows that the possible file types are TEXT and BINARY and if the command ends after the word TYPE, TEXT will be used. If you see braces that are not italic, { such as the ones around this phrase }, these are actually part of the command.

. . .
> An ellipsis (three dots) means that the preceding item can be repeated. Example:
>
> **MSEND** *file [file [file [. . .]]]*
>
> or, more compactly:
>
> **MSEND** *file . . .*
>
> This means the MSEND (multiple send) command can be given with one or more filenames separated by spaces.

Commonly used C-Kermit command parameters include:

number
> A decimal (base 10) number, like 31 or 9024. You also can enter small positive numbers (0–255) in octal (base 8) or hexadecimal (base 16) using backslash notation. If you don't know what octal or hexadecimal notation are, don't worry about it—skip the rest of this paragraph. Use \o*nnn* for an octal number; that is, backslash followed by the letter *O* (upper- or lowercase) followed by one to three octal digits (which are 0 through 7). For a hexadecimal number, use \x*nn*; that is, backslash followed by the letter *X* (upper or lower), followed by exactly two hexadecimal digits, which are 0 through 9 and A through F. The letters A–F can be in uppercase or lowercase. Example:
>
> **SET RETRY** *number*
>
> means you can type commands such as:
>
> ```
> C-Kermit>set retry 13          (A decimal number)
> C-Kermit>set retry \13         (A decimal number)
> C-Kermit>set retry \d13        (A decimal number)
> C-Kermit>set retry \o15        (An octal number)
> C-Kermit>set retry \x0D        (A hexadecimal number)
> ```
>
> The allowable range for the number depends on the command. If you enter a number that is out of range, an error message is given and the command has no effect:
>
> ```
> C-Kermit>set window 793
> ?Sorry, 31 is the maximum
> C-Kermit>
> ```

Describing Kermit's Commands 27

filename
> The name of a file on the computer where you are running C-Kermit. The name can, but need not, include device and/or directory information. Upper- and lowercase letters are treated differently in UNIX filenames, but case does not matter in VMS, OpenVMS, OS/2, AOS/VS, and most other operating systems. The filename may not contain wildcard characters. For example:
>
> **TAKE** *filename*
>
> means that the TAKE command needs the name of a file on your computer:
>
> ```
> C-Kermit>take oofa.*
> ?Wildcards not allowed in command file name
> C-Kermit>take oofa.cmd
> C-Kermit>take $disk2:[olga]oofa.cmd      (A VMS or OpenVMS file)
> C-Kermit>take /usr/ivan/kermit/oofa.cmd  (A UNIX or Amiga file)
> C-Kermit>take f:\\olaf\\kermit\\oofa.cmd (An OS/2 or Atari file)
> ```
>
> Note the double backslashes in the OS/2 or Atari ST filename.

filespec
> A file specification applying to the computer where you are running C-Kermit. Just like a *filename*, except it is allowed to (but need not) contain wildcard characters to indicate a group of files. Example:
>
> **SEND** *filespec*
>
> means you can give commands like:
>
> ```
> C-Kermit>send oofa.txt                 (A single file)
> C-Kermit>send oofa.*                   (A group of files)
> C-Kermit>send *.*                      (A bigger group of files)
> C-Kermit>send $disk2:[olga]*.cmd       (VMS or OpenVMS files)
> C-Kermit>take /usr/ivan/kermit/*.ini   (UNIX, OS-9, Amiga files)
> C-Kermit>take f:\\olaf\\kermit\\*.*    (OS/2 or Atari ST files)
> ```
>
> File specifications can also include device, directory, or other identifying fields meaningful to your operating system.

remote-filename
> The name of a file on another computer, in whatever form the other computer requires. It should not contain wildcard characters. Example:
>
> **REMOTE TYPE** *remote-filename*
>
> lets us give commands like:
>
> ```
> C-Kermit>remote type oofa txt a              (A VM/CMS file)
> C-Kermit>remote type f:\\olaf\\oofa.txt      (MS-DOS or OS/2)
> C-Kermit>remote type $disk2:[olaf]oofa.txt;17 (VMS or OpenVMS)
> C-Kermit>remote type :udd:olaf:oofa.txt      (AOS/VS)
> C-Kermit>remote type ~olaf/oofa.txt          (UNIX or OS-9)
> C-Kermit>remote type diska:/olaf/oofa.txt    (Amiga)
> ```

remote-filespec

Just like *remote-filename*, but wildcard characters may (but need not) be included. Wildcards, if used, should be in a format acceptable to the other computer. Example:

GET *remote-filespec*

allows:

```
C-Kermit>get * exec                       (Files from VM/CMS)
C-Kermit>get f:\\olaf\\oofa.*             (From MS-DOS or OS/2)
C-Kermit>get $disk2:[olaf]oofa.*;0        (From VMS or OpenVMS)
C-Kermit>remote type :udd:olaf:oofa.-     (From AOS/VS)
```

directory-name

The name of a directory on the computer where C-Kermit is running. Upper- and lowercase letters are distinct in UNIX directory names, but case does not matter in most other operating systems. Example:

CD *directory-name*

allows:

```
C-Kermit>cd /usr/olga/           (UNIX)
C-Kermit>cd c:\\usr\\olga        (OS/2)
C-Kermit>cd sys$help:            (VMS or OpenVMS)
C-Kermit>cd :udd:olga            (AOS/VS)
```

remote-directory-name

The name of a directory on another computer, in whatever form the other computer requires. Example:

REMOTE CD *remote-directory-name*

allows:

```
C-Kermit>remote cd c1            (VM/CMS)
C-Kermit>remote cd f:\\public    (OS/2 or MS-DOS)
C-Kermit>remote cd [-.programs]  (VMS or OpenVMS)
C-Kermit>remote cd ^:programs    (AOS/VS)
```

command

In most contexts, a system command on the computer where C-Kermit is running, such as you would type to the UNIX shell, to DCL in VMS or OpenVMS, or to the CLI in AOS/VS. Alphabetic case matters in UNIX, but it does not matter in most other operating systems. Example:

RUN *command*

allows:

```
C-Kermit>run diff oofa.old oofa.new    (A UNIX command)
C-Kermit>run purge/log oofa.*          (A VMS command)
C-Kermit>run more < ckermit.ini        (An OS/2 command)
C-Kermit>run help/v copy               (An AOS/VS command)
```

```
C-Kermit>run status                    (An Amiga command)
C-Kermit>run deldir test               (An OS-9 command)
```

In other contexts, *command* stands for a C-Kermit command.

remote-command

The name of a command or program on another computer, in the form required by the other computer. Example:

REMOTE HOST *remote-command*

allows:

```
C-Kermit>remote host lf oofa * (date   (A command for VM/CMS)
C-Kermit>remote host mkdir hw2         (A command for UNIX)
```

text

Any old text. Zero or more words, everything you type up to the end of the command. As in all C-Kermit commands, trailing comments are ignored. Example:

ECHO *text*

allows:

```
C-Kermit>echo                          (No words)
                                       (A blank line appears)
C-Kermit>echo Hi ; This is a comment   (One word, with comment)
Hi
C-Kermit>echo Time to go home          (Several words)
Time to go home
C-Kermit>
```

Some Basic C-Kermit Commands

You already know Kermit's EXIT command. C-Kermit also includes a few other commands that you can experiment with right now, before you learn how to use the program for data communication and file transfer. These commands, listed in Table 2-2, give you access to file management and other functions of your computer's operating system. Use these commands to practice the features you've read about in this chapter: question mark to get help, completion, abbreviation, correction, continuation, and comments. Within a few minutes you should be comfortable with C-Kermit's command style and an expert navigator of Kermit commands.

The Kermit command shown in the first column of the table is the form used in C-Kermit and most other Kermit programs. The equivalent commands in UNIX, VMS, OpenVMS, AOS/VS, and other operating systems might have different names, but in many cases these names are accepted by Kermit too, so you don't have to remember two different commands for the same task.

Table 2-2 Basic C-Kermit Commands

Kermit	UNIX	VMS, OpenVMS	AOS/VS	Description
`cd`	`cd`	`set default`	`directory`	Change directory
`delete`	`rm`	`delete`	`delete`	Delete files
`directory`	`ls -l`	`directory`	`filestatus`	List files
`echo`	`echo`	`write`	`write`	Display text on screen
`help`	`man`	`help`	`help`	Display help messages
`pause`	`sleep`	`wait`	`pause`	Sleep for some seconds
`print`	`lp, lpr`	`print`	`print`	Print files on a printer
`push`	`sh, csh, ksh`	`spawn, @`	`push`	Enter system
`pwd`	`pwd`	`show default`	`dir`	Show current directory
`rename`	`mv`	`rename`	`rename`	Rename files
`run`	`command`	`[ run ] command`	`[ xeq ]`	Run a command or program
`space`	`df`	`show quota`	`space`	Show disk space
`type`	`cat`	`type`	`type`	Display contents of a text file

Here are the descriptions of the commands from the table:

CD [*directory-name*]

Changes your default directory (CD stands for Change Directory). If you specify a directory name, it becomes your new default directory for all file-related Kermit commands. The directory name can be fully specified or it can be relative to your current directory. If you omit the directory name, most versions of C-Kermit put you back in your login directory. Examples:

```
C-Kermit>cd $disk1:[olga.letters]   (Fully specified, VMS)
C-Kermit>cd [.letters]              (Relative directory, VMS)
C-Kermit>cd /usr/olga/letters       (Fully specified, UNIX)
C-Kermit>cd :udd:olga:letters       (Fully specified, AOS/VS)
C-Kermit>cd c:\\olga\\letters       (Fully specified, OS/2)
C-Kermit>cd c:/olga/letters         (Alternate form, OS/2)
C-Kermit>cd c:\\olga\\letters       (Fully specified, Atari)
C-Kermit>cd c:/olga/letters         (Fully specified, Amiga)
C-Kermit>cd ~olaf                   (User's home directory, UNIX)
C-Kermit>cd letters                 (Relative directory)
C-Kermit>cd                         (Login (home) directory)
```

The CD command applies only within Kermit itself and any programs that Kermit runs. When you EXIT from Kermit, you should find yourself back where you started. Synonyms: **CWD** (Change Working Directory), **SET DEFAULT**.

DELETE *filespec*

Deletes (removes, erases, destroys) all files that match the *filespec*, which may contain wildcards, directory names, and/or device designators. Successful execution of this command requires that you have appropriate access rights to the specified file or files. UNIX examples:

```
C-Kermit>delete oofa.txt       (One file in current directory)
C-Kermit>del *                 (All files in current directory)
C-Kermit>del /usr/olaf/kermit/a.txt
                               (Fully specified UNIX file)
```

VMS and OpenVMS examples:

```
C-Kermit>delete oofa.txt;3     (One file in current directory)
C-Kermit>del *.*;*             (All files in current directory)
C-Kermit>del $disk1:[olaf.kermit]a.txt;7
                               (Fully specified VMS file)
```

Synonym: **RM**.

DIRECTORY *[{ filespec, directory-name }]*

Lists files. If no filespec or directory name is given, lists all files in the current directory. If a directory name is given, lists all files in the specified directory. If a filespec is given, lists all files that match it. Examples for UNIX:

```
C-Kermit>directory        (List all files in current directory)
C-Kermit>dir ~olga        (All files in olga's login directory)
C-Kermit>dir ~/kermit     (All files in my kermit directory)
C-Kermit>dir kermit       (All files in kermit subdirectory)
C-Kermit>dir ck*.*        (Files whose names match)
C-Kermit>dir ..           (All files in superior directory)
C-Kermit>dir ../a*.*      (Matching files in superior directory)
```

Corresponding VMS and OpenVMS examples:

```
C-Kermit>dir              (List all files in current directory)
C-Kermit>dir $disk:[olga] (All files in olga's login directory)
C-Kermit>dir [olga.kermit] (and in olga's kermit subdirectory)
C-Kermit>dir [.kermit]    (All files in my kermit subdirectory)
C-Kermit>dir ck*.*        (Files whose names match)
C-Kermit>dir [-]          (All files in superior directory)
C-Kermit>dir [-]a*.*      ("a" files in superior directory)
```

Corresponding AOS/VS examples:

```
C-Kermit>dir              (List all files in current directory)
C-Kermit>dir :udd:olga:+  (All files in olga's login directory)
C-Kermit>dir :udd:olga:kermit:+ (in olga's kermit subdirectory)
C-Kermit>dir kermit:+     (All files in my kermit subdirectory)
C-Kermit>dir ck+.+        (Files whose names match)
C-Kermit>dir ^+           (All files in superior directory)
C-Kermit>dir ^:a+         ("a" files in superior directory)
```

Synonym: **LS**.

ECHO *[text]*

Displays the *text* on the screen. The text may contain imbedded backslash codes to be interpreted. If the *text* is omitted, an empty line is displayed. Examples:

```
C-Kermit>echo Good morning.
Good morning.
C-Kermit>echo \7Wake up!\7   ; Comment won't echo
<BEEP>Wake up!<BEEP>
C-Kermit>
```

Leading and trailing spaces are removed unless the *text* is enclosed in curly braces:

```
C-Kermit>echo      Testing
Testing
C-Kermit>echo {    Testing    }
   Testing
C-Kermit>
```

Synonym: **WRITE SYS$OUTPUT**. Related: **WRITE SCREEN**.

HELP *[command]*

Displays a help message. The *command* is a C-Kermit command, one or two words at most, such as COMMENT, ECHO, or SET DUPLEX. Example:

```
C-Kermit>help set duplex
```

```
Syntax: SET DUPLEX { FULL, HALF }

During CONNECT: FULL means remote host echoes, HALF means
C-Kermit does its own echoing.
```

```
C-Kermit>
```

If you do not include any text after the word HELP, a brief overview is displayed. Use question mark to get menus within the HELP command. Synonym: **MAN**.

PAUSE *[number=1]*

This command tells Kermit to do nothing for the given number of seconds. The prompt returns after the time has expired or if you type something (any character) in the meantime. Examples:

```
C-Kermit>pause                      (Pause for one second)
C-Kermit>pau 30                     (Pause for 30 seconds)
```

Synonyms: **WAIT** (when used without modem signals), **SLEEP**.
Related: **MSLEEP**. Like PAUSE, but number is in milliseconds.

PRINT *[local-options] filename*

Prints the local file on a local printer, if your computer has one. Local options can be included for your computer's printing command. Examples:

```
C-Kermit>print oofa.txt             (Print a file)
C-Kermit>print /copies=3 oofa.txt   (VMS or OpenVMS options)
C-Kermit>print -#3 oofa.txt         (UNIX options)
C-Kermit>print /copies=3 oofa.txt   (AOS/VS options)
```

PUSH

Invokes your system's command processor "underneath" Kermit interactively in such a way that you can return to Kermit later.

```
C-Kermit>push
%
% who ivan
% watsun!ivan   ttyh9   Aug 11 14:21
% write ivan ttyh9
Hi there!
Ctrl-D
% exit
C-Kermit>
```

To return from the "inferior" command processor to C-Kermit, use the `exit` or `Ctrl-D` command in UNIX or OS-9, the EXIT command in OS/2, LOGOUT in VMS and OpenVMS, POP in AOS/VS, ENDCLI on the Amiga. Synonyms: **!**, **@**, **RUN**.

PWD

PWD stands for Print Working Directory. It displays the name of your current default (working) directory. Examples:

```
C-Kermit>pwd
/usr/olga/letters            (UNIX, OS-9, or Amiga)
$DISK1:[OLGA.LETTERS]        (VMS or OpenVMS)
:UDD:OLGA:LETTERS            (AOS/VS)
C:\OLGA                      (OS/2 or Atari ST)
```

Synonym: **SHOW DEFAULT**.

RENAME *filename1 filename2*

Changes the name of the file whose name is *filename1* to *filename2*, for example:

```
C-Kermit>ren space-adventure.exe spreadsheet.exe
```

The ability of the RENAME command to operate across directories or devices depends on the capabilities of the underlying operating system. Synonym: **MV**.

RUN *[command]*

Runs the named system command or program and returns to the C-Kermit prompt automatically when the command or program is finished. If no command name is given, the RUN command is exactly like the PUSH command. Examples:

```
C-Kermit>run fortune
Who messed with my anti-paranoia shot?
```

Synonyms: **PUSH**, **!**, **@**. Examples:

```
C-Kermit>@show system                         (VMS or OpenVMS)
C-Kermit>@search area-codes.txt Chicago       (VMS or OpenVMS)
C-Kermit>!date                                (UNIX or OS-9)
C-Kermit>!grep Chicago area-codes.txt         (UNIX or OS-9)
C-Kermit>!time                                (AOS/VS)
C-Kermit>!find "Chicago" areacode.txt         (OS/2)
```

SPACE *[device]*
  Displays information indicating how much space is available on the current or given disk device, or in the current directory, or remaining in your quota, depending on the operating system.

TYPE *filename*
  Displays the contents of the file on the screen. The TYPE command does not pause at the end of each screenful, like UNIX more or VMS TYPE/PAGE. If you need this effect in UNIX, use !more. In VMS, PUSH to DCL and use TYPE/PAGE instead.

The C-Kermit Initialization File

The initialization file is a command file that C-Kermit executes automatically when it starts. Its name and location depend on which type of computer system you have (see Table 2-3 on the next page), normally .kermrc (UNIX and OS-9) or CKERMIT.INI (all the others).

The initialization file should contain the commands that you want to be executed every time you start the C-Kermit program. For example, if you have a UNIX workstation whose serial communication device is connected to a Hayes 2400 modem and you always use C-Kermit to dial out on this device, your initialization file, .kermrc, might contain commands like these:

```
set modem hayes                     ; So DIAL command works right
set line /dev/ttyb                  ; Use ttyb for communication
set speed 2400                      ; Modem's highest speed
echo Ready for Hayes dialing at 2400 bps on /dev/ttyb.
echo Remember to turn on your modem!
```

(The SET commands are explained in the next chapter.) Note the use of trailing comments for documentation. With this initialization file, the only command you need to give Kermit to dial up another computer is DIAL (also explained in the next chapter):

```
$ kermit                                (Start Kermit)
Ready for Hayes dialing at 2400 bps on /dev/ttyb.
Remember to turn on your modem!
C-Kermit>show communications            (Check effect of init file)
Communications Parameters:
 Line: /dev/ttyb, speed: 2400, mode: local, modem: hayes
 ...
C-Kermit>dial 9876543                   (Dial another computer)
Call completed.                         (So easy!)
C-Kermit>                               (Kermit awaits your command)
```

As you progress through this book, other likely candidates will suggest themselves for inclusion in your "init" file—terminal settings (Chapter 4), file transfer protocol settings (Chapters 5–7), character-set selections (Chapter 9), macro definitions (Chapters 11–13).

Table 2-3 C-Kermit Initialization File Name

System	File Name	Remarks
Atari ST	`CKERMIT.INI`	C-Kermit looks first in the current directory, then in your home directory, and finally in the root directory.
Commodore Amiga	`CKERMIT.INI`	C-Kermit looks first in the `s:` directory, then in the current directory.
Data General AOS/VS	`CKERMIT.INI`	C-Kermit looks in your home directory.
OS/2	`ckermit.ini`	C-Kermit checks the directories defined by the OS/2 environment variables INIT, PATH, and DPATH, in that order, and if the file is not found, then looks in the current directory.
OS-9	`.kermrc`	C-Kermit looks in your home directory first, then in the current directory.
UNIX (all versions)	`.kermrc`	Your home directory, period.
VMS, OpenVMS	`CKERMIT.INI`	C-Kermit looks for `CKERMIT_INI:CKERMIT.INI`, then for the file defined by the symbol `CKERMIT_INIT`, and finally in your home directory, `SYS$LOGIN`, for `CKERMIT.INI`.

If you want Kermit to use a specific command file for initialization instead of the default command file shown in Table 2-3, you can specify an alternate initialization-file name on the command line, using the -y (lowercase) command-line option:

`$ kermit -y special.cmd`

If you want to run C-Kermit without any initialization file at all, use the -Y (uppercase) command-line option:

```
$ kermit -Y                    (UNIX, OS/2, etc.)
$ kermit "-Y"                  (VMS or OpenVMS, quotes required)
```

If you want C-Kermit to execute a particular command file *after* it executes the initialization file, but before it issues its first prompt, include the filename as the first word after *kermit* when you invoke C-Kermit from the system prompt:

`$ kermit tuesday.tak`

See the Appendix particular to your operating system for details about the initialization file, as well as Chapter 11 for further information about command files in general.

We recommend that you use the standard initialization file, `CKERMIT.INI`, that is distributed with C-Kermit 5A, and that you make any desired modifications or customizations in the accompanying `CKERMOD.INI` file.

Chapter 3

Getting Connected

In Chapter 2 you learned how to operate C-Kermit within the safe and circumscribed environment of a single computer, much like you would use most other computer software applications. But unlike those applications, the purpose of Kermit software is to let you use *two* computers at once, such as the PC on your desk and a large mainframe located elsewhere.

Before we proceed, let's refresh our memories about *remote* and *local*. A Kermit program is in local mode if you are using it to establish a connection to another computer. Otherwise, it is in remote mode. For example, if you are using an MS-DOS PC on your desk to access a remote UNIX computer where C-Kermit resides, you will be using MS-DOS Kermit in *local mode* and C-Kermit in *remote mode*, as illustrated in Figure 3-1 on the next page. The PC establishes the connection, so it's the local computer. The UNIX system receives the connection, so it's the remote computer.

○ ○ ○ ○ ⟵ *(Stepping stones)*
If you will be using C-Kermit *only* in remote mode, you don't need to read this chapter or the next one. Skip ahead to Chapter 5, page 95, to learn how to transfer files. If necessary, also consult the "Getting Online" section of the documentation for your local Kermit program, for example, Chapter 7 of *Using MS-DOS Kermit* [29].

There are two ways to use C-Kermit in local mode, depending on what kind of computer you have. The first method is used when you have a workstation on your desk from which you establish a connection to a remote computer. Figure 3-2 shows your local computer

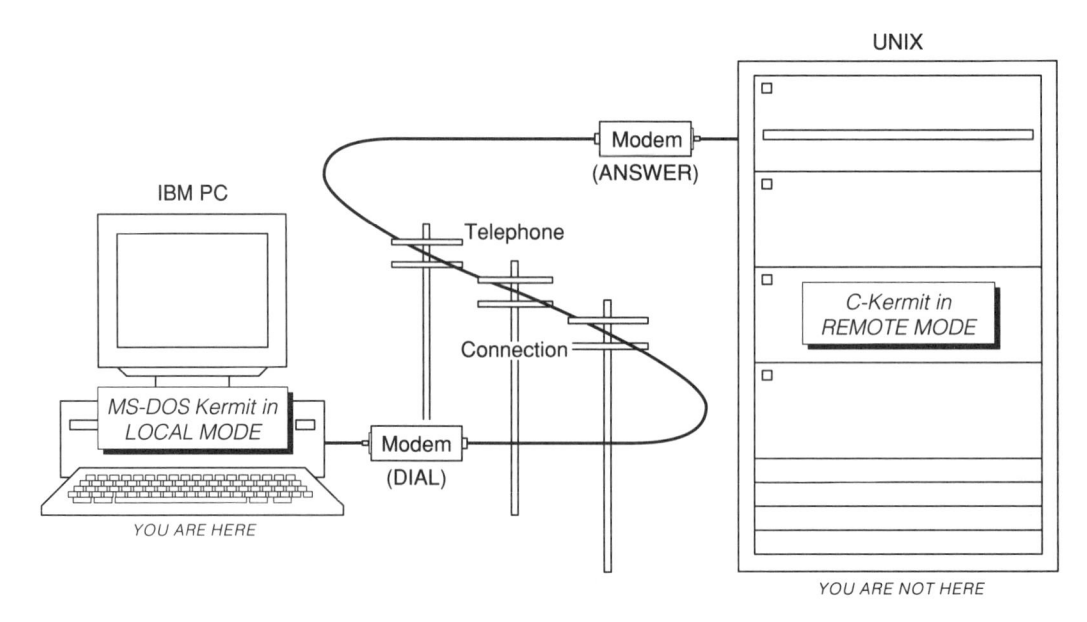

Figure 3-1 C-Kermit in Remote Mode

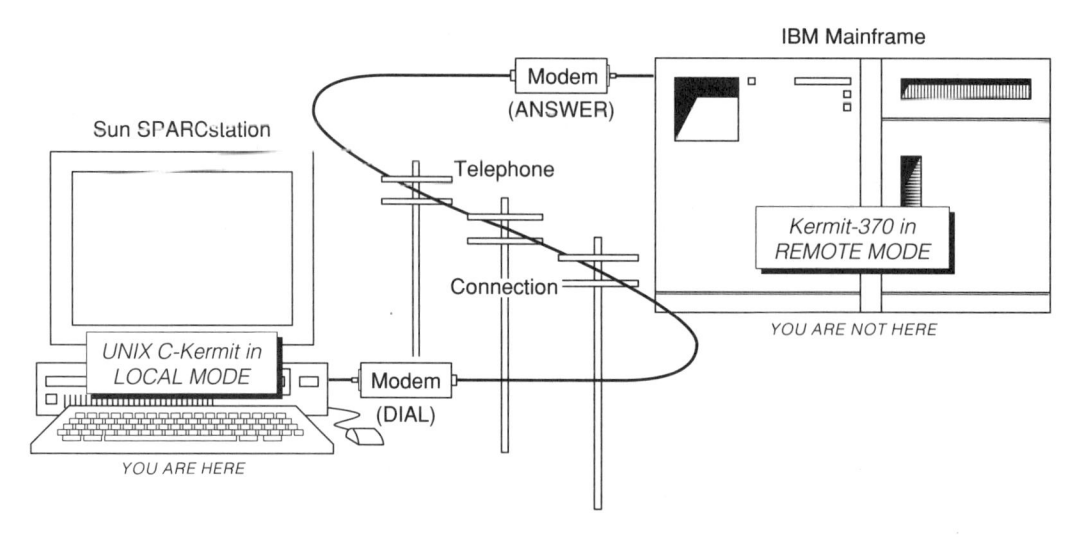

Figure 3-2 C-Kermit in Local Mode

as a Sun SPARCstation, with a modem connection to a remote IBM mainframe. The workstation could be any UNIX or OS-9 workstation, a VAXstation, a PC with OS/2 or UNIX, an Amiga, or an Atari ST. Any of these computers could use C-Kermit to establish the connection to the remote computer.

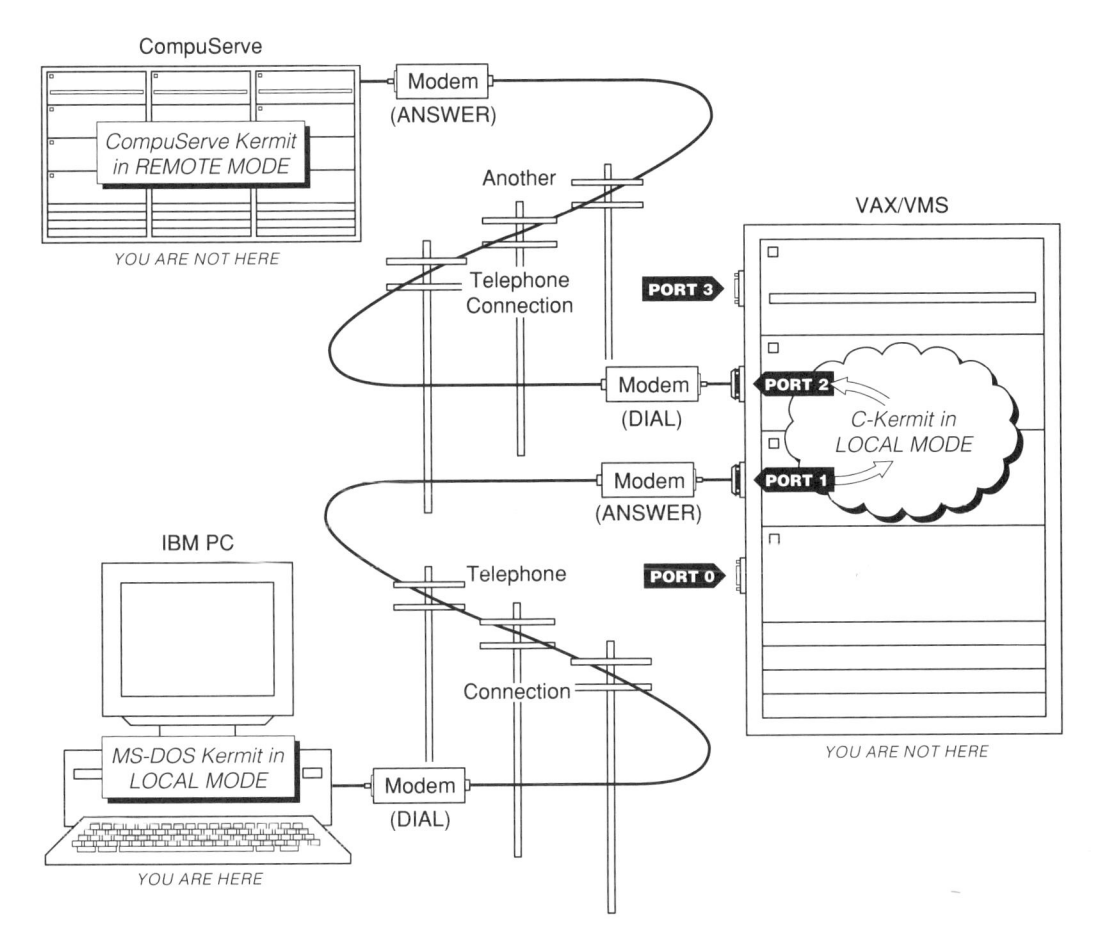

Figure 3-3 C-Kermit in the Middle

In the second scenario, illustrated in Figure 3-3, you are accessing a multiuser UNIX, VMS, OpenVMS, or AOS/VS timesharing system from a PC, Macintosh, workstation, or terminal on your desk, and you are using C-Kermit on the multiuser computer to connect to a third computer. You would use this method if the multiuser computer has a connection method not available to your desktop computer, or if the multiuser computer is where you do most of your work.

Figure 3-3 shows an IBM PC with MS-DOS Kermit calling a VAX/VMS computer and using C-Kermit on the VAX to place a call to CompuServe. As you can see, you are using two communication ports on the VAX: the first for logging in and the second for dialing out. This illustrates how a *local* Kermit program uses a *separate device*, having nothing to do with your keyboard and screen, to communicate with the remote computer.

Getting Connected 39

Using C-Kermit in Local Mode

Local mode operation of C-Kermit has four phases: setting the appropriate communication parameters, making the connection, using the connection, and releasing the connection. The process can be easy or difficult, depending on your local computer, the connection method used, and the remote computer or service. C-Kermit is set up to handle the easy cases automatically, but the hard cases require a little extra effort.

○ ○ ○ ○
This chapter assumes you are familiar with data communication concepts such as modem, null modem, speed, parity, cable, and connector. If you aren't, please turn to Appendix II on page 359 for a tutorial.

Before you can make two computers communicate, you have to learn certain essential facts about them and the connection between them. What is the connection method —dialup, direct, or network? For dialup and direct connections, what is the name of the communication device on the local computer and what speeds are permitted? For dialup connections, what type of dialout modem is on the local computer and what is the remote computer's telephone number? Use C-Kermit's SET command to supply these facts. C-Kermit tries to give you reasonable defaults; if your connection to the other computer fits the defaults, you need just a few SET commands and connecting is easy.

A Test Drive

To show you just how easy a connection can be, let's use C-Kermit to dial the Digital Equipment Corporation Electronic Store. In this example, we're running C-Kermit on a DEC UNIX workstation (DECstation) in a terminal window, which provides VT terminal emulation. We dial out using a Hayes Smartmodem 2400 at 2400 bits per second. This same example should work on practically any other computer where C-Kermit runs, but you probably will have to substitute a different device name in the SET LINE command, and possibly a different modem type.

How do you know the name of the communication device? If you have a desktop workstation, look in your workstation's user manual. Some sample workstation dialout device names are listed in Table 3-1, in which the modem is assumed to be attached to the first serial device on each computer.[8] If you are dialing out from a multiuser computer, you'll have to consult your site-specific documentation or ask the system support staff. This demonstration is available only in the North American calling area, and it works only if C-Kermit is running in an environment that supports DEC VT100, VT200, VT300, or

---

[8]If your workstation has a serial mouse, the modem might be attached to the *second* serial device.

Table 3-1 Sample Dialout Device Names

System	Default Device	Dialout Device Name
Apple A/UX	*console*	`/dev/modem`
AmigaDOS	`serial.device/0`	`serial.device/0`
Amiga UNIX	*console*	`/dev/term/ser` or `/dev/term/ql00`
AT&T 6300 PLUS	*console*	`/dev/tty1`
AT&T 7300 UNIX PC	*console*	`/dev/ph0`
Atari ST GEMDOS	`AUX:`	`AUX:`
Data General Aviion	*console*	`/dev/tty00`
Data General AOS/VS	*console*	`@con1`
DECstation ULTRIX	*console*	`/dev/tty00`
Dell UNIX	*console*	`/dev/tty01` (if mouse on `/dev/tty00`). For RTS/CTS, use `/dev/tty01h`.
HP-9000 HP-UX	*console*	`/dev/culd0`
IBM RS/6000 AIX	*console*	`/dev/tty0`
Interactive UNIX/386	*console*	`/dev/tty0` or `/dev/acu0`
NeXT	*console*	`/dev/cua`. Use `/dev/cufa` for RTS/CTS.
OS/2	`COM1`	`COM1`
OS-9	*console*	`/t1`
SCO UNIX	*console*	`/dev/tty1A` (uppercase A selects modem control)
SCO Xenix	*console*	`/dev/tty1a`
Sun SPARCstation	*console*	`/dev/cua0` or `/dev/cua1`
VMS, OpenVMS	*console*	`TXA0:`, `TTA0:`, or `LTA0:`

higher VT terminal emulation, such as a true VT terminal or emulator connected to the system where C-Kermit is running, a DECterm or xterm window on a workstation, the console driver on a PC-based UNIX system, or you are using OS/2 C-Kermit, which provides its own VT100 emulation.

```
$ kermit                              (Start Kermit on the DECstation)
C-Kermit 5A(188), 23 Nov 92, ULTRIX 4.2
Type ? or HELP for help
C-Kermit>set modem hayes              (What kind of modem you have)
C-Kermit>set line /dev/cua0           (Communication device to use)
C-Kermit>set speed 2400               (Dialing speed)
C-Kermit>dial 1-800-234-1998          (Place the call)
 Dialing 1-800-234-1998               (Messages from C-Kermit...)
 Device=/dev/cua0, modem=hayes, speed=2400
 Call completed.<BEEP>
```

```
C-Kermit>connect                    (Make the connection)
Connecting to /dev/cua, speed 2400.
The escape character is Ctrl-\ (ASCII 28, FS).
Type the escape character followed by C to get back,
or followed by ? to see other options.

Welcome to Digital's Electronic Store.  Please wait a moment ...

  (Follow the directions,
    browse around for a while, and then...)
```

To get back to C-Kermit at any time after connecting to the remote service, type Ctrl-Backslash and then the letter C. That is, hold down the Ctrl (or Control) key and press the backslash key,[9] then let go of the control key and press the C key.

```
Ctrl-\C                             (Escape back to C-Kermit)
C-Kermit>exit                       (All done, exit to UNIX)
$
```

Wasn't that easy? Here's hoping that all your connections are so easy! In this case, all you had to do was tell C-Kermit what kind of modem to use, the name of the communication device that the modem was connected to, and the speed to use for dialing. Then you dialed the phone number, connected, did some window shopping, got back to C-Kermit, and then returned to your operating system.

Establishing a Serial Connection

The rest of this chapter discusses C-Kermit's different methods for connection establishment: direct connections, dialout modem connections, and network connections. Terminal connection is covered in Chapter 4.

○ ○ ○ ○
If you will not be making serial connections, but you will be making network connections, please skip ahead to page 67.

A serial connection is made over an asynchronous serial communication device, also called a serial port, terminal port, tty port, RS-232 port, V.24 device, EIA port, asynchronous adapter, or internal modem. If the port is connected directly to another computer, which would normally be done with a null modem cable, the connection is *direct*. If it is connected to a modem that is, in turn, connected to a telephone line that must be dialed, the connection is *dialed*.

---

[9]On the NeXT workstation, substitute the right bracket key for the backslash key. Most NeXT keyboards do not support the Control-Backslash key combination. On PCs running OS/2, use either Control-Rightbracket or Alt-X (hold down the Alt key and press the X key).

Selecting the Communication Device

For any type of serial connection, you must tell Kermit the name of the serial device. The SET LINE command opens a serial communication device so you can use it:

SET LINE *[device]*
Opens the serial communication device through which you will be communicating. If you give the SET LINE command without including a device name, C-Kermit closes any currently open communication device and returns to the default communication device, which in most cases is your controlling terminal (*console*) and remote mode, or to the default dialout device, as shown in Table 3-1. Synonym: **SET PORT**. Examples:

```
C-Kermit>set line /dev/cua        (UNIX)
C-Kermit>set line txa4:           (VMS or OpenVMS)
C-Kermit>set line @con2:          (AOS/VS)
C-Kermit>set line com2            (OS/2)
C-Kermit>set line 2               (OS/2, same as line com2)
C-Kermit>set port 2               (OS/2, same as line 2)
C-Kermit>set line                 (All, default device)
```

Whenever you give a SET LINE command, C-Kermit closes any currently open communication device before attempting to open the new one. The SET LINE command can fail for any of the following reasons, which are printed as error messages on your screen:

Sorry, access to device denied
The communication device is protected against you. Contact your system administrator to see if you can get the required access.

Sorry, access to lock denied
(UNIX only) The lock mechanism that prevents more than one person from using the same communication device at the same time is protected against you. Contact your system administrator.

Sorry, device is in use
Somebody else is currently using the communication device you have specified. If you get the "device is in use" message in UNIX, C-Kermit attempts to show you who is using it:

```
C-Kermit>set line /dev/ttyh8
-r--r--r--  1 olga   11  Feb 24 15:17 /var/spool/locks/LCK..ttyh8
pid = 15688
/dev/ttyh8: Sorry, device is in use
C-Kermit>
```

The first line is a directory listing of the lock file showing who created it (Olga). The "pid" is the process ID of the program that created the lockfile. If you know where Olga is, you can ask her when she will be finished with the device you need.

Sorry, can't open connection
> Kermit encountered some other kind of error or difficulty when trying to open the device. The appropriate system error message is also printed, for example:
>
> ```
> No such file or directory
> ```

Timed out, no carrier
> You have given a SET CARRIER ON command (see page 46) that specified a time limit for SET LINE to wait for carrier, but carrier did not appear within the time limit.

If a SET LINE command appears to be stuck, it means that the operating system is having difficulty opening the device. You should be able to get back to the C-Kermit prompt by typing Ctrl-C.

If a new prompt appears and there is no error message, C-Kermit has opened the serial communication device successfully.

Specifying the Communication Speed

Before using the serial communication device that you specified in your SET LINE command, you should select the transmission speed. This should be the same speed as the remote computer or service uses. Two serial devices can't communicate at all if they are not using the same speed.

SET SPEED *number*
> Specifies the transmission speed, in bits per second, to use on the serial communication device specified in your most recent SET LINE command. If you don't give a SET SPEED command, Kermit tries to learn the device's current speed and use it. Only certain speeds are available; type SET SPEED ? to find out what they are. The list can vary from computer to computer. Here is a typical example:

```
C-Kermit>set speed ?
Transmission rate in bits per second, one of the following:
  110            1200                150            19200
  200            2400                300            3600
  38400          4800                50             600
  75             75/1200             9600
C-Kermit>set speed 2400
C-Kermit>
```

Notice that the speeds are arranged in "alphabetical" rather than numeric order. Because they are keywords, you can use abbreviation and completion with them, and you cannot enter an illegal value by mistake. Examples:

```
C-Kermit>set speed 9600        (9600 bits per second)
C-Kermit>set sp 9              (9600 bits per second)
C-Kermit>set sp 9500           (Not in the list)
?No keywords match - 9500
C-Kermit>
```

The 75/1200 entry is for use with split-speed modems, found mostly in Europe. Split speed operation is supported only in C-Kermit versions where the underlying computer operating system and hardware also support it. 75/1200 means C-Kermit transmits at 75 bps and receives at 1200 bps.

Remember, SET SPEED applies to the device given in the most recent SET LINE command. Kermit must know which device's speed you are setting. So the rule is: SET LINE first, then SET SPEED.

You can't use C-Kermit's SET SPEED command to change your login terminal's speed. If you issue the SET SPEED command while Kermit is in remote mode, you'll get an error message:

```
C-Kermit>set speed 2400
?Sorry, you must SET LINE first
```

Hanging up the Connection

To terminate a connection, use the HANGUP command:

HANGUP

Breaks the connection. If you have given a SET MODEM command, the HANGUP command attempts to put your modem in command mode and then issue the modem's hangup command, for example ATH0 for Hayes modems. If this does not work, or if you have not given a SET MODEM command, C-Kermit attempts to lower the Data Terminal Ready (DTR) signal for about half a second.

On a dialed modem connection, HANGUP should cause the modem to terminate (hang up) the telephone, which should, in turn, cause the remote computer or service to terminate your session if it is still in progress. A properly wired direct connection should simulate these same actions.

Normally, the HANGUP command need not be used. When you log out from a remote computer or service, it hangs up its end of the connection, and C-Kermit should automatically pop back to its prompt. Use the HANGUP command in situations where this does not happen, or when you want to be sure that the connection is broken.

The Carrier Signal

Serial communication devices might not allow themselves to be opened if the software and hardware don't agree about the RS-232 Carrier Detect (CD) signal, a signal from the modem to the computer (see Appendix II).

Most versions of C-Kermit assume that CD is off during dialing, that it is on when the connection has been made and is in use, and that it goes off again when the connection is broken. But your modem might be configured to keep carrier on (or off) all the time, or the cable connecting the modem to your serial port might not convey the carrier signal correctly. The SET CARRIER command lets you adjust Kermit to such situations:

SET CARRIER { AUTO, OFF, ON [*number*] }

Successful operation of SET CARRIER is highly dependent on the capabilities of your operating system and version, and Kermit's knowledge of them, as well as the configuration of your serial port, modem, and cable. The SET CARRIER command takes effect on the *next* SET LINE command. Thus you should SET CARRIER first, then SET LINE. Here are the SET CARRIER options:

SET CARRIER AUTO
Requires carrier during CONNECT but not at other times. AUTO is the default.

SET CARRIER OFF
C-Kermit is to ignore carrier at all times. This option is useful for direct connections, misbehaving modem connections, miswired or misconfigured modems, or buggy serial device drivers. It should be used only when necessary because it takes away Kermit's ability to automatically detect a broken connection.

SET CARRIER ON [*number*]
C-Kermit is to require carrier for all communication. An error is diagnosed if carrier disappears during CONNECT or file transfer, and C-Kermit should give an error message and pop back to its prompt automatically. When SET CARRIER ON is in effect, CD must be present when you give the SET LINE command. If it is not, Kermit waits for the carrier signal to appear. This allows the SET LINE command to wait for an incoming telephone call.

If you want to set a limit on how long SET LINE should wait for carrier, you can include an optional number after SET CARRIER ON that indicates how many seconds to wait before timing out and returning to the prompt, for example:

`C-Kermit>`<u>`SET CARRIER ON 30`</u>

You can also type Ctrl-C to interrupt a SET LINE command that is taking too long. In both cases (timeout and Ctrl-C interruption), the device is not successfully assigned.

Flow Control

Flow control is the process by which one computer (or other device) can request another computer (or device) to stop sending data, allowing time for the data received so far to be processed, and then request it to start sending again. Flow control is especially important to Kermit during file transfer operations and is covered in greater detail in Chapter 6.

Flow control prevents buffer overflows and data loss, *if* it is used effectively, meaning the computers or devices on each end of the connection must be configured to use the same type of flow control. There are two major types of flow control, software and hardware. Software flow control, also called Xon/Xoff flow control, is accomplished by inserting special control characters, Ctrl-S (Xoff) and Ctrl-Q (Xon), into the transmitted data. Xoff means stop sending and Xon means resume sending. Software flow control is generally used end-to-end, that is, between the computers at the two ends of the connection, rather than between a computer and the device it is immediately connected to.

Hardware flow control generally occurs between a computer and the communication device (modem, terminal server) directly connected to it. It uses separate wires in the cable, usually the RTS and CTS circuits. Hardware flow control should be used whenever available, because it is far more effective than software flow control. The flow control signals take effect immediately and are not subject to loss or corruption.

The C-Kermit command to select the flow control method is:

SET FLOW-CONTROL { KEEP, NONE, RTS/CTS, XON/XOFF }

The options are:

KEEP
   Use whatever type of flow control the device was configured with at the time that C-Kermit first opened it.

NONE
   Don't use any method of serial-connection flow control. Use this option when the two computers or devices do not share a flow control method in common, or when the two computers or devices are both so fast they don't need to use flow control, or when the connection is not serial at all, for example a TCP/IP network connection, in which case the underlying network protocol provides the flow control.

RTS/CTS
   Hardware flow control using the RTS and CTS RS-232 signals. This option is not available in all versions of C-Kermit because certain operating systems do not support it. If it is available, it will show up in the keyword menu if you type "SET FLOW ?". Use this option with high-speed modems, terminal servers, or other devices that also support it, and on direct serial connections when the two serial devices and their driver software also support it, and when the null modem cable is properly wired to convey these signals (Model B in Figure II-6, Appendix II, page 372).

XON/XOFF
   Software flow control using Ctrl-S and Ctrl-Q. Use this method when both end systems support it and RTS/CTS is not available. This method is effective only on full

duplex connections and should not be used on half duplex (local echo) connections. XON/XOFF is the default flow control method, so be sure to SET FLOW NONE if you are making a half duplex connection.

RTS/CTS flow control is sometimes available to you even when C-Kermit's SET FLOW command does not offer it. For example, in certain UNIX systems, such as a NeXT workstation, or Dell UNIX, it can be selected by using special device names (see Table 3-1 on page 41). On other systems it can be enabled by giving a system command before starting C-Kermit, for example:

% `stty crtscts`

on certain UNIX systems, or:

) `characteristics /on/ifc/ofc`

in AOS/VS. Consult your system documentation for further information.

Certain versions of C-Kermit might also support less common hardware flow-control options, such as DTR/CD or DTR/CTS. If your version of C-Kermit, and the underlying device and driver software, and the directly connected communication device, support these options, then you can use them in place of RTS/CTS. Use them with caution, however; the CD signal normally tells C-Kermit the connection is broken, so you should SET CARRIER OFF before attempting to use DTR/CD flow control. Also, when using either DTR/CD or DTR/CTS, make sure your communication device is configured not to hang up the connection if your computer turns off the DTR signal!

Displaying Communication Settings

To find out your current communication device, speed, carrier, flow control, and other settings, use the SHOW COMMUNICATIONS command, as in this example for UNIX:

```
C-Kermit>show comm
 Line: /dev/ttyh8, speed: 9600, mode: local, modem: direct
 Terminal bits: 7, parity: none, duplex: full, flow: xon/xoff
 Carrier: auto, lockfile: /var/spool/locks/LCK..ttyh8
 Escape character: 28 (^\)
C-Kermit>
```

Direct Serial Connections

Figure 3-4 shows a direct serial connection from a DEC VAXstation to a remote computer using a null modem cable. The VAXstation could also be any other kind of computer where you are running C-Kermit in local mode. This kind of connection is relatively easy to use because no modems are involved and dialing is not required. All you have to do is tell C-Kermit the name of the communication device that the cable is connected to and the communication speed to use. The other end of the cable should be connected to a port on

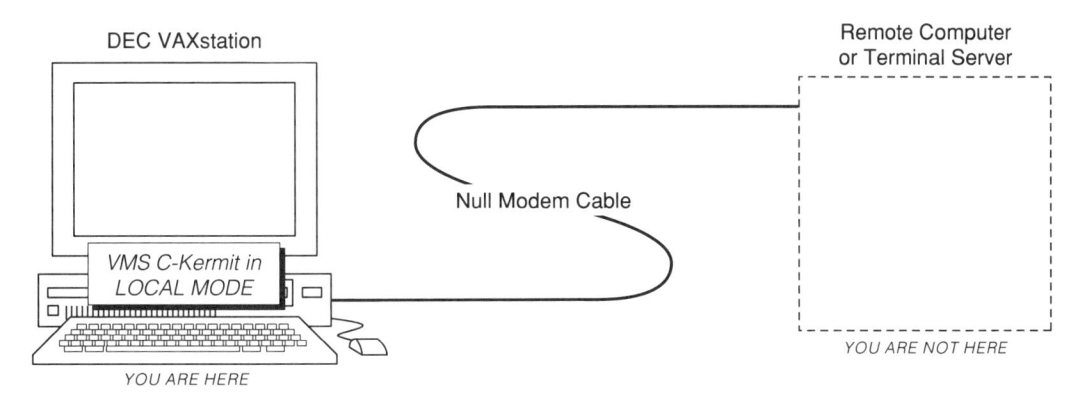

Figure 3-4 A Direct Connection

the remote computer that has been set up to let you log in. The remote computer in the figure also can be a terminal server or similar device with which you have a brief dialog to select a computer or service and which then connects you to it.

The only commands C-Kermit should need to establish a direct connection are SET LINE and SET SPEED. Here is an example of setting C-Kermit up for a local-mode direct connection, showing the order in which you should give the commands:

```
C-Kermit>set speed 9600            (Set the speed)
?Sorry, you must SET LINE first    (Oops)
C-Kermit>set line txa5             (Select communication device)
C-Kermit>set speed 9600            (Now set the speed)
C-Kermit>                          (No complaint)
```

If you have trouble establishing a direct connection:

- Make sure the port on the remote computer is set up to allow logins (or it is a port on a PC or workstation controlled by a Kermit server).

- Make sure the serial devices on the two computers are configured to use the same communication speed.

- Make sure you have used a null modem cable rather than a modem cable (see Figure II-6 on page 372), and that each computer's serial port asserts the DTR signal and receives all the signals it requires, usually DSR, CTS, and CD.

- Make sure the total length of the cable does not exceed 15 meters or 50 feet. For direct connections over longer distances, use powered line drivers or limited distance modems (LDMs) at each end of the cable, or use a shielded low-capacitance cable.

- Try SET CARRIER OFF before SET LINE.

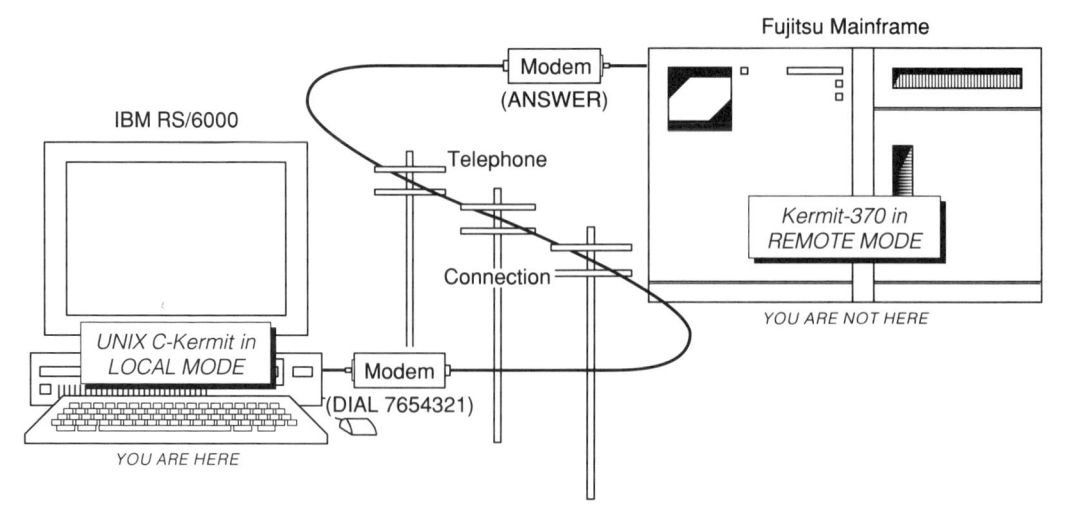

Figure 3-5 A Dialed Connection

REMEMBER: SET CARRIER first (only if necessary), then SET LINE, then SET SPEED. In that order.

If your direct connection is wired with a true null modem cable (such as the one shown in Figure II-6, Model B), Kermit should notice when the remote computer crashes or when you log out from it, and return you automatically to the local C-Kermit prompt with a message like "communications disconnect". If you have used a "fakeout" cable (like Model A in the figure), Kermit does not notice, and the connection remains open.

○ ○ ○ ○

The rest of this chapter tells how to make dialed and network connections. If you will not be making dialed connections, but you will be making network connections, turn to page 67 in this chapter. If you will not be making dialed or network connections, turn to Chapter 4 to learn how to make a terminal connection.

Dialed Serial Connections

When you can't connect two computers with a direct cable (or with a network), you can do it with modems and the telephone system, as illustrated in Figure 3-5. With C-Kermit and an appropriate modem, your computer can call any computer or data service in the world that accepts modem calls and has a modem compatible with yours. C-Kermit sends dialing commands to the modem, the modem places the call and tells Kermit whether it was answered, and Kermit tells you whether the call was placed successfully.

Let's demonstrate the simple steps that should work in most situations. Find out what kind of modem you will be dialing with, the name of the communication device it is attached to, the phone number of the computer or service you will be dialing, and the speed at which its modem answers calls (you should dial at the same speed). Follow this example, substituting your own particulars for the ones shown, but issue the given commands in exactly this order:[10]

```
C-Kermit>set modem telebit      (Identify the modem type)
C-Kermit>set line /dev/cua      (Identify the communication device)
C-Kermit>set speed 2400         (Select the dialing speed)
C-Kermit>dial 93,1-800-555-1234 (Dial the phone number)
```

REMEMBER: SET MODEM first, SET LINE second, SET SPEED third, and then DIAL.

NOTE: A different technique is used for dialing a modem that is connected to a TCP/IP modem server. It is described on p. 74 in the network section of this chapter.

The SET MODEM Command

The SET MODEM command lets you tell C-Kermit whether you will be using a modem, and if so, which dialing language it uses.

SET MODEM [*type*=NONE]

If you are dialing out with an autodial modem, you must specify which type of modem is to be used so Kermit will know what kinds of commands to give it and how to read its responses. You must give the SET MODEM command *before* you open the communication device so the operating system doesn't block waiting for the CD signal when trying to open the device.

There are three categories of modem types:

NONE (or DIRECT)

This is the default modem type. Use NONE when there is no modem and therefore no modem signals and no dialing, as on a directly wired connection, or to cancel a previously established modem type. Examples:

```
C-Kermit>set modem none         (Direct connection)
C-Kermit>set modem direct       (Same as above)
C-Kermit>set modem              (Same as above)
```

CCITT, HAYES, TELEBIT, ...

If you name a specific type of modem, Kermit uses its built-in knowledge of the dialing language and conventions for that modem when you issue a DIAL command, and it declares the connection complete or failed based upon responses from the modem.

---

[10] All telephone numbers shown in this book are fictitious unless noted otherwise.

Dialed Serial Connections 51

The modems known to C-Kermit are listed in Table 3-2. In case new modems have been added since this book was printed, type SET MODEM ? to see an up-to-date list, for example:

```
C-Kermit>set modem ?          (See what's available)
  attdtdm          attisn           attmodem      att7300
  ccitt-v25bis     cermetek         concord       df03-ac
  df100-series     df200-series     direct        gendatacomm
  hayes            Many more...
C-Kermit>set modem hayes      (Hayes Smartmodem)
```

IMPORTANT: The modem type is not necessarily the same as the modem brand. For example, if you have a Microcom modem that is configured to use the Hayes command set rather than the Microcom-specific command set, you should SET MODEM HAYES rather than SET MODEM MICROCOM. Most modern modems are (or can be configured to be) "Hayes compatible." So if your modem is not listed or if dialing with a non-Hayes modem does not work, try SET MODEM HAYES.

UNKNOWN

This means that there is a modem, but it is of a type unknown to C-Kermit (or to you). You must specify the modem's entire dialing sequence in C-Kermit's DIAL command. Modem signals are ignored while dialing, but Kermit, after dialing, waits for the CD signal to indicate the call was completed. Example:

```
C-Kermit>set modem unknown
C-Kermit>dial ATDT7654321
```

If your computer has a type of modem that is not directly supported by C-Kermit, you still have ways to dial:

1. SET MODEM UNKNOWN and specify the complete dialing string in your DIAL command.

2. Dial *manually*. SET CARRIER OFF, then CONNECT, then interact with the modem directly, typing the dialing commands and monitoring the result codes (see p. 65 for details).

3. Write a script program to dial your modem. Script programming is explained in Chapters 11–13.

4. If you are a C programmer, modify the module `ckudia.c` to include support for your modem (and send the code back to Columbia University).

Having selected a modem type, you can SET LINE and SET SPEED in the normal way. If the SET LINE command succeeds, the DTR signal of the computer's communication device is turned on to enable communication with the modem. If SET LINE fails, you'll get an informative error message (see page 43 for a list of them). Set the communication speed to the highest speed supported by both modems, and select RTS/CTS hardware flow control if it is available, as in the example on page 54.

Table 3-2 Modem Types Known to C-Kermit

Name	Description
ATTDTDM	AT&T Digital Terminal Data Module
ATTISN	AT&T ISN Network
ATTMODEM	AT&T switched network modems
ATT7300	AT&T 7300 UNIX PC (3B1) internal modem
CCITT	CCITT V.25*bis*-compliant modem
CERMETEK	Cermetek Info-Mate 212A
CONCORD	Concord Condor CDS 220 2400b
DF03-AC	DEC DF03-AC
DF100-SERIES	DEC DF100 Series
DF200-SERIES	DEC DF200 Series
DIGITEL-DT22	Digitel DT-22 (Brazil)
DIRECT	No modem at all, direct connection (= NONE)
GENDATACOMM	General Datacomm 212A/ED
HAYES	Hayes Smartmodem 1200, 2400, 9600, compatible, or Rolm 244PC
HST-COURIER	Courier10PitchBT-Roman HST modems
MICROCOM	Microcom modems in native (SX) mode
NONE	No modem at all, direct connection (= DIRECT)
PENRIL	Penril modems
PEP-TELEBIT	Telebit modem insisting on PEP protocol
RACALVADIC	Racal Vadic (Racal Milgo) modems
ROLM	IBM/Rolm 8000, 9000, or 9751 CBX DCM
SLOW-TELEBIT	Telebit modem with PEP, MNP, etc, disabled
TELEBIT	Telebit modem allowing PEP, Bell, or CCITT protocols
UNKNOWN	Unknown (generic) modem type
USROBOTICS-212A	US Robotics 212A
V32-TELEBIT	Telebit dialing in V.32 mode
V42-TELEBIT	Telebit dialing in V.42 mode
VENTEL	Ventel modems

```
C-Kermit>set modem telebit     (Modem type)
C-Kermit>set line /dev/cua     (Device)
C-Kermit>set speed 38400       (Speed)
C-Kermit>set flow rts/cts      (Flow control)
```

The DIAL and REDIAL Commands

At last, you are ready to dial. C-Kermit's DIAL command dials the given number, and the REDIAL command dials the previous number again.

DIAL *dial-string*

Dials the given telephone number using C-Kermit's built-in method for operating the type of modem you identified in your last SET MODEM command. If a particular modem type is set, just include the phone number and C-Kermit issues the appropriate dialing instructions and reads the responses:

```
C-Kermit>dial 7654321
```

If no modem type is set, this command gives an error message ("Sorry, you must SET MODEM first"). If the modem type is UNKNOWN, you must include the modem's dialing command in the phone number, for example:

```
C-Kermit>dial at&c1dp7654321
```

The *dial-string* is a telephone number or access code expressed in the syntax of your telephone system or PBX, possibly with other characters added that are meaningful to the modem. Example:

```
C-Kermit>dial T 93,1 (212) 555-4321
```

In this example, the modem is a Hayes or compatible, which ignores parentheses, spaces, and hyphens, so these may be included for clarity. The T tells the Hayes modem to use Tone dialing,[11] 93 is a PBX code to get an outside line, the comma is a Hayes command to allow time for the secondary dialtone to appear, and the 1 requests a long distance call (in the North American dialing region). Consult Table II-2 on page 366 for details about the special characters allowed in Hayes modem dial strings, or read your modem manual.

REDIAL

Dial the number specified in your most recent DIAL command again. Example:

```
C-Kermit>dial 7654321          (Dial the number)
Failed ("BUSY")                (Get a busy signal)
C-Kermit>redial                (A few minutes later...)
```

Repeat as needed.

---

[11]Rather than Pulse dialing. C-Kermit does not tell Hayes modems which type of dialing to use, but instead lets the modem dial using its normal dialing method. You only need to insert a T or P here to override the modem's normal behavior, or for Hayes-like devices that actually *require* the T or P in the dialing command, such as the Rolm 244PC.

A DIAL Example

Here is an example of normal, problem-free, straightforward dialing, using a Hayes modem attached to a UNIX computer's `ttyh4` device:

```
C-Kermit>set modem hayes              (Set the modem type)
C-Kermit>set line /dev/ttyh4          (Then open the serial device)
C-Kermit>set speed 2400               (Set the speed for dialing)
C-Kermit>dial 765-4321                (Dial the number)
 Dialing 765-4321
 Device=/dev/ttyh4, modem=hayes, speed=2400
 The timeout for completing the call is 64 seconds.
 To cancel: type your interrupt character (normally Ctrl-C).
 Call completed.
C-Kermit>
```

The Dialing Directory

If you don't want to remember (or type) lots of long telephone numbers, you can store your frequently called numbers in a *dialing directory*, a plain-text file containing entries of the form:

name   number   speed   parity   comments

Create the dialing directory file using your system's CREATE command, or a text editor or word processor (be sure to save it in ASCII or plain-text format).

To use the dialing directory, first tell C-Kermit the name of your dialing directory file:

SET DIAL DIRECTORY *[filename]*

Specifies the name of the dialing directory file. If C-Kermit can find the file and has read access to it, it is opened and kept open until you EXIT from C-Kermit or give a subsequent SET DIAL DIRECTORY command. If the *filename* is omitted, any currently open dialing directory file is closed. Examples:

```
C-Kermit>set dial directory ~/.kdd        (UNIX or OS/9)
C-Kermit>set dial dir c:/ckermit/ckermit.kdd  (OS/2)
C-Kermit>set dial dir ckermit.kdd         (Current directory)
C-Kermit>set dial dir                     (Close directory file)
```

Now, whenever you give a DIAL command, C-Kermit tries to match your *dial-string* with a *name* in the file. When there is a match, the associated *number* is substituted and your SPEED and PARITY settings are changed automatically if they are specified in the dialing directory entry. If the *dial-string* is not found in the directory, it is used exactly as given.

The dialing directory fields are separated by one or more spaces or tabs. A field can include spaces if it is surrounded by curly braces. Trailing fields after the *number* field can be omitted, in which case the corresponding settings are not changed. The comments, of course, are optional. You can put an = sign in a particular speed or parity field to leave it unchanged. This format is compatible with the MS-DOS Kermit dialing directory. Here is a sample (all numbers are fictitious except the DIGITAL Store):

```
sprintnet   7654321        2400   mark   
oofanet     6543210        1200   odd    This entry has a comment
tymnet      93,876-5432    2400   even   Punctuation allowed
decstore    1-800-2341998  2400   none   The DIGITAL Store
hometone    T5551212       1200   none   T forces Hayes tone dialing
homepulse   P5551212       1200   none   P forces Hayes pulse dialing
home        5551212        1200   none   Default dialing method
anyspeed    999-9999       =      none   Use current speed
anyparity   888-8888       9600   =      Use current parity
whocares    777-7777       =      =      Use current speed and parity
{my sun}    {987 6543}     2400   none   With word grouping
defaults    987-6543
```

Words may be entered in the directory, and in the DIAL command itself, in any combination of uppercase and lowercase.

You can abbreviate the name in your DIAL command; C-Kermit searches for an exact (but case-independent) match, and uses it if found. Otherwise, the directory is searched from top to bottom and the first entry that matches your abbreviation is used. So for example, DIAL D would dial the DIGITAL Store, DIAL H would dial the HOMETONE number, and DIAL HOME would dial the HOME number. Assuming the file is called CKERMIT.KDD (KDD means Kermit Dialing Directory), and it is in the current directory, it can be used like this:

```
C-Kermit>set dial dir ckermit.kdd    (Specify the directory file)
C-Kermit>dial hometone               (Use name instead of number)
C-Kermit>dial HOMETONE               (Case doesn't matter)
C-Kermit>dial sprint                 (Abbreviations are OK)
C-Kermit>dial my sun                 (A two-word entry)
C-Kermit>dial 8765432                (A number not in the directory)
```

If you have a dialing directory file, you can put a SET DIAL DIRECTORY command for it in your C-Kermit initialization file so you don't have to type this command every time you run C-Kermit, for example:[12]

```
set dial directory \v(home)ckermit.kdd
```

The notation \v(home) means "my home directory." It is explained in Chapter 11, but there is no need to read ahead—just use it. It lets C-Kermit find your dialing directory file, no matter what your current directory is. Of course, you can also give a system-specific file specification, and you can use different filenames:

```
set dial directory ~olga/.kdd
set dial directory /usr/olga/my-dialing-directory
set dial directory $disk1:[olga]ckermit.kdd
set dial directory :udd:olga:olga.kdd
```

---

[12]The standard C-Kermit initialization file already includes a command like this.

but then your initialization file won't be portable among UNIX, VMS, OpenVMS, AOS/VS, OS/2, and so on.

C-Kermit also supports a more sophisticated *services directory*, which not only dials a particular number, but also logs you in to the host or service of your choice automatically. The services directory is explained in Chapters 11 through 13.

The Finer Points of Dialing

○ ○ ○ ○

If dialing works for you with what you have learned so far, there is no need to read anything further about serial connections. Skip ahead to Network Connections on page 67 (if you plan to use them), or go directly to Chapter 4 to learn about terminal connection.

When you encounter problems with dialing, C-Kermit has some commands that can help you diagnose and overcome them. Use the SHOW DIAL command first. It gives you a quick summary of all the settings that are likely to affect dialing, including the current LINE, MODEM, and SPEED values:

```
C-Kermit>set modem telebit      (First select a modem type)
C-Kermit>set line /dev/cua      (Then a serial device)
C-Kermit>set speed 2400         (Then the speed)
C-Kermit>show dial              (Now let's take a look...)
 Line: /dev/cua, modem: telebit, speed: 2400
 Dial directory: (none)
 Dial hangup: on, dial timeout: auto
 Dial kermit-spoof: off, dial display: on
 Dial speed-matching: off, dial mnp-enable: off
 Dial init-string: ATF1M1Q4X3S2=43\{13}
 Redial number: none
 Carrier: auto
/dev/ttyh8 modem signals:
 Carrier Detect      (CD):  Off
 Dataset Ready       (DSR): On
 Clear To Send       (CTS): On
 Ring Indicator      (RI):  Off
 Data Terminal Ready (DTR): On
 Request to Send     (RTS): On
C-Kermit>
```

This is the first place to look for something obviously wrong: wrong line, wrong speed, wrong modem type. If any of these are incorrect, use SET commands to fix them and try dialing again (hint: use the REDIAL command).

If dialing still doesn't work, we'll have to dig deeper. The next command to use is SET DIAL DISPLAY ON. It doesn't fix anything, but it lets you watch what goes on between Kermit and the modem and might give you an idea of what needs to be changed.

SET DIAL DISPLAY *[{ OFF, ON }]*
> Tells whether C-Kermit should display its dialog with the modem on your screen during the dialing process. Normally DIAL DISPLAY is OFF. When it is ON, you can watch Kermit's commands to the modem and the modem's responses, except that characters ignored by C-Kermit are not displayed.

Let's continue our example with the Telebit modem. We have already SET MODEM, SET LINE, and SET SPEED. Now let's watch a successful DIAL command in action:

```
C-Kermit>set dial display on      (Watch dialing actions)
C-Kermit>dial T741-8100           (Dial the number)
 Dialing T741-8100
 Device=/dev/cua, modem=telebit, speed=2400
 The timeout for completing the call is 69 seconds.
 To cancel: type your interrupt character (normally Ctrl-C).
 Hangup OK
ATF1M1Q4X3S2=43                              (Kermit sends)
OK                                           (Modem responds)
ATS48=1 S51=255 S52=2 S54=2 ATS7=69 S58=0    (Kermit sends)
OK                                           (Modem responds)
S55=0 S66=0 S68=255 S95=0 ATS50=0 S110=0     (Kermit sends)
OK                                           (Modem responds)
ATDT741-8100                                 (Kermit sends)
CONNECT 1200                                 (Modem responds)
 Speed changed to 1200                       (Kermit message)
 Call completed.                             (Kermit message)
C-Kermit>                                    (Prompt returns)
```

There are many items of interest here, each of which can affect the success of the DIAL command. Kermit tells us that it will allow 69 seconds for the call to be completed. If the modem has not responded by that time, Kermit closes the call and gives an error message: Timed out. What if more time is needed?

SET DIAL TIMEOUT *number*
> When you give a DIAL command, C-Kermit waits a certain number of seconds for a report from the modem telling whether the call succeeded or failed. The time limit is computed automatically based on the communication speed, the length of the phone number, the type of modem, and other factors. In some cases, the timeout might not be long enough, for example for an international call or for an advanced type of modem that must go through protracted negotiations with a different type of remote modem. Use this command to make Kermit skip its dial timeout calculation and use your value instead. Example:
>
> ```
> C-Kermit>set dial timeout 200    (200 seconds)
> ```

When you have SET MODEM to HAYES or one of the TELEBIT models, C-Kermit also sets modem switch S7 (see Table II-2 on page 366) correspondingly, so the modem waits at least as long as C-Kermit does for the call to be completed.

The message "Hangup OK" means that Kermit hung up the phone connection as a first step. This ensures that the modem is in command mode rather than online mode from a previous connection; otherwise, the modem might totally ignore Kermit's dialing commands. Unfortunately, this seemingly proper and innocent measure can sometimes result in unwanted problems caused by improper configuration or wiring, or by the inability of the underlying operating system to handle the hangup request correctly, in which case you will see a "Hangup failed" message, or worse. Here are two commands to work around such situations:

SET DIAL HANGUP *[{ OFF, ON }]*
> Tells Kermit whether to hang up the phone at the beginning of the dialing process. Use SET DIAL HANGUP OFF only if you get hangup-related error messages during the DIAL command or if dialing doesn't work with DIAL HANGUP ON.

SET DIAL MODEM-HANGUP *[{ OFF, ON }]*
> Applies only when DIAL HANGUP is ON. When MODEM-HANGUP is OFF, C-Kermit uses the "hardware" method of hanging up, namely turning off the DTR signal to the modem for about half a second. Experience has shown that this often fails to achieve the desired effect, so SET MODEM-HANGUP ON tells C-Kermit to try hanging up by using a modem-specific command (such as Hayes ATH0), and turning off DTR only if a confirmation (such as OK) fails to appear from the modem. MODEM-HANGUP is ON by default.

Back to our Telebit dialing example. The lines beginning with `AT` are commands from Kermit to the modem. Space does not permit describing what they do, but if you have a Telebit modem manual you can look them up. The `OK` and `CONNECT` lines are responses from the modem to Kermit.

`ATF1M1Q4X3S2=43` is the *initialization string* sent by Kermit to the modem; it puts the modem in the command and response modes that Kermit needs to control it (this command contains mostly Hayes-like options that you can look up in Table II-2 on p. 366). It is sometimes possible to overcome dialing difficulties by changing the initialization string. Here's how:

SET DIAL INIT-STRING *[text]*
> C-Kermit's DIAL command sends a preprogrammed sequence of characters to your modem to initialize it. Each of Kermit's modem types has its own initialization string. You can use this command to substitute your own initialization string, such as `ATZ\13` or `AT&F&D3\13` or `ATS0=1\13`. This command is particularly useful for forcing your modem to dial using certain modulation, error-correction, or compression techniques. See your modem manual. The *text* can be any reasonable length, and it can include imbedded carriage returns or other characters encoded in backslash notation (such as \13 for carriage return), so it can even contain more than one modem command. It

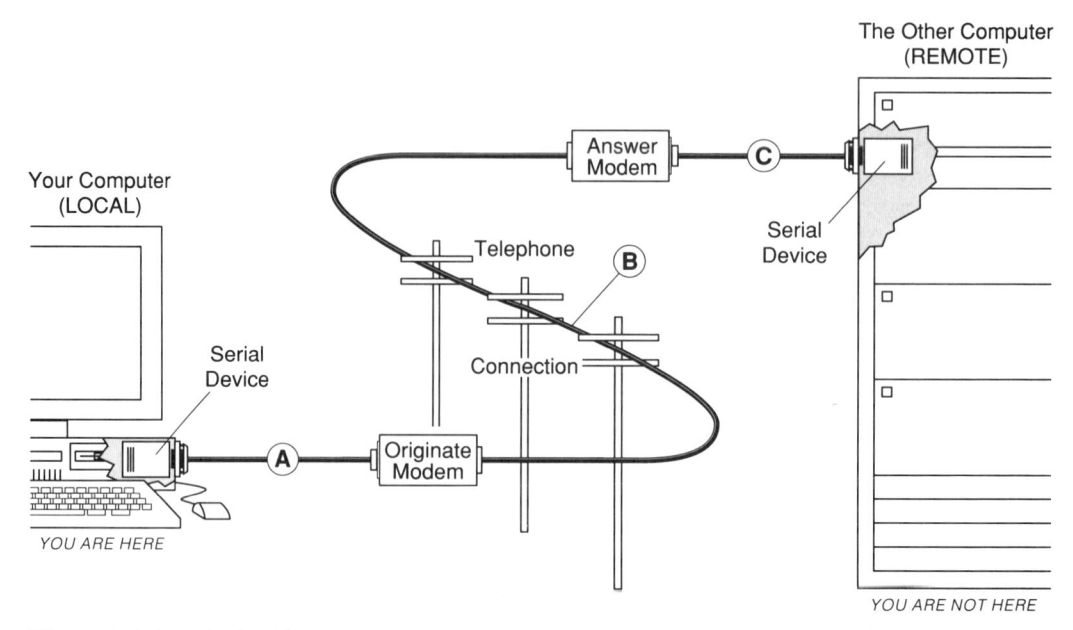

Figure 3-6 Speed Matching

should normally end with \13. If you give the SET DIAL INIT-STRING command without any *text*, Kermit's default initialization string is restored.

Use the SET DIAL INIT-STRING command with caution. Mistakes can put your modem into undesired and disreputable modes. If you are doing this to a modem that other people use, you should make sure to put it back in its normal state when you are finished using it (hint: read about the ON_EXIT macro in Chapter 11).

In the next few lines of our example, Kermit sets numerous "S-Registers" in the Telebit modem. These are simply SET commands expressed in the modem's own language. This modem has many options (maybe even more than Kermit!); see your modem manual. Finally, Kermit dials the number:

```
ATDT741-8100
```

The modem response, CONNECT 1200, tells Kermit that the remote modem answered the call, but at a lower speed than the one we dialed at. Kermit noticed this and changed its own transmission speed to 1200 by doing a SET SPEED 1200 command internally, and informed you with a message, "Speed changed to 1200." Very nice!

Or maybe not so nice. Hayes 1200, higher-model Hayes modems, and compatibles report the speed of the connection (labeled B in Figure 3-6) between themselves and the other modem in their CONNECT messages. But this does not necessarily mean that the interface speed between the modem and C-Kermit (A in the figure) also changed. Some newer-model modems have a feature called *speed matching*, which keeps the interface speed (A) constant when the connection speed (B) changes. Unfortunately, speed-matching modems might report the *connection* speed (B) in the CONNECT message, rather than the *interface* speed (A). How does Kermit know how to react to the speed given in the modem's CONNECT message? You must tell it:

SET DIAL SPEED-MATCHING *[{ OFF, ON }=OFF]*
   This command tells C-Kermit whether to believe the connection speed reported by your modem. The default setting is ON, which tells Kermit to believe it and to adjust its interface speed according to the modem's CONNECT report. SET DIAL SPEED-MATCHING OFF tells C-Kermit that the modem's interface speed is locked, so C-Kermit should ignore the CONNECT speed reported by the modem. See your modem manual for further information about speed matching. As of this writing, the SET DIAL SPEED-MATCHING command works only for Hayes and Telebit modem types.

More Dialing Controls

The SET DIAL INIT-STRING command gives you a way to override C-Kermit's built-in modem initialization and setup. However, it is sometimes necessary to change other dialing actions too.

SET DIAL DIAL-COMMAND *[text]*
   Overrides C-Kermit's built-in modem dialing command. For example, the default dialing command for Hayes and compatible modems is ATD followed by the phone number. You can use SET DIAL DIAL-COMMAND, for example, to add a T to force Tone dialing (or a P to force Pulse dialing), so you don't have to put modem-specific codes in your dialing directory. The *text* must contain the characters %s, which C-Kermit's DIAL command replaces by the telephone number. Example:

   ```
   C-Kermit>set dial dial-command ATDT%s\13
   C-Kermit>dial 7654321
   ```

   This results in ATDT7654321 followed by carriage return (\13). Of course, you can also use this command to alter the modem-dialing command in any other way. If you omit the *text* from this command, C-Kermit's built-in dialing method is restored.

SET DIAL PREFIX *[text]*
   Tells C-Kermit to add the given *text* as a prefix to any telephone number before dialing; for example, as an area code or an access prefix to get an outside line from a PBX. This allows your dialing directory file to be independent of where you are dialing from. Here is an example that shows how to use your dial directory to dial out from a PBX that needs a 93 prefix for outside calls:

   ```
   C-Kermit>set dial prefix 93
   C-Kermit>dial decstore
   ```

Dialed Serial Connections   61

Multi-Stage Dialing

When placing long-distance modem calls, it is sometimes necessary to dial two numbers: one to place the desired call and the other to gain access to a long-distance carrier service or charge the call to another phone.

When performing such operations with C-Kermit's DIAL command, you must accomplish all phases of the call in a single DIAL command. You can't use more than one DIAL command, because the first one will fail when carrier fails to appear, and the connection will be dropped. Multi-stage dialing usually can be accomplished by including special codes in the telephone number for interpretation by your modem. For example, Hayes modems allow codes to pause, to wait for ringing to stop, to wait for dialtone, to perform a hook flash, and so on (see Table II-2 on page 366, or your modem manual).

However, multi-stage dialing will often take longer than Kermit's (or even the modem's) time limit on waiting for carrier. So you might also have to use the SET DIAL TIMEOUT command to increase the limit. Here's an example in which a long-distance call is placed using a calling-card number:

```
C-Kermit>set modem hayes
C-Kermit>set line /dev/cua
C-Kermit>set speed 2400
C-Kermit>set dial timeout 75
C-Kermit>dial *70-0212-555-1234,,,,,,,,000 000 0000 0000
```

In this example, each comma pauses two seconds, enough time for the long-distance service provider to become ready to receive the calling-card number (shown as all zeros). Do not put calling-card numbers in your dialing directory. If anybody else gains access to your dialing directory file, they can learn your calling-card number and use it to charge calls to your account.

Special Modem Features

Kermit's SET DIAL command also lets you turn special features of your modem on and off without having to know the cryptic modem commands.

SET DIAL KERMIT-SPOOF [{ OFF, ON }=ON]

Certain modems made by Telebit, US Robotics, and perhaps others include a "Kermit spoof." The modem itself executes the Kermit file transfer protocol. C-Kermit thinks it is transferring a file with the remote computer, but really it is exchanging Kermit packets with your local modem. The modem uses its own internal protocol to send the data to the remote modem, which in turn uses a Kermit spoof to transfer the data to the remote computer. If your modem has this feature, you can SET KERMIT-SPOOF ON to enable it and SET KERMIT-SPOOF OFF to disable it. You should use the Kermit spoof if it results in better performance and you should turn it off if file transfer is faster without it. This setting is OFF by default.

SET DIAL MNP-ENABLE *[{ OFF, ON }=ON]*

Many modern modems include a feature called Microcom Networking Protocol, or MNP. It comes in various levels; 1 through 4 for error correction, 5 for compression, and others. When both modems support MNP, the highest level they share in common is typically used. Question: How does an MNP modem know whether to use its MNP features, and at what level? Answer: It "negotiates" with the other modem.

Problem: when the calling modem supports MNP but the called modem does not, the MNP negotiation material sent by the called modem passes through the called modem to the remote computer or service. The remote computer might mistake this data for your user ID. In the worst case, the remote device is waiting for you to type a particular character, such as carriage return, for speed recognition. When it receives the MNP negotiation burst instead, it picks the wrong speed and you can't communicate at all even though you have a connection.

Solution: SET DIAL MNP-ENABLE OFF. If C-Kermit knows how to disable your modem's MNP feature, this command will do it. If not, look in your modem manual to find the appropriate command and use SET DIAL INIT-STRING to redefine your modem's initialization command to include it.

More DIAL Examples

REMEMBER: when dialing out, you must specify a modem type, a communication device, and a speed *in that order*. Then dial the number using Kermit's DIAL command. Here is an example showing how to use SET DIAL HANGUP OFF to get around system errors that occur when Kermit tries to hang up the phone in preparation for dialing:

```
C-Kermit>set modem microcom              (Set the modem type)
C-Kermit>set line /dev/ttyh9             (Open the tty device)
C-Kermit>set speed 2400                  (Set desired speed)
C-Kermit>dial 7654321                    (Try to dial)
Sorry, can't hang up communication device: device or data error
C-Kermit>set dial hangup off             (Let's try again)
C-Kermit>set line /dev/ttyh9             (Close and reopen the device)
C-Kermit>set speed 2400                  (Set speed again)
C-Kermit>redial                          (Dial again)
Call completed.
C-Kermit>
```

Here is an example of using the UNKNOWN modem type, in which you must supply the entire modem dialing sequence, shown using a Hayes modem for illustrative purposes:

```
C-Kermit>set modem unknown               (Specify generic modem dialing)
C-Kermit>set line /dev/ttyh9             (Open the device)
C-Kermit>set speed 2400                  (Set the speed)
C-Kermit>dial ATDT7654321                (Dial)
Call completed.
C-Kermit>
```

Note that Kermit supplies a carriage return at the end of the dial string. When the modem type is UNKNOWN, Kermit waits for carrier to appear from the modem if the modem, cable, and operating system cooperate to pass this information along to Kermit; if not, the DIAL command times out and you get an error message.

Here is an example in which we place an international call that takes a long time to answer, using a Telebit modem that does speed matching and that has a Kermit spoof:

```
C-Kermit>set modem pep-telebit        (Select modem type)
C-Kermit>set dial speed-match off     (Ignore modem's speed reports)
C-Kermit>set dial kermit-spoof on     (Use modem's Kermit spoof)
C-Kermit>set dial timeout 150         (Wait this long for an answer)
C-Kermit>set line txa5:               (Select communication port)
C-Kermit>set speed 19200              (Specify the speed)
C-Kermit>dial t0,05,11,765-4321       (Tone-dial the number)
Dialing t0,05,11,765-4321
 Device=_TXA5:, modem=pep-telebit, speed=19200
 The timeout for completing the call is 150 seconds.
 To cancel: type your interrupt character (normally Ctrl-C).
 Call completed.
C-Kermit>
```

In the next example we use C-Kermit to dial from the modem pool of a Rolm Computerized Branch Exchange (CBX) to the DEC Store, whose number is in our dialing directory. We enjoy watching the progress of the dialing operation so we SET DIAL DISPLAY ON.

```
C-Kermit>set dial dir ckermit.kdd     (Dial directory)
C-Kermit>set modem rolm               (Modem type first)
C-Kermit>set line txa4:               (Then communication line)
C-Kermit>set speed 1200               (Then speed)
C-Kermit>set dial display on          (Watch what's happening)
C-Kermit>set dial prefix 93           (Prefix for outside line)
C-Kermit>dial decstore                (Dial the number)
Dialing 931-800-2341998
 Device=_TXA4:, modem=rolm, speed=2400
 The timeout for completing the call is 54 seconds.
 To cancel: type your interrupt character (normally Ctrl-C).
 Hangup OK
TYPE "CALL HELP" +SEVERAL RETURNS FOR INFO   (Messages from CBX...)

CALL, DISPLAY OR MODIFY? CALL 931-800-2341998
CALLING 931-800-2341998. MODEM 77274.
CALL COMPLETE
 Call completed.                      (Kermit's message)
C-Kermit>
```

The dial display lets us see the CBX modem number, an essential item when reporting failures to the modem pool administrators.

Manual Dialing

You can also dial a modem by hand. This might be necessary if you have a type of modem that C-Kermit doesn't know about or if you want to talk to the modem directly for any other reason, for example to change or query its configuration. Here is an example, using a Hayes modem:

```
C-Kermit>set carrier off        (Ignore the carrier signal)
C-Kermit>set modem none         (Pretend there is no modem)
C-Kermit>set line /dev/cua      (Select communication device)
C-Kermit>set speed 2400         (Set the communication speed)
C-Kermit>connect                (Begin terminal connection)
Connecting to /dev/cua, speed 2400.
The escape character is Ctrl-\ (ASCII 28, FS).
Type the escape character followed by C to get back,
or followed by ? to see other options.
+++                             (Get the modem's attention)
OK                              (Modem responds OK)
ATDT7654321                     (Type the dialing command)
CONNECT 2400                    (Modem confirms the connection)

  (Conduct a session with the remote computer or service)

Ctrl-\C                         (Escape back to the prompt)
C-Kermit>
```

Troubleshooting Dialed Connections

For communication to work in general, and Kermit's DIAL command to work at all, you have to ensure proper setup and configuration of Kermit, your computer, the modem, the modem cable, and the telephone line. And it doesn't hurt if all the stars and planets are in perfect alignment too. If you can't seem to complete a dialed call, follow these seventeen easy steps:

1. Make sure your modem is turned on and connected to the phone line.

2. Make sure your modem is connected to your computer with a straight-through modem cable (not with a null modem cable, see Appendix II), and that the cable has not wiggled loose at one or both ends.

3. Make sure your modem cable conveys (has wires for) all the necessary signals, including SG, TD, RD, DSR, RTS, CTS, CD, and DTR (see Appendix II).

4. Make sure the wires in the cable and the pins in the connector are not broken and that the pins are all sticking straight out.

5. Make sure Kermit's CARRIER setting agrees with your modem's configuration. SET CARRIER OFF if necessary. The recommended configuration for the modem is to assert carrier only while it is successfully engaged with the other modem and to hang up the phone connection if your computer's DTR signal goes down. Read your modem

Dialed Serial Connections 65

manual to find out how to configure the modem this way. If it can be done with commands from the computer, you can use Kermit's SET DIAL INIT-STRING command or you can CONNECT to the modem and do it by hand. In some cases, it might be necessary to change some (physical) switch settings—see your modem manual.

6. Make sure your modem supports at least one modulation technique (Bell 103, Bell 212, CCITT V.22, V.32, V.32*bis*, Telebit PEP, etc.) in common with the modem you are calling.

7. Make sure you have SET SPEED to a speed supported by both the local (calling) and remote (called) modems.

8. Make sure your DIAL settings, especially SPEED-MATCHING, correspond with your modem's configuration. Increase the DIAL TIMEOUT if necessary.

9. The hangup operation might be causing problems. Try SET DIAL MODEM-HANGUP OFF or SET DIAL HANGUP OFF before dialing.

10. Make sure you give the appropriate SET MODEM command *first*, then a SET LINE command for the device the modem is actually connected to, and then a SET SPEED command for a speed that your modem's dialer can handle. These commands must be given in the proper order.

11. Make sure your modem's escape sequence is not a character or sequence that you would need to send to the remote computer during terminal emulation or that Kermit would send in a file transfer packet. The default Hayes sequence, for example, is safe: +++ preceded and followed by at least one full second of silence. Other modems have been known to use unsafe sequences like a single Ctrl-A (which happens to be Kermit's start-of-packet character) without any guard time; in cases like this, change your modem's escape character or disable it entirely (or change Kermit's start-of-packet character; see Chapter 6).

12. If your modem has MNP or other error-correcting or compression protocols enabled, try turning them off. In particular, MNP modems send characters to each other *after* carrier has been established to negotiate protocol level and features. These characters can interfere with the remote host's speed detection or login procedures if the answering modem doesn't support MNP. In general, take your modem down to its least sophisticated level and work up from there one feature at a time.

13. Read your modem manual. Perhaps there are modem-specific characters you can insert in the dialing string to help the process along. For example, Hayes 2400 Smartmodems allow W (wait for dialtone), @ (wait for silence), comma (pause), and so forth. Make sure your modem's carrier wait time is not too short, that it is set for originate mode, and so forth.

14. On the other hand, maybe you inserted spacing or punctuation into your phone number that is not permitted by your modem. Try reissuing the DIAL command without the spacing and punctuation.

15. As a semifinal resort, study your modem manual carefully to learn how to control its selection of modulation technique, error correction, and compression, and its fallback schemes for each. Experiment with different combinations of settings until you find one that works.

16. If all else fails, SET CARRIER OFF, CONNECT to the modem, and try to dial manually by typing dialing commands in the modem's own syntax directly at it (see your modem manual). If this doesn't work, check your modem's configuration and then repeat the previous steps.

17. As a last resort, try configuring your modem to ignore DTR and always assert carrier. Read your modem manual to find out how to do this.

Using Network Connections

○ ○ ○ ○
If your computer is not on a TCP/IP or X.25 network, please feel free to skip ahead to Chapter 4 to learn how to make and use a C-Kermit terminal connection to a remote computer.

C-Kermit can be used in two ways in a computer network. You can use a network to access C-Kermit on a remote host and transfer files or you can have C-Kermit establish network connections itself. C-Kermit has certain advantages over other network virtual terminal and file transfer software:

- The Kermit file transfer protocol can be more flexible than network file transfer. Kermit can be more adept at converting text files into useful form when transferring them between unlike computers. In particular, Kermit is probably unique in its ability to translate national and international character sets during file transfer (Chapter 9).

- C-Kermit's terminal connection includes features not found in most network virtual terminal programs, including character-set translation, key mapping, session logging, and support for Shift-In/Shift-Out for transmitting 8-bit characters across 7-bit connections (Chapters 4 and 9).

- Kermit's built-in script programming language can be used to automate network file transfers and to set up unattended or repeated operations (Chapters 11–13).

- Kermit's logging facilities can be used in combination with its script programming language for network monitoring and reporting.

Remote Mode

Using C-Kermit in remote mode over a network connection is just like using C-Kermit in remote mode over a direct or dialed serial connection, except that you establish the connection from your local Kermit program by using a networking communication method rather than a serial one. The following example uses MS-DOS Kermit 3.11 or later and assumes all the necessary SET TCP/IP information has already been supplied:

```
MS-Kermit>set port tcp/ip 128.59.39.2
MS-Kermit>connect
```

In this case, the SET PORT TCP/IP command takes the place of SET PORT COM1 (or COM2, etc.) and DIAL. Once the connection is made, you can conduct a terminal session and transfer files in the normal manner.

Local Mode

Setting up a network connection from C-Kermit to another network host is similar to setting up a dialed connection, but with different commands. C-Kermit presently supports several network types, TCP/IP [17], X.25 [11], and DECnet.[13] The SET MODEM, SET CARRIER, SET SPEED, SET DIAL, and DIAL commands have no effect on network connections. The only commands needed to set up a network connection are:

SET NETWORK { TCP/IP, X.25, DECNET }

This command tells C-Kermit which type of network to use. This is analogous to the SET MODEM command that is used on dialed serial connections to tell Kermit which kind of modem to use. The available network types depend on your computer and operating system and, of course, whether your computer is attached to a network at all:

```
C-Kermit>set network ? One of the following:
 tcp/ip      x.25
C-Kermit>set network tcp
```

If you give a SET HOST command without a prior SET NETWORK command, a TCP/IP network is assumed, if it is supported.

SHOW NETWORK

This command shows the types of network connections and protocols available, plus information about the currently active network connection, if any:

```
C-Kermit>sho net
Supported networks:
 X.25
 TCP/IP, TELNET protocol
```

---

[13] As of this writing, TCP/IP support is available in the AOS/VS II version as well as in selected VMS, OpenVMS, and UNIX versions. X.25 support is currently available only for Sun computers equipped with the SunLink X.25 product. DECnet support is available only for OS/2 systems equipped with DEC PATHWORKS.

```
SET TELNET parameters
 echo: local
 newline-mode: on
 terminal-type: vt100

Current network type:
 TCP/IP

Active SET HOST connection:
 None

C-Kermit>
```

SET HOST [*host*]

This command tells C-Kermit that you want to make a network connection rather than use a serial communication device, and it gives the name or address of the other computer you want to communicate with on the currently selected type of network. When you are making a network connection, use SET HOST instead of SET LINE and DIAL. The *host* is a network host name or number. If no host name is given, the currently open network connection (if any) is closed and Kermit reverts to its default communication device. The SET HOST command attempts to open a connection to the specified host immediately. If the connection cannot be established, an error message is printed.

HANGUP

When the current connection is via TCP/IP, X.25, or some other type of network, the HANGUP command closes the network connection.

TCP/IP Networks

TCP/IP network hosts address each other using a protocol called IP (Internet Protocol). Each computer on a TCP/IP network has a 32-bit IP address, written as four decimal numbers separated by periods, with each number between 0 and 255 (inclusive), for example:

`128.59.39.2`

The IP address is like the address on a letter; it lets an IP message travel through a complicated network to its destination.

People aren't particularly good at remembering long numbers, so IP hosts can also have names that stand for their numeric addresses. An IP hostname is usually a series of words separated by periods, for example:

`watsun.cc.columbia.edu`

The fields in the name don't have any particular relationship to the fields in the numeric address. The dotted fields represent a hierarchy from left to right, called a domain name. The example identifies the computer called "watsun" on the Computer Center (cc) network, which has many computers; at Columbia University (columbia), which has many local area networks; on the educational portion of the Internet (edu), which also includes many other educational institutions. The Internet has other major subdivisions besides "edu," including "com" for the commercial portion, "gov" for the government portion, "it" for the Italian portion, and so on.

Host names are translated to numeric IP addresses by network servers called domain name resolvers, or, more simply, name servers. The name server can be on your own computer, on some other computer on your network, or even on a distant computer outside your organization.

People tend to prefer short names to long ones. Therefore IP hosts can have nicknames, like "watsun" or "w" for `watsun.cc.columbia.edu`. Nicknames are generally valid only within an organization's local network and are translated to IP numbers by a local name server.

C-Kermit's SET HOST command accepts any of these forms. If you give a name, C-Kermit attempts to find a name server that will supply the corresponding address. If you give a numeric address, C-Kermit uses it directly, without attempting to contact a name server. Thus if you have trouble making a TCP/IP connection to a host by name, try its IP address instead if you know it. Here are some examples showing how to establish connections with the SET HOST command:

```
C-Kermit>set net tcp                         (Choose network type)
C-Kermit>set host ? IP host name or number,
 or carriage return to close an open connection
C-Kermit>set host watsun                     (Unknown nickname)
 Can't get address for watsun
C-Kermit>set host watsun.cc.columbia.edu     (Full domain name)
C-Kermit>set host 128.59.39.2                (IP address)
C-Kermit>set host                            (Close the connection)
 Closing Connection
C-Kermit>
```

You should use names rather than numbers when possible, because numbers can change without your knowledge. The name server, however, is supposed to have a current number for each name.

C-Kermit connects to the TELNET server (TCP port 23) on the remote host by default, but you can specify any desired TCP port or service after the IP host name or address:

SET HOST *host service*

or you can append it to the *host* field with a colon (no spaces):

SET HOST *host*:*service*

As with addresses, Kermit calls upon the operating system to translate a service name (like telnet) into a TCP port number. If you give a port number, it is used as is. Here are some examples:

```
C-Kermit>set host watsun                        (Default is port 23)
C-Kermit>set host watsun 23                     (Port 23 specified)
C-Kermit>set host 128.59.39.2 telnet            (TELNET is port 23)
C-Kermit>set host martini.eecs.umich.edu:3000   (Port 3000)
C-Kermit>set host 141.212.196.79 3000           (Port 3000)
C-Kermit>set host marvin.cs.buffalo.edu:2000    (Port 2000)
```

The SET HOST command displays the translation from IP host name to numeric IP address:

```
C-Kermit>set host marvin.cs.buffalo.edu:2000
 Trying 128.205.32.4...
```

and then tries to establish the connection. If the connection cannot be made, you will get an informative error message. Examples:

```
C-Kermit>set host 123.123.123.123
 Trying 123.123.123.123...
Sorry, can't open connection: Network is unreachable
C-Kermit>set host watsun foo
 Trying 128.59.39.2...
Sorry, can't open connection: Cannot find port for service foo
C-Kermit>set host watsun 2345
 Trying 128.59.39.2...
Sorry, can't open connection: Connection refused
```

The first message means either that there is no such IP address, or that the network implied by the IP address cannot be located or reached. The second message means that the TCP service-name database did not contain an entry for a service called *foo*. The last message indicates that there is no server on TCP port 2345 at host watsun.

Use the SHOW NETWORK command to display the name, address, service, network, and protocol of an active connection:

```
C-Kermit>sho net
Supported networks:
 X.25
 TCP/IP, TELNET protocol

SET TELNET parameters:
 echo: local
 newline-mode: on
 terminal-type: vt300

Current network type:
 TCP/IP

Active SET HOST connection:
 marvin.cs.buffalo.edu:3000 [128.205.32.4]
 Via: TCP/IP (sockets)
 TELNET protocol

C-Kermit>
```

The TELNET command combines the functions of SET NETWORK TCP/IP, SET HOST, and CONNECT (explained in Chapter 4) into one convenient command:

TELNET [*host* [*service*]]
> Opens a connection to the specified IP host on the designated TCP port (23 = TELNET by default). If successful, C-Kermit enters CONNECT mode automatically, otherwise it issues an appropriate error message and remains at the prompt. If a host is not specified, the currently active TCP/IP connection, if any, is resumed. Examples:
> ```
> C-Kermit>telnet ?  IP host name or number,
>  or carriage return to resume an open connection
> C-Kermit>telnet watsun ? TCP service name or number,
>  or carriage return for telnet (23)
> C-Kermit>telnet watsun 2000
> C-Kermit>telnet                    (Resume an open connection)
> ```

C-Kermit performs TELNET option negotiation protocol [51] automatically. These negotiations are used to inform the remote host of your terminal type and to determine which side does the echoing. If the TCP service port is TELNET (23), Kermit sends the initial negotiations. Otherwise, Kermit sends no TELNET negotiations, but is prepared to handle them if they should arrive from the remote host. Negotiations can take place at any time during the connection: in CONNECT mode (for example, to turn echoing off and on around password entry), during script program execution, and so on.

The SET TELNET command can be used to alter C-Kermit's initial TELNET configuration:

SET TELNET ECHO { REMOTE, LOCAL }
> In accordance with the TELNET Network Virtual Terminal specification [51], C-Kermit begins a TELNET connection in local-echo mode, meaning C-Kermit itself echoes the characters that you type on the keyboard. In the rare cases where this causes problems (for example with a remote server that does not properly follow the TELNET protocol), you can use this command to change C-Kermit's initial echoing state.

SET TELNET NEWLINE-MODE { ON, OFF }
> The TELNET specification also states that when you press the Return or Enter key, this should be transmitted to the TELNET server as a carriage-return and linefeed pair (CRLF). This is what C-Kermit does unless you give the command SET TELNET NEWLINE-MODE OFF, in which case C-Kermit sends the Return or Enter key as a carriage return followed by the null character. Use this command only if your TELNET session doesn't behave normally without it.

SET TELNET TERMINAL-TYPE *text*
> The remote TELNET server might request C-Kermit to send your local terminal type. Unless you say otherwise, C-Kermit sends what it believes your terminal type to be. In UNIX, VMS, and OpenVMS, for example, this is based on the value of the TERM

environment variable. But if the remote system does not support your terminal type or recognize its name, it won't be able to set your terminal type automatically. Use this command to tell C-Kermit the terminal name to use in TELNET negotiations. Example:

```
C-Kermit>set telnet term vt100
```

This command does not affect your local terminal type.

Here is an example showing how to use C-Kermit to connect from a TCP/IP host to the Internet Network Information Center (NIC), a source of information about the Internet.

```
$ kermit                                (Start Kermit)
C-Kermit 5A(188) 23 Nov 92, SunOS 4.1
Type ? or HELP for help
C-Kermit>telnet nic.ddn.mil             (Connect to host)
 Trying  192.112.36.5...
Connecting to host nic.ddn.mil:23
The escape character is Ctrl-\ (ASCII 28, FS).
Type the escape character followed by C to get back,
or followed by ? to see other options.

SunOS UNIX (nic.ddn.mil) (ttyp0)
*
* For TAC news, type:                            TACNEWS <return>
* For user and host information, type:  WHOIS <return>
* For NIC information, type:            NIC <return>
*
* Please report system problems to ACTION@NIC.DDN.MIL

NIC, SunOS Release 4.1.1 (NIC) #1:
Cmdinter Ver 1.2 Sun Jun  7 18:55:09 1992 EST

    (Have a session)

@logout
Communication disconnect (Back at Local System)
C-Kermit>exit                           (Leave Kermit)
$                                       (Back where we started)
```

Several special features are available for testing and managing your TCP/IP connection. At the C-Kermit prompt, you can use the PING command:

PING *[host]*

to send an IP message to see if the host is reachable and responsive. If a host is not specified, the message is sent to the current SET HOST or TELNET host. This command simply runs your system's PING command, so the response depends on your system:

```
C-Kermit>set host spacelink.msfc.nasa.gov
C-Kermit>ping
spacelink.msfc.nasa.gov is alive
C-Kermit>
```

The other special features are available as CONNECT-mode escape commands and are described in Chapter 4, but they are also listed here for completeness:

A   Send a TELNET "Are You There?" command.

B   Send a TELNET Break command.

I   Send a TELNET Interrupt Process command.

How to Dial Using a TCP/IP Modem Server

If your site maintains a pool of dialout modems on a "reverse terminal server" that is on your TCP/IP network, you can use C-Kermit to dial out by following these steps *in the order given:*

1. Give a SET HOST (not TELNET) command, specifying the IP host name or numeric address of the terminal server.

2. Give a SET MODEM command to specify the type of modem.

3. Issue any necessary SET DIAL commands.

4. Give a DIAL command for the desired phone number.

If the connection succeeds but echoing is incorrect, you can try giving a SET TELNET ECHO REMOTE (or LOCAL) command as a first step, or else give a SET TERMINAL ECHO REMOTE (or LOCAL) command after the connection is made.

X.25 Networks

As of this writing, X.25 connections are supported only for Sun computers that have the SunLink X.25 package and a connection to an X.25 network, such as the public data networks found in many countries (SprintNet or Tymnet in the US, Datapac in Canada, for example). Use the SHOW NETWORK command to find out if X.25 support is available in your version of C-Kermit.

For X.25 connections, an X.121 [14] address is used in the SET HOST command; this is a many-digit number usually consisting of a 1-digit prefix, a 4-digit DNIC (Data Network Identification Code) followed by an NTN (Network Terminal Number) up to 10 digits in length, or a 3-digit DCC (Data Country Code) followed by a country-dependent NN (National Number) up to 11 digits in length. For example, the following sequence might set up a connection to a hypothetical host in Brazil (Country Code 724):

```
C-Kermit>set parity mark
C-Kermit>set net x.25
C-Kermit>set host 07240987654321
```

In most cases, you should SET PARITY to MARK (or some other value besides NONE) before attempting to transfer files over an X.25 connection.

Before giving a SET HOST command for an X.25 connection, you can issue the following commands to specify how the connection is to be made:

SET X.25 CALL-USER-DATA *{ OFF, ON text }*
Lets you specify up to 12 characters of "call user data," usually an identifier or password required by the host you are calling. Consult the instructions from your service provider to see if you need to send call user data and what it should be.

SET X.25 CLOSED-USER-GROUP *{ OFF, ON n }*
Membership in a closed user group gives you access to addresses that might otherwise be off limits. C-Kermit assumes no user group. If you need to access a service that is in a closed user group, use SET X.25 CLOSED-USER-GROUP ON *n* to specify a closed user group number, 0 to 99.

SET X.25 REVERSE-CHARGE *{ OFF, ON }*
Normally, the caller pays for an X.25 call. If the remote host or service is willing to pay for your call, use SET X.25 REVERSE-CHARGE ON. The default is OFF.

An X.25 terminal connection goes through a PAD (Packet Assembler Disassembler), which is something like an autodial modem or a terminal server. You can converse with it directly (in *command mode*) or have it pass your data through to the selected host (*data mode*). When your local host is connected directly to the X.25 network (as opposed to dialing up a PAD), it takes the place of the PAD, and you have to use C-Kermit commands to control the simulated PAD:

PAD CLEAR
Clears the X.25 virtual circuit. Discards any information that might be in transit.

PAD INTERRUPT
Sends an X.25 interrupt packet.

PAD RESET
Resets the X.25 virtual circuit.

PAD STATUS
Requests a status report from the PAD.

C-Kermit also sets the PAD parameters itself. Each of these commands controls a different PAD parameter. The numbers correspond to CCITT X.3 parameters [10]. X.3 parameter numbers higher than 12 are not necessarily available on all X.25 networks.

SET PAD BREAK-ACTION *n*
X.3 Parameter 7, or what the PAD should do if it receives a BREAK signal (escape-character followed by B) from C-Kermit. *n* is the sum of the following digits: 0 means nothing, 1 means send an X.25 Interrupt packet, 2 means reset the connec-

Using Network Connections 75

tion, 4 means send an Indication of Break message, 8 means escape back to the PAD, 16 means discard pending output. The default is 21 (= 16 + 4 + 1).

SET PAD CHARACTER-DELETE *n*
X.3 Parameter 16. *n* = 0–127, the ASCII value of the character to be used for erasing a character during terminal emulation. The default is 8 (Ctrl-H, Backspace).

SET PAD CR-PADDING *n*
X.3 Parameter 9, Padding After Carriage Return (CR). *n* = 0–255, the number of padding characters the PAD should send to C-Kermit after sending a CR, default 0.

SET PAD DISCARD-OUTPUT { 0, 1 }
X.3 Parameter 8. 0 means normal data delivery, 1 means discard output, default 0.

SET PAD ECHO { 0, 1 }
X.3 Parameter 2. 0 means the PAD will not echo, 1 means the PAD will echo. The default is 1 (Kermit assumes the PAD will echo). This command also changes Kermit's DUPLEX setting.

SET PAD EDITING { 0, 1 }
X.3 Parameter 15. 0 means you can't edit the lines you type at the PAD before it sends them to the host, 1 means editing is allowed. The default is 1.

SET PAD ESCAPE { 0, 1 }
X.3 Parameter 1. 0 means escaping back to the PAD is not possible, 1 means you can use Ctrl-P to escape to the PAD. The default is 1.

SET PAD FORWARD *n*
X.3 Parameter 3, Data Forwarding Characters. The PAD forwards the characters it has received to the remote host as soon as it sees the packet forwarding character. *n* = 0 means none, 2 means carriage return. The default is 2, to make X.25 packets correspond as much as possible with Kermit packets.

SET PAD LF-PADDING *n*
X.3 Parameter 14. *n* = 0–255, the number of padding characters to be sent by the PAD after it sends a linefeed. The default is 0.

SET PAD LF-INSERT *n*
X.3 Parameter 13, Linefeed (LF) Insertion after Carriage Return (CR). *n* = 0 means no LF insertion, 1 means the PAD inserts a LF after each CR sent to C-Kermit, 2 means the PAD inserts a LF after each CR received from C-Kermit, 4 means the PAD echoes LF as CRLF. The default is 0.

SET PAD LINE-DELETE *n*
X.3 Parameter 17. *n* = 0–127, the ASCII value of the character to be used for erasing a line. The default is 21 (Ctrl-U).

SET PAD LINE-DISPLAY *n*
X.3 Parameter 18. *n* = 0–127, the ASCII value of the character you can type to redisplay an edited line. The default is 18 (Ctrl-R).

SET PAD LINE-FOLD *n*
X.3 Parameter 10, Line Folding, or what to do when a line is too long to fit on your screen. *n* = 0 means no line folding, 1–255 specifies the number of graphic characters per line after which the PAD should insert folding characters. The default is 0, and should be kept at 0 during file transfer to prevent damage to Kermit's file transfer packets.

SET PAD PAD-FLOW-CONTROL { 0, 1 }
X.3 Parameter 5. 0 means no flow control by the PAD, 1 means the PAD may send Xon/Xoff flow control to C-Kermit. The default is 0, which allows Xon/Xoff flow control to work end-to-end.

SET PAD SERVICE-SIGNALS { 0, 1 }
X.3 Parameter 6, PAD Service and Command Signals. 0 means PAD service signals are not sent to C-Kermit, 1 means PAD service signals sent. The default is 1.

SET PAD TIMEOUT *n*
X.3 Parameter 4, Data Forwarding Timeout. *n* = 0–255 (twentieths of a second), how long the PAD should wait for its packet buffer to fill up or for a forwarding character to appear before it times out and transmits what it has so far. The default is 0, no data forwarding on timeout.

SET PAD USER-FLOW-CONTROL { 0, 1 }
X.3 Parameter 12. 0 means the PAD should ignore any flow control characters sent by C-Kermit, 1 means the PAD should pay attention to them. The default is 0.

During CONNECT mode, the following X.25-specific keyboard escape options are available. Type these letters in after typing the CONNECT-mode escape character (normally Control-Backslash):

I   Send an X.25 Interrupt packet. Equivalent to PAD INTERRUPT.

R   (X.25 only) Reset the X.25 connection. Equivalent to PAD RESET.

It is beyond the scope of this book to go into any more detail about X.25 networks. See the manual from your X.25 service provider, the relevant CCITT Recommendations [10, 11, 12, 13, 14], or *Kermit, A File Transfer Protocol* [18, pp. 98–102].

Chapter 4

Terminal Connection

○ ○ ○ ○
If you will not be using C-Kermit in local mode to establish connections to other computers, skip this chapter and proceed to Chapter 5 on page 95 to learn how to transfer files.

C-Kermit's CONNECT command lets you carry on an interactive dialog with a remote computer or service. It works in both the 7-bit and 8-bit communication environments, on both full and half duplex connections. It includes a mechanism for shifting back and forth between the remote and local computer, a way to record the remote session, character-set conversion, and a key mapping feature.

When you use C-Kermit in local mode, no matter what your connection method—dialup, direct, or network—the method of shifting back and forth between the two computers is the same: use the CONNECT command at the C-Kermit prompt to go to the remote computer, and type a special character sequence to get back to C-Kermit.

The CONNECT Command

The CONNECT command makes C-Kermit act like a terminal connected to the remote computer. The characters you type on your keyboard are sent to the remote computer, and all the characters that arrive from the remote computer are sent to your screen, as shown in Figure 4-1 on the next page. *HINT:* The CONNECT command can be abbreviated by a single letter, C, even though several other Kermit commands also begin with C.

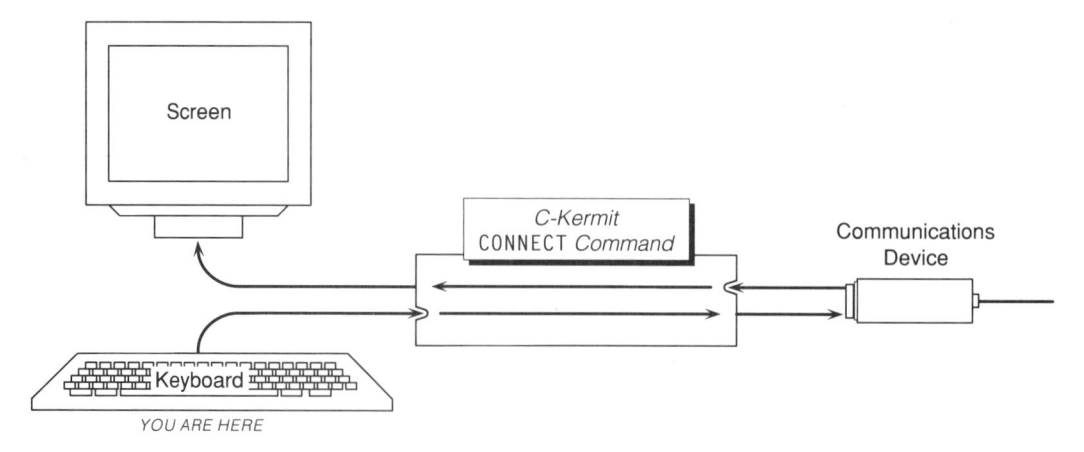

Figure 4-1 Terminal Connection

The Escape Character

Typing the escape character regains the attention of the local C-Kermit program during a CONNECT session. When you give the CONNECT command, C-Kermit tells you what the escape character is:

```
C-Kermit>connect                        (Begin terminal connection)
Connecting to ttxa0:, speed 19200.      (Messages from C-Kermit...)
The escape character is Ctrl-\ (ASCII 28, FS).
Type the escape character followed by C to get back,
or followed by ? to see other options.
```

Ctrl-\ (Control-Backslash) is C-Kermit's normal escape character. It is produced by holding down the Ctrl (or Control) key and pressing the backslash (\) key.[14] This gets C-Kermit's attention. Now follow the escape character by a second character that tells C-Kermit what to do, such as the letter *C* to return to the C-Kermit prompt without breaking the connection.

SET ESCAPE *number*

Changes the escape character to the control character of your choice; *number* is the numeric value of an ASCII control character, as listed in Table VIII-2. Example:

```
C-Kermit>set esc 2
C-Kermit>show escape
 CONNECT-mode escape character: Ctrl-B (ASCII 2, STX)
C-Kermit>
```

---

[14]The keyboards on most NeXT workstations do not generate the Control-Backslash character. The NeXT version of C-Kermit uses Control-Rightbracket as its escape character. OS/2 C-Kermit also uses Ctrl-Rightbracket. Be sure to pay attention to the CONNECT message.

This changes your CONNECT-mode escape characer to Control-B (ASCII character number 2, called STX). Only 7-bit control characters (codes 0 through 31 and 127) may be used for this purpose. You should select a character that you are unlikely to use at the remote host and that you are able to generate on your local keyboard. You can use SHOW ESCAPE or SHOW TERMINAL to find out the current escape character.

The mechanics of terminal connection are easy after a few minutes of practice. Use CONNECT to go to the remote host and use Ctrl-Backslash C (hold down the Ctrl key, press the backslash (\) key, then let go of both these keys, then press the C key) to escape back to C-Kermit. If your escape character isn't Ctrl-Backslash, make the appropriate substitution. Now practice going back and forth a few times. In this example, we have a direct connection from a VAX workstation to a central computer:

```
C-Kermit>set line ttxa0:         (Direct connection)
C-Kermit>set speed 19200         (Set the speed)
C-Kermit>connect                 (Begin terminal connection)
Connecting to ttxa0:, speed 19200.
The escape character is Ctrl-\ (ASCII 28, FS).
Type the escape character followed by C to get back,
or followed by ? to see other options.
WELCOME TO RALPH'S ACADEMY OF BRAIN SURGERY
EARN WHILE YOU LEARN!
Username: olaf                   (Log in)
Password:                        (Supply your password)
$ Ctrl-\c                        (Escape back)
C-Kermit>pwd                     (Give a C-Kermit command)
  $DUA0:[OLAF]
C-Kermit>set esc 22              (Change the escape character)
C-Kermit>c                       (Connect again)
Connecting to ttxa0:, speed 19200.
The escape character is Ctrl-V (ASCII 22, SYN).
Type the escape character followed by C to get back,
or followed by ? to see other options.
$                                (Back at Ralph's)
$ show time                      (Give a command)
  11-JUN-92 19:44:00
$ Ctrl-Vc                        (Escape back again)
C-Kermit>run fortune             (Give a C-Kermit command)
The brain is a wonderful organ; it starts working the moment you
get up in the morning and does not stop until you get to school.
C-Kermit>c                       (Connect again)
```

You can connect and escape back as often as you like. Escaping back does not break the connection. If characters arrive from the remote computer or service while you are not CONNECTed, they are buffered to the capacity of the underlying operating system. If the operating system's buffer becomes too full, flow control, if in effect, should prevent any loss of characters.

Closing the Connection

When you're finished using the remote computer, you should close the connection. There are several ways to do this. You should try them in this order:

1. If you were logged in to the remote computer or service, log out from it. This should pop you back to the C-Kermit prompt automatically. Example:

    ```
    $ logout
    Communications disconnect (Back at local system)
    C-Kermit>
    ```

2. If you're not back at the C-Kermit prompt yet, type *Ctrl-\H* (your CONNECT-mode escape character followed by the letter *H*) to hang up the connection:

    ```
    Ctrl-\h
    Communications disconnect (Back at local system)
    C-Kermit>
    ```

3. If you're still not back at the C-Kermit prompt yet, type *Ctrl-\C* to return to the C-Kermit prompt and give the SET LINE command to close the communication device:

    ```
    Ctrl-\c
    (Back at local system)
    C-Kermit>set line
    C-Kermit>
    ```

CONNECT-Mode Keyboard Escape Commands

C-Kermit's escape-character functions are listed in Table 4-1. Let's look at them in detail. When the CONNECT command is active, C-Kermit monitors the keyboard for its CONNECT-mode escape character, which (in most versions) is Ctrl-Backslash unless you have used the SET ESCAPE command to change it (OS/2 C-Kermit also accepts certain Alt-key equivalents; see Appendix V). When Kermit sees its escape character, it interprets the next character from the keyboard as a special CONNECT-mode command. If you press a key that is not a valid CONNECT-mode command, Kermit beeps, ignores the key, and remains in CONNECT mode.

If you type the escape character and then decide you didn't mean to do it, just press the space bar. C-Kermit ignores the escape character and the space bar, and does not beep at you. No characters are transmitted to the remote computer, and Kermit remains in CONNECT mode.

Kermit's CONNECT-mode escape commands are described in the following sections. Letters are shown in uppercase, but they may be entered in either upper- or lowercase. Each command must be preceded by Kermit's CONNECT-mode escape character.

Table 4-1 C-Kermit CONNECT-Mode Escapes

Character	Description
?	Help—prints the available CONNECT-mode escape options.
!	(also @) Enters the local system command processor. EXIT or LOGOUT to return to C-Kermit CONNECT mode.
0	(the digit zero) Transmits a NUL (ASCII 0).
A	Sends "Are You There?" (TELNET only).
B	Transmits a BREAK signal.
C	Returns to the C-Kermit prompt without breaking the connection.
H	Hangs up the phone or network connection.
I	Sends a network Interrupt request.
L	Transmits a Long BREAK signal.
Q	Hangs up, closes the connection, and quits from C-Kermit.
R	(X.25 only) Resets an X.25 connection.
S	Shows the status of the connection: device name, speed, parity, etc.
Z	(UNIX only) Suspends Kermit. Use the UNIX `fg` command to continue Kermit's CONNECT session.
SP	(Space) Sends nothing, stays in CONNECT mode.
\	(Backslash) Introduces a backslash code that translates into a single character, for example \127 or \xff.
Ctrl-\	(or whatever your escape character is) Type the escape character twice to send one copy of it to the remote computer.

Getting Help: ?

Typing the escape character followed by question mark lists the available CONNECT-mode escape options. These can vary depending on the C-Kermit version and the features it was built with. This message tells you which ones are available in your version. Example:

```
Ctrl-\?
Press C to return to the C-Kermit prompt, or:
 ? for this message
 0 (zero) to send a null
 B to send a BREAK
 L to send a Long BREAK
 H to hangup and close the connection
 Q to hangup and quit Kermit
 S for status
 ! to push to local shell
 Z to suspend
 \ backslash code:
```

```
      \nnn   decimal character code
      \Onnn  octal character code
      \Xhh   hexadecimal character code
      terminate with carriage return.
 Type the escape character again to send the escape character, or
 press the space-bar to resume the CONNECT command.
Command>
```

After printing the help text, C-Kermit prints a prompt, `Command>`, and waits for you to enter one of the options just listed.

Returning to the C-Kermit Prompt: C

Typing the escape character followed by the letter *C* returns you to the C-Kermit prompt without breaking the connection to the remote computer. This is called escaping back. After escaping back, you can give commands to C-Kermit to change its settings, transfer files, and so forth. Give another CONNECT command to get back to the remote computer. Example:

```
C-Kermit>connect              (Connect to remote computer)
$                             (Remote computer's prompt)
$ ^\c                         (Escape back to C-Kermit)
C-Kermit>                     (C-Kermit's prompt)
C-Kermit>connect              (Return to remote computer)
$                             (Remote computer's prompt)
```

Status Inquiry: S

Typing the escape character followed by the letter *S* tells Kermit to print a brief message showing the status of the connection and then resume the CONNECT session. Example:

```
C-Kermit>connect
$
$ ^\s
Connected through /dev/ttyh8, speed 9600
Terminal bytesize: 7, Command bytesize: 7, Parity: none
Terminal echo: remote
  Carrier Detect       (CD):  On
  Dataset Ready        (DSR): Off
  Clear To Send        (CTS): Off
  Ring Indicator       (RI):  Off
  Data Terminal Ready  (DTR): On
  Request to Send      (RTS): On
$
```

The report includes the communication device name and relevant parameters, plus (for serial devices only, and only if your system supports it) a report of the RS-232 modem signals (listed and explained briefly in Table II-1 on page 364). The status report is useful if you have trouble communicating during CONNECT mode. The information shown here might indicate the cause: wrong device, wrong speed, a missing modem signal, and so on.

Escape to Local System: !, @

Typing the escape character followed by an exclamation mark (!) or at-sign (@) tells C-Kermit to start an "inferior" copy of your system's command processor, such as the UNIX shell or VMS or AOS/VS command line interpreter, leaving your Kermit connection open.[15] This is similar to putting a telephone call on hold. You can have an interactive dialog with your system for as long as you like without disturbing your Kermit connection. To return to your Kermit CONNECT session, use the appropriate command to exit from the system command processor (EXIT in UNIX or OS/2, LOGOUT in VMS, POP in AOS/VS, and so on). Example:

```
$ kermit                              (Start Kermit)
C-Kermit>set line /dev/tty1           (Select communication device)
C-Kermit>set speed 19200              (and speed)
C-Kermit>connect                      (Start CONNECT session)
Connecting to /dev/tty1:, speed 19200, etc...

login: ivan                           (Log in)
Password: _____                       (Enter password)
%
% send olga Hi, are you ordering pizza for lunch?
% message from olga: OK, but I need the phone number.
% send olga OK, wait a second...
%
% ^\!                                 (Escape to local shell)
$
$ grep "Yummy Pizza" phones.txt       (Look up phone number)
Yummy Pizza: 765-4321
$ exit                                (Exit local shell)
%                                     (Resume CONNECT session)
% send olga It's 765-4321.
%
```

In UNIX only, you can also follow the escape character by the letter Z to suspend Kermit, if SUSPEND is SET to ON. See Appendix III for details.

Sending BREAK Signals: B and L

Typing the escape character followed by the letter *B* tells C-Kermit to transmit a BREAK signal. On serial (terminal device or modem) connections, BREAK is a spacing (0) condition lasting about 275 milliseconds (slightly more than a quarter of a second), required by some hosts, services, and communication processors for transmission speed recognition, to get their attention, or to interrupt a runaway or stuck process. Here's an example showing how to log in to an IBM VM/CMS mainframe over a linemode connection, in which you are instructed to "press BREAK key." The setup and connection details are omitted.

---

[15] If this feature is missing from your version of C-Kermit, then it has been built with the NOPUSH option to prevent users from directly accessing the system from within Kermit.

```
C-Kermit>connect
Connecting to /dev/cua, speed 9600...
VIRTUAL MACHINE/SYSTEM PRODUCT--CUVMB     --PRESS BREAK KEY
^\b
!
Enter one of the following commands:
   LOGON userid              (Example:  LOGON VMUSER1)
   LOGOFF
.logon olga
Enter password: _____
.
```

Typing the letter *L* instead of *B* after the escape character tells C-Kermit to transmit a Long BREAK signal. On serial connections, this is a spacing condition lasting about 1.5 seconds that is used to get the attention of certain communication devices.

Network Functions

On network connections, some of the CONNECT-mode escapes behave differently and some additional ones are available. Type the escape character followed by:

A (TELNET only) Send a TELNET "Are You There" message. If the remote TELNET server is active, it will send back a message like "[Yes]." This usually works only on true port-23 TELNET connections, not when you TELNET to non-TELNET ports.

I Send an Interrupt message (X.25 Interrupt or TELNET Interrupt Process). The action taken depends on the network and the remote host. Sending a TELNET interrupt is usually equivalent to typing the remote host's interrupt character.

B Send a network BREAK. Again, the interpretation depends on the network and the remote host. On TELNET connections, a TELNET protocol Break message is sent, which might be interpreted by the remote TELNET server as a stand-in for the BREAK signal as it is used on serial connections, or as an interruption command.

L On network connections, L is treated exactly like B.

Sending Special Characters

Several methods are provided for sending special characters to the remote host during a CONNECT session. Type the CONNECT-mode escape character followed by:

0 (the digit zero) Transmit a NUL (ASCII 0). This is useful if your remote computer or application wants you to send a NUL character, but your keyboard doesn't give you a way to type it.

^ (Ctrl-Backslash, or whatever you have set the escape character to be) Type the escape character twice in a row to send one copy of it to the remote computer.

A more general technique lets you transmit any character at all. If you follow the CONNECT-mode escape character with a Backslash (\) (not Control-Backslash) character, then you can enter a number representing any 7- or 8-bit code for Kermit to send.

The backslash is followed by an optional base indicator: *d* for decimal, *o* for octal, or *x* for hexadecimal, and then a 1-, 2-, or 3-digit number in the indicated base (hexadecimal numbers must be exactly two characters long), which Kermit interprets as a character code between 0 and 255 inclusive. If there is no base indicator, base 10 is assumed.

Terminate the code by pressing the Return or Enter key, and Kermit sends the character represented by the code. The carriage return itself is not sent. If you type an ungrammatical backslash code, Kermit beeps and sends nothing. In all cases, Kermit leaves you in CONNECT mode after processing the backslash code.

Suppose your keyboard has a broken A key. The ASCII code for uppercase A is 65 decimal, 101 octal, or 41 hexadecimal (see Table VIII-1). During a CONNECT session, you can transmit it in any of these ways:

```
^\\65
^\\d65
^\\o101
^\\x41
```

For example:

```
I wish my ^\\65
 key worked.
```

The host will receive:

```
I wish my A key worked.
```

Hanging Up and Quitting: H and Q

Typing the escape character followed by the letter *H* tells C-Kermit to hang up. On dialed serial connections when DIAL MODEM-HANGUP is ON, Kermit attempts to put the modem in command mode and then gives it the command to hang up the phone. If MODEM-HANGUP is OFF, or if it doesn't work, or if the modem type is DIRECT, Kermit turns off the Data Terminal Ready (DTR) signal for about half a second. If your serial communication device is connected to a modem, this is supposed to signal the modem to hang up the phone connection. Network connections are simply closed. If you are running C-Kermit in interactive mode, a successful hangup should return you automatically to the C-Kermit prompt. If you started C-Kermit with the -c or -n command-line option, hanging up should return you to the system prompt (see Chapter 14).

Typing *Q* instead of *H* after the escape character tells C-Kermit to hang up and then quit (exit), returning you to the system prompt no matter how you started C-Kermit.

Terminal Emulation

The OS/2 version of C-Kermit has its own built-in emulator for DEC VT102, VT100, and VT52 terminals and includes several capabilities not described in this chapter. See Appendix V for OS/2-specific information. In other C-Kermit versions, most screen formatting and other terminal-specific operations during CONNECT sessions are handled externally to C-Kermit.

If you have a UNIX, VMS, OpenVMS, OS-9, Atari, or Amiga workstation on your desk, the specific terminal emulation is provided by workstation services. For example, on a DEC VAXstation running VMS, OpenVMS, or ULTRIX with DECwindows, your access to the system command parser (VMS DCL or UNIX shell) is through a character-mode terminal emulation window that emulates a DEC VT terminal. When you run C-Kermit in this window the VT terminal emulation remains in effect, so escape sequences sent by the remote host are processed correctly in CONNECT mode. Workstation terminal windows can also provide services like scroll bars to view material that has scrolled off the screen, printing, resizing, cut and paste, font selection, and so on.

Similar comments apply to Sun Workstations (using the standard console driver or the VTTOOL or CRTTOOL programs under SunView), NeXT workstations using the TERMINAL or STUART window), X Window System stations (using *xterm*) [49], SCO Xenix or UNIX workstations (using the ANSI terminal driver), the IBM RS/6000 with AIX Windows, and so forth. System V consoles on PC-based or other workstations generally follow VT100 (ANSI) conventions via a terminfo entry (such as AT386). On the Commodore Amiga, the console device automatically provides ANSI terminal emulation, similar to VT100. On the Atari ST, the console driver provides a superset of VT52 emulation.

Setting Terminal Parameters

The following commands control the number of data and parity bits used during C-Kermit's CONNECT command and other terminal-oriented operations.

SET COMMAND BYTESIZE { 7, 8 }
Tells whether to use 7 or 8 data bits per character on the connection between C-Kermit and your keyboard and screen, shown in Figure 4-2 as (A). The default is to use 7 data bits and ignore the 8th bit. This setting applies to both command mode (when you see the C-Kermit prompt) and CONNECT mode.

SET TERMINAL BYTESIZE { 7, 8 }
Tells whether the CONNECT command should use 7 or 8 data bits per character on the connection between C-Kermit and the other computer, shown in Figure 4-2 as (B). The default is to use 7 data bits. If you give a value of 8, then 8-bit characters are used if PARITY is set to NONE, otherwise 7-bit characters are used.

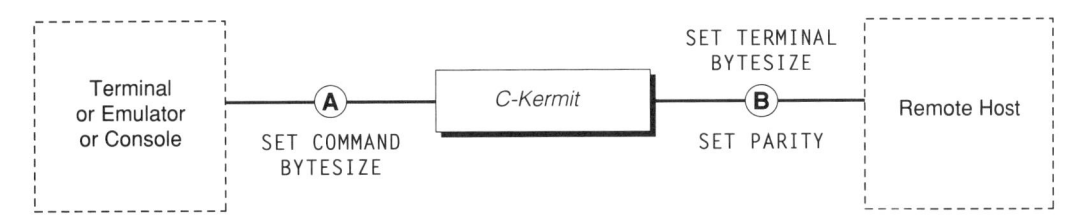

Figure 4-2 Command and Terminal Bytesize

SET PARITY *[{ EVEN, ODD, MARK, SPACE, NONE }]*
Tells which kind of parity to use on the connection between C-Kermit and the remote computer, (B). The default parity is NONE. A PARITY setting of EVEN, ODD, MARK, or SPACE causes C-Kermit to use 7 data bits per character, regardless of the TERMINAL BYTESIZE setting. A PARITY setting of NONE allows the TERMINAL BYTESIZE setting to determine the number of data bits per character.

Remember, the default setting for PARITY is NONE, and the default setting for both COMMAND and TERMINAL BYTESIZE is 7. This is because it is common for remote hosts or services, or the devices that connect you to them, to use (add or strip) parity. And it is just as common for users to be unaware of it.

If the bytesizes were set to 8 rather than 7 by default, parity bits on characters arriving from the remote host or service would change them into other characters and you would see gibberish on your screen. If C-Kermit's default parity was not NONE, this could prevent non-parity connections from working.

The default settings allow the initial connection to be made successfully in most cases. If your connection needs parity, then SET the appropriate kind. If you need to use 8-bit characters, be sure to read Chapter 9.

SET TERMINAL CHARACTER-SET *remote-cset [local-cset]*
Specifies the remote and local character sets so C-Kermit can translate between them during CONNECT sessions. The default terminal character-set is TRANSPARENT, which means that characters are not translated during terminal connection. This command and character sets in general are discussed in Chapter 9.

SET TERMINAL ECHO *{ LOCAL, REMOTE }*
Tells whether C-Kermit should echo the characters you type locally (LOCAL) or let the remote computer echo them (REMOTE). The default is REMOTE except for TELNET network connections, where it is LOCAL until and unless renegotiated by TELNET protocol or overriden by a SET TELNET ECHO command (see Chapter 3). If characters don't echo when you type them, you should SET TERMINAL ECHO LOCAL. If characters echo

twice when you type them, then SET TERMINAL ECHO REMOTE. The SET DUPLEX and SET LOCAL-ECHO commands perform the same functions as this command.

SET TERMINAL LOCKING-SHIFT { ON, OFF }
Tells whether C-Kermit should use Shift-In and Shift-Out control characters (Ctrl-N and Ctrl-O) for transmitting 8-bit characters on a 7-bit connection between C-Kermit and the remote computer during a CONNECT session (see Chapter 9 for a fuller discussion of this feature). This setting applies in both directions: to characters you type at the keyboard and to characters arriving from the remote computer or service.

SET TERMINAL NEWLINE-MODE { ON, OFF }
Tells whether C-Kermit should automatically convert carriage return (CR, ASCII 13) characters typed at the keyboard into carriage-return-linefeed (CRLF, ASCII 13 and ASCII 10) combinations before transmission. Normally OFF. Don't use this one unless your CONNECT-mode screens look like they need it. The normal indications are that the remote host does not respond to your commands, or that your commands overwrite one another.

SET TERMINAL CR-DISPLAY { CRLF, NORMAL }
This is like SET TERMINAL NEWLINE-MODE, but in the opposite direction. It tells whether carriage return characters received from the communication device should be displayed as carriage return only (NORMAL, the default) or as carriage return and linefeed (CRLF). Use the CRLF option when connected to a device that terminates its output lines with bare carriage returns.

SHOW TERMINAL
Displays your current terminal settings:

```
C-Kermit>sho term
  Command bytesize:  7 bits
  Terminal bytesize: 7 bits
  Terminal echo: remote
  Terminal locking-shift: off
  Terminal newline-mode:  off
  Terminal cr-display:    cr-only
  Terminal character-set: transparent
  CONNECT-mode escape character: Ctrl-\ (ASCII 28, FS)
  Suspend: on
C-Kermit>
```

In this example, the SHOW TERMINAL display shows all the default terminal settings for UNIX C-Kermit. The *Suspend: on* line applies only to UNIX (see Appendix III) and does not appear in other operating systems.

Key Mapping

C-Kermit can substitute any character or character string for any key that you press during a CONNECT session. For keys that produce 7- or 8-bit codes, the default assignment for each key is itself, that is, the key transmits the code that it produces when you press it. You can use the following commands to change the default assignments.

SHOW KEY

This command tells Kermit to ask you to press a key. When you do, Kermit shows you the code value of the key and the key's current definition. The codes and their character assignments are necessarily system-dependent. Here is an example using a NeXT workstation:

```
C-Kermit>set command bytesize 8
C-Kermit>show key
 Press key: Alt-s
 Key code \251 => Character: ß \251 (self, no translation)
```

The user types Alt-s (holds down the Alternate key and presses the s key). On the NeXT, this produces "German sharp s" (ß, Ess-Zet). 251 is the key code. It is shown in decimal. In most C-Kermit versions, only 7-bit or 8-bit code values are accessible. Under OS/2, additional codes are available for Alt, function, and arrow keys.

SET KEY *key-code [definition]*

This assigns the given definition to any (and all) key(s) that produce the given key code. The *key-code* may be a simple decimal number or a backslash code used to express the number in decimal, octal, or hexadecimal notation (Table I-2). Normally you would use the same notation for the key as SHOW KEY displays for it. The *definition* can be a single character, expressed literally (if possible) or in backslash notation, or a string of characters (possibly containing backslash codes). If the definition is omitted, the key's default definition is restored. Here are some examples, in which we assign various values to the NeXT Alt-s key:

```
C-Kermit>set key \251 \29           (Ctrl-Rightbracket)
C-Kermit>set key \251 x             (The single character 'x')
C-Kermit>set key \251 ss            (Double 's')
C-Kermit>set key \251 Oh my, this is a wordy keystroke!\13
C-Kermit>set key \251               (Restore default value)
```

C-Kermit's SET KEY command has several restrictions:

- To use 8-bit key codes, you must first SET COMMAND BYTESIZE 8. The method for entering 8-bit characters depends on your computer, operating system, terminal emulator (if any), keyboard, and keyboard driver.

- If you use SET KEY to assign CONNECT-mode escape commands to single keys, the characters assigned to the key are transmitted, rather than treated as escapes.

- If you include a NUL (ASCII 0, \0) value in a key definition, it terminates the definition, and the NUL character itself will not be transmitted when you press the key.

A common use for the SET KEY command is to relocate inconveniently placed keys for easy typing. For example, some keyboards have the Esc (Escape) key far off in right field, out of reach, and the accent-grave (backquote) key where you want the Esc key to be. Use SET KEY to swap them:

```
C-Kermit>set key \96 \27
C-Kermit>set key \27 \96
```

Another common use of SET KEY is to change what is sent by your BACKSPACE key. Some hosts expect DEL (Delete, ASCII 127), others expect BS (Backspace, Ctrl-H, ASCII 8). This example assigns ASCII BS to the NeXT's backspace key, whose key code (and therefore default assignment) is 127:

```
C-Kermit>set key \127 \8
C-Kermit>set key \8 \127
```

Here again, we swap keys. In case we actually have to transmit a real DEL, it is assigned to the Ctrl-H key.

C-Kermit's SET KEY assignments are effective only while the CONNECT command is active. When you press a key that has been given a definition with SET KEY, all terminal and communication settings are applied to the characters in its definition before they are sent, just as if you had typed the characters on the keyboard during CONNECT mode.

Logging and Debugging Your Terminal Session

You can have C-Kermit copy all the characters that appear on your screen during a CONNECT session to a file called the session log. You can also make C-Kermit display control characters graphically rather than passing them directly to your terminal emulator or console driver. Here are the commands:

LOG SESSION *[[filename] { APPEND, NEW }]*
This command tells C-Kermit to copy the characters that are sent to your screen into the file whose name is given. If no name is given, Kermit creates a new file called SESSION.LOG in your current directory. The trailing keyword, APPEND or NEW, tells whether to write the session log to the end of an existing file or to create a new file. The default is NEW (in VMS and OpenVMS, a new file version is always created). Characters are recorded in their 8-bit form if PARITY is NONE and TERMINAL BYTESIZE is 8. Otherwise only 7-bit characters are logged. If the terminal character set is not TRANSPARENT, the characters are recorded after translation. The SHOW FILE command displays the name of your current session log file. It is also shown in the CONNECT message and by the CONNECT-mode status-display request:

```
C-Kermit>log ses            (Start a session log)
C-Kermit>connect            (Begin terminal connection)
Connecting to /dev/ttyh8, speed 9600
...
(Session logged to session.log, text)
login: Ctrl-\S              (Status request)
...
Logging to: session.log
```

CLOSE SESSION

Terminates session logging and closes your session log file. The log file is also closed automatically when you EXIT from C-Kermit.

SET SESSION-LOG { BINARY, TEXT }

(UNIX and AOS/VS only) A binary-mode session log contains every character that is received from the remote computer, including NUL and DEL padding characters, as well as carriage returns. When the session-log type is TEXT, C-Kermit discards NUL, DEL, and CR characters, so the result is more likely to be usable as a UNIX or AOS/VS text file (this command has no effect in VMS, OS/2, or C-Kermit's other operating systems). TEXT is the default type of session log.

SET DEBUG { SESSION, OFF }

The SET DEBUG SESSION command changes your CONNECT-mode screen into a kind of data analyzer. Control and 8-bit characters are displayed graphically. For example, Ctrl-A is displayed as ^A, ESC is displayed as ^[, etc. (see Table VIII-2). An 8-bit character is shown as a tilde (~) followed by the 7-bit version of the character, for example the letter *A* with its parity bit set looks like ~A. On a network connection, TELNET protocol negotiations are displayed on the screen. Terminal character sets are not translated during session debugging. Session debugging is normally OFF.

Here is an example of a debugging display on a TELNET connection, in which both TELNET negotiations and control characters are displayed symbolically:

```
C-Kermit>set debug session
C-Kermit>telnet foo.bar.com
[WILL TERMINAL TYPE][DO SUPPRESS GO AHEAD]<DO TERMINAL TYPE><WIL
L SUPPRESS GO AHEAD><SB TERMINAL TYPE 01 IAC SE>[SB TERMINAL TYP
E 00 VT300 IAC SE]<WILL ECHO>[DO ECHO]<DO ECHO>^M^J^M^JSunOS UNI
X (watsun)^M^J^M^@^M^J^M^@login: olaf^M^JPassword:^M^JLast login
: Sat Jul  4 16:20:45 from watsun^M^JSunOS Release 4.1.1 (WATSUN
) #1: Mon Sep 23 20:11:19 EDT 1991^M^J^M^J^[[1;24r^[[24;1H^M^@We
lcome to /dev/ttyp6^M^J$ exit^M^J[WONT ECHO]<DONT ECHO>
```

The TELNET options that Kermit sends are enclosed in square brackets and the ones it receives are enclosed in angle brackets. ^[[1;24r^[[24;1H is a screen setup command for a VT terminal. ^M^J is a carriage return and linefeed sequence, and ^@ is a NUL.

Chapter 5

The Basics of File Transfer

○ ○ ○ ○
This chapter explains the basic method for transferring ordinary text and binary files using the Kermit protocol. If you encounter difficulties, read Chapter 6 to learn how to solve them. If you need to transfer text files containing national or international characters, also read Chapter 9. VMS and OpenVMS users who need to cope with special file formats also should read Appendix IV. To transfer files with other computers or services that do not have Kermit file transfer available, consult Chapter 10. After you have mastered basic file transfer, you can stop reading for a while. Later, when you find yourself wanting easier or faster ways to transfer data, read Chapters 7 and 8. And if you want to automate yourself out of business, read about script programming in Chapters 11–13.

Basic File Transfer Commands

The Kermit protocol transfers files from one computer to another and it requires **Kermit** software on both computers. Kermit programs communicate with each other using formatted messages called packets. If packets are lost, duplicated, or damaged during transmission, the receiving Kermit notifies the sending Kermit and corrective action is taken automatically to ensure your files are transferred without error. For a detailed description of the Kermit protocol, see the book *Kermit, A File Transfer Protocol* [18]. We assume you understand the terms "local computer" and "remote computer," and you are able to connect your local computer to the remote one with Kermit communications software. If

Table 5-1 Special Characters in C-Kermit File Specifications

Field or Pattern	UNIX	VMS	AOS/VS	OS/2	OS-9	Amiga	Atari
Username	~				~		~
The directory separator	/	[.]	:	\ or /	/	/	\
The current directory	.	[ ]	=	.	.		.
The superior directory	..	-	^	..	..	/	..
* Inferior directories		...	#				
* Any string of characters	*		+		*	*	
* Any string not containing "."		*	-	*			*
* Any single character	?				?	?	
* Any character but "."		%	*	?			?
* Any character from a set	[abc] [a-z]						
* Any string from a set	{foo,bar}						
* Exception string			\				

necessary, please review Chapter 3 or consult the documentation for your local Kermit program if it is not C-Kermit.

The basic file transfer commands are SEND and RECEIVE. One computer's Kermit must be told to send a file and the other computer's Kermit program must be told to receive it.

The SEND Command

SEND *filespec*
    The SEND command sends the file or files denoted by *filespec* to the Kermit program on the other computer, which must be given a RECEIVE command.

The *filespec* is allowed to contain "wildcard" characters to send all the files whose names match. A wildcard is a special character used in a filename to denote a group of files whose names match a given pattern. Wildcards are also called *metacharacters* (in UNIX) or *templates* (in AOS/VS). Wildcard syntax can vary from system to system. Table 5-1 gives a summary of special characters that can be used in filenames on systems supported by C-Kermit; the items marked by asterisk (*) in the first column are considered wildcards. Consult the system-specific appendices of this book for details.

The name of each file, converted to uppercase if necessary, is transmitted to the receiving Kermit program so the file can be stored with its own name automatically when it arrives.

SEND can be abbreviated to the single letter S, even though other C-Kermit commands
begin with S. Examples:

```
C-Kermit>send oofa.txt       (A single file)
C-Kermit>sen oofa.+          (All AOS/VS oofa files)
C-Kermit>sen oofa.*          (All oofa files, other systems)
C-Kermit>s \?\?              (UNIX files with 2-char names)
C-Kermit>s %%                (VMS files with 2-char names)
```

The default directory for filenames is the one where you started C-Kermit or the one given in the most recent CD command. You can include disk and/or directory information in the *filespec* for files that are not in your current directory. During transmission, filenames are stripped of any device, directory, or version information. For example, when the following file is sent by VMS C-Kermit:

```
C-Kermit>send $disk1:[olga]login.com;5
```

the receiver is told that its name is simply LOGIN.COM.

The RECEIVE Command

RECEIVE *[filename]*
The RECEIVE command tells C-Kermit to wait for one or more files to arrive from the other Kermit program, which must be given a SEND command.

Incoming filenames are converted to the format of C-Kermit's underlying operating system; for example, UNIX C-Kermit converts uppercase letters in the filename to lowercase. If the incoming filename includes a device or directory, C-Kermit tries to store the file there. The RECEIVE command can be abbreviated by the single letter R. Examples:

```
C-Kermit>receive             (Receive one or more files)
C-Kermit>r                   (Receive one or more files)
```

If the optional *filename* is included, the arriving file is stored under that name rather than the name it was sent with:

```
C-Kermit>receive oofa.txt    (Store incoming file as oofa.txt)
```

The "as-name" can include disk and directory information so you can store the incoming file somewhere other than your current directory, and it can also denote a device such as a printer if your operating system allows. It may not contain wildcard characters. If more than one file arrives, only the first one is renamed; the rest are stored under their own names. UNIX creates the file with the as-name just as you typed it, but VMS, OpenVMS, AOS/VS, and other systems create the file with an uppercase name even if you typed it with lowercase letters.

The RECEIVE command requires that you have write access to the device and directory in which the arriving file is to be stored. C-Kermit will not create files for you that you could not otherwise create yourself.

Other Commands for Sending Files

A variation on the SEND command lets you supply a list of files to be sent, rather than just one file specification:

MSEND *filespec [filespec [...]]*
> Multiple Send. This command sends all the files in the list in a single operation, so you only have to give one RECEIVE command to the other Kermit. The names are separated by spaces. Each file is sent under its own name. Each item in the list can be the name of a single file or a wildcard file group specification. The files can be on different devices and in different directories. Examples:

```
C-Kermit>msend oofa.txt oofa.new    (Two files or...)
C-Kermit>mse ~olga/*.c ~olaf/*.h    (from different directories)
C-Kermit>ms [olga]*.c [ivan]*.h     (Ditto, VMS and OpenVMS)
C-Kermit>ms ckc*.c cku*.c ckw*.c ck*.h makefile
```

A final variation on the SEND command lets you send a single file under an assumed name:

SEND *filename [remote-filename]*
> Sends the file specified by *filename*, which must not contain wildcards, transmitting it under the name *remote-filename*. Example:

```
C-Kermit>send night.txt day.txt
```

> This sends the file `night.txt` but tells the receiving Kermit that its name is `day.txt`. The *remote-filename* field should be a filename in the syntax of the remote computer. It can contain any printable characters, even spaces. C-Kermit does not (and can not) check it for syntax, and does not convert it in any way. If you do not supply a *remote-filename* field, the file is sent with its own name.

Easy File Transfer Examples

Let's introduce two new words, illustrated in Figure 5-1: *upload* and *download*. Upload means to send a file from your local computer to the remote computer. Download means to transfer a file from the remote computer to your local computer.

All Kermit programs are set up to transfer ordinary 7-bit US ASCII text files unless you say otherwise, so let's begin by doing that. The procedure for *uploading* is:

1. Start Kermit on your local computer.

2. Make a connection to the remote computer.

3. CONNECT to the remote computer and log in.

4. Start Kermit on the remote computer and tell it to RECEIVE the desired file.

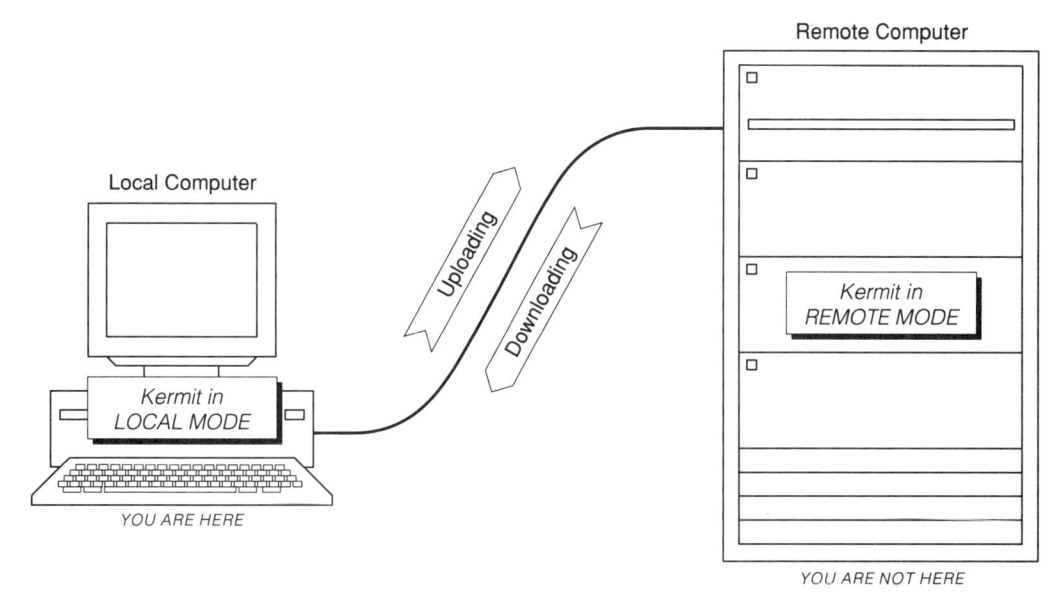

Figure 5-1 Upload and Download

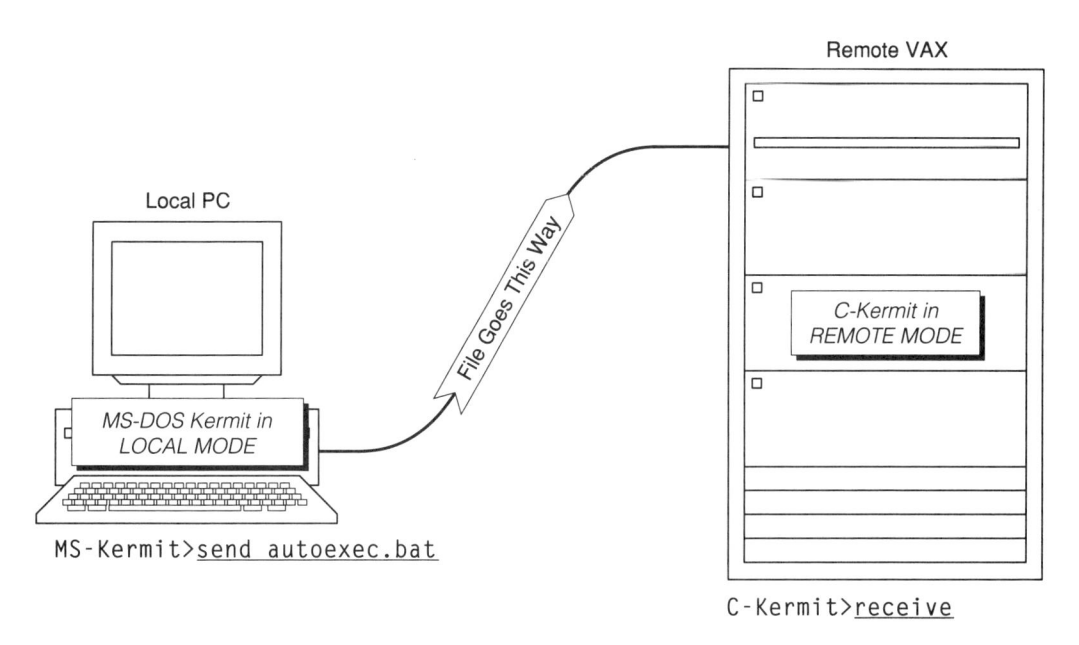

Figure 5-2 Uploading a File

Easy File Transfer Examples 99

5. If necessary, escape back to Kermit on the local computer.

6. Tell the local Kermit to SEND the file.

7. Watch the file transfer display.

8. Wait for the beep or message that says the transfer is complete.

9. CONNECT back to the remote computer, conduct any further business you might have there, and then log out from it when you're finished.

10. Escape back to your local Kermit (if necessary) and exit from it.

In our first example, shown in Figure 5-2, you are sitting at a PC equipped with MS-DOS Kermit. You will connect to a VAX computer over a direct line and upload a file to C-Kermit on the VAX.

```
C:\>kermit                            (Start Kermit on the PC)
MS-Kermit>set speed 9600              (Set the desired speed)
MS-Kermit>connect                     (Begin terminal emulation)

Username: olga                        (Log in on the VAX)
Password: _____                       (Type your password)

$ kermit                              (Start Kermit on the VAX)
C-Kermit 5A(188), 23 Nov 92, OpenVMS VAX
Type ? or HELP for help
C-Kermit>receive                      (C-Kermit receives the file)
Return to your local Kermit and give a SEND command.
KERMIT READY TO RECEIVE...
Alt-X                                 (Escape back to the PC)
                                      (Hold down Alt key and press X)
MS-Kermit>send autoexec.bat           (Tell the PC to send the file)
   (The file is transferred...)
MS-Kermit>                            (Beep, all done)
```

Presto, the file is transferred. Notice that you only have to tell the sending Kermit the name of the file to be sent. It tells the receiving Kermit so the file is automatically stored with the right name. For completeness, let's go back to the VAX and properly finish our session:

```
MS-Kermit>connect                     (Connect back to the VAX)
C-Kermit>dir /size/date autoexec      (Is the file really there?)
Directory $DISK1:[OLGA]
AUOTEXEC.BAT;1    3    31-DEC-92 23:59:59
C-Kermit>exit                         (Exit from C-Kermit on the VAX)
$ logout                              (Log out from the VAX)
Alt-X                                 (Escape back to the PC)
MS-Kermit>exit                        (Exit from MS-DOS Kermit)
C:\>                                  (Back to the DOS prompt)
```

Now you're back where you started.

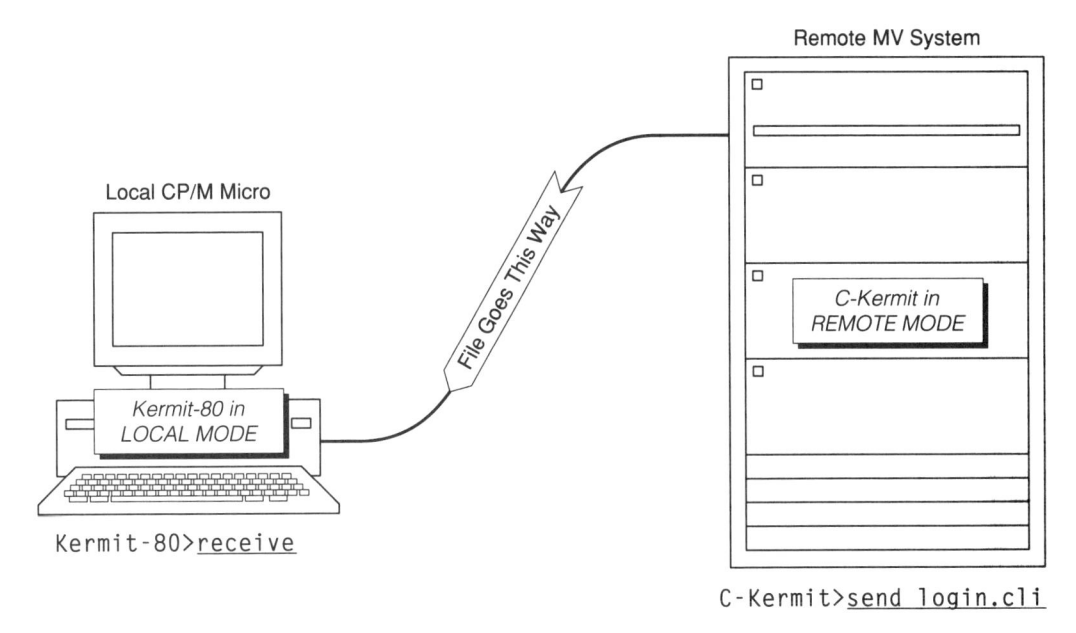

```
                                            Remote MV System


   Local CP/M Micro

                              File Goes This Way
                                                  C-Kermit in
                                                  REMOTE MODE


      Kermit-80 in
      LOCAL MODE


Kermit-80>receive
                                            C-Kermit>send login.cli
```

Figure 5-3 Downloading a File

HINT: If the file transfer didn't work, it's probably because of a communication parameter called *parity*. Try giving the command:

C-Kermit>set parity even

(or SET PARITY SPACE) to C-Kermit before you give the SEND command, escape back, and give the same SET command to your local Kermit before giving the RECEIVE command. We'll cover parity and other difficulties in Chapter 6.

Downloading

Downloading is just like uploading, except with the SEND and RECEIVE commands exchanged. In this example, illustrated in Figure 5-3, we connect from a desktop CP/M microcomputer to a remote Data General MV AOS/VS system. The micro is the local computer, the MV is the remote, and they have a direct connection:

```
B>a:kermit                             (Start Kermit on the micro)
Kermit-80 v4.11
Kermit-80>set speed 9600               (Set the desired speed)
Kermit-80>connect                      (Begin terminal emulation)
Username: ivan                         (Log in to the MV system)
Password:                              (Type your password)
) kermit                               (Start Kermit on the MV system)
C-Kermit 5A(188), 23 Nov 92, AOS/VS
Type ? or HELP for help
C-Kermit>                              (AOS/VS C-Kermit prompt)
```

Easy File Transfer Examples **101**

```
C-Kermit>send login.cli          (C-Kermit sends the file)
Return to your local Kermit and give a RECEIVE command.

KERMIT READY TO SEND...
Ctrl-]C                          (Escape back to the micro)
Kermit-80>rec                    (The micro receives the file)

  (The file is transferred...)

Kermit-80>                       (Beep, finished)
Kermit-80>dir login              (Check it)
LOGIN  CLI    3
Kermit-80>
```

See, the file is really on your micro's disk, stored automatically under the correct name. Now connect back to the remote computer, finish your session, and log out:

```
Kermit-80>c                      (Connect back)
C-Kermit>exit                    (Exit from C-Kermit)
) bye                            (Log out from AOS/VS)
Ctrl-]C                          (Escape back)
Kermit-80>
```

What Are Those Squiggles?

When you give the SEND command to the remote Kermit, as in the previous example, it waits for a few seconds to give you time to escape back to the local Kermit program and issue a RECEIVE command. Then it sends its first file transfer packet. The normal waiting time is about 5 seconds. If you fail to escape back quickly enough, you will see the first packet on your screen, looking something like this:[16]

```
C-Kermit>send oofa.txt
Return to your local Kermit and give a RECEIVE command.

KERMIT READY TO SEND...
^A0 Sz* @-#Y1~*   yE
```

No harm is done; you have about a full minute to escape back and engage the receiving Kermit before the remote Kermit loses patience and returns to its prompt. But if you are disconcerted by the appearance of this packet on your screen, you may lengthen the delay interval:

SET DELAY *number*

Tells C-Kermit how many seconds to wait before sending its first packet after it has been given a SEND command, when it is in remote mode. Example:

```
C-Kermit>set delay 10
```

---

[16]If you have given a RECEIVE command and did not escape back fast enough, you will see a packet that looks like this: "# N3".

Once you have become highly dextrous and proficient at escaping back and typing RECEIVE, the normal 5-second hiatus can be surprisingly annoying, so you can also shorten C-Kermit's waiting time:

```
C-Kermit>set delay 1
```

The SET DELAY command has no effect when receiving files, or when uploading files from C-Kermit on your local computer.

Network File Transfer

If you are accessing the remote computer with a true high-speed network connection, C-Kermit works the same as in the previous examples, but much faster. In this example we access a UNIX host computer via a TCP/IP Ethernet connection from MS-DOS Kermit on a PC and *download* a file:

```
MS-Kermit>set port tcp kermit.cc.columbia.edu
MS-Kermit>connect

login: olaf
Password: _____

$ Kermit                           (Start UNIX Kermit)
C-Kermit 5A(188), 23 Nov 92, SunOS 4.1
Type ? or HELP for help
C-Kermit>send mailing.lst         (Send a file)
Alt-X                              (Escape back to the PC)
MS-Kermit>r                        (Receive the file)

  (The file is transferred...)

MS-Kermit>c                        (Connect back to UNIX)
C-Kermit>exit                      (Exit from C-Kermit)
$ exit                             (Log out from UNIX)
```

If the file transfer failed, SET PARITY to SPACE (for TELNET), or to MARK, EVEN, or ODD (on other types of connections), and start the file transfer again.

File Transfer through Terminal Servers

If you have made a serial connection to a terminal server or similar device that makes a network connection to the computer where C-Kermit resides, the host operating system probably does not know your true connection speed, and therefore neither does C-Kermit. For example, suppose you have dialed up a terminal server at 2400 bps and then used it to access a UNIX host computer. The host computer probably thinks your speed is much higher, most likely 38400 bps.[17] Kermit uses the host computer's idea of the speed to calculate its packet timeouts, so you should be sure the host computer knows your true connection speed before you start C-Kermit, or file transfer might fail:

---

[17]This is the speed that most UNIX hosts associate with /dev/tty when it is not a real terminal device.

```
    $ stty 2400                        (UNIX)
    $ set terminal /speed=2400         (VMS and OpenVMS)
```

Here is an example in which we use MS-DOS Kermit to dial up a terminal server, connect from there to an IBM RS/6000 host, and then transfer a file from the PC to the RS/6000:

```
C:\>kermit                             (Start Kermit on the PC)
MS-Kermit>set speed 2400               (Set the desired speed)
MS-Kermit>dial 7654321                 (Dial the terminal server)
MS-Kermit>connect                      (Begin terminal emulation)

Please enter a hostname                (Terminal server greeting)

Hostname? unixa                        (Specify hostname)
Trying UNIXA...                        (Connection is established)

Welcome to UNIXA.  AIX 3.2             (UNIX greeting)

login: ivan                            (Log in to UNIX)
Password: _____                      (Type your password)

    $ stty 2400                        (Before starting C-Kermit!)
    $
    $ kermit                           (Start Kermit on UNIX)
C-Kermit 5A(188), 23 Nov 92, IBM RS/6000
Type ? or HELP for help
C-Kermit>receive                       (C-Kermit receives the file)
Return to your local Kermit and give a SEND command.

KERMIT READY TO RECEIVE...
Alt-X                                  (Escape back to the PC)
MS-Kermit>send read.me                 (MS-DOS Kermit sends the file)

   (The file is transferred...)

MS-Kermit>                             (All done)
```

Local-Mode File Transfer

In this example, you are running C-Kermit on your *local* computer, a UNIX workstation or timesharing system, and you are dialing up a remote computer to download some files. Note the use of the wildcard character * to denote a file group.

```
$ kermit                               (Start Kermit on UNIX)
C-Kermit 5A(188), 23 Nov 92, SunOS 4.1
Type ? or HELP for help
C-Kermit>set modem hayes               (Specify modem type)
C-Kermit>set line /dev/ttyh8           (and communication device)
C-Kermit>set speed 2400                (and speed)
C-Kermit>dial 5551234                  (Dial the number)
Connection completed.                  (Call completed)
```

```
C-Kermit>connect                    (Begin terminal emulation)
Connecting through /dev/ttyh8, speed 2400.
The escape character is Ctrl-\ (ASCII 28, FS).
Type the escape character followed by C to get back,
or followed by ? to see other options.
ELECTRO-BRAIN 9000
LOGIN: olaf                         (Type your username)
PASSWORD: _____                    (and your password)

WELCOME. CHOOSE:
1. Chess
2. World Domination
3. Kermit
4. Logout

YOUR CHOICE? 3                      (Kermit, of course)
Electro-Kermit>send plan*.txt       (Send some files)
Ctrl-\c                             (Escape back to C-Kermit)
C-Kermit>receive                    (Receive the files)

   (The files are transferred...)

C-Kermit>connect                    (Go back to the remote computer)
Electro-Kermit>exit                 (Exit from the remote Kermit)
YOUR CHOICE? 4                      (Log out)
ELECTRO-BRAIN 9000 HAS TERMINATED YOUR SESSION.
GOOD BYE.
Communications disconnect (back at local system)
C-Kermit>dir plan*.txt              (List the received files)

-rw-rw----   1 olaf         42378 Aug  8 19:21 plan1.txt
-rw-rw----   1 olaf          5986 Aug  8 19:21 plan2.txt
-rw-rw----   1 olaf         12873 Aug  8 19:21 plan3.txt

C-Kermit>exit                       (Exit from C-Kermit)
$
```

Here is another example, in which you use C-Kermit to make a TCP/IP TELNET connection to a remote Internet host and upload some files to it. Both computers have C-Kermit, so you take advantage of the SET PROMPT command to keep yourself oriented:

```
C-Kermit>set prompt Local>          (Prompt for local Kermit)
Local>telnet hq                     (Go to the remote host)

login: olaf                         (Log in)
Password: _____                    (Enter your password)

$ kermit                            (Start Kermit on remote computer)
C-Kermit 5A(188), 23 Nov 92, HP 9000 Series HP-UX
Type ? or HELP for help
C-Kermit>set prompt Remote>         (Prompt for remote Kermit)
Remote>r                            (Receive some files)
Ctrl-\c                             (Escape back to local C-Kermit)
```

```
Local>s /usr/include/t*.h        (Send some files)

  (The files are transferred...)

Local>c                          (Connect back to remote computer)
Remote>exit                      (Exit from remote Kermit)
$ exit                           (Log out from remote computer)
Communications disconnect (back at local system)
Local>
```

The File Transfer Display

When C-Kermit is used in local mode, it displays the progress of the file transfer on your screen in one of several formats: fullscreen, serial, crt, or none at all. The command to select the display style is:

SET FILE DISPLAY { CRT, FULLSCREEN, NONE, SERIAL }

The default type of display is SERIAL.

The FULLSCREEN display, available in VMS, OpenVMS, OS/2, OS-9, Amiga, and most UNIX C-Kermit versions, produces a formatted report on a 24-line by 80-column screen:

```
C-Kermit 5A(188), 23 Nov 92, MYVAX

      Current Directory: $DISK1:[OLAF.TMP]
    Communication Device:  TXA5:
     Communication Speed: 2400
                 Parity: none

                Sending: OOFA.TMP;6 => OOFA.TMP => oofa.tmp
              File Type: text
              File Size: 40918
           Percent Done: 39
     Estimated Time Left: 00:01:44
           Window Slots: 3 of 4
            Packet Type: D
           Packet Count: 20
          Packet Length: 1000
     Packet Retry Count: 1
     Packet Block Check: 2

             Last Error:
           Last Message:

X to cancel file, Z to cancel group, <CR> to resend packet,
E to send Error packet, or Ctrl-C to quit immediately.
```

The fields on the right are updated continuously to keep you informed of the progress of the transfer. The top line shows the Kermit version number, release date, and the name of your local computer (if known). The estimated time remaining to transfer the current file is updated continuously and can fluctuate as the speed of the transfer changes. The "Sending" line shows the local filename, the name used in the packet, and the name used on the remote computer. At the end of a successful transfer, the Last Message field changes to a summary report, a beep is sounded, and the C-Kermit prompt reappears:

```
        Last Error:
      Last Message: Files: 4, Total Bytes: 1432371, 229 cps
C-Kermit>
```

"cps" means characters per second, an indication of the efficiency of the file transfer (discussed more fully in Chapter 8). To check whether the FULLSCREEN display is available:

```
C-Kermit>check fullscreen
 Available
C-Kermit>
```

Even when available, the fullscreen display won't work if your terminal type is set incorrectly or is not supported.

The SERIAL file transfer display, which is used unless you specify otherwise, works with all kinds of display devices, including video and hardcopy terminals as well as Braille and speech units. It looks like this:

```
SF
X to cancel file,  CR to resend current packet
Z to cancel group, A for status report
E to send Error packet, Ctrl-C to quit immediately:
A
Receiving: PLAN1.TXT => plan1.txt
Size: 8113, Type: text
........Z [OK]
F A
Receiving: PLAN2.TXT => plan2.txt
Size: 12341, Type: text
..........T%..N%..Z [OK]
F A
Receiving: PLAN3.TXT => plan3.txt
Size: 10001, Type: text
..........Z [OK]
B
```

The single letters like S, F, A, Z, and B are Kermit protocol packet types, listed in Table 5-2 on the next page. If there is any information to report, it is shown after the packet letter. For example, after the F packet, C-Kermit reports the file name, such as **PLAN1.TXT**. When the A packet arrives, which contains the file's size, C-Kermit shows the reported size. => `plan1.txt` shows the local name for file.

Table 5-2 Kermit Packet Types

Type	Name	Function
A	Attributes	Attributes of file.
B	Bye	End of transmission.
C	Command	Host command for a server.
D	Data	Data from file.
E	Error	Fatal error, contains message.
F	File Header	Start of file, contains filename.
G	Generic	File management command for a server.
I	Information	Protocol parameters.
N	NAK	Negative acknowledgement, requests retransmission.
R	Receive Initiate	Asks server to send a file.
S	Send Initiate	Negotiates parameters and starts sending.
T	Timeout	(Pseudopacket) Indicates a timeout waiting for a packet.
Y	ACK	Acknowledgement.
Z	End of File	Tells receiver to close the file.
X	Text Header	Precedes screen data.
%	Retransmission	(Pseudopacket) Indicates that a packet was retransmitted.

When the file starts to arrive, C-Kermit prints a period for every K (1024 characters) of data successfully received. If an expected packet does not arrive within a per-packet timeout interval, a T is printed. If a negative acknowledgement is sent or received, an N is printed. If a packet is retransmitted, a percent sign (%) is displayed.

If FILE DISPLAY is set to CRT, the dots are replaced by a line continuously showing the bytes (characters) transferred so far, the percentage done, the current transfer rate in characters per second (CPS), and the length of the current packet. This line is refreshed by simple overstriking, and so should work on any CRT (video) terminal:

```
Sending: ckuxla.h => CKUXLA.H
Size: 2599, Type: text
    File    Percent         Packet
    Bytes   Done      CPS   Length
    2599    89%       229      998
```

When FILE DISPLAY is OFF, C-Kermit skips the display and transfers files silently. The file-transfer interruption characters (X, Z, E) are disabled, but you can still get back to the C-Kermit prompt by typing Ctrl-C. The file transfer display is turned off automatically if C-Kermit is transferring files in the background.

Interrupting a File Transfer

While files are being transferred, you can interrupt the transfer or query its progress. This is done from the *local* Kermit program by pressing a key, a key combination, a sequence of keys, or, in some cases (as in Macintosh Kermit), a mouse button.

When C-Kermit is the local Kermit program, in most cases you need only type a single key, such as X. In others, notably those based on AT&T System V UNIX, you must type the CONNECT-mode escape character (normally Ctrl-Backslash) before you type the interruption key.[18]

C-Kermit's file transfer interruption keys are available to you when C-Kermit is in local mode and its file transfer display is active. When the file transfer begins, C-Kermit tells you what the available interruption keys are. In most C-Kermit versions, the message looks like this:

```
X to cancel a file,  CR to resend current packet
Z to cancel group, A for status report
E to send Error packet, Ctrl-C to quit immediately.
```

In versions that require you to type the CONNECT-mode escape character before the interruption key, the message might look like this:

```
Type escape character (^\) followed by:
X to cancel a file,  CR to resend current packet
Z to cancel group, A for status report
E to send Error packet, Ctrl-C to quit immediately.
```

or like this:

```
<^\>X to cancel file, <^\>Z to cancel group, <^\><CR> to resend packet,
<^\>E to send Error packet, or Ctrl-C to quit immediately.
```

Most of the interruption keys also have control-character equivalents and possibly other synonyms. For example, to interrupt transfer of a single file, you can type X, F, Ctrl-X, or Ctrl-F. The X or F can be either upper- or lowercase.

The same interruptions can be sent to a *remote* C-Kermit program from your local PC, Macintosh, or other Kermit program. They work the same way, but you might have to enter them differently; for example, the Macintosh Kermit file transfer display has interruption boxes that you can click on with your mouse. Consult the documentation for your local Kermit program.

---

[18]The control-character prefix is required because of limitations in the System V terminal driver. Nevertheless, certain System-V based C-Kermit versions include a workaround, so also try entering the interruption characters without the control-character prefix.

Cancelling a Single File: X

The X key (or, if required, escape-character followed by X) cancels the file currently being transferred. If a group of files is being sent, Kermit skips ahead to the next one.

```
C-Kermit>s ckuusr.*
SF
X to cancel file,  CR to resend current packet
Z to cancel group, A for status report
E to send Error packet, Ctrl-C to quit immediately:
A
Sending: ckuusr.c => CKUUSR.C,
Size: 41152, Type: text
.......X
Cancelling File [discarded]
F A
Sending: ckuusr.h => CKUUSR.H
Size: 17773, Type: text
...............Z [OK]
C-Kermit>
```

If C-Kermit is sending a file, it tells the remote receiver to close and discard the file. If C-Kermit is receiving a file, it tells the sender to cancel the transfer, then closes and discards the portion of the file received so far.

Cancelling a Group of Files: Z

If you type Z instead of X and more than one file is being transferred, the entire file group is cancelled and C-Kermit should return to its prompt. If only one file is being transferred, Z works exactly like X.

Retransmitting a Packet: Carriage Return

If the file transfer appears to be stuck, you can type a carriage return (press the Return or Enter key) to resend the most recent packet. This does no harm because packets are numbered and duplicates are automatically discarded.

Requesting a Status Report: A

If you type the letter A, C-Kermit prints a brief summary of how the transfer has progressed so far, then continues with the transfer:

```
....................A
Status report:
  file type: text          block check: 1
  file number: 1           compression: 1
  size: 50532              8th-bit prefixing: 0
  characters so far: 20761 packet length: 89
  percent done: 41         window slots: 1
........................... [OK]
```

The A command is ignored if you are using the FULLSCREEN file transfer display, since most of this information is already on the screen.

Suspending C-Kermit: Ctrl-Z

On UNIX computers with job control, you can type Ctrl-Z to suspend Kermit during local-mode file transfer in such a way that the file transfer can be continued in either the foreground or the background. See Appendix III for details.

Interrupting C-Kermit: Ctrl-C

You can always type Ctrl-C to interrupt any file transfer. In local mode you only need to type one Ctrl-C to get back to the prompt immediately. A remote mode C-Kermit can be returned to its prompt by typing two Ctrl-C's in a row:

```
C-Kermit>send me.away       (Send a file)
^A0 Sz* @-#Y1~*   yE        (See the Kermit packet)
Ctrl-C Ctrl-C               (Type two Control-C's)
^C...                       (Kermit confirms that it got them)
C-Kermit>                   (and returns to its prompt)
```

When you interrupt a local-mode file transfer with Ctrl-C, no protocol messages are sent to the remote Kermit (if any), and it remains in packet mode. Therefore, use this method only as a last resort or if you forgot to start the Kermit program on the other end.

Sending an Error Packet: E

You can cancel any kind of transfer and put the remote Kermit back into a known state by typing the letter *E* (or escape-character followed by E) while your file transfer display screen is active. This makes C-Kermit send an error (E) packet.

This is useful, for example, if the remote Kermit does not respond to the X or Z cancellation messages; most popular Kermit programs do (see Table 1-1 on page 8). If the remote Kermit was started interactively and was given a SEND or RECEIVE command, the error packet should make it return to its prompt. If the remote Kermit is in server mode (explained in Chapter 7), the error packet makes it ready to receive a new command.

You can also send an error packet by issuing the following command at the C-Kermit prompt or from a command file:

E-PACKET
    Send an Error packet to the other Kermit. Example:

```
C-Kermit>e-packet           (Send an error packet)
```

This command is useful when you mistakenly type Ctrl-C to interrupt a local-mode file transfer. If C-Kermit is not in local mode, the error packet appears on your screen containing the text "User cancelled." It does no harm.

Interrupting a File Transfer   *111*

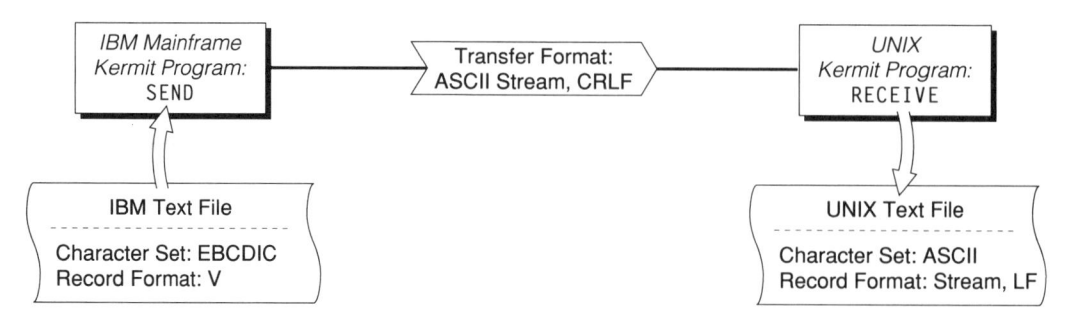

Figure 5-4 Kermit Text File Conversion

Transferring Text Files

○ ○ ○ ○
Transfer of text files that contain accented letters, non-Roman letters, or other national or international characters is described in Chapter 9.

○ ○ ○ ○
The VMS and OpenVMS file system is far more complex than the simple model presented here, and VMS C-Kermit's handling of the VMS file system is quite different. VMS C-Kermit users should be sure to read Appendix IV in addition to this and the next few chapters.

A text file is one that you can read on your screen without using any special kind of formatting software such as a word processor or electronic publishing package. If you can display a file with your computer's TYPE (or equivalent) command and it looks right, then it's most likely a text file.

Text files are made up of lines containing ordinary printable characters such as letters, digits, spaces, and punctuation marks, without special effects like boldface and italics. Different computers have different ways of representing text files: different codes to represent the characters (the character set) and different ways of separating the lines (the record format). On an ASCII-stream-based file system, for example, text files are generally made up of ASCII (or national or international) printing characters, with lines separated by carriage return, linefeed, or both, and containing no other control characters or formatting codes except perhaps for tab, backspace, and formfeed.

Kermit automatically converts ordinary text files into a useful and appropriate format when you transfer them between unlike computers. It does this by using a standard representation for text within its file transfer packets, which is normally ASCII (ISO 646 USA version) character codes (listed in Table VIII-1 on page 461) with Carriage-Return

Linefeed (CRLF) line terminators. The sending Kermit translates from the local computer's text file conventions to this form, and the receiving Kermit converts back to its own local conventions, as in the example shown in Figure 5-4.

No special commands are needed to take advantage of Kermit's text file conversion. It happens automatically unless you say otherwise. To be certain that Kermit will transfer files in text mode, however, you can use this command:

SET FILE TYPE TEXT
   Tells Kermit to perform character set and record format conversions during file transfer, storing files in conventional and useful text format on the receiving computer. This is Kermit's default file transfer mode.

Transferring Binary Files

Files that are not text files are called *binary files*. Our own peculiar definition of a binary file is a file that is not to be converted in any way during transfer. A good example would be an executable program image. Kermit does not know and cannot guess (except on VMS and OpenVMS) which files you want converted and which ones you don't. You must tell it. The command is:

SET FILE TYPE BINARY
   This command tells Kermit that no conversions of any kind are to be performed upon the file during transfer.

Let's look at an example of binary file transfer in which we upload a copy of a PC ZIP archive to a UNIX computer, making it available for other people to download to their PCs:

```
C>kermit                            (Start Kermit on the PC)
MS-DOS Kermit 3.11
Type ? or HELP for help
MS-Kermit>dir oofa.zip              (Check the file's size)
  OOFA     ZIP     192488  2-08-92  3:28p
MS-Kermit>set speed 2400            (Set the dialing speed)
MS-Kermit>dial 555-1234             (Dial the UNIX computer)
MS-Kermit>connect                   (Begin terminal emulation)
                                    (Press Enter to begin)
login: olaf                         (Type your username)
Password: _____                    (and password)

Welcome to UNIX.

$ kermit                            (Start C-Kermit)
C-Kermit 5A(188), 23 Nov 92, UNIX System V R4
Type ? or HELP for help
C-Kermit>set file type binary       (Use BINARY mode)
C-Kermit>receive                    (Tell C-Kermit to receive the file)
```

```
Alt-x                           (Escape back to MS-DOS Kermit)
MS-Kermit>set file type binary  (Use BINARY mode)
MS-Kermit>send oofa.zip         (Send the file)

    (The file is transferred...)

MS-Kermit>connect               (Connect back to UNIX)
C-Kermit>dir oofa.zip           (Check file file's size)
-rw-rw-r--   1 olaf       192488 Feb  8 13:28 oofa.zip
C-Kermit>
```

The two directory listings show that the received file on UNIX is exactly the same size as the original, which is a good indication that no conversions have taken place.

To download the file from UNIX, follow the same procedure, but give a SEND command to UNIX C-Kermit first and then a RECEIVE command to MS-DOS Kermit:

```
C-Kermit>set file type binary   (Use binary mode)
C-Kermit>send oofa.zip          (Tell C-Kermit to send the file)
Alt-x                           (Escape back to the PC)
MS-Kermit>set file type binary  (Binary mode here too)
MS-Kermit>receive               (Tell MS-DOS Kermit to receive)
```

It is not always necessary to give the SET FILE TYPE command to both Kermit programs. It is often sufficient to give it only to the sender, and then the sender informs the receiver of the file type automatically by means of an *attribute packet*, explained in Chapter 8. Attribute packets are an optional feature of the Kermit protocol, and are not supported by all Kermit software programs (see Table 1-1 on page 8).

File Names

Kermit transfers not just a file's contents, but also its name. By default, file names are converted to a simple standard form on the assumption that the file is being transferred to a computer that has different file naming conventions. Kermit's normal form for names should be inoffensive enough to agree with all kinds of computers. You can alter Kermit's treatment of file names with the SET FILE NAMES command:

SET FILE NAMES CONVERTED

When sending files, C-Kermit translates the file name into uppercase if necessary and ensures that there is no more than one dot (period) in it. Extra dots or unusual characters like spaces or punctuation are translated to X or underscore (_) and if a dot is the first character, an X is placed in front of it. In addition, all device, directory, and path names, as well as version numbers, are removed. For example:

```
The file:                       Is sent as:
oofa.txt                        OOFA.TXT
/usr/olga/oofa.txt              OOFA.TXT
$DISK1:[OLGA]OOFA.TXT;3         OOFA.TXT
```

114   The Basics of File Transfer / Chapter 5

```
oofa.txt.new                          OOFA.TXTXNEW
oofa.txt.~3~                          OOFA.TXTXX3X
.login                                X.LOGIN
```

When receiving files, UNIX C-Kermit converts the name to lowercase, but does not alter it otherwise. Other C-Kermit implementations attempt to use the incoming filename as is.

SET FILE NAMES LITERAL

Leave file names alone. Do not change the case of letters, do not remove extra dots, do not strip device, directory, or path names, and do not strip version numbers. This option should be used only between like operating systems, and then only when they have the same directory structure and you have the appropriate access to the specified directories.

In both cases, if an incoming filename contains device, directory, or version information, C-Kermit attempts to use it. For example, suppose you want to send a file from UNIX to a particular device and directory on VMS or OpenVMS. If you give this command to send the file:

```
C-Kermit>send oofa.txt $disk1:[olga.new]oofa.txt;7
```

VMS C-Kermit attempts to store the file on the given device in the given directory, with the given name and version number. If the device or directory doesn't exist or you don't have write access to them, the transfer would fail with a message like "Can't open file".

No matter what your FILE NAMES setting, the receiving computer still might have to make some changes in the name. For example, MS-DOS restricts a file name to eight characters before the dot and three after, so, if necessary, MS-DOS Kermit shortens the incoming name. Examples:

```
The file sent as:                     Is stored in MS-DOS as:
OOFA.TXT                              OOFA.TXT
OOFA.TXTXNEW                          OOFA.TXT
OOFA.TXTXX3X                          OOFA.TXT
X.LOGIN                               X.LOG
FILEWITHVERYLONGNAME.ANDALONGTYPE     FILEWITH.AND
```

Thus a file can have up to three names in its passage: its original name, the name it is sent with, and the name it is stored under on the receiving system. Hence the three names shown in the fullscreen file transfer display:

```
Sending: OOFA.TMP;6 => OOFA.TMP => oofa.tmp
```

To accomplish effects not possible with SET FILE NAMES, use the "as-name" option of the SEND or RECEIVE command, for example:

```
C-Kermit>receive oofa.new Oofa.Old
```

File Names 115

Filename Collisions

What should C-Kermit do if it receives a file that has the same name as an existing file? Should it silently overwrite the existing file? Should it make an effort to preserve the existing file? Should it reject the incoming file? These are called file collision actions, and you have six to choose from:

SET FILE COLLISION BACKUP
> This setting, which is C-Kermit's default file collision action, allows the file to arrive and to be stored under the name it was sent with, without destroying any previously existing file that has the same name. The existing file is given a new, unique name that fits within the operating system's file naming restrictions, generally by adding digits to the name; for example, in UNIX `oofa.txt` becomes `oofa.txt.~1~`. See the appropriate appendix for details.

SET FILE COLLISION OVERWRITE
> Overwrites (replaces) the existing file. Use this setting with caution.

SET FILE COLLISION APPEND
> Adds the incoming file to the end of the existing file. This option is useful for appending information to a log file, but it should be used with caution to avoid, for example, joining two files of different types (like text and binary).

SET FILE COLLISION DISCARD
> Refuses and/or discards the incoming file and preserves the existing file. This option is handy for resuming multi-file transmissions that were broken. Only those files that do not have a counterpart on the receiving system are transferred.

SET FILE COLLISION RENAME
> This is just like the BACKUP option, except that the *incoming* file gets the new name, rather than the existing file.

SET FILE COLLISION UPDATE
> Accepts the incoming file only if it is newer than the existing file, in which case the existing file is overwritten. This feature depends on the file creation date field in the attribute packet (explained in Chapter 8), and requires the other Kermit to support attribute packets (Table 1-1, p. 8). The UPDATE option is handy for keeping a parallel collection of files up to date on another computer; only those that have changed since the last update are sent.

The SET FILE COLLISION command is effective only when given to the file *receiver*. The VMS and OpenVMS versions of C-Kermit always create a new version of any incoming file that is not rejected, preserving earlier versions according to the file's version limit, which makes the BACKUP, OVERWRITE, APPEND, and RENAME options identical in VMS and OpenVMS.

Incomplete Transfers

If a file transfer fails in the middle of a file for any reason—the connection is broken or a disk write fails—there is no way to resume it and the data transferred so far is lost. This can be frustrating if you are transferring a very long file. But it's the proper behavior; you should not be led to believe that an incomplete file is the result of a successful transfer. Nevertheless, C-Kermit gives you the option of keeping incompletely received files. However, you must ask for it explicitly:

SET FILE INCOMPLETE { KEEP, DISCARD }
This setting tells whether a partially received file is to be kept if the transfer is interrupted for any reason, including intentional cancellation. To keep incomplete files:

```
C-Kermit>set file incomplete keep
```

The SET FILE INCOMPLETE command is effective only when given to the file *receiver*; it has no effect when given to the file sender. Synonym: **SET INCOMPLETE**.

If you can go back to the system you were sending the file from, break out the part of the file that was not sent (using a text editor or other utility), and send the remainder using SET FILE COLLISION APPEND on the receiving end, the result should be pretty close to what you wanted.

Keeping a Record of Your File Transfers

During a long multi-file transfer, you probably have better things to do than keep your eyes glued to the screen. But then how will you know what happened? You can ask C-Kermit to keep a record for you, called a *transaction log*:

LOG TRANSACTIONS *[filespec [{ APPEND, NEW }]]*
Records information about the file transfer, including the date and time, file name, file type (text or binary), statistics, and error messages, in the given log file. The default log file name is TRANSACT.LOG (lowercase on UNIX) on the current disk and directory. C-Kermit creates a new log file, overwriting any existing file of the same name, unless you include the keyword APPEND after the filename. Examples:

```
C-Kermit>log trans                  (transact.log, new)
C-Kermit>log t tuesday.log new      (A new daily log)
C-Kermit>log t february.log append  (Add to a monthly log)
```

CLOSE TRANSACTIONS
Closes the current transaction log file, if any. The transaction log is also closed automatically when you EXIT from C-Kermit.

Summary

First-time Kermit users sometimes find the mechanics of file transfer confusing. But it's not very hard if you keep a few basic points in mind. First, establish a connection from the Kermit program on your local computer to the remote computer and, if necessary, log in on the remote computer.

Second, start the Kermit program on the remote computer. A Kermit program can't transfer a file unless it has another Kermit program to transfer it with! Now, just follow these three easy steps:

1. While still connected to the remote computer, tell the *remote* Kermit what to do: SEND or RECEIVE.

2. Return to your local Kermit program by typing its CONNECT-mode escape sequence, such as `Ctrl-\C` (usually) for C-Kermit or `Alt-X` for MS-DOS Kermit. Note that some communication software programs are always in "CONNECT mode," and therefore do not require you to escape back.

3. At your local Kermit's prompt, tell it what to do: RECEIVE or SEND, or select RECEIVE or SEND from your local software's file transfer menu. This is the opposite of what you told the remote Kermit to do. If you told the remote Kermit to SEND, you should tell the local Kermit to RECEIVE, and vice versa.

When you are finished using the remote computer, remember to CONNECT back to it (if necessary) and log out.

You can transfer groups of files by including wildcard characters in the SEND-command file specification, you can record the progress of your file transfers in a transaction log, and you can use SET FILE commands to select text or binary transfers, the treatment of filenames, the handling of filename collisions, and the disposition of incomplete transfers. Here is a quick summary of the SET FILE commands presented in this chapter:

SET FILE COLLISION
Options: APPEND, BACKUP, DISCARD, OVERWRTE, RENAME, UPDATE. Default: BACKUP. Function: Specifies action to be taken when a file arrives that has the same name as an existing file. Give this command to the file *receiver*.

SET FILE DISPLAY
Options: CRT, FULLSCREEN, SERIAL, or NONE. Default: SERIAL. Function: Selects format for file transfer display. For use when C-Kermit is in *local* mode.

SET FILE INCOMPLETE
Options: DISCARD, KEEP. Default: DISCARD. Function: Tells what to do with a file incompletely received. Give this command to the file *receiver*.

SET FILE NAMES

Options: CONVERTED, LITERAL. Default: CONVERTED. Function: Specifies how to handle file names during transfer. Meaningful to both the file sender and the file receiver.

SET FILE TYPE

Options: TEXT or BINARY. Default: TEXT. Function: Selects text or binary mode for file transfer. Give this command to the file *sender* and, if necessary, also to the file receiver.

PROBLEMS: If a file transfer fails, use the SET PARITY command and try again. If it still fails, read Chapter 6. If file transfer works but the transferred file has the wrong format, issue the appropriate SET FILE TYPE command and try again. If file transfers work but seem inefficient, read Chapter 8.

Use the SHOW FILE command to display C-Kermit's file type, collision action, file naming, incomplete file treatment, transaction log, initialization file name, and other file-related settings:

```
C-Kermit>sho file

File parameters:
 Attributes: on
 Names:      converted    Debugging Log:    none
 Type:       text         Packet Log:       none
 Collide:    backup       Session Log:      none
 Display:    fullscreen   Transaction Log:  none
 Incomplete: discard      Init file:        .kermrc
C-Kermit>
```

These are the ABCs of Kermit file transfer, suitable for use between any two Kermit programs. More advanced and simpler techniques, which you can use once you have mastered the basic techniques, are described in the following chapters.

Chapter 6

Solving File Transfer Problems

○ ○ ○ ○
If you had no trouble transferring files using the basic techniques given in Chapter 5, please do not feel compelled to read this chapter. But don't tear these pages out of the book and rip them into tiny shreds; some day you might need them. For now, skip ahead to Chapter 7 on page 139, which shows you how to turn C-Kermit into a file server and how to use C-Kermit as a client of another C-Kermit server—much easier than the SEND/RECEIVE style of operation you have been using up till now. Then go on to Chapter 8 to learn how to transfer files more efficiently.

Like people, computers have different languages, conflicting customs, competing ideologies, quirks, idiosyncracies, and bad habits. Telecommunications systems punch holes in our data. Sensible data on one computer becomes incomprehensible gibberish on another. To transfer files in a diverse, and sometimes hostile, computing and communications environment, Kermit software programs use the *Kermit protocol*, a set of rules and procedures for exchanging structured, error-checked messages with each other.

Kermit's default settings for all kinds of communications-, file-, and protocol-related items are based on the most common situations. But there are hundreds of different kinds of computers in the world with different styles of communication and different file formats, and there are many different ways to connect these computers. You should expect to encounter some combinations where the defaults don't work.

```
  7 Data Bits, 1 Parity Bit                    8 Data Bits
┌─┐┌─┐┌─┐┌─┐┌─┐┌─┐┌─┐┌─┐        ┌─┐┌─┐┌─┐┌─┐┌─┐┌─┐┌─┐┌─┐
│1││1││0││0││0││1││0││1│        │1││1││0││0││0││1││0││1│
└─┘└─┘└─┘└─┘└─┘└─┘└─┘└─┘        └─┘└─┘└─┘└─┘└─┘└─┘└─┘└─┘
 ↑
**Even Parity Bit**                             **No Parity**
```

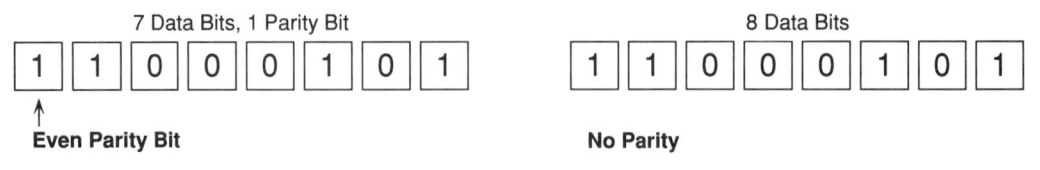

Figure 6-1 Character Formats

Because C-Kermit lets you control virtually every aspect of its operation, you can teach it to overcome computer-related incompatibilities and communications impediments, and you can help it achieve maximum efficiency under all sorts of conditions. Let's look at the effects of the communications environment on file transfer and how you can use the SET command to adapt C-Kermit to them.

Parity

The most common cause for file transfer failure is *parity*. Let's say that once again, with emphasis:

The most common cause for file transfer failure is parity.

Computers store characters in 8-bit "bytes." Some computers prefer to transmit these bytes as 7 bits of data plus one bit of error-checking information, called the parity bit. The parity bit *replaces* one of the data bits.[19] The parity bit is set to 0 or 1 based on the values of the remaining seven data bits. There are five kinds of parity: even, odd, mark, space, and none. Even parity sets the parity bit to make the overall number of 1-bits in the transmitted character even. Odd parity makes the overall number of 1-bits odd. Mark parity always sets the parity bit to 1, and space parity always sets it to 0.

Parity is an unpleasant fact of life in data communications. The receiver of a transmitted character can't tell from looking at it whether it has 7 data bits and 1 parity bit, or 8 data bits. (See Figure 6-1.) Can you? Parity prevents the transmission of 8-bit data bytes, such as we find in binary data or international character codes.

During terminal emulation, C-Kermit ignores parity unless you tell it otherwise, on the assumption that only 7-bit ASCII or ISO 646 characters are being transmitted and the 8th bit carries no useful information. That is, C-Kermit assumes parity is probably in effect without the user's knowledge.

---

[19]Other arrangements are possible but occur rarely in practice. In the most common case, and the one supported by Kermit, a byte is always transmitted as 8 bits: either 8 data bits and no parity bit, or 7 data bits and a parity bit.

122   *Solving File Transfer Problems / Chapter 6*

During file transfer, C-Kermit normally puts the communication line into 8-bit no-parity mode so it can transmit 8-bit data, on the assumption that the other Kermit program can do this too. Most Kermit programs can. The major exception is IBM mainframe Kermit, due to limitations of the IBM mainframe communication architecture.

However, it can—and often does—happen that a network or communication device between C-Kermit and the other computer might be using parity, even when both computers are not.

File transfers can fail when parity is in use but the Kermit programs do not know about it, because Kermit might misinterpret the parity bits as data bits. Luckily, this situation is caught by Kermit's own error-checking procedure so parity will not cause files to be transferred incorrectly—it simply prevents them from being transferred at all. Usually the error message is something like "Failure to receive acknowledgement" or "Too many retries." If this happens to you, use the SET PARITY command to tell the Kermit program what the parity is:

SET PARITY { EVEN, ODD, MARK, SPACE, NONE }
> This command, when given with any of its options other than NONE, tells Kermit to actually add the selected type of parity bit to all characters it sends, during both CONNECT mode and file transfer, and to remove the 8th bit of incoming characters.

If you don't know which kind of parity to use, don't worry. Just pick one. EVEN is a good first choice for serial connections; try SPACE for TCP/IP TELNET or RLOGIN connections. Give matching SET PARITY commands to the two Kermit programs and file transfer should work smoothly:

```
C-Kermit>receive                    (Receive a file)
Alt-x                               (Escape back)
MS-Kermit>set file type binary      (Binary transfer mode)
MS-Kermit>send budget.wks           (Send a spreadsheet file)
                                    (Many retries, and then...)
?Unable to receive acknowledgement from host

MS-Kermit>connect                   (Let's try it again)
C-Kermit>set parity even            (Once more, with parity)
C-Kermit>receive
Alt-x                               (Escape back again)
MS-Kermit>set parity even           (Here too)
MS-Kermit>send budget.wks           (Send it again)

   (The file is transferred)

Transfer complete.                  (This time it works)
MS-Kermit>
```

If EVEN or SPACE parity doesn't do the trick, try MARK or ODD. MARK is used with some mainframes and X.25 networks. ODD is rarely, if ever, used in data communications.

When PARITY is used during file transfer, data characters whose 8th bit is 1 are transmitted as 2-character sequences: the data character itself has its 8th bit replaced by a parity bit, and the result is preceded by an ampersand (&) character, which also has the appropriate parity bit applied to it. The receiving Kermit removes the 8th bit from each arriving character and converts the special 2-character sequences back to a single 8-bit character. As you can imagine, this can add a lot of transmission overhead. But it does allow Kermit to transfer 8-bit data through a 7-bit connection, a claim that other protocols cannot make.

HINT: Some Kermit programs, including C-Kermit and MS-DOS Kermit, attempt to detect parity *automatically* during packet operations, so even if you forget to SET PARITY there is a chance the transfer will work correctly anyway. This technique is not totally dependable because there is no way to tell the difference between space parity and no parity at all. So it is still better to SET PARITY explicitly, on *both* ends of the transfer, if your connection does not allow 8-bit data to pass through. But in case you had your PARITY set to NONE and found it changed to, say, EVEN after a file transfer, now you know why.

Speed and Flow Control in the Full Duplex Environment

During file transfer, Kermit programs compose a packet and send it as a unit, all at once. But the receiving computer might not be able to swallow that many bytes in one gulp, in which case the file transfer could fail. Like when your sink backs up—the water doesn't go down the drain as fast as it comes out of the faucet and eventually it spills onto the floor. With computers, this condition is called a buffer overflow.

Buffer overflows rarely occur on network connections, but are common on serial (direct or dialed) connections. One way to cope with buffer overflows is to connect the two computers at a lower transmission speed. The slower the data bytes arrive, the more time the computer has to process them. However, reducing transmission speed increases the time it takes to transfer a file, and therefore also your phone bill and your aggravation level.

If your serial transmission speed is too high, buffer overflows can result in lost characters and therefore packet retransmissions and reduced efficiency. If the speed is too low, transmission capacity is wasted. But there is no way to pick the perfect speed—speeds, like clothes, only come in certain sizes: 1200, 2400, 4800, ... (those are speeds, not waist sizes). And conditions change: computers can slow down and speed up depending on what other tasks they are working on.

If you have a *full duplex* connection between your computers, you may be in luck. While one computer is sending a packet, the other computer can talk back to it: "Stop!" "OK, I'm caught up, continue." This is called flow control. It works if both computers know how to do it and are told in advance that they *should* do it. There are two major types of flow control:

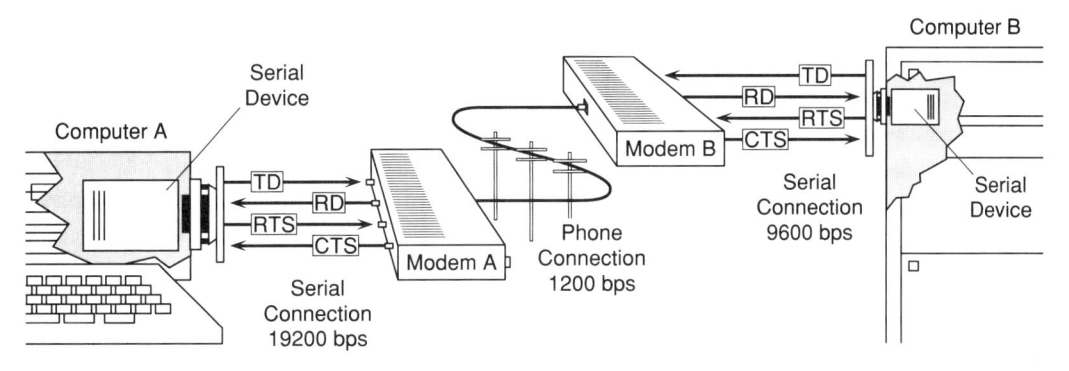

Figure 6-2 Hardware Flow Control

Software flow control
> is accomplished by inserting special characters into the data stream. These characters are normally Ctrl-S (XOFF), and Ctrl-Q (XON). The data receiver sends an XOFF to tell the sender to stop sending, and an XON to tell it to resume sending.

Hardware flow control
> occurs between the computer and the device it is immediately connected to, for example, a terminal server or a high-speed modem. It is accomplished using special wires, normally the RS-232 Request To Send (RTS) and Clear To Send (CTS) circuits. When both devices are properly configured for the same type of hardware flow control, its effect is immediate.

To illustrate, Figure 6-2 shows a modem connection between two computers. Computer A is connected to its modem at 19200 bps, but the two modems are connected at only 1200 bps. Modem A takes care of the speed discrepancy with its speed matching feature. But now Computer A can send data into Modem A much faster than Modem A can send it to Modem B. So Modem A stems the flow of data from Computer A by turning off its CTS signal, and then turns it back on when it is ready for more data. This type of flow control is often used by error-correcting modems; if the telephone connection is noisy, the modems might be retransmitting data between themselves, and therefore must block further data arriving from the computer.

Now let's turn the tables. Suppose Computer A isn't fast enough to keep up with the data coming in from Modem A. Computer A turns off its RTS signal to make the modem stop sending. But Computer B doesn't know about this, so it continues to send data. Somehow Modem A has to tell Modem B to stop sending, then Modem B has to tell Computer B. For all this to work, there must be some kind of higher-level protocol going on between the two modems (such as MNP or V.42), and local flow control of some kind must be enabled between Modem B and Computer B. Thus, for hardware flow control to function effectively, it must take place on all segments of the connection and it should propagate rapidly from one end to the other.

When flow control is in effect and working properly, you can set the transmission speed to the highest value offered by the physical connection and you shouldn't have to worry about buffer overflows. Assuming the flow control signals are delivered promptly and correctly, the effective data rate will be as high as it could possibly be at any given moment, adjusting itself automatically to varying conditions of load on the two computers and the communication medium.

The command governing flow control is:

SET FLOW-CONTROL { DTR/CD, DTR/CTS, KEEP, NONE, RTS/CTS, XON/XOFF }

Selects the desired type of flow control: Xon/Xoff (software), DTR/CD, DTR/CTS, or RTS/CTS (hardware), no change (KEEP), or none at all (NONE). Xon/Xoff flow control is used during file transfer when the underlying operating system supports it, unless you tell Kermit otherwise. Hardware flow control options are available only in Kermit implementations where the underlying operating system supports them, and they are effective only for serial communication devices. Type a question mark after SET FLOW to see which options are offered by your version of C-Kermit:

```
C-Kermit>set flow ? One of the following:
  none     keep     rts/cts    xon/xoff
```

Software flow control generally operates *end to end;* that is, between C-Kermit and the computer on the other end of the connection. The Xon and Xoff characters are subject to delay and corruption, just like any other transmitted characters. If you have a long-delay connection, for example one where it takes a second or two for your characters to echo, software flow control probably will not be very effective.

Hardware flow control solves these problems and should be used when available. Even when C-Kermit's SET FLOW-CONTROL command does not offer RTS/CTS or other hardware flow control methods, it still might be possible for you to use hardware flow control on your connection by issuing an operating system command before you start C-Kermit, or by using a special device name in the SET LINE command, in conjunction with C-Kermit's SET FLOW-CONTROL KEEP option. See the appendix for your operating system (Appendix III for UNIX, IV for VMS and OpenVMS, and so on).

On most network connections, particularly TCP/IP, it might be beneficial to SET FLOW NONE. The network takes care of flow control itself, so Kermit (or the underlying operating system's terminal device driver) doesn't need to duplicate the effort, and this can make your file transfers go faster.

Half Duplex Communication

Half duplex communication should be familiar to anyone who has used CB radio, but may seem unnatural to the rest of us who are accustomed to immediately blurting out any thoughts that come into our heads. It works just like CB: while you are talking, the other person can't talk until you release your talk button. When the direction of transmission is reversed, you have to wait until the other person is finished. If you talk out of turn, your partner won't hear you.

The talk button is the key to this process. When computers are connected with a half duplex communication channel, they too have a talk button. It is usually a special control character. A computer can send a message of any length at all, and the communication line cannot turn around until this character, called a *handshake*, is sent.

Certain kinds of mainframes communicate with their terminals in half duplex. The person at the terminal types a command and terminates it with the Enter key (which sends a carriage return character). The carriage return turns the communication channel over to the mainframe. The mainframe responds to the command, possibly sending many lines or screens full of who knows what, and when it is done sends its own handshake character, such as an XON (Control-Q) character. The carriage return is the terminal's handshake, and the XON is the mainframe's.

Kermit's commands for half duplex communication are:

SET DUPLEX HALF
   Enables local echoing during terminal connection. This command does not affect file transfer, but is listed here for completeness. Synonyms: **SET LOCAL-ECHO ON**, **SET TERMINAL ECHO ON**.

SET FLOW-CONTROL NONE
   Disables full-duplex flow control. Xon or Xoff characters sent out of turn by C-Kermit to a half-duplex computer could interfere with successful communication. However, it might still be possible to use hardware flow control, such as RTS/CTS, for example, if you are using a high-speed modem that supports it.

SET HANDSHAKE [{ BELL, CR, ESC, LF, NONE, XOFF, XON, CODE *number* **}]**
   During file transfer, C-Kermit should wait for the specified character after a packet has been received before sending the next packet, so as not to send the packet before the other Kermit program is prepared to read it. C-Kermit's default handshake is NONE. The most common handshake character on half duplex connections is XON.

If you have made a connection to a remote computer and found that you had to SET DUPLEX HALF before you could see your characters echo during CONNECT mode, and then you found that file transfer didn't work and that SETting PARITY was not enough to cure the problem, try SET HANDSHAKE XON or one of the other HANDSHAKE options. For example, the following settings are typical for a linemode connection to an IBM mainframe:

```
C-Kermit>set parity mark        (Parity is mark)
C-Kermit>set duplex half        (Local echo is needed)
C-Kermit>set flow none          (No full-duplex flow control)
C-Kermit>set handshake xon      (Handshake is xon)
```

How do you know what the handshake character is? One way to find out is to use C-Kermit's session-debugging feature, which displays control characters on your screen in printable form during CONNECT mode. Here is an example in which we give a command to an IBM mainframe and then observe the last character it sends after executing the command. This is most likely the handshake character:

```
C-Kermit>set debug session
C-Kermit>connect
.query time^J^M^@TIME IS 15:28:00 EST MONDAY 11/23/92^M^J^@
Ready; T=0.01/0.01 15:28:01^M^J^@.^Q
```

The final character is "`^Q`"—Control-Q (XON), and that's your handshake character: SET HANDSHAKE XON.

Noise and Interference

Once you have found a common "language" for the two computers, you still have no guarantee that they can communicate, any more than the fact that two people speak the same language guarantees they can talk at a party with loud music and other people shouting in their ears. If I ask you "Are you having fun?" and you respond "Tomatoes and lemons," I know you didn't receive my message correctly and I repeat my question.

Data signals are subject to distortion, interference, and loss as they travel through the wires. One of Kermit's most important jobs is to detect when this happens and retransmit any portions of your data that were damaged. Kermit does this by including a *block check* in each Kermit packet. The packet sender computes the block check when constructing the packet, and the packet receiver computes its own version when reading the packet. If the two don't agree, the packet is rejected by the receiver and retransmitted.

Block Check Options

Unless you say otherwise, Kermit includes only one block check character per packet. Although this is sufficient for most occasions, there is always a probability that certain kinds of damage can occur that won't be detected by this method. This probability increases with the packet length, and is also higher for 8-bit data than for 7-bit data. Therefore, Kermit offers a selection of block checks:

SET BLOCK-CHECK 1
> A single-character block check, the 8-bit sum of all the other characters in the packet, folded into 6 bits. This is the default.

SET BLOCK-CHECK 2
> A two-character block check, the 12-bit sum of all the other characters in the packet.

SET BLOCK-CHECK BLANK-FREE-2
> A two-character block check, the 12-bit sum of all the other characters in the packet, exactly like type 2, except encoded in such a way that neither of the two characters can be a blank. For use on connections where "trailing blanks" might be stripped.

SET BLOCK-CHECK 3
> A three-character block check, the 16-bit cyclic redundancy check (CRC) [47] of all the other characters in the packet.

The higher the block check number, the stronger the error detection, but (there's a price for everything) file transfer is slightly less efficient. Block check types 2, B, or 3 are recommended when using long packets, transferring 8-bit data, or when the connection is particularly noisy.

The single-character block check is supported by all Kermit programs. It is sufficient for relatively clean serial connections and connections provided by error-correcting modems or networks. The two- and three-character block checks are optional features of the Kermit protocol (but supported by most Kermit programs—see Table 1-1, p. 8); if the other Kermit doesn't support them, the single-character block check is used automatically, even if you ask for a higher one.

The Retry Limit

Damaged packets are recovered by automatic retransmission. But there is a limit to the number of times each packet can be retransmitted. If the limit is exceeded, Kermit concludes that the connection is unusable and gives up with an error message like "Too many retries" or "Unable to receive acknowledgement". C-Kermit allows 10 retries per packet. You can use the SET RETRY command to change this number:

SET RETRY *number*
> Specifies the maximum number of retransmissions allowed for each packet. Example:
> ```
> C-Kermit>set retry 20
> ```

The purpose of the SET RETRY command is to help Kermit decide when a connection is unusable. Increase the retry limit if you know that the connection is very noisy and you want Kermit to make every effort to push the file through, even if the cost in retransmissions (and the size of your phone bill) is high. Reduce the number if you want Kermit to detect and give up on a bad connection quickly.

Timeouts

C-Kermit expects to receive each packet within a reasonable amount of time, the *timeout interval*. At the beginning of a file transfer, each Kermit program tells the other the timeout interval to use. Thus C-Kermit's timeout interval is normally determined by the other Kermit. The timeout interval that C-Kermit tells the other Kermit to use depends on the type of connection.

When you make a SET HOST or TELNET network connection, C-Kermit has no way to know the connection speed, and so it uses a built-in default timeout value of 10 seconds.

On a serial connection, C-Kermit calculates a timeout interval based on the communication speed and packet length. For example, if the speed is 1200 bps (=120 characters per second)[20] and the packet length is 6000, it would take:

$$\frac{6000\ chars}{120\ chars/sec} = 50\ seconds$$

to transmit a packet. C-Kermit adds 10 percent for safety, raising the interval to 55 seconds.

But some connections might be slower than C-Kermit expects. For example, a 9600 bps serial connection might be routed through a congested wide-area network, where each packet must queue up at a succession of overloaded packet-switch nodes and wait its turn to be relayed to the next node until it reaches its final destination, resulting in a transfer rate far slower than 9600 bps.

When a packet doesn't arrive in time, an alarm goes off. The file sender retransmits its previous packet or the file receiver sends a request for the expected packet that did not arrive. But if the tardy packet was already on the way, it will arrive eventually, followed by a second, redundant copy of itself resulting from the timeout. The process can repeat throughout the transfer, slowing the pace to a crawl or even causing the transfer to fail. The solution is to adjust the timeout interval:

SET { SEND, RECEIVE } TIMEOUT *number*
    This command tells C-Kermit to set the timeout interval to the given number of seconds, rather than calculating it automatically. SET RECEIVE TIMEOUT tells C-Kermit to tell the other Kermit what timeout interval to use, bypassing C-Kermit's timeout calculation. SET SEND TIMEOUT tells C-Kermit to use the given timeout, regardless of what the other Kermit requests.

---

[20] In asynchronous serial transmission, there are 10 bits per character because of the stop bit and start bit. See Appendix II.

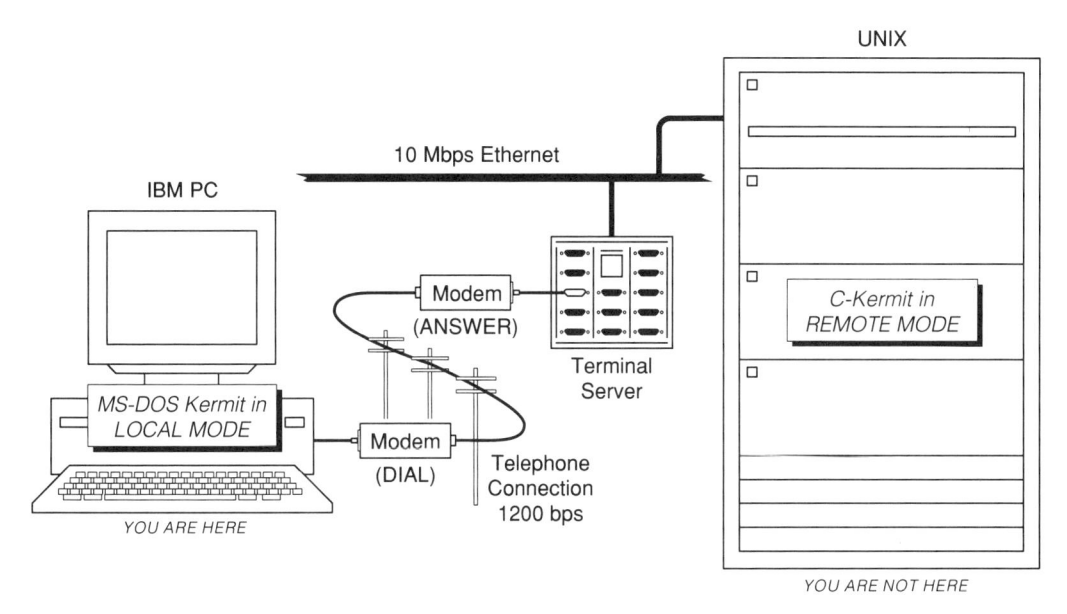

Figure 6-3 Terminal Server Connection

Here is a real-life example, in which scientific and survival data is sent from an Antarctic outpost to a relay station in Florida via an aging earth satellite, which can cut out for periods as long as a minute and a half, transmitting through such exotic sources of noise interference as aurora borealis [20]:

```
C-Kermit>set send timeout 120    (A 2-minute timeout)
C-Kermit>set rec time 120        (In both directions)
C-Kermit>set retry 100           (Allow many retries)
C-Kermit>set block 3             (Use strongest error checking)
C-Kermit>send ozone.dat          (Send ozone-layer data)
```

Premature timeouts can also occur if C-Kermit does not know what your true communication speed is. A common scenario is shown in Figure 6-3, in which you are dialed at 1200 bps to a terminal server that hides your true connection speed from C-Kermit. You can inform the operating system of your true speed before starting C-Kermit, as explained in Chapter 5, or you can tell C-Kermit to use a longer timeout based on the packet length you are using and your true communication speed, for example:

`C-Kermit>set receive timeout 10` *(For 1000-byte packets)*

10 seconds should allow enough time for a 1000-character packet to be transmitted at 120 characters per second.

To override the timeouts calculated by *both* Kermit programs, you can either (a) give each Kermit a SET RECEIVE TIMEOUT command, or (b) give both a SET RECEIVE TIMEOUT and a SET SEND TIMEOUT to one of them.

Transparency Problems

Kermit packets are normally framed by a Control-A character (Start of Header) at the beginning and Carriage Return (Control-M) at the end. In between, there are no control characters at all. Control characters in your file data are encoded as printable character sequences (for example, Control-S is encoded as #S) to prevent their interception by devices or drivers along the communication pathway (which is why Xon/Xoff flow control can work during file transfer).

But some computers or communication processors won't let even these two innocent control characters pass by unscathed. For example, we have heard of at least one modem that uses Control-A as its escape character: send your first Kermit packet and you're back talking to your modem dialer instead of to the other computer! For pathological cases like this, C-Kermit lets you adjust the framing of the packets:

SET { SEND, RECEIVE } START-OF-PACKET *number*
> Changes the packet-start character from Control-A to something else, which can be any 7-bit ASCII character. A control character should be used unless the communication path refuses to allow any control characters at all to pass through. Give the ASCII code for the character (see Table VIII-1, page 461); for example, 2 for Ctrl-B, 5 for Ctrl-E. You must give corresponding commands to both Kermit programs:

```
MS-Kermit>set send start-of-packet 7    (PC sends Ctrl-G)
MS-Kermit>connect                       (Connect to remote)
C-Kermit>set receive start 7            (C-Kermit receives Ctrl-G)
C-Kermit>send oofa.txt                  (Start the transfer)
Alt-x                                   (Escape back to the PC)
MS-Kermit>receive                       (Receive the file)
```

> Here we change the packet-start character only for the packets that are being sent by the PC to C-Kermit; Control-A is still used to start the packets send by C-Kermit to the PC. You can also change the packet-start character in the other direction, or in both directions. Just remember to give the corresponding SET SEND START-OF-PACKET and SET RECEIVE START-OF-PACKET commands to both Kermit programs.

SET { SEND, RECEIVE } END-OF-PACKET *number*
> Changes the packet-end character from Carriage Return to something else, which must be an ASCII 7-bit control character. Give corresponding commands to both Kermits, for example:

```
MS-Kermit>set send end-of-packet 10     (PC sends Ctrl-J)
MS-Kermit>connect                       (Connect to remote)
C-Kermit>set receive end 10             (C-Kermit receives Ctrl-J)
C-Kermit>receive                        (Wait for files)
Alt-x                                   (Escape back to the PC)
MS-Kermit>send *.txt                    (Send some files)
```

> This changes the packet terminator in the PC-to-C-Kermit direction.

In addition to changing the packet start and end characters, you can also tell C-Kermit to send additional characters *between* the packets:

SET { SEND, RECEIVE } PAD-CHARACTER *number*
Specifies an additional character to insert before the start-of-packet character. It must be different from the start-of-packet character. Pad characters are ignored by the Kermit protocol, but can be useful to give the receiving computer time to prepare to read the packet. There is at least one case where the pad character is used to put the packet receiver's front end into a special "transparency mode." Without this the packet itself could not pass through. SET SEND PAD-CHARACTER tells C-Kermit which character to send for padding; SET RECEIVE PAD-CHARACTER tells C-Kermit to tell the other computer's Kermit program which character to *send* as padding.

SET { SEND, RECEIVE } PADDING *number*
This tells how many copies of the pad character to insert before each packet.

Here, for example, is the series of commands that allows C-Kermit to transfer files with a Cray supercomputer running the CTSS operating system and Cray Kermit:

```
C-Kermit>set parity even         (Even parity required)
C-Kermit>set send end 23         (Packet end is Ctrl-W)
C-Kermit>set send padding 1      (Use 1 pad character)
C-Kermit>set send pad-char 26    (Pad char is Ctrl-Z)
C-Kermit>send animation.txt      (Now send a file)
```

IBM Mainframe Linemode Communication

There are two types of connections to IBM mainframes: full screen and linemode. A full-screen connection goes through a device that converts between IBM 3270 EBCDIC block-mode terminal and asynchronous ASCII character-mode terminal conventions. For brevity, we call this device a 3270 protocol converter. It masks all the peculiarities of IBM mainframe-style communication from the user and can be used (usually) with little extra effort.

IBM mainframe linemode connections, on the other hand, require Kermit to jump through more than a few hoops. Nearly every communication parameter—duplex, parity, flow control, handshake—is contrary to C-Kermit's defaults, and so must be set explicitly.

The next page shows an example of a C-Kermit local-mode file transfer with an IBM mainframe running the VM/CMS operating system. To add a little spice, the modem intercepts the Ctrl-A character, so Kermit's packet-start character must be changed (the modem name below is fictional, to avoid lawsuits).

To complicate matters further, the login process reveals the connection to be very noisy, so the user prudently adjusts communication parameters for extra noise resistance.

```
$ kermit                                (Start Kermit on UNIX)
C-Kermit 5A(188) 23 Nov 92, SunOS 4.1
Type ? or HELP for help
C-Kermit>set modem xyz                  (Specify modem type)
C-Kermit>set line /dev/ttyh8            (and communication device)
C-Kermit>set speed 2400                 (and speed)
C-Kermit>set parity mark                (Mainframe needs mark parity)
C-Kermit>set duplex half                (Connection is half duplex)
C-Kermit>set flow none                  (No full duplex flow control)
C-Kermit>set handshake xon              (Use XON for line turnaround)
C-Kermit>set send start 2               (Change out-packet start to ^B)
C-Kermit>dial 5551234                   (Dial the number)
Connection completed.                   (The call is answered)
C-Kermit>connect                        (Connect to the mainframe)
VIRTUAL MAC~xINE/S{{TEM PRODU=T         (Notice the noisy herald)
.login olga                             (Log in)
Enter password:XXXXXXXX
LOGON AT 22:00:52 EDT SU~~{Y 08/11/92
VM/SP REL 5 04/19/88 19:39
.
Ready; T=0.07/0.11 2~~{{:55
CMS
.
.kermit                                 (Run Kermit on the mainframe)
Kermit-CMS Versi%x 4.2.4
Enter ? for a ~~st of valid commands

Kermit-CMS>set retry 20                 (Allow many retries)
Kermit-CMS>set block 3                  (Use strongest error checking)
Kermit-CMS>set receive start 2          (Change in-packet start to ^B)
Kermit-CMS>send profile exec            (Send a file)
Kermit-CMS ready to send.
Please escape to local Kermit now to RECEIVE the file(s).

KERMIT READY TO SEND...
Ctrl-\c                                 (Escape back to C-Kermit)

C-Kermit>set retry 20                   (Allow many retries)
C-Kermit>receive                        (Tell it to receive the file)
SF
PROFILE.EXEC A Size: 18113
=> profile.exec ..N%N%..T%..N%..T%T%T%N%......T%..N%..Z [OK]
B
C-Kermit>connect                        (Connect back to the mainframe)

Kermit-CMS>exit                         (Leave mainframe Kermit)
Ready; T=0.02/0.08 22:01:37
.logoff                                 (Log out)
Ctrl-\c                                 (Escape back to C-Kermit)
C-Kermit>exit                           (Exit from C-Kermit)
$
```

IBM Mainframe Full-Screen Communication

Full-screen Kermit connections to IBM mainframes go through 3270 protocol converters. These devices translate between normal ASCII and the IBM EBCDIC character sets, they translate IBM 3270 screen directives into escape sequences for your terminal, and they generally fool the parties on either end of the connection into thinking they are dealing with their own familiar world.

The techniques used by C-Kermit to transfer files with an IBM mainframe through a protocol converter depends on whether the protocol converter can be put into transparent mode by IBM mainframe Kermit. Transparent means the protocol conversion functions are turned off, and the device passes data through without modification. Some protocol converters, such as the IBM 7171, allow this. Others, such as the IBM 3708 or certain terminal servers with built-in 3270 emulation, do not.

A connection to a protocol converter is just like a connection to a full-duplex computer host or service, except that even parity is usually a requirement.

File Transfer with Transparent Mode

Most 3270 protocol converters allow transparent mode operation, which is preferred because it makes for simpler and more efficient file transfer. Common examples include the IBM Series/1, 7171, 4994, 3174 AEA, and 938x ASCII subsystem, as well as many non-IBM products. Kermit-370 on the IBM mainframe attempts to detect transparent-mode capability automatically and use it. When automatic detection doesn't work, IBM mainframe Kermit's SET CONTROLLER command can be used to force a specific style of transparency when it is available.

When the protocol converter can be put into transparent mode, file transfer works normally:

```
C-Kermit>set parity even
C-Kermit>show communications
 Line: ttx4, speed 19200, parity: even
 duplex: full, flow: xon/xoff, handshake: none, ...
C-Kermit>connect                (Connect to the mainframe)
.
.kermit                         (Start mainframe Kermit)
Kermit-CMS Version 4.2.4
Enter ? for a list of valid commands
Kermit-CMS>send maketape exec   (Send a file)
Please escape to local Kermit now to RECEIVE the file(s).

KERMIT READY TO SEND...
Ctrl-\c                         (Escape back)
C-Kermit>receive                (Receive the file)
```

If this example does not work for you, use IBM mainframe Kermit's SHOW CONTROLLER command to find out what kind of transparency, if any, is being used, and then try using different SET CONTROLLER commands to achieve transparency:

```
Kermit-CMS>set controller series1
Kermit-CMS>set controller graphics
Kermit-CMS>set controller aea
```

and then try the file transfer again. If none of these works, consult the IBM mainframe Kermit documentation for further information or ask the IBM mainframe system administrators for help. If all else fails, you can access the mainframe in linemode (if that is possible at your site) rather than full-screen mode when you need to transfer files, or else you can use the non-transparent technique.

File Transfer without Transparent Mode

When the protocol converter can *not* be put into transparent mode, it is impossible to send a normal Kermit packet through it because *all* control characters are filtered out, including Kermit's packet-start and -end characters. Lines (packets) longer than the screen width are broken and wrapped, blanks might be discarded, the protocol converter can engage in screen optimizations that interfere with packets sent by the mainframe, and each packet sent to the mainframe can be echoed once, twice, or more by the protocol converter.

By switching to a slightly modified version of the Kermit protocol, in which there are no distinguished characters to mark the beginning and end of a packet, and with a special type of block check that never includes blanks, even these obstacles can be overcome. IBM mainframe Kermit version 4.2.3 or later is required.

The trick is to tell IBM mainframe Kermit to operate in fullscreen mode, rather than transparent mode, then set the packet-start character to be a printable ASCII character, avoid the use of handshake characters, and use the "blank-free-2" block check:

```
C-Kermit>set parity even            (Even parity)
C-Kermit>set send start 58          (Packet start is ":")
C-Kermit>set receive start 58       (in both directions)
C-Kermit>set block-check b          (Type B block check)
C-Kermit>set handshake none         (No handshake)
C-Kermit>connect                    (Now go to the mainframe)
.
. kermit                            (Start mainframe Kermit)
Kermit-CMS Version 4.2.3
Enter ? for a list of valid commands
Kermit-CMS>set controller fullscreen  (No transparent mode)
Kermit-CMS>set send start 58        (Packet start is ":")
Kermit-CMS>set receive start 58     (in both directions)
Kermit-CMS>set block-check b        (Type B block check)
Kermit-CMS>set handshake 0          (Do not send handshake)
Kermit-CMS>send data sas b          (Send a file...)
```

NOTE: All four start-of-packet characters must be the same.

The file is transferred more slowly than with transparent mode, but at least it can be done. Short packets are used automatically to avoid "formatting assistance" by the protocol converter, and various other trickery goes on behind the scenes. In some cases, mainframe Kermit's ASCII/EBCDIC translation tables might need to be altered, depending on the make, model, and configuration of the protocol converter. For detailed information about which protocol converters are transparent and which are not, and about file transfer through non-transparent 3270 protocol converters, consult the IBM mainframe Kermit documentation [15].

For X.25 Users Only

If you have connected to the remote computer through an X.25 network PAD, your connection is probably set up for character-mode interactive operation. In the normal setup, each character you type is sent to the remote computer in a separate X.25 packet so it can be processed and echoed immediately. You want this to happen when you are conducting an interactive session with the remote computer. However, this mode of operation can be very inefficient during Kermit file transfer. Transfers can proceed much faster if you change your network connection to make Kermit packets correspond as much as possible with X.25 packets. A detailed discussion of X.25 networking is beyond the scope of this book,[21] but you might try escaping back to the PAD (normally by typing Ctrl-P) and issuing X.3 commands to put the PAD into a mode suitable for Kermit packet transmission:

```
Kermit-11>send report.txt              (Send file from remote Kermit)
Ctrl-P                                 (Escape back to the PAD)
@PAR?                                  (See your current PAD settings)
PAR1:1,2:1,3:0,4:80,5:0,6:1,7:0,8:0,9:0,10:80,11:3,12:0
@SET 2:0,3:2,4:0,5:1,6:0,10:0,12:1     (Change them)
@continue                              (Connect back to remote host)
Ctrl-\c                                (Escape back to C-Kermit)
C-Kermit>receive                       (Receive the file)
```

These commands tell the PAD not to echo, to forward characters sent by the terminal (that is, your local Kermit program) only after a carriage return (Kermit's normal packet termination character) has been received, to use no packet forwarding timeout, to enable Xon/Xoff flow control between the terminal and the PAD (rather than end-to-end), to suppress network messages that might interfere with the Kermit packets, and to do no line folding. If your local Kermit has built-in X.25 network support, you can use the corresponding SET PAD Kermit commands instead.

When you connect back after the file transfer, your PAD connection will no longer be suitable for interactive use, so you must restore the original PAD parameters, as in the following example:

---

[21]Read the literature provided by your X.25 service provider, for example, *How to Use SprintNet Asynchronous Dial Service*, or consult references [10, 11, 12, 13].

```
C-Kermit>connect                        (Connect back to remote)
Ctrl-P                                  (Escape back to the PAD)
@SET 2:1,3:2,4:80,5:0,6:1,10:80,12:0 (Restore old settings)
@continue                               (Connect back to remote host)
Kermit-11>
```

Or if you have an X.25-capable version of C-Kermit, use its built-in SET PAD commands. *Hint:* After you read the chapters on macros and scripts, you will be able to write macro commands that make this procedure a lot easier and faster. *Another Hint:* Certain networks have built-in commands to condition your connection for file transfer, for example SprintNet's DTAPE command. See the literature from your network service provider.

Collecting the Evidence

If you have file transfer problems, check your protocol-related settings with the SHOW PROTOCOL command:

```
C-Kermit>show proto
Protocol Parameters:    Send    Receive
  Timeout (used= 8):    10      7
  Padding:              0       0           Block Check:    2
  Pad Character:        0       0           Delay:          1
  Packet Start:         1       1           Max Retries:    10
  Packet End:           13      13
C-Kermit>
```

Make any desired adjustments and try again. The timeout values are the current SEND and RECEIVE TIMEOUT settings; the "used=" value is the (possibly adjusted) interval that C-Kermit actually used in the most recent transfer. An asterisk (*) next to the SEND timeout means you have given a SET SEND TIMEOUT command.

If all else fails, you can capture C-Kermit's (mis)behavior in two types of log files:

LOG PACKETS *[filespec=PACKET.LOG [{ APPEND, NEW }=NEW]]*
Records Kermit's file transfer packets in the specified file. Use this option to track down problems. Show the packet log to a Kermit guru or decode the packets yourself if you have a copy of *Kermit, A File Transfer Protocol* [18], which spells out the details of Kermit packet format and protocol rules.

LOG DEBUG *[filespec=DEBUG.LOG [{ APPEND, NEW }=NEW]]*
Records voluminous information about C-Kermit's inner workings in the specified file. For Kermit gurus only. Used for serious late-night marathon debugging sessions in combination with the C-Kermit source code. Knowledge of the C programming language [46] is a plus.

These log files are closed automatically when you EXIT from C-Kermit. You can also close them at any desired time with the CLOSE PACKETS or CLOSE DEBUG commands.

Chapter 7

Using a Kermit Server

By now you should be a wiz at Kermit file transfer. You can use SET commands to adapt Kermit programs to all sorts of different conditions and you can send files back and forth successfully. In this chapter, you'll learn an easier way to transfer files, in which you won't have to give commands to *both* Kermit programs. And you'll see that Kermit not only transfers files, but can help you manage them too.

In Kermit's basic mode of operation, you tell the remote Kermit what to do, then escape back to the local Kermit and tell the local Kermit what to do. If you are only transferring one file or one group of files, this is not a major inconvenience—no more than, say, cooking a simple dinner for yourself at home. But if you want to upload some files, download some others, delete some, print some, and so on, repeated connecting and escaping back can become tiresome. This is more like hosting a dinner party. For such occasions, you might prefer to take your friends to a restaurant and eat out.

A *Kermit server* is a Kermit program running in a special way. You tell your local Kermit program what you want and it tells the Kermit server what to do, like your waiter gives your order to the chef. The server performs the required tasks silently, out of sight in the kitchen, and relays the results back to your local Kermit program, just as your waiter brings your dinner once the chef has prepared it.

The difference between using a Kermit server and eating in a restaurant is that with Kermit, before you can order anything you have to visit the kitchen briefly and install the chef. Once installed, your chef no longer talks to you directly, but only to the waiter, who translates your order into the colorful restaurant jargon that only the chef understands.

Before you can "eat out," you need two things: one Kermit program that can act as a server (the chef), and another one (the waiter) that knows how to talk to the server. The computer jargon for the waiter is "client." The Kermit client is usually the local Kermit, and the server is usually on the remote end. C-Kermit can act as either a client or a server.

Starting the Server

Here is the one and only command you need to put your chef to work:

SERVER
> Tells the Kermit program to enter server mode using current communication and protocol settings. The prompt disappears, and all further communication takes place using Kermit protocol packets.

Here's an example in which your local computer is a PC running MS-DOS Kermit, and you start a C-Kermit server on a *remote* UNIX computer:

```
MS-Kermit>connect                       (Connect to the remote computer)
login: olga                             (Login if necessary)
Password:

$ kermit                                (Start Kermit)
C-Kermit>server                         (Put it in server mode)
Entering server mode.  If your local Kermit software is menu driven, use
the menus to send commands to the server.  Otherwise, enter the escape
sequence to return to your local Kermit prompt and issue commands from
there.  Use SEND and GET for file transfer.  Use REMOTE HELP for a list of
other available services.  Use BYE or FINISH to end server mode.
KERMIT READY TO SERVE...
Alt-X                                   (Escape back to PC)
MS-Kermit>
```

From this point, you may conduct all further business from your local Kermit's prompt. If you try typing commands before you escape back, nothing will happen: the characters you type are not likely to be valid Kermit packets, so the server ignores them. In an emergency, however, you can get back to the C-Kermit command prompt by typing two Ctrl-C's in a row:

```
C-Kermit>server                         (Put C-Kermit in server mode)
Entering server mode.  If your local Kermit software is menu driven, use
the menus to send commands to the server.  Otherwise, enter the escape
sequence to return to your local Kermit prompt and issue commands from
there.  Use SEND and GET for file transfer.  Use REMOTE HELP for a list of
other available services.  Use BYE or FINISH to end server mode.
KERMIT READY TO SERVE...
Ctrl-C Ctrl-C                           (Type Ctrl-C twice)
^C...
C-Kermit>                               (The prompt comes back)
```

Sending Commands to Kermit Servers

To use the server, you must know what services it offers:

REMOTE HELP

Tells the local Kermit to ask the remote server for a list of the services it offers. In this example, an MS-DOS Kermit client queries a C-Kermit server:

```
MS-Kermit>remote help
C-Kermit Server REMOTE Commands:

GET files     REMOTE CD [dir]        REMOTE DIRECTORY [files]
SEND files    REMOTE SPACE [dir]     REMOTE HOST command
MAIL files    REMOTE DELETE files    REMOTE WHO [user]
BYE           REMOTE PRINT files     REMOTE TYPE files
FINISH        REMOTE HELP            REMOTE SET parameter value
```

If the client Kermit has these commands, the C-Kermit server will obey them. Other Kermit servers might have different menus.

The first interactive Kermit command you learned was EXIT. The first command you should learn for controlling a Kermit server is the one that takes it out of server mode:

FINISH

Sends a command packet from a Kermit client to a Kermit server. This packet instructs the server to exit server mode and return to its interactive Kermit prompt. Example:

```
MS-Kermit>finish           (Shut down the server)
MS-Kermit>connect          (Go back)
C-Kermit>                  (C-Kermit's prompt has returned)
```

A similar command makes the entire remote session just go away:

BYE

Tells the client Kermit program to send a command packet to a Kermit server. This packet tells the server to destroy itself and log out the session or job under which it is running and hang up the connection.

Let's practice starting and stopping a remote C-Kermit server a few times from a PC:

```
MS-Kermit>connect          (Connect to the remote computer)
login: olga                (Log in)
Password:                  (Supply your password)

$ kermit                   (Start Kermit)
C-Kermit>server            (Put it in server mode)
```

Entering server mode. If your local Kermit software is menu driven, use the menus to send commands to the server. Otherwise, enter the escape sequence to return to your local Kermit prompt and issue commands from there. Use SEND and GET for file transfer. Use REMOTE HELP for a list of other available services. Use BYE or FINISH to end server mode.

```
KERMIT READY TO SERVE...
help                              (Type commands to the server)
exit                              (See how it ignores them)

Alt-X                             (Escape back to PC)
MS-Kermit>finish                  (Shut down the server)
MS-Kermit>connect                 (Connect again)
C-Kermit server done
C-Kermit>                         (The prompt is back)
C-Kermit>server                   (Start the server again)
```

Entering server mode. If your local Kermit software is menu driven, use the menus to send commands to the server. Otherwise, enter the escape sequence to return to your local Kermit prompt and issue commands from there. Use SEND and GET for file transfer. Use REMOTE HELP for a list of other available services. Use BYE or FINISH to end server mode.

```
KERMIT READY TO SERVE...
Ctrl-C Ctrl-C                     (Type 2 Ctrl-C's)
^C^C...
C-Kermit>                         (Prompt reappears)
C-Kermit>server                   (Start the server again)
```

Entering server mode. If your local Kermit software is menu driven, use the menus to send commands to the server. Otherwise, enter the escape sequence to return to your local Kermit prompt and issue commands from there. Use SEND and GET for file transfer. Use REMOTE HELP for a list of other available services. Use BYE or FINISH to end server mode.

```
KERMIT READY TO SERVE...
Alt-X                             (Escape back to PC)
MS-Kermit>bye                     (Terminate the remote session)
C>
```

Transferring Files with a Server

Now that you know how to start and stop the server, let's put it to work. Here are the basic commands for transferring files, which you would give to your *local* client Kermit program's prompt, *after* putting the *remote* Kermit program in server mode and escaping back to the local Kermit program:

SEND *filespec [remote-filename]*

Sends the file or group of files named by *filespec* to the server. This is exactly the same command that you use to send files to a Kermit program that has been given the RECEIVE command and it works the same way in every respect (see Chapter 5).

MSEND *filespec [filespec [. . .]]*

You can also use the MSEND command to send a selected group of files to the server, each under its own name.

GET *filespec*

Asks the Kermit server to send the file or file group specified by *filespec*. The file specification is expressed in the syntax of the server's computer.

The GET command is quite different from the RECEIVE command. Unlike the RECEIVE command, which passively waits for a file to arrive from another Kermit that has been given a SEND command, the GET command actively requests a particular file with a "please send me" protocol message containing the file's name. If you give a RECEIVE command instead, the server doesn't know what file you want:

```
MS-Kermit>receive                     (This should have been GET)
Protocol Error: Did you say RECEIVE instead of GET?
MS-Kermit>
```

A special form of the GET command lets you ask for a file and then store it under a different name. Just type carriage return (press the key marked Return or Enter) immediately after the word GET, and Kermit prompts you for the remote and local names separately:

```
MS-Kermit>get
 Remote source file: foo bar b
 Local destination file: foo.bar
```

You can use wildcards in both SEND and GET commands. Wildcards in the GET command must be in the notation of the computer that the server is running on.

When C-Kermit itself is the server, your GET command can include a single filename, a wildcard filename, or a list of any mixture of these. The C-Kermit server will send all the files in a single operation:

```
MS-Kermit>get ck*.c *.h ~olga/oofa.doc
```

The file specifications are separated by spaces. If you need to include a space in a filename, use \32 (backslash followed by the ASCII code for space), for example (when asking a VMS C-Kermit server to send a file that resides on another DECnet node):

```
MS-Kermit>get node"USER\32PASSWD"::dev:[dir]name.ext
```

If you need to include a backslash in the filename, use two of them.

When both Kermit programs are capable of transmitting the file type in an Attribute packet (see Chapter 8), you can switch between text and binary mode as often as you like when sending files to the server:

```
MS-Kermit>set file type text          (Text files)
MS-Kermit>send oofa.txt               (Send a file)
MS-Kermit>send a:mskermit.ini         (Send another file)
MS-Kermit>send \autoexec.bat          (And another)
MS-Kermit>set file type binary        (Now send binary files)
MS-Kermit>send *.exe                  (Send all my exe files)
MS-Kermit>send *.com                  (Send all my com files)
```

When the C-Kermit server is running on a VMS or OpenVMS system, it can send a mixture of text and binary files in a single operation:

```
MS-Kermit>get kermit.*                (A mixture)
```

Sending Commands to Kermit Servers   143

When sending files in response to the GET command on other operating systems (such as UNIX), the C-Kermit server has no way to differentiate between text and binary files automatically, so it sends them in its current mode, TEXT or BINARY.

The SET SERVER Command

Normally the C-Kermit server silently waits for commands to arrive from the client program. You can make it time out and send NAK packets at periodic intervals during this period by using the command:

SET SERVER TIMEOUT *seconds*

This is useful if the client program is not capable of timing out. If SECONDS is 0, there are no timeouts during server command wait.

If C-Kermit is in local mode and has been given a SERVER command, it normally does not produce a file transfer display. If you want it to, tell it:

SET SERVER DISPLAY ON

This enables whatever type of display you have chosen in your most recent SET FILE DISPLAY command (SERIAL by default).

File Management Services

So far, we've only seen the Kermit server as a new way of doing the same old thing—transferring files. But you can also use the server for remote file management, just as you can use C-Kermit for local file management by giving it DIRECTORY, DELETE, and similar commands. The difference is the word REMOTE. The REMOTE prefix lets you send the commands to the remote Kermit server instead of executing them locally:

```
MS-Kermit>delete data.tmp          (Delete a local file)
MS-Kermit>remote delete data.tmp   (Delete a remote file)
```

The DELETE command deletes a file on your local computer; the REMOTE DELETE command asks the remote Kermit server to delete a file on *its* computer.

REMOTE HELP

This command asks the server to send you a list of all the commands it can respond to, as in the example on page 141.

REMOTE CD [*directory*]

Tells the client Kermit program to ask the Kermit server to change its default (working) directory to the one given. If none is given, it changes to your home or login directory on the server's computer. Examples:

```
MS-Kermit>remote cd /usr/include   (UNIX)
MS-Kermit>remote cd sys$system     (VMS or OpenVMS)
MS-Kermit>remote cd                (Default directory)
```

REMOTE DELETE *filespec*
> Tells the client Kermit program to ask the Kermit server to delete the specified file or files on the server's computer. Normal access restrictions apply—the server can't delete a file that you could not delete yourself. Example:
>
> ```
> MS-Kermit>remo del *.tmp          (Delete all my .tmp files)
> ```

REMOTE DIRECTORY *[filespec)]*
> Tells the client Kermit program to ask the Kermit server to send a directory listing of the specified file or files to your screen. The *filespec* is in the syntax of the Kermit server's operating system. If no *filespec* is given, the server sends a directory listing of all files in its current directory. The format of the listing depends on the server Kermit's underlying operating system.
>
> ```
> MS-Kermit>remo dir *.txt          (List all my txt files)
> MS-Kermit>rem dir                 (All files in current dir)
> MS-Kermit>rem dir [ivan]          (A different directory)
> ```
>
> When the server is C-Kermit running under UNIX, VMS, OpenVMS, or OS/2, you can include directory command qualifiers in your REMOTE DIRECTORY command after the words REMOTE DIRECTORY and before the file specification (if any):
>
> ```
> MS-Kermit>remo dir -t *.txt       (UNIX, reverse time order)
> MS-Kermit>rem dir /o-d *.txt      (OS/2, reverse time order)
> MS-Kermit>rem dir /size /date     (VMS, include size and date)
> ```

REMOTE SPACE *[device/directory]*
> Tells the client Kermit program to ask the Kermit to give a brief report on space used or available on the given device or directory, or if none is given, in the server's current device or directory. Examples:
>
> ```
> MS-Kermit>remot space /usr        (UNIX, /usr partition)
> MS-Kermit>remo spac sys$login     (VMS, login disk)
> MS-Kermit>rem spa a:              (OS/2, A: disk)
> MS-Kermit>rem spa                 (Any, current disk)
> ```

REMOTE TYPE *filespec*
> Tells the client Kermit program to ask the Kermit server to display the specified file on your screen. The file is assumed to be a text file. Example:
>
> ```
> MS-Kermit>remote type oofa.txt
> ```

These commands are the same regardless of the machine or operating system of the server. They are translated by your local Kermit into standard protocol messages understood by all Kermit servers that support these commands. If you send a command that is not in the server's repertoire, the server responds with a message like "Unimplemented server command."

Sending Commands to Kermit Servers 145

Fun with Servers

Kermit servers have a few extra capabilities besides ordinary file transfer and management. You can use the following commands if both your local Kermit and the remote server support them:

REMOTE WHO *[user]*

Tells the client Kermit program to ask the Kermit server to send information about a particular user of its computer, or if the computer is on a network, about any user on any computer on the network. If no user is specified, the server sends a list of all users who are currently logged in. Examples:

```
MS-Kermit>remote who                   (All logged-in users)
MS-Kermit>remote who olaf              (A particular user)
MS-Kermit>remote who kermit@watsun     (A user on the network)
```

REMOTE HOST *command*

Tells the client Kermit program to ask the server to ask its host operating system to execute the given command and return the results to your screen. The command must not require a dialog; it has to be the sort of command that you can give to your host operating system completely on one line and that responds by printing a message on your screen using ordinary characters—not graphics—or by not printing anything, and then exits. Examples:

```
MS-Kermit>remote host copy oofa.old oofa.new
MS-Kermit>remo hos date                (UNIX date and time)
Sat Jul  4 18:42:43 EDT 1992
MS-Kermit>rem ho show time             (VMS date and time)
   4-JUL-1992 18:42:43
MS-Kermit>remote host mkdir temp       (Create UNIX directory)
MS-Kermit>remo ho create/dir temp      (Create VMS directory)
```

If you invoke any other kind of program with REMOTE HOST, the results are unpredictable, and probably not what you wanted.

REMOTE KERMIT *text*

Tells the client Kermit program to send the text to the server, which is to interpret it as if it were a Kermit command typed at its own Kermit prompt. C-Kermit can send this command as a client, but a C-Kermit server cannot respond to it.

REMOTE LOGIN *name password [account]*

Tells the client Kermit program to send user ID and password (and optionally, account) information to a Kermit server. Some Kermit servers (C-Kermit not among them) can be set up to require login before they will respond to any other commands.

REMOTE LOGOUT

Terminates your access rights with a Kermit server that you have previously accessed via REMOTE LOGIN.

REMOTE PRINT *filespec [options]*
Sends the specified local file to the Kermit server and asks the Kermit server to print it using the specified options, if any. The options are in the syntax of the server's host operating system. If no options are specified, the server system's defaults are used:

```
MS-Kermit>remote print oofa.txt /queue=laser /copies=3    (VMS)
MS-Kermit>remo prin oofa.txt -Plaser -#3                  (UNIX)
MS-Kermit>rem pri oofa.txt
```

MAIL *filespec address*
Sends the specified local file to the Kermit server, and asks the server to deliver it as electronic mail to the specified address rather than storing it on disk. Examples:

```
MS-Kermit>mail oofa.txt olga, ivan
MS-Kermit>mail message.txt info-kermit@watsun
```

Interrupting Server Operations

SEND, MSEND, and GET can be interrupted in the normal way: X to cancel a file, Z to cancel a group, and so on (see Chapter 5). Most REMOTE commands can be interrupted in this way too. You can also CONNECT to the C-Kermit server and type two Ctrl-C's.

Changing the Server's Settings

If your server allows it (as C-Kermit does), and your local Kermit program has the commands for it (both C-Kermit and MS-DOS Kermit do), you can change the remote server's settings by giving commands to the client program:

REMOTE SET *parameter value*
Tells the Kermit client to ask the remote Kermit server to set the given parameter to the specified value. The parameters include many of the same ones used in the SET command, like BLOCK-CHECK, FILE TYPE, and so forth. Issuing the REMOTE SET command to your local Kermit program is exactly like issuing the corresponding SET command to the remote Kermit program if it were in interactive command mode. Here is an example in which we switch a Kermit server from sending files in text mode to binary mode (remember, it is the file *sender* that controls the transfer mode):

```
MS-Kermit>get *.txt                     (Get text files)
MS-Kermit>remote set file type binary
MS-Kermit>get *.bin                     (Get binary files)
```

To see a complete list of REMOTE SET commands supported by your client Kermit program, just type REMOTE SET followed by a space and a question mark. Here is an example for MS-DOS Kermit:

```
MS-Kermit>remote set ? One of the following:
 attributes   file       incomplete   block-check   receive    retry
 server                  transfer     window-slots
MS-Kermit>remote set attributes date off
```

Sending Commands to Kermit Servers **147**

These are the REMOTE SET commands an MS-DOS Kermit client can send to a Kermit server. As with the local SET command, some of these commands have further options:

```
MS-Kermit>remote set receive ? One of the following:
 packet-length   timeout
MS-Kermit>remote set receive timeout 8
MS-Kermit>
```

When C-Kermit itself is the client, it can send the following REMOTE SET commands to a Kermit server:

```
C-Kermit>remote set ? One of the following:
 attributes        block-check      file            incomplete
 receive           retry            server          transfer
 window
C-Kermit>
```

And when C-Kermit is the server, it also allows these commands to be sent to it. If you send a REMOTE SET command to a Kermit server that does not support this feature, it replies with an error message like "Unimplemented server function" or "Unknown REMOTE SET parameter."

Server Security

You can control access to the C-Kermit server's services on an individual basis with the DISABLE and ENABLE commands. All services are enabled by default.

DISABLE *service*
   Instructs the server not to perform the named service.

ENABLE *service*
   Reinstates a service that was previously disabled.

Here are the services that can be disabled and enabled. The effect of disabling each service is described. Enabling a service removes all restrictions that were imposed when you DISABLEd it. If you want to disable certain functions, be sure to give the appropriate DISABLE commands *before* you give the SERVER command.

DISABLE BYE

   Ignore BYE commands; remain in server mode. Example:

```
C-Kermit>disable bye              (Don't let them log me out)
C-Kermit>server                   (Enter server mode)
C-Kermit server starting, blah blah blah ...
Alt-x                             (Escape back)
MS-Kermit>bye                     (Try to log out the server)
Protocol Error: BYE disabled
MS-Kermit>
```

The server remains in server mode, ready to accept any commands that have not been disabled.

DISABLE CD

Disallow changing of the default device and/or directory. Don't allow files to be transferred into or out of any but the current device/directory. Don't allow files outside the current directory to be listed, deleted, or typed.

DISABLE DELETE

Ignore REMOTE DELETE commands.

DISABLE DIRECTORY

Ignore REMOTE DIRECTORY commands.

DISABLE FINISH

Ignore FINISH commands; remain in server mode.

DISABLE GET

Ignore GET commands; don't send files.

DISABLE HOST

Ignore REMOTE HOST commands.

DISABLE SEND

Refuse to receive files when the client Kermit tries to SEND them.

DISABLE SET

Ignore REMOTE SET commands.

DISABLE SPACE

Ignore REMOTE SPACE commands.

DISABLE TYPE

Ignore REMOTE TYPE commands.

DISABLE WHO

Ignore REMOTE WHO commands.

You can find out which services are enabled and disabled with the SHOW SERVER command. For example, in C-Kermit:

```
C-Kermit>sho server
Function            Status:
 GET                enabled
 SEND               enabled
 REMOTE CD/CWD      enabled
 REMOTE DELETE      enabled
 REMOTE DIRECTORY   enabled
 REMOTE HOST        enabled
```

```
  REMOTE SET          enabled
  REMOTE SPACE        enabled
  REMOTE TYPE         enabled
  REMOTE WHO          enabled
  BYE                 disabled
  FINISH              enabled
Server timeout: 0
Server display: off
```

CAUTION: Some of these commands, including DELETE, DIRECTORY, SPACE, TYPE, and WHO, are also accessible via REMOTE HOST. If you want to prevent users from accessing these services through the server, you must DISABLE HOST too.

Turning the Tables

Now that you can control a remote Kermit server from your local computer, can you think of a reason why you might want to control a *local* Kermit server from a *remote* Kermit client? Suppose you want to send a mixture of text and binary files from a remote UNIX computer to your local PC. Here is one way to do it. Connect and login to the remote computer from your local PC. Then use your UNIX text editor to create a *command file* for UNIX C-Kermit containing the necessary SET FILE TYPE and SEND commands, as in this example, called `xfer.tak`:

```
echo Return to your local Kermit and give the SERVER command.
set delay 5             ; Allow time to escape back
set file type binary    ; Binary for object and executable files
msend *.o wermit
set file type text      ; Text for source files
msend *.c *.h
finish                  ; Return the PC to normal
```

The FINISH command makes the MS-DOS Kermit's prompt reappear after all the files have been transferred.

Now start C-Kermit on the VAX, have it TAKE the command file, then escape back to the PC and put MS-DOS Kermit into server mode:

```
C-Kermit>take xfer.tak              (TAKE the command file)
Return to your local Kermit and give the SERVER command.
Alt-x                               (Escape back to the PC)
MS-Kermit>serve                     (Put it in server mode)
```

And now go to lunch while all the files are being transferred. This has been our first glimpse into Kermit's capabilities for unattended operations. If you are intrigued, be sure not to skip Chapters 11 through 13.

Chapter 8

File Transfer Power Tools

In this chapter, we'll take a look at some advanced features of the Kermit protocol that can save you time and effort: efficiency boosters like long packets, sliding windows, and locking shifts, and the Attribute-Packet mechanism that one Kermit uses to tell the other some key facts about the files that are being transferred. But before you can use these features, you need to know a little bit about the Kermit protocol itself.

Overview of the Kermit Protocol

When you transfer a file, Kermit breaks it up into a series of messages called packets. Each packet consists of distinct start and end markers; a length field for framing; a sequence number for detection of missing, duplicated, or out-of-sequence packets; a packet type; some data; and a checksum for error detection, as shown in Figure 8-1.

Except for the start and end markers (normally Control-A and Carriage Return, respectively), the packets are encoded by the sender as simple lines of printable text to survive even the most hostile communication environments, and decoded by the receiver into the appropriate form.

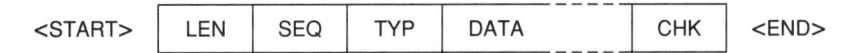

<START>	LEN	SEQ	TYP	DATA	CHK	<END>

Figure 8-1 Kermit Packet Format

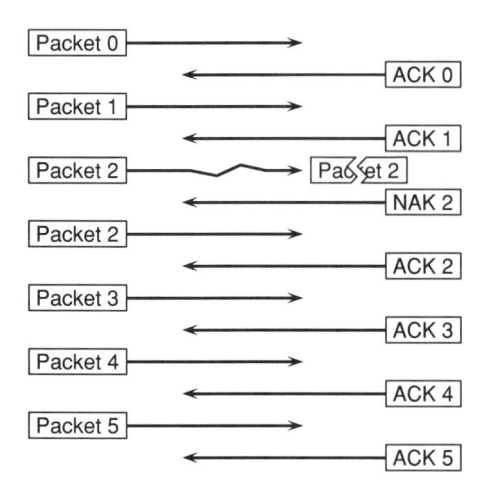

```
Packet 0 ──────────▶
         ◀────────── ACK 0
Packet 1 ──────────▶
         ◀────────── ACK 1
Packet 2 ────∿────▶ Packet 2
         ◀────────── NAK 2
Packet 2 ──────────▶
         ◀────────── ACK 2
Packet 3 ──────────▶
         ◀────────── ACK 3
Packet 4 ──────────▶
         ◀────────── ACK 4
Packet 5 ──────────▶
         ◀────────── ACK 5
```

Figure 8-2 Stop-and-Wait Packet Exchange

The file sender sends packets of various types, and the file receiver replies to each packet with an acknowledgement (ACK) to indicate that the packet was received correctly, or a negative acknowledgement (NAK) that tells the sender a packet was received in damaged condition—or not received at all—and therefore needs to be retransmitted. Because the file sender waits for an acknowledgement before sending the next packet, the rate at which packets are exchanged is controlled by the receiver, which prevents a fast sender from overrunning a slower receiver. This style of packet exchange is called "stop and wait," and is illustrated in Figure 8-2. Of course, neither Kermit program stops and waits forever. If an expected packet does not arrive within the timeout interval, there is an automatic timeout and retransmission to break the deadlock.

The packet exchange proceeds through the following phases, each of which is associated with a particular packet type, shown in parentheses (see Table 5-2 on page 108 for a more complete list of Kermit packet types):

1. (S) Feature negotiation. By exchanging special packets, the two Kermits determine which features they have in common and agree to use them. This allows the newest, most full-featured version of Kermit to work automatically with even the oldest barest-bones version.

2. (F) The file sender sends the file name so the receiver can create the new file with the same name.

3. (A) The file sender sends information about the file (file attributes) so the receiver can create the file with the appropriate attributes, including size, creation date, type (text or binary), character set, and so forth.

4. (D) The file sender sends the contents (data) of the file, usually requiring many packets. During the data phase, the Kermit protocol accomplishes the necessary conversions by translating between the local computer's character codes and file formats and the standard ones specified by the protocol, so each computer only needs to know its own local conventions and the standard ones.

5. (Z) When all the file's data has been sent, the file sender sends an end-of-file packet so the receiving computer knows the file has been completely received and can close it.

If there are more files to send, steps 2–5 are repeated for each file.

6. (B) When all the files have been sent, the file sender terminates the operation by sending a "Bye" packet, causing each Kermit program to leave packet mode and return control to the user, with the local Kermit program notifying the user that the file has been completely transferred.

Analyzing Kermit's Performance

After the file transfer is finished, you can use the STATISTICS command to get information about its efficiency and what parameters were used:

```
C-Kermit>stat
Most recent transaction --
 files: 6
 characters last file    : 109313
 total file characters   : 452992
 communication line in   : 25989
 communication line out  : 489226
 packets sent            : 5180
 packets received        : 5187
 damaged packets rec'd   : 4
 timeouts                : 2
 retransmissions         : 7
 parity                  : none
 8th bit prefixing       : no
 locking shifts          : no
 window slots used       : 1 of 1
 packet length           : 94 (send), 94 (receive)
 compression             : yes [~] (79010)
 block check type used   : 1
 elapsed time            : 681 sec
 transmission rate       : 9600 bps
 effective data rate     : 665 cps
 efficiency (percent)    : 69
C-Kermit>
```

Let's take a brief look at this report. It contains all the information needed to tune Kermit's peformance.

```
files: 6
characters last file  : 109313
total file characters : 452992      (f)
```
This tells you how many files were transferred, as well as how many characters were in the last file, and in all the files. Let's call this last number f.

```
communication line in  : 25989      (p_i)
communication line out : 489226     (p_o)
```
This tells you how many characters were received (p_i) and transmitted (p_o) on the communication device. The number of extra characters introduced by the Kermit protocol is:

$$p_i + p_o - f$$

The encoding efficiency is the ratio of the file size to the total number of characters sent and received:

$$\frac{f}{p_i + p_o}$$

which, in this case, comes out to $452992/(25989+489226) = 0.88$. If this number is less than 1, there is a net expansion, and therefore a loss of efficiency. If it's greater than 1, the data must have been compressed more than enough to compensate for the packet overhead.

```
packets sent          : 5180
packets received      : 5187
damaged packets rec'd : 4
timeouts              : 2
retransmissions       : 7
```
This tells us how many packets were sent and received. The number of damaged packets is a good indicator of the cleanliness of the connection. A perfectly clean connection should have none. Timeouts can indicate either a very poor connection (bad enough to make a packet indistinguishable from line noise), long delays, or a timeout value based on an incorrect perception of the communication speed. The number of retransmissions is the number of times packets had to be sent again because of a timeout, because a NAK was received, or because a damaged packet was received.

```
parity            : none
8th bit prefixing : no
locking shifts    : no
```
These items tell whether C-Kermit is operating in 7-bit or 8-bit mode. If PARITY is not NONE, you have a 7-bit connection, and 8-bit data is transmitted using single shifts (8th-bit prefixing) or locking shifts (described later) if these features are successfully negotiated (see Table 8-1 on page 168). Both of these methods add additional overhead and should be avoided when possible.

```
window slots used       : 1 of 1
packet length           : 94 (send), 94 (receive)
compression             : yes [~] (79010)
```

These are Kermit's performance boosters. Keep reading this chapter to find out how to use them.

```
elapsed time            : 681 sec      (t)
transmission rate       : 9600 bps     (r)
effective data rate     : 665 cps
efficiency (percent)    : 69           (e)
```

This is Kermit's report card: 69 percent. We'll improve our score shortly, but first let's see how it was calculated [19]:

$$e = \frac{f \times 10}{r \times t}$$

where:

e = efficiency, 1.00 is perfection
f = file size in characters
t = elapsed time in seconds
r = transmission rate, bits per second

That is, the ratio of total file bits actually transferred to the number of bits that could possibly be transferred in the elapsed time. In our example, this is:

$$\frac{452992 \times 10}{9600 \times 681} = 0.6929$$

or about 69 percent.

Kermit's small packet size and stop-and-wait technique of exchanging packets tend to result in this kind of performance. But this design lets Kermit protocol work on many types of connections where other protocols fail to work at all. Of course other factors must be considered in the performance too: the speed of the computers (CPU power, load on the system, disk access time, and so on), the quality of the connection (the number of retransmissions), and the delay properties of the connection.

Improving File Transfer Performance

There are several ways to improve the performance of Kermit file transfer:

- Turn off the file transfer display
- Increase the ratio of real data to packet overhead characters
- Eliminate the wait between packets
- Compress the data

In this section we present the tools you will need to accomplish each of these feats, one at a time or in any combination.

The File Transfer Display

C-Kermit's local-mode FULLSCREEN file transfer display can slow down the transfer measurably, particularly on high-speed network connections. You can often speed up the transfer by selecting a simpler display, such as CRT or SERIAL, or, for maximum transfer speed, NONE. When C-Kermit is the remote, try similar techniques with your local Kermit program. For example, tell MS-DOS Kermit to SET DISPLAY QUIET.

Long Packets

Kermit data packets can be any length between about 20 and 9000 characters.[22] Normal Kermit packets are about 94 characters long, and C-Kermit uses this length unless told otherwise. As Figure 8-1 shows, each packet has five control fields in addition to the data, and each packet must be acknowledged by another packet that includes five control fields of its own, but (usually) no data.

Kermit's packet length is a major factor in its performance. The longer the packet, the higher the proportion of actual data to protocol overhead characters, and the fewer acknowledgements required. Under a certain set of conditions, you can increase Kermit's file transfer efficiency as much as 800 percent by using longer packets (reference [19], page 13, Table 4). The trick is to find the ideal packet length for a given connection. The command that governs Kermit's packet length is:

SET RECEIVE PACKET-LENGTH *number*
> Give this command to the file receiver before the transfer starts. The file receiver gives permission to the file sender to send packets up to the given *number* of bytes (characters) in length. When you are using long packets, you should also use a stronger error-checking method, since the probability of undetected errors goes up with the packet length. Example:

```
C-Kermit>set rec pack 2000      (Set the packet length)
C-Kermit>receive                (Receive a file)
Alt-x                           (Escape back to the PC)
MS-Kermit>set block-check 3     (Use strong error checking)
MS-Kermit>send oofa.txt         (Send a file)
```

Remember, the SET RECEIVE PACKET-LENGTH command works only when you give it to the *file receiver*. Of course, the file sender can decide to use shorter packets anyway, for

---

[22]The absolute limit is $95^2 - 1 = 9024$, but some Kermit programs have a lower limit because of memory or addressing limitations. Use the SHOW PROTOCOL command to find the maximum packet length of your Kermit program.

example if its maximum packet length is less than what the receiver asked for, or if it doesn't support the long-packet extension to the Kermit protocol at all; see Table 1-1 on page 8. For that matter, you can even tell the file sender yourself:

SET SEND PACKET-LENGTH *number*
> Give this command to the file sender. This is the maximum length packet to send. When the file transfer begins, the file receiver tells the sender the longest packet it is prepared to receive. The smaller of that number and the sender's SET SEND PACKET-LENGTH value is used.

Thus, it is impossible to force a Kermit program to send packets longer than the receiver asks for, but it is possible to force shorter ones.

To find the optimum packet length for a given connection, select a moderate-size file and transfer it using different packet lengths. Note the efficiency (or, when the speed is not accurately known, as on a network connection, the effective data rate) reported by C-Kermit's STATISTICS command after each transfer. Use whatever packet length results in the highest performance. In this example, we use 2000-byte packets to transfer a 53,000-byte text file:

```
C-Kermit>set receive packet-len 2000   (Try 2000-byte packets)
C-Kermit>r                              (Receive a file)
Alt-x                                   (Escape back to PC)
MS-Kermit>set block 2                   (Use 2-byte checksum)
MS-Kermit>s test.txt                    (Send the file)

  (The file is transferred)

MS-Kermit>c                             (Connect back)
C-Kermit>stat                           (Get statistics)
  ...
 packet length            : 94 (send), 2000 (receive)
 elapsed time             : 61 sec
 transmission rate        : 9600 bps
 effective data rate      : 870 cps
 efficiency (percent)     : 90           (Better than 69!)
C-Kermit>
```

Dynamic Packet Length

In a perfect world, it would make sense to use the longest possible packets all the time. But this is the real world. On a noisy connection, long packets can actually *reduce* the efficiency of a file transfer:

> *The longer a packet, the more likely it is to be damaged and the longer it takes to retransmit.*

When C-Kermit is sending a file, it tries to compensate for noise on the communication line by reducing the packet length automatically whenever a packet is damaged or a timeout occurs, and then slowly increasing it again for each packet that is transmitted successfully: the packet length adjusts to the noise level [15]. This trick is not foolproof, however. If a packet is absolutely, positively too long for the receiver's or network's buffers, it will never get through. The only remedy in this case is to start again with a shorter maximum packet length.

Sliding Windows

On a clean direct or dialed connection, long packets are probably all you need to achieve good performance. But suppose you have a long-distance connection through a public packet-switched network or an earth satellite. It might take a second or more for a packet to reach its destination and just as much time for an acknowledgement to make the return trip. Or suppose you have a no-delay connection that is noisy or in which there are buffer-size limitations. Kermit's *sliding window* option is designed for these situations.

Kermit's normal packet protocol is: send packet number n, wait for an acknowledgement for packet n, then send packet $n+1$, and so on, as you saw in Figure 8-2. When the connection has a long round-trip delay, the waiting time destroys the efficiency of the protocol. For example, on a 9600 bps connection with 1 second delay, where one tenth of a second is required to transmit a 94-byte packet, the waiting time could have been used to transmit 9 more packets. Efficiency plummets to about 10 percent, as in this example, using the same 53K file as before:

```
C-Kermit>set rec pack 94      (No long packets)
C-Kermit>c                    (Receive a file)
Alt-x                         (Escape back to PC)
MS-Kermit>send test.txt       (Send a test file)

  (The file is transferred)

MS-Kermit>c                   (Connect back)
C-Kermit>stat                 (Get statistics)
 ...
 packet length            : 94 (send), 94 (receive)
 elapsed time             : 686 sec
 transmission rate        : 9600 bps
 effective data rate      : 77 cps
 efficiency (percent)     : 8     (Terrible!)
C-Kermit>
```

That's 11 minutes to transfer the file at 8 percent efficiency, when you would expect to be able to transfer it in about a minute. If you are using a modem, you can watch the receive and transmit lights to appreciate what's happening: the transmit light blinks on for a brief moment, then both lights go dark. After a long pause, you get a blip on the receive light, followed immediately by a blip on the transmit light, then another long pause. And so on. More than 90 percent of the time is wasted.

Let's try the same transfer again with 1000-character packets to see how much long packets might help. Here we just show the statistics:

```
C-Kermit>stat                   (Get statistics)
...
  packet length           : 94 (send), 1000 (receive)
  window slots used       : 1 of 1
  elapsed time            : 117 sec
  transmission rate       : 9600 bps
  effective data rate     : 451 cps
  efficiency (percent)    : 47
C-Kermit>
```

Much better, but still less than half the transmission speed. The long intervals of dead air remain between each packet, only now we have fewer of them.

The inter-packet waiting time can be eliminated if the normal stop-and-wait rule is relaxed to let Kermit send packet *n*+1 before packet *n*'s acknowledgement arrives. C-Kermit is so relaxed about this rule it can happily tolerate as many as 31 outstanding packets, using the sliding window technique [18] illustrated in Figure 8-3.

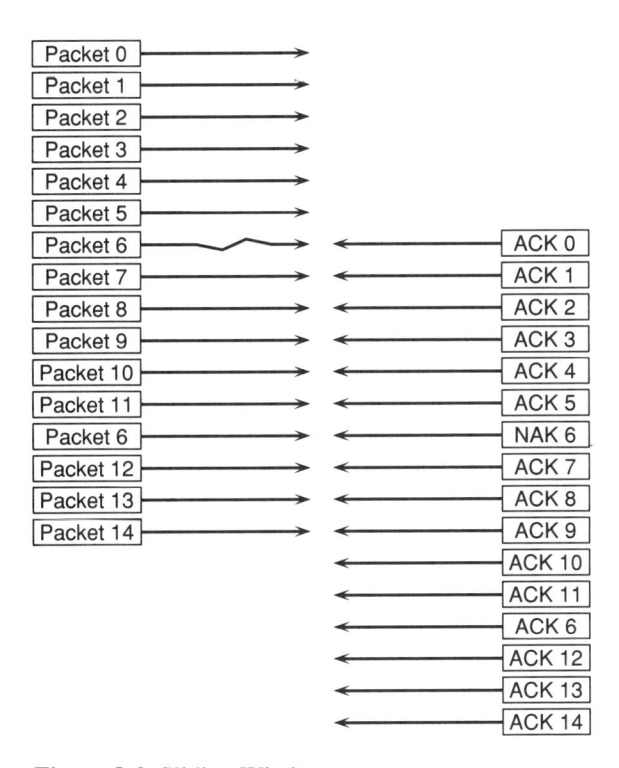

Figure 8-3 Sliding Windows

Improving File Transfer Performance 159

SET WINDOW *number*

    Specifies how many packets, 1 to 31, may be transmitted before acknowledgements arrive. With a sufficiently large window size, Kermit can (usually) transfer packets continuously. It is necessary to give a SET WINDOW command to *both* Kermit programs in order to make this feature work. If the window sizes differ, the smaller of the two is used. If the other Kermit does not support sliding windows at all, normal stop-and-wait packet exchange is used automatically, which is equivalent to using a window size of 1.

Let's see if we can pep up our connection with a combination of long packets and sliding windows. Here we transfer the same file again, over the same long-distance connection:

```
C-Kermit>set rec pack 500        (Packet-length is 500)
C-Kermit>set window 4            (Use four window slots)
C-Kermit>r                       (Receive a file)
Alt-x                            (Escape back to PC)
MS-Kermit>set window 4           (Select window size)
MS-Kermit>send test.txt          (Send the file)

  (The file is transferred)

MS-Kermit>c                      (Connect back)
C-Kermit>stat                    (Get statistics)
 ...
 packet length             : 94 (send), 500 (receive)
 window slots used         : 2 of 4
 elapsed time              : 65 sec
 transmission rate         : 9600 bps
 effective data rate       : 816 cps
 efficiency (percent)      : 85
C-Kermit>
```

That's more like it! Don't be alarmed if the file receiver reports a smaller number of window slots used than the file sender. This is normal. The file sender sends packets as fast as it can until its window fills up or an ACK arrives; the file receiver, however, gets the packets in order and ACKs each one when it arrives. The receiver's window is used only when packets are received in damaged condition or out of order.

Sliding windows can be beneficial even when the connection has no delays at all. First, sliding windows eliminate the ACK/NAK overhead. The ACKs and NAKs are on the wire simultaneously with the data packets, so they don't take up any extra time. Second, sliding windows can give better results than long packets on noisy connections. Remember the rule for long packets: *The longer a packet, the more likely it is to be damaged and the longer it takes to retransmit.*

When sliding windows are in effect and a packet is damaged or lost (perhaps it was stolen by a pick-packet?), the Kermit protocol recovers by selective retransmission, meaning that only the damaged packet is retransmitted, as with Packet 6 in Figure 8-3. If packets are short, they are *less* likely to be damaged and take *less* time to retransmit.

But when the connection is clean and unobstructed, we can use long packets and sliding windows together to obtain optimum results, as in this example with a window size of 2 and a packet length of 4000:

```
C-Kermit>stat
 ...
 packet length           : 94 (send), 4000 (receive)
 window slots used       : 2 of 2
 elapsed time            : 57 sec
 transmission rate       : 9600 bps
 effective data rate     : 921 cps
 efficiency (percent)    : 96
C-Kermit>
```

For typical text files, 96 percent is just about the optimum Kermit file transfer efficiency. To achieve this level on a particular connection, experiment with different combinations of packet length and window size.

Windows and Buffers

If sliding windows are so beneficial, perhaps you are wondering why the SET WINDOW command is necessary at all. Why not use a window size of 31 all the time? First of all, many packets sent in a continuous stream could have the same ill effect as a very long packet when computers or networks have small buffers: fatal indigestion.

Second, most Kermit programs have a limited amount of memory for packet buffers. To use sliding windows, Kermit must keep all windowed packets in memory simultaneously so selected packets can be retransmitted and out-of-order packets can be sorted before writing their contents to disk. If the total packet buffer memory available is less than the product of the maximum packet size and the maximum window size ($9024 \times 31 = 279744$ bytes plus some extra), then the window size or the packet size must be reduced.

Most implementations of C-Kermit are set up to allow packet buffers to be allocated dynamically. You can increase the overall packet buffer size using the command:

SET BUFFERS *send-length receive-length*
   Allocates the specified number of bytes of memory for send and receive packet buffers, respectively. Example:

```
C-Kermit>set receive packet-len 9000
C-Kermit>set window 31
 Adjusting receive packet-length to 286 for 31 window slots
C-Kermit>show protocol
 Receive packet-length: 286, Windows: 31, Buffers: 9065 9065
C-Kermit>set buffers 280000 280000
C-Kermit>set rec pack 9000
C-Kermit>show protocol
 Receive Packet-length: 9000, Windows: 31, Buffers: 280015 280015
C-Kermit>
```

If Kermit can't find the memory you asked for, the command fails. If the SET BUFFERS command gives a syntax error, your version of C-Kermit does not have this feature at all:

```
C-Kermit>set buffers 280000 280000
?No keywords match - buffers
C-Kermit>check dynamic
 Not available
C-Kermit>
```

Now perhaps you are wondering why the SET BUFFERS command is necessary. Why not always allocate 279744 bytes of memory for each kind of buffer and be done with it? The answer is simple: different computers have different amounts of memory available, different memory allocation strategies, different strategies for paging and swapping, and so forth. On some computers (but not others), allocating a lot of memory for packet buffers can result in extremely poor performance: just the opposite of what you wanted. So once again the onus is on you to find the numbers that are *just right* for your computer.

Single Shifts

When Kermit transfers 8-bit data over a 7-bit connection, it uses a single-shift method. Each 8-bit character is preceded by a special prefix character, normally ampersand (&), that tells the receiving Kermit to put back the 8th bit. This 8-bit transparency technique is supported by virtually all Kermit versions (see Table 1-1 on page 8). It is negotiated automatically; C-Kermit bids to use this option if its PARITY is set to any value other than NONE, and agrees to use it whenever the other Kermit asks for it. Otherwise, the 8th bit of each data byte is preserved. C-Kermit has no command, other than SET PARITY, to control the use of single shifts.

Since 8-bit characters occur either not at all, or else more or less randomly, in most types of files, this simple approach lets the data get through without too much extra overhead. The penalty is approximately zero for ASCII text, about 5 percent for text written in European languages, and 50 percent for non-textual binary files that contain a uniform distribution of 8-bit byte values.

Locking Shifts

Certain types of files can have long sequences of 8-bit bytes. The most common examples are text files written in a non-Roman alphabet and encoded in character sets like Latin/Cyrillic, Latin/Greek, Latin/Hebrew, Latin/Arabic, and especially the EUC encoding for Japanese Kanji.[23] The penalty for single-shift encoding in typical Cyrillic text is about 80 percent, and for EUC Kanji it is very close to 100 percent.

---

[23]Character sets are explained in Chapter 9.

When you need to transfer this type of file over a 7-bit connection, C-Kermit uses locking shifts [31] as well as single shifts if the other Kermit program agrees. A locking shift is a special character, Ctrl-N (Shift-Out, SO), that means that all the following characters up to the next Ctrl-O (Shift-In, SI) are to have their 8th bits set to 1 upon receipt:[24]

```
Seven-bit-text<SO>Eight-bit-text<SI>Seven-bit-text
```

While encoding data to be sent, in each case C-Kermit decides whether it is more efficient to use a locking shift or single shift.

The use of this option is almost never bad. At worst, performance is the same with it as without it (as with 7-bit text files and 8-bit binary files). In some cases (particularly for Kanji and Cyrillic text), it produces a dramatic increase in efficiency, as much as 100 percent. The use of locking shifts is controlled by a SET command:

SET TRANSFER LOCKING-SHIFT { OFF, ON, FORCED }
Specifies whether or how locking shifts should be used by Kermit for encoding and decoding packets. Synonym: **SET XFER LOCKING-SHIFT**. The options are:

ON: This is the default setting. If PARITY is *not* NONE C-Kermit tries to negotiate the use of locking-shift protocol with the other Kermit, and uses it if the other Kermit agrees. If PARITY *is* NONE, locking shifts aren't used unless the other Kermit requests them.

OFF: Don't use locking shifts, regardless of the PARITY setting. If the other Kermit asks for locking shifts, C-Kermit refuses.

FORCED: Use locking shifts, regardless of the PARITY setting and negotiations. For the file sender, this command lets data be sent to a receiver that doesn't understand locking shift protocol; the embedded SO and SI characters are stored in the received file, where they can be processed by terminals, printers, and other devices. For the file receiver, this command forces the treatment of SO and SI characters in the data as shift commands. This option automatically disables the use of single shifts.

To illustrate the usefulness of locking shifts, let's try transferring a Japanese Kanji text file through a 7-bit connection without them (notice how the STATISTICS command tells whether locking shifts were actually used):

```
C-Kermit>set parity even
C-Kermit>set file character-set shift-jis
C-Kermit>set xfer character-set japanese
C-Kermit>set xfer locking-shift off
```

---

[24]The Ctrl-N and Ctrl-O characters are, of course, encoded as printable characters, #N and #O, during packet transmission.

```
C-Kermit>send kanji.txt
 ...
C-Kermit>statistics
 total file characters   : 29440
 communication line out  : 58451
 8th bit prefixing       : yes [&]
 locking shifts          : no
 elapsed time            : 61 sec
 efficiency (percent)    : 50
C-Kermit>
```

and with them:

```
C-Kermit>set parity even
C-Kermit>set file character-set shift-jis
C-Kermit>set xfer character-set japanese
C-Kermit>set xfer locking-shift on
C-Kermit>send kanji.txt
 ...
C-Kermit>stat
 total file characters   : 29440
 communication line out  : 32404
 8th bit prefixing       : yes [&]
 locking shifts          : yes
 elapsed time            : 34 sec
 efficiency (percent)    : 90
C-Kermit>
```

Nearly twice as fast. So...

> When you're in Japan or the (ex)-USSR
> And your file transfers need a lift,
> Remember the old football cheer:
> Lock that Shift! Lock that Shift! Lock that Shift!

Data Compression

Long packets, sliding windows, and locking shifts have SET commands to govern whether, how, or how much they are to be used because each one has drawbacks as well as advantages. But there is one feature you get for free: *data compression*. It has no disadvantages, so there is no SET command to turn it on and off. Whenever you initiate a file transfer, the sending Kermit asks the receiving Kermit if it can accept compressed data. If there is agreement, the file sender collapses repeated bytes into a sequence composed of a special compression lead-in character, a repeat count, and then the character itself. For example:

~@C

stands for 32 letter *C*'s in a row (~ is the lead-in character, @ is the encoded repeat count, and C is the letter *C* itself).

Text files with long strings of blanks and binary files with repeated null characters turn out to be quite common. The average file—text or binary—is compressed about 15 percent during transmission using this simple method [18, pp. 248–250], which tends to offset most other types of overhead introduced by the Kermit protocol. As an extreme example, we transfer a Sun SPARC executable program ("Hello World"), 24576 bytes in length:

```
C-Kermit>set file type binary
C-Kermit>s hello
 ...
C-Kermit>statistics
  total file characters  : 24576
  communication line out : 3032
  compression            : yes [~] (23504)
  elapsed time           : 4 sec
  transmission rate:     : 9600 bps
  effective data rate:   : 6144 cps
  efficiency (percent)   : 647
```

File Attributes

We are finished with Kermit protocol efficiency. Now let's spend a few pages on *your* efficiency, where we present features that let the sending Kermit tell the receiving Kermit certain facts about the file (so you don't have to yourself), and that can prevent files from being transferred unnecessarily or in the wrong mode.

The Kermit protocol has the ability to convey and process information about a file, called the file's *attributes*, along with the file's name and contents, if both Kermit programs support this option and agree to use it. The attributes are sent in a special *attribute packet* (A-packet). Attribute information includes the file's character set (see Chapter 9), the file's creation date, length, type (text or binary), disposition, and an identifier for the sending system. Attribute packets are supported by (at least) C-Kermit, MS-DOS Kermit, Macintosh Kermit, and IBM Mainframe Kermit (see Table 1-1 on page 8).

When the file arrives at the other Kermit, it introduces itself with a capsule biography: "Hi, my name is OOFA, I was born in MS-DOS on January 9, 1986, at 10:28:00 AM, I am 12345 bytes long, I am made of ASCII text, and I would like you to print me," or, translated into Attribute-packet language:

```
A+!P1%12345!!1#119860109 10:28:00."U8"#AMJ*!A
```

Based on this information, the receiver can decide whether to accept or refuse the file, how to interpret it, and what to do with it. Here are the attributes supported by C-Kermit:

TYPE
> The sending Kermit tells the receiving Kermit whether the file is being sent in text (A) or binary (B) mode. This allows the receiving Kermit to switch between text and binary modes automatically. UNIX and most other C-Kermit versions send the text or binary file type attribute according to your most recent SET FILE TYPE command. When receiving a file, the incoming file type attribute takes precedence over whatever you have set. For VMS and OpenVMS, see Appendix IV.

DATE
> When sending a file, C-Kermit includes its creation or last modification date and time (given in local time) in the attribute packet. When receiving a file whose creation date and time is given in the Attribute packet, C-Kermit stores the file with the given creation date and time (or refuses to accept it if FILE COLLISION is set to UPDATE and the arriving file is not newer than an existing file of the same name). Time zone information is not conveyed.

LENGTH
> When sending a file, C-Kermit includes its length in the attribute packet. If the receiving computer notices that the file is bigger than its available disk space or the user's disk quota, it may refuse the file, which can save you a lot of wasted time and phone charges. When there is sufficient disk space, this information allows the receiving Kermit (if it is in local mode) to continuously display the percent done while the file is being transferred. When receiving a file, the OS/2, VMS, Commodore Amiga, and Atari ST versions of C-Kermit reject a file that is too large to fit in the available disk space (in VMS, the user's quota is not checked). The UNIX, AOS/VS, and OS-9 versions of C-Kermit currently do not check the reported file size against available disk space, and always accept the file.

CHARACTER-SET
> This is the TRANSFER CHARACTER-SET (explained in Chapter 9). When sending a file in text mode and when the TRANSFER CHARACTER-SET is not TRANSPARENT (which is the default), C-Kermit translates from the current FILE CHARACTER-SET to the TRANSFER CHARACTER-SET and includes a code to identify the TRANSFER CHARACTER-SET in the Attribute packet. Codes contain registration numbers from the ISO Register [42]. They include:
>
> | | |
> |---|---|
> | I6/100 | ISO 8859-1 Latin Alphabet 1 |
> | I6/101 | ISO 8859-2 Latin Alphabet 2 |
> | I6/144 | ISO 8859-5 Latin/Cyrillic Alphabet |
> | I114/13/87 | Japanese EUC |
>
> When receiving a text file, C-Kermit learns the TRANSFER CHARACTER-SET from the Attribute packet and translates from it into the current FILE CHARACTER-SET.

DISPOSITION
> What to do with the file. Normally, transferred files are simply stored on disk. This attribute is used by the MAIL and REMOTE PRINT commands, presented in Chapter 7, to request that a file be sent as electronic mail or that it be printed, rather than stored on disk.

SYSTEM-ID
> The file sender includes a code identifying its computer and operating system, in case the file receiver wants to use this information in any way. C-Kermit sends this item when sending files and ignores it when receiving files. System IDs are listed in [18, pp. 275–278].

If the other Kermit does not support the exchange of attribute packets, C-Kermit does not send them. This is settled automatically when the two Kermits first say hello to each other with the S or I packet.

But when the two Kermits agree to exchange attribute information, you might find that the effects are not what you desire. For example, you might not want arriving files stored with their original dates because this causes your backup system to skip over them. Or you may find that Kermit's estimate of available disk space is too conservative and it refuses a file that you believe will fit. So C-Kermit gives you the ability to turn each attribute on or off:

SET ATTRIBUTE { CHARACTER-SET, DATE, DISPOSITION, LENGTH, SYSTEM-ID, TYPE } { ON, OFF }
> Turns a particular attribute on or off, leaving the others undisturbed. The individual settings are used only if the entire attribute mechanism is on.

And if the attribute mechanism itself—as opposed to one or more particular attributes—is causing problems, you can disable and enable it with this command:

SET ATTRIBUTE { ON, OFF }
> Turns the entire attribute mechanism on or off. When it is off, C-Kermit will not engage in attribute packet exchange with the other Kermit.

You can also use SET ATTRIBUTE ALL ON or OFF to turn all individual attributes on or off at once without affecting whether the attribute mechanism itself is enabled or disabled. For example, to turn off all attributes except type, you could:

```
C-Kermit>set attr all off      (Turn 'em all off)
C-Kermit>set attr type on      (Turn this one back on)
```

The SHOW ATTRIBUTES command displays C-Kermit's current attribute-related settings.

Displaying and Controlling File Transfer Options

Use the SHOW PROTOCOL command to list C-Kermit's current file transfer protocol-related settings:

```
C-Kermit>show protocol
Protocol Parameters:  Send   Receive
  Timeout:             10      7       Server Timeout:   0
  Padding:              0      0       Block Check:      3
  Pad Character:        0      0       Delay:            4
  Packet Start:         1      1       Max Retries:     10
  Packet End:          13     13       8th-bit Prefix:  '&'
  Packet Length:       90    1000      Repeat Prefix:   '~'
  Maximum Length:    9024    9024      Window Size:     2 set, 1 used
  Buffer Size:       9065    9065      Locking-Shift:   enabled, used

C-Kermit>
```

Some of the protocol options are controlled by the file sender, others by the receiver, others can be elected by either one, still others require both to agree. There are some principles at work here, but they are not worth explaining. Instead, to reduce the confusion, Table 8-1 summarizes the major protocol options, who controls them, and with what commands. The File Type and Transfer Character-Set entries assume that the Attribute-Packet mechanism is active. If it isn't, the appropriate SET commands must be given to *both* Kermits, rather than only to the file sender.

Table 8-1 Kermit File Transfer Feature Summary

Feature	Controlled By	Command
File Collision	Receiver	SET FILE COLLISION to *receiving* Kermit
File Type	Sender	SET FILE TYPE to *sending* Kermit
File Character-Set	Both	SET FILE CHARACTER-SET to *both* Kermits
Incomplete Transfers	Receiver	SET FILE INCOMPLETE to *receiver*
Transfer Character-Set	Sender	SET XFER CHARACTER-SET to *sending* Kermit
Block Check	Sender	SET BLOCK-CHECK to *sending* Kermit
8th-Bit Prefixing	Either	SET PARITY to *either* Kermit
Locking Shifts	Either	SET PARITY to *either* Kermit
Packet Length	Receiver	SET RECEIVE PACKET-LENGTH to *receiving* Kermit
Sliding Windows	Both	SET WINDOW to *both* Kermits
Compression	Automatic	*(none)*
Attributes	Automatic	SET ATTRIBUTE . . . OFF to disable

Chapter 9

International Character Sets

○ ○ ○ ○
If you have no need to transfer text files that contain accented or non-Roman characters and you never need to display these characters on your screen at C-Kermit command level or during CONNECT mode, skip ahead to Chapter 10 on page 199.

All the different computers and operating systems supported by C-Kermit use the ASCII character set, the American Standard Code for Information Interchange [1], listed in Table VIII-1 on page 461.[25] Command and file names, messages and help text—all textual matter is encoded in ASCII.

ASCII contains uppercase and lowercase Roman letters, decimal digits, and punctuation marks sufficient for representing English text and most computer commands and programming languages. But it does not contain the accented or special letters needed for Italian, Norwegian, French, German, or other languages written using Roman-based alphabets, let alone the non-Roman characters of languages like Russian or Japanese.

Although C-Kermit's user interface is strictly English and ASCII, you can use C-Kermit to conduct terminal sessions using a wide variety of Roman and non-Roman character sets and to transfer text files written in languages using most Roman, as well as Cyrillic and Japanese, character sets. This chapter tells you how.

---

[25] ASCII is the United States version of ISO 646 [36].

Table 9-1 Decimal Character Codes for Accented Capital Letter A

Character		IBM PC CP 850	Macintosh Quickdraw	Data General DGI	DECstation DEC MCS	NeXT Workstation
A-Grave	À	183	231	193	192	129
A-Acute	Á	181	203	192	193	130
A-Circumflex	Â	182	229	194	194	131
A-Tilde	Ã	199	204	196	195	132
A-Diaeresis	Ä	142	128	195	196	133
A-Ring	Å	143	129	197	197	134

Proprietary Character Sets

There are hundreds of different languages in the world, hundreds of different kinds of computers, and a potentially vast number of ways to represent the characters of each language on each computer. If we consider only the written languages based on the Roman alphabet, such as Italian, Portuguese, or Norwegian, we find that different computers, such as the IBM PC, the Apple Macintosh, the Data General MV system, the DECstation, and the NeXT workstation represent the accented letters and other special symbols in completely different ways internally. Table 9-1 shows the codes for the uppercase letter A with various accents used by each of these computers.

CP850 is IBM's ASCII-based multilingual code page for PCs, Quickdraw is the character set most commonly used on Apple Macintosh computers, DGI is the Data General International character set, DEC MCS is DEC's Multinational Character Set, and the NeXT character set is used on NeXT computers (see Table VIII-4 on page 464 for a fuller listing). These are just a few of the many proprietary character sets in current use.

Most modern equipment supports some form of national or international text. As long as you stick with a particular manufacturer's equipment—display, keyboard, printer—you can create, read, and print text in any language supported by your equipment. This is a great leap forward from the ASCII-only days. But what if you need to access a different kind of equipment from within your own computing environment? What if you need to exchange text with users of a different kind of equipment?

There are several ways to cope with this problem. The traditional solution has been to ban the use of accented Roman letters as well as all letters from languages like Russian or Hebrew that have non-Roman alphabets. Since computers everywhere support the letters A–Z, transportability of data is assured. But the nature of the data is severely limited, and non-English speaking computer users justifiably resent this approach.

At the other extreme, we could attempt to translate directly between each character set and all the others. This works adequately when the number of sets is small, but quickly becomes unwieldy and unmanageable as the number increases. If the number of character sets is n, the number of translations is $n \times (n-1)$ (the number of pairs chosen from a set of size n, sampling without replacement; see any statistics book [54]).

So if we have two character sets, A and B, we need two translations, one from A to B and one from B to A. If we have three sets—A, B, and C—we need $3 \times 2 = 6$ translations: AB, BA, AC, CA, BC, and CB. And so on. Each translation is typically a pair of tables, 256 bytes in each.

Now consider that IBM alone lists 276 different coded character set identifiers in its registry [35]. If we needed translations between every pair of IBM character sets, we would require 75,900 of them, or about 4 megabytes of tables. Now add in all the other companies and their character sets to appreciate the magnitude of the problem.

A more reasonable approach is to represent characters in a *standard* intermediate character set during transmission. The sender translates from its local codes to the standard ones, the receiver translates from the standard codes to its local ones. This cuts the problem down to a manageable size; each computer needs to know only its own character sets plus a handful of standard sets.

Standard Character Sets

Standard character sets come in 7-bit and 8-bit single-byte varieties, as well as multibyte sets for Chinese, Japanese, and Korean.

The 7-bit sets include US ASCII and other national sets provided for by ISO Standard 646 [36]. The more flexible 8-bit international standard character sets include ISO 8859 Latin Alphabets 1 and 2 for Western and Eastern European languages, respectively, and the ISO 8859-5 Latin/Cyrillic[26] Alphabet [39]. Multibyte character sets include the Chinese, Japanese, and Korean national standard sets.

ISO 646 is the international standard for 7-bit character sets. It is identical to ASCII except that 12 of its positions are set aside for the characters needed for each national language. In ASCII itself, the US version of ISO 646, these 12 positions are occupied by the familiar brackets, braces, bars, and so on, used in many programming languages. In other ISO 646 national versions, these character positions are occupied by national characters.

---

[26]"Cyrillic" refers to the family of alphabets used for Russian, Ukrainian, and other Slavic languages, created by Saint Cyril in the 9th century A.D.

Table 9-2 ISO 646 National Character Sets, Differences from ASCII

	2/03	4/00	5/11	5/12	5/13	5/14	5/15	6/00	7/11	7/12	7/13	7/14
decimal	35	64	91	92	93	94	95	96	123	124	125	126
US ASCII	#	@	[	\	]	^	_	'	{	|	}	~
British	£	@	[	\	]	^	_	'	{	|	}	~
Canadian-French	#	à	â	ç	ê	î	_	ô	é	ù	è	û
Chinese Roman	#	@	[	¥	]	^	_	'	{	|	}	‾
Danish	#	@	Æ	Ø	Å	^	_	'	æ	ø	å	~
Dutch	£	¾	ÿ	½	|	^	_	'	¨	ƒ	¼	'
Finnish	#	@	Ä	Ö	Å	Ü	_	é	ä	ö	å	ü
French	£	à	°	ç	§	^	_	µ	é	ù	è	¨
German	#	§	Ä	Ö	Ü	^	_	'	ä	ö	ü	ß
Hungarian	#	Á	É	Ö	Ü	^	_	ú	é	ö	ü	″
Icelandic	#	Þ	Ð	\	Æ	Ö	_	þ	ð	|	æ	ö
Italian	£	§	°	ç	é	^	_	ù	à	ò	è	ì
Japanese Roman	#	@	[	¥	]	^	_	'	{	|	}	‾
Norwegian	§	@	Æ	Ø	Å	^	_	'	æ	ø	å	|
Portuguese	#	'	Ã	Ç	Õ	^	_	'	ã	ç	õ	~
Spanish	£	§	¡	Ñ	¿	^	_	'	°	ñ	ç	~
Swedish	#	É	Ä	Ö	Å	Ü	_	é	ä	ö	å	ü
Swiss	ù	à	é	ç	ê	î	è	ô	ä	ö	ü	û

For example, the character that occupies position 91, left bracket ([) in ASCII, is replaced by Æ in Danish, ÿ in Dutch, Ä in Finnish, Þ in Icelandic, and so on, as shown in Table 9-2.

The Latin alphabets are 8-bit, 256-character sets. As shown in Figure 9-1, the left half (first 128 characters) of each Latin alphabet is the same as ASCII. It includes 32 7-bit control characters (C0), the Space (SP) character, 94 7-bit graphic characters (GL), and the additional control character, DEL. The right half contains 32 8-bit (C1) control characters and 96 graphic characters (GR) for a particular group of languages. Table 9-3 lists the Latin alphabets.

Table 9-4 on p. 174 shows the graphic characters (columns 10–15) of the right half of Latin Alphabet 1. The DEC Multinational Character Set is very similar to Latin-1, as you can see by comparing Tables 9-4 and 9-5.

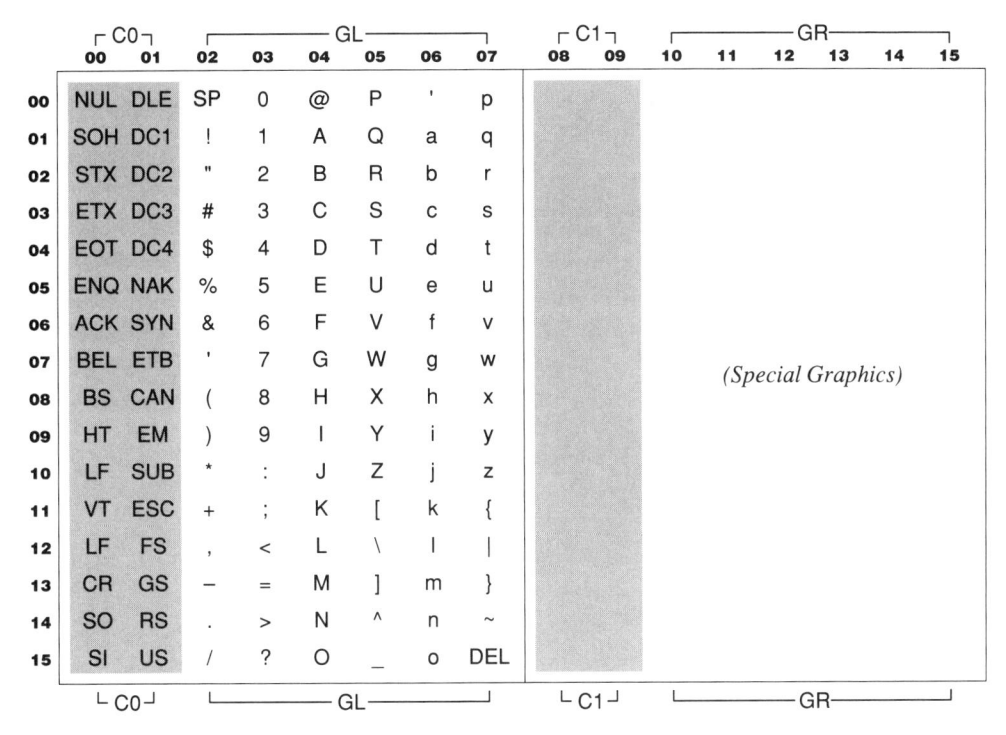

	00	01	02	03	04	05	06	07	08	09	10	11	12	13	14	15
00	NUL	DLE	SP	0	@	P	`	p								
01	SOH	DC1	!	1	A	Q	a	q								
02	STX	DC2	"	2	B	R	b	r								
03	ETX	DC3	#	3	C	S	c	s								
04	EOT	DC4	$	4	D	T	d	t								
05	ENQ	NAK	%	5	E	U	e	u								
06	ACK	SYN	&	6	F	V	f	v								
07	BEL	ETB	'	7	G	W	g	w								
08	BS	CAN	(	8	H	X	h	x						*(Special Graphics)*			
09	HT	EM	)	9	I	Y	i	y								
10	LF	SUB	*	:	J	Z	j	z								
11	VT	ESC	+	;	K	[	k	{								
12	LF	FS	,	<	L	\	l	|								
13	CR	GS	–	=	M	]	m	}								
14	SO	RS	.	>	N	^	n	~								
15	SI	US	/	?	O	_	o	DEL								

Columns 00–01 = C0, 02–07 = GL, 08–09 = C1, 10–15 = GR.

Figure 9-1 Structure of an 8-Bit Latin Alphabet

Table 9-3 The ISO Latin Alphabets

Character Set	Standard	Languages
Latin-1	ISO 8859-1	Danish, Dutch, English, Faeroese, Finnish, French, German, Icelandic, Irish, Italian, Norwegian, Portuguese, Spanish, Swedish
Latin-2	ISO 8859-2	Albanian, Czech, English, German, Hungarian, Polish, Romanian, Serbocroatian (Croatian), Slovak, Slovene
Latin-3	ISO 8859-3	Afrikaans, Catalan, English, Esperanto, French, Galician, German, Italian, Maltese, and Turkish
Latin-4	ISO 8859-4	Danish, English, Estonian, Finnish, German, Greenlandic, Lappish, Latvian, Lithuanian, Norwegian, and Swedish
Latin/Cyrillic	ISO 8859-5	Bulgarian, Bielorussian, English, Macedonian, Russian, Serbocroatian (Serbian), and Ukrainian
Latin/Arabic	ISO 8859-6	Arabic, English
Latin/Greek	ISO 8859-7	Greek, English
Latin/Hebrew	ISO 8859-8	Hebrew, English
Latin-5	ISO 8859-9	Dutch, English, Faeroese, Finnish, French, German, Irish, Italian, Norwegian, Portuguese, Spanish, Swedish, Turkish

Table 9-4 Right Half of Latin Alphabet 1

	10	11	12	13	14	15
00		°	À	Ð	à	ð
01	¡	±	Á	Ñ	á	ñ
02	¢	²	Â	Ò	â	ò
03	£	³	Ã	Ó	ã	ó
04	¤	´	Ä	Ô	ä	ô
05	¥	µ	Å	Õ	å	õ
06	¦	¶	Æ	Ö	æ	ö
07	§	•	Ç	×	ç	÷
08	¨	,	È	Ø	è	ø
09	©	¹	É	Ù	é	ù
10	ª	º	Ê	Ú	ê	ú
11	«	»	Ë	Û	ë	û
12	¬	¼	Ì	Ü	ì	ü
13		½	Í	Ý	í	ý
14	®	¾	Î	Þ	î	þ
15	¯	¿	Ï	ß	ï	ÿ

Table 9-5 DEC Multinational Character Set

	10	11	12	13	14	15
00		°	À		à	
01	¡	±	Á	Ñ	á	ñ
02	¢	²	Â	Ò	â	ò
03	£	³	Ã	Ó	ã	ó
04			Ä	Ô	ä	ô
05	¥	µ	Å	Õ	å	õ
06		¶	Æ	Ö	æ	ö
07	§	•	Ç	Œ	ç	œ
08	¤		È	Ø	è	ø
09	©	¹	É	Ù	é	ù
10	ª	º	Ê	Ú	ê	ú
11	«	»	Ë	Û	ë	û
12		¼	Ì	Ü	ì	ü
13		½	Í	Ÿ	í	ÿ
14			Î		î	
15		¿	Ï	ß	ï	

International Characters in Commands

If you have an 8-bit communication link (no parity) between your terminal (keyboard and screen) and C-Kermit, or if you are running C-Kermit on a workstation, use the following command to tell C-Kermit to allow 8-bit characters in your commands:

SET COMMAND BYTESIZE { 7, 8 }
  Specifies the character size, in bits, to be used in C-Kermit's commands and messages. The default is 7, allowing only 7-bit character sets.

For example, suppose you have a German keyboard and an 8-bit connection to C-Kermit. SET COMMAND BYTESIZE 8 lets you use German letters in your commands. Correct display of 8-bit characters depends, of course, on your terminal emulator or console driver.

```
C-Kermit>set command bytesize 8
C-Kermit>echo grüße aus Köln!
grüße aus Köln!
C-Kermit>
```

International Characters in Terminal Emulation

Most versions of C-Kermit provide no particular kind of terminal emulation during CONNECT mode. Kermit just passes all characters received from the remote host along to your screen and passes your keystrokes to the remote host. The responsibility for most terminal-oriented functions—escape sequence interpretation, function keys, screen roll-back, and so on—lies in your terminal, emulator, or workstation window.

Character-set translation is an exception to this rule. If the remote computer or service uses a character set different from your local computer and it is known to C-Kermit, you can ask C-Kermit to translate between the remote character set and the one used by your terminal or emulator so the characters sent by the remote computer will have the correct appearance on your screen and the characters you type will be translated into the remote computer's character set before being sent.

Choosing the Terminal Character Set

C-Kermit usually has no way of knowing which character sets are in use. You must tell it by giving the following command:

SET TERMINAL CHARACTER-SET *remote-cset [local-cset]*
  Specifies the character set used on the remote computer (*remote-cset*) and the character set used by your terminal or emulator (*local-cset*). If *local-cset* is not specified, C-Kermit's current FILE CHARACTER-SET (explained on page 182) is used. To disable terminal character-set translation, use SET TERMINAL CHARACTER-SET TRANSPARENT, which is the default.

To find out which character sets are available, type a question mark in either one of the character-set name fields:

```
C-Kermit>set terminal character-set ?
remote terminal character-set, one of the following:
 ascii           british          canadian-french  cp437
 cp850           cp852            cp866-cyrillic   cyrillic-iso
 danish          dec-multinational dg-international dutch
 finnish         french           german           hungarian
 italian         koi8-cyrillic    latin1-iso       latin2-iso
 macintosh-latin next-multinational norwegian      portuguese
 short-koi       spanish          swedish          swiss
 transparent
C-Kermit>set terminal character-set spanish
C-Kermit>
```

Table 9-7 on page 181 tells you exactly which character sets these names refer to. The sets with "national" names, like French, Dutch, Finnish, and so on, are 7-bit ISO 646 national sets, which are shown in Table 9-2 on page 172. The Roman 8-bit sets (Latin-1, DEC Multinational, NeXT, etc.) are shown in Tables VIII-4 and VIII-5, and the Cyrillic codes are listed in Table VIII-6. These tables begin on page 464.

Here is an example in which we CONNECT from C-Kermit on a PC running SCO UNIX and using IBM Code Page 437 to a remote Mailbox (BBS) in Cologne, Germany, that uses the German ISO 646 set.

```
C-Kermit>connect
Gr}~e aus K|ln!

F}r Mailbox "gast" eingeben...
login:
```

If this does not look like German to you, it's because the remote computer is using a different character set than your local one. Let's try it again, but this time with C-Kermit providing the translation:

```
C-Kermit>set terminal char german cp437
C-Kermit>connect
Grüße aus Köln!

Für Mailbox "gast" eingeben...
login:
```

When terminal character-set translation is in effect, C-Kermit uses a standard character set (such as Latin-1), if necessary, as an intermediate step between the local and remote sets. Otherwise, C-Kermit's 28 terminal character sets would require 756 translation functions! But by choosing an appropriate intermediate set for each pair, we have about 100, and these also happen to be the same ones we use for file transfer. However, as a result of this ecologically sound design, we can lose characters that the local and remote character sets do not have in common with the intermediate set. For example, both the Macintosh and NeXT character sets have a Florin sign (f), but since Latin-1 doesn't have one (see Table VIII-4), it is replaced by something else along the way, most likely a question mark.

Using a 7-Bit Terminal Character Set

If both the remote and local terminal character sets are 7-bit sets (ASCII, Short KOI, or one of the ISO 646 national sets like Italian, Portuguese, or Norwegian), you should be able to operate in both the 7-bit and 8-bit communication environments equally well.

However, a word of warning is required. If the remote computer sends escape sequences to control the appearance of your screen, these sequences might contain 7-bit graphic characters that would normally be translated before they reach your screen. For example, many ANSI and therefore VT100, VT200, and VT300 escape sequences [4, 53] include the left bracket ([) character, as in:[27]

```
ESC [ 24 ; 40 H
```

---

[27] ESC is the ASCII Escape character. Spaces are shown for clarity, but are not part of the escape sequence.

Table 9-6 ANSI Escape Sequence Formats

Introducer	Type	Terminator
ESC [	Control Sequence	64–126
ESC P	Device Control String	ESC \
ESC]	Operating System Command	ESC \
ESC ^	Privacy Message	ESC \
ESC _	Application Program Command	ESC \
ESC *other*	Escape Sequence	48–126

which moves the cursor to column 40 of line 24 on the screen. But the left bracket is an ISO 646 national character and would be translated as shown in Table 9-2 on page 172, thus destroying the escape sequence and interfering with your screen display.

C-Kermit does its best to avoid this effect by skipping translation of ANSI escape sequences during CONNECT mode. ANSI escape sequences begin with the ESC (Escape) character, ASCII 27, and terminate under various conditions, depending on the character that follows the Escape, as shown in Table 9-6. Whenever C-Kermit sees an Escape character under these conditions, it reads the ensuing characters up to and including the final character or sequence, listed in the *Terminator* column in the table, and sends them to the screen without translation. In the example:

ESC [24 ; 40 H

ESC [is a Control Sequence Introducer, which means that the escape sequence continues until a terminating character in the range 64–126 appears. The first such character in the example is H.

This technique is used only when translation of a 7-bit character set is requested, and so 8-bit escape sequences are not, and don't need to be, recognized. C-Kermit makes no attempt to handle non-ANSI terminal control codes.

Using an 8-Bit Terminal Character Set

During C-Kermit CONNECT mode, there are two components to the connection between your desktop terminal or computer and the remote computer or service: the one between C-Kermit and your keyboard and screen, and the one between C-Kermit and the remote host or service. Each component can be either a 7-bit or an 8-bit connection. Unless you tell C-Kermit otherwise, it treats both as 7-bit connections. This is to prevent parity from being mistaken for real data, a sensible default given the widespread use of parity and the equally widespread lack of awareness about it. But this default prevents the use of 8-bit character sets during a CONNECT session.

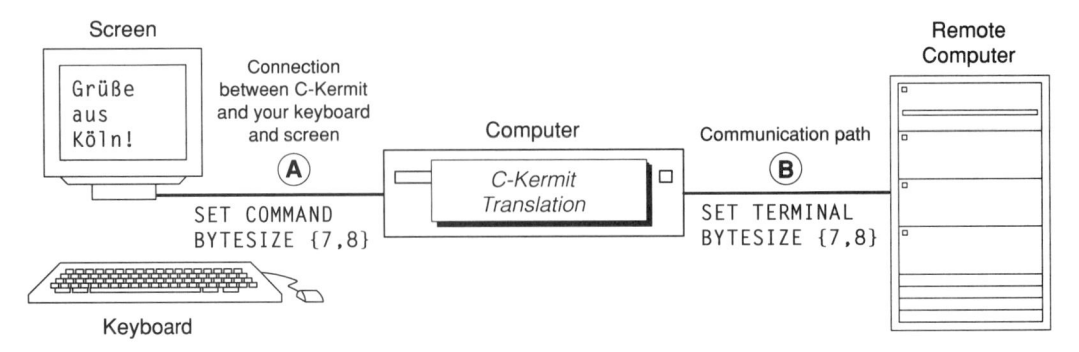

Figure 9-2 Terminal Character Set Translation

Figure 9-2 shows the two components of the CONNECT-mode connection. If the communication path between your terminal or emulator and C-Kermit (A in the figure) is truly 8-bits-no-parity, you can give the command SET COMMAND BYTESIZE 8 to tell C-Kermit not to strip the 8th bit from each character that comes in from your keyboard and goes out to your screen.

Similarly, if the path between C-Kermit and the remote host (B in the figure) is really 8 bits, give the commands SET TERMINAL BYTESIZE 8 and (if necessary) SET PARITY NONE to prevent Kermit from stripping the 8th bit of characters that go in to and out of the communication device. Now you can use 8-bit terminal character sets with no further ado.

Using an 8-Bit Terminal Character Set on a 7-Bit Connection

If the connection between C-Kermit and the remote host (B) is normally 7 bits, but you need to transmit and receive 8-bit characters, you might still be able to do so. Explore the terminal- and communication-related commands of the remote host and of any communication equipment or networks in between: SET TERMINAL /EIGHT on VMS or OpenVMS, `stty pass8` or `stty -parity` on some UNIX systems, `rsh -8` *host* when making "rshell" connections from one UNIX system to another; check the configuration of your modem, terminal server, network PAD, and so on. Do whatever you can to achieve an 8-bit connection.

If all else fails, the C-Kermit CONNECT command supports a terminal-oriented protocol, known as shift-in/shift-out, that allows it to exchange 8-bit data over a 7-bit terminal connection. The remote host must also be using this protocol. It works like this: if an 8-bit character (a character with its 8th bit set to 1) must be sent on a 7-bit connection, an SO character (Shift Out, Control-N, ASCII 14) is sent first, then the 8-bit character is sent with its 8th bit replaced by the required parity bit. When the receiver gets the SO, it knows to set the 8th bit of subsequently received characters to 1 before interpreting them. The next time a 7-bit character must be sent, an SI character (Shift-In, Control-O, ASCII character 15) is sent first. This tells the receiver to set the 8th bit of subsequently received characters to 0. Thus, SO applies to all subsequent characters until an SI is received, and vice versa. To illustrate, suppose we have the German phrase:

Grüße aus Köln!

encoded in Latin Alphabet 1. Using SO/SI, it would be transmitted like this:

Gr<SO>|_<SI>e aus K<SO>v<SI>ln!

where <SO> and <SI> represent the Shift-Out and Shift-In control characters. The "funny" characters are obtained by removing the 8th bit from the Latin-1 special characters, which is equivalent to subtracting 128 from their code values. For example, the Latin-1 code for ü is 252, minus 128 is 124, which is the code for vertical bar, |.

Here is the C-Kermit command that controls the use of Shift-In/Shift-Out during terminal connection:

SET TERMINAL LOCKING-SHIFT { OFF, ON }
This setting, which is normally OFF, applies to the portion of the connection between C-Kermit and the remote host. If you plan to use an 8-bit character set on the remote host, but you only have a 7-bit connection, *and* the remote host can use Shift-In and Shift-Out codes to switch between 7-bit and 8-bit characters, set this option to ON. When TERMINAL LOCKING-SHIFT is ON, C-Kermit interprets incoming characters according to the current shift state and automatically shifts the characters you type on your keyboard before sending them to the remote host.

If the remote host uses an 8-bit character set, but you can't get an 8-bit connection to it, and it does not support shift-in/shift-out, all is not necessarily lost. For example, on a remote UNIX host, you can pipe your 8-bit files through a shift-in/shift-out filter like the one in Appendix XI, for example:

$ cat latin1.txt | so | more

Key Mapping

C-Kermit translates the keys you press into the remote host's character set before transmitting them, according to your most recent SET TERMINAL CHARACTER-SET command. These translations also apply to any key redefinitions you have made with the SET KEY command.

National or international characters in your key definitions should use the coding of your *local* character set, not the remote coding. This is the more natural arrangement and it allows you to access different remote computers that use different character sets without having to change your key mappings.

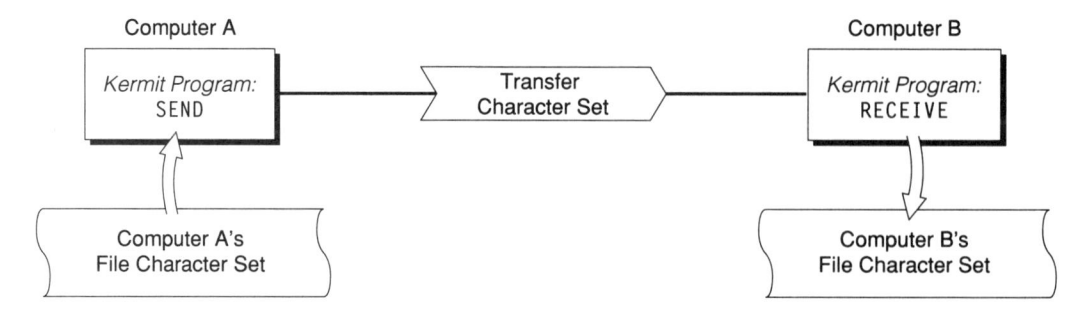

Figure 9-3 International Text File Transfer

Transferring International Text Files

The Kermit protocol distinguishes between vendor-specific codes, used in storing and displaying files on each computer, and the codes used within Kermit's packets when transferring a file [30]. The vendor-specific file encoding is called the *file character-set*; the file character-sets known to C-Kermit are listed in Table 9-7. The code used during file transfer is called the *transfer character-set*. The Kermit protocol supports only a small number of transfer character-sets, namely those that are well-established as international standards, such as ISO 8859-1 Latin Alphabets 1 and 2 or ISO 8859-5 Latin/Cyrillic.[28] The sender translates the file from its local code to the standard transfer code, and the receiver translates from the transfer code to its own local code, as shown in Figure 9-3.

Specifying Character Sets for File Transfer

If your computer supports international character sets at all, it probably does so only as an afterthought. Most computers and operating systems were designed to support only a single character code such as ASCII or EBCDIC, suitable only for representing English. As computer users in non-English-speaking countries began to demand support for their own languages, IBM, DEC, Apple, and other manufacturers introduced terminals, printers, and PCs capable of displaying French, German, Italian, Russian, Hebrew, Arabic, Japanese, and other languages, but in most cases they did this without significantly changing the computers themselves. Text is still stored on the disk in undistinguished, anonymous 8-bit bytes, and the terminal or printer must be told how to interpret them. Files are stored on most computers without any indication of character set.

To send or receive a file containing international characters, you must tell C-Kermit which character sets to use: which character set the original file is encoded in, which standard

---

[28]Eventually, there will be a single standard encoding that encompasses most of the world's character sets [40].

Table 9-7 C-Kermit File Character Sets

Name	Bits	Description
ascii	7	ISO 646 United States Version, ASCII, ANSI X3.4-1986 [1]
british	7	ISO 646, British Version, BSI 4730 [7]
canadian-french	7	French-Canadian NRC (DEC) [26]
cp437	8	IBM Code Page 437, used on PCs [34]
cp850	8	IBM/Microsoft Code Page 850, used on PCs [34]
cp852	8	IBM/Microsoft Code Page 852 for Eastern Europe [34]
cp866	8	Microsoft Code Page 866 Cyrillic, used on PCs [48]
cyrillic-iso	8	ISO 8859-5 Latin/Cyrillic Alphabet [39]
danish	7	(Same as Norwegian) [42]
dec-multinational	8	DEC Multinational Character Set [26]
dg-international	8	Data General International Character Set [23]
dec-kanji	M	DEC multibyte Japanese Kanji
dutch	7	Dutch NRC (DEC) [26]
finnish	7	Finnish NRC (DEC) [26]
french	7	ISO 646, French Version, NF Z 62010-1982 [42]
german	7	ISO 646, German Version, DIN 66083 [42]
hungarian	7	ISO 646, Hungarian Version, HS 7795/3 [42]
italian	7	ISO 646, Italian Version [42]
japanese-euc	M	Japanese Extended UNIX Code, JIS X 0201 + JIS X 0208
jis7-kanji	M	Japanese 7-bit JIS Encoding
koi8-cyrillic	8	"Old KOI-8" Cyrillic (GOST 19768-74) [50]
latin1-iso	8	ISO 8859-1 Latin Alphabet 1 [39]
latin2-iso	8	ISO 8859-2 Latin Alphabet 2 [39]
macintosh-latin	8	Apple Quickdraw extended
next-multinational	8	NeXT Workstation
norwegian	7	ISO 646, Norwegian Version, NS 4551 [42]
portuguese	7	ISO 646, Portuguese Version [42]
shift-jis-kanji	M	Code Page 932 Kanji, used on PCs
short-koi	7	7-bit Roman and Cyrillic, uppercase only [50]
spanish	7	ISO 646, Spanish Version [42]
swedish	7	ISO 646, Swedish Version, SEN 850200 [42]
swiss	7	Swiss NRC (DEC) [26]

character set is to be used during transfer, and which character set is to be used in the new copy of the file. The first command you need is:

SET FILE CHARACTER-SET *name*
> Identifies the character set to be used for file input or output. The file sender translates from the file character set to the transfer character set, and the file receiver translates from the transfer character set to its own file character set. In most cases, the default file character-set is ASCII. In certain versions of C-Kermit, the local character set is known, so that is your default file character-set. For example, on the NeXT, it is the NeXT character set; on AOS/VS systems, it is DG-International; in OS/2, it is your current PC code page.

Your version of C-Kermit does not necessarily support all of the file character-sets listed in Table 9-7. C-Kermit can be configured to omit one or more character-set families: East European, Cyrillic, or Japanese Kanji. You can use the SHOW FEATURES and CHECK commands to obtain configuration information:

```
C-Kermit>show features
...
 No Kanji character-set translation
C-Kermit>check latin2
 Available
C-Kermit>
```

To see the list of supported file character-sets, use a question mark in the SET FILE CHARACTER-SET command:

```
C-Kermit>set file char ? local file code, one of the following:
 ascii              british           canadian-french    cp437
 cp850              cp852             cp866-cyrillic     cyrillic-iso
 danish             dec-kanji         dec-multinational  dg-international
 dutch              finnish           french             german
 hungarian          italian           japanese-euc       jis7-kanji
 koi8-cyrillic      latin1-iso        latin2-iso         macintosh-latin
 next-multinational norwegian         portuguese         shift-jis-kanji
 short-koi          spanish           swedish            swiss
C-Kermit>set file char hungarian
```

This is the list you would see with a fully-configured C-Kermit program.

Choosing the appropriate file character-sets for the two computers solves two-thirds of the puzzle. To complete the puzzle, you must choose the transfer character-set that is best capable of representing the characters in your file character-sets:

SET TRANSFER CHARACTER-SET *name*
> Identifies the intermediate character set to be used in Kermit-to-Kermit communication, that is, in Kermit's data packets. Synonym: **SET XFER CHARACTER-SET**.

The default transfer character-set is TRANSPARENT, meaning that no translation takes place during file transfer.

C-Kermit supports the following transfer character-sets:

LATIN1-ISO
> is ISO 8859-1 Latin Alphabet 1 [39], or Latin-1 for short. This is the usual choice for Western European languages based on the Roman alphabet, such as Italian, Portuguese, Norwegian, French, and Spanish, because it is capable of representing all the characters used in about 15 of these languages (see Table 9-3). Latin Alphabet 1 is listed in Table VIII-4.

LATIN2-ISO
> is ISO 8859-2 Latin Alphabet 2, or Latin-2 for short. This is the usual choice for Eastern European languages based on the Roman alphabet, such as Czech, Polish, Romanian, and Hungarian (see Table 9-3). Latin Alphabet 2 is listed in Table VIII-5.

CYRILLIC-ISO
> is ISO 8859-5, the Latin/Cyrillic Alphabet [39], also known as ECMA-113 [27], which can represent Russian, Ukrainian, and other languages written in Cyrillic and (because it includes ASCII as its left half) English. Listed in Table VIII-6.

JAPANESE-EUC should be used for Japanese text.

ASCII
> means to render each character as its closest ASCII equivalent, for example by removing diacritical marks from accented Roman vowels, or by converting Cyrillic characters "by sound." Use this option when your computer does not have a way to display the file's characters correctly (these conversions don't work for Japanese).

TRANSPARENT
> means that no character translation occurs; each code is sent as-is. For compatibility with earlier releases of C-Kermit, this is the default transfer character-set. This option can also be used whenever both computers use the same character set.

Your version of C-Kermit might be configured differently. To find out which transfer character-sets are available to you:

```
C-Kermit>set transfer char ?
 ascii      latin1-iso      transparent
```

When you specify the file and transfer character-sets, Kermit picks the appropriate translation function and uses it as shown in Figure 9-4 on the next page, which illustrates what happens when you transfer an Italian language text file from a PC with MS-DOS Kermit to a Data General Aviion workstation with C-Kermit.

It's your job to use the SET FILE CHARACTER-SET and SET TRANSFER CHARACTER-SET commands to pick the translation you need. Kermit can't do this for you because it doesn't know what you are trying to accomplish. To illustrate this point, let's suppose you want

```
Local PC Kermit Commands                Remote C-Kermit Commands
MS-Kermit>set file char cp437           C-Kermit>set file char dg
MS-Kermit>set transfer char latin1      C-Kermit>set xfer char latin1
MS-Kermit>send linguini.txt             C-Kermit>receive
```

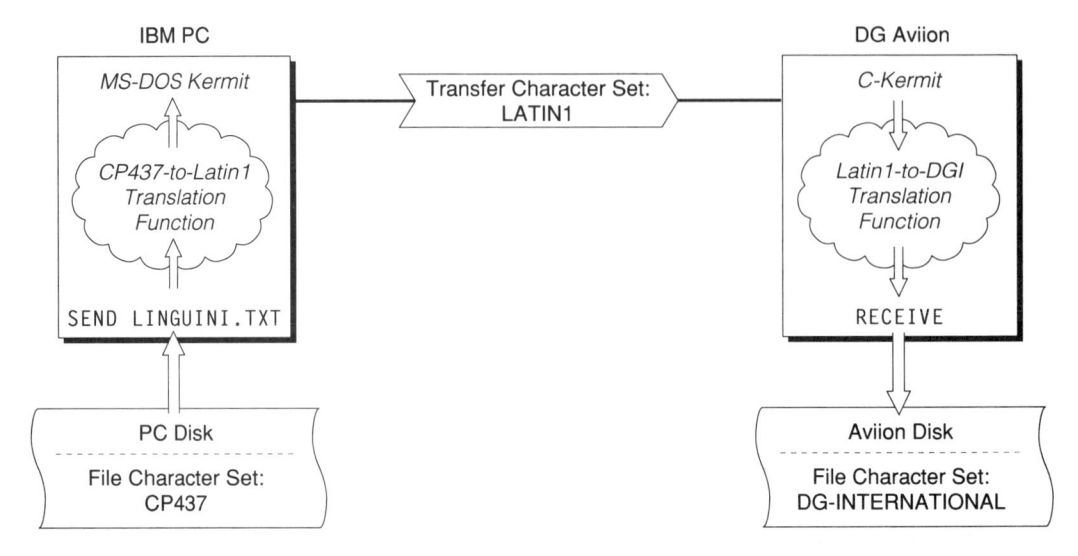

Figure 9-4 Linguini Transfer

to receive a French-language text file with C-Kermit on an SCO UNIX system running on an IBM or compatible PC. The TRANSFER CHARACTER-SET is LATIN1. Your PC uses Code Page 437. You can choose your FILE CHARACTER-SET to be:

- CP437 if you want the file to display correctly on your PC screen

- CP850 if you want to copy the file to a tape cartridge for an IBM RS/6000

- LATIN1 if you want to keep the Latin-1 encoding intact for an application on your PC that requires Latin-1 rather than CP437

- FRENCH if you want to print the file on your PC printer, but your printer only supports the French ISO 646 character set

- ASCII if you want to convert the special characters to plain ASCII, for example because your PC-based e-mail system only supports ASCII

- NEXT if you want to copy the file to a DOS-format diskette to be read on a NeXT workstation

And so on...

Use the SHOW CHARACTER-SETS command to see C-Kermit's current terminal, file, and transfer character-sets:

```
C-Kermit>sho char
 File Character-Set: US ASCII (7-bit)
 Transfer Character-Set: Transparent
 Unknown-Char-Set: Keep
 Terminal character-set: transparent

   (Now change them...)
C-Kermit>set file char next
C-Kermit>set xfer char latin1
C-Kermit>set term char dg next
C-Kermit>set unkn discard
C-Kermit>sho char
 File Character-Set: NeXT Multinational (8-bit)
 Transfer Character-Set: LATIN1, ISO 8859-1
 Unknown-Char-Set: Discard
 Terminal character-sets:
   Remote: dg-international
   Local: next-multinational
   Via:    latin1-iso
C-Kermit>
```

The UNKNOWN-CHAR-SET setting tells C-Kermit what to do if a file arrives announcing itself with a character set that C-Kermit doesn't support. Normally the file is accepted (KEEP) without translation, but you can also instruct C-Kermit to reject such files:

```
C-Kermit>sent unknown-char-set discard
```

The SET UNKNOWN-CHAR-SET command is effective only when given to the file receiver.

Transferring Roman Text

Let's try a simple example. Suppose we have a German-language file stored on an IBM PC using PC Code Page 437. The file is called `modem.txt` and it looks like this:

```
Wer ein Selbstwähl-Modem hat, muß zur Herstellung der Verbindung
mit dem anderen Rechner die Wählkommandos eintippen. Man kann zur
Kermit-Kommandoebene zurückgelangen durch Eintippen der
'Rückkehrsequenz'.
```

Let's transfer this file from the PC to a UNIX system that uses the 7-bit German character set. Assume we're already logged in. The Kermit program on *each* computer must be told which file character-set to use, but only the file sender has to be told the transfer character-set because the sender automatically informs the receiver in the attribute packet. First tell MS-DOS Kermit on the PC which character sets to use:

```
MS-Kermit>set file character-set cp437
MS-Kermit>set transfer character-set latin1
```

Now go to the UNIX system, start C-Kermit, tell it which file character-set to use, and then tell it to wait for the file:

```
MS-Kermit>connect
$ kermit
C-Kermit>set file character-set german
C-Kermit>receive
```

Now escape back to the PC and send the file. MS-DOS Kermit automatically tells C-Kermit that the transfer character-set is Latin-1.

```
Alt-X                              (Escape back)
MS-Kermit>send modem.txt           (Send the file)
  (The file is transferred...)
```

Now the file is stored on the UNIX system with German ISO 646 encoding. To check that it was transferred correctly, tell MS-DOS Kermit's terminal emulator about the character set and then connect back to UNIX and display the file on your screen:

```
MS-Kermit>set terminal character-set german
MS-Kermit>connect
C-Kermit>type modem.txt
Wer ein Selbstwähl-Modem hat, muß zur Herstellung der Verbindung
mit dem anderen Rechner die Wählkommandos eintippen. Man kann zur
Kermit-Kommandoebene zurückgelangen durch Eintippen der
'Rückkehrsequenz'.
$
```

As you can see, the file arrived with its special characters intact. Now let's transfer the same file from UNIX to another PC. But this time it is to be printed on a device that does not have German characters. Here we choose ASCII as the transfer character-set to translate the special characters to their closest ASCII equivalents, rather than into gibberish:

```
C-Kermit>set file char german      (Translate from this)
C-Kermit>set xfer char ascii       (to this)
C-Kermit>send modem.txt            (Send the file from UNIX)
alt<X>                             (Escape back)
MS-Kermit>receive                  (Wait for the file on the PC)
  (The file is transferred...)
MS-Kermit>type modem.txt           (Take a look...)
Wer ein Selbstwahl-Modem hat, mus zur Herstellung der Verbindung
mit dem anderen Rechner die Wahlkommandos eintippen. Man kann zur
Kermit-Kommandoebene zuruckgelangen durch Eintippen der
'Ruckkehrsequenz'.
$
```

Notice how ä has become simply a, ü has become u, and ß has become s. Without these translations, the text would have been printed like this:

```
Wer ein Selbstw{hl-Modem hat, mu~ zur Herstellung der Verbindung
mit dem anderen Rechner die W{hlkommandos eintippen. Man kann zur
Kermit-Kommandoebene zur}ckgelangen durch Eintippen der
'R}ckkehrsequenz'.
```

Transferring Cyrillic Text

Cyrillic text (Russian, Ukrainian, Bielorussian, and so on) can be encoded using a variety of different and incompatible character sets, including at least the following:

- Microsoft Code Page 866 [48], used on PCs, which, like other PC code pages, has ASCII in the left half and the special characters in the right. Supported by MS-DOS Kermit and C-Kermit.

- Alternative Cyrillic, a precursor to Code Page 866, developed for PCs in the Soviet Union by Bryabin, et al. [6].

- IBM Code Page 855 for PCs [34]. Like Code Page 866, but with different encoding.

- Old KOI-8, an 8-bit Soviet government standard (GOST 19768-74) [50] character set consisting of full upper- and lowercase Latin and Cyrillic alphabets, in which the 8-bit Cyrillic letters run parallel to their 7-bit ASCII phonetic equivalents. KOI stands for Код для Обмена Информатсии —Kod dlia Obmiena Informatsii (Code for Information Interchange, like the CII in ASCII).

- New KOI-8, a newer standard (GOST 19768-87) that is supposed to replace Old KOI-8. Old KOI-8 is still in wide use.

- Short KOI [50], a 7-bit code containing the uppercase Roman and Cyrillic letters, but no lowercase. The Roman letters are in ASCII order, and Cyrillic letters parallel the Roman letters phonetically.

- DKOI [50], similar to KOI-8, but with an EBCDIC-style layout, used on IBM compatible mainframes and supported by IBM mainframe Kermit [16].

- IBM Code Page 880 [34], IBM's EBCDIC-based Cyrillic Multilingual Code Page for IBM mainframes, totally different from DKOI, supported by IBM mainframe Kermit [16].

- IBM Code Page 1025, a newer revision of IBM Code Page 880.

- ISO 8859-5 Latin/Cyrillic, similar to Latin-1, but with Cyrillic characters in the right half. This is the international standard Cyrillic character set.

Each of these sets is capable of representing both Roman and Cyrillic letters. The Kermit protocol uses ISO 8859-5 Latin/Cyrillic as the transfer character-set for Cyrillic text, supported, as of this writing, by MS-DOS Kermit, IBM mainframe Kermit, and C-Kermit. Use this command:

SET TRANSFER CHARACTER-SET CYRILLIC

to select the Latin/Cyrillic transfer character-set.

C-Kermit supports the following Cyrillic file character-sets:

SET FILE CHARACTER-SET CYRILLIC
    ISO 8859-5 Latin/Cyrillic.

SET FILE CHARACTER-SET CP866
    Microsoft PC Code Page 866.

SET FILE CHARACTER-SET KOI8
    Old KOI-8.

SET FILE CHARACTER-SET SHORT-KOI
    Short KOI.

These character sets are listed in Table VIII-6 on page 470. The method for transferring Cyrillic files is the same as for Roman text. You have to identify the file character-set to be used on each computer and you also must tell the file sender which transfer character-set to use. Here is an example in which we send a KOI-8 file from C-Kermit to an IBM-compatible mainframe, where it is to be stored using EBCDIC CECP 880:

```
Kermit-CMS>set file char cp880     (Translate to IBM code page)
Kermit-CMS>receive                 (Receive the file)
Ctrl-\c                            (Escape back to C-Kermit)
C-Kermit>set file char koi8        (Identify the file character-set)
C-Kermit>set xfer char cyrillic    (Translate to Latin/Cyrillic)
C-Kermit>send icsti.txt            (Send the file)
```

C-Kermit tells IBM Mainframe Kermit that the transfer character-set is Latin/Cyrillic, and IBM Mainframe Kermit translates from this to Code Page 880.

Suppose you need to look at Cyrillic text on a computer that does not have a Cyrillic display device available. Use Short KOI, in which all Roman letters are converted to uppercase, and Cyrillic letters are converted to their lowercase Roman phonetic equivalents, listed in Table VIII-6 on page 470. In this example, we send a copy of Pushkin's poem *Bronze Horseman* from a PC, where it is stored using CP866, to C-Kermit, where it is stored in Short KOI format.

```
MS-Kermit>type horseman.txt        (Read it in Russian)
    На берегу пустынных волн
    Стоял он, дум великих полн,
    И вдаль глядел. Пред ним широко
    Река неслася; бедный чёлн
    По ней стремился одиноко.
    ...
MS-Kermit>connect                  (Go to UNIX)
C-Kermit>set file char short-koi   (Translate to Short KOI)
C-Kermit>receive                   (Wait for the file)
Alt-X                              (Escape back)
```

188 International Character Sets / Chapter 9

```
MS-Kermit>set file char cp866      (Translate from this...)
MS-Kermit>set transf char cyr      (to this)
MS-Kermit>send horseman.txt        (Send the file)

   (The file is transferred...)

MS-Kermit>connect                  (Go back to UNIX)
C-Kermit>type horseman.txt         (Look at the result)

 na beregu pustynnyh woln
stoql on, dum welikih poln,
i wdalx glqdel.  pred nim {iroko
reka neslasq; bednyj ~eln
po nej stremilsq odinoko.
  ...
```

You can mix Roman-based and Cyrillic-based character sets during file transfer, but then you lose the Cyrillic characters. For example, if you translate from KOI-8 to Latin-1, the ASCII text survives, but the Cyrillic characters all become question marks (but see page 193 before giving up on this idea).

Similarly, if you translate from Latin-1 to Latin/Cyrillic, it is the same as translating from Latin-1 to ASCII. All accents and other diacritical marks are lost.

Transferring Japanese Text

Japanese writing combines several different elements:

- Kanji, ideograms similar to those used in China and Korea, with each ideogram standing for a word. More than 6,000 Kanji symbols are in common use.

- Kana, a phonetic writing system, containing 50–60 characters, including punctuation and sound symbols. Kana comes in two major varieties, Katakana and Hiragana, the latter being a more cursive and stylized form.

- Roman letters, digits, and punctuation.

As you might expect, there is more than one character set for representing Japanese text:

- JIS (Japan Industrial Standard) X 0201 [43] combines Roman and Katakana in a Latin-alphabet-like 8-bit single-byte character set. It differs from a Latin alphabet in that the left half is not exactly ASCII (backslash is replaced by Yen sign, tilde by overbar), and the right half has some empty positions.

- JIS X 0208 [44] is a set of 6877 two-byte characters including Roman, Cyrillic, Greek, Katakana, Hiragana, and Kanji characters, plus special symbol and line-drawing characters.

- JIS X 0212 [45] is a newer revision of JIS X 0208.

- Japanese EUC (Extended UNIX Code) combines JIS X 0201 and 0208 in a single code in which single-byte Roman characters have their 8th bits set to zero, double-byte JIS X 0208 codes have their 8th bits set to 1, and single-byte JIS X 0201 Katakana codes are invoked via a single-shift mechanism.

- Shift-JIS (Code Page 932) is used on PCs and includes single-byte Roman and Katakana and 2-byte Kanji, but at different code points than the standard sets or EUC.

- DEC Kanji is used on VMS and OpenVMS and is equivalent to EUC, but without single-byte Katakana.

- Various "EBCDIC" Kanji codes are used on IBM, Hitachi, and Fujitsu mainframes, supported by IBM mainframe Kermit [16].

To complicate matters, we have 7-bit transmission media and e-mail to contend with. For this, a variation of EUC called JIS-7 is used, in which all characters are represented by 7-bit bytes, and switching among JIS Roman, JIS Katakana, and JIS X 0208 is done by locking shifts [30, 37] imbedded in the data stream.

C-Kermit uses Japanese-EUC as the transfer character-set for Japanese text, since it accommodates the three major writing methods and still distinguishes between single- and double-width Roman and Katakana characters:

SET TRANSFER CHARACTER-SET JAPANESE-EUC

C-Kermit supports the following Japanese file character-sets:

SHIFT-JIS
Shift-JIS (CP932) on PCs.

DEC-KANJI
DEC Kanji, used primarily on VMS and OpenVMS.

JIS-7
The code most commonly used in electronic mail.

JAPANESE-EUC
Japanese Extended UNIX code itself, commonly found on UNIX computers.

Here we use C-Kermit on a PC-based UNIX system (which uses Shift-JIS) to send a Kanji file to C-Kermit on a remote VAX (which uses DEC-Kanji). We also use the SET PROMPT command to distinguish between the two C-Kermit prompts.

```
C-Kermit>set prompt Kyoto>        (Local PC Kermit prompt)
Kyoto>set file char shift-jis     (Translate from this...)
Kyoto>set xfer char japan         (to this)
Kyoto>connect                     (Go to the VAX)
```

```
    $ kermit                              (Start Kermit)
    C-Kermit>set prompt Tokyo>            (Change the prompt)
    Tokyo>set file char dec-kanji         (Translate to this)
    Tokyo>r                               (Receive the file)
    Ctrl-\c                               (Escape back)
    Kyoto>send genji.txt                  (Send the file)
```

There is no mechanism for translating Japanese into Roman characters or vice versa. C-Kermit lets you combine Japanese and non-Japanese transfer and file character-sets, but only the Roman letters are preserved. C-Kermit does not support Japanese character set translation during terminal emulation.

Language-Specific Translations

When C-Kermit is receiving a file encoded in the Latin-1 transfer character-set but has been told to store the file as ASCII, or when it is sending a file encoded in a national or international character set but has been told to use ASCII as its transfer character-set, it strips diacritical marks and stores or sends the bare letters; for example, *à côté* becomes *a cote* (French), *Füße* becomes *Fuse* (German). For most Romance languages (Italian, Spanish, etc.), not much else can be done.

Languages like Dutch, Norwegian, Danish, Swedish, and German, however, have rules for changing accented or other special characters into the plain letters A–Z. These rules are shown in Table 9-8 (in which Scandinavian means Danish, Finnish, Norwegian, or Swedish). Since Kermit does not know what language a file is written in, you must tell it. Here's the command:

SET LANGUAGE *name*

Tells C-Kermit which language text files are written in so it can apply language-specific transliteration rules when converting between ASCII and a national or international character set. Type a question mark to see which languages are supported by your C-Kermit program, for example:

```
C-Kermit>set language ? One of the following:
 danish          dutch              finnish          french
 german          icelandic          norwegian        none
 russian         swedish
C-Kermit>set language finnish
```

NONE, which is the default, means that no special language rules should be applied.

If you SET LANGUAGE to DUTCH, FRENCH, GERMAN, ICELANDIC, or any of the Scandinavian languages DANISH, FINNISH, NORWEGIAN, or SWEDISH, you get the effects shown in Table 9-8 when translating into ASCII from an 8-bit character set or from a 7-bit ISO 646 national version, but *not* in the other direction. The language-specific translations are not invertible.

Table 9-8 Language-Specific Transliteration Rules

Character	Dutch	French	German	Icelandic	Scandinavian
Å	–	–	–	–	Aa
å	–	–	–	–	aa
Ä	–	–	Ae	–	Ae
ä	–	–	ae	–	ae
Æ	–	–	–	Ae	Ae
æ	–	–	–	ae	ae
Ö	–	–	Oe	Oe	Oe
ö	–	–	oe	oe	oe
Œ	–	Oe	–	–	–
œ	–	oe	–	–	–
Ø	–	–	–	–	Oe
ø	–	–	–	–	oe
Ü	–	–	Ue	–	Ue
ü	–	–	ue	–	ue
ÿ	ij	–	–	–	–
ß	–	–	ss	–	–
Ð	–	–	–	D	–
ð	–	–	–	d	–
Þ	–	–	–	Th	–
þ	–	–	–	th	–

You can find out your current character sets and language with the SHOW FILE, SHOW LANGUAGES, or SHOW CHARACTER-SETS commands, for example:

```
C-Kermit>set xfer ch latin1
C-Kermit>show lang
  Language-specific translation rules: Icelandic
  File Character-Set: ASCII
  Transfer Character-Set: Latin-1
C-Kermit>
```

To illustrate the use of the SET LANGUAGE command, let's transfer our German file again, and suppose again that the file is to be printed on a device that does not have the German special characters. We can convert the German characters to ASCII without any loss of information by using our special language rules:

```
MS-Kermit>set file character-set cp437
MS-Kermit>set transfer character-set latin1
MS-Kermit>connect
$ kermit
C-Kermit>set file character-set ascii
C-Kermit>set language german
C-Kermit>receive
Alt-X
MS-Kermit>send modem.txt
MS-Kermit>connect
C-Kermit>type modem.txt
Wer ein Selbstwaehl-Modem hat, muss zur Herstellung der Verbindung
mit dem anderen Rechner die Waehlkommandos eintippen. Man kann zur
Kermit-Kommandoebene zurueckgelangen durch Eintippen der
'Rueckkehrsequenz'.
$
```

The umlaut-a's have become ae's, the umlaut-u's are now ue's, and the German double-s is two s's—perfectly acceptable and proper German. Note, however, that these rules can not be applied in the opposite direction. For example, if oe were always translated to ö, then *Kommandoebene* would be improperly written as *Kommandöbene*.

SET LANGUAGE RUSSIAN has a special meaning. If C-Kermit's file character-set is one of the Cyrillic ones (KOI8, Cyrillic-ISO, etc.), but the transfer character-set is ASCII, C-Kermit uses Short KOI in place of ASCII in the Kermit packets. This lets you send, for example, a Latin-Cyrillic file in Short-KOI form, or receive a file in Short-KOI form and store it in a proper 8-bit Cyrillic character set. This is useful when the one of the two computers does not support Cyrillic characters. For example, here we send a short file composed of both Roman and Cyrillic characters from a Russian computer running C-Kermit to a CP/M microcomputer running Kermit-80:

```
C-Kermit>set file character-set koi8      (Translate from this)
C-Kermit>set xfer character-set ascii     (to this)
C-Kermit>set language russian             (using Short KOI)
C-Kermit>send kepmit.txt                  (Send a file)
Ctrl-C]                                   (Escape back to micro)
Kermit-80>receive                         (Receive the file)

   (The file is transferred)

Kermit-80>type kepmit.txt                 (Take a look at it)
protokol pereda~i fajlow KERMIT.
ppf razrabotan w sootwetstwii so standartom ISO 7498 "|talonnaq
modelx wzaimodejstwiq otzayplh sistemy princip raboty ppf
zakl'~aetsq w obmene paketami KERMIT mevdu kompxywerami. format
paketow KERMIT:
   +------+-----+-----+------+--  --  --  ---+-------+
   ? MARK ? LEN ? SEQ ? TYPE ?     DATA      ? CHECK ?
   +------+-----+-----+------+--  --  --  ---+-------+
```

Transferring International Text Files 193

```
MARK       - marker paketow KERMIT;
LEN        - dlina paketa;
SEQ        - nomer paketa;
TYPE       - tip paketa;
DATA       - dannye;
CHECK      - kontrolxnaq summa.
Kermit-80>
```

In the Short-KOI result, the uppercase words are English and the lowercase words are Russian. Question marks indicate characters that could not be translated. For example, the original text had vertical bars (|) in the diagram, but since vertical bar is the Short KOI notation for the Cyrillic letter Э (see Table VIII-6), we can't use vertical bars to represent themselves.

Transferring 8-Bit Text Files in the 7-Bit Environment

The Japanese-EUC and Latin/Cyrillic transfer character sets contain a preponderance of 8-bit characters. Does this mean that you must pay a heavy performance penalty when transferring Japanese or Russian text over a 7-bit connection?

As part of its international text transfer capability, the Kermit protocol has been fitted with a locking shift mechanism, explained in Chapter 8, pages 162–164. Rather than prefix each 8-bit byte with an additional character, Kermit shifts into and out of 8-bit character sequences much as you push the Caps Lock key on your keyboard. Locking shifts are used automatically whenever you have told Kermit to SET PARITY to anything but NONE and the other Kermit agrees to use them.[29]

Translating without Transferring

Since the facilities for translation are already in place for CONNECT sessions and file transfer, C-Kermit includes—at no extra cost—a command to translate a local file from one character set to another:

TRANSLATE *file1 cs1 cs2* [*file2*]
Translate the local file *file1* from the character set *cs1* into the character set *cs2*. Both character sets may be selected from C-Kermit's repertoire of file character sets. The result is stored in *file2* or (if *file2* is not specified), displayed on your screen.
Synonym: **XLATE**.

As with terminal connection and file transfer, an intermediate standard character set is used in translation. If the target character-set (*cs2*) is Cyrillic (CP866, KOI8, Short KOI,

---

[29]Other Kermit programs that support this feature include MS-DOS Kermit and IBM Mainframe Kermit. See Table 1-1 on page 8 for a comparison of the capabilities of different Kermit programs.

etc.), Latin/Cyrillic is the intermediate set. Japanese EUC is used as the intermediate set if either one of the files is Japanese. If either one of the sets is Latin-2 or CP852, Latin-2 is used. Otherwise, if it is Roman-based, Latin-1 is used.

Here's an example in which a Swedish-language electronic mail message has been received and then saved to disk. It is encoded in Swedish 7-bit ISO 646, but needs to be converted to Latin-1 for printing:

```
C-Kermit>xla diab.msg swedish latin1 diab.lat   (Translate)
C-Kermit>type diab.lat                          (Check it)
From: bl@diab.se (Benny Löfgren)
Subject: C-Kermit 5a(177)
Date: Thu, 30 Jan 92 12:55:58 MET

Är det annonserat någon nyare C-Kermit än 5A(177)? Jag har
kompilerat upp den med TCP/IP-stöd på DS90, och det verkar
fungera bra.  Kan lägga upp binären på klubben.  Följande
entry har jag lagt till i makefilen:
========= cut ========= cut ========= cut ======== cut =========
#DIAB DS90, DNIX 5.3 or later, with HDB UUCP, nap, rdchk, TCP/IP
dnix5r3net:
...
C-Kermit>print diab.lat         (Looks good, print it)
```

In case you are not lucky enough to have a Latin-1 capable printer, you can use the SET LANGUAGE command with the TRANSLATE command in exactly the same way it is used in file transfer. Here we convert the Swedish message for printing on an ASCII-only printer:

```
C-Kermit>set language swedish
C-Kermit>xla diab.msg swedish ascii diab.asc    (Translate)
C-Kermit>type diab.lat                          (Check it)
From: bl@diab.se (Benny Loefgren)
Subject: C-Kermit 5a(177)
Date: Thu, 30 Jan 92 12:55:58 MET

Aer det annonserat naagon nyare C-Kermit aen 5A(177)? Jag har
kompilerat upp den med TCP/IP-stoed paa DS90, och det verkar
fungera bra.  Kan laegga upp binaeren paa klubben.  Foeljande
entry har jag lagt till i makefilen:
========= cut ========= cut ========= cut ======== cut =========
#DIAB DS90, DNIX 5.3 or later, with HDB UUCP, nap, rdchk, TCP/IP
dnix5r3net:
...
C-Kermit>print diab.asc         (Looks OK, print it)
```

See how the special characters were converted according to the rules listed in Table 9-8: a-ring to aa, and so on.

One-Sided Translation

International character-set support is a relatively recent addition to the Kermit file transfer protocol, and you won't find it in every Kermit program. As of this writing, it is available in MS-DOS Kermit 3.0 and later, in Kermit-370 4.2 and later for the major IBM mainframe operating systems, and in C-Kermit itself.

That doesn't mean you can't use C-Kermit's translation features with other Kermit programs that don't support this feature. Whenever you send a file from C-Kermit to a non-internationalized Kermit on a computer that happens to support one of Kermit's transfer character-sets, have C-Kermit translate the file in the normal way, for example:

```
C-Kermit>set file char cp437
C-Kermit>set xfer char latin1
C-Kermit>sen oofa.txt
```

The other Kermit does no translating, but it doesn't have to.

If a local file is encoded in any character set that is also supported by the other computer, you can use the TRANSPARENT transfer character-set to send it from C-Kermit, in which case your current file character-set setting is ignored.

You can also use C-Kermit's TRANSLATE command to pre- and/or postprocess transferred files. In this example, C-Kermit running on an Apple Macintosh with A/UX uploads an Icelandic-language file to a bulletin board system (BBS) that has Kermit protocol built in, but which does not support character-set translation. The BBS is on a PC that uses Code Page 850. C-Kermit translates the file from Macintosh Latin to CP850 and then sends it without further translation:

```
C-Kermit>type kermit.txt

Af hverju er Kermit svona vinsæll?  Hann er ódýr og góður.  Með
Kermit getur þú tengst tölvum, stórum eða litlum, nær og fjær.
Þú getur skiptst á upplýsingum, á þægilegan og öruggan hátt, við
næstum hvaða tölvu sem er.  Þú getur tengst fréttakerfum,
verslunum, póstkerfum, bönkum, verðbréfabönkum og sent og tekið á
móti skrám.  Þú getur skiptst á gögnum við vini og nágranna, þó
þeir eigi öðruvísi tölvu en þú.  Þú getur unnið heiman frá þér.
Kermit getur tengt þig við "netið."  Notið ímyndunaraflið.  Með
nútíma alþjóðlegu símakerfi og ört vaxandi tækni í síma
og tölvumálum eru ykkur engin takmörk sett.

C-Kermit>translate kermit.txt macintosh-latin cp850 kermit.850
C-Kermit>set transfer character-set transparent
C-Kermit>send kermit.850
```

When the remote computer supports only ASCII, C-Kermit can send files to it using ASCII as the transfer character-set, perhaps together with C-Kermit's SET LANGUAGE command for language-specific rules. In this example, we upload the same Icelandic text file to another BBS, but this BBS supports neither the Kermit protocol nor any 8-bit character sets, so we use the rules from Table 9-8 to transliterate the Icelandic letters to ASCII:

```
C-Kermit>set file char mac        (Macintosh-Latin)
C-Kermit>set xfer char asc        (ASCII)
C-Kermit>set lang icelandic       (Icelandic rules)
C-Kermit>transmit kermit.txt      (Unguarded upload)

Af hverju er Kermit svona vinsaell? Hann er odyr og godur.  Med
Kermit getur thu tengst toelvum, storum eda litlum, naer og fjaer.
Thu getur skiptst a upplysingum, a thaegilegan og oeruggan hatt, vid
naestum hvada toelvu sem er.  Thu getur tengst frettakerfum,
verslunum, postkerfum, boenkum, verdbrefaboenkum og sent og tekid a
moti skram.  Thu getur skiptst a goegnum vid vini og nagranna, tho
their eigi oedruvisi toelvu en thu.  Thu getur unnid heiman fra ther.
Kermit getur tengt thig vid "netid." Notid imyndunaraflid.  Med
nutima althjodlegu simakerfi og oert vaxandi taekni i sima
og toelvumalum eru ykkur engin takmoerk sett.

C-Kermit>
```

Finally, it is conceivable that a Kermit program attempts to perform character-set translation but does so incorrectly, or at least not according to your preferences. You can prevent two Kermit programs from negotiating automatic translation with each other by issuing the command SET ATTRIBUTES CHARACTER-SET OFF, which forces the transfer character-set to be TRANSPARENT.

Labor-Saving Devices

If you always work in a particular language and character-set environment, you can save yourself some work by putting the appropriate commands in your C-Kermit initialization file so they will be in effect whenever you run C-Kermit. Say, for example, you always use the Italian character set on the computer where you run C-Kermit and you often transfer Italian-language text files from there to your MS-DOS PC, where they must be encoded in the PC's character set, CP437. Put the following commands in your C-Kermit initialization file (CKERMIT.INI or .kermrc):

```
set file character-set italian
set transfer character-set latin1
```

If you add the corresponding commands to the initialization file for Kermit on your PC (MSKERMIT.INI):

```
set file character-set cp437
set transfer character-set latin1
set terminal character-set italian
```

you will never have to worry about character sets again and you can forget everything you have read in this chapter.

Chapter 10

Transferring Files without the Kermit Protocol

Not all computers have Kermit software available. For example, certain dialup data services, bulletin board systems (BBSs), and remote typesetting services don't offer Kermit file transfer capability. The same might be true of various types of data-taking and laboratory devices, as well as of certain application software, particularly electronic mail and text editors, found on the hosts or services that you access with C-Kermit.

In such situations, C-Kermit lets you transmit files to and capture files from computers, services, or applications that don't support Kermit file transfer. This is done *without error detection or correction of any kind*:

> Data transferred without error correction is subject to corruption, loss, interference, misinterpretation, duplication, and other types of damage.

In most cases, only textual data can be transferred using the methods described here, and often only 7-bit text. In general, these methods work only for a single file, not for a group of files.

Before proceeding, consider the alternatives. Can you get Kermit for the other computer? (See page 9.) Or can you persuade the proprietors of the remote service to support the Kermit protocol? Is a network connection available with its own file transfer or sharing method? Is there some kind of removeable storage medium common to both computers—compatible diskettes or tapes? If none of these options is viable, read on.

Downloading to C-Kermit

Unguarded downloading is the act of capturing a file from a remote computer without its knowledge. It thinks it is simply displaying the file on your screen. You, however, are surreptitiously recording the screen characters on your disk during your C-Kermit CONNECT session. Here are the commands to use:

LOG SESSION *[filespec [{ APPEND, NEW }]]*
> The characters that are sent to C-Kermit during CONNECT mode are recorded in the specified file. The default filename is SESSION.LOG. All current communication settings are used, including duplex, flow control, shift-in/shift-out, and parity. Xon/Xoff flow control can be used to help prevent loss of data. If parity is in use or the terminal bytesize is set to seven, the 8th bit of each character is discarded. Character-set translations implied by your TERMINAL CHARACTER-SET settings are performed. A new session log file is created unless you include the APPEND option, which adds the recorded material to the end of the named file, if it exists, and otherwise creates a new one. When a new log is created, any previously existing file with the same name (on the same device, in the same directory, on the same computer) is destroyed, unless the underlying operating system supports multiple versions of the same file (as do VMS and OpenVMS).

SET SESSION-LOG *{ BINARY, TEXT }*
> (UNIX only) Specifies the recording format for the session log. TEXT is the default, meaning that certain control characters are discarded, including Carriage Return (ASCII 13), Null (ASCII 0), and Delete (ASCII 127). BINARY means that every character that arrives is recorded. Character-set translations are done in both cases unless you use SET TERMINAL CHARACTER-SET TRANSPARENT to disable them. SET SESSION-LOG BINARY does *not* mean you can capture binary files such as executable programs.

To capture a remote file, display it on the other computer while logging your session with C-Kermit. The trick is to avoid capturing an excessive amount of extraneous data, such as commands, system prompts, and so forth. Here is an example in which you use C-Kermit to log in to a VAX and copy a coveted recipe. The SET FLOW, PARITY, and SESSION-LOG commands are included for emphasis; the settings shown are the defaults, so you won't need to give these commands unless you have previously changed the settings:

```
C-Kermit>set modem hayes           (Select modem type)
C-Kermit>set line /dev/ttyh8       (Select communication device)
C-Kermit>set speed 2400            (and speed)
C-Kermit>set flow xon/xoff         (and flow control)
C-Kermit>set parity even           (and parity)
C-Kermit>set session-log text      (and session log format)
C-Kermit>dial 7654321              (Dial the phone number)
Connection completed.
```

```
C-Kermit>connect                        (Begin terminal emulation)
BON GIORNO!

Username: garfield                      (Login)
Password: _____                      (Supply your password)
```

So far everything is normal. Now comes the tricky part. You must type the command to display the text file you want to capture, *but without the terminating carriage return* (for UNIX, the command is `cat`, for most other systems it is TYPE). Then escape back, turn on the session log, CONNECT again, and *then* type the carriage return. When the system's prompt reappears, escape back again, close the session log, and you've got the file, or at least as much of it as appeared on your screen, plus one system prompt at the end, which you can remove with a text editor.

```
$ type lasagna.recipe                   (Don't press Return yet!)
Ctrl-\C                                 (Escape back)
C-Kermit>log sess lasagna.recipe        (Start the session log)
C-Kermit>connect                        (Go back)
<RETURN>                                (and press carriage return)
Ingredients:                            (The characters that appear)
1 lb Moozarel'                          (on your screen are being)
1 lb Rigotha                            (recorded in the session log)
1 lb tiny meatballs
...                                     (etc etc)
$                                       (Prompt reappears)
Ctrl-\C                                 (Escape back again)
C-Kermit>close session                  (Close the session log)
C-Kermit>type lasagna.recipe            (Check it out)
Ingredients:                            (Looks good, mmmmmm!)
1 lb Moozarel'
1 lb Rigotha
1 lb tiny meatballs
...                                     (etc etc, good it worked)
$                                       (Notice the system prompt)
C-Kermit>
```

Now edit the file to remove or correct any unwanted material—system dialog, prompts, messages, noise interference, and so on.

To ensure that the captured file is as close to the original as possible, you should make sure the host is not sending any characters that are not part of the file. For example, you should take whatever measures the host allows to turn off services like line or word wrap, tab expansion, pausing at end of each screenful, and so on, as well as eliminating other possible sources of interference such as messages from other users, e-mail notifications, alarm clocks, or host-generated mode lines.

HINT: This process includes quite a few routine steps that could be easily automated in a script program. Chapters 11–13 cover script programming.

Uploading from C-Kermit

How do you create a text file on a computer? You set up a process on the computer that copies your keystrokes to a disk file. This could be a simple copy process, or it could be a text editor. When you have finished entering characters into the file, you type a special key or sequence to tell the copy process or text editor to close the file. The simplest way to create a file in UNIX is like this:

```
$ cat > file.new                       (Start the copy process)
I am typing some characters.           (Type characters into the file)
They are being copied into
file.new.
Ctrl-D                                 (Ctrl-D closes the file)
$                                      (and returns you to the prompt)
```

and in VMS and OpenVMS it is:

```
$ create file.new                      (Start the copy process)
I am typing some characters.           (Type characters into the file)
They are being copied into
file.new.
Ctrl-Z                                 (Ctrl-Z closes the file)
$                                      (and returns you to the prompt)
```

Other systems, of course, have other methods.

Now suppose you have a text file on your computer that you want to send to a remote computer that doesn't have its own copy of Kermit. Instead of retyping the characters of the text file with your own fingers, you can set up the remote computer for creating a file, as shown in the previous examples, and then tell C-Kermit to imitate what you would do if you were typing the file at your keyboard. The remote computer should never know the difference. The command is:

TRANSMIT *filename*
Sends the characters of the file out the current communication device, just as if you were typing them in CONNECT mode. The TRANSMIT command obeys all current (and relevant) communications and terminal settings, including echo, parity, flow control, and shift-in/shift-out. Unless you say otherwise, the TRANSMIT command also displays the transmitted data on your screen according to the current TERMINAL ECHO setting. Synonym: **XMIT**.

The most important factor affecting how the TRANSMIT command works is the current FILE TYPE setting:

SET FILE TYPE TEXT
If the current file type is TEXT, the TRANSMIT command treats each line of the file as an individual record. It reads a line, strips off the line termination characters (such as LF for UNIX or AOS/VS, CRLF for VMS or OS/2, CR for OS-9), and sends a single

carriage return at the end of each line, just as you would do if you were typing the line yourself. Then it waits a certain amount of time for the remote system to echo a linefeed before sending the next line (so if your file contains long lines, be sure the remote host or service has been told not to wrap them). Characters are translated according to the current TERMINAL CHARACTER-SET setting. If you want to avoid translation, SET TERMINAL CHARACTER-SET TRANSPARENT before giving the TRANSMIT command.

SET FILE TYPE BINARY

The file's bytes are sent exactly as they are stored on the disk with no conversion at all, and there is no synchronization between the two sides as there is with text file transmission. Use binary transmission with caution and skepticism.

The standard text and binary transmission procedures might not work in every case, so C-Kermit also offers you the customary selection of SET commands to modify their operation as needed:

SET TRANSMIT ECHO { OFF, ON }

Tells C-Kermit whether you want to see the transmitted characters echoed on your screen. The default setting is ON, in which case echoing is done according to the current TERMINAL ECHO (DUPLEX) setting. If the computer or device on the other end of the connection does not echo, you should SET TERMINAL ECHO ON (or SET DUPLEX HALF, same thing) if you want C-Kermit itself to display each character it sends, or SET TRANSMIT ECHO OFF if you don't want the characters displayed. No echoing is more efficient. Synonym: **SET XMIT ECHO**.[30]

SET TRANSMIT EOF *[string]*

Tells C-Kermit the character or characters to send after it sends the last line of the file, or when you type Ctrl-C to interrupt a transmission. Normally, nothing is sent at the end of the file. To include control characters in the *string*, use backslash codes such as \4 for Ctrl-D or \26 for Ctrl-Z (see Table VIII-2 on page 462). To cancel a previous TRANSMIT EOF setting, type this command without specifying a *string*. Examples:

```
C-Kermit>set transmit eof \4       (Send Ctrl-D on EOF)
C-Kermit>set transm eof \26        (Send Ctrl-Z on EOF)
C-Kermit>set xfer eof              (Send nothing on EOF)
```

The next example shows a typical sequence that might be sent to a text editor to exit from text insert mode, save the file, and exit:

```
C-Kermit>set xf eof \26save\13\exit\13
```

The TRANSMIT EOF setting applies to both text and binary file transmission.

---

[30] All the SET TRANSMIT commands can also be entered as SET XMIT.

SET TRANSMIT FILL *number*

The TRANSMIT command normally sends a blank line as a sequence of two carriage returns. Some computer text entry systems, however, treat two carriage returns in a row as an "end of file." This command lets you specify a single character to insert into each blank line so it won't be blank any more. The *number* is the code for the character, such as 32 for ASCII space (blank). This setting applies only in text mode. Examples:

```
C-Kermit>set transmit fill 32     (Add space to empty lines)
C-Kermit>set transm fill          (Don't fill empty lines)
```

SET TRANSMIT LINEFEED { OFF, ON }

SET TRANSMIT LINEFEED ON tells C-Kermit to send both carriage return *and* linefeed at the end of each line, rather than just a carriage return. This command applies only in text mode. The default is OFF, meaning that only a carriage return is sent at the end of each line. Examples:

```
C-Kermit>set transmit linefeed on
C-Kermit>set xm li off
```

SET TRANSMIT LOCKING-SHIFT { OFF, ON }

If you want to transmit 8-bit data over a 7-bit connection, and the remote computer or service supports Shift-In and Shift-Out (Ctrl-N and Ctrl-O) as a way of shifting between 7-bit data and 8-bit data, you can use SET TRANSMIT LOCKING-SHIFT ON to have Kermit provide the shifting. Use SET TRANSMIT LOCKING-SHIFT OFF to cancel a previous SET TRANSMIT LOCKING-SHIFT ON command. Applies only in text mode.

SET TRANSMIT PAUSE *number*

If the FILE TYPE is TEXT, this command tells C-Kermit to pause the given number of milliseconds (1/1000 of a second) after sending each line. If the FILE TYPE is BINARY, the pause occurs between each character.

SET TRANSMIT PROMPT *number*

Use this command to tell C-Kermit to wait for some character other than linefeed as permission to send the next line. The number is the code for the character to wait for, such as 17 for Control-Q (Xon). A value of zero tells C-Kermit not to wait at all, but to send all the characters of the file without waiting for any response, which is useful for transmitting text to devices that do not echo a suitable, unique character at the end of each line. This command applies only in text mode. In binary mode, the TRANSMIT command never waits for a response.

```
C-Kermit>set file type text          (Use text mode)
C-Kermit>set transmit prompt 17      (Wait for Xon)
C-Kermit>set transm pr 0             (Don't wait for anything)
```

You can examine SET TRANSMIT settings with the SHOW TRANSMIT (or SHOW XMIT) command:

```
C-Kermit>show xmit
 File type: text
 Terminal echo: remote
 Terminal character-set: transparent
 Transmit EOF: none
 Transmit Fill: none
 Transmit Linefeed: off
 Transmit Prompt: 10 (host line end character)
 Transmit Echo: on
 Transmit Locking-Shift: off
 Transmit Pause: 0 milliseconds
C-Kermit>
```

TRANSMIT Examples

Now let's work through two examples. In the first, we upload a text file to a UNIX computer. On the UNIX end we simply `cat` (type) from the keyboard to a file. C-Kermit is told to transmit the file, followed by a Ctrl-D to close it.

```
$ kermit                          (Start Kermit)
C-Kermit>set modem hayes          (Select modem type)
C-Kermit>set line /dev/ttyh8      (Select communication device)
C-Kermit>set speed 2400           (and speed)
C-Kermit>set flow xon/xoff        (and flow control)
C-Kermit>dial 7654321             (Dial the phone number)
C-Kermit>connect                  (Begin terminal emulation)
WELCOME TO THE HOLLYWOOD SCRIPT AGENCY

login: olga                       (Log in)
Password: _____

$ cat > stormy.txt                (Start the copy process)
Ctrl-\c                           (Escape back to C-Kermit)
C-Kermit>set transm eof \4        (Send Ctrl-D when done)
C-Kermit>transmit stormy.txt      (Transmit the file)
THE DARK AND STORMY NIGHT         (The lines are displayed)

It was a dark and stormy night in Plainville. Everyone was huddled
inside their houses, safe and dry.  In the old abandoned house on
Main Street, a sinister light shone from the attic window...
etc etc

C-Kermit>                         (C-Kermit prompt returns)
C-Kermit>connect                  (Go back to the remote system)
$ cat stormy.txt                  (Look at the file)
THE DARK AND STORMY NIGHT

It was a dark and stormy night in Plainville. Everyone was huddled
inside their houses, safe and dry.  In the old abandoned house on
Main Street, a sinister light shone from the attic window...
etc etc
```

Uploading from C-Kermit

```
$
$ exit                                  (Log out)
Communications disconnect.
C-Kermit>exit                           (All done)
$
```

This example was easy because C-Kermit's default settings are well suited for a direct dialup connection to the remote UNIX system. The UNIX system has a simple mechanism for entering text from the keyboard into a file; it does not react adversely to blank lines and it echoes a linefeed whenever it receives a carriage return to indicate it is ready for another line.

Now let's see how far we can push C-Kermit by trying to upload the same file to an IBM mainframe with the VM/CMS operating system, using a text editor on the mainframe. The connection is linemode and half duplex, so we must wait for the editor's prompt (which is a period followed by an Xon, or Ctrl-Q) before sending the next line or else data will be lost. The text editor, Xedit, leaves text insertion mode if it gets a blank line and therefore must have a fill character in case the file contains blank lines. The fill character is chosen to be capital X (ASCII 88) because a printable character is required—blank won't do. The EOF string is set to be a carriage return (\13), which sends a blank line, putting the editor back into command mode, followed by the commands to save the file (`save\13`) and exit (`qq\13`).

```
$ kermit                                (Start C-Kermit)
C-Kermit>set modem hayes                (Select modem type)
C-Kermit>set line /dev/ttyh8            (Select communication device)
C-Kermit>set speed 2400                 (and speed)
C-Kermit>set duplex half                (Connection is half duplex)
C-Kermit>set flow none                  (No Xon/Xoff flow control)
C-Kermit>set parity mark                (Mainframe uses MARK parity)
C-Kermit>dial 8765432                   (Dial the phone number)
Connection completed.
C-Kermit>connect                        (Begin terminal emulation)

VIRTUAL MACHINE/SYSTEM PRODUCT--CUVMB --PRESS BREAK KEY

Ctrl-\B                                 (Send BREAK)
!
.login olga                             (Log in)

Enter password: XXXXXXXX                (Half duplex; password echoes)

LOGON AT 15:28:14 EDT THURSDAY 09/21/92
VM/SP REL 5 04/19/88 19:39
.
CMS
.xedit stormy txt                       (Start the editor)
.i                                      (Put it in text input mode)
DMSXMD573I Input mode:
Ctrl-\C                                 (Escape back to C-Kermit)
```

```
C-Kermit>set transm fill 88      (Fill blank lines with X)
C-Kermit>set transm prompt \17   (Wait for Xon)
C-Kermit>set transm eof \13save\13qq\13
C-Kermit>transmit stormy.txt     (Send the file)
THE DARK AND STORMY NIGHT        (The echoed lines are displayed)
X
It was a dark and stormy night in Plainville. Everyone was huddled
inside their houses, safe and dry.  In the old abandoned house on
Main Street, a sinister light shone from the attic window...
etc etc

C-Kermit>                        (Prompt returns when done)
C-Kermit>connect                 (Return to the mainframe)
.
Ready; T=0.02/0.06 15:29:11
.lf stormy                       (Make sure file is there)
STORMY    TXT                    (It is)
Ready; T=0.01/0.01 15:29:16
.type stormy txt                 (Take a peek)
THE DARK AND STORMY NIGHT
X
It was a dark and stormy night in Plainville. Everyone was huddled
inside their houses, safe and dry.  In the old abandoned house on
Main Street, a sinister light shone from the attic window...
etc etc

Ready; T=0.01/0.01 15:29:20
.logout                          (Log out from the mainframe)
CONNECT= 00:01:11 VIRTCPU= 000:00.12 TOTCPU= 000:00.32
LOGOFF AT 15:29:25 EDT THURSDAY 09/21/92
Ctrl-\C                          (Escape back to C-Kermit)
C-Kermit>exit
$
```

The X's can be removed with a text editor (such as Xedit, the same editor that made you put them there in the first place).

Encoding 8-Bit Data Files for Transmission

Unguarded transfer of binary files or 8-bit text files is an iffy proposition at best. If even one byte is lost or corrupted, terrible damage could result. And it is usually not easy to repair a damaged binary file with a text editor, as you can do with a text file. It is often better to convert a binary or 8-bit text file into simple lines of printable ASCII text, then up- or download it in text mode, and then convert it back into its original form. The easiest, most reliable, and most portable format is called "hex" (hexadecimal), in which each 8-bit byte is translated into two printable hexadecimal digits taken from the set 0123456789ABCDEF. Short lines are formed, composed of only these characters. A file of this form is slightly more than twice the length of the original, but it is immune to any known translation or transparency problems. A pair of short C-language programs for hexifying and dehexifying is included in Appendix X.

Other encoding methods might be more efficient. For example, a pair of programs, uuencode and uudecode, is available on most UNIX computers, but not necessarily on other systems. The encoding is more efficient than hex, but also uses a bigger alphabet that might cause transparency or translation problems, for example with EBCDIC hosts.

There are many other file encoding, compaction, and archiving techniques available too. Use whatever works best for you. The primary considerations are transparency (can the encoded data survive the passage to the other computer?) and portability (can you reconstruct the original data after transmitting to another computer?).

Chapter 11

Command Files, Macros, and Variables

○ ○ ○ ○
If you have digested the material in the preceding chapters and applied the examples to your own connections, you should be comfortable using C-Kermit to accomplish your communication chores by hand. But manually operating communications software does not make the best use of your time. In these three chapters, you'll see how to automate all the procedures you have learned so far. By the end of Chapter 13 you will be able to create and use commands that make the connection for you, carry on scripted dialogs with remote hosts or services, and transfer data automatically, even when you are elsewhere.

This chapter shows you how to group commands together into command files and macros so you can execute many commands by issuing a single command. It also introduces the concept of *variables* and describes the kinds of variables offered by C-Kermit.

Chapter 12 shows you how to "program" C-Kermit to make decisions, execute commands repeatedly in loops, read and write files, and so on, using C-Kermit commands very similar to the ones you're already accustomed to. Finally, in Chapter 13 these somewhat abstract concepts are put to practical use. The remainder of the book is devoted to reference material.

Command Files Revisited

You first encountered command files back in Chapter 2. There you learned that you could put any Kermit commands at all in a file and then execute all of them by giving a single command, TAKE, at the C-Kermit prompt. In this example we compose a short command file on a VAX, where VMS's CREATE command is the easiest way to make a short text file. Of course you could also use any text editor or word processor that is capable of creating a plain-text file.

```
$ create escape.tak            (Create a command file)
set escape 29                  (Enter text from the keyboard)
show escape
^Z                             (Ctrl-Z closes the file)
$
```

Now we execute the command file by telling C-Kermit to TAKE it:

```
$ kermit                            (Start C-Kermit)
C-Kermit 5A(188), 23 Nov 92, OpenVMS VAX
Type ? or HELP for help
C-Kermit>take escape.tak
 Escape character: Ctrl-] (ASCII 29, GS)
C-Kermit>
```

If the command file is not in your current directory, you have to supply the complete file specification:

```
C-Kermit>take $disk1:[olga]escape.tak
```

A command file can include as many C-Kermit commands as you like, including TAKE commands for other command files. The TAKE command normally executes all the commands in the file, from the beginning to the end, or up to the first command that tells it to stop, such as EXIT or QUIT. If a command has a syntax or execution error, C-Kermit prints an error message and goes on to the next command in the file. For example, if you executed a command file called TOAST.TAK that looked like this:

```
echo Making toast...           ; Valid command
set toaster dark               ; Invalid command
toast two slices               ; Invalid command
echo Time for breakfast.       ; Valid command
```

The result would be:

```
C-Kermit>take toast.tak
Making toast...
?No keywords match - toaster
?Invalid: toast two slices
Time for breakfast.
C-Kermit>
```

But you might not want C-Kermit to be so tolerant of failing commands.

The SET TAKE command can be used to change how the TAKE command works:

SET TAKE ECHO { ON, OFF }

OFF means that lines from the command file are not displayed on your screen. This is the normal and default setting. ON means that each command is displayed on your screen at the time C-Kermit reads it from the file. This is useful to help you locate errors in command files.

SET TAKE ERROR { ON, OFF }

OFF, the normal and default setting, means that errors in command files do not cause termination. ON means that any command in the file that has a syntax or execution error terminates execution of the command file.

Execution errors occur when a command is syntactically (grammatically) correct but C-Kermit can't carry it out successfully, for example, if you tell C-Kermit to TAKE, TYPE, or SEND a file that you don't have read access to.

Command File Example

To illustrate the usefulness of the TAKE command, suppose that on a certain day you need to upload and download an odd mixture of text and binary files totaling many millions of bytes in size. How much time are you willing to devote to this task? If you do it interactively, you'll have to sit and watch your screen constantly and enter new commands at the right times. It could take all day. With a command file, each command is executed when the previous one completes, no sooner, no later; no time is wasted, and while all this is happening you can be off somewhere else doing something that *may* be more fun than watching Kermit's file transfer display. Here's a sample command file for the job; let's call it BIGJOB.TAK:[31]

```
set take error on          ; Quit if there's an error
log transactions           ; Keep a record of what happened
set file type text         ; Transferring text files
send daily.*               ; Upload daily reports
send weekly.*              ; Upload weekly reports
send monthly.*             ; Upload monthly reports
get orders.new             ; Download new orders
set file type binary       ; Switch to binary mode
send budget.wks            ; Upload budget worksheet
send salary.wks            ; Send salary worksheet
set file type text         ; Back to text mode
mail ok.txt boss           ; Send e-mail when done
bye                        ; Logout remote job
```

---

[31] Switching between text and binary mode in this way depends on the remote server's ability to read the file type from C-Kermit's attribute packet. See Table 1-1 on page 8. C-Kermit, MS-DOS Kermit, and IBM Mainframe Kermit have this capability.

After you've composed this file with a text editor and saved it on disk, you can start Kermit, make your connection to the remote computer, log in, start Kermit there, put it in server mode, escape back to C-Kermit, and TAKE the command file:

```
$ kermit                            (Start kermit)
Ready to dial...                    (Message from init file)
C-Kermit>dial 765-4321              (Dial the number)
C-Kermit>c                          (CONNECT to remote computer)
. login olga                        (Enter username)
Password:                           (Enter password)

. kermit                            (Start Kermit on remote computer)
Kermit-CMS>server                   (Put it in server mode)
Ctrl-\C                             (Escape back to C-Kermit)
C-Kermit>take bigjob.tak            (TAKE the command file)
```

Later, when you come back from wherever you went, you can examine the transaction log to see what happened. Your electronic mail message (composed previously and stored in the file OK.TXT) is sent to the boss only if all the files were transferred successfully. The SET TAKE ERROR ON command ensures that any errors terminate the command file before the message is sent so you won't look like a fool.

Nested Command Files

When a command file itself contains TAKE commands, the command files are said to be *nested,* one within the other. Any C-Kermit command is legal in a command file, including TAKE. In fact, one command file can TAKE another, which TAKEs yet another, which TAKEs still another, and so on, to a nesting depth of about 20. This feature lets you create building-block command files that can be pieced together in different ways, possibly saving you much duplication of effort over the years.

But there can be more down-to-earth, if less obvious, reasons for nesting command files. Suppose, for example, BIGJOB.TAK encountered an error. The command file would terminate immediately, the C-Kermit prompt would return, but the connection to the remote computer would not necessarily be broken. If your absence from the office was longer than expected, you might have run up a large phone bill for nothing. But if you invoke BIGJOB.TAK from a superior TAKE file, it would regain control as soon as BIGJOB.TAK completed—successfully or not. Such a file might look like this:

```
take bigjob.tak             ; TAKE the command file
hangup                      ; Hang up the phone when done
```

Call this two-line superior command file BIGGERJOB.TAK and start it like this:

```
C-Kermit>take biggerjob.tak
```

Then, no matter how BIGJOB.TAK may terminate, C-Kermit hangs up the phone without delay.

The C-Kermit Initialization File

C-Kermit issues an automatic TAKE command for your initialization file whenever you start it. Your initialization file should contain commands that you wish to be executed whenever you start Kermit. For example, to select a particular modem type, communication device, and speed, and to tell Kermit where to find your dialing directory, use:

```
set modem ccitt                  ; My workstation has a CCITT modem
set line /dev/cua                ; Attached to this serial device
set speed 2400                   ; My dialing speed is 2400 bps
set dial directory /usr/olga/phone-numbers
```

In previous chapters, some other commands were suggested as likely candidates for your initialization file. Suppose, for example, you always want to use long packets, sliding windows, and a type-3 block check during file transfer. It is usually safe to set these protocol parameters all the time, because C-Kermit negotiates them downwards automatically if the other Kermit program can't handle them. You could add these lines:

```
set receive packet-length 1000   ; Long packets
set window 4                     ; Four window slots
set block 3                      ; 3-character CRC error checking
```

Language and character-set related items might also be suitable for your initialization file. For example, if all your text files are written in Finnish using the Finnish version of ISO 646, you would add these lines to ensure that your text files are always translated correctly during file transfer:

```
set file character-set finnish   ; I use Finnish on my computer,
set xfer character-set latin1    ; Latin-1 for transfer, and
```

and this one to take care of terminal emulation to a Data General host:

```
set term character-set dg        ; DG International for CONNECT
set term byte 8                  ; 8-bit path to the host
set command byte 7               ; and 7 bits to my terminal
```

Practically any SET command is appropriate for your initialization file, as long as it is a setting you want in effect at all times, no matter which computers or services you are communicating with. Here are a few examples:

```
set delay 1                      ; I can escape back quickly
set attrib date off              ; New files get current date
set dial hangup off              ; "ON" confuses my modem
set escape 31                    ; Escape = Ctrl-Underscore
```

But if you use C-Kermit to connect to many different hosts or services, using a variety of connection methods, a single collection of settings is not enough. Instead, you need a way to switch quickly among a variety of environments, and this is where macros come in.

Command Macros

"Macro" usually means "big," but in computer language it means something small that stands for something bigger. Kermit macros are new commands that you create by combining existing commands (or even other macros). Like command files, macros give you a way to group commands together so you can execute a bunch of them with a single word. The command for making macros is:

DEFINE *name [text]*
> This command creates a macro called *name*. The macro's definition is the *text* following its name. This is normally a list of C-Kermit commands (possibly including names of other macros), separated by commas, but it can be any text at all. No interpretation, evaluation, or verification of the commands is done; the definition is taken literally. If a macro of the given name already exists, its definition is replaced by the one given. If no text follows the macro name, the named macro (if it exists) is removed from C-Kermit's "macro dictionary" and becomes undefined.

You can type the DEFINE command at the C-Kermit prompt, put DEFINE commands in command files, and even put them inside of other macro definitions. If you have taken the trouble to construct a macro that you want to use frequently, the best place to put its definition is in your C-Kermit initialization file.

The macro name can be any reasonable character string that contains no spaces or control characters. Uppercase and lowercase letters are treated equivalently. The macro definition can be up to about 1,000 characters in length. Here is an example you can try if you have C-Kermit running next to your bed:

```
define alarm echo Good night!, sleep 28800, echo \7\7\7Wake up!
```

The macro's name is:

```
alarm
```

The definition is:

```
echo Good night., sleep 28800, echo \7\7\7Wake up!
```

The DEFINE command puts the ALARM macro in C-Kermit's macro dictionary, turning it into a new C-Kermit command:

```
C-Kermit>alarm
Good night.
```

Eight hours later:

```
<BEEP><BEEP><BEEP>Wake up!
C-Kermit>
```

The following command destroys the definition of the ALARM macro so you can't use it any more:

```
C-Kermit>define alarm
```

(This is like throwing your alarm clock out the window.)

A common and straightforward use for macros is to group SET commands together to allow rapid switching among different kinds of connections, for example:

```
define vax set parity none, set duplux full,-
  set flow xon/xoff, set handshake none
def ibm-linemode set parity mark, set dupl half,-
  set handsh xon, set flow none
```

Here two macros are created, the first named VAX and the second IBM-LINEMODE.

Pay careful attention to punctuation: use commas to separate commands, and hyphen (dash) to continue a line. The final line of the definition, of course, must *not* end with a hyphen. If you accidentally omit a hyphen, the next line is taken as a new command, rather than part of the macro definition.

If your macro definition is in a command file (including your initialization file), you can add trailing comments to each line:

```
define vax -                      ; Macro for connecting to a VAX
  set parity none,-               ; No parity
  set command byte 8,-            ; 8-bit data,
  set terminal byte 8,-           ; from end to end
  set terminal echo remote,-      ; The VAX echoes
  set flow xon/xoff,-             ; Use Xon/Xoff flow control
  set handshake none              ; No line turnaround handshake
```

When a line is continued, trailing comments must come *after* the continuation character, not before it, and must be preceded by at least one space or tab. If you put a hyphen at the end of a trailing comment, the next line is considered part of the same comment.

You can find out the definition of a macro with the SHOW MACRO command:

```
C-Kermit>show macro ibm-linemode
ibm-linemode = set parity mark,-
 set dupl half,-
 set handsh xon,-
 set flow none
```

The definition is shown one command per line, with commas separating the commands and hyphens showing line continuation. If you type SHOW MACRO without giving the name of a macro, C-Kermit shows you all the currently defined macros and their definitions. Even if you haven't defined any macros, you will still see definitions for some of C-Kermit *predefined* macros, such as FATAL (explained in Chapter 12).

Command Macros

Using Macros

Now that you know how to create macros, you might also want to know how to use them. There are two ways to use (invoke) a macro. The first and most natural way is simply to type its name at the C-Kermit prompt, either in full:

`C-Kermit>ibm-linemode`

or abbreviated unambiguously:

`C-Kermit>ib`

This way works as long as your macro does not have the same name as, and is not an abbreviation of, a built-in C-Kermit command.

The second way is with the DO command:

DO *macro-name*
> Invokes the macro whose name is given. The macro name may be abbreviated to any length that still distinguishes it from the names of all other defined macros. Examples:
>
> `C-Kermit>do ibm-linemode`
> `C-Kermit>do ibm`

The DO command removes any possible confusion between macros and built-in commands because it looks only in the macro dictionary. If you type a question mark at the C-Kermit prompt, the macro names are not listed. But if you type DO followed by a space and a question mark, the names of all defined macros are listed:

```
C-Kermit>do ? macro, one of the following:
 ibm-linemode      vax
C-Kermit>
```

If you have defined a macro with the same name as a built-in command, the DO command is the only way to invoke it because C-Kermit gives priority to its built-in commands. If you always pick original names for your macros, there is no ambiguity and the DO command need never be used.

Macro execution can be controlled in the same ways as command file execution:

SET MACRO ECHO { OFF, ON }
> Controls whether commands from the macro definition are echoed on your screen as C-Kermit reads them. MACRO ECHO is normally OFF, meaning that the commands are not shown. You can use SET MACRO ECHO ON for debugging.

SET MACRO ERROR { OFF, ON }
> Controls whether an error—syntax or execution—in a command causes C-Kermit to terminate execution of the macro. Normally MACRO ERROR is OFF.

Macro execution can be interrupted at any time by typing Ctrl-C.

Macros that Invoke Macros

Like command files, macros can be nested to any reasonable level. Just as command files can TAKE other command files, macros can invoke other macros. For example:

```
define modem set modem hayes, set speed 2400
define computer set parity even, set flow xon
define communication modem, computer
define protocol set window 4, set rec packet-len 2000, set block 3
define setup communication, protocol
```

After you have executed these definitions, invoking the SETUP macro will invoke the COMMUNICATION and PROTOCOL macros. The COMMUNICATION macro will, in turn, invoke the MODEM and COMPUTER macros.

Macros that Define Macros

Before proceeding, let's stop and ask ourselves the vital question: Can we define a macro that defines other macros? Suppose you use C-Kermit on a PC with OS/2 to access two different remote computers, one of them running the VMS operating system and the other running UNIX. Suppose also that on each computer you switch back and forth between Italian and Russian text. But the two computers use different character sets for each of these languages. You want to have one set of macros called VMS and UNIX for switching between the two computer systems, and another set called ITALIAN and RUSSIAN for switching between the two languages appropriately for each machine. To illustrate how to construct macros that define macros, let's make the VMS and UNIX macros each define their own appropriate ITALIAN and RUSSIAN macros. But first we must solve a small syntax problem. In the command:

```
def unix def italian set xfer char latin1, set file char italian
```

which macro, UNIX or ITALIAN, does the SET FILE CHAR ITALIAN command belong to? We need a way of grouping commands inside a macro definition so Kermit can tell which definition the commands belong to. For this, we use curly braces. First, the VMS macro:

```
define vms -
  set parity none, -
  set terminal display 8, -
  define italian { -
    set terminal character-set dec-mcs, -
    set file character-set cp850, -
    set transfer character-set latin1 -
  }, -
  define russian { -
    set terminal character-set koi8 cp866, -
    set file character-set cp866, -
    set transfer character-set cyrillic -
  }
```

When you execute the VMS macro, it sets the parity and terminal display parameters immediately and defines ITALIAN and RUSSIAN macros for later use. The curly braces tell

Kermit which commands are part of the VMS macro and which ones are part of the ITALIAN and RUSSIAN macros. Now here is the UNIX macro:

```
define unix -
  set parity even, -
  set terminal display 7, -
  define italian { -
    set terminal character-set italian, -
    set file character-set cp850, -
    set transfer character-set latin1 -
  }, -
  define russian { -
    set terminal character-set short-koi cp866, -
    set file character-set cp866, -
    set transfer character-set cyrillic -
  }
```

First you invoke the VMS or UNIX macro to tell which kind of system you're talking to. Then you can invoke the ITALIAN or RUSSIAN to set up the proper character sets for the given language on the computer you are using.

The On_Exit Macro

Just as C-Kermit has an initialization file for commands that you want executed every time Kermit starts, it also has a way to execute commands of your choice automatically when it exits. If you have defined a macro called ON_EXIT, Kermit executes it when you give the EXIT or QUIT command, just before it does its final acts of cleaning up and self destruction. The ON_EXIT macro should be defined in your C-Kermit initialization file. Here's a sample that can be used by someone who always uses C-Kermit to dial out:

```
define on_exit hangup, echo Remember to turn off your modem!
```

To illustrate its use:

```
$ kermit                                  (Start Kermit)
  (Transfer some files, etc...)
C-Kermit>exit                             (EXIT hangs up the phone)
Remember to turn off your modem!          (and prints a reminder)
$
```

Macros versus Command Files

Command files and macros can be mixed in every conceivable way. Macros can be (and typically are) DEFINEd in command files, macros can be invoked from command files, command files can be TAKEn from inside a macro, a macro can DEFINE another macro, and so on. What are the differences between command files and macros?

- A command file can be any length at all, whereas a macro definition is restricted to the length of C-Kermit's command buffer, which is about 1000 characters.

- Macros, once defined, are available at all times while C-Kermit is running and can be invoked simply by name, regardless of C-Kermit's current directory, whereas the command for invoking a command file changes when C-Kermit's default directory changes.

- Macro execution is faster, because C-Kermit executes macros out of its own memory rather than by opening and reading a disk file.

- You can define all your macros in a single command file, which usually is preferable to cluttering up your disk with lots of command files.

- Most importantly, macros can have *arguments*.

Macro Arguments

You can furnish a macro with additional information in the form of operands, or *arguments*, by including them after the macro name when you invoke it and separating each argument by whitespace (one or more spaces or tabs). You can think of a macro as a verb to which you can give different objects, like "eat spaghetti," "eat corn," "eat salad." Eating is a routine operation, but it can be performed on a variety of foods.

```
C-Kermit>define eat echo Thank you for the \%1. It tastes good.
C-Kermit>eat bread
Thank you for the bread. It tastes good.
C-Kermit>eat calzone
Thank you for the calzone. It tastes good.
C-Kermit>
```

The arguments are real data—words, numbers, filenames, and so on—that are plugged into special place-holders in the macro definition (\%1 in the previous example) before the commands in the macro are executed.

Here is a more complete, formal, and precise description of macro invocation:

[**DO**] *macro-name* [*arg1* [*arg2* [... [*arg9*]]]]
    Sets the variable \%0 to the name of the macro. Copies the text of the arguments into the variables \%1, \%2, ..., \%9. Sets the variable \v(argc) (explained later in this chapter) to the number of arguments plus 1, and then executes the commands defined for the named macro, substituting any occurrences of these variable names in the macro definition with the values just assigned.

Let's try that again in English. When you invoke a macro, you can also type some other stuff—up to nine words—after the macro's name. Each word is assigned to a *variable* that has a funny-looking name: backslash-percent-digit. For example: \%2. The digit tells the position of the word in the command you just typed: 0 for the name of the macro itself, 1 for the first word after its name (the first argument), 2 for the second word, and so on. If there are more than 9 words, the extra words are ignored. If there are fewer than 9 words, the extra variables are given a null (empty) value. Argument variable names (`\%0`, `\%1`, etc.) that occur anywhere in your macro definition are replaced by the assigned values when the commands in the macro are executed.

Maybe another example will help. Here is a macro definition that adds a COPY command to the UNIX version of C-Kermit:

```
C-Kermit>define copy run cp \%1 \%2
```

(for VMS or OS/2, just change `cp` to `copy`).[32] Invoke this macro by typing its name, followed by the name of the file you want to copy and the name of the file you want to copy it to:

```
C-Kermit>copy oofa.old oofa.new
```

When the macro is executed, `\%1` is replaced by `oofa.old` and `\%2` is replaced by `oofa.new`, so the command that Kermit actually executes is:

```
run cp oofa.old oofa.new
```

Kermit's argument-passing scheme should be crystal clear to you now—so clear that you put this book down between the last paragraph and this one, ran to your terminal, added even more new commands, and then translated all of Kermit's built-in commands into Hungarian simply by defining macros for them. If you didn't do all that, go do it now.

Format of Macro Arguments

A macro argument is a string of characters surrounded by whitespace (spaces or tabs). The final macro argument can be either the final string of non-whitespace characters on the command line, or it can be followed by a trailing comment, which is ignored. To illustrate, we define a macro, ARGLIST, that prints its first four arguments, and then we invoke it in various ways:

```
C-Kermit>def arglist echo 1=(\%1) 2=(\%2) 3=(\%3) 4=(\%4)
C-Kermit>arglist amethyst blue red yellow green
1=(amethyst) 2=(blue) 3=(red) 4=(yellow)
C-Kermit>arglist one two
1=(one) 2=(two) 3=() 4=()
C-Kermit>arglist one two ; with a comment
1=(one) 2=(two) 3=() 4=()
C-Kermit>
```

---

[32]This example does not apply to AOS/VS, whose COPY command reverses the order of the filenames. We'll see how to cope with that problem in the next chapter.

If you want an argument to include spaces, enclose it in curly braces:

```
C-Kermit>arglist {this one has four words} abc xyz
1=(this one has four words) 2=(abc) 3=(xyz) 4=()
```

As you can see, the braces are removed. If you want the braces kept, use two pair:

```
C-Kermit>arglist {{abc def}} xyz
1=({abc def}) 2=(xyz) 3=() 4=()
```

The command SHOW ARGUMENTS, given inside a macro, displays the macro's arguments:

```
C-Kermit>define shoargs show arguments
C-Kermit>shoargs one two {three and} four
Macro arguments at level 0
 \%0 = shoargs
 \%1 = one
 \%2 = two
 \%3 = three and
 \%4 = four
C-Kermit>
```

Scope of Macro Arguments

The argument variables \%0 through \%9 are created when the macro is invoked and are available to the macro throughout its execution. Arguments that are not specified are set to null (empty) values, as shown in the previous examples.

If macro A invokes macro B, macro B gets a whole new set of arguments \%0 through \%9, and it does not have access to macro A's arguments at all. When macro B terminates, macro A still has its own original copies of these variables. This process is replicated as deeply as macro invocations can be nested. To illustrate:

```
C-Kermit>def top show arg, middle Testing, show arg
C-Kermit>def middle show arg, bottom XXX, show arg
C-Kermit>def bottom show arg
C-Kermit>top Hello                  (Invoke TOP macro with arg "Hello")
Macro arguments at level 0          (Now we're in the TOP macro)
 \%0 = top                          (TOP macro shows its arguments)
 \%1 = Hello                        (This is what I typed)
Macro arguments at level 1          (TOP macro invokes MIDDLE macro)
 \%0 = middle                       (MIDDLE macro shows its name)
 \%1 = Testing                      (and its argument)
Macro arguments at level 2          (MIDDLE invokes BOTTOM)
 \%0 = bottom                       (BOTTOM macro shows its name)
 \%1 = XXX                          (and its argument)
Macro arguments at level 1          (Now back to MIDDLE macro)
 \%0 = middle                       (Its name is still the same)
 \%1 = Testing                      (and so is its argument)
Macro arguments at level 0          (Now back to TOP macro)
 \%0 = top                          (Its name is still the same)
 \%1 = Hello                        (and its argument is too)
C-Kermit>
```

If a macro definition happens to include a TAKE command, the macro's arguments are available to the command file too. To illustrate, suppose the file HAYES.TAK contains:

```
set modem hayes           ; Specify modem type
set line /dev/cua         ; Specify communication device
set speed 2400            ; Set the speed
dial \%1
```

Also suppose you define the following macro and then invoke it:

```
C-Kermit>define hayes take hayes.tak
C-Kermit>hayes 7654321
```

C-Kermit executes the commands in the HAYES macro, replacing all the backslash-percent variables by the macro's actual arguments. Because the HAYES macro is still active while the command file is being executed, the \%1 variable is available in the command file too, and the HAYES.TAK command:

```
dial \%1
```

becomes:

```
dial 7654321
```

before C-Kermit executes it.

A Macro Sampler

To bring the concepts of macros and arguments down to earth, here is a brief sampling of connection and file-transfer macros that real C-Kermit users actually use in everyday life.

Dialing Macros

Suppose that whenever you dial out, you always use a particular modem on a certain device. Here is a macro called MYDIAL that issues all the needed SET commands, dials your number, and puts you in CONNECT mode if the call is completed successfully. Put these commands in your C-Kermit initialization file, substituting your own modem type, device name, and speed.

```
; MYDIAL - All the steps needed for dialing out in one command.
define mydial -
  set macro error on,-       ; Quit on failure
  set modem hayes,-          ; Modem type
  set line /dev/cua,-        ; Device name
  set speed 2400,-           ; Speed
  dial \%1,-                 ; Dial the number
  connect,-                  ; Only if the call is completed
  set macro error off        ; Back to normal
```

You can use this macro to call any number at all:

```
C-Kermit>mydial 765-4321         ; A phone number
C-Kermit>mydial 1-800-555-555    ; Another phone number
```

Here are sample macros that use MYDIAL to call specific numbers (the numbers shown are fictitious, except the last one).

```
define compuserve mydial 7654321
define mcimail    mydial 8765432
define dowjones   mydial 9876543
define decstore   mydial 1-800-234-1998
```

(You can also use names from your dialing directory in place of actual phone numbers.) You can use these macros to call a host or service by typing just the macro name at the C-Kermit prompt. You can even abbreviate the name:

C-Kermit>mci

Adapt the macros in this section to your own setup and the hosts or services that you use and put their definitions in your C-Kermit initialization file. Then let *Kermit's* fingers do the walking!

Network Macros

If you're a network user, you can add similar macros for the network connections you commonly make to your C-Kermit initialization file. Here are macros to make the appropriate settings for TCP/IP and X.25 networks.

```
define tcp -
  set net tcp/ip, set flow none, set parity none, -
  set receive packet-length 2000, set window 4, -
  telnet \%1

define x25 -
  set net x.25, set flow xon/xoff, set parity mark, -
  set receive packet-length 250, set window 8, -
  set host \%1, if success connect
```

IF SUCCESS is explained in the next chapter. The communications and file transfer parameters are samples only, and not necessarily optimal for all connections.

And here are macros to make the desired connections just by typing their names (host names and numbers are fictitious):

```
define chemvax tcp vax.chem.xxx.edu
define catalog tcp library.xxx.edu
define mcimail x25 1234567890
```

File Transfer Macros

Finally, here are two macros for selecting and initiating text or binary mode file transfer:

```
define bsend set file type binary, send \%1 \%2
define tsend set file type text, send \%1 \%2
```

The second argument, \%2, is the name the file is to be sent under. If the second argument is omitted, the file is sent under its own name.

A Macro Sampler 223

Variables

Variables are things that stand for other things. At different times, the same variable might take on different values. Its value can *vary*, which is why it's called a variable, but its name always stays the same. Macro arguments are one type of C-Kermit variable, accessible only to the macro they were given to. This section describes several other kinds of variables, which, unlike macro arguments, are *global*, meaning they are accessible to all commands at all levels: at the C-Kermit prompt, in command files, and in macros, no matter how deeply nested.

Global Variables

Global variable names are like macro argument names, but spelled with unaccented Roman letters instead of digits: \%a, \%b, \%c, ..., \%z. The case of the letter doesn't matter; \%a is the same variable as \%A, so there are 26 global variables available for your use. All of these variables have the null (empty) value until a value is given to them with the DEFINE or ASSIGN command:

```
C-Kermit>define \%n Fred C. Dobbs
C-Kermit>defin \%d 1(212)555-1212
C-Kermit>def \%f oofa.txt
```

You can find out which global variables are defined and what their values are with the SHOW GLOBALS command:

```
C-Kermit>show glob
Global variables:
 \%f = oofa.txt
 \%d = 1(212)555-1212
 \%n = Fred C. Dobbs
C-Kermit>
```

You can use a variable almost anywhere in any Kermit command. Simply place it where you want its value inserted:

```
C-Kermit>echo \%n calling \%d to transfer \%f...
Fred C. Dobbs calling 1(212)555-1212 to transfer oofa.txt...
C-Kermit>dial \%d              (dial 1(212)555-1212)
C-Kermit>send \%f              (send oofa.txt)
C-Kermit>
```

Evaluation of variables is simply a matter of text substitution. Variables do not have types, like numeric versus character string. They are substituted in place at the time they are evaluated. If the result is illegal, an error is diagnosed in the same way it would be you had typed the illegal value in directly. Example:

```
C-Kermit>define \%x oofa        (A non-numeric value)
C-Kermit>set block-check \%x    (Use it in a numeric context)
?Invalid - set block oofa       (Kermit doesn't understand)
```

```
C-Kermit>define \%x 2            (Try a numeric value)
C-Kermit>set block-check \%x     (Use it in the same context)
C-Kermit>                        (No complaint)
```

If you want to use a variable name itself literally in a command, precede its name with a backslash:

```
C-Kermit>define \%a Hello again
C-Kermit>echo My name is "\\%a".  My value is "\%a".
My name is "\%a".  My value is "Hello again".
C-Kermit>
```

You should keep in mind one restriction on C-Kermit's text substitution. You can't place a variable that expands into multiple words in a command field that is required to be a single word. For example:

```
C-Kermit>def \%a file type binary
C-Kermit>set \%a
?More fields required
C-Kermit>
```

But:

```
C-Kermit>def \%b file             (Define each word separately)
C-Kermit>def \%c type
C-Kermit>def \%d binary
C-Kermit>set \%b \%c \%d
C-Kermit>                         (No complaint)
```

Assigning versus Defining

Variable definitions can be nested, meaning that the definition of one variable can contain the names of other variables:

```
C-Kermit>define \%a My name is \%b.
C-Kermit>define \%b not \%c
C-Kermit>define \%c Olga
C-Kermit>echo \%a
My name is not Olga.
C-Kermit>
```

This raises an interesting question: what happens if we define a variable in terms of itself?

```
C-Kermit>define \%a 5             (\%a is defined to be "5")
C-Kermit>define \%a -\%a          (\%a defined to be "-\%a")
C-Kermit>echo \%a                 (What does this do?)
```

Luckily, you'll never know. This is called a circular definition, and would result in the construction of an infinitely long string of dashes in front of the 5, quickly filling up the computer's memory if C-Kermit didn't notice and put a stop to it:

```
?Definition circular or too deep
C-Kermit>
```

Variables 225

But what if all we really wanted to do was replace the definition of \%a by itself with a dash in front of it, for example to turn a positive number into a negative one? We need a way to tell C-Kermit to copy the *value* of the variable(s) in the definition, rather than their names. This capability is provided by the ASSIGN command:

ASSIGN *name [text]*
> This command is like the DEFINE command, and, like DEFINE, can be used to create or give new values to either macros or variables. Unlike DEFINE, it evaluates any variables in the *text* before making it the value of the variable or macro. Synonym: **ASG**. Example:
>
> ```
> C-Kermit>define \%a 5
> C-Kermit>assign \%a -\%a
> C-Kermit>echo \%a
> -5
> C-Kermit>
> ```

The difference between DEFINE and ASSIGN is important when the definition text contains backslash-prefixed items such as variable names whose values might change before they are used. DEFINE copies them literally, postponing their evaluation until a command actually refers to them, allowing future references to pick up the new values, whereas ASSIGN evaluates them at the time the assignment is made, preserving their *current* values.

Macros as Variables

Macros can be used as variables too. Define a macro in the normal way, but if you intend to use it as a variable rather than as a list of commands, it can contain any text at all:

```
C-Kermit>define phone-number 1(212)555-1212
```

You can refer to it using special notation: precede its name by \m and enclose it in parentheses. C-Kermit replaces this construction with the macro's definition:

```
C-Kermit>echo \m(phone-number)
1(212)555-1212
C-Kermit>dial \m(phone-number)
```

A macro used in this way is exactly like a global variable, except it can have a long descriptive name. Obviously, you can't execute macros whose definitions are not Kermit commands:

```
C-Kermit>phone-number
?Invalid: 1(212)555-1212
C-Kermit>
```

It is usually a better idea to name variables in this way than to use the global variables \%a through \%z because there is less chance that they will be accidentally superseded by new definitions. See the standard C-Kermit initialization file, CKERMIT.INI or .kermrc, for examples.

Arrays

An array is a global variable that has a list of values, each one with its own *index*, a number ranging from 0 to a maximum that you choose. An array name looks like a global variable name, except with an ampersand instead of a percent sign: \&a, \&b, ..., \&z. As with other variable names, case doesn't matter: \&a is the same array as \&A. The index goes in square brackets appended to the name: \&a[0] is the "zeroth" element, \&a[1] is the first element, and so on.

Before you can use an array, you must DECLARE its size so Kermit can allocate memory for it:

DECLARE *array-name*[*number*]

Creates an array of the given name, with *number*+1 elements, 0 through *number*. For example, the command:

```
C-Kermit>declare \&x[200]
```

creates an array named \&x that has 201 elements, numbered 0 through 200.

Array elements, like any other variable, can be created with the DEFINE or ASSIGN command. An array index can be a constant or any type of variable, including another array element:

```
C-Kermit>dcl \&x[1023]          (Declare array \&x, size 1024)
C-Kermit>def \&x[100] HUNDRED   (Define 100th element of \&x)
C-Kermit>def \%i 100            (Define a global variable)
C-Kermit>ech \&x[\%i]           (Use it as an index)
HUNDRED
C-Kermit>asg \&x[99] \%i        (Define another array element)
C-Kermit>ech \&x[\&x[99]]       (Use it as an index)
HUNDRED
C-Kermit>
```

C-Kermit arrays are one-dimensional. That is, you cannot create or use an array that has more than one index. A declaration for an array that already exists destroys the previous array, and allocates a new empty one with the same name and with the given size. A declaration with a size of zero destroys the array and releases its memory:

```
C-Kermit>declare \&x[0]
```

You can find out what arrays are declared with the SHOW ARRAYS command:

```
C-Kermit>sho arra
Declared arrays:
 \&@[4]
 \&a[3]
 \&x[200]
```

We'll see some uses for arrays in the coming chapters.

Variables 227

The C-Kermit Argument Vector Array

The array \&@ is special. It is created automatically when Kermit starts up, and it contains the program's "argument vector"—the command you gave to start C-Kermit. For example, suppose you started C-Kermit by giving the following command at the UNIX shell prompt:[33]

```
$ kermit -l /dev/ttya
C-Kermit>echo \&@[0]
kermit
C-Kermit>echo \&@[1]
-l
C-Kermit>echo \&@[2]
/dev/ttya
C-Kermit>
```

Kermit does not let you change the values of the \&@ array. They are read-only.

Built-in Variables

C-Kermit offers a selection of built-in, read-only, named variables. Read-only means that C-Kermit itself gives them their values. You can't DEFINE or ASSIGN them yourself, you can only use the values Kermit gives them or test them with IF DEFINED. Built-in variables have names that look like this:

\v(*name*)

that is, a backslash, the letter v, and then the variable name in parentheses. Either upper- or lowercase letters can be used. C-Kermit's built-in read-only variables include:

\v(argc)
> The number of arguments to the current macro, including its name. Example:
> ```
> C-Kermit>define countwords echo Arguments: \v(argc)
> C-Kermit>countwords here are some words
> Arguments: 5
> C-Kermit>
> ```

\v(args)
> The number of "words" you typed when you invoked C-Kermit:
> ```
> $ kermit -p e -l /dev/acu -b 2400
> C-Kermit>echo \v(args)
> 7
> C-Kermit>
> ```

\v(cmdlevel)
> Current command level; 0 means interactive. Anything greater than zero means C-Kermit is getting its commands from a command file or a macro definition.

---

[33]Command-line arguments are explained in Chapter 14.

\v(cmdfile)
> The name of the current command file, if any. If a macro is currently executing, its name is available as \%0. Example:
> ```
> Echo Greetings from \v(cmdfile)!
> ```

\v(cmdsource)
> The current source of commands: PROMPT (if interactive), FILE (if a command file), or MACRO (if a macro definition).

\v(count)
> The current SET COUNT value (explained in Chapter 12).

\v(cpu)
> The type of CPU for which C-Kermit was built (which is not necessarily the same as the type of CPU on which it is running). Examples include mc68000 for the Motorola 68000 series, i386 for the Intel 80386, sparc for the Sun SPARC RISC processor, and so on. If not known, the value is simply "unknown".

\v(date)
> The current date, for example 8 Aug 1992. The month is the first three letters of the month's name (your operating system might be configured to return month names in your local language). The date string contains imbedded spaces (see \v(ndate) for an alternative). Example:
> ```
> C-Kermit>echo Today is \v(date).
> Today is 8 Aug 1992.
> C-Kermit>
> ```

\v(day)
> The day of the week, written as the first three letters of the weekday: Sun, Mon, ..., Sat (your operating system might be configured to return day names in your local language). Example:
> ```
> C-Kermit>echo Today is \v(day), \v(date).
> Today is Sat, 8 Aug 1992.
> C-Kermit>
> ```

\v(directory)
> The current (default) directory. Example:
> ```
> C-Kermit>set prompt [\v(dir)] C-Kermit>
> [/usr/olga/correspondence] C-Kermit>
> ```

\v(exitstatus)
> The numeric return code that C-Kermit would give to your computer's host operating system if you gave it the EXIT command right now. This code indicates the success or failure in various operations (see page 323).

\v(filespec)
: The file specification from your most recent file transfer. Useful for referring to the same group of files again for other purposes, for example:

```
C-Kermit>send x*.*
C-Kermit>echo \v(filespec)
x*.*
C-Kermit>remote dir \v(filespec)
```

\v(fsize)
: The size of the file most recently transferred.

\v(home)
: Your home (login) directory. For UNIX, something like /usr/olga/. For VMS, something like $DISK1:[OLGA]. \v(home) is a portable construction suitable for concatenation with a filename without any intervening characters; a construction like \v(home)oofa.txt should work on all operating systems where C-Kermit runs.

\v(host)
: The network host name, if any, of the computer where C-Kermit is running:

```
C-Kermit>set prompt Kermit-at-\v(host)>
Kermit-at-watsun>
```

\v(inchar)
: The last character that was read by the INPUT command (explained in Chapter 13).

\v(incount)
: The number of characters read by the most recent INPUT command (Chapter 13).

\v(input)
: The contents of the INPUT buffer (Chapter 13).

\v(line)
: The current communication line or device or network host name or number (the most recent SET LINE or SET HOST value).

\v(local)
: 1 if Kermit is in local mode; that is, you have given a SET LINE, SET HOST, or TELNET command to initiate a connection from the computer where C-Kermit is running to another, remote computer. 0 otherwise.

\v(ndate)
: The current date in numeric yyyymmdd format, e.g. 19920208, suitable for sorting or comparison with IF EQUAL, IF LLT, IF LGT (explained Chapter 12), or for making filenames. For example:

```
C-Kermit>log transactions \v(ndate).log
```

`\v(nday)`
: The numeric value of the day of the week. 0 is Sunday, 1 is Monday, and so on until Saturday, which is 6.

`\v(ntime)`
: Numeric time. The current time in seconds since midnight, local time. For example, 10:00 p.m. would be 79200.

`\v(platform)`
: The specific platform for which your version of C-Kermit was built, such as `AT&T_System_V_R4`, `NeXT`, etc. This is the same as the end part of C-Kermit's version herald, but with spaces replaced by underscores to allow convenient use of this variable in commands without introducing unwanted field delimiters.

`\v(program)`
: The name of this program, C-Kermit.

`\v(return)`
: The return value of the most recently called macro or user-defined function (explained in Chapter 12).

`\v(speed)`
: The communication device transmission speed, if known. Be careful, the value reported is misleading if the communication device is not a true serial communication device. For example, most UNIX systems report the speed of a pseudoterminal device as 38400 bps.

`\v(status)`
: Zero (0) if the previous command succeeded, nonzero if it failed. Use this variable to access a command's status so you can save it for later reference. For example:

```
send oofa.a
assign \%a \v(status)
send oofa.b
assign \%b \v(status)
echo Status: oofa.a \%a, oofa.b \%b.
```

`\v(system)`
: The generic name for the host operating system or environment: UNIX, VMS, or OS/2.

`\v(tfsize)`
: The total number of file bytes transferred in the most recent file transfer. If a group of files was transferred, `\v(tfsize)` shows their total size, whereas `\v(fsize)` shows the size of only the last file transferred.

`\v(time)`
: The current local time in 24-hour `hh:mm:ss` format. Example: `15:28:00`.

\v(ttyfd)
: (UNIX only) The file descriptor of the communication device selected in the most recent SET LINE or SET HOST command. Use this to construct command lines to invoke exterior protocols or communication programs with the RUN command, for example:

```
C-Kermit>set modem microcom
C-Kermit>set line /dev/cua
C-Kermit>set speed 2400
C-Kermit>dial 7654321
C-Kermit>run xyzcom -f \v(ttyfd)
```

\v(version)
: The Kermit program's numeric version number. For example, version 5A(188) is 501188. Use this in IF EQUAL, IF LLT, IF LGT statements (explained later) to construct scripts that can take advantage of commands in new releases of C-Kermit that aren't present in old releases.

C-Kermit's built-in variables can be used in any context where they make sense:

```
C-Kermit>echo It's \v(time) on \v(date)
It's 17:56:04 on 11 Mar 1992
C-Kermit>
```

You can find out what built-in variables are available and their current values with the command SHOW VARIABLES (this example does not show a complete list):

```
C-Kermit>show var
 \v(argc) = 0
 \v(args) = 2
 \v(cmdfile) =
 \v(cmdlevel) = 0
 \v(cmdsource) = prompt
 \v(cpu) = sparc
 \v(date) = 12 Jul 1992
 \v(day) = Sun
 \v(directory) = /usr/olga
 \v(home) = /usr/olga/
 \v(host) = watsun
 \v(line) = /dev/tty
 \v(local) = 0
 \v(ndate) = 19920712
 \v(nday) = 0
 \v(ntime) = 82463
 \v(platform) = SunOS_4.1_(BSD)
 \v(program) = C-Kermit
 \v(speed) = 38400
 \v(status) = 0
 \v(system) = UNIX
 \v(time) = 22:54:24
C-Kermit>
```

Environment Variables

Environment variables are variables that certain computer operating systems or application environments make available to application software (such as C-Kermit) at runtime. An environment variable has a name and a value. C-Kermit gives you access to your computer's environment variables (if it has any) with variables of the form:

\$(*name*)

that is, backslash and dollar sign followed by the name of the environment variable enclosed in parentheses. Which, if any, variables are available depends on your computer system and your own setup, which is entirely unknown to C-Kermit. Those commonly available on UNIX and VMS include:

\$(HOME)   Your home directory

\$(USER)   Your login username

\$(TERM)   Your terminal type

Note that alphabetic case *is* significant in environment variable names. Example (with results shown for both UNIX and VMS):

```
C-Kermit>echo HOME=\$(HOME), USER=\$(USER), TERM=\$(TERM)
HOME=/usr/olga, USER=olga, TERM=vt300
HOME=$disk1:[olga], USER=OLGA, TERM=vt300
```

In UNIX and OS/2, you can find out what environment variables are currently defined by issuing the command `set` at the shell prompt, or by using the C-Kermit command:

```
C-Kermit>run set
```

In UNIX, you can define an environment variable like this:

```
$ MYNAME=Olaf ; export MYNAME     (sh or ksh)
% setenv MYNAME Olaf              (csh)
```

In VMS and OpenVMS, C-Kermit treats logical names as environment variables:

```
C-Kermit>echo \$(SYS$SYSTEM)
SYS$SYSROOT:[SYSEXE]
```

You can find out your logical names with the VMS SHOW LOGICALS command and you can define new ones with the VMS DEFINE command:

```
$ define MYNAME "Olaf"
$ show logical myname
    "MYNAME" = "Olaf" (LNM$PROCESS_TABLE)
$ kermit
C-Kermit>echo Hello there, \$(MYNAME).
Hello there, Olaf.
C-Kermit>
```

Defining versus Assigning Revisited

Some of C-Kermit's \v() variables change depending on conditions. For example, \v(directory) changes whenever you give a CD command; the \v(time) variable changes every second, all by itself. These variables serve nicely to illustrate the distinction between DEFINE and ASSIGN, in case it is still in doubt. Let's create a variable \%a that includes a reference to \v(time) in its value. First with the DEFINE command, which copies the *name* of the \v(time) variable into the definition of \%a:

```
C-Kermit>DEFINE \%a The time is \v(time)
C-Kermit>show globals              (Check the value of \%a)
 \%a = The time is \v(time)
C-Kermit>echo \%a                  (Evaluate it)
The time is 13:25:03
C-Kermit>sleep 60                  (Let one minute pass)
C-Kermit>echo \%a                  (Look again)
The time is 13:26:03               (See how it changed)
```

And again, but with the ASSIGN command, which evaluates the \v(time) variable and copies its *value* into the \%a definition:

```
C-Kermit>ASSIGN \%a The time is \v(time)
C-Kermit>sho globals               (Check the value)
 \%a = The time is 13:31:47        (No \v(time))
C-Kermit>echo \%a                  (Evaluate \%a)
The time is 13:31:47
C-Kermit>sleep 60                  (Sleep one minute)
C-Kermit>echo \%a                  (Check again)
The time is 13:31:47               (Time stands still!)
```

So, once again, the rule is: use ASSIGN to get the current value of a variable whose value might change before you want to use it. Use DEFINE to ensure that whenever you reference a variable, you get its latest value. When the definition text does not contain variables, DEFINE and ASSIGN are equivalent.

Chapter 12

Programming Commands

Command files, macros, and variables are useful tools, but by themselves they are little more than conveniences. However, if they are used within the framework of a programming language, they can open up all sorts of new possibilities. *Programming language?* If you're not a programmer, don't be alarmed. The language we're talking about is nothing more than the Kermit commands you are already familiar with, plus a few additional elements: commands for decision-making, for skipping other commands, for repeatedly executing groups of commands, for reading and writing file data, and for interacting directly with the user.

The IF Command

Let's begin by introducing Kermit's decision-making command.

IF *condition command*
　　If the *condition* is true, the *command* is executed. If the condition is not true, the command is ignored; that is, it is treated as a comment.

IF NOT *condition command*
　　If the *condition* is *not* true, the *command* is executed. If the condition is true, the command is ignored.

The *command* can be any C-Kermit command, including another IF command, but not an ELSE command (see page 237), and it can also be a macro invocation or a TAKE command. It is on the same line as the IF command, and is separated from it by one or more spaces, no commas or other punctuation. The *condition* is a statement that can be true or false, consisting of one to four "words" separated by spaces. Example:

```
if equal "\%a" "Rumpelstiltskin" echo You guessed my name!
```

The *condition* is:

```
equal "\%a" "Rumpelstiltskin"
```

and the *command* is:

```
echo You guessed my name!
```

The following sections describe C-Kermit's IF conditions.

Comparing Numbers

Let's begin with the IF commands that compare numbers. The numbers in the following IF conditions can be constants (literal numbers) or variables of any kind whose values are whole numbers, positive or negative. If these comparisons are used with nonnumeric values, or numbers containing decimal points, they give a syntax error message and fail.

IF = *number1 number2 command*

If *number1* is equal to *number2*, the *command* is executed. Example:

```
C-Kermit>define \%a 2
C-Kermit>if = ? First number or variable name
C-Kermit>if = \%a ? Second number or variable name
C-Kermit>if = \%a 3 echo They are equal    (Nothing happens)
C-Kermit>if = \%a 2 echo They are equal    (Condition is true)
They are equal                             (Command is executed)
C-Kermit>
```

IF NOT = *number1 number2 command*

If *number1* is not equal to *number2*, the *command* is executed. Example:

```
C-Kermit>define \%a 2
C-Kermit>if not = \%a 2 echo Not equal     (Nothing happens)
C-Kermit>if not = \%a 3 echo Not equal     (Condition is true)
Not equal                                  (Command is executed)
C-Kermit>
```

IF < *number1 number2 command*

If *number1* is less than *number2*, the *command* is executed. Example:

```
C-Kermit>define \%a 2
C-Kermit>if < \%a -5 echo It's less        (Nothing happens)
C-Kermit>if < \%a 100 echo It's less       (Condition is true)
It's less                                  (Command is executed)
C-Kermit>
```

IF NOT < *number1 number2 command*

If *number1* is not less than (is greater than or equal to) *number2*, the *command* is executed. Example:

```
C-Kermit>define \%a 2
C-Kermit>if not < \%a 1 echo Not less     (Condition is true)
Not less                                   (Command is executed)
C-Kermit>if not < \%a 2 echo Not less     (Nothing happens)
C-Kermit>
```

IF > *number1 number2 command*

If *number1* is greater than *number2*, the *command* is executed. Example:

```
C-Kermit>define \%a 2
C-Kermit>if > \%a 1 echo Greater          (Condition is true)
Greater                                    (Command is executed)
C-Kermit>if > \%a 2 echo Greater          (Nothing happens)
C-Kermit>
```

IF NOT > *number1 number2 command*

If *number1* is not greater than (is less than or equal to) *number2*, the *command* is executed. Example:

```
C-Kermit>define \%a 2
C-Kermit>if not > \%a 2 echo Not greater   (Condition is true)
Not greater                                 (Command is executed)
C-Kermit>if not > \%a 1 echo Not greater   (Nothing happens)
C-Kermit>
```

Here is an example of using "IF <" to construct a timely greeting message:

```
if < \v(ntime) 43200 def \%x morning       (Before noon)
if not < \v(ntime) 43200 def \%x afternoon (Before 5)
if not < \v(ntime) 61200 def \%x evening   (After 5)
echo Good \%x!
```

The ELSE Command

The IF command can be followed on the next line by an ELSE command:

ELSE *command*

Executes the *command* if the preceding command was an IF command and its condition was not true.

Example:

```
C-Kermit>if = 1 2 echo 1 = 2               (Not true)
C-Kermit>else echo 1 is not 2              (So ELSE is executed)
1 is not 2
C-Kermit>
```

The ELSE command causes an error if it is executed after any command other than IF. IF and ELSE are separate commands, not two parts of the same command. They are intended primarily for use within command files and macros, but they can also be executed at the C-Kermit prompt, in which case you should not be alarmed if another prompt suddenly appears after the IF condition:

```
C-Kermit>if = 1 2 echo Strange...    (False, nothing happens)
C-Kermit>if = 1 1                    (True, new prompt appears)
C-Kermit>echo As expected...         (ECHO command is executed)
As expected...
C-Kermit>
```

When the condition is true, C-Kermit prompts you for a command to be executed. If the condition is not true, C-Kermit treats the rest of the IF command as a comment. Here is an example of using IF and ELSE in a macro:

```
C-Kermit>def add if = \%1 1 if = \%2 1 echo 2, else echo Too hard!
C-Kermit>add 1 1
2
C-Kermit>add 2 2
Too hard!
```

The comma separating the IF and ELSE commands is necessary because IF and ELSE are separate commands. This example also shows how an AND effect can be achieved by combining multiple IF commands on the same line. A more structured "extended IF" command is presented later.

String Comparisons

The following commands compare character strings just as the IF =, IF <, and IF > commands compare numbers, and you can use NOT in these commands the same way.

IF EQUAL *string1 string2 command*

Executes the *command* if the two character strings are equal, meaning they are the same length and they contain the same characters in the same order. A string may be either a literal string or a variable containing a string. Examples:

```
if equal \%1 secret echo You guessed the secret word!
if not equ \%1 secret echo Sorry, wrong again.
```

If a variable is not defined, or has an empty value, a command field will be missing, causing a command error:

```
C-Kermit>define \%1              (\%1 is undefined)
C-Kermit>if equal \%1 ?Text required
C-Kermit>
```

To handle this situation, put *string1* and *string2* in identical quotes or parentheses:

```
C-Kermit>define \%1              (\%1 is undefined)
C-Kermit>if equal "\%1" "oofa" echo You guessed the secret word!
C-Kermit>
```

If \%1 has not been defined, C-Kermit sees this as:

```
if equal "" "oofa" echo You guessed the secret word!
```

which makes the desired comparison, rather than as:

```
if equal oofa echo You guessed the secret word!
```

which compares "secret" with "echo".

IF LLT *string1 string2 command*
Executes the *command* if *string1* is "lexically" less than (LLT) *string2*, in other words; if *string1* would be alphabetized before *string2*. Example:

```
if llt "\%a" "zyzzniak" echo It's less.
```

IF NOT LLT means "lexically greater than or equal to."

IF LGT *string1 string2 command*
Executes the *command* if *string1* is lexically greater than (LGT) *string2*. Example:

```
if lgt "\%a" "aardvark" echo It's greater.
```

IF NOT LGT means "lexically less than or equal to."

In these commands, literal strings to be compared must not contain any spaces, or else C-Kermit will think the characters after the space are the beginning of the command to be executed. For example, the following command compares the value of the variable \%a with the word *The* and if they are equal attempts to execute the END command, probably not what was intended:

```
if equal \%a The End echo All finished.
```

You can get around this limitation by putting multiword character strings in variables:

```
C-Kermit>define \%b The End
C-Kermit>if equal \%a \%b echo All finished.
```

The treatment of alphabetic case in string comparisons is governed by the command:

SET CASE OFF
In all C-Kermit's string comparison and matching commands—IF and others still to come—treats uppercase and lowercase letters as equivalent: "A" is the same as "a", "aardvark" equals "AARDVARK", etc.

SET CASE ON
Treats upper- and lowercase as distinct: "A" and "a" are different characters.

Unless you tell Kermit otherwise, alphabetic case is ignored. *WARNING:* caseless string comparisons, for example in the IF EQUAL, IF LLT, and IF LGT commands, work only for 7-bit ASCII characters. For international (accented and/or non-Roman) characters, you must use case-sensitive comparisons. Even then, there is no guarantee that IF LLT or IF LGT will work correctly (but IF EQUAL will).

Checking for Success and Failure

One of the most useful features of C-Kermit's programming language is the ability to take different actions depending on whether a command succeeded or failed. For example, if a command doesn't work as expected, you might want to print a message or try a different command instead of just going on to the next command.

IF SUCCESS *command*

Executes the *command* if the previous command succeeded. Equivalent to IF NOT FAILURE. Example:

```
send oofa.txt
if success echo The SEND command succeeded.
else echo The SEND command failed.
```

Every C-Kermit command except COMMENT sets the SUCCESS indicator when it completes. You can inquire about the success or failure of the previous command with the SHOW STATUS command:

```
C-Kermit>type oofa.txt
?File not found - oofa.txt
C-Kermit>show status
  FAILURE
C-Kermit>set file type binary
C-Kermit>show status
  SUCCESS
C-Kermit>
```

IF FAILURE *command*

Executes the *command* if the previous command failed. Equivalent to IF NOT SUCCESS. A command fails not only if it doesn't work, but also if it has a syntax error. Synonym: **IF ERROR**.

Other IF Commands

C-Kermit's IF command also lets you check the existence and format of variables and files, as well as various aspects of C-Kermit's operation.

IF DEFINED *name command*

Executes the *command* if *name* is the name of a macro, a macro argument, a global variable, a built-in variable, an environment variable, an invocation of a built-in function, or an array element that is defined and has a non-empty value. Example:

```
C-Kermit>define \%a foo              (Define a variable)
C-Kermit>if def \%a echo It's defined
It's defined
C-Kermit>define \%a                  (Undefine it)
C-Kermit>if def \%a echo It's defined
C-Kermit>if not def \%a echo Not defined
Not defined
C-Kermit>
```

IF NUMERIC *name command*

Executes the *command* if *name* consists only of digits, or is a variable whose value consists only of digits, possibly with a leading plus or minus sign.

IF EXIST *filename command*

Executes the *command* if a single, regular, readable file of the given name exists, and it is not a directory, not a wildcard file group specification. Here's an example in which we add the UNIX more command to the UNIX version of C-Kermit:

```
define more -
  if exist \%1 run more \%1, -
  else echo File \%1 not found
```

IF FOREGROUND *command*

Executes the *command* if Kermit is running in the foreground; that is, if its standard input is coming from the keyboard and its standard output is going to the screen. Example:

```
send oofa.txt
if success if foreground echo Transfer succeeded.
```

This command can be used to control whether messages are printed on the screen during execution of a command file or macro. If Kermit is running in the background, you probably don't want messages interfering with your foreground work.

IF BACKGROUND *command*

Executes the *command* if Kermit is running in the background, and/or with its standard input and/or output redirected. IF BACKGROUND is the same as IF NOT FOREGROUND.

IF COUNT *command*

This command is used for counted loops (explained later in this chapter). The COUNT variable may be referred to only as an IF condition, whereas the variable \v(count) can be used anywhere.

IF VERSION *number command*

Executes the *command* if C-Kermit's numeric version number is greater than or equal to the *number* given. The numeric version number is displayed by the VERSION command:

```
C-Kermit>version
C-Kermit 5A(188), 23 Nov 92
 Numeric: 501188
C-Kermit>
```

The IF VERSION command gives C-Kermit command files and macros independence from the program version. For example, suppose a future release of C-Kermit—say, 502200—has a new command SET BLOCK-CHECK 6 (the current release does not). If you guard new commands within IF VERSION statements, older releases of C-Kermit will not attempt to execute them:

```
if version 502200 set block-check 6,
else set block-check 3
```

This would let the same macro or command file run on both newer and older versions of C-Kermit and select the highest available block check type. You can refer to C-Kermit's numeric version number in other contexts with the built-in variable \v(version):

```
if not < \v(version) 502200 set block-check 6
else echo No block-check 6 in version \v(version).
```

An EDIT Macro

Now we have all the tools we need to construct a somewhat smarter macro, one that is both useful and friendly. The macro is called EDIT, and it lets you edit a file directly from C-Kermit command level, returning you to the C-Kermit prompt when you are finished editing.[34] The first time you use the EDIT macro, you must furnish the name of a file to edit. The next time, if you leave out the filename, the macro will use the same name as before. If you supply a new filename, the macro will use that one instead of the old one.

```
define myeditor emacs            (Name of my editor)
define myfile                    (No edit file specified yet)
define edit -                    (Define the EDIT macro)
  if = \v(argc) 2 assign myfile \%1,-
  if not defined myfile echo Edit what?,-
  else run \m(myeditor) \m(myfile)
```

What's happening here? First we defined a macro, myeditor, to be the name of the system command that starts our favorite editor. If yours isn't EMACS, replace the word emacs with whatever you want. Then we ensured that the macro, MYFILE, starts out with no definition.

The next command (continued on several lines) defines the EDIT macro itself. If the argument count \v(argc) is exactly 2—the macro name itself plus one argument—the argument \%1 is taken as the name of a file to edit, and the value of this variable is assigned to the macro, MYFILE, which will hold our filename even after the EDIT macro completes. Next, we check to see if the MYFILE variable is defined. If it isn't, the user must have typed EDIT without giving the name of a file to edit and had not specified a file name in an earlier EDIT command. So we just print a message and quit. But if MYFILE is defined, we execute the ELSE command, which runs our chosen editor on the file. Examples:

```
$ kermit                         (Start Kermit)
C-Kermit>edit                    (No previous filename)
Edit what?                       (Error message)
C-Kermit>edit oofa.txt
```

---

[34]You will find a somewhat more sophisticated version of the EDIT macro in the distributed sample files.

```
  (oofa.txt is edited...)
C-Kermit>edit                        (No filename given)
  (oofa.txt is edited, EDIT macro remembers last filename...)
C-Kermit>
```

Notice that we did not use IF EXIST to check if the argument was a real file. That was on purpose, to allow the EDIT command to create new files.

The STOP and END Commands

Macros and command files are normally terminated after C-Kermit reads and executes their final command, or if they contain an EXIT command, or if an error occurs and you have SET MACRO ERROR ON or SET TAKE ERROR ON. There are also two other ways to explicitly terminate a macro or command file prematurely:

STOP [*number* [*text*]]
> This command returns you to the C-Kermit command prompt immediately from any level of command file or macro execution, no matter how deeply nested. When given at the C-Kermit prompt, the STOP command has no effect. If C-Kermit is not running interactively, the STOP command halts the program entirely. If a *number* is given, it is used as a return code. If *text* is also given, it is printed on the screen. For example, here is a command file called TESTSTOP.TAK:
>
> ```
> echo Testing the STOP command...
> stop 1 This is an error message from the STOP command.
> echo You shouldn't see this.
> ```
>
> Now we execute it:
>
> ```
> C-Kermit>take teststop.tak
> Testing the STOP command...
> This is an error message from the STOP command.
> C-Kermit>show status
>   FAILURE
> C-Kermit>
> ```

END [*number* [*text*]]
> This command causes C-Kermit to return immediately to the command level from which the current command file or macro was invoked. The optional *number* is a return code, and the optional *text* is a message to be printed.

The default *number* is 0 (for success) for both commands. The *text* message cannot be printed unless a number is included before it.

The return code lets a macro or command file declare whether it succeeded or failed. For example, suppose you have defined a macro called SENDLOTSAFILES and you invoke it from inside a command file:

```
C-Kermit>take daily.tak
```

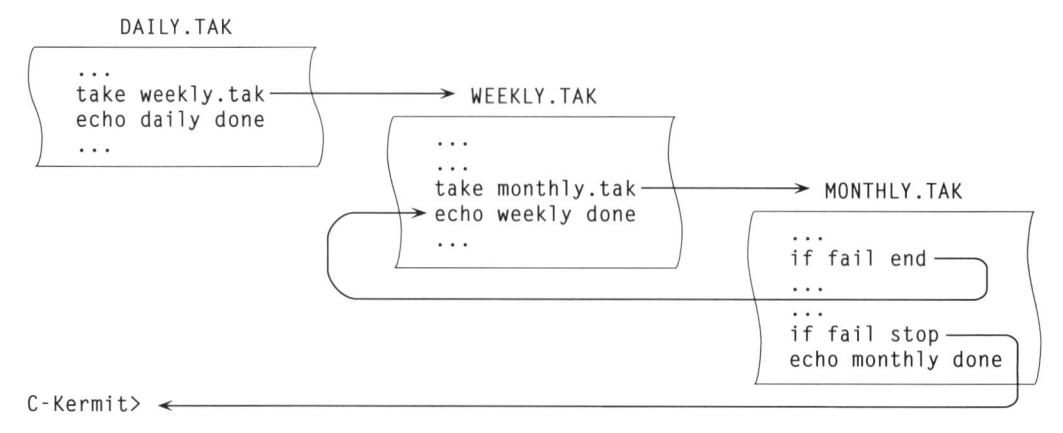

```
       DAILY.TAK
   ...
   take weekly.tak  ──────▶  WEEKLY.TAK
   echo daily done                ...
   ...                            ...
                                  take monthly.tak  ──────▶  MONTHLY.TAK
                               ▶  echo weekly done                ...
                                  ...                             if fail end ──┐
                                                                  ...           │
                                                                  ...           │
                                                                  if fail stop ─┤
                                                                  echo monthly done
C-Kermit> ◀────────────────────────────────────────────────────────────────────┘
```

Figure 12-1 Returning from Nested Command Files

```
sendlotsafiles
if success echo Macro succeeded.
```

The message will always appear, even if the macro failed, because the (implied) DO command itself succeeded. DO or TAKE commands only fail when the given macro or command file can't be found. To make the macro pass along a failure code, use the END or STOP command with a nonzero return code, as in this macro definition:

```
define sendlotsafiles -
  send oofa.txt, -
  if failure end 1 Can't send oofa.txt, -
  set file type binary, -
  send oofa.exe, -
  if fail end 1 Can't send oofa.exe,-
  else end 0
```

To illustrate the difference between STOP and END, suppose we have a command file called DAILY.TAK, which we run every day. This command file performs its daily tasks and then checks (using \v(day) or \v(nday)) to see if it is Friday. If so, it TAKEs another command file, WEEKLY.TAK, which in turn checks to see if it is the first week of the month,[35] and if so TAKEs MONTHLY.TAK. So our command files are nested 3 deep. Now suppose MONTHLY.TAK encountered an error and could not continue. If it gives the END command, WEEKLY.TAK will resume executing after its TAKE MONTHLY.TAK command. If MONTHLY.TAK gives the STOP command, C-Kermit will cancel all the command files and return to its prompt, as shown in Figure 12-1.

---

[35] By extracting the day of the month from \v(date) or \v(ndate). We'll learn about substrings later in this chapter.

A Helpful COPY Macro

Remember our earlier COPY macro from page 220?

```
define copy run cp \%1 \%2
```

It was so easy to write, it seems a shame to complicate it. Nevertheless, much can go wrong with our original version. In the first place, it isn't portable. The ideal C-Kermit COPY macro should work on every computer that C-Kermit runs on: UNIX, VMS, OpenVMS, OS/2, AOS/VS, and so on. These systems can have different names for their COPY commands (UNIX calls it cp, the others call it COPY), and the filenames might be given in a different order (AOS/VS puts the destination file first, then the source; the others have the source file first, then the destination). So let's make a new COPY macro, incorporating what we have learned about decision making and built-in variables. It has the following form, no matter where it runs:

COPY *filename1 filename2*

> The COPY macro makes a copy of the file whose name is *filename1*, which must exist and must be a single, readable file. The copy is a new file called *filename2*. If a file called *filename2* already exists, the COPY macro fails.

Here is our new COPY macro. Study it as a not totally serious example of compulsive verification of user input. Informative error messages are issued for every conceivable condition where the copy operation could fail.

```
define COPY -
  if > \v(argc) 3 -                        ; Too many arguments given?
    end 1 \%0: too many arguments,-        ;   Too many, fail.
  if not def \%1 -                         ; Was a source file given?
    end 1 copy what?,-                     ;   No, nothing to copy.
  if not exist \%1 -                       ; Does source file exist?
    end 1 file "\%1" doesn't exist,-       ;   No, it can't be copied.
  if not def \%2 -                         ; Destination file given?
    end 1 copy \%1 to what?,-              ;   No, it can't be created.
  if not = \ffiles(\%2) 0 -                ; Does it already exist?
    end 1 file \%2 already exists,-        ;   Yes, don't write over it.
  if equal "\v(system)" "AOS/VS" -         ; For AOS/VS:
    run COPY \%2 \%1,-                     ;    COPY dest source
  else if equal "\v(system)" "UNIX" -      ; COPY command for UNIX:
    run cp \%1 \%2,-                       ;    cp source dest
  else run COPY \%1 \%2,-                  ; Others: COPY source dest
  if exist \%2 end 0 \%1 copied OK,-       ; Check work, return SUCCESS
    else end 1 COPY failed.                ;   or FAILURE.
```

Install this macro, run it with every imaginable type and combination of improper arguments, and see if it lets you get away with anything.

The GOTO Command

So far we've used the decision-making capability of the IF statement in a very limited way: to execute or not execute a single command. In more general cases, we would like to decide whether to execute whole groups of commands. There are two ways to do this. The way you know already is to group statements in macros or command files, because DO and TAKE count as single commands. Examples:

```
if equal \%a yes do something   ; "something" is a macro name
else take something.tak         ; "something.tak" is a command file
```

The new way is the GOTO command. It changes the order in which Kermit executes commands in a command file or a macro:

GOTO *label-name*
   In a command file or a macro, go immediately to the first command after the first occurrence of the *label* in the current macro or command file and begin executing commands at that point. If the label is not found, return to the previous level (macro or command file) and look there. Repeat this process until the label is found or the search fails. If the label is never found, C-Kermit returns to its prompt and issues an error message. In case of duplicate labels within a command file or macro, Kermit uses the first one.

The GOTO command has no effect as an interactive command. And when piped into C-Kermit's command processor from standard input, it does nothing except issue an error message:

```
C-Kermit>goto sleep
?Sorry, GOTO only works in a command file or macro
C-Kermit>
```

A *label* is a character string of your choosing. It must begin with a colon (:), and it must be on a line by itself (but it can have a trailing comment). Here is an example of a command file that uses GOTO commands and labels:

```
send oofa.txt
if failure goto bad
echo oofa.txt was sent ok.
echo Deleting oofa.txt
delete oofa.txt
goto done
:bad
echo oofa.txt was not sent.
echo Keeping oofa.txt.
:done
echo Finished.
```

In this example, BAD and DONE are labels. If the file is sent successfully, it is deleted and the messages in the BAD section are skipped. If the file was not sent, it is not deleted and the messages in the BAD section are displayed. In both cases, the "Finished" message is displayed. Here is the same example converted to a macro that takes the filename as an argument:

```
define mysend send \%1,-
  if failure goto bad,
  echo \%1 was sent ok.,-
  echo Deleting \%1, delete \%1,-
  goto done,-
:bad,-
  echo \%1 was not sent., echo Keeping \%1.,-
:done,-
  echo Finished.
```

You can use the MYSEND macro to send and delete any file:

```
C-Kermit>mysend oofa.txt
C-Kermit>mysend ckermit.ini
```

The *label-name* by which the GOTO command refers to the label should be the same as the label, except that the colon can be omitted. Alphabetic case is always ignored when searching for labels. The following GOTO statements are all equivalent, meaning they all look for the same label, BEGIN:

```
goto begin
GoTo :begin
GOTO :BEGIN
```

GOTO label references can be variables. This lets you execute different groups of commands depending on the value of a variable:

```
define spellnum if not def \%1 end,-
  else if not numeric \%1 end 1 { Sorry, not a number},-
  else if > \%1 9 end 1 { Sorry, too hard},-
  else if < \%1 0 end 1 { Sorry, I can't spell negative numbers},-
  else goto \%1,-
:0,echo zero,end,-
:1,echo one,end,-
:2,echo two,end,-
:3,echo three,end,-
:4,echo four,end,-
:5,echo five,end,-
:6,echo six,end,-
:7,echo seven,end,-
:8,echo eight,end,-
:9,echo nine,end
```

Execute this definition and then:

```
C-Kermit>spellnum 0
zero
C-Kermit>spellnum 8
eight
```

and so on.

Finally, here is an example that shows how Kermit peels back macro invocation levels to find the GOTO label:

```
define first :loop, echo \%0, do second
define second echo \%0, do third
define third echo \%0, goto loop
do first
```

If you put these commands into a command file and then TAKE it, you will soon see that it repeats forever: first, second, third, first, second, third, first, and so on. This is called a *loop*. Programmers call loops that go on forever *infinite loops*. You can terminate this infinite loop by typing Ctrl-C. But a way is also needed to terminate loops automatically, without human intervention.

Counted Loops

A somewhat more practical use of the GOTO command lets you repeat selected portions of a command file or macro a specified number of times. Before you can do this, you must have a counting mechanism. C-Kermit offers several of these. The simplest one is the SET COUNT / IF COUNT construction:

SET COUNT *number*

Sets the variable called COUNT to the given number, which must be greater than zero, for example:

```
C-Kermit>set count 5
```

IF COUNT *command*

Subtracts one from the COUNT variable. If the new value of COUNT is greater than zero, the *command* is executed.

The SET COUNT and IF COUNT commands can be combined with the GOTO command to form a counted loop:

```
set count 10
:loop
echo \v(count)
if count goto loop
echo Zero!
```

If you put these commands in a command file and TAKE the file, they print "10, 9, 8, 7, 6, 5, 4, 3, 2, 1, Zero!" You can do the same thing in a macro:

```
def count -
  set count 10,:loop,echo \v(count),if count goto loop,echo Zero!
```

The COUNT "variable" is usable only as the condition of an IF statement. In other contexts, use the \v(count) variable, as shown. Referring to the \v(count) variable does not change its value; only IF COUNT can do that.

Structured Programming

The SET COUNT / IF COUNT / GOTO mechanism is easy to use, but programming purists may prefer a more structured approach. C-Kermit offers three structured programming constructs, the XIF (extended IF) command, the FOR loop, and the WHILE loop. Each of these allows groups of statements to be executed conditionally or repeatedly without the use of labels and GOTOs.

XIF *condition* { *command [, command...] } [ELSE { command [, command...] }]*

If the condition is true, execute the command or commands enclosed in the first set of curly braces. If an ELSE-part is provided, and the *condition* is not true, execute the commands inside the second set of curly braces. The conditions are the same as for the regular IF command. Examples:

```
xif not exist oofa.txt { echo no oofa.txt!, stop } -
  else { send oofa.txt, echo oofa.txt sent ok. }
xif < \%a \%b { echo \%a } else { echo \%b }
```

The differences between the XIF and IF commands are summarized in Table 12-1.

FOR *variable* initial final increment >{ *command [, command...] }*

Repeats the *commands* that are enclosed in braces a certain number of times. The *initial* value is assigned to the *variable*. If the value is not greater than the *final* value, the *commands* are executed. Then the *increment* is added to the *variable* and the process is repeated until the *variable* finally exceeds the *final* value. The number of times the commands are executed is:

$$n = \frac{final - initial}{increment} + 1$$

If *n* is zero or less, the commands are not executed at all.

Table 12-1 Comparison of IF and XIF Commands

Feature	IF Command	XIF Command
Braces	Not allowed. Example: `IF = \%a 1 echo Equal`	Required. Example: `XIF = \%a 1 { echo Equal }`

ELSE Part	Separate Command, optional.
	`IF = \%a 1 echo Equal`
	`ELSE echo Not equal`
		Part of XIF Command, optional.
		`XIF = \%a 1 { echo Equal } -`
		`ELSE { echo Not Equal }`

Object Commands	Only one allowed.
	`IF = \%a 1 echo Equal`
	`ELSE echo Not Equal`
		Multiple commands allowed.
		`XIF = \%a 1 { echo Equal, -`
		`goto xxx -`
		`} ELSE { -`
		`echo Not Equal, stop }`

Here are some examples of FOR loops:

```
for \%i 1 5 1 { echo hello }     ; Prints "hello" five times
```

You can read this as, "Counting from one to five by ones, echo the word hello."

```
for \%j 2 10 2 { echo \%j }      ; Counts to ten by twos
```

Meaning: "Counting from 2 to 10 by twos, echo the counter." It prints 2, 4, 6, 8, and 10.

```
for \%k 10 0 -1 { echo \%k }     ; Counts backwards
```

This one means "Counting backwards from 10 to 0 by –1, print the counter." It prints 10, 9, 8, ... 0.

Here's an example in which we have an array \&f[] containing the names of files to be sent and then deleted. There are \%n filenames in the array. A file is deleted only if it is sent successfully.

```
for \%i 1 \%n 1 { send \&f[\%i], if success delete \&f[\%i] }
```

Finally, here is a loop that prints the C-Kermit program's command line from the argument vector array, \&@[]. The size of the argument vector array is given by the \v(args) built-in variable:

```
for \%k 0 \v(args) 1 { echo \\&@[\%k] = "\&@[\%k]" }
```

The last two examples show how to use a variable to index the elements of an array. The value of the loop variable changes with each trip through the loop, thus accessing the next array element.

The WHILE Command

The SET COUNT / IF COUNT and FOR-loop constructions let you execute groups of commands a certain number of times. But it is also sometimes desirable to loop based on some other criterion, such as a certain condition being satisfied. The WHILE command serves this need:

WHILE *condition* { *command* [, *command*...] }

Executes the *commands* as long as the *condition* is true.

Here is an example of a "polling loop" that periodically checks the time of day until a certain time is reached:

```
while not lgt \v(time) 23:59:59 { echo \v(time), pause 3600 }
while not lgt \v(time) 07:30:00 { echo \v(time), pause 60 }
dial 87654321
hangup
```

This example gives you a wakeup call at 7:30 a.m. Start it up when you leave work; it checks the time every hour until midnight, then it checks the time every minute until 7:30 a.m. arrives, then it calls your phone number.

In an XIF, FOR, or WHILE command, the part within the braces is called the *object command list*. In case you're curious, the XIF, FOR, and WHILE commands are implemented as Kermit macros (SHOW MACROS will display their definitions—don't try to understand them or you'll get a headache). The object command list is the single macro argument (now you know why it's enclosed in braces).

Altering Loop Execution

The following commands let you exit from FOR or WHILE loops early, or skip parts of them and continue execution:

BREAK

Exits immediately from a FOR or WHILE loop. The following example tries to send a file until it succeeds, or until it fails 10 times in row, whichever comes first:

```
for \%i 1 10 1 { send oofa.txt, if success break }
```

If loops are nested, BREAK exits from the innermost enclosing loop. BREAK is an illegal command if it is executed outside a FOR or WHILE loop.

CONTINUE

Causes the next cycle of the enclosing FOR or WHILE loop to begin immediately, skipping any commands between the CONTINUE command and the end of the loop. Here's an example in which the array \&f[50] contains names of files, some of which might exist, others might not. This loop transfers the files that exist:

```
for \%i 1 50 1 { if not exist \&f[\%i] continue, send \&f[\%i] }
```

Like BREAK, CONTINUE is illegal outside of a FOR or WHILE command.

Structured Programming Examples

FOR and WHILE loops can contain many commands and they can be nested. This example, written on multiple lines and indented for neatness and comprehensibility (???), sorts the array \&x, which has \%n text elements, using the "Programming 101" bubble sort algorithm. Pay careful attention to the use of commas, braces, and hyphens (and recall that ASG is our tasteful abbreviation for ASSIGN).

```
for %i 1 \feval(\%n-1) 1 { -         ; Outer loop: i from 1 to n-1
  for %j \%i \%n 1 { -                ; Inner loop: j from i to n
    xif lgt \&x[\%i] \&x[\%j] { -     ; Compare array elements
      asg \%t \&x[\%i], -             ; If out of order,
      asg \&x[\%i] \&x[\%j], -        ; exchange them
      asg \&x[\%j] \%t -
    } -
  } -
}
```

\feval() is a built-in function for evaluating arithmetic expressions, explained on page 257. Here it subtracts 1 from the value \%n.

Finally, here is a truly silly example of a macro that uses a nested, multipart XIF command to find the smallest of its three arguments:

```
def smallest xif < \%1 \%2 {-         ; Compare first two arguments
  echo \%1 is less than \%2,-         ; The first one is smaller
  xif < \%1 \%3 {-                    ; Compare it with the third
    echo \%1 is less than \%3,-       ; The first one is smaller
    def \%a \%1-                      ; Copy it to \%a
  } else {-                           ; The third is smaller
    echo \%1 is not less than \%3,-
    def \%a \%3-                      ; Copy it to \%a
  }-
} else {-                             ; Otherwise
  echo \%1 is not less than \%2,-     ; The second is smaller
  xif < \%2 \%3 {-                    ; Compare it with the third
    echo \%2 is less than \%3,-       ; The second is smaller
    def \%a \%2-                      ; Copy it to \%a
  } else {-                           ; The third is smaller
    echo \%2 is not less than \%3,-
    def \%a \%3-                      ; Copy it to \%a
  }-
}, echo So the smallest is \%a.       ; Announce the winner
```

If you have stored this macro definition in a file called `smallest.tak`, you can issue a TAKE command to read the definition, and then you can try it out:

```
C-Kermit>take smallest.tak       (This defines the macro)
C-Kermit>smallest 6 4 9          (Try it)
6 is not less than 4
4 is less than 9
So the smallest is 4.
C-Kermit>
```

C-Kermit's structured programming constructs are intended for use within command files or macros, and are not very handy to type interactively, but you can do it if you want to. You will find that question-mark help does not work on object commands, because they are just text passed as arguments to macros.

Built-in Functions

You're almost a full-fledged Kermit programmer. You have mastered decision making, GOTOs, loops, and structured programming. Next comes the *function call*. All programming languages offer a variety of built-in functions to perform operations on numbers or character strings, and C-Kermit's language is no exception.

A function is a kind of "black box" into which you place some information, and which returns a result based on that information. The items you give to the function are called the *function arguments*. There can be zero, one, two, or more arguments, but there is only one result.

C-Kermit's built-in functions have names that look like this:

\fname()

That is, backslash, the letter F, the name of the function, and then a pair of parentheses to hold its arguments. The F and the name can be upper- or lowercase. The name can be abbreviated to any length that distinguishes it from other built-in function names. The *arguments* are separated by commas. For example, in:

\fmax(\%a,100)

there are two arguments, \%a and 100. The function reference is replaced by its result. In this example, \fmax() is a function that returns the larger of its two arguments, which must be numeric:

```
C-Kermit>define \%a 333
C-Kermit>echo The maximum of \%a and 100 is \fmax(\%a,100).
The maximum of 333 and 100 is 333.
C-Kermit>
```

If the function call is illegal in any way, its result is null (empty):

```
C-Kermit>define \%a oofa
C-Kermit>echo The maximum of \%a and 333 is "\fmax(\%a,333)".
The maximum of oofa and 333 is "".
C-Kermit>
```

Function arguments can be literal strings of characters, variable names, macro arguments, array elements, backslash codes, invocations of other functions, or any combination of these, but they are legal only if they represent the type of data required for the particular function argument. The result is always a character string.

C-Kermit has functions that operate on strings of characters, numbers, and filenames. You can get a list of C-Kermit's built-in functions by issuing the command SHOW FUNCTIONS.

Character String Functions

The following functions are used for processing character strings:

\Fliteral(*arg*)
  Copies its argument literally, preventing any evaluation of variables (or other functions) from taking place. Example:

```
C-Kermit>def \%a foo
C-Kermit>echo \flit(\%a) = \%a
\%a = foo
C-Kermit>
```

\Fcharacter(*number*)
  Returns the single character corresponding to its argument, which must be numeric. For example, \fchar(65) is the ASCII letter A, \fchar(193) is Latin-1 A-acute.

If you give a negative number or a number larger than 255, only the low-order 8 bits are used. Example:

```
C-Kermit>echo \fchar(79)\fchar(79)\fchar(70)\fchar(65)!
OOFA!
C-Kermit>
```

Characters in the range 128–255 depend on the character set. Here is a way to display your terminal's 8-bit character set (if you have an 8-bit connection to C-Kermit):

```
set command bytesize 8
for \%i 0 255 1 { echo \%i: [\fchar(\%i)] }
```

\Fcode(*character*)

Returns the numeric code of the given character, for example \fcode(A) is 65, the ASCII value of uppercase letter A. If the argument is longer than one character, the numeric value of the first character is returned. If there is no argument, the null value is returned.

\Fsubstring(*text,start,length*)

The result of this function is the portion of the *text* argument that starts at position *start* and is *length* characters long. *text* can be any text and can also be, or include, variable names, other functions, etc.; *start* and *length* must be numbers or variables that have numeric values. The start position is 1 for the first character, 2 for the second, and so on. Example:

```
C-Kermit>echo \fsubst(hello there,7,3)
the
C-Kermit>
```

If the length argument is omitted, all of the characters from the starting position to the end are returned:

```
C-Kermit>def \%a 123456789
C-Kermit>ech \fsub(\%a,4)
456789
C-Kermit>
```

\Fright(*text,length*)

Is replaced by the rightmost *length* characters of the *text*, or the entire *text*, whichever is shorter. Example:

```
C-Kermit>echo "\Fright(kermit.exe,4)"
".exe"
C-Kermit>
```

\Flower(*text*)

Converts all uppercase letters in its argument text to lowercase, for example:

```
C-Kermit>define \%a FINE
C-Kermit>echo This is a \Flower(\%a Mess).
This is a fine mess.
```

\Fupper(text)
   Converts all lowercase letters in its text argument to uppercase.

\Freverse(text)
   Reverses the order of the characters in its text argument, for example:
   \frev(mupeen) is neepum.

\Frepeat(text,number)
   Repeats the first argument the number of times given by the second argument.
   Examples:
   ```
   C-Kermit>echo \frepeat(=,10)
   ==========
   C-Kermit>echo +\frep(-+,10)
   +-+-+-+-+-+-+-+-+-+-+
   ```

\Flpad(text,number,character)
   Left-pads the *text* to length *number* with *character*. If the *character* is omitted, blank (space) is used. Handy for lining things up. Examples:
   ```
   C-Kermit>def xx echo \flpad(\%1,10)
   C-Kermit>xx 20
           20
   C-Kermit>xx 1992
         1992
   C-Kermit>echo \flpad($50,10,*)
   *******$50
   C-Kermit>
   ```

\Frpad(text,number,character)
   Right-pads the *text* to length *number* with *character*. If *character* is omitted, blank (space) is used.

\Fexecute(macroname arguments)
   Executes the named macro with the given arguments (if any) and returns the macro's RETURN value (if any). This function has a single argument, which is the macro name followed by its arguments. \fexec() is discussed more fully later in this chapter in the section on User-Defined Functions.

\Fcontents(variable-name)
   Returns the current definition (contents) of a variable. If the definition includes variable names or function references, these are copied literally, not replaced by their values. Example:
   ```
   C-Kermit>def \%a I like \%b.
   C-Kermit>def \%b pizza
   C-Kermit>echo \%a
   I like pizza.
   C-Kermit>echo \fcont(\%a)
   I like \%b.
   C-Kermit>
   ```

Built-in Functions   255

\Fdefinition(*macro-name*)

Returns the literal definition of the named macro. This is equivalent to the \m( ) notation for macro names. Example:

```
C-Kermit>define xxx echo \%a
C-Kermit>echo \fdef(xxx)
echo \%a

C-Kermit>echo \m(xxx)
echo \%a
C-Kermit>
```

Note how different degrees of textual replacement can be achieved by using (or not using) the \fliteral() and \fcontents() functions:

```
C-Kermit>def \%a foo            (\%a is "foo")
C-Kermit>def \%b I like \%ad.   (\%b includes \%a)
C-Kermit>echo \%b               (Full replacement)
I like food.                    (Nested variables are handled)
C-Kermit>echo \fcont(\%b)       (Contents of \%b)
I like \%ad.                    (Nested variables not handled)
C-Kermit>echo \flit(\%b)        (Take it literally)
\%b                             (No replacement at all)
C-Kermit>
```

Each of the following character-string related functions returns a numeric character string (a string of digits). Recall that their handling of alphabetic case is governed by the most recent SET CASE command. By default, alphabetic case is ignored.

\Flength(*string*)

Returns the length of the argument string, after evaluation of any variables or functions it might contain. Example:

```
C-Kermit>def \%a oofa!       (Define a variable)
C-Kermit>echo \flen(\%a)     (Length of its value)
5                            (The length is 5)
C-Kermit>
```

\Findex(*arg1,arg2* [*,arg3*])

Looks for a string, *arg1*, in another string, *arg2*, and tells its starting position:

```
C-Kermit>echo \find(ss,Mississippi)   (Find "ss" in Mississippi)
3
C-Kermit>
```

This means that the first occurrence of the string "ss" starts at position 3 in the string "Mississippi". You can also make this function start looking at a specified position in the string instead of starting from the beginning, by including the optional third argument, *arg3*, which must be numeric:

```
C-Kermit>echo \findex(ss,Mississippi,4)   (Find second "ss")
6
C-Kermit>
```

Character positions are numbered starting from 1. The first character is at position 1, the second character at position 2, and so on. If the string *arg1* is not found in *arg2*, the return value is zero:

```
C-Kermit>echo \findex(sss,Mississippi)
0
C-Kermit>
```

Any of the arguments can be variables of any kind (macro arguments, global variables, array elements, or built-in variables), or even functions. In this example we find the position of the first "i" in "Mississippi" that comes after the first "s":

```
C-Kermit>def \%a Mississippi
C-Kermit>echo \findex(i,\%a,\findex(s,\%a))
5
C-Kermit>
```

The last example shows the \Findex function calling itself, which is permissible.

Integer Arithmetic Functions and Commands

These functions require numeric arguments (numeric strings or variables whose values are numeric strings), representing integer (whole) numbers, which can be positive or negative. If the arguments are illegal in any way, these functions return the null (empty) string.

\Fmax(*arg1,arg2*)

Returns the maximum of its two numeric arguments. Examples:

```
C-Kermit>define \%x 9
C-Kermit>echo \fmax(12,\%x)
12
```

\Fmin(*arg1,arg2*)

Returns the minimum of its two numeric arguments.

\Feval(*expression*)

Evaluates the given arithmetic expression. The precedence is the normal, intuitive algebraic (or programming) precedence, and can be altered by the use of parentheses, which have higher precedence than any other operator. Spaces may be used to separate operators from operands, but they are not required. Examples:

```
C-Kermit>def \%x 6
C-Kermit>def \%y 10
C-Kermit>echo \feval(\%x)
6
C-Kermit>echo \feval(\%x + 2)
8
C-Kermit>echo \feval((\%x+2) * \%y)
80
C-Kermit>echo \feval(\%x + (2*\%y))
26
```

Built-in Functions 257

Table 12-2 \Feval( ) Operators

Operator	Fix	Precedence	Operation	Example	Result
\%a = 2,	\%b = -3,	\%c = 7,	\%d = 27		
( )	circum	1	Group	(\%a + 3) * (\%b-5)	-40
!	post	2	Factorial	\%c!	5040
~	pre	3	Logical NOT	~1	-2
-	pre	3	Negate	-\%a	-2
^	in	4	Raise to power	2^\%c	128
*	in	5	Multiply	\%c * 5	35
/	in	5	Divide	\%d / 5	5
%	in	5	Modulus	\%d % 5	2
&	in	5	Logical AND	\%d & 7	3
+	in	6	Add	\%a + \%c	9
-	in	6	Subtract	31 - \%c	24
|	in	6	Logical OR	\%c | 4	4
#	in	6	Exclusive OR	\%d#7	28
@	in	6	Greatest Common Divisor	\%d @ 51	3

Table 12-2 shows the mathematical operators accepted by \feval(). The heading marked *Fix* tells where the operator goes in relation to its operands. The choices are *in* (the operator goes in between its operands, for example 2+2); *pre* (it goes before its operand, for example -1, minus one); *post* (it goes after its operand, for example 3!, three factorial); or *circum* (it goes around its operands, for example (2+2), two plus two in parentheses). The "Precedence" column shows the precedence of the operator: the lower the number, the higher the precedence. For example, * has higher precedence than + so:

\feval(2 * 3 + 4 * 5)

is 26 because the multiplications are done before the addition (just like you learned in school).

As you can see from the table, parentheses have the highest precedence of all, so you can use them to change the order of evaluation:

\feval(2 * (3 + 4) * 5)

This makes Kermit evaluate the expression in parentheses, (3+4), first, so the result is 70 rather than 26.

Only integer arithmetic is available: no fractions, no decimals, no scientific notation. The remainder of an integer division operation is discarded (except, of course, by the modulus operator, which discards the quotient).

Note that the # Exclusive OR operator is the same as one of Kermit's comment introducers, so you can't use it in an \feval() function unless you make sure it is not followed by a space:

```
C-Kermit>echo \feval(7 # 2)
?Invalid - echo \feval(7 #
C-Kermit>echo \feval(7#2)
5
```

See the rules for comments on page 23.

Two Kermit commands are also available to perform simple arithmetic on variables:

INCREMENT *name [value]*
  Adds the *value* to the named variable. If the *value* is omitted, adds 1. If the variable does not have a numeric value, prints an error message and fails. Examples:

```
C-Kermit>def \%a 9
C-Kermit>increment \%a
C-Kermit>echo \%a
10
C-Kermit>incr \%a 5
C-Kermit>echo \%a
15
C-Kermit>incr \%a -20
C-Kermit>echo \%a
-5
C-Kermit>
```

DECREMENT *name [value]*
  Subtracts the *value* from the named variable. If the *value* is omitted, subtracts 1. If the variable does not have a numeric value, prints an error message and fails. This example is a loop that counts down from 10 to 0:

```
def \%i 10
while not < \%i 0 { echo \%i, decr \%i }
```

The *value* given in the INCREMENT and DECREMENT commands need not be a constant. You can include variables:

```
C-Kermit>define \%n 1
C-Kermit>while < \%n 5000 { echo \%n, increment \%n \%n }
 1 2 4 8 16 32 64 128 256 512 1024 2048 4096
C-Kermit>
```

And you can use any other item that C-Kermit can evaluate into a number: backslash character-codes, array references, function invocations, environment variables, or built-in variables.

File Functions

C-Kermit offers two functions for dealing with files. The first, \Ffiles(), returns the number of files that match a given file specification, possibly containing wildcard characters. The second, \Fnextfile(), returns the names, one by one, of each file that matched the file specification given to \Ffiles().

\Ffiles(*filespec*)

Returns the number of files that match the given file specification, for example:

```
C-Kermit>echo \ffiles(ck*.c)
37
C-Kermit>
```

If no files match, the result is 0. If too many files match, the result is –1.

\Fnextfile()

Returns the next filename that matches the \Ffiles() file specification, until there are none left, or until you use \Ffiles() again, or until you execute any command (such as SEND, TYPE, or OPEN) that parses a filename. \Ffiles() and \Fnextfile let you write loops that process a selected group of files.

Here is an example that defines a macro called AUTOSEND that you can use to send a wildcard group of files to a Kermit server, switching between text and binary mode automatically for each file. In this case, binary mode is used if the last four characters of the file's name are .exe.

```
define autosend -
assign \%n \ffiles(\%1),-              ; How many files match
echo files = \%n,-                     ; Print a message
declare \&f[\%n],-                     ; Make an array for names
for \%i 1 \%n 1 { -                    ; Copy names into array
    asg \&f[\%i] \fnextfile() -
},-
for \%i 1 \%n 1 { -                    ; Loop for each file
    xif eq ".exe" "\fright(\&f[\%i],4)" {- ; If suffix is ".exe"
        set file type binary,-         ; use binary mode,
        echo Sending \&f[\%i] (binary),- ; print a message,
        send \&f[\%i] -                ; and send the file
    } else {-                          ; Otherwise,
        set file type text,-           ; use text mode,
        echo Sending \&f[\%i] (text),- ; print a message
        send \&f[\%i] -                ; and send the file
    },-
}
```

Invoke this macro with a command like:

```
C-Kermit>autosend oofa.*
```

Replace oofa.* with the file specification of your choice. Of course, this example depends on the receiving Kermit's ability to switch automatically between text and binary mode based on the Attribute packet sent by C-Kermit (see Table 1-1).

Can We Talk?

You can already carry on a dialog with C-Kermit. It prompts you for a command, you type a command, it prompts you for another one, and so on. You can do this because you're a Kermit expert. But suppose you want to set up a procedure for someone who is not a Kermit expert. Here are the commands you can use to issue prompts on the screen and read responses from the keyboard:

ASK *variable text*
Prints the text on the screen and reads what the user types in response, up to a carriage return. Stores what the user types in the named variable, without the terminator. The variable can be a global variable (\%a-z), a macro argument (\%1-9), or an array element (\&a-z[ ]). The user's characters echo on the screen as they are typed.

ASKQ *variable text*
"Ask Quietly." Just like ASK, but does not echo what the user types. Use ASKQ to read passwords or other sensitive information.

Example:
```
C-Kermit>ask \%n   What is your name\?
What is your name?Olaf
C-Kermit>askq \%p Hello, \%n, what's your password\?
Hello Olaf, what's your password?_____
C-Kermit>
```

As you can see, Kermit strips leading and trailing blanks from the ASK and ASKQ prompts, and it requires you to quote any question marks with backslash (an unquoted question mark gives a help message). If you want to have leading or trailing spaces in the prompt, enclose it in curly braces:

```
C-Kermit>ask \%n {   What is your name\? }
   What is your name? Olga
C-Kermit>
```

When the user responds to the prompt, all of Kermit's special command editing keys are active: Delete, Backspace, Ctrl-W, Ctrl-U, Ctrl-R, etc., so the user doesn't have to worry about typing a perfect response. As always, the question mark key is used to request a help message. If the user types a question mark with the intention of including it in the response, a helpful message is printed that says to type \? to include a question mark literally:

```
C-Kermit>ask \%f { What files do you want to send\? }
 What files do you want to send? oofa.? Please respond.
 Type \? to include a question mark in your response.
 What files do you want to send? oofa.\?
C-Kermit>echo OK, I will send \%f
OK, I will send oofa.?
C-Kermit>
```

In an interactive dialog with a user, it is common to ask a question that requires a Yes or No answer. A friendly program does not care if the user spells these words out in full or abbreviates them, nor about their alphabetic case. And neither does C-Kermit's GETOK command:

GETOK *[text]*
> Asks the user a yes-or-no question. The *text* is the question. If you omit the text, Kermit supplies the question "Yes or no?". The user can answer by typing Yes, No, or OK in upper- or lowercase, abbreviated or in full. Any other answer results in an error message and a repetition of the question. The GETOK command succeeds if the user gives an affirmative answer and fails if the answer is negative. Here is an example in which the user is asked whether temporary files should be deleted, and then the files are deleted or not according to the answer:
>
> ```
> getok Should I delete your temporary files\?
> xif success { -
>     echo Deleting temporary files *.tmp...,-
>     delete *.tmp -
> } else {-
>     echo OK, I won't.-
> }
> ```

To include leading or trailing blanks, enclose the question *text* in curly braces:

```
C-Kermit>getok \%a { OK to proceed? }
  OK to proceed? ok
C-Kermit>sho status
  SUCCESS
C-Kermit>
```

Calculators and Adding Machines

Here is a macro you can use to have Kermit evaluate arithmetic expressions for you interactively. Kermit's answer to the pocket calculator:

```
define CALC -
echo Press Return to exit,-         ; Say how to exit
def \%1 1,-                          ; Initial condition for loop
while defined \%1 { -                ; Loop until they want to exit
    ask \%1 { expression: },-        ; Ask for an expression
    echo \flpad(\feval(\%1),10)-     ; Evaluate and print answer
},-
echo Back to...                      ; All done
```

To use the calculator, first execute this macro definition.[36] Then just type CALC at any time to the C-Kermit prompt. You can type any kind of arithmetic expression listed in Table 12-2, and the operands can be either integer constants or variables with integer values.

---

[36]You'll find a copy in the command demonstration file, CKEDEMO.INI, that is distributed with C-Kermit.

```
$ kermit                                (Start Kermit)
C-Kermit 5A(188), 23 Nov 92
Type ? or HELP for help
C-Kermit>def \%a 7                      (Define some variables)
C-Kermit>def \%b 9
C-Kermit>calc                           (Start the calculator)
Press Return to exit
  expression: 1+1                       (Add 1 and 1)
        2
  expression: 6!                        (6 factorial)
       720
  expression: 2^16                      (2 to the 16th power)
     65536
  expression: (\%a + 3) * (\%b - 5)     (Expression with variables)
        40
  expression:                           (Press Return to exit)
Back to...
C-Kermit>
```

Here is a small interactive program that imitates an adding machine, illustrating the use of ASKQ along with functions that line things up, WHILE loops, and other items you learned in this chapter:

```
define ADDINGMACHINE -
echo Adding machine.,-
echo Type numbers or press Return to quit...,-
assign \%3 0,-                                   ; Initialize the sum
while = 1 1 {-                                   ; Loop till done
    askq \%1,-                                   ; Wait for a number
    if not def \%1 break,-                       ; Return quits loop
    increment \%3 \%1,-                          ; Add it to the sum
    write screen \flpad(\%1,10)\flpad(\%3,10),-  ; Print results
},-
echo Total\flpad(\%3,15,.)
```

Once this macro is defined (for example, by TAKEing the C-Kermit demo file) you can add up a column of numbers any time you want (integers only, positive or negative): just type ADDINGMACHINE at the C-Kermit prompt.

Special Effects

When commands like ECHO and ASK print your text on the screen, they evaluate all variables and other backslash codes first. This lets you achieve special effects on the screen. For example, you can send escape sequences for clearing the screen, positioning the cursor, highlighting text, changing colors, and so on. Kermit itself has no built-in knowledge of terminal control sequences, so you're on your own for this. A common terminal type is the DEC VT100 series [25], and some useful escape sequences (which also apply to the VT200, 300, and 400 series) are listed in Table 12-3. For other types of terminals, see your terminal manual.

Table 12-3 Selected VT100 Escape Sequences

Escape Sequence	Kermit Notation	Description
Ctrl-H	\8	Backspace cursor
Ctrl-I	\9	Horizontal tab
ESC # 3	\27#3	Double height/width line, top half
ESC # 4	\27#4	Double height/width line, bottom half
ESC # 6	\27#4	Double width line
ESC D	\27D	Moves cursor down one line
ESC M	\27M	Moves cursor up one line
ESC [r ; c H	\27[r;cH	Moves cursor to row r, column c
ESC [r ; c r	\27[r;cr	Sets scrolling region to row r, column c
ESC [0 J	\27[0J	Erases from cursor to end of screen
ESC [1 J	\27[1J	Erases from start of screen to cursor
ESC [2 J	\27[2J	Erases entire screen
ESC [0 K	\27[0K	Erases from cursor to end of line
ESC [1 K	\27[1K	Erases from start of line to cursor
ESC [2 K	\27[1K	Erases entire line
ESC [? 5 h	\27[\?5h	Reverse video, whole screen
ESC [? 5 l	\27[\?5l	Normal video, whole screen
ESC [0 i	\27[0i	Prints current screen
ESC [4 i	\27[0i	Stops transparent printing
ESC [5 i	\27[0i	Starts transparent printing
ESC [0 m	\27[0m	Regular characters
ESC [1 m	\27[1m	Bold characters
ESC [2 m	\27[2m	Underscored characters
ESC [5 m	\27[5m	Blinking characters
ESC [7 m	\27[7m	Reverse-video characters
ESC [3x m	\27[3xm	Selects foreground color (see Table V-9)
ESC [4x m	\27[4xm	Selects background color (see Table V-9)
ESC Z	\27Z	Terminal type query (host to terminal)
ESC [? 1 c	\27[\?1c	VT100 terminal ID (terminal to host)
ESC [? 6 c	\27[\?6c	VT102 terminal ID (terminal to host)
ESC [? 6 c	\27[\?62c	VT200 terminal ID (terminal to host)
ESC [? 6 c	\27[\?63c	VT300 terminal ID (terminal to host)
ESC [3 4 h	\27[34h	Executes MS-DOS Kermit TERMINALS macro
ESC [3 4 l	\27[34l	Executes MS-DOS Kermit TERMINALR macro

Several of the entries in the table require you to insert specific values. The escape sequence to position the cursor to a specific row and column needs the row and column number, separated by a semicolon (;). The rows and columns are numbered from one. So to position the cursor in the upper left corner of the screen:

\27[1;1H

and to put it in row 17, column 53:

\27[17;53H

To "home" the cursor and clear the screen:

\27[1;1H\27[2J

The escape sequence for setting the scrolling region requires the row numbers of the top and bottom lines; for example, to use lines 7 through 24:

\27[7;24r

To make the whole screen the scrolling region, use:

\27[r

The escape sequences for setting foreground and background color are specific to the MS-DOS Kermit and OS/2 C-Kermit VT terminal emulators running on PCs with color monitors and adapters. The *x* in the escape sequence is replaced by a digit between 0 and 7 to select the color (0 = black, 1 = red, 2 = green, 3 = orange, 4 = blue, 5 = amethyst, 6 = turquoise, 7 = white), for example:

\27[36m\27[45m

results in turquoise characters on an amethyst background.

Here is an example for you to try. If you have an IBM PC or compatible with a color monitor running MS-DOS Kermit 3.0 or later or OS/2 C-Kermit, the results will be in technicolor. Put these commands in a file and TAKE the file from C-Kermit:[37]

```
define on_exit echo \27[r\27[0m\27[1;1H\27[2JGoodbye!
define \%g \27[0m\27[32m\27[7m\frepeat(=,80)\27[0m\27[34m
echo \27[1;1H\27[2J\%g\27[47m
ask \%n { What is your name\? \27[30m\27[7m}
echo \%g
echo \27[35m\27[5m Welcome to Kermit, \27[30m\27[5m\%n\13\10\%g
echo \13\10\27[0J\27[7;24r\27[22;1H
set prompt {\%g\13\10 \27[33mWhat is your command\? \27[34m}
```

Without giving away any secrets, it can be observed that this program does some unusual things to VT-series terminals. Note the use of the ON_EXIT macro to put the terminal back to normal when C-Kermit exits.

---

[37] A copy of this file is distributed with C-Kermit as CKEVT.INI.

PC Printing

Here is a simpler but a somewhat more useful example of using escape sequences. It lets C-Kermit print a file on your local printer if you have a VT100-series terminal (VT102 or higher) or compatible, or an IBM PC or compatible with MS-DOS Kermit. It sends the escape sequence to turn on transparent printing, then displays the file, which should cause your terminal or emulator to send the text to the printer instead of the screen, and then sends the escape sequence to turn off transparent printing.

```
define vtprint echo \27[5i, type \%1, echo \27[4i
```

Execute this macro definition, and then print files on your local printer like this:

```
C-Kermit>vtprint oofa.txt
```

File Transfer Shortcuts

Here is a set of easy file-transfer macros you can use between C-Kermit and a PC with MS-DOS Kermit. They let you initiate file transfers from C-Kermit while in MS-DOS Kermit CONNECT mode, without having to escape back to MS-DOS Kermit.

MS-DOS Kermit recognizes a special pair of VT terminal escape sequences that it associates with MS-DOS Kermit macros named TERMINALS and TERMINALR,[38] which you can define as follows:[39]

```
define TERMINALS server, connect    ; Respond to PCGET
define TERMINALR receive, connect   ; Respond to PCSEND
```

These definitions tell MS-DOS Kermit to enter the appropriate file transfer mode automatically upon receipt of the TERMINALS or TERMINALR escape sequences, and then to CONNECT back to the host when the file transfer is complete.

Also add these lines to your C-Kermit initialization file:

```
define PCGET echo \27[\?34h,-         ; Send TERMINALS escape sequence
  get \%1,-                           ; GET the files
  finish                              ; FINISH MS-DOS Kermit server

define PCSEND asg \%9 \ffiles(\%1),-     ; How many files match?
  if = 0 \%9 end 1 {\?File not found},-  ; None, fail
  set delay 1, echo \27[\?34l,-          ; Send TERMINALR sequence
  if = 1 \%9 send \%1 \%2,-              ; Send single file with as-name
  else send \%1                          ; or file group with no as-name
```

---

[38] See Table 12-3. MS-DOS Kermit must be emulating a VT100 or higher VT-series terminal for these sequences to be recognized.

[39] TERMINALR and TERMINALS are defined this way in the standard initialization for MS-DOS Kermit, MSKERMIT.INI.

The PCGET macro sends the TERMINALS sequence to the PC, which activates its TERMINALS macro, which in turn puts MS-DOS Kermit in server mode. Then a GET command is sent to the PC for the desired files, and when the transfer is complete, a FINISH command is sent to take MS-DOS Kermit back out of server mode. Then MS-DOS Kermit executes the next command from the TERMINALS definition, which is CONNECT, so you are automatically back where you started.

The PCSEND macro works in a similar way, but it also does a bit of extra checking to see whether you are sending one file or a group of files, so it can use the appropriate form of the SEND command.

Now, at the C-Kermit prompt you can use PCSEND to send a file to your PC and PCGET to get a file from your PC without ever having to escape back to the MS-DOS Kermit prompt. Try it! Remember, if a C-Kermit command needs to include directory fields in a PC filename, be sure to double the backslashes. Examples:

```
C-Kermit>pcget mskermit.ini
C-Kermit>pcget c:\\dos\\config.sys
C-Kermit>pcsend ckermit.ini
C-Kermit>pcsend ckermit.ini c:\\ckermit\\ckermit.ini
```

User-Defined Functions

You've seen Kermit's built-in functions. Now you'll learn to write your own. A user-defined function is a macro that returns a value. To return a value, a new command is needed:

RETURN [*value*]

Terminates the execution of the current macro and makes the *value* available to the caller (that is, the command level from which the macro was invoked). If the RETURN command is used in a command file, it can not return a value; only macros may return values. The RETURN command can not be used in the command list of a FOR, WHILE, or XIF command. Here is a user-defined function that returns the first character of its argument:

```
define first return \fsubstr(\%1,1,1)
```

The RETURN command can also be used without a value, in which case an empty (null) value is returned, in which case it is equivalent to the END 0 command.

But exactly how is the function's value returned? It is returned in two ways: first, it is stored in the built-in variable \v(return):

```
C-Kermit>define first return \fsubstr(\%1,1,1)
C-Kermit>ask \%a { Type something: }
 Type something: oofa
```

```
C-Kermit>first \%a
C-Kermit>echo The first character of \%a is "\v(return)".
The first character of oofa is "o".
C-Kermit>
```

Second, if you put the macro invocation (that is, the macro name followed by its arguments) inside the parentheses of the \fexecute() function, the macro's RETURN value becomes the result of \fexecute():

```
C-Kermit>echo The first character of \%a is "\fexec(first \%a)".
The first character of oofa is "o".
C-Kermit>
```

If a macro does not include a RETURN statement, or it omits the RETURN value, \fexecute() and \v(return) return the null (empty) value.

Functions that Call Themselves

User-defined functions can refer to macro arguments, global or built-in variables. They can call upon built-in functions and other user-defined functions, and they can even call upon themselves. Here, for example, is a function that adds all the numbers from 1 up to and including its argument:[40]

```
def sum if not def \%1 return,-    ; Make sure there is an argument
  if not numeric \%1 return,-      ; Make sure argument is numeric
  if not > \%1 0 return,-          ; Make sure argument is positive
  if = \%1 1 return 1,-            ; If argument is 1, the sum is 1
  else return \feval(\%1 + \fexecute(sum \feval(\%1 - 1)))
```

Translated into English, it reads something like this: If you ask me to add up all the numbers from 1 to 1, I can tell you right away the answer is 1. If the number is larger than one, the answer is the number you gave me plus the sum of all the numbers less than that. The process repeats to get the sum of "all the numbers less than that," until we reach 1. This process is called *recursion*. To give yourself a better idea how it works, try working through the process for the number 3.

You can write a simple macro to call the sum function and print its value:

```
C-Kermit>def addemup echo sum = \fexec(sum \%1)
C-Kermit>addemup 6
sum = 21
C-Kermit>addem 11
sum = 66
C-Kermit>
```

The sum function will not work with numbers larger than C-Kermit's maximum recursion depth (which is 20 by default) plus one.

---

[40]Of course, we all know there is a closed solution to this problem: $(n \times (n + 1)) / 2$, compliments of the 7-year-old Karl Friedrich Gauss (1777-1855).

One final note about user-defined functions: any Kermit action commands (like SEND, MSEND, RECEIVE, CONNECT, SERVER, GET, REMOTE, FINISH, BYE, or MAIL) that you include in a macro to be executed by \fexecute() will be ignored. This is because the \fexecute() function is parsed and executed in the middle of another command, and affairs would become quite confused if a file transfer display or terminal emulation screen suddenly popped up before the command containing the \fexecute() was finished.

Reading and Writing Files and Commands

Like any conventional programming language, C-Kermit lets you open, read, write, and close files. Computer people call this I/O (Input/Output). The commands, not surprisingly, are OPEN, READ, WRITE, and CLOSE.

OPEN { READ, WRITE, APPEND } *filename*

Opens the given file in READ, WRITE, or APPEND mode. A READ file must already exist and is opened for reading only. A WRITE file is created as a new file, overwriting any existing file of the same name. An APPEND file, if it already exists, will have new information added to the end of it. If it does not exist, it is created as a new file.

```
open read oofa.txt          ; Read from the file oofa.txt
open write oofa.new         ; Create the file oofa.new
open append oofa.log        ; Write to end of oofa.log
```

These commands fail if the file can't be found or can't be opened in the desired mode, for example if a file is protected against you.

OPEN { !READ, !WRITE } *command*

You also can open files that are not really files at all, but system commands, programs, or applications, and then read from their output or write to their input. Examples:

```
open !read dir /except=(*.doc,*.hlp) /after=yesterday ck*.*
```

The example causes VMS or OpenVMS to produce a list of all the files in the current directory whose names start with CK, except the ones with filetypes of .DOC or .HLP, that were created since yesterday. C-Kermit can read this list and use it, for example, to send the selected files.

The next example shows how Kermit can write lines of text to the UNIX, OS/2, or OS-9 SORT utilities directing the sorted output to the file `alpha.txt`:

```
open !write sort > alpha.txt
```

Only one READ or !READ file can be open at once, and only one WRITE, !WRITE, or APPEND file can be open at once. Reading from and writing to subprocesses only works under operating systems that support straightforward methods of input and output redirection.

Now that we know how to open files and processes for reading and writing, we also need to get data in and out of them. For this, we use the READ and WRITE commands:

READ *variable-name*

Reads the next line from the current OPEN READ or OPEN !READ file and makes it the value of the named variable, for example:

```
read \%a
```

If no more lines remain in the file, the command fails and the file is closed automatically. Here is an example that reads and displays an entire file:

```
open read oofa.txt
read \%a
while success { echo \%a, read \%a }
```

WRITE *file text*

Writes the given text to the indicated log or file. The *text* can include backslash codes, variables, etc., which are fully evaluated before the text is written. The *text* is not terminated by a line terminator in the output file unless you include the appropriate backslash code(s). Example:

```
write debug-log { Here is where the trouble starts...\13\10}
```

The *file* can be any of the following files or logs, which must already be open:

DEBUG-LOG

The C-Kermit debugging log (opened with LOG DEBUG).

FILE

The currently open WRITE, !WRITE, or APPEND file.

PACKET-LOG

C-Kermit's packet log (opened with LOG PACKETS).

SCREEN

Your screen. WRITE SCREEN is just like ECHO except that WRITE does not supply a line terminator at the end. The SCREEN "file" is always open, so C-Kermit does not give you a command to open or close it.

ERROR

Just like WRITE screen, but using standard error rather than standard output. Useful on systems like UNIX that separate the two, especially when output redirection has been done on standard output.

SESSION-LOG

C-Kermit's session log (opened with LOG SESSION).

TRANSACTION-LOG

C-Kermit's file transfer transaction log (opened with LOG TRANSACTIONS).

When you are finished reading or writing a file (or process), you should close it. The command is:

CLOSE *name*
> Closes the named file: DEBUG-LOG, PACKET-LOG, SESSION-LOG, TRANSACTION-LOG, READ, !READ, WRITE, !WRITE, or APPEND. A READ or !READ file is closed automatically when end-of-file (EOF) is encountered during a READ operation, but it does no harm to close it again. WRITE, !WRITE, and APPEND files should be closed explicitly. All files are closed automatically when you EXIT or QUIT from C-Kermit.

Here is a C-Kermit program that reads lines from one file, OOFA.TXT, and writes them into another file, NUMBERED.TXT, with line numbers added:

```
set take error off                  ; So EOF can be handled
open read oofa.txt                  ; Open input file "oofa.txt"
open write numbered.txt             ; Open output file "numbered.txt"
define \%c 0                        ; Start line counter at zero
:loop                               ; Loop to read all lines
read \%a                            ; Read one line into \%a
if fail goto done                   ; Catch EOF this way
increment \%c                       ; Count the line
write file \flpad(\%c,3). \%a\10    ; Format and write it
goto loop                           ; Go back and get more
:done
close write                         ; Finished, close the files
echo Lines copied: \%c.             ; Print a message
```

A Mass Mailing

In this example we use C-Kermit's file input/output feature on a UNIX computer to send annual review letters to our employees via electronic mail—the personal touch! These are form letters that look like this:

```
Dear \m(name),
You have done a \m(word) job this year.
Keep up the \m(word) work.
```

This is called a *boilerplate*, and we have stored it in a file called BOILER. It contains C-Kermit variables that will be filled in by our program for each employee, based on records in another file called EMPLOYEES that look like this:

name address comment

In each record, *name* is the employee's name, *address* is the employee's electronic mail address, and *comment* is a word characterizing the employee's performance for the year, for example:

```
Olga ole great
Olaf oop swell
Ivan itt terrible
```

Here is the program that reads and processes the records, sending personalized mail to each employee. Store this in a file called REVIEWS and then TAKE REVIEWS.

```
define \%d 100              ; Maximum lines in a letter
declare \&z[\%d]            ; Array for lines
def split asg name \%1,-    ; SPLIT macro assigns words in its
   asg user \%2,-           ; argument to separate variables
   asg word \%3
open read boiler            ; Open the boilerplate file
if fail stop 1 Can't open boilerplate file

; Loop to read each line of boilerplate file.
;
for \%n 1 \%d 1 {-          ; \%n is the line number
   read \&z[\%n],-          ; Store this line in the array
   if fail break-           ; Stop at end of file
}
if = \%i \%d -              ; If too many lines before end of file,
   end 1 Your letter is too long ; stop here

; Read employee records
;
def \%m 0                   ; Employee counter
open read employees         ; Open the employee file
if fail -                   ; Handle failure
   end 1 Can't open employee file
:loop                       ; Loop for each employee
read \%e                    ; Read a record
if fail goto done           ; Failure means we're done
increment \%m               ; Got a record, count the employee

split \%e                   ; Get name, address, and comment

; Write boilerplate lines to mail program, making substitutions
;
open !write mail \m(user)   ; Start the mail program
for \%i 1 \%n 1 {-          ; Write lines 1 through n
   write file \&z[\%i]\10-  ; to the mail program "file"
}
close write                 ; Close the mail program
goto loop                   ; Go back for next employee
:done                       ; Come here when finished
echo Done, letters: \%m     ; Print completion message
```

Now you have fulfilled your managerial responsibilities, spending mere seconds on a task that normally takes weeks. While your employees are contemplating their review letters, you can go back to playing Space Adventure on your computer.

Chapter 13

Script Programming

You're probably wondering what Chapters 11 and 12 have to do with data communications and file transfer. On the surface, not much. But the programming techniques introduced there—repetitive loops, decision making, and so on—resemble the things you do yourself when you are interacting with a remote computer. In this chapter, you will use these techniques to teach C-Kermit to do automatically exactly what you do when you use it by hand to connect to, log in to, and use a remote computer or service.

Anything you do with Kermit—whether at the command prompt or in CONNECT mode—in a routine and repetitive way is a good candidate for automation. A certain sequence of commands is always required for dialing out or for making a network connection. A certain dialog is required for logging in to a particular remote computer or service. Automating these routine procedures has all sorts of benefits. It makes them easier, it makes them easily accessible to the computer-shy, and it lets computers talk to each other even when no humans are around: late at night when phone rates are lowest, the computers can call each other up and exchange data automatically.

○ ○ ○ ○
The material in this chapter is primarily for those who use C-Kermit in *local mode*; that is, for dialing out or making network connections from C-Kermit to remote computers or services. If you will be using C-Kermit only in *remote* mode, you might want to skip this chapter.

Automated Connection Establishment

Before you can use a remote computer or service, you must establish a connection to it from your local computer. C-Kermit supports three types of connections: direct, network, and dialed. These methods are described in Chapter 3.

Let's write three general-purpose macros to automate the connection task, one for each type of connection. First we'll handle direct serial connections. For this kind of connection, Kermit only needs to know the device name and the connection speed. Let's define a macro that takes these two items as arguments, issues the appropriate commands, and checks to make sure the commands were successful:

```
COMMENT - SERIAL macro.  Arguments:
; \%1 = device name
; \%2 = speed
;
define SERIAL -
  if < \v(argc) 3 -                              ; All arguments given?
    end 1 Usage: SERIAL device speed,-           ; No
  set line \%1,-                                 ; OK, try to SET LINE
  if failure -                                   ; If this failed,
    end 1 Can't open device: \%1,-               ; print message, quit
  set speed \%2,-                                ; Try to set the speed
  if fail end 1 Unsupported speed: \%2,-         ; Failed
  echo Connection successful.                    ; Succeeded
```

The macro parameter \%1 is the device name and \%2 is the connection speed in bits per second. Both parameters are required; there is no default device or speed. If you omit any arguments, the macro gives a helpful usage message and fails. If you give too many arguments, the extra ones are ignored. Use the SERIAL macro like this:

```
C-Kermit>serial /dev/tty01 9600       (Direct connection from UNIX)
C-Kermit>serial txa5 2400             (Direct connection from VMS)
C-Kermit>serial com1 19200            (Direct connection from OS/2)
Connection successful.
C-Kermit>
```

Now let's define a NET macro for making network connections. The required items are the network type (such as TCP/IP or X.25) and the network host name or address:

```
COMMENT - NET macro.  Arguments:
; \%1 = network type
; \%2 = host name or address
;
define NET -
  if < \v(argc) 3 -                              ; Check arguments
    end 1 Usage: NET network host,-              ; Something missing
  set network \%1,-                              ; OK, set network type
  if fail -                                      ; Did it work?
    end 1 unsupported network: \%1,-             ; No, fail
```

274 Script Programming / Chapter 13

```
    set host \%2,-                    ; Make the connection
    if fail -                         ; Did it work?
       end 1 can't reach host: \%2,-  ; No, fail
    echo Connection successful.       ; Yes, done
```

You can use the NET macro like this:

```
C-Kermit>net tcp/ip foo.com          (Internet)
C-Kermit>net x.25 31182120010300
Connection successful.
C-Kermit>
```

For dialed connections, Kermit needs to know the modem type, the name of the device the modem is connected to, the speed for dialing, and the phone number. Since the called number might be busy, we will have our dialup procedure try dialing up to 10 times, waiting a full minute between each try.[41] If you are running the CALL macro interactively, you can press any key during the 60-second wait to wake it up and try again (this is a property of the PAUSE command). Here is our CALL macro:

```
COMMENT - CALL macro.   Arguments:
; \%1 = modem type
; \%2 = device name
; \%3 = speed
; \%4 = phone number
;
define CALL -
    if < \v(argc) 5 -            ; All arguments present?
       end 1 Usage: CALL modem device speed number,-
    set modem \%1,-              ; Set modem type
    if fail end 1 unknown modem type: \%1,-
    set line \%2,-               ; Communication device
    if fail end 1 can't open device: \%2,-
    set speed \%3,-              ; Communication speed
    if fail end 1 unsupported speed: \%3,-
    for \%i 1 10 1 { -           ; Try up to 10 times
        xif > \%i 1 { -          ; Not first time, so ...
            echo Will redial in 1 minute: please wait...,-
            pause 60,-           ; Give message, wait one minute
            echo Redialing: try number \%i...,-
        },-
        dial \%4,-               ; Dial the number
        if success goto ok,-     ; If it answered, we're done
        hangup,-                 ; Hangup and continue the loop
    } -
    end 1 Can't place call: \%4,-
    :ok,-
    pause 1,-
    echo Connection successful.
```

---

[41] Adapt this to your own needs and local regulations if necessary. Note: the phone number can also be a dialing directory entry.

Again, all parameters are required:

```
C-Kermit>call
Usage: CALL modem device speed number
C-Kermit>call telebit /dev/acu 19200 555-9876
Connection successful.
C-Kermit>
```

The macro issues the DIAL-related commands in the proper order, verifies that each command was executed successfully, and then places the call. If the call completed successfully, the macro exits the FOR loop, pauses for one second, and issues the "Connection successful" message. Otherwise, the FOR loop is continued: a message is printed, Kermit waits for one minute, and then redials. If the connection is not made within 10 tries, the CALL macro fails.

When you give a LINE, NET, or CALL command and receive the "Connection successful" message in return, Kermit is ready to communicate with the remote host or service. Now you can give a CONNECT command and go through your normal login procedure.

These three macros, which are included in the standard C-Kermit initialization file, allow you to make different kinds of connections quite easily. For example, you don't have to remember the precise order of commands required for dialing out; the CALL macro takes care of the details for you.

Synchronization Commands

The connection-establishment macros are useful in their own right, but they are only the first step in the automation process. Now let's take the next step and automate the login procedure, in which you get the remote computer's attention and identify yourself to it. The method differs for each type of host or service, but each time you connect to a particular one, you usually perform the same steps.

How do you know what to put in a login script? The best way to construct a successful script is to go through the connection and login procedure once by hand, observing exactly which characters are sent and received, in what order, and with what timing. For example, let's use our new CALL macro to dial a VMS computer, then CONNECT to it and log in:

```
C-Kermit>call hayes /dev/cua 2400 7654321
Connection successful.              (Get confirmation message)
C-Kermit>connect                    (Connect to the VMS system)
<CR>                                (Type a carriage return)
Welcome to the Complaint Department
The more you complain, the longer you live.

Username: olga                      (See prompt, type username)
Password: _____                     (See prompt, type password)

Welcome to VMS V5.3
```

```
Last interactive login on Saturday, 14-MAR-1992 11:47
Last non-interactive login on Friday, 8-FEB-1992 20:02
$                              (See system prompt)
```

Observe what you type and what VMS sends back in return. The VMS system sends two types of text to your terminal: informational or greeting messages, and prompts that you should reply to. In this example, the prompts are:

`Username:`

and:

`Password:`

The login process is complete when you see the system prompt:

`$`

That's a dollar sign, followed by a space, on the left margin (\13\10$\32).

How can we automate this procedure? Let's clear up one misconception right away. You can't use the CONNECT command to send precomposed text to the remote computer. The CONNECT command always reads from the keyboard, never from a file. To illustrate, the following command file:

```
set line /dev/ttyh8
set speed 9600
connect
olga
secret
```

will *NOT* log the user Olga in to the remote computer. It will *not* send the strings "olga" and "secret" out the communication device. When you put a CONNECT command in a command file or macro, it does exactly what it does when you issue it interactively: it connects your keyboard and screen to the remote computer. The previous example will do just that, and then when you escape back from CONNECT mode, Kermit will try to execute the commands "olga" and "secret," which are not C-Kermit commands at all.

We can't simply blast text at the remote computer, expecting it to be processed correctly and at the right time. We have no guarantee this will happen. Instead, we want Kermit to do exactly what we do when we log in to the remote computer: look for a particular prompt, send the appropriate text, look for the next prompt, and so on, ignoring (just as we do) all the informational and greeting messages. We should *synchronize* our responses with the remote computer's prompts; we should *not* send text to the remote computer until it has issued a prompt for it.

Synchronization is important for many reasons. For example, you must not send characters on a half-duplex connection until the remote system has given you permission by sending you its line turnaround character, such as Ctrl-Q (Xon). If you (or Kermit) do not wait for the Xon, the characters sent prematurely are lost.

Even on full duplex connections there might be times when "typeahead" is not allowed. When you log in to UNIX, for example, the login program clears the input buffer of typeahead after issuing the "Password:" prompt and before reading your password, as a security measure; any part of your password that you send before the prompt appears is lost and your login fails.

So before we can write our login scripts, we must learn how to synchronize Kermit's responses with the prompts and actions of the remote computer.

The OUTPUT and INPUT Commands

A script program is a lot like a movie script containing a dialog between two actors. In a C-Kermit script, the actors are the two computers, and their lines are spoken and read, respectively, by C-Kermit's OUTPUT and INPUT commands. These commands do what you would do if you were interacting manually with the other computer during a CONNECT session: CONNECT requires a person at the controls, whereas INPUT and OUTPUT work on automatic pilot. OUTPUT "types" what you would type and INPUT reads the computer's response.

```
output \13              (Send a carriage return)
input 5 login:          (Wait 5 seconds for login prompt)
output olaf\13          (Send my user ID and <CR>)
input 5 Password:       (Wait for password prompt)
```

OUTPUT *text*

Sends the text out the currently selected communication device (serial port or network). Example:

C-Kermit>output I am not really typing this text.

The text may contain any of the backslash codes, variables, or functions described in Chapters 11–12.

C-Kermit>out The local time is \v(time).\13

It can also include the special code \B, which means to send a BREAK signal (the letter B can be upper- or lowercase), or the code \L (upper- or lowercase) to send a Long BREAK signal:[42]

C-Kermit>output \b   (Send a BREAK signal)

If you want to include leading or trailing spaces in the text, enclose it within curly braces:

C-Kermit>output { hello }

---

[42] On a serial connection, a BREAK is a 0.275-second spacing (0) condition and a Long BREAK is a 1.5-second spacing condition. On a TCP/IP TELNET connection, both \B and \L send the TELNET BREAK command to the remote TELNET server.

The enclosing braces are removed by C-Kermit's command processor, so the command just shown sends the word *hello* with a leading blank and a trailing blank. If you want to output text that actually begins and ends with curly braces, use two of each:

`C-Kermit>`<u>`output {{ hello }}`</u>   *(sends "{ hello }")*

Kermit does not add a carriage return or linefeed to the end of the OUTPUT text. You must include the appropriate backslash code, for example:

`C-Kermit>`<u>`output hello\13`</u>   *(Include a carriage return)*

The OUTPUT command succeeds unless there is a device output error, for example if the connection was broken.

INPUT *number [text]*

This command waits up to the given *number* seconds for the specified *text* to arrive from the communication device. The *text* may contain backslash codes, variables, or functions, which are evaluated before the arriving characters are scanned, but it may not include NUL (ASCII 0) characters, which serve only to terminate the text. To include leading or trailing spaces in the text, enclose it in curly braces. Alphabetic case in the text is ignored unless you have SET CASE ON. The 8th bit of each character is ignored if your current PARITY setting is anything but NONE (NONE is the default) or if your TERMINAL BYTESIZE is set to 7 (which is the default). If the text arrives within the specified interval, the command succeeds. If the specified number of seconds passes without the text arriving, the command terminates automatically and fails. Here is an example of how to test whether INPUT succeeds or fails:

```
input 10 login:                         ; Wait for login prompt
if failure end 1 No login prompt
```

If you omit the *text* from the INPUT command, it waits the given interval for any character at all, including NUL:

```
input 10                                ; Wait for any character
if failure end 1 No input
```

The last character that was read by the INPUT command, whether it succeeded or not, is available in the `\v(inchar)` variable. The number of characters read by the most recent INPUT command is given by the `\v(incount)` variable.

The INPUT and OUTPUT commands are hooked into the session log. If you have given a LOG SESSION command, all characters processed by INPUT AND OUTPUT are recorded in the session log, just as if they had been captured during CONNECT mode, except that no conversions take place (character-set translation, removal of linefeeds, and so on).

When you combine the INPUT and OUTPUT commands with the decision-making powers of the IF command, you can make Kermit imitate your own behavior: it "types" what you would have typed, it reads the responses, and makes the same decisions you would make.

Synchronization Commands **279**

Using the INPUT Buffer

Characters that are read by the INPUT command are copied into a special place called the INPUT buffer. You can refer to the contents of the INPUT buffer at any time using the built-in variable \v(input), and you can also look at the results of previous INPUT commands with the REINPUT command:

REINPUT *number text*

This command works like INPUT except that it scans the INPUT buffer for the text rather than reading new characters from the communication device. In other words, it reexamines the characters read by recent INPUT commands. If the requested text is present, REINPUT succeeds immediately, otherwise it fails immediately. Thus the timeout interval is ignored.

Here's a small script program in which Kermit dials a Hayes modem, reads the modem's response, and takes various actions depending on the response. The modem's response is a string of characters surrounded by linefeed characters (\10).

```
set speed 2400                      ; Use 2400 bps
output atdt7654321\13               ; Dial the number
input 40 \10                        ; Wait 40 sec for first linefeed
if failure -                        ; Did it come?
  end 1 No response                 ; Timed out, quit
input 20 \10                        ; Wait 20 sec for next linefeed
if failure -                        ; Did it come?
  end 1 Incomplete response         ; No
reinput 0 BUSY                      ; Got response, was it "BUSY"?
if success -                        ; Yes
  end 1 Line is busy                ; Quit with message
reinput 0 CONNECT                   ; Was it "CONNECT"?
if failure -                        ; No
  end 1 No CONNECT                  ; Give up
reinput 0 CONNECT 1200              ; Yes, did modem speed change?
if success set speed 1200           ; Yes, change Kermit's too
```

A script program can contain any Kermit commands at all, not just INPUT, REINPUT, IF, OUTPUT, and ECHO; for example, the SET SPEED command used in the example.

The INPUT buffer has a fixed size of 256 characters. Each INPUT command adds new material where the last INPUT command left off. When the end of the buffer is reached, new material wraps around to the beginning, overwriting what was there before (computer folks call this a *circular buffer*). Thus, the words or phrases you are looking for might have wrapped around too. The INPUT and REINPUT commands know how to cope with this situation, but if you are searching the \v(input) variable yourself with \findex(), you can use a trick like this:

```
assign \%i \findex(Enter Username:,\v(input)\v(input))
if = \%i 0 echo Not found
else echo Found at \%i
```

To handle the possibility that the phrase we are searching for, "Enter Username:", wrapped around, we concatenate the input buffer to itself. This pastes the beginning of the phrase at the end of the buffer to the end of the phrase at the beginning of the buffer, in case the phrase you are looking for is split in half (clear?). Speaking of clear, you can erase the entire INPUT buffer with the CLEAR command:

CLEAR *[{ INPUT-BUFFER, DEVICE-BUFFER, BOTH }]*
> The CLEAR command erases the contents of the INPUT command buffer, the communications device input buffer, or both (the default is BOTH).

In the following example, the CLEAR command ensures that each line that is INPUT from the communication device starts at the beginning of the input buffer, so it can be processed as a line of text (in this case, simply displayed) without any extraneous characters before or after it.

```
set input echo off              ; Echo lines ourselves
:loop                           ; Loop for each line
clear input-buffer              ; Clear INPUT buffer
input 5 \10                     ; Read a line
if eq \fsubstr(\v(input),1,1) $ -
  stop                          ; Stop if line starts with "$"
write screen \v(input)          ; Display the line
goto loop                       ; Go back for more
```

Controlling the INPUT Command

You can use the SET INPUT command to control how the INPUT and REINPUT commands match character sequences, display their progress, and so forth:

SET INPUT CASE { IGNORE, OBSERVE }
> Tells whether the INPUT command should pay attention to alphabetic case when comparing its text to the characters that arrive from the communication device. The default is IGNORE. Caseless comparison is possible only for unaccented Roman letters (A–Z = a–z). Synonym: **SET CASE { OFF, ON }**.

SET INPUT ECHO { OFF, ON }
> Tells whether the INPUT command should display the characters from the communication device on your screen as it receives them. The default is ON, meaning that arriving characters are displayed.

SET INPUT SILENCE *number*
> This command tells C-Kermit the longest interval of silence, in seconds, that will be tolerated by the INPUT command. If *number* is less than the timeout interval given in the INPUT command, and if *number* seconds pass without any characters arriving at all during the INPUT timeout interval, the INPUT command fails. If *number* is zero (0), which is the default, there is no silence constraint and only the INPUT timeout interval applies. Silence is broken by the arrival of any character at all, including NUL.

SET INPUT TIMEOUT-ACTION { PROCEED, QUIT }
> Tells whether a failure of the INPUT command to match its text within the specified timeout interval should cause the current macro or command file to be terminated automatically. SET INPUT TIMEOUT QUIT is equivalent to following every INPUT command with IF FAILURE END 1. The default is PROCEED, so you can use IF SUCCESS or IF FAILURE to decide what to do after each INPUT command.

If a command file or macro is terminated automatically because of an INPUT failure, the TAKE or (implied) DO command also fails.

International Character Sets

Character set translation is *not* done by INPUT, REINPUT, and OUTPUT commands. If you want to OUTPUT a non-ASCII character, include a backslash code for its numeric value in the OUTPUT command, for example:

```
output Gr\252\233e\13
```

to send *Grüße* and a carriage return to a host that uses the Latin-1 alphabet. Similarly, if you need to match international characters from the remote host in an INPUT command, you should also use backslash codes to express their values in the character set used on the remote host. See Tables VIII-4–VIII-6.

Translation is avoided in script commands because it would introduce more problems than it could solve: unwanted mistranslations, character-set dependent case conversion, scrambling of host-generated escape sequences, plus the possibility that the remote host is using a character set that Kermit doesn't know about. It's better for you to have total control in this critical area.

The PAUSE and WAIT Commands

Kermit scripts are often used to navigate through a series of devices until the final destination is reached. For example, suppose Kermit tells the local modem to dial a number; the call is answered by a port selection unit which, after a dialog, connects Kermit to a terminal server for another dialog, and from there to a front end, more dialog, and finally the remote host. Switching from device to device can take time, and if Kermit sends characters before the switching is finished, they might be lost. You can use the PAUSE and WAIT commands to allow for these periods of transition:

PAUSE [*number*]
> This command does absolutely nothing for the specified number of seconds. It pauses for 1 second if the *number* is omitted. Synonym: **SLEEP**. Examples:
>
> ```
> C-Kermit>pause 10              (Pause 10 seconds)
> C-Kermit>paus \%s              (Use value of variable)
> C-Kermit>pau                   (Pause 1 second)
> ```

The PAUSE command can be interrupted by typing any character on your keyboard.
Interruptions can be detected by an IF FAILURE command:

```
echo Please wait for 20 seconds...
pause 20
if failure end 1 Please don't touch the keyboard!
else echo Thank you for your patience.
```

The PAUSE command turns out to be surprisingly useful. Many a nonfunctioning script can be made to work by inserting PAUSEs at strategic locations.

MSLEEP *[number]*

This command sleeps (pauses) for the given number of *milliseconds* (thousandths of seconds). It is not interruptible from the keyboard except by Ctrl-C. Synonym: **MPAUSE**.

WAIT *[number=1 [{ CD, CTS, DSR } ...]]*

This command waits up to the specified number of seconds for all of the given modem signals to appear on the currently selected (SET LINE) serial communication device. If no modem signals are included, WAIT is equivalent to PAUSE. If all the specified modem signals don't appear within the prescribed interval, or if there is an interruption from the keyboard, the WAIT command fails. Examples:

```
wait 10 dsr
if fail end 1 Please turn on your modem
wait 45 cd
if fail end 1 No carrier
wait 5 dsr cts
if fail end 1 Modem not ready
```

The WAIT command fails immediately if the communication device is not a serial device, if the underlying operating system is not capable of reporting modem signal status, or if a system error occurs while trying to obtain the modem signals.

Constructing a Login Script for VMS

Let's look again at the procedure for logging in to a VMS computer:

```
C-Kermit>call hayes /dev/cua 2400 7654321
Connection successful.           (Get confirmation message)
C-Kermit>connect                 (Connect to VMS)
<CR>                             (Type a carriage return)
Welcome to the Complaint Department
The more you complain, the longer you live.

Username: olga                   (See prompt, type username)
Password: _____                  (See prompt, type password)

Welcome to VMS V5.3
```

```
Last interactive login on Saturday, 14-MAR-1992 11:47
Last non-interactive login on Friday, 8-FEB-1992 20:02
$                                       (See system prompt)
```

Now let's see if we can use the INPUT and OUTPUT commands to automate the process. We'll begin by writing a C-Kermit command file called VMS.SCR:

```
set input timeout quit          ; INPUT failures are fatal
set input echo off              ; Work quietly
output \13                      ; Send a carriage return
input 10 Username:              ; Wait 10 sec for username prompt
output olga\13                  ; Send username and carriage return
input 5 Password:               ; Wait 5 sec for password prompt
output secret\13                ; Send password and carriage return
input 100 {\13\10$ }            ; Wait 100 sec for system prompt
```

This is a straightforward translation of our actions and decisions into a Kermit script program. We don't know yet whether it actually works, but even on the surface it has one *extremely serious* flaw: the user's password is stored in the command file.

Never store a password in a file!

This is easy to fix. Just have the script program prompt for the password:

```
askq \%p Password:              ; Make the user type the password
```

and then use this variable when it is needed:

```
input 5 Password:               ; Wait 5 sec for password prompt
output \%p\13                   ; Send password and carriage return
```

Now let's run our script and see what happens:

```
C-Kermit>call hayes /dev/cua 2400 T987-6543
Connection successful.
C-Kermit>take vms.scr
Password:_____
?Input timed out
C-Kermit>
```

It didn't work, but we don't know why.

The first step in debugging a script program is to SET INPUT ECHO ON so we can watch it in action. Since there was a SET INPUT ECHO OFF command in the VMS.SCR file, we simply remove it and TAKE the file again:

```
C-Kermit>call hayes /dev/cua 2400 T987-6543
Connection successful.
C-Kermit>take vms.scr
Password:_____
Welcome to the Complaint Department
The more you complain, the longer you live.
```

```
login: olga
Password:

Welcome to VMS V5.3

Last interactive login on Saturday, 14-MAR-1992 11:48
Last non-interactive login on Friday, 8-FEB-1992 20:02

?Input timed out
C-Kermit>
```

It looks like the script program logged us in correctly, but we never got the system prompt. Don't panic. Scripts like this usually work. The failure of this one gives us a chance to track down and fix a subtle problem. In this case, there was an INVISIBLE CONVERSATION between VMS and your terminal, using control characters and escape sequences that did not appear on your screen when you logged in by hand.

To view these elusive fragments, use Kermit's SET DEBUG SESSION command to display control characters in ^X notation rather than passing them along to your terminal emulator. In this example, we log in to a VMS computer again:

```
C-Kermit>set line /dev/ttyb
C-Kermit>set debug session
C-Kermit>connect
Connecting to /dev/ttyb, speed 9600.
The escape character is CTRL-\ (ASCII 28).
Type the escape character followed by C to get back,
or followed by ? to see other options.
(Debugging Display...)
^M^J^G^M^J^M^JWelcome to the Complaint Department^M^JThe mor
e you complain, the longer you live.^M^J^M^JUsername: OLGA^M
^J^MPassword:          ^M^JYou again? Welcome to VMS V5.3
^M^J^M^JLast interactive login on Saturday, 14-MAR-1992 11:5
2^M^JLast non-interactive login on Friday, 8-FEB-1992 20:02^
M^J^[Z^[[c^[[0c^M^J%SET-W-NOTSET, error modifying TWA26:^M^J
-SET-I-UNKTERM, unknown terminal type^M^J$Ctrl-\C
(Back at Local System)
C-Kermit>
```

^M represents Carriage Return, ^J is Linefeed, and ^[is Escape (see Table VIII-1 on page 461). The user typed in her username and password, and then after the "last login" messages were printed, the characters ^[Z appeared on the screen: Escape followed by the letter Z, which is VMS's terminal identification query. Normally, you don't see this; your terminal or terminal emulator intercepts it and replies automatically with its ID (see Table 12-3 on page 264).

But your terminal did not respond this time because the Escape character was translated by Kermit's debugging display to ^[(Circumflex and Left Bracket), so VMS timed out after several seconds and sent additional terminal ID requests in different formats. Finally VMS gave up and complained that your terminal type was unknown. Meanwhile, we've learned all we need to correct our script program and automate our VMS logins. The new vms.scr file handles the terminal ID request and it also includes several other improvements. For example, it tries three times to get the VMS Username: prompt in case there was noise on the communication line.

```
COMMENT - C-Kermit command file VMS.SCR.
;
; Log in to a VMS system
;
askq \%p Password:                 ; Make user type in password
set count 3                        ; Allow 3 tries to log in
:getlogin
output \13                         ; Send a carriage return
input 5 Username:                  ; Wait for login prompt
if success goto dologin            ; Got it
if not count end 1 No Username prompt
goto getlogin                      ; Try again
:dologin
output olga\13                     ; Send my username
input 5 Password:                  ; Wait for password prompt
if fail end 1 No password prompt
output \%p\13                      ; Send password, carriage return
input 10 \27Z                      ; Get terminal ID query
if success output \27[\?1c         ; Send VT102 terminal ID
input 200 {\13\10$ }               ; Wait for system prompt
echo Login successful.
```

This command file should work. Let's try it:

```
C-Kermit>call hayes /dev/cua 2400 T987-6543
Connection successful.
C-Kermit>take vms.scr
Password:_____
Login successful.
C-Kermit>
```

It works, but it still has some shortcomings. First, it works only for user Olga. Each user would have to edit this file to substitute the appropriate username. And then there is the fact that the script is a command file. Suppose you change your default directory and try to run it again:

```
C-Kermit>cd articles
C-Kermit>call hayes /dev/cua 2400 T987-6543
Connection successful.
C-Kermit>take vms.scr
?No files match - vms.scr
C-Kermit>
```

Kermit can't find it. You could solve this problem by giving the full pathname of the command file in your TAKE command. Or you could define a macro to do it:

```
define govms take ~olga/kermit/vms.scr      ; (UNIX)
define govms take [olga.kermit]:vms.scr     ; (VMS or OpenVMS)
define govms take c:\\kermit\\vms.scr       ; (OS/2)
define govms take :udd:olga:kermit:vms.scr  ; (AOS/VS)
etc...
```

But now you need different definitions of the VMS macro depending on the operating system. If you keep the file in your home (login) directory, you can use C-Kermit's portable notation:

```
define govms take \v(home)vms.scr     ; (All systems)
```

This statement should work on any computer that C-Kermit runs on.

But you can fix the problems with this command file even more simply by rewriting it as a macro and putting its definition in your C-Kermit initialization file. That way, it is always ready for use, and the username and password can be passed to it as macro parameters.

```
COMMENT - VMSLOGIN macro.  Arguments:
; \%1 = VMS user ID
; \%2 = Password.  If password not supplied, it is prompted for.
;
define VMSLOGIN -
    if < \v(argc) 2 end 1 Usage: \%0 userid password,-
    while equal "\%2" "" { -
        askq \%2 { \%1's password: } -
    },
    set parity none,-              ; Set communication parameters
    set duplex full,-
    set handshake none,-
    set flow xon/xoff,-
    set term byte 8,-
    set comm byte 8,-
    set input timeout quit,
    for \%i 1 3 1 { -              ; Try 3 times to get prompt
        out \13,-                  ; Send carriage return
        in 5 Username:,-           ; Look for prompt
        if success goto dologin -  ; Success, go log in
    },-
    end 1 No Username prompt,
:dologin,-                         ; Come here to log in
    out \%1\13,-                   ; Send username, carriage return
    inp 5 Password:,-              ; Wait 5 sec for this prompt
    if fail end 1 No password prompt,-
    out \%2\13,-                   ; Send password
    def \%2,                       ; Quickly erase it from memory
    set input echo off,-           ; Protect terminal from this
    inp 10 \27Z,-                  ; Look for terminal ID query
    if success output \27[\?1c,-   ; Send response
    set input echo on,-            ; Echo input again
    inp 200 {\13\10$ },-           ; Wait for system prompt
    echo Login successful.
```

Shall we dissect this macro definition? The first command in the definition:

```
if < \v(argc) 2 end 1 Usage: \%0 userid password,-
```

checks to make sure you specified a user ID. If not, it gives you a usage message and fails. The next command is a WHILE loop:

```
while not defined \%2 { -
    askq \%2 { \%1's password: } -
},-
```

If the \%2 password variable is not already defined, C-Kermit prompts for a password and reads it from the keyboard into the \%2 variable without echoing it. A WHILE loop is used here rather than a simple IF command to make sure the user actually types in a password. If the user just hits the Return (Enter) key, the password prompt comes back, and the process repeats until some nonblank characters have been entered. The next section:

```
set parity none,-
set duplex full,-
set handshake none,-
set flow xon/xoff,-
set term byte 8,-
set comm byte 8,-
```

establishes the appropriate communication parameters. Some of them happen to be identical to C-Kermit's defaults, but we set them here deliberately to ensure the right settings in case they have been changed. Now we can start to send and read characters. The following section:

```
for \%i 1 3 1 { -            ; Try 3 times to get prompt
    out \13,-                ; Send carriage return
    in 5 Username:,-         ; Look for prompt
    if success goto dologin - ; Success, go log in
},-
end 1 No Username prompt,-
```

sends a carriage return and waits 5 seconds for the Username: prompt. If the prompt does not appear within the 5-second interval, the process is repeated up to 3 times. If the prompt does not appear after 3 tries, the VMSLOGIN macro fails. If it does appear, we go to the final section:

```
:dologin,-                        ; Come here to log in
    out \%1\13,-                  ; Send username, carriage return
    inp 5 Password:,-             ; Wait 5 sec for this prompt
    if fail end 1 No password prompt,-
    out \%2\13,-                  ; Send password
    def \%2,                      ; Quickly erase it from memory
    set input echo off,-          ; Protect terminal from this
    inp 10 \27Z,-                 ; Look for terminal ID query
    if success output \27[\?1c,-  ; Send response
    set input echo on,-           ; Echo input again
    inp 200 {\13\10$ },-          ; Wait for system prompt
    echo Login successful.
```

which sends the user ID and a carriage return (`\%1` is the user ID and `\13` is the carriage return), waits five seconds for the Password: prompt, sends the password that you had typed in previously, waits 10 seconds for the terminal type query (`\27Z`), responds with the VT-100 terminal ID (`\27[\?1c`, that is, escape-left-bracket-question-mark-one-c). INPUT ECHO is turned off during this period to prevent your terminal from seeing the terminal type query. The macro then waits up to a minute for the system prompt, dollar sign on the left margin followed by space (`{\13\10$ }`), to appear. If it does, the VMSLOGIN macro completes successfully.

The 200-second wait should allow ample time for system messages to be displayed and your login command procedure to be executed. Of course, the script continues as soon as the prompt appears; it doesn't always wait 200 seconds (and if it did, it would fail). If your system's prompt is anything other than dollar sign on the left margin followed by space, you'll have to change the INPUT command accordingly.

And so we have constructed our first login script. Before writing more of them, let's reflect on how it fits in to the big picture. The only prerequisite for VMSLOGIN is that the connection is already established. VMSLOGIN doesn't care what kind of connection it is. If you have defined this macro (for example, in your C-Kermit initialization file), you can use it after any of the connection-establishment macros, SERIAL, NET, or CALL:

```
C-Kermit>serial /dev/ttyh8 19200
Connection successful.
C-Kermit>vmslogin ivan
 ivan's password: _____
Login successful.
C-Kermit>
```

In the next few sections, we will write login scripts for several other kinds of computers and services. When we are done, we will have quite a versatile set of building blocks, allowing us to make many kinds of connections to many kinds of computers and services, and they will be completely portable among all implementations of C-Kermit. And then we will see what we can build with these blocks. But first let's look at how to log in to a few more common computers and services.

A UNIX Login Script

The normal procedure for logging in to a UNIX computer is to type a carriage return (press the Enter key), type a username in response to the `login:` prompt, and then type a password in response to the Password: prompt. But unlike VMS, most UNIX systems do not use your initial carriage return for speed recognition. Therefore, it is possible that the speeds on the two ends don't agree: the login prompt appears to you as garbage, and whatever you type looks like garbage to UNIX.

You can't be expected to change your connection speed to match that of the remote UNIX system because your communication device might not support the UNIX speed. For example, you might have dialed from a 2400 bps modem, but the UNIX system answers at 9600 bps. Therefore you have to get the UNIX system to change its communication speed to match yours. There is a time-honored ritual to accomplish this: when you send a BREAK signal, which comes through as a BREAK at any speed, UNIX changes its speed and reprints its login prompt. If you can't read it, send another BREAK, and so on until the login prompt appears legibly.

Here is our UNIXLOGIN macro. It is similar to the VMSLOGIN macro, except it includes the BREAK speed-changing trick and it omits the terminal ID inquiry and response, since most UNIX systems don't do this. BREAK is sent up to 15 times, to try each of the communication speeds supported by UNIX:

```
COMMENT - UNIXLOGIN macro.  Arguments:
;  \%1 = user ID
;  \%2 = password
;
define UNIXLOGIN -
    if < \v(argc) 2 end 1 Usage: \%0 userid password,-
    while not defined \%2 { -
        askq \%2 { \%1's password: } -
    },-
    set terminal echo remote,-    ; Set communication parameters
    set terminal byte 7,-         ; Most UNIXes use even parity
    set command byte 7,-
    set parity none,-             ; But not for file transfer
    set handshake none,-
    set flow xon/xoff,-
    set case on,-                 ; Case is important in UNIX
    out \13,-                     ; Send a carriage return
    for \%i 1 15 1 { -            ; Try up to 15 times
        in 5 login:,-             ; to get login prompt
        if success goto dologin,-
        output \B -               ; Send BREAK to change speed
    },-
    end 1 No login prompt,-
:dologin,-                        ; Have login prompt
    out \%1\13,-                  ; Send user ID
    inp 5 Password:,-             ; Get Password prompt
    if fail end 1 No password prompt,-
    out \%2\13,-                  ; Send password
    def \%2,-                     ; Erase password
    inp 60 {\13\10$ },-           ; Wait for prompt "$ "
    if fail end 1 No system prompt,-
    echo Login successful.
```

Like the VMSLOGIN macro, the UNIXLOGIN macro can be used after any of the connection-establishment macros: SERIAL, NET, or CALL. If your UNIX prompt is not a dollar sign on the left margin followed by space, change the final INPUT command accordingly.

An IBM Mainframe Linemode Login Script

This example shows an interactive login to an IBM mainframe running the VM/CMS operating system over a half-duplex line-at-a-time connection. The login process looks like this:

```
VIRTUAL MACHINE/SYSTEM PRODUCT--CUVMB     --PRESS BREAK KEY
!(Press BREAK key here)
 Enter one of the following commands:
   LOGON userid              (Example:  LOGON VMUSER1)
   DIAL userid               (Example:  DIAL VMUSER2)
   LOGOFF
.<Ctrl-Q>logon olaf
Enter password:
 ************************
 HHHHHHHHHHHHHHHHHHHHHHHHH
 SSSSSSSSSSSSSSSSSSSSSSSSS
.<Ctrl-Q>_____
```

In response to the message PRESS BREAK KEY, you have to send a BREAK signal. Then at the dot prompt (which happens to be followed by a Ctrl-Q line turnaround character, which you can verify using SET DEBUG SESSION) you enter your user ID. Then you are given a password prompt, which includes a lot of overprinted asterisks, H's, and S's to cover your password (in case you are logging in from a hardcopy terminal), followed by the dot prompt and Ctrl-Q. Once you have supplied a correct password, greeting messages are printed and you must type a carriage return in response to the system prompt two times before you can begin to do any work. (At least, that's how our local VM/CMS system operates.) Here is a VMLINELOGIN macro that takes care of all this:

```
COMMENT - VMLINELOGIN macro.  Arguments:
; \%1 = User ID
; \%2 = Password
;
define VMLINELOGIN -
    if < \v(argc) 2 end 1 Usage: \%0 userid password,-
    while not defined \%2 { -
        askq \%2 { \%1's password: } -
    },-
    set parity mark,-              ; Set communication parameters
    set flow none,-
    set handshake xon,-
    set duplex half,-
    set input timeout quit,-       ; Don't bother with IF FAILURE
    input 10 BREAK KEY,-           ; Look for BREAK KEY prompt
    pause 1,-                      ; Wait a second
    output \B,-                    ; Send BREAK
    input 10 .\17, output logon \%1\13,-  ; Now log in
    input 10 .\17, output \%2\13,-        ; Send password
    input 10 .\17, output \13,-           ; Send carriage return
    input 10 .\17, output \13,-           ; Send another one
    echo Login successful.
```

Once we have made sure we have the user ID and password, we set the IBM mainframe linemode communication parameters, which are very different from Kermit's defaults. Then we send the BREAK signal and the required material in response to each of four identical prompts (period followed by Control-Q). For variety as well as compactness, we have omitted the IF FAILURE commands after each INPUT command. Instead, we have simply SET INPUT TIMEOUT QUIT to force the entire macro to fail automatically if any of its INPUT commands failed, in which case the FAILURE status is returned. Like the other login macros, the VMLINELOGIN macro can be used in conjunction with any of the connection-establishment macros.

An IBM Mainframe Fullscreen Login Script

The more popular style of communication with IBM mainframes is called *block mode* or *full screen*, in which the IBM mainframe believes it is connected to a 3270-style terminal, but in reality the connection goes through a *protocol converter* (such as an IBM 7171 or 3174 AEA) that converts the 3270 screens to your ASCII terminal type. These devices generally use full duplex communication, Xon/Xoff flow control, and even parity.

For the screen to be painted correctly, the protocol emulator must know your terminal type. In general the procedure is to type a carriage return (for speed recognition). In response, the protocol emulator prompts you for a terminal type with a message like this:

ENTER TERMINAL TYPE:

and you respond with a terminal type, such as:

ENTER TERMINAL TYPE: vt-100

Then a login screen like the one in Figure 13-1 is displayed. The mainframe login screen contains fields for the ID and password, which you must fill in. You should send this information only after the screen is completely painted and the mainframe is waiting for input. This is indicated by the word RUNNING somewhere near the lower right corner, as shown in the figure.

When the RUNNING message appears in the lower right, you may type your user ID and password, separated by a tab character. As in the linemode example, a couple of carriage returns are needed after that. Here is the macro, VMFULLOGIN, that automates the process:

```
COMMENT - VMFULLOGIN macro.  Arguments:
; \%1 = User ID
; \%2 = Password
;
define VMFULLOGIN -
    if < \v(argc) 2 end 1 Usage: \%0 userid password,-
    while not defined \%2 { -
        askq \%2 { \%1's password: } -
    },-
```

```
VIRTUAL MACHINE/SYSTEM PRODUCT


                   CCCCCC   UU      UU VV      VV MM        MM BBBBBB
                  CCCCCCCC  UU      UU VV      VV MMM      MMM BBBBBBB
                  CC    CC  UU      UU VV      VV MMMM    MMMM BB   BB
                  CC        UU      UU VV      VV MM MMMM MM BB    BB
                  CC        UU      UU VV      VV MM  MM  MM BBBBBBB
                  CC        UU      UU VV      VV MM      MM BB   BB
                  CC    CC  UU      UU  VV    VV  MM      MM BB   BB
                  CCCCCCCC  UUUUUUUU     VVVV     MM      MM BBBBBBB
                   CCCCCC    UUUUUU       VV      MM      MM BBBBBB


                        C O L U M B I A    U N I V E R S I T Y
                             Center for Computing Activities


Fill in your USERID and PASSWORD and press ENTER
(Your password will not appear when you type it)
USERID    ===>
PASSWORD  ===>

COMMAND   ===>
                                                            RUNNING   CUVMB
```

Figure 13-1 Sample IBM 3270 Login Screen

```
    set input timeout quit,-      ; Quit if INPUT fails
    set parity even,-             ; Set communication parameters
    set duplex full,-
    set handshake none,-
    set flow xon/xoff,-
    out \13,-                     ; Send carriage return
    inp 5 TERMINAL TYPE:,-        ; Get terminal-type prompt
    out vt-100\13,-               ; Just send "vt-100"
    inp 20 RUNNING,-              ; Get RUNNING message
    pau 1,-                       ; Wait one second
    out \%1\9\%2\13,-             ; Send user ID, tab, password
    out \13\13,-                  ; Two more carriage returns
    echo Login successful.
```

Here again we use SET INPUT TIMEOUT QUIT to keep the macro short and we are careful to set all relevant communication parameters. Like our other login scripts, this one works with any of the connection-establishment macros.[43] Note that the SET INPUT TIMEOUT QUIT command applies only to the current command level (macro or command file) and is inherited by those below it. When the VMFULLOGIN macro terminates, the previous INPUT TIMEOUT setting is restored.

---

[43]Except NET, because C-Kermit does not, itself, perform 3270 terminal emulation. But if you can TELNET to a terminal server or protocol converter, or make an X.25 connection to a device, that provides 3270 emulation, then you can make network full-screen connections after all.

Login Scripts for Commercial Data Services

A very common use of communication software is to log in to commercial information services like CompuServe, MCI Mail, or Dow Jones News/Retrieval. In many cases, the connection and login procedure is very similar to that for UNIX and VMS: dial the phone number, type a carriage return, and then supply your user ID and password in response to the prompts. For example, a CompuServe login might look like this:

```
C-Kermit>set modem hayes
C-Kermit>set line /dev/ttya
C-Kermit>set speed 1200
C-Kermit>dial 5551212
Connection completed.
C-Kermit>connect
Type CR here
  01NMS

Host Name: CIS
User ID: 00000,0000
Password:
```

and then you get a greeting, a menu, and the prompt, ending with:

```
Enter choice !
```

The login script is straightforward:

```
COMMENT - CISLOGIN macro.  Arguments:
; \%1 = CompuServe User ID
; \%2 = Password
;
define CISLOGIN -
    if < \v(argc) 2 end 1 Usage: \%0 userid password,-
    while not defined \%2 { -
        askq \%2 { \%1's password: } -
    },-
    set input timeout quit,-    ; No IF FAILURE's
    output \13,-                 ; Send initial carriage return
    input 5 Host Name:,-         ; Look for Host Name prompt
    output cis\13,-              ; Send "cis" and carriage return
    input 5 User ID:,-           ; Look for User ID prompt
    output \%2\13,-              ; Send ID and carriage return
    input Password:,-            ; Look for Password prompt
    output \%3\13,-              ; Send password and CR
    input 20 Enter Choice!,-     ; Look for menu prompt
    echo Login successful.
```

Sometimes it is preferable to go through a public data network to access the desired service, rather than dialing it directly. In the following example, we dial a SprintNet node and tell it to connect us to Dow Jones News/Retrieval.

```
C-Kermit>set modem hayes          (Choose modem type)
C-Kermit>set line /dev/ttya       (Communication device)
C-Kermit>set speed 1200           (Communication speed)
C-Kermit>dial 5551212             (Dial the number)
Connection completed.             (Call is answered)
C-Kermit>connect                  (Connect to SprintNet)
Type CR here
Type CR here
TELENET                           (SprintNet greeting)
212 517A

TERMINAL=D1                       (Enter terminal type)

@c dow                            (Connect to Dow)

DOW CONNECTED                     (Dow greeting)

WHAT SERVICE PLEASE????           (Dow service prompt)
djnr                              (Enter "djnr")
ENTER PASSWORD                    (Password prompt)
WWWWWWWWWWWWWWW
MMMMMMMMMMMMMMM
@@@@@@@@@@@@@@@<Ctrl-Q>   <Ctrl-Q>
```

As you can see, the procedure is to type two carriage returns, get a greeting and the TERMINAL= prompt, enter D1, then get the SprintNet @ prompt. At this point, you tell it to connect (c) you to "dow". Once you have been put through, Dow asks you which service you want. You reply "djnr" (Dow Jones News/Retrieval) and then supply your password in response to a rather tricky prompt, which ends with two Ctrl-Q's separated by some spaces. This is quite different from our other examples, because we have to make what amounts to *two* calls, rather than one. The first call is to SprintNet, and the second call is from SprintNet to DJNR. Naturally, you can also call other hosts and services from SprintNet, and it is conceivable that DJNR can also be reached in other ways besides SprintNet. So let's separate the two functions.

First, we write the macro that asks SprintNet to call a given service:

```
COMMENT - SPRINT macro.  Arguments:
; \%1 = Service name or address
;
define SPRINT -
    if < \v(argc) 2 end 1 Usage: \%0 service,-
    set input timeout proceed,-            ; Use IF FAILURE
    output \13\13,-                        ; Send two CRs
    input 10 TERMINAL=,-                   ; Get TERMINAL= prompt
    if fail end 1 No terminal prompt,-     ; Fail if it doesn't come
    out D1\13,-                            ; Send terminal type, CR
    inp 10 @,-                             ; Look for atsign prompt
    if fail end 1 No atsign prompt,-       ; Fail if it doesn't come
    output c \%1\13,-                      ; Connect to  service
    input 10 CONNECTED,-                   ; Look for confirmation
    if fail end 1 Can't access \%1 from SprintNet
```

Login Scripts for Commercial Data Services

Here is the Dow login macro, which can be used after the service has been reached, independent of the communication method:

```
COMMENT - DOWLOGIN macro.  Arguments:
; \%1 = Dow Jones Password
;
define DOWLOGIN -
    while not defined \%1 { -                ; Get password
        askq \%1 { Dow Jones password: } -
    },-
    input 20 SERVICE PLEASE\?\?\?\?,-        ; Look for Dow prompt
    if fail -
        end 1 No service prompt,-
    out djnr\13,-                            ; Select DJNR
    input 10 @@@@,-                          ; Get password prompt
    if fail -
        end 1 No password prompt,-
    pause 1,-                                ; Wait a second, then...
    output \%1\13,-                          ; send password and CR
    input 20 ENTER QUERY,-                   ; Get DJNR query prompt
    if fail -
        end 1 No main query prompt,-
    pause 1,-
    echo Login successful.
```

The PAUSE commands towards the end of the script allow time for the invisible characters (control characters and spaces) to arrive before the password is sent.

Here is how we use our macros to access DJNR via dialup:

```
C-Kermit>call hayes /dev/tty01 2400 7418100
C-Kermit>sprint dow
C-Kermit>dowlogin
 Dow Jones password: _____
```

But suppose you want to use only one macro for logging in to Dow Jones through SprintNet, rather than two. Easy. Add this definition to your C-Kermit initialization file:

```
define djnrsprint sprint dow, dowlogin
```

Finally, let's consider hosts or services that don't require any login at all. For these, we define a special macro that does nothing:

```
COMMENT - NOLOGIN macro.
;
define NOLOGIN comment
```

What were these last two items for? Keep reading.

A Directory of Services

Wouldn't it be nice if you could have one single file that describes all the computers and services that you connect to with C-Kermit? One file that would allow you to refer to any service simply by name, and Kermit would take care of the connection establishment and logging in automatically? A plain text file that is easy to create, read, and modify?

Let's design such a file and a series of short macros that use it. For simplicity, let's call the file CKERMIT.KSD (KSD = Kermit Services Directory) and keep it in our home directory. In reality, the file can have various names (such as .ksd in UNIX and OS-9) and locations. These details are handled in the standard C-Kermit initialization file. Here is how our services directory file might look:

```
XXVMA       vmlinelogin   olaf        serial /dev/ttyh8 9600
XXVMB       vmfullogin    olaf        call   hayes /dev/cua 2400 765-4321
CUMIN       vmslogin      olaf        net    tcp/ip cumin
WATSUN      unixlogin     olaf        net    tcp/ip watsun.cc.columbia.edu
COMPUSERVE  cislogin      000,0000    call   hayes /dev/cua 2400 876-5432
DJNR        djnrsprint    xxxx        call   hayes /dev/cua 2400 741-8100
GEOGRAPHY   nologin       xxxx        net    tcp/ip 141.212.99.9:3000
CONGRESS    nologin       xxxx        net    tcp/ip dra.com
```

The file has one line for each service, and each line contains four items:

1. The name of the computer or service

2. The name of the macro used to log in to it

3. Your user ID on the computer or service

4. The name of the macro used to establish a connection to the computer or service, followed by its arguments

The items in each line are separated by one or more spaces or tabs. Whenever you want to add, delete, or modify a service, just use a text editor to make the changes.

Our job now is to design a macro that lets you access any of these services by name. We will call it ACCESS and use it like this:

```
C-Kermit>access compuserve
C-Kermit>access watsun
C-Kermit>access djnrsprint
```

How might the ACCESS macro work? The straightforward, but less efficient, way would be for it to read the services file every time you use it, searching for the service name. Let's try a slightly more complicated but more efficient approach. We will read the services file only once, copying it to an internal array that can be searched quickly.

First we add the following commands to the C-Kermit initialization file. These commands tell Kermit to read the services directory file into an array \&d[ ] whenever you start C-Kermit. Let us assume that the C-Kermit initialization file has already assigned the file specification of the services directory to the _servicedir variable:

```
def max_svcs 50                      ; Maximum number of entries
set take error off                   ; So we can use IF FAIL
if not exist \m(_servicedir) -       ; Have directory?
  goto noservices                    ; No
open read \m(_servicedir)            ; Yes, try to open it
if fail -                            ; Failed?
  end 1 Can't open CKERMIT.KSD       ; Give message and quit
declare \&d[\m(max_svcs)]            ; Open, declare an array
for \%i 1 \m(max_svcs) 1 { -         ; Read the entries
  read \&d[\%i],-                    ; into the array
  if fail goto done-                 ; Check for end of file
}
end 1 Too many entries in directory
:DONE
asg \&d[0] \feval(\%i - 1)           ; Remember how many
end 0                                ; Finished
:NOSERVICES                          ; No directory
define access -                      ; So change these commands...
  echo Services directory not available
define list -
  echo Services directory not available
```

In this example, we're allowing up to 50 entries. If you want to have more, just change 50 to a bigger number in the first line. Notice that the number of entries actually found in the directory is stored in the "zeroth" element of the array, \&d[0].

Next, we define a macro, called LIST, to list the services directory. In the simple form shown here, it prints all the entries. A somewhat more flexible version, which also accepts a service name and lists only that entry, appears in the standard CKERMIT.INI file. Here is the simple version:

```
define list echo \&d[0] items in directory:,-
  for \%i 1 \&d[0] 1 { echo \&d[\%i] }
```

Which you can use like this:

```
C-Kermit>list
8 items in directory:
XXVMA        vmlinelogin   olaf       serial /dev/ttyh8 9600
XXVMB        vmfulllogin   olaf       call hayes /dev/cua 2400 765-4321
CUMIN        vmslogin      olaf       net tcp/ip cumin
WATSUN       unixlogin     olaf       net tcp/ip watsun.cc.columbia.edu
COMPUSERVE   cislogin      000,0000   call hayes /dev/cua 2400 876-5432
DJNR         djnrsprint    xxxx       call hayes /dev/cua 2400 741-8100
GEOGRAPHY    nologin       xxxx       net tcp/ip 141.212.99.9:3000
CONGRESS     nologin       xxxx       net tcp/ip dra.com
```

Now we define the ACCESS macro. Its two arguments are a service name and a password:

```
COMMENT - ACCESS macro.  Arguments:
; 1 = service name
; 2 = password (optional)
;
define ACCESS -
    if not defined \%1 end 1 access what?,-     ; Check service
    lookup \%1,-                                ; Look it up
    if success doaccess { \%2} \v(return),-     ; OK, try it
    else end 1 "\%1" not in service directory,- ; Not found
    if fail stop 1
```

The ACCESS macro uses two other macros, which we define in a moment. The LOOKUP macro looks up the service name in the service directory. If it is found, the entire directory entry—that is, the line that starts with the desired name—is returned and assigned to the local temporary variable \%9 and the DOACCESS macro is invoked with the password and the directory entry. Otherwise the ACCESS macro fails (STOP 1).

For security reasons, the service directory does not contain passwords. The ACCESS macro is designed to accept a password as a second argument after the service name:

```
C-Kermit>access compuserve mypassword
C-Kermit>acces djnr mypassword
C-Kermit>acc watsun mypassword
```

Notice that the service names can be abbreviated and that passwords echo when you type them on the ACCESS command line. You can also omit your password:

```
C-Kermit>access compu
C-Kermit>acces djnr
C-Kermit>acc wat
```

If you omit the password, the LOGIN macro prompts you for it and it does not echo when you type it:

```
C-Kermit>access watsun
 olaf's password: _____
```

When you omit the password, the \%2 argument is undefined. Therefore the ACCESS macro prepends a space to it before passing it to the DOACCESS macro to ensure that DOACCESS will always get a password (even an empty one) as its first argument:

```
    if def \%9 doaccess { \%2} \%9
```

The second argument, \%9, is expanded *before* it is passed to DOACCESS, so although it looks like one argument here, DOACCESS sees one argument for each word in the directory entry.

Here is the LOOKUP macro. It searches the \&d[ ] array, which contains the services directory, one line per array element, and returns the first matching line, or if no matches were found, the null (empty) string:

```
COMMENT - LOOKUP macro.  Argument:
;  \%1 = Service name to look for in services directory
;
define LOOKUP -
    set case off,-             ; Case doesn't matter
    for \%i 1 \&d[0] 1 { -     ; Loop through services directory
        if eq \%1 \fsubstr(\&d[\%i],1,\flen(\%1)) -   ; Compare
            break -
    },-
    if not > \%i \&d[0] return \&d[\%i]
```

The command:

```
if eq \%1 \fsubstr(\&d[\%i],1,\flen(\%1))
```

compares the name that you typed with a substring of each services-directory entry, starting at the first character, with the same number of characters as you typed. If they are equal (except for the case of the letters), the BREAK command terminates FOR-loop and LOOKUP returns the entire line of text from the directory.

Finally, here is DOACCESS. Its purpose is simply to pick apart the words from the services directory entry into separate macro parameters and call the connection establishment and login macros with them. It is called with a password followed by the services directory entry, so the password is argument \%1, the service name is \%2, the login macro name is \%3, the user ID is \%4, the connection-establishment macro name is \%5, and the connection-establishment macro arguments are \%6 through \%9:

```
define DOACCESS -
    asg \%1 \fsubstr(\%1,2),-
    do \%5 \%6 \%7 \%8 \%9,-
    if success do \%3 \%4 \%1
```

The first command:

```
    asg \%1 \fsubstr(\%1,2)
```

removes the space that was prepended to the password, so now the password is either truly empty or else it is the one you typed on the ACCESS command line. The next command:

```
    do \%5 \%6 \%7 \%8 \%9
```

executes the connection-establishment macro from the services directory entry, together with its arguments. \%5 is the name of the macro, and the rest are the arguments. If connection establishment is successful:

```
    if success do \%3 \%4 \%1
```

the associated login macro (\%3) is executed, with the user name (\%4) and password (\%1) as its arguments. If the password is empty, the login macro prompts you for it.

Using the Services Directory

The CKERMIT.INI file that comes with C-Kermit 5A already contains all the pieces you have read about in this chapter. Just install this file as your own C-Kermit initialization file (see Table 2-3 on page 36 for proper name and location).

Now you should create a CKERMIT.KSD or .ksd file of your own, using a text editor capable of creating plain ASCII text files. Once you have your services directory in place, C-Kermit reads it automatically upon startup and then you can log in to any desired computer or service using any connection method available to your computer. Simply type ACCESS followed by the service name and then supply your password.

Automated File Transfer

Establishing the connection and logging in is only the beginning of the story. Once logged in to a remote computer or service, you can program Kermit to do automatically just about anything that you would do by hand. For example, let's dial up a remote VMS computer, start Kermit there, send a file to it, then log out and hang up. We can easily construct a command file out of the building blocks from previous sections. Let's call it SENDOOFA.TAK:

```
access cumin                  ; Access a VMS computer
set input timeout quit
output kermit\13              ; Run C-Kermit on VMS
input 5 C-Kermit>             ; Get its prompt
out server\13                 ; Put it in server mode
input 5 READY TO SERVE...     ; Get READY message
send oofa.txt                 ; Send the file
bye                           ; Log out the VMS job
exit                          ; Finished
```

The first line makes the connection and logs you in.

Nightly Polling

Let's construct a more ambitious example, in which we call up all our franchises at night, get their daily reports and inventories, and send them our new recipes. Using the building blocks we have already constructed, this is a relatively simple matter. We'll use our services directory for this purpose, which has already been read into memory by the C-Kermit initialization file. The list of franchises to be accessed is in another file, which we will call FRANCHISES.TXT, and which might look like this:

```
Anaheim
Boston
Milano
Moscow
Nashville
Paris
```

```
Stuttgart
Tokyo
```

Each name in this list corresponds to a services directory entry, for example:

```
Anaheim   vmslogin  hq   call hayes     /dev/cua   2400  1-213-555-0123
Boston    unixlogin hq   call telebit   /dev/cub  19200  1-617-555-1234
```

Here is the script program, written as a command file. Let's name it NIGHTLY.SCR:

```
open read franchises.txt                ; Open the list of franchises
if error   end 1 Can't open franchises.txt
open write nightly.log                  ; Keep a record of what happens
if error   end 1 Can't open nightly.log
write file  Polling franchises: \v(date) \v(time)
:loop                                   ; Loop for each franchise
read \%a                                ; Read a franchise name
if fail goto done                       ; No more left, we're done
write file \v(time): calling \%a
access \%a                              ; Access the franchise
xif fail { -                            ; Check for failure
    write file Can't access \%a.,-
    goto loop -
}
output kermit\13                        ; Start Kermit there
input 10 >                              ; Get its prompt
output server\13                        ; Put it in server mode
pause 2                                 ; Give it time to get ready
get inventory                           ; Get the inventory file
xif success { -
  rename inventory inventory.\%a,-
  write file \v(time): got inventory.\%a,-
} else { -
  write file \v(time): can't get inventory -
}
send recipes                            ; Send the new recipes
if fail write file \v(time): can't send recipes
else write file \v(time): sent recipes ok
bye                                     ; Log out from the franchise
goto loop                               ; Go do the next one
:done                                   ; Come here when finished
write file \v(time): done               ; Make final log entry
close write                             ; Close the log
end 0                                   ; Succeeded
```

To poll the franchises, just start C-Kermit and tell it to TAKE this file:

```
$ kermit                                (Start Kermit)
C-Kermit>take nightly.scr               (TAKE the command file)
```

Passwords and Security versus Automation

The problem with NIGHTLY.SCR is that it prompts you for the password of each franchise when the franchise is dialed, which could keep you sitting at the terminal all night! This difficulty could be solved easily by including all of the franchise passwords in the FRANCHISES.TXT file, along with the franchise names. But passwords in files pose an unacceptable security risk.

There is no perfect solution to this problem. One approach would be for NIGHTLY.SCR to read the entire FRANCHISES.TXT file into an array before it begins calling the franchises. As part of this process, it prompts you for each franchise's password and stores it in a parallel array, as in this example (which allows up to 50 franchises):

```
open read franchises.txt            ; The list of franchises
if error end 1 Can't open franchises.txt
define n_franchises 50              ; Change if you need more
declare \&f[\m(n_franchises)]       ; Array for franchise names
declare \&p[\m(n_franchises)]       ; Array for passwords
for \%i 1 \m(n_franchises) 1 { -
    read \&f[\%i], -
    if fail break, -
    askq \&p[\%i] Password for \&f[\%i]: -
}
close read                          ; Close the file
decrement \%i                       ; Number of entries
assign \&f[0] \%i                   ; Record it here
```

Notice the use of ASKQ to request the passwords without echoing them. It is unsafe to echo passwords; someone might be spying on your terminal.

Now you can change the main loop of NIGHTLY.SCR into a counted loop, from 1 to \&f[0], and when you ACCESS a franchise, you can provide both the service name and the password:

`access \&f[\%i] \&p[\%i]`

There are drawbacks to this approach. First, you still have to type the whole list of passwords every night, a tedious and error-prone process, especially when they don't echo! If you make a typographical error in a franchise password, NIGHTLY.SCR will not be able to access the franchise and business can suffer.

Second, we have not really removed the security risk. The passwords are in an array in Kermit's memory for as long as NIGHTLY.SCR is running. A computer-literate burglar could break in after you leave, interrupt Kermit, and have it display the two arrays with a few simple keystrokes:

```
Ctrl-C ^C...
C-Kermit>for \%i 1 \&f[0] 1 { echo \&f[\%i]: \&p[\%i] }
```

Encryption

A second method is to store the franchise names and passwords together in the `FRANCHISES.TXT` file, but to encrypt the file with an encryption key known only to yourself. First, create the file in plain text. Each line has the name of a franchise (corresponding to a name in your services directory) and the password, separated by one or more spaces. Suppose your `FRANCHISES.TXT` file now looks like this:

```
Anaheim      goofy
Boston       beans
Milano       bongiorno
Moscow       priwjet
Nashville    howdy
Paris        pernod
Stuttgart    gruessgott
Tokyo        saki
```

If it does, you're already in trouble! Before you start worrying about how to make your C-Kermit script more secure, rush to the phone, call up your franchises, and have them fix their passwords to be harder to guess. Random combinations of upper- and lowercase letters and digits are recommended, as well as punctuation marks if the system allows them.

The rest of this section is aimed at UNIX users. We'd have said this earlier, but we wanted you to read about passwords first. This is the 90s!

Assuming your passwords are not easily guessable, encrypt the `FRANCHISES.TXT` file with the UNIX `crypt` program and then remove the plain-text version:

```
$ crypt keyword < franchises.txt > franchises.x
$ rm franchises.txt                   (Delete the original)
$ mv franchises.x franchises.txt      (Rename)
```

The *keyword* is your encryption key, a string of characters that, like a password, should not be easily guessable. If you want to decrypt the file, just give the same `crypt` command again with the same keyword. For example, to view the file on your screen:

```
$ crypt keyword < franchises.txt
```

Now modify `NIGHTLY.SCR` to prompt you for the encryption key and then read the encrypted file through the crypt program. Now you only have to type in one password instead of many. This mitigates the consequences of both error and theft. Note that the key stays in Kermit's memory for only a brief instant, presumably while you are still present and *en garde*:

```
askq \%8 Encryption key:            ; Ask for key
open !read crypt \%8 < franchises.txt  ; Read file through crypt
if fail end 1 Can't decrypt franchises.txt
define \%8                          ; Erase key from memory
```

But what if you make a typographical error when entering the key? The entire nightly polling run would be wasted. You can avoid this by adding commands to check the key by displaying the first few lines of the FRANCHISES.TXT file:

```
:GETKEY
askq \%8 { Encryption key: }          ; Ask for key
run crypt \%8 < franchises.txt | head ; Display a few lines
getok { Is this correct\? }           ; Make sure key is correct
if fail goto getkey                   ; If not, try again
```

We get past this loop only when a working encryption key has been entered.

Next we modify NIGHTLY.SCR to make it as secure as possible. All the commands that deal with login passwords are moved into a macro, and we keep the login password in a temporary variable local to the macro, an unused macro argument. Should burglars interrupt C-Kermit, all local temporary variables are automatically erased from memory before the prompt returns.

Here is the secure version of the NIGHTLY.SCR file, for UNIX only.

```
COMMENT - File NIGHTLY.SCR, nightly franchise-polling program.

define GETNAME -                      ; Macro to extract service name
    assign franchise \%1              ; from franchises.txt entry

define SECUREACCESS -                 ; Secure wrapper for ACCESS
    read \%9,-                        ; Read a line from franchises.txt
    if fail goto done,-               ; If none left, we are done
    getname \%9,-                     ; Get service name
    write file -                      ; Make a log entry
      \v(time): calling \m(franchise)\10,-
    access \%9,-                      ; Access <name> <password>
    xif fail { -
        write file Can't access \m(franchise)\10,-
        goto loop -
    }

COMMENT - Program begins here.
;
open write \v(ndate).log              ; Start a log file
if fail -
    end 1 Can't write \v(ndate).log

:GETKEY                               ; Encryption key section

askq \%8 { Encryption key: }          ; Ask for encryption key
;
; Use UNIX "head" program to display the top of the file
; and ask whether it looks right.
;
run crypt \%8 < franchises.txt | head ; Display a few lines
getok { Is this correct\? }           ; Ask if they look OK
if fail goto getkey                   ; If not, try again
```

```
; We have the encryption key.  Open and read the franchises file.
;
open !read crypt \%8 < franchises.txt   ; Read & decrypt file
assign \%8 \v(status)                   ; Get status, erase key
if not = \%8 0 -                        ; Check status
    end 1 Can't read franchises.txt

write file Polling franchises: \v(date) \v(time)\10

:LOOP                                   ; Loop for each franchise
secureaccess                            ; Access next franchise
output kermit\13                        ; Start Kermit there
input 10 Kermit>                        ; Get its prompt
output server\13                        ; Put it in server mode
pause 2                                 ; Give it time to get ready
get inventory                           ; Get the inventory file
xif success { -
  rename inventory inventory.\m(franchise),-
  write file \v(time): got inventory.\m(franchise)\10,-
} else { -
  write file \v(time): can't get inventory from \m(franchise)\10 -
}
send recipes                            ; Send the new recipes
if fail write file \v(time): recipes NOT sent to \m(franchise)\10
else write file \v(time): recipes sent to \m(franchise)\10
bye                                     ; Log out from the franchise
goto loop                               ; Go do the next one

:DONE                                   ; Come here when done
write file \v(time): done\10            ; Make final log entry
close write                             ; Close the log
end 0                                   ; Succeeded
```

To run this secure version of NIGHTLY.SCR, an additional security is required; rather than typing:

C-Kermit><u>take nightly.scr</u>

define a macro to TAKE the command file:

C-Kermit>ptext>define nightly take nightly.scr   (Define the macro)
C-Kermit><u>nightly</u>   (and execute it)

This way the variable \%8, which briefly holds the encryption key, is safe from program interruption. Should anyone Ctrl-C the program at a crucial moment—for example while it is asking "Is this correct?"—the key disappears from memory automatically.

Remember, however, that no computer program can be totally secure; not our script program, not C-Kermit itself, not the underlying operating system or its utilities. While it is always better to take precautions like those we have used here, it is also wise not to have too much faith in them.

The SCRIPT Command

The SCRIPT command is shorthand for a series of INPUT and OUTPUT commands, allowing an entire login script to be executed in a single short (but cryptic) command. Strictly speaking, the SCRIPT command is not needed. There is nothing it can do that cannot be done by the methods already described. The SCRIPT command has been a part of C-Kermit since 1985 and is carried forward for compatibility with previous releases. The other programming features described in this and the previous chapters are new to C-Kermit version 5A.

A SCRIPT consists of a series of *expect* and *send* strings, separated by spaces. Kermit waits for the first *expect* string; when it comes Kermit sends its first *send* string and then waits for its next *expect* string, and so on:

SCRIPT *expect send [expect send [...]]*
    Executes the given series of *expect* and *send* strings. If an *expect* string does not arrive, the command fails. If all the *expect* strings arrive, the command succeeds.

The *send* and *expect* strings can contain special sequences prefixed by tilde (~), listed in Table 13-1 on the next page. Most of these can also be adequately represented by Kermit's normal backslash codes.

Kermit automatically includes a carriage return at the end of each *send* string unless it ends with ~c. Only the last seven characters in each *expect* are matched. A null *expect*, ~o or two adjacent dashes, causes a short delay before proceeding to the next *send* sequence. A null *expect* always succeeds.

If there is a chance that an *expect* sequence might not arrive, you can express conditional sequences in the form:

`-send-expect[-send-expect[...]]`

where dashed sequences are followed until an *expect* succeeds. For example, on a noisy connection:

`script ~0 login\32olaf-ssword:-login\32olaf-ssword:`

sends "login olaf" followed by a carriage return. If the Password: prompt does not arrive within the default timeout interval, "login olaf" is sent again.

expect-send transactions can be debugged by logging transactions (LOG TRANSACTIONS). This records all exchanges, both expected and actual. The script execution is also logged in the session log, if that is activated.

Script execution can be interrupted by typing your interrupt character, normally Ctrl-C.

Table 13-1 Notation for SCRIPT Command

Notation	Description
~b	Backspace (you can also use \8)
~s	Space (= \32)
~q	Question mark (= \?)
~n	Linefeed (= \10)
~r	Carriage return (= \13)
~t	Tab (= \9)
~~	Tilde (= \126)
~x	XON (Control-Q) (= \17)
~c	Don't append a carriage return to a send string.
~n[n[n]]	Octal representation of an ASCII character code (= \onnn)
~0	(zero) When used as an *expect* string, this means "expect nothing" and proceed immediately to the next *send* string. When used by itself as a *send* string, it means to send nothing followed by a carriage return.
~d	Delay approximately 1/3 second during send.
~w[d[d]]	Wait the specified number of seconds during expect, then time out. The default waiting interval is 15 seconds.

The progress of a SCRIPT command is normally displayed on your screen, but you can control the display with the following command:

SET SCRIPT ECHO { ON, OFF }

Controls whether the characters sent and received during script execution are to be echoed on your screen. The default, ON, echoes the characters.

Here is an example in which the SCRIPT command is used to log in to a VMS computer, similar to our VMSLOGIN macro from page 287:

`script ~0 ~0 name:--name: \%1 word: \%2 \27Z \27[\?1c $--$--$`

In this example, we expect nothing, then send a carriage return, then wait for name: from the Username: prompt. If we don't get it, we send another carriage return and wait for it again. If we get it, we send our username (which is contained in the variable \%1), then wait for the Password: prompt. If it comes, we send our password \%2, wait for the terminal ID query, send a VT100 terminal ID, then wait for the VMS dollar sign prompt. If it doesn't come, we send a carriage return and wait again, and so on. The example demonstrates how a single SCRIPT command can replace a long series of OUTPUT, INPUT, and IF SUCCESS commands, accomplishing the same actions in a more compact (and more cryptic) form. The SCRIPT command, however, does not allow intermixture of *expect-send* items with regular Kermit commands such as SET PARITY, SEND, RECEIVE, and so on, but SCRIPT commands themselves can be intermixed with any other C-Kermit commands.

Script Programming Ideas

This chapter describes only a few of the many applications for C-Kermit's script programming language. If you have the urge to program, here are some other ideas that might interest you:

1. Define a CAPTURE macro that simplifies the job of using LOG SESSION to capture a file from a remote host or service that does not have the Kermit protocol.

2. Construct a NEWDIAL macro that supports a new type of modem that is not directly supported by C-Kermit's built-in DIAL command. *HINT:* use SET CARRIER OFF before SET LINE, and then SET CARRIER AUTO after dialing.

3. Change the CALL macro to accept a list of phone numbers, rather than just one. If a call fails, have it try the next number in the list. This is useful for calling services that can be reached at several different phone numbers.

4. If you have a multiuser computer with several shared dialout devices, try modifying the CALL macro to search for the first one that is not in use, rather than giving up right away if the given device can't be used.

5. Test your modem pool. Read a list of phone numbers from a file, dial them all up, monitor whether they answer or not, and summarize the results in a report file.

6. Check your network hosts. Write a script that SETs HOST to the computers on your network, and keeps a log of which ones were reachable and which ones were not.

7. Check your network gateways. Write a script that logs in to each of your gateways and gathers statistics about their use, and appends the statistics report to a log file that can be read by other programs to produce usage summaries or graphs.

Chapter 14

Command-Line Options

Until now, you have communicated with C-Kermit *interactively*: you start Kermit, Kermit issues its prompt, you give it a command, it issues another prompt, and so on until you EXIT from the program. In some circumstances, however, you might want to—or be required to—give Kermit its commands as part of the system command that starts it. The following example shows an alternative way of telling Kermit to send the file `oofa.exe` in binary mode using even parity:

```
$ kermit -i -p e -s oofa.exe
```

The command with which you start Kermit is called the command line. Any items included after the program's name on the command line are called command-line options. Command-line options can be useful for various reasons:

1. Certain UNIX C-Kermit programs are configured for command-line operation only. This must be done for systems, primarily 286-or-lower PCs that have limited address space, or compilers or linkers that are not capable of building an interactive version.

2. Interactive program dialog might be unfamiliar to some UNIX users. In UNIX, most applications are invoked by giving their names and possibly some operands, and they automatically exit back to the UNIX prompt without any dialog when done.

3. In UNIX, you might want to use Kermit in a command pipeline, sending files from standard input or receiving them to standard output, for example to transfer a file in compressed and/or encrypted form between two UNIX systems.

4. You might want to change Kermit's normal startup actions, for example specifying a different initialization file or no initialization file at all.

A selection of C-Kermit commands is available on the command line in environments that support passing of command-line options to programs through the C-language "argv, argc" mechanism [46], provided that Kermit has been configured to use them. In VMS, Kermit must be installed as a foreign command so VMS will make the command line options available to Kermit, for example:

```
KERMIT :== $SYS$SYSTEM:KERMIT.EXE
```

Command-line options allow you to define convenient command macros or aliases for starting Kermit in certain ways. For example, using the UNIX K-Shell [5], you could define aliases like these in your `.env` file:

```
alias "kr=kermit -r"    # to receive files, just type 'kr'
alias "ks=kermit -s"    # to send text files, type 'ks filename'
alias "kb=kermit -is"   # to send binary files, type 'kb filename'
```

C-Kermit's command-line options conform to the normal UNIX conventions [33]:

- Command names (like "kermit") must be between 2 and 9 characters long.

- Command names must include lowercase letters (in UNIX) and digits only.

- An option name is a single character.

- Options are delimited by " -", for example " -q -z".

- Options with no arguments may be grouped (bundled) behind one delimiter, for example " -s oofa.txt -qt".

- Option-arguments cannot be optional.

- A group of bundled options may end with an option that has an argument, for example " -qzs oofa.txt".

- Arguments immediately follow options, separated by whitespace.

- The order of options does not matter.

- "-" preceded and followed by whitespace means standard input.

C-Kermit's command-line options are summarized in Table 14-1.

Table 14-1 C-Kermit Command-Line Option Summary

Option	Argument	Action	Description
=		N	Ignore the rest of the command line
-a	filename	N	As-name for transferred file
-b	number	N	Transmission rate, bits per second
-C	"command-list"	N	Interactive-mode Kermit commands to execute
-c		Y	CONNECT before file transfer
-d		N	Create a debugging log file, DEBUG.LOG
-e	number	N	Set receive packet-length
-f		Y	Send a FINISH command to a Kermit server
-g	filespec	Y	Send a GET command to a Kermit server
-h		Y	Print a help message listing the command-line arguments
-i		N	Binary file transfer
-j	host	N	TCP/IP host name or address
-k		Y	Receive to standard output
-l	device-name	N	SET LINE to specified serial device
-m	modem-type	N	SET MODEM to specified modem type
-n		Y	CONNECT after file transfer
-o	number	N	X.25 closed user group number
-p	letter	N	Parity: e(ven), o(dd), m(ark), s(pace), or n(one)
-q		N	Quiet mode, suppress messages and file transfer display
-r		Y	RECEIVE files
-S		N	Stay, enter command mode even if action options specified
-s	filespec	Y	SEND files
-t		N	Local echo, XON handshake for file transfer
-U	text	N	Specify X.25 call user data
-u		N	Specify X.25 reverse-charge call
-v	number	N	Specify file transfer sliding window size
-w		N	Incoming files write over existing files with same name
-X	number	N	Specify an X.25 host (X.121) address
-x		Y	Enter server mode
-Y		N	Do not execute the initialization file
-y	filename	N	Execute *filename* instead of the normal initialization file
-Z	number	N	Specify the file descriptor of an open X.25 connection
-z		N	Force foreground operation

Command-Line Options

Option List

C-Kermit's command-line options fall into two categories: action options and non-action options. If you give one or more action options on the command line, C-Kermit exits after performing them, returning an appropriate exit status code to your system's command processor (shell, DCL, etc.), *unless* you also specified the -S (uppercase) "Stay" option. If your command-line includes no action options, C-Kermit issues its prompt after executing the command-line options. The action options are primarily those for entering CONNECT mode and for transferring files. The non-action options correspond mostly to SET commands.

In VMS, uppercase options must be enclosed in doublequotes to prevent them from being converted to lowercase before C-Kermit sees them.

Program Management Options

The first group of options is concerned with program management:

-h Help. Action option. Displays a brief synopsis of the command line options.
Example:

```
$ kermit -h
```

-y *filename*
Executes commands from the specified file instead of the standard initialization file. Applies only to interactive versions. Examples:

```
% kermit -y /usr/olga/special.ini     (UNIX)
$ kermit -y sys$login:special.ini     (VMS or OpenVMS)
) kermit -y :udd:olga:special.ini     (AOS/VS)
F:\>kermit -y c:\kermit\special.ini   (OS/2)
```

-Y (uppercase Y) Do not read or execute any initialization file. Applies only to interactive versions. Examples:

```
$ kermit "-Y"                         (VMS - Note doublequotes)
% kermit -Y                           (Elsewhere)
```

filename
If the first item on C-Kermit's command line is a filename, C-Kermit executes commands from the named file after it finishes the initialization file, if any. Applies only to interactive versions. Example:

```
% kermit sendmyfiles
```

In UNIX only, C-Kermit command files can be constructed to be run as if they were programs, starting C-Kermit automatically. To do this, include a line like the following as the first line of the command file:

```
#!/usr/local/bin/kermit
```

where /usr/local/bin/kermit is the full pathname of the Kermit program on your computer. Add execute permission to the command file:

% chmod +x sendmyfiles

and then you can run it as if it were any other UNIX command, program, or shell script:

% sendmyfiles

In VMS, you can define convenient aliases to run Kermit easily with different command files, by using VMS's DEFINE command, for example:

```
$ define compuserve $sys$system:kermit.exe sys$login:compuserve.cmd
$ define sprintnet  $sys$system:kermit.exe sys$login:sprintnet.cmd
```

-C *"command, command, ..."*

(uppercase C) Executes the interactive-mode commands after the initialization file (if any), the other command-line options (if any), and the command file (if any). Applies to interactive versions only. The command list must be enclosed in doublequotes, with commands separated by commas. Examples:

```
$ kermit "-C" "set block-check 3, send oofa.txt"    (VMS)
$ kermit -C "set block-check 3, send oofa.txt"      (Elsewhere)
```

This option lets you give any commands at all to C-Kermit from the command line. The maximum length of the command line is your operating system's command line buffer size. The maximum length for the command-list is 1024.

When you use the -C option, the command list is assigned to a macro called CL_COMMANDS (command-line commands), so you can also execute these commands later during your session simply by typing the name of this macro:

C-Kermit>cl_commands

The -C option is not considered an action option, even if the command list contains action commands. Therefore, if there are no other action commands among the command-line arguments, the C-Kermit prompt appears when the last command in the list has finished executing. To defeat this behavior, include EXIT as the last command, as in this example, which uses all the power of C-Kermit to clear a VT100 terminal screen:

kermit -C "echo \27[2J\27H, exit"

The -C option is available only if C-Kermit includes the script programming language; that is, if it has a DEFINE command.

-q Quiet. Suppresses screen messages during local-mode file transfer as well as most other screen writing. This option is used to allow a file transfer to take place in the background. It is equivalent to the interactive-mode command SET QUIET ON.

- **-z** Force foreground operation. Even if Kermit thinks it is running in the background, it should behave as if it were in the foreground, issuing its normal prompts and messages, and so on. You can use this option whenever you start C-Kermit in some unusual way and its prompt fails to appear. It is equivalent to the interactive-mode command SET BACKGROUND OFF.

- **-d** Debug. Equivalent to the interactive-mode command LOG DEBUG. Records debugging information in the file DEBUG.LOG in the current directory. Use this option if you believe Kermit is misbehaving, and show the resulting log file to your local Kermit maintainer.

- **-S** (uppercase S) Stay. This option tells C-Kermit to issue its prompt and enter interactive command mode even if the command line included action options. Applies to interactive versions only. Examples:

  ```
  $ kermit -s oofa.txt "-S"      (VMS or OpenVMS)
  $ kermit -r -a oofa.txt -S     (Elsewhere)
  ```

- **= text**
  Tells C-Kermit to ignore all command-line options that follow but (in an interactive version of C-Kermit that includes the script programming feature) make them available, along with all the other items from the command line, in the array \&@[ ]. In VMS, this option must be enclosed in doublequotes if it is the first option. Examples:

  ```
  $ kermit -z = this is some text  (Anywhere)
  $ kermit "=" this is some text   (VMS or OpenVMS)
  $ kermit = this is some text     (Elsewhere)
  ```

Communications Options

These are the options for selecting and configuring your communication device. You won't need any of these, except perhaps **-p**, if you are using C-Kermit in remote mode.

- **-l** *device*
  Specifies a serial communication device to use for file transfer and terminal connection. Equivalent to the SET LINE command (see page 43). Examples:

  ```
  % kermit -l /dev/ttyi5     (UNIX)
  $ kermit -l txa5:          (VMS or OpenVMS)
  ) kermit -l @con5          (AOS/VS)
  C:\>kermit -l com1         (OS/2)
  ```

  You can also give a numeric file descriptor for a serial communication (tty) device that is already open:

  ```
  $ kermit -l 6
  ```

  This is useful for starting Kermit from some other communication software that already has opened the device.

When a serial communication device is being used, you also need some additional options for successful communication:

-b *number*
: Bits per second. Specifies the transmission speed in bits per second ("baud rate") for the serial communication device given in the -l option, as in:

    ```
    $ kermit -l /dev/ttyi5 -b 9600
    ```

    This option, equivalent to the SET SPEED command (p. 44), should always be included with the -l option since the speed of a device is not necessarily what you expect.

-p *letter*
: Parity. Selects the type of parity for use on the selected communication device. The argument is a single letter, e, o, m, s, or n, identifying the type of parity: even, odd, mark, space, or none. The default is n, none. Equivalent to SET PARITY (page 89).

-t Specifies local echoing during CONNECT mode and half-duplex line turnaround with XON as the handshake character during file transfer. Used for communicating with IBM mainframes in linemode. Equivalent to SET TERMINAL ECHO ON (page 89) and SET HANDSHAKE XON (page 127).

-m *name*
: Modem type: hayes, penril, vadic, etc. (see Table 3-2 on page 53). Use this option in conjunction with the -l and -b options if you want to use C-Kermit to dial out. If you don't specify a modem type, and the modem is not asserting the carrier signal, Kermit might not be able to open the device given in the -l option. The modem name must be given in lowercase, but can be abbreviated, e.g. "hay" for "hayes." Equivalent to SET MODEM (page 51). Example:

    ```
    $ kermit -m telebit -l /dev/cub -b 2400
    ```

    You can also use the -C option to include a dialing command:

    ```
    $ kermit -m telebit -l /dev/cub -b 2400 -C "dial 7654321"
    ```

If you want to use a network connection (see pages 67–77) rather than a serial terminal device for communication, use the following options rather than -l, -b, and -m. Parity is usually not required. The speed (-b) option has no effect on network connections.

-j *host*
: Host. Specifies a TCP/IP network host. Equivalent to the SET NETWORK TCP/IP and SET HOST commands. The *host* can be an IP host name, an IP host number (containing dots), or either one of these followed by a colon and then a TCP service name or number (the default service is 23, which is TELNET). The following examples all connect to the TCP TELNET port on the same host:

    ```
    $ kermit -j kermit.columbia.edu
    $ kermit -j kermit.columbia.edu:23
    ```

```
$ kermit -j kermit.columbia.edu:telnet
$ kermit -j 128.59.39.2
$ kermit -j 128.59.39.2:23
$ kermit -j 128.59.39.2:telnet
```

If you get a message like:

```
?Invalid argument, type 'kermit -h' for help
```

it means your Kermit version was not built with TCP/IP network support.

The following example connects to a non-TELNET information server:

```
$ kermit -j martini.eecs.umich.edu:3000
```

The *host* field can also be just a number, in which case it is assumed to be a file descriptor for an open TCP/IP TELNET connection:

```
$ kermit -j 4
```

For X.25 connections only, you also have four additional options:

-X *address*
: (uppercase X) X.25 address. Specifies an X.25 network address.

-Z *number*
: (uppercase Z) X.25 file descriptor. Specifies a file descriptor for an X.25 connection that is already open.

-o *index*
: X.25 closed user group call.

-u X.25 reverse-charge call.

Here are C-Kermit's terminal connection options:

-c Establishes a terminal connection over the communication device before any Kermit protocol activity takes place. Get back to your local computer by typing the escape character (normally Control-Backslash) followed by the letter c. A communication device must also be specified. Equivalent to the CONNECT command (page 79). Examples:

```
% kermit -l /dev/ttya1 -b 2400 -c      (UNIX)
$ kermit -l txa4: -b 1200 -c           (VMS or OpenVMS)
C:\>kermit -l com2 -b 9600 -c          (OS/2)
$ kermit -j watsun.cc.columbia.edu -c  (Network)
```

-n Like -c, but *after* Kermit protocol activity; -c and -n may both be used in the same command line. For example, the -c option lets you connect to the other computer, log in, and start a file transfer, and the -n option lets you connect back after the file transfer and log out.

File Transfer Options

The following command-line options are available to perform C-Kermit's basic text and binary file transfer operations, described fully in Chapters 5–8:

-s *filespec*
    Send. Action option. Sends the specified file or files to a Kermit program that is in RECEIVE or SERVER mode. In UNIX, if *filename* contains wildcard (meta) characters, the UNIX shell expands it into a list of filenames. The *filespec* can also be a list of files, as in:

    `kermit -s ckcmai.c ckuker.h oofa.txt`

    Thus, this option is equivalent to the interactive-mode command MSEND. If the *filename* is - (a hyphen), Kermit sends from its standard input, which may come from a file:

    `kermit -s - < foo.bar`

    or piped in from a process:

    `ls -l | grep Tokyo | kermit -s -`

    You cannot use this mechanism to send characters from your terminal's keyboard. If you want to send a file whose actual name is -, you can precede it with a path name, as in:

    `kermit -s ./-`

    To use standard input as a source for sending files in VMS, you must redefine SYS$INPUT to be the desired file, for example:

```
$ define sys$input login.com
$ kermit -s "-"
$ deassign sys$input
```

    Note that the final hyphen must be quoted; otherwise VMS interprets it as a DCL command-continuation character.

-r Receive. Action option. Waits passively for files to arrive from another Kermit program, which must be told to send the file(s). This option is equivalent to the RECEIVE command.

-k Receive to standard output. Action option. Receives a file or files from another Kermit, which must be told to send the file(s), and writes them to standard output. This option can be used in several ways:

    `kermit -k`
        Displays the incoming files on your screen; to be used only in local mode.

`kermit -k > `*filename*
> (UNIX and other operating systems that support standard-output redirection via the > operator) Sends the incoming file or files to the named file, *filename*. If more than one file arrives, all are concatenated together into the single file, *filename*.

`kermit -k | `*command*
> (UNIX and other operating systems that support command pipelines via |) Pipes the incoming file or files to the indicated command, as in:
>
> `kermit -k | sort > sorted.stuff`

-a *filename*
> As-name. If you have specified a file transfer option, you may give an alternate name for a single file with the -a option. For example,
>
> `kermit -s foo -a bar`
>
> sends the file `foo`, telling the receiver that its name is `bar` ("send foo as bar"). If more than one file arrives or is sent, only the first file is affected by the -a option:
>
> `kermit -ra baz`
>
> stores the first incoming file under the name `baz` and any others under their own names.

-x Server. Action option. Become a Kermit server. This is equivalent to the SERVER command.

Here are the options for sending commands to Kermit servers:

-g *remote-filename*
> Get. Action option. Actively requests a Kermit server to send the named file or files; *remote-filename* is a file specification in the remote host's own syntax. In UNIX, if *remote-filename* happens to contain any special shell characters, like space, *, [, ~, etc., these must be quoted using the UNIX shell's quoting mechanisms, as in:
>
> `kermit -g x\*.\?`
>
> or:
>
> `kermit -g "profile exec"`
>
> The -g option is equivalent to the GET command.

-f Finish. Action option. Sends a FINISH command to a remote server, equivalent to the FINISH command.

The command line may contain no more than one protocol action option; that is, only one of these: s, r, x, g, f, or k.

The following modifier options can be included with file-transfer action options:

-i Binary mode; equivalent to the SET FILE TYPE BINARY command. Specifies that files should be sent or received with no conversions. See Chapter 5.

-w Writeover. If an incoming file has the same name as an existing file, it replaces the existing file. This changes the default behavior, which is to preserve the old file by changing the name of the existing file before creating the new one. Equivalent to SET FILE COLLISION OVERWRITE.

-e *number*
   Receive packet-length. Specifies that C-Kermit is allowed to receive packets up to the specified length, between 10 and some large number, like 1,000 or 2,000, or even 9,000, depending on how C-Kermit was configured. The default maximum length for received packets is 94. Packets longer than 94 are used only if the other Kermit supports and agrees to use the long packet protocol extension. This command is equivalent to SET RECEIVE PACKET-LENGTH.

-v *number*
   Window size. Specifies that C-Kermit is allowed to send and receive files using a window size up to the given number. Window sizes greater than 1 speed up transfers in most situations, especially long-distance network connections. The default window size is 1, the maximum is 31. Sizes greater than 1 work only if the other Kermit supports this option and has been told to use it. Equivalent to the SET WINDOW command.

Command-Line Examples

`kermit -l /dev/ttyi5 -b 1200 -rcn`
   This command connects you (the c in -rcn) to another computer through the ttyi5 device at 1200 bps, where you presumably log in, run Kermit, and give it a SEND command. After you escape back, C-Kermit waits for a file (or files) to arrive (the r in -rcn). When the file transfer is complete, you are reconnected (the n in -rcn) to the remote system so you can logout. This example illustrates the principles that the order of options does not matter and that options with no arguments can be grouped.

`kermit -l /dev/ttyi5 -b 1200 -cntp m -r -a foo`
   This command is like the preceding one, except the remote system in this case uses half-duplex communication (the t in -cntp) with mark parity (-...p m). This illustrates how the final option (p) in an option bundle -cntp can take an argument. The first file that arrives is stored under the name foo (-a foo).

`kermit -ix`
   This command starts up C-Kermit as a server (note the bundling of the options -i and -x). Files are sent in binary (image) mode.

```
kermit -l /dev/ttyi6 -b 9600
```
    This command sets the communication line and speed. Since no action is specified, C-Kermit issues a prompt and enters an interactive dialog with you. Any settings given on the command line remain in force during the dialog, unless explicitly changed.

```
kermit
```
    This command starts up Kermit interactively with all default settings.

The next example shows how UNIX C-Kermit might be used to send an entire directory tree from one UNIX system to another, using the *tar* (tape archive) program as Kermit's standard input and output. On the originating system, in this case the remote, type (for instance):

```
tar cf - /usr/olga | kermit -is -
```

This causes tar to send the directory /usr/olga (and all its files and all its subdirectories and all their files...) to standard output rather than to a tape; C-Kermit receives this as standard input and sends it as a binary file. On the receiving system, in this case the local one, type (for instance):

```
kermit -il /dev/ttya -b 9600 -k | tar xf -
```

Kermit receives the tape archive and sends it via standard output to its own copy of tar, which extracts from it a replica of the original directory tree.

This example shows how the UNIX compression utility might be used to speed up Kermit file transfers between two UNIX computers:

```
kermit -cnikl /dev/cua -b 9600 | uncompress > foo   (local receiver)
compress < file | kermit -is -                      (remote sender)
```

And the final example combines the previous two to give you the fastest serial line backup ever:

```
kermit -cnil /dev/ttya -b 9600 -k | uncompress | tar xf -
tar cf - /usr/olga | compress | kermit -is -
```

Appendix I

C-Kermit Command Reference

When you start C-Kermit, it performs commands in this order:

1. The -d command-line option, if any.

2. The initialization file. If -Y (uppercase) was used, the initialization file is skipped. If -y (lowercase) was used to specify an alternative initialization file, it is executed instead of the standard file.

3. If a filename was given as the first command-line argument, the commands in that file.

4. Command-line options (except -y and -c), if any.

5. The command list given in the -c command-line option.

6. Interactive commands if no action commands were given on the command line, or if action commands were given and the -s option was included on the command line.

The interactive commands in (6) include commands piped in or redirected from files, in which case Kermit exits upon the end of the file. For truly interactive operation from the keyboard, Kermit keeps prompting you until you type the EXIT or QUIT command.

When C-Kermit exits, it returns a numeric code that can be tested by batch files, shell scripts, etc. The values are shown in Table I-1. A nonzero return code can be the sum of any combination of these values; for example, a code of 6 means both a SEND and a RECEIVE command failed. The return codes that C-Kermit supplies automatically can be overridden by supplying a return code with the EXIT or QUIT command.

Table I-1 C-Kermit Return Codes

Code	Meaning
0	Overall success
1	A program error occurred
2	A SEND command failed
4	A RECEIVE command failed
8	A REMOTE command failed

Command Summary

This section lists C-Kermit's commands alphabetically, with the syntax notation described in Chapter 2, and with concise descriptions of their actions. All commands set the SUCCESS or FAILURE flag for explicit testing by the IF SUCCESS and IF FAILURE commands, as well as implicit testing by the command file reader (according to SET TAKE ERROR) and the macro expander (SET MACRO ERROR), unless otherwise noted.

Variables, functions, and other quantities introduced by backslash (\) are fully evaluated before a command is executed, except in fields that require *variable-names* or unless otherwise noted. C-Kermit's backslash codes are summarized in Table I-2 on p. 325, built-in variables are listed in Table I-3 on p. 326, and built-in functions are listed in Table I-4 on p. 327. File transfer interruption characters are listed in Table I-5 on p. 328.

; (followed by at least one space)
   Introduces a comment. Chapter 2. Synonym: #.

! [*command*]
   Runs the local host operating system command or program denoted by *command*. If no command is given, the local system's command processor is entered in such a way that exiting from it returns you to the C-Kermit prompt. The command may include trailing arguments, i/o redirection symbols, and so on, as permitted by the underlying operating system. Chapter 2. Synonyms: **@**, **RUN**, **PUSH**, **SPAWN**.

\# Synonym for ; .

:*name*
   A label, to be used as a target of the GOTO command. Chapter 12.

@ [*command*]
   Synonym for !.

ASG
   Synonym for ASSIGN.

Table I-2 Summary of Backslash Codes

Code	Example	Meaning
\		(at end of command) Line continuation
\{	\{27}3	Braces are used for grouping
\%	\%a	A user-defined simple variable
\&	\&a[4]	An array reference
\$	\$(TERM)	An environment variable
\b	\b	The BREAK signal (OUTPUT command only)
\d	\d123	A decimal number
\f	\feval(2+2)	A built-in function
\l	\l	The LONG BREAK signal (OUTPUT command only)
\m	\m(oofa)	A macro used as a variable
\o	\o123	An octal number
\v	\v(time)	A built-in variable
\x	\x0f	A hexadecimal number
\\	\\	The backslash character itself
	\123	Decimal digit: a 1- to 3-digit decimal number
	\?	Anything else: quote the next character

ASK *variable-name text*

   Prints the text as a prompt, and stores the line typed by the user in the named variable, echoing the user's keystrokes on the screen. Leading and trailing spaces are trimmed from the *text* prompt unless it is enclosed in { braces }. Chapter 13.

ASKQ *variable-name text*

   Exactly like ASK, but without echoing. Chapter 13.

ASSIGN *{ variable-name, macro-name } text*

   Evaluates the *text*, expanding any variables or function references it might contain, and makes the result the value of the named variable or macro. If the *text* is surrounded by { braces }, they are discarded. Chapter 11. Synonym: **ASG**.

BUG

   Displays a brief message describing how to report C-Kermit bugs.

BYE

   Requests a Kermit server to terminate itself and log out its job. When a C-Kermit server receives a BYE command packet, it does everything that the EXIT command does, and then logs out its own job and hangs up the connection. Chapter 7.

Table I-3 Summary of Built-in Variables

Name	Description
\v(argc)	Number of arguments passed to currently active macro
\v(args)	Number of program command-line arguments
\v(cmdfile)	Name of current command file, if any
\v(cmdlevel)	Command level, 0 = top
\v(cmdsource)	PROMPT, FILE, or MACRO
\v(count)	Current value of SET COUNT variable
\v(cpu)	CPU type for which C-Kermit was compiled
\v(date)	Current date in dd mmm yyyy format
\v(day)	Day of the week: Sun, Mon, Tue, ... , Sat
\v(directory)	Current directory
\v(exitstatus)	Program exit status (return code)
\v(filespec)	File specification from most recent file transfer
\v(fsize)	Size of file most recently transferred
\v(home)	Home (login) directory
\v(host)	The network host name of this computer
\v(inchar)	Most recent INPUT character
\v(incount)	Number of characters read by most recent INPUT
\v(input)	Current INPUT buffer contents
\v(line)	Current communication device or remote network host name
\v(local)	1 in local mode, 0 in remote mode
\v(macro)	Name of currently executing macro
\v(ndate)	Date in numeric form, for example 19901007
\v(nday)	Day of week in numeric form, 0 (Sun) through 6 (Sat)
\v(time)	Time of day, seconds since midnight
\v(platform)	Specific machine and/or OS C-Kermit was built for
\v(program)	Name of this program: C-Kermit
\v(return)	Most recent RETURN value
\v(speed)	Transmission device speed, or "unknown"
\v(status)	0 = success, nonzero = failure of previous command
\v(system)	Generic operating system for which C-Kermit was built
\v(tfsize)	Total size of most recently transferred file group
\v(time)	Current time in hh:mm:ss 24-hour clock format
\v(ttyfd)	(UNIX only) File descriptor of communication device
\v(version)	Numeric C-Kermit version number

Table I-4 Summary of Built-in Functions

Name	Returns	Description
\Fcharacter(*n*)	*character*	Character whose numeric code is given
\Fcode(*c*)	*number*	Numeric code value of character *c*
\Fcontents(*variable*)	*text*	Value of *variable*
\Fdefinition(*macro*)	*text*	Definition of *macro*
\Fevaluate(*expression*)	*number*	Value of arithmetic *expression*
\Fexecute(*macro args*)	*any*	Return value of macro execution
\Ffiles(*filespec*)	*number*	Number of files that match *filespec*
\Findex(*text1,text2,n*)	*number*	Position of *text1* in *text2* starting at *n*
\Flength(*text*)	*number*	Length of *text*
\Fliteral(*text*)	*text*	Literal *text*, no evaluation
\Flower(*text*)	*text*	Letters in *text* converted to lowercase
\Flpad(*text,n,c*)	*text*	*text* left-padded to length *n* with char *c*
\Fmaximum(*n,n*)	*number*	Larger of the two numbers
\Fminimum(*n,n*)	*number*	Smaller of the two numbers
\Fnextfile()	*text*	Next filename from \Ffiles() list
\Frepeat(*text,n*)	*text*	*n* repetitions of *text*
\Freverse(*text*)	*text*	*text* reversed
\Fright(*text,n*)	*text*	Rightmost *n* characters of *text*
\Frpad(*text,n,c*)	*text*	*text* right-padded to length *n* with char *c*
\Fsubstr(*text,n1,n2*)	*text*	Substring of *text* starting at *n1*, length *n2*
\Fupper(*text*)	*text*	Letters in *text* converted to uppercase

C Synonym for CONNECT.

CAT *filename*

Displays the file on the screen. Synonym for TYPE.

CD *[directory]*

Changes C-Kermit's current (default) directory. Chapter 2. File specifications that do not include full device and directory names will be in or relative to the specified directory. If the *directory* is omitted, returns to your home or root directory or, on some operating systems, prints the name of the current directory. Synonyms: **CWD**, **SET DEFAULT**.

CHECK *feature-name*

Checks whether C-Kermit was configured to include the given feature; for example CHECK IF-COMMAND for the script programming language. If the feature is available,

Table I-5 Summary of File Transfer Interruption Keys

Key	Description
X	Attempts to cancel the current file (also Ctrl-X, F, Ctrl-F).
Z	Attempts to cancel the rest of the file group (also B, Ctrl-B).
R	Resends the previous packet (also Carriage Return, Ctrl-R).
A	Prints a short status report (also Ctrl-A).
E	Forces a fatal error by sending an Error packet (also Ctrl-E).
Ctrl-C	Returns to the C-Kermit prompt immediately without sending any kind of protocol message to the other computer. This is your system's interrupt character, which might be something besides Ctrl-C.
Ctrl-Z	Suspends Kermit in a way that allows it to be continued (only on UNIX systems with job control).
Ctrl-Y	Equivalent to Ctrl-C on VMS and OpenVMS. Equivalent to Ctrl-Z on certain UNIX systems.

the command succeeds, otherwise it fails. If the CHECK command is issued from top level, a message is printed telling whether the feature is available. If it is issued from a command file or macro and the feature is not available, it fails. Type CHECK ? for a list of feature-names that can be checked. Use this command for constructing configuration-independent command files.

CLEAR *[{ INPUT-BUFFER, DEVICE-BUFFER, BOTH }]*

The CLEAR command erases the contents of the INPUT command buffer, the communication device input buffer, or both (the default is BOTH). Chapter 13.

CLOSE *file*

Closes the indicated file: DEBUG-LOG, PACKET-LOG, READ-FILE, SESSION-LOG, TRANSACTION-LOG, or WRITE-FILE. Chapters 4, 5, 10, 13.

COMMENT *[text]*

Does nothing. The text is ignored.

CONNECT

(Also –c on the command line) Makes a terminal connection through the serial communication device given in the most recent SET LINE command or to the network host in the most recent SET HOST or TELNET command. May be abbreviated as C. Return to C-Kermit by typing the escape character, normally Ctrl-\ (Control-Backslash), and then the letter C. See also SET ESCAPE, SET TERMINAL. Chapter 4. Escape-character commands are listed in Table I-6.

CWD

Change Working Directory. Synonym for CD.

Table I-6 C-Kermit CONNECT-Mode Escapes

Character	Description
?	Help—Prints the available CONNECT-mode escape options.
!	(also @) Enters the local system command processor. Use EXIT or LOGOUT to return to C-Kermit CONNECT mode.
0	(the digit zero) Transmits a NUL (ASCII 0).
A	Sends an Are You There request (TELNET only).
B	Transmits a BREAK signal.
C	Returns to the C-Kermit prompt without breaking the connection to the remote computer.
H	Hangs up the phone or network connection.
I	Sends a network Interrupt request.
L	Transmits a Long BREAK signal.
Q	Hangs up and closes the connection, then quits from C-Kermit.
R	(X.25 only) Resets the X.25 connection.
S	Shows the status of the connection: device name, speed, parity, and so on.
Z	(UNIX only) Suspends Kermit. Use the UNIX `fg` command to continue Kermit's CONNECT session.
SP	(Space) Nothing, resumes CONNECT mode.
\	(Backslash) Introduces a backslash code that translates into a single character, for example \127 or \xff.
Ctrl-\	(or whatever your escape character is) Type the escape character twice to send one copy of it to the remote computer.

DCL
Synonym for DECLARE.

DECLARE *array-name[number]*
Creates an array with *number* + 1 elements, 0 through *number*. Example: `declare \&x[100]`. Chapter 11. Synonym: **DCL**.

DECREMENT *variable-name [number]*
Subtracts *number* from the named variable, if it has a numeric value. If the *number* is omitted, 1 is subtracted. If the variable does not have a numeric value, this command fails. Chapter 12.

DEFINE *{ variable-name, macro-name } text*
> Makes the *text* be the value of the named variable or macro. Variable and function names in the *text* are copied literally and not evaluated. If the text is enclosed in curly braces, the braces are discarded. Chapter 11.

DELETE *filespec*
> Deletes the specified file or files on the local computer. Chapter 2. Synonym: **RM**.

DIAL *string*
> Using the methods implied by the most recent SET MODEM and SET DIAL commands, instructs the modem connected to the device specified in the most recent SET LINE command to dial the telephone number or other character sequence specified by *string*. If a SET DIAL DIRECTORY command has been given, the DIAL command looks up the *string* in the dialing directory file and makes the appropriate substitution. Chapter 3.

DIRECTORY *[options] [filespec]*
> Lists files that match *filespec* on the local computer by running the underlying operating system's file-listing command with the given options, if any. If no *filespec* given, lists all files in the current directory. System-specific command modifiers may be given before the filespec in (at least) the UNIX, VMS, OpenVMS, and OS/2 versions. Chapter 2. Synonym: **LS**.

DISABLE *{ ALL, BYE, CD, DELETE, DIRECTORY, FINISH, GET, HOST, SEND, SET, SPACE, TYPE, WHO }*
> Instructs C-Kermit, when acting as a server, to refuse or restrict the given command. Chapter 7.

[**DO** *] macro-name [argument [argument [...]]]*
> Executes the commands from the definition of the named macro until the end of the macro definition is reached, a STOP, EXIT, END, RETURN, or equivalant command is encountered, or a GOTO command is executed for a label that is not in the macro definition, or a command error occurs and MACRO ERROR is ON. The macro arguments (of which there may be zero to nine) replace the corresponding argument variables (\%1, \%2, ... \%9) in the macro definition, and the macro name replaces the variable \%0. The macro is created with the DEFINE or ASSIGN command. Commands within the macro definition are separated by commas, except when enclosed in curly braces. Chapter 11.

ECHO *[{] text [}]*
> Displays the *text* on the screen. All backslash codes, variables, and functions are evaluated first. Leading and trailing spaces are discarded unless the text is enclosed in { braces }, in which case the braces themselves are discarded. In a macro definition, braces must also be used to surround the text if it includes commas. A line terminator is supplied automatically at the end of the text. Chapter 2. Also see WRITE SCREEN.

ELSE *command*
Executes the C-Kermit *command* if the preceding command was an IF command and its condition was not true. Chapter 12.

ENABLE { **ALL, BYE, CD, DELETE, DIRECTORY, FINISH, GET, HOST, SEND, SET, SPACE, TYPE, WHO** }
Instructs C-Kermit, when acting as a server, to allow itself to execute the given command. Chapter 7.

END *[number [text]]*
Returns immediately from the current command file or macro to the command level (command file, macro, interactive command, or host system command line) that invoked it. If a *number* is included, it becomes the return code of the invoking TAKE or (implied) DO command: 0 for success, nonzero for failure. If *text* is included, it is printed on the screen. The text may be enclosed in braces to include leading or trailing spaces. Chapter 12. Synonym: **POP**.

E-PACKET
Sends a Kermit Error packet on the currently selected communication device, to cancel any Kermit protocol operation that might be underway. Chapter 8.

EXIT *[number]*
Closes all open files and devices, hangs up any dialed or network connection, restores the command terminal to its normal state, executes the macro named ON_EXIT if one is defined, and returns to the system. If a *number* is included, it is C-Kermit's exit status code, otherwise C-Kermit returns a status code whose format depends on the host operating system, but which summarizes the overall success of its file transfer operations. Normal exit codes are 0 (overall success), 1 (program error), 2 (a SEND command failed), 4 (a RECEIVE or GET command failed), 8 (a REMOTE command failed). A nonzero return code can be the sum of any combination of these. Chapter 2. Synonym: **QUIT**.

EXTPROC
(OS/2 only) When included as the first command in a command file, this allows self-running OS/2 C-Kermit scripts. EXTPROC should be followed by the full pathname of the C-Kermit program, for example EXTPROC C:\CKERMIT\CKERMIT. The EXTPROC command is treated by C-Kermit exactly like the COMMENT command, and it may be used in non-OS/2 versions (where it has no effect at all).

FINISH
(Also -f on the command line) Tells C-Kermit to tell a Kermit server to leave server mode and return to wherever server mode was invoked from the Kermit command prompt or the host system prompt. Chapter 7.

FOR *variable-name initial final increment { command [, command [, . . .]] }*
Sets the named variable to the *initial* value. If the variable's value is not greater than the *final* value (less than the final value, if the *increment* is negative), executes the list of commands, then adds the *increment* to the variable, and repeats the process until the variable's value passes the final value. Chapter 12.

FOT
Synonym for DIRECTORY.

GET *[remote-filespec]*
(Also -g on the command line) Tells C-Kermit to tell a Kermit server to send, using the Kermit file transfer protocol, the specified file or files, whose names are given in the remote host's filename syntax. If the *remote-filespec* is omitted, C-Kermit prompts for it on a second line, and then prompts for a local name to store the file under on a third line. May be abbreviated by the single letter G. To include leading or trailing spaces in the *remote-filespec*, enclose it in braces. Chapter 7.

GETOK *[text]*
Prints the *text*, a question whose answer should be Yes or No. The default question is "Yes or no?". The user must answer by typing Yes, No, or OK in upper- or lower-case, abbreviated or in full. The GETOK command succeeds if the user gives an affirmative answer, and fails if the answer is negative. Chapter 13.

GOTO *label-name*
Finds the label in the current macro or command file and begins executing the commands after the label. If the label is not found, returns to the next-higher command level and repeats the process all the way up to top level. GOTO commands issued at top level, either at the prompt or in a command file that has been redirected to C-Kermit's standard input, have no effect. Chapter 12.

HANGUP
On a serial connection, momentarily turns off the Data Terminal Ready (DTR) modem signal in an attempt to break a dialed or null-modem RS-232 connection. Correct operation depends on cable and modem configuration, and on the underlying operating system. Network connections are simply closed. This command has no effect in remote mode (without a prior SET LINE or SET HOST command). Chapter 3.

HELP *[command]*
Asks C-Kermit to print a brief message describing the given C-Kermit COMMAND. If the COMMAND is omitted, a brief overview is displayed. Otherwise, you may include the name of a command, or, for SET and REMOTE commands only, an optional third command word such as HELP SET PARITY or HELP REMOTE DIRECTORY. Chapter 2. Synonym: **MAN**.

IF [NOT] *condition command*
> If the *condition* is (not) true, the Kermit *command* is executed. The IF command may be followed immediately (on the next line) by an ELSE command. Chapter 12. The conditions are:

IF < *arg1 arg2*
> *arg1* and *arg2* both have integer numeric values that are within the precision of the underlying computer architecture, and *arg1* is arithmetically less than *arg2*. The results are unpredictable if the values exceed the precision or range of the underlying computer architecture.

IF = *arg1 arg2*
> *arg1* is arithmetically equal to *arg2*.

IF > *arg1 arg2*
> *arg1* is arithmetically greater than *arg2*.

IF BACKGROUND
> C-Kermit is running in the background.

IF COUNT
> This statement subtracts 1 from the COUNT (\v(count)) variable. The condition is true if the result is greater than zero. Also see SET COUNT.

IF DEFINED *{ variable-name, macro-name }*
> The named variable or macro is defined.

IF EQUAL *arg1 arg2*
> The two text string arguments are the same. Alphabetic case is treated according to SET CASE.

IF ERROR
> Synonym for IF FAILURE.

IF EXIST *filename*
> The named file exists.

IF FAILURE
> The previous command failed.

IF FOREGROUND
> C-Kermit is executing in the foreground.

IF LLT *arg1 arg2*
> *arg1* is lexically less than *arg2*. Alphabetic case is treated according to SET CASE.

IF LGT *arg1 arg2*
: *arg1* is lexically greater than *arg2*. Alphabetic case treated according to SET CASE.

IF NUMERIC *text*
: The *text* consists only of decimal digits, 0–9, possibly preceded by a minus sign (-). Variables and functions in the *text* are evaluated before the decision is made.

IF SUCCESS
: The previous command succeeded.

INCREMENT *variable-name [number=1]*
: Adds *number* to the named variable, if it has a numeric value. If *number* omitted, 1 is used. If the variable does not have a numeric value, this command fails. Chapter 12.

INPUT *number [text]*
: Waits up to *number* seconds for the given *text* to arrive from the current communication device or network connection. Sets SUCCESS if the text arrives within the interval, and FAILURE otherwise. Alphabetic case in the text is treated according to SET CASE. Leading and trailing blanks are ignored in the *text* unless it is enclosed in curly braces, in which case the braces are discarded. If the *text* is omitted, arrival of any character at all within the timeout interval causes the INPUT command to succeed. Also see SET INPUT. Chapter 13.

INTRODUCTION
: Displays a brief introduction to C-Kermit on the screen.

LOG DEBUG *[filename]*
: (Also -d on the command line) Records internal program debugging information in the named file, or if no filename is given, in the file DEBUG.LOG in the current directory. Also see CLOSE. Chapter 6. Synonym: **SET DEBUG ON**.

LOG PACKETS *[filename]*
: Records Kermit's file transfer packets in the specified file, or in PACKET.LOG if no name is given. Also see CLOSE. Chapter 6.

LOG SESSION *[filename]*
: Records the characters that appear on the terminal screen during CONNECT in the specified file, or in `session.log` if no filename given. Chapter 4. Also see CLOSE, SET SESSION-LOG.

LOG TRANSACTIONS *[filename]*
: Records information about Kermit file transfers and SCRIPT command execution in the named file, TRANSACT.LOG by default. Also see CLOSE. Chapter 5.

LS *[options] [filespec]*
: Synonym for DIRECTORY.

MAIL *filespec address*
Tells C-Kermit to send the specified local file(s) to the other Kermit, which must be in RECEIVE or SERVER mode, and to ask the receiving Kermit to deliver the file as electronic mail to the given e-mail address. Chapter 7.

MAN *command*
Synonym for HELP.

MGET *remote-filespec*
Synonym for GET.

MPAUSE
Synonym for MSLEEP.

MPUT *filespec* ...
Synonym for MSEND.

MSEND *filespec [filespec [...]]*
(Also -s on the command line) Sends the specified file or files to the other Kermit program, which must be in RECEIVE or SERVER mode. Chapter 5.

MSLEEP *[number=100]*
Does nothing for (at least) the indicated number of milliseconds (thousandths of seconds). Chapter 13. Synonym: **MPAUSE**.

MV
Synonym for RENAME.

O Synonym for OUTPUT.

OPEN !READ *command*
Starts the specified system command in a way that allows subsequent C-Kermit READ commands to read its output a line at a time. Chapter 12.

OPEN !WRITE *command*
Starts the specified system command with its standard input reading from the output produced by subsequent C-Kermit WRITE commands. Chapter 12.

OPEN *{ APPEND, READ, WRITE } filename*
Opens the specified file for the given type of access. Only one READ OR !READ file, and only one WRITE, !WRITE, or APPEND file, may be open at once. READ files must exist. WRITE files are created, overwriting existing files of the same name. APPEND files are appended to, if they exist, otherwise a new file is created. Chapter 12.

OUTPUT *[{] text [}]*
Sends the *text* out the currently selected communication device. May be abbreviated as O. In addition to the normal backslash codes, variables, and functions, the *text* may

include the special codes \B to send a BREAK signal and \L to send a Long BREAK signal. Leading and trailing blanks are ignored in the *text* unless it is enclosed in { braces }, in which case the braces are discarded. Chapter 13.

PAD CLEAR
Clears the X.25 virtual circuit. Chapter 3.

PAD INTERRUPT
Sends an X.25 interrupt packet. Chapter 3.

PAD RESET
Resets the X.25 virtual circuit. Chapter 3.

PAD STATUS
Requests an X.25 status report. Chapter 3.

PAUSE *[number=1]*
Does nothing for the indicated number of seconds, or until interrupted from the keyboard. Fails if interrupted. Chapter 13. Synonym: **SLEEP**.

PING *[host]*
(TCP/IP only) Sends an ICMP ECHO request to the given host, or if no host is given, to the one specified in the most recent SET HOST or TELNET command. System-dependent options can be given with C-Kermit's PING command, according to the syntax of your system's PING command. Chapter 3.

POP
Synonym for END.

PRINT *[options] [filename]*
Prints the given file on a local printer, using the local operating system's printing command, with the given options, if any. Chapter 2.

PUSH *[command]*
Runs the local host operating system *command*. If no command is given, enters the local host command processor in such a way that exiting or logging out from it returns to the C-Kermit prompt. Chapter 2. Synonyms: !, @, **RUN**, **SPAWN**.

PUT
Synonym for SEND.

PWD
Print Working Directory. Shows the current default directory. Chapter 2. Synonym: **SHOW DEFAULT**.

QUIT
Synonym for EXIT.

READ *variable-name*
> Reads a line from the current OPEN !READ subprocess or OPEN READ file into the named variable. Succeeds if a line is successfully read. Fails if a !READ or READ file is not open or is at end of file, or upon subprocess termination, or if a line cannot be read for any other reason. Upon failure, closes the READ file or terminates the !READ process. Chapter 12.

RECEIVE *[filename]*
> File reception using the Kermit file transfer protocol. Waits for one or more files to arrive from another Kermit program, which must be given a SEND command. If a *filename* is given, the first file that arrives is stored under that name instead of the name it was sent with. Chapter 5.

REDIAL
> Dials the phone number given in the most recent DIAL command. Chapter 3.

REINPUT *number text*
> Checks whether text that has already been processed by the INPUT command contains the given *text*. Alphabetic case is handled according to SET CASE. The *number* is required but ignored. Only works if no more than 256 characters have been INPUT since the *text* first entered the INPUT buffer. Chapter 13. Also see INPUT, SET INPUT.

REMOTE *command [operands]*
> Tells C-Kermit to tell a Kermit server to execute the given command. The results, if any, are sent back, using the Kermit file transfer protocol, for display on your screen if C-Kermit is in local mode, otherwise they are discarded. Chapter 7.

REMOTE CD *[remote-directory-name]*
> Requests the Kermit server to change its default directory to the given directory, or if none is given, to its default or login remote directory. Synonym: **REMOTE CWD**.

REMOTE DELETE *remote-filespec*
> Requests the Kermit server to delete the specified file or files.

REMOTE DIRECTORY *[options] [remote-filespec]*
> Requests the Kermit server to list the specified files, or if none specified, to list all files in the current remote directory, using the file-listing command of its underlying operating system, with the given *options*, if any.

REMOTE HELP
> Requests the Kermit server to list the commands it can respond to.

REMOTE HOST *remote-command*
> Requests the Kermit server to ask the remote operating system to execute the given command. This works only if the *remote-command* prints its output on the screen (standard output) and does not request any input, and the output is plain text.

REMOTE KERMIT *remote-kermit-command*
Requests the Kermit server to execute the given Kermit command, which must be given in the Kermit server's own interactive command syntax.

REMOTE LOGIN *userid password [account]*
Identifies you to a Kermit server that requires authentication.

REMOTE LOGOUT
Removes your login and access rights from a Kermit server to which you have previously given a REMOTE LOGIN command.

REMOTE PRINT *filespec [options]*
Sends the named file or files to the Kermit server and asks it to print them, using any specified printer options, which should be given in syntax appropriate for the remote computer's printing command.

REMOTE SET *parameter value*
Requests the Kermit server to set the given parameter to the specified value. Parameters include ATTRIBUTES, BLOCK-CHECK, FILE, INCOMPLETE, RECEIVE, RETRY, SERVER, TRANSFER, WINDOW. See descriptions of corresponding SET commands.

REMOTE SPACE *[{ remote-device-name, remote-directory-name }]*
Requests the Kermit server to report on available space in the specified area, or if none is given, its current disk and/or directory.

REMOTE TYPE *remote-filespec*
Requests the Kermit server to display the contents of the specified file(s) on your screen. This is equivalent to having the remote server transfer the file to C-Kermit in text mode, except the file is shown on the screen rather than being stored on the disk.

REMOTE WHO *[remote-user]*
Requests the Kermit server to send a brief report about the specified user, or if no user is specified, about the users who are currently logged in on the server's system.

RENAME *filename new-name*
Changes the name of the specified local file to *new-name*. The rules of the server's underlying operating system apply. Chapter 2.

RETURN *[value]*
Returns immediately from the current macro to the command level (command file, macro, interactive command, or host system command line) that invoked it. If a *value* is given, it is made available to the invoking level in the \v(return) variable. If the RETURN command is executed within a macro that was invoked via the \fexecute() function, the given *value* is returned as the result of that function. If this command is executed outside of a macro, the *value* is ignored and the command behaves like the END command. The RETURN command should not be used in the command list of a

FOR, WHILE, or XIF command; if it is, the results are unpredictable. Also see STOP, END, BREAK, CONTINUE. Chapter 12.

RM *filename*
Synonym for DELETE.

RUN *[command]*
Runs the local host operating system *command*. The command may including trailing operands. If no command is given, enters the local host command processor in such a way that exiting or logging out from it returns to the C-Kermit prompt. Chapter 2. Synonyms: **!**, **@**, **PUSH**, **SPAWN**.

SCRIPT *text*
Executes the line of *text* as a series of *expect* and *send* strings over the currently selected communication device or network connection. See Chapter 13, page 307.

SEND *filespec [alternate-name]*
(Also -s on the command line) Sends the specified file or files, using the Kermit file transfer protocol, to another Kermit program, which must be given a RECEIVE or SERVER command. If *filespec* does not contain wildcards, an *alternate-name* can be given to send it with. May be abbreviated as S. Chapter 5. Synonym: **PUT**.

SERVER
(Also -x on the command line) Tells C-Kermit to become a Kermit server, and accept further commands only in the form of Kermit packets containing SEND, MSEND, GET, MAIL, REMOTE, FINISH, and BYE commands. In an emergency, you can return to the C-Kermit prompt by typing two `Ctrl-C`'s in a row. Chapter 7.

SET ATTRIBUTES { OFF, ON }
Turns file attribute packet processing off or on. When ATTRIBUTES are OFF, C-Kermit does not send Attribute packets and does not indicate its ability to process them to the other Kermit. The attribute mechanism is ON by default. Chapter 8.

SET ATTRIBUTES ALL { OFF, ON }
Disables or enables all of the file attributes supported by C-Kermit without disabling the file attribute mechanism itself. All attributes are ON by default.

SET ATTRIBUTES CHARACTER-SET { OFF, ON }
Turns processing of the file character-set attribute off or on. Turning it off inhibits automatic character set notification, but still allows translation that is explicitly requested via SET { FILE, TRANSFER } CHARACTER-SET. Chapter 8.

SET ATTRIBUTES DATE { OFF, ON }
Controls processing of the file creation date attribute. When receiving files, OFF prevents incoming files from being stored with their original creation dates (the current date and time is used instead) and prevents SET FILE COLLISION UPDATE from

rejecting incoming files based on date. When sending files, OFF prevents C-Kermit from telling the receiving Kermit the file's creation date and time. Chapter 8.

SET ATTRIBUTES DISPOSITION { OFF, ON }
Turns processing of the file distribution attribute off or on. If it is OFF, MAIL and REMOTE PRINT commands cannot be executed, nor will C-Kermit honor incoming MAIL or REMOTE PRINT requests. Chapter 8.

SET ATTRIBUTES LENGTH { OFF, ON }
Turns processing of the file length attribute off or on. OFF prevents files from being rejected when the receiving Kermit thinks they are too big to fit in the available disk space. Chapter 8.

SET ATTRIBUTES SYSTEM-ID { OFF, ON }
Turns notification of the file system ID attribute off or on. Chapter 8.

SET ATTRIBUTES TYPE { OFF, ON }
Turns processing of the file type (text or binary) attribute off or on. OFF prevents the file receiver from automatically switching between text and binary mode based on the file type attribute supplied by the file sender. Chapter 8.

SET BACKGROUND { OFF, ON }
Forces C-Kermit into foreground (OFF) or background (ON) mode. In background mode, there are no prompts or information messages and no file transfer display. Use SET BACKGROUND OFF if C-Kermit's prompt fails to appear. Chapter 8.

SET BAUD *number*
Synonym for SET SPEED.

SET BLOCK-CHECK { 1, 2, BLANK-FREE-2, 3 }
Establishes the file transfer protocol error checking level. 1 is weakest but most efficient, 3 is strongest but least efficient. 1 is the default. 2 and BLANK-FREE-2 are equivalent, but the latter is encoded to use only non-blank printable characters. See pages 128 and 136 in Chapter 6.

SET BUFFERS *number1 number2*
In versions of C-Kermit that have been configured for dynamic memory allocation, this command allocates *number1* bytes of memory for send-packet buffers and *number2* bytes for receive-packet buffers. Chapter 8.

SET CARRIER
Specifies the desired treatment of the carrier signal during local-mode serial (SET LINE) connections. Chapter 3.

SET CARRIER AUTO
Requires carrier during CONNECT only.

SET CARRIER OFF
Tells C-Kermit to ignore carrier at all times.

SET CARRIER ON [number]
Requires carrier at all times except while dialing. The optional number tells C-Kermit how long to wait for carrier to appear when the SET LINE command is given for a modem-controlled device. If no number is given, C-Kermit waits forever (or until the command is cancelled via Ctrl-C from the keyboard).

SET CASE { OFF, ON }
Ignores (OFF) or pays attention to (ON) upper- and lowercase in letters when comparing character strings. Pertains to IF, XIF, and INPUT commands and works reliably with ASCII letters (A–Z) only, not 8-bit international characters. Applies only to the current command level and below; if this command is given in a macro or command file, the previous CASE setting is restored when the macro or command file exits. Chapters 12 and 13. Synonym: **SET INPUT CASE**.

SET COMMAND BYTESIZE { 7, 8 }
The bytesize to be used by C-Kermit's command interpreter and between C-Kermit and your terminal during CONNECT. 7 bits by default. Use 8 to allow transmission of 8-bit characters between C-Kermit and your keyboard and screen. Chapters 2 and 4.

SET COUNT number
Initializes a loop execution counter for use with IF COUNT. The number must be greater than 0. Chapter 12.

SET DEBUG { ON, OFF }
ON is a synonym for **LOG DEBUG**. OFF is a synonym for **CLOSE DEBUG**.

SET DEFAULT directory
Synonym for CD.

SET DELAY number
The number of seconds to wait after a SEND command is given before sending the first packet, in remote mode only. Gives you time to escape back to your local Kermit before the first packet comes. Chapter 5.

SET DIAL
Controls aspects of the DIAL command. Display these settings with SHOW DIAL.

SET DIAL DIAL-COMMAND [text]
Changes the modem's dialing command to the given *text*, which must contain %s to be replaced by telephone numbers from the DIAL command. The text may contain backslash codes to represent control characters and it may be enclosed in braces to preserve leading and/or trailing spaces. If the *text* is omitted, C-Kermit's built-in modem-specific dialing command is used. Chapter 3.

SET DIAL DIRECTORY *[filename]*
> Designates the named file as a directory in which the DIAL command should look up phone numbers. If the filename is omitted, the dialing directory feature is disabled. Chapter 3.

SET DIAL DISPLAY { ON, OFF }
> Shows selected portions of dialing activity on screen. Normally OFF. Chapter 3.

SET DIAL HANGUP { OFF, ON }
> Tells C-Kermit whether to hang up the phone on the communication device in preparation for dialing, using the hangup method prescribed by SET DIAL MODEM-HANGUP. Normally ON. Use OFF if you have trouble with ON. Chapter 3.

SET DIAL INIT-STRING *[text]*
> Substitutes the given *text* for Kermit's built-in modem dialer initialization string. The text may contain backslash codes to represent control characters and it may be enclosed in braces to preserve leading and/or trailing spaces. If no text is given, Kermit's default modem-specific initialization string is restored. Chapter 3.

SET DIAL KERMIT-SPOOF { OFF, ON }
> Disables or enables the modem's "Kermit spoof" if it has one (as Telebit modems do). Chapter 3.

SET DIAL MNP-ENABLE { OFF, ON }
> Enables or disables the modem's MNP features and negotiation, if it has MNP (and if Kermit knows how to do this). Normally, Kermit does not alter the modem's MNP settings. A modem's MNP features might need to be turned off when dialing to a non-MNP modem. Chapter 3.

SET DIAL MODEM-HANGUP { OFF, ON }
> When DIAL HANGUP is ON, this command determines the hangup method. When DIAL MODEM-HANGUP is OFF (the default), C-Kermit attempts to turn off the DTR signal for about half a second. When DIAL MODEM-HANGUP is ON, C-Kermit issues the modem's escape sequence to put it into command mode, then issues the modem's hangup command. If that doesn't work, C-Kermit drops DTR. Chapter 3.

SET DIAL PREFIX *[text]*
> Inserts the given *text* at the beginning of any phone number that you DIAL, for example as an access or area code. The text may contain backslash codes to represent control characters and it may be enclosed in braces to preserve leading and/or trailing spaces. If no text is given, any previously specified prefix is canceled. Chapter 3.

SET DIAL SPEED-MATCHING { OFF, ON }
> Normally, C-Kermit's DIAL command changes the communication line speed automatically if the modem reports connection at a different speed than the one dialed.

However, some modems keep the interface speed constant, even when the connection speed changes, but still report the connection speed. To use Kermit with such modems, SET DIAL SPEED-MATCHING OFF. Chapter 3.

SET DIAL TIMEOUT *number*
The number of seconds to wait for a response from the modem when dialing, overriding Kermit's built-in timeout calculation. Chapter 3.

SET DUPLEX { FULL, HALF }
Determines which side of a serial terminal connection does the echoing of typed characters during CONNECT: the remote computer (FULL) or C-Kermit itself (HALF). Echoing on TCP/IP TELNET connections is negotiated automatically. Chapter 4. Synonyms: **SET LOCAL-ECHO**, **SET TERMINAL ECHO**.

SET ESCAPE-CHARACTER *number*
Changes C-Kermit's CONNECT-mode escape character to the ASCII control character whose ASCII code is specified by *number*, which must be 0–31 or 127. Chapter 4.

SET FILE *parameter value*
Alters Kermit's file-related settings. Chapters 5–10.

SET FILE BYTESIZE { 7, 8 }
Normally 8, meaning that all the bits in each file byte are considered data. If 7, the 8th bit of each file byte is considered extraneous and is stripped during file transfer.

SET FILE CHARACTER-SET *name*
Selects the character-set of the file(s) to be sent or received so Kermit can make the appropriate translation to or from the transfer character-set. Choices include ASCII, BRITISH, CANADIAN-FRENCH, CP437, CP850, CP852, CP866-CYRILLIC, CYRILLIC-ISO, DANISH, DEC-KANJI, DEC-MULTINATIONAL, DG-INTERNATIONAL, DUTCH, FINNISH, FRENCH, GERMAN, HUNGARIAN, ITALIAN, JAPANESE-EUC, JIS7-KANJI, KOI8-CYRILLIC, LATIN1, LATIN2, MACINTOSH-LATIN, NEXT-MULTINATIONAL, NORWEGIAN, PORTUGUESE, SHIFT-JIS-KANJI, SHORT-KOI, SPANISH, SWEDISH, and SWISS. Chapter 9.

SET FILE COLLISION *option*
Tells what C-Kermit should do if a file arrives that has the same name as an existing file. Chapter 5.

SET FILE COLLISION APPEND
Appends the incoming file to the end of the existing file. (In VMS and OpenVMS, a new version of the file is created.)

SET FILE COLLISION BACKUP
Renames the old file to a new, unique name and stores the incoming file under the name it arrived with. This is the default file collision action. (In VMS and OpenVMS, a new version of the file is created.)

SET FILE COLLISION DISCARD
Refuses and/or discards the incoming file and preserves the existing file.

SET FILE COLLISION OVERWRITE
Overwrites (replaces) the existing file (in VMS a new version is created).

SET FILE COLLISION RENAME
Gives the incoming file a unique name (in VMS and OpenVMS a new version is created), preserving the existing file with its original name.

SET FILE COLLISION UPDATE
Accepts the incoming file only if its creation date, as reported in the accompanying file attribute packet (if any) is later than that of the existing file.

SET FILE DISPLAY { CRT, FULLSCREEN, NONE, SERIAL }
Selects the style of file transfer screen display for local-mode file transfers. The default style is SERIAL. OFF is accepted as a synonym for NONE and ON is a synonym for SERIAL. Chapter 5.

SET FILE INCOMPLETE { DISCARD, KEEP }
Tells C-Kermit what to do if receipt of a file terminates with an error or is interrupted intentionally. C-Kermit's normal action is DISCARD: delete the partially received file. Chapter 5.

SET FILE LABEL *parameter* **{ OFF, ON }**
(VMS and OpenVMS only) Tells C-Kermit which items are to be handled in labeled-file transfer, for use with SET FILE TYPE LABELED. Parameters are: ACL, BACKUP-DATE, NAME, OWNER, and PATH. Appendix IV.

SET FILE NAMES { CONVERTED, LITERAL }
Tells C-Kermit whether to convert file names to "normal form" (all uppercase, no strange characters, no device or directory specifications) during file transfer or to use them literally. CONVERTED is the default. Chapter 5.

SET FILE RECORD-LENGTH *number*
(VMS and OpenVMS only) Specifies the record length, in bytes, for incoming binary or image files. 512 is the default. Appendix IV.

SET FILE TYPE BINARY
Tells C-Kermit to perform no conversions on file data during file transfer. When receiving files, this setting can be overridden by the file type in an incoming Attribute packet. Chapter 5, Appendix IV.

SET FILE TYPE BINARY [{ FIXED, UNDEFINED }]
(VMS and OpenVMS only) Specifies that no conversions be done on incoming files. SET FILE TYPE BINARY is ignored when sending files. An optional record format for

incoming files, FIXED or UNDEFINED, can be specified after the word **BINARY**. The default record format for creating binary files is FIXED. Can be overridden by the file type in the incoming Attribute packet. Has no effect when sending files. Appendix IV.

SET FILE TYPE IMAGE
(VMS and OpenVMS only) Tells C-Kermit to perform no conversions on file data during file transfer and to ignore VMS record attributes. When receiving files, this setting overrides the file type in incoming Attribute packets. Appendix IV.

SET FILE TYPE LABELED
(VMS and OpenVMS only) Tells C-Kermit that RMS and other VMS-specific information is (to be) included with the file data. This data can be stored (archived) by non-VMS systems, or interpreted by VMS systems to allow reconstruction of complex formatted VMS files. The data itself is processed like IMAGE. Appendix IV.

SET FILE TYPE TEXT
Tells C-Kermit to perform record format and character-set conversions on file data during file transfer to make the file useful as text on the receiving computer. When receiving, this setting can be overridden on a per-file basis by the file type attribute in the incoming Attribute packet. Chapter 5.

SET FILE TYPE TEXT
(VMS and OpenVMS only) This command is operational only when receiving files, but it can be superseded on a per-file basis by the file type attribute in the incoming Attribute packet. When sending files, VMS C-Kermit determines automatically whether they are text or binary (but this behavior can be overridden by using file types of IMAGE or LABELED). Appendix IV.

SET FLOW-CONTROL { DTR/CD, KEEP, NONE, RTS/CTS, XON/XOFF }
Tells C-Kermit what kind of flow control to use during file transfer. Xon/Xoff (software flow control) is the default, but it is only usable on full duplex connections. Use NONE for half duplex or other connections that do not support Xon/Xoff flow control. RTS/CTS (hardware flow control) is useful with high-speed modems or other locally attached high-speed devices. KEEP means to use whatever flow-control method the device was configured with when C-Kermit first opened it. Type SET FLOW ? to see which options are available in your version of C-Kermit. Chapters 3, 6.

SET HANDSHAKE { BELL, CR, ESC, LF, NONE, XOFF, XON, CODE *number* **}**
Tells C-Kermit which character to use for line turnaround during file transfer, meaning that C-Kermit will wait for the given character after receiving a packet before it sends its next packet. If you specify NONE, Kermit does not wait for any special character after the packet. If you specify CODE, you may enter the numeric ASCII value of the handshake character to be used, which must be between 1 and 31, or else 127. Normally used only in half duplex connections. Chapter 6.

SET HOST *[host [service]]*
> Tells C-Kermit to use the current network protocol (TCP/IP by default) to establish a connection with the host whose name or network number is given. If a *service* is given, use it instead of the default service. Host and service names and numbers depend on the type of network. If the connection is established, the command succeeds. If it cannot be established, an error message is printed and the command fails. If no name or number is given, the current connection (if any) is closed. Chapter 3.

SET INCOMPLETE *{ DISCARD, KEEP }*
> Synonym for SET FILE INCOMPLETE. Chapter 5.

SET INPUT *option value*
> Controls for the INPUT command. Use SHOW SCRIPTS to display. Chapter 13.

SET INPUT CASE *{ IGNORE, OBSERVE }*
> Synonym for SET CASE { OFF, ON }.

SET INPUT ECHO *{ OFF, ON }*
> Tells C-Kermit whether to echo text on your screen that is read by the INPUT command. Normally ON, meaning the text is displayed. Chapter 13.

SET INPUT SILENCE *seconds*
> The number of seconds before the INPUT command times out before any characters at all arrive from the communication device, if *seconds* is less than the INPUT timeout interval. Chapter 13.

SET INPUT TIMEOUT-ACTION *{ PROCEED, QUIT }*
> Tells C-Kermit whether to proceed to the next command in a command file or macro definition if an INPUT command fails (times out). The default action is PROCEED. SET INPUT TIMEOUT QUIT takes precedence over SET MACRO ERROR ON and SET TAKE ERROR ON, but SET MACRO ERROR ON and SET TAKE ERROR ON have precedence over SET INPUT TIMEOUT PROCEED. Applies only to the current command level and below; if this command is given in a macro or command file, the previous INPUT TIMEOUT setting is restored when the macro or command file exits. Chapter 13.

SET KEY *number [text]*
> Assigns the *text* to the key whose key-press code is *number*. The key-press code can be obtained using SHOW KEY. The *text* can be a single character or backslash code, or any string of characters. Key mappings accomplished by SET KEY are effective during CONNECT mode. Chapters 4, 9; Appendix V.

SET LANGUAGE *name*
> Enables language-specific transliterations during text file transfer when either file or transfer character-set is ASCII. Type SHOW LANGUAGE for a list of available languages. Chapter 9.

SET LINE [*device-name*]
Opens a serial communication device for local-mode connections. If the device name is omitted, any currently open device is closed and Kermit returns to its default communication device (normally the job's controlling terminal). Chapter 3.

SET LOCAL-ECHO { OFF, ON }
Synonym for SET DUPLEX, SET TERMINAL ECHO.

SET MACRO ECHO { OFF, ON }
Tells C-Kermit whether to echo commands as it reads and executes them from a macro definition. Normally OFF, meaning macro definitions are not echoed during execution. Chapter 11.

SET MACRO ERROR { OFF, ON }
Tells C-Kermit whether to terminate execution of the current macro automatically if it encounters a syntax or execution error. Normally OFF, meaning errors do not terminate the execution of a macro. Chapter 11.

SET MODEM *name*
Tells C-Kermit the kind of autodial modem you will be using, if any, in local-mode communication. NONE (the default) means there is no autodial modem. If you are using a modem, this command must be given *before* the SET LINE command, so C-Kermit can activate the proper modem controls when opening the device. Type a question mark or see Table 3-2 on page 53 for a list of supported modems. Chapter 3.

SET NETWORK *name*
Tells C-Kermit the type of network to be used when establishing SET HOST connections, such as TCP/IP or X.25. Type SHOW NETWORK to see which network types are supported by your copy of C-Kermit. If you get an error message, there is no network support at all. Chapter 3.

SET PAD *option* `value`
X.25 PAD settings. Chapter 3.

SET PAD BREAK-ACTION *n*
(X.25 only) X.3 Parameter 7. What C-Kermit's simulated PAD should do if it receives a BREAK signal from your keyboard. 0 = nothing, 1 = send Interrupt packet, 2 = reset, 4 = send Indication of Break PAD message, 8 = escape to PAD, 16 = discard output. Default = 21 (= 16 + 4 + 1).

SET PAD BREAK-CHARACTER *n*
(X.25 only) Default 0.

SET PAD CHARACTER-DELETE *n*
(X.25 only) X.3 Parameter 16. 0–127 = ASCII value of the character to be used for erasing a character. Default = 8 (Ctrl-H = Backspace).

SET PAD CR-PADDING *n*
> (X.25 only) X.3 Parameter 9, Padding After Carriage Return (CR). 0–255. Number of padding characters PAD should send to DTE after sending a CR. Default = 0.

SET PAD DISCARD-OUTPUT { 0, 1 }
> (X.25 only) X.3 Parameter 8. 0 = normal data delivery (default), 1 = discard output.

SET PAD ECHO { 0, 1 }
> (X.25 only) X.3 Parameter 2. 0 = PAD will not echo, 1 = PAD will echo. Default = 1.

SET PAD EDITING { 0, 1 }
> (X.25 only) X.3 Parameter 15. 0 = No editing, 1 = editing allowed. Default = 1.

SET PAD ESCAPE { 0, 1 }
> (X.25 only) X.3 Parameter 1. 0 = Escape to PAD not possible, 1 = use Ctrl-P.

SET PAD FORWARD *n*
> (X.25 only) X.3 Parameter 3, Data Forwarding Characters. 0 = none, 1 = any alphanumeric, 2 = carriage return, others. Default = 2.

SET PAD LF-INSERT *n*
> (X.25 only) X.3 Parameter 13, Linefeed (LF) insertion after carriage return (CR). 0 = no LF insertion, 1 = PAD inserts LF after each CR sent to DTE, 2 = PAD inserts LF after each CR received from DTE, 4 = PAD echoes LF as CRLF. Default = 0.

SET PAD LF-PADDING *n*
> (X.25 only) X.3 Parameter 14. 0–255 padding characters to be sent by PAD after linefeed. Default = 0.

SET PAD LINE-DELETE *n*
> (X.25 only) X.3 Parameter 17. 0–127 = ASCII value of the character to be used for erasing a line. Default = 21 (Ctrl-U).

SET PAD LINE-DISPLAY *n*
> (X.25 only) X.3 Parameter 18. 0–127 = ASCII value of the character to redisplay an edited line. Default = 18 (Ctrl-R).

SET PAD LINE-FOLD *n*
> (X.25 only) X.3 Parameter 10, Line Folding. 0 = none, 1–255 = number of graphic characters per line after which to insert folding characters. Default = 0.

SET PAD PAD-FLOW-CONTROL { 0, 1 }
> (X.25 only) X.3 Parameter 5. 0 = No flow control by PAD, 1 = PAD may send Xon/Xoff flow control to user. Default = 0.

SET PAD SERVICE-SIGNALS { 0, 1 }
> (X.25 only) X.3 parameter 6, PAD Service and Command Signals. 0 = PAD service signals are not sent to DTE, 1 = PAD service signals sent. Default = 1.

SET PAD TIMEOUT *n*
> (X.25 only) X.3 Parameter 4, Data forwarding timeout, 0–255 (twentieths of a second). Default = 0 (no data forwarding on timeout).

SET PAD USER-FLOW-CONTROL { 0, 1 }
> (X.25 only) X.3 Parameter 12. 0 = no flow control by user, 1 = user device may send Xon/Xoff flow control to PAD. Default = 0.

SET PARITY { EVEN, MARK, NONE, ODD, SPACE }
> Selects the type of parity to be used on the communication device during terminal connection, script program execution, and file transfer. NONE allows transmission of 8-bit data. Any of the others restricts communication to 7-bit data and forces C-Kermit to use shifting techniques for 8-bit data during file transfer. Also see SET COMMAND BYTESIZE and SET TERMINAL BYTESIZE. Chapters 4, 6, 8, 9.

SET PORT
> Synonym for SET LINE.

SET PROMPT *[text]*
> Changes C-Kermit's interactive command prompt to *text*. Leading and trailing blanks are ignored in the *text* unless it is enclosed in curly braces, in which case the braces are discarded. If the *text* is omitted, C-Kermit's default prompt is restored. Variables in the *text* are evaluated every time the prompt is issued so, for example, your prompt string can contain variables like \v(dir) or \v(time) to have Kermit always display its current directory or the current time. Chapter 2.

SET QUIET { OFF, ON }
> Controls the display of C-Kermit's informational (but not error) messages. SET QUIET OFF (the default) enables them, SET QUIET ON suppresses them.

SET RECEIVE END-OF-PACKET *number*
> Specifies the numeric ASCII value of the character to be used by the other Kermit to terminate the packets it sends to C-Kermit, normally Carriage Return (ASCII 13). The *number* must be the code for an ASCII control character, 0–31 or 127. Chapter 6.

SET RECEIVE PACKET-LENGTH *number*
> Specifies the maximum length for packets to be sent to C-Kermit by the other Kermit, up to 9024, depending on C-Kermit's configuration. Chapters 6, 8.

SET RECEIVE PAD-CHARACTER *number*
> Specifies the numeric ASCII value of the character to be sent to C-Kermit by the other Kermit before the beginning of each packet. Chapter 6.

SET RECEIVE PADDING *number*
> Specifies the number of pad characters to be sent to C-Kermit by the other Kermit (normally 0). Chapter 6.

SET RECEIVE START-OF-PACKET *number*

Tells C-Kermit the numeric ASCII value of the character that the other Kermit will use to indicate the start of a packet. The *number* can be the code for any ASCII character, but a control character, 0–31 or 127, should be used whenever possible. The normal START-OF-PACKET character is Control-A (= 1). Chapter 6.

SET RECEIVE TIMEOUT *number*

Tells C-Kermit the amount of time the other Kermit should wait for a packet before timing out and taking corrective action. Chapter 6.

SET RETRY *number*

Tells C-Kermit how many times any particular packet may be retransmitted (or NAK'd) before the file transfer is declared a failure. Chapter 6.

SET SCRIPT ECHO { OFF, ON }

Tells whether SCRIPT commands should echo their progress on the screen. Normally ON. Chapter 13.

SET SEND END-OF-PACKET *number*

Specifies the numeric ASCII value of the character to be used by C-Kermit to terminate the packets it sends to the other Kermit, normally Carriage Return (ASCII 13). Must be a control character. Chapter 6.

SET SEND PACKET-LENGTH *number*

Specifies the maximum length packet C-Kermit may send to the other Kermit, even if the other Kermit requests longer ones. This command will not make C-Kermit send packets longer than the other Kermit requests. Chapters 6, 8.

SET SEND PAD-CHARACTER *number*

Specifies the numeric ASCII value of the character to be sent by C-Kermit to the other Kermit before the beginning of each packet, no matter what pad-character the other Kermit asks for. Chapter 6.

SET SEND PADDING *number*

The number of padding characters C-Kermit is to send to the other Kermit (normally 0), overriding the number of pad-characters the other Kermit requests. Chapter 6.

SET SEND START-OF-PACKET *number*

Tells C-Kermit the numeric character code value of the character that it should use to mark the beginning of packets it sends. Can be any ASCII character. Normally Control-A (ASCII 1), and should normally be in the control range. Chapter 6.

SET SEND TIMEOUT *number*

Tells C-Kermit the amount of time to wait for a packet from the other Kermit before timing out and resending a packet (or sending a NAK), even if the other Kermit asks for a different timeout value. Chapter 6.

SET SERVER DISPLAY { OFF, ON }
When C-Kermit is running as a server in local mode, it normally does not produce a file transfer display. Use SET SERVER DISPLAY ON to enable the display. Chapter 7.

SET SERVER TIMEOUT *number*
Tells the C-Kermit server the number of seconds to wait for a command packet from the other Kermit before timing out and sending a NAK packet. The normal value is 0, meaning not to time out at all during server command wait. Use a nonzero value only if the client Kermit program is not capable of timeouts and automatic retransmission. Chapter 7.

SET SESSION-LOG { BINARY, TEXT }
(UNIX only) How the session log is recorded. TEXT, which is the default, means not to record certain characters (such as carriage returns, NUL, and DEL) that are inconsistent with UNIX text file format. BINARY means to record all arriving characters. Character-set translation, if elected, is done in both cases. Chapters 4, 10.

SET SPEED *number*
The speed (in bits per second) to use on a serial communication device selected by SET LINE. Common values include 1200, 2400, 9600, and 19200. Chapter 3.

SET SUSPEND { OFF, ON }
(UNIX only) Tells C-Kermit whether it is allowed to be suspended by keyboard signal (normally Ctrl-Z), or by its own SUSPEND or Z command. SUSPEND is ON by default in most UNIX implementations. Set this to OFF if suspending Kermit doesn't work right on your computer. Appendix III.

SET TAKE ECHO { OFF, ON }
Tells C-Kermit whether to display commands from command files on your screen as it executes them. Normally OFF, meaning the commands are not displayed. Chapter 11.

SET TAKE ERROR { OFF, ON }
Tells C-Kermit whether to terminate a command file automatically if it encounters a syntax or execution error. Normally OFF, meaning the command file is not terminated. Applies to current command level and below. Chapter 11.

SET TELNET ECHO { LOCAL, REMOTE }
Controls the initial echoing state when making TCP/IP SET HOST or TELNET connections. After the connection is made, the echoing state can be changed by TELNET protocol negotiations. The default is LOCAL. Chapter 3.

SET TELNET NEWLINE-MODE { ON, OFF }
When ON, which is the default, C-Kermit sends carriage return (CR) characters from your keyboard to the remote TELNET server as CR-linefeed (CRLF) combinations, according to the TELNET specification [51]. Use OFF to send CR as CR alone, followed

by NUL (ASCII 0; the NUL is required by the TELNET specification); this should be necessary only when the remote TELNET server does not conform to the TELNET specification.

SET TELNET TERMINAL-TYPE *text*
The terminal-type string to send if requested by the remote TELNET server. By default, your local terminal type is sent. Chapter 3.

SET TERMINAL *option value*
Changes settings for terminal connection. Chapter 4.

SET TERMINAL BYTESIZE *{ 7, 8 }*
Specifies the byte size to use during CONNECT, INPUT, OUTPUT, TRANSMIT, and similar nonprotocol communication commands between C-Kermit and the remote computer. Normally 7, meaning that each byte is stripped of its 8th bit. 8 bits are used only if TERMINAL BYTESIZE is 8 and PARITY is NONE. Chapters 4, 9.

SET TERMINAL CHARACTER-SET *remote-cset [local-cset]*
Specifies the character sets used on the local and remote computers, respectively, during CONNECT, LOG SESSION, and TRANSMIT, so C-Kermit can translate between them. The list of character sets should be the same as that for SET FILE CHARACTER-SET, but with the addition of TRANSPARENT for no translation. TRANSPARENT is the default. If the *local-cset* is not specified, C-Kermit's current FILE CHARACTER-SET is used. Chapter 9.

SET TERMINAL COLOR *{ HELP, NORMAL, REVERSE, STATUS, UNDERLINED } foreground-color background-color*
(OS/2 only) Sets the foreground and background colors for the specified types of text during VT102 terminal emulation. Color choices include BLACK, BLUE, BROWN, CYAN, DGRAY (dark gray), GREEN, LBLUE (light blue), LCYAN (light cyan), LGREEN (light green), LRED (light red), MAGENTA, RED, WHITE, and YELLOW. Appendix V.

SET TERMINAL CR-DISPLAY *{ CRLF, NORMAL }*
Controls the display of carriage return (CR) characters that arrive from the remote system. NORMAL (the default) displays CR as itself. CRLF displays CR as CR plus linefeed. Chapter 4.

SET TERMINAL CURSOR *{ FULL, HALF, UNDERLINE }*
(OS/2 only) Selects the cursor shape for terminal emulation. Appendix V.

SET TERMINAL ECHO *{ LOCAL, REMOTE }*
Tells C-Kermit whether it should echo keyboard characters locally during CONNECT. TERMINAL ECHO is REMOTE by default, meaning C-Kermit expects the remote device to echo. Synonyms: SET DUPLEX, SET LOCAL-ECHO. Chapter 4.

SET TERMINAL LOCKING-SHIFT { **OFF, ON** }
  Tells C-Kermit whether to use shift-in/shift-out protocol during CONNECT and TRANSMIT for 8-bit transparency over 7-bit connections. Chapters 4, 9.

SET TERMINAL NEWLINE-MODE { **OFF, ON** }
  Normally when you press the Return or Enter key during CONNECT mode, C-Kermit sends a carriage return (CR) character, ASCII 13. SET TERMINAL NEWLINE-MODE ON tells C-Kermit to send CR and linefeed (LF, ASCII 10) instead. Chapter 4.

SET TRANSFER CHARACTER-SET { **ASCII, CYRILLIC-ISO, JAPANESE-EUC, LATIN1, LATIN2, TRANSPARENT** }
  Specifies the character set to be used by C-Kermit when transferring text files. When sending files, C-Kermit translates from the current file character-set to the selected transfer character-set. When receiving files, C-Kermit translates from the specified transfer character-set to the current file character-set or, if the sending Kermit has included a character-set attribute in a file's Attribute packet and if ATTRIBUTE CHARACTER-SET is ON, C-Kermit uses the transfer character-set specified in the Attribute packet. Chapter 9. Synonym: **SET XFER CHARACTER-SET**.

SET TRANSFER LOCKING-SHIFT { **OFF, ON, FORCED** }
  Tells C-Kermit whether to use locking-shift protocol during file transfers when PARITY is not NONE. Normally ON. Chapters 8 and 9. Synonym: **SET XFER LOCKING-SHIFT**.

SET TRANSMIT *parameter value*
  Modifies the default behavior of the TRANSMIT command. You can display these settings with SHOW TRANSMIT. Chapter 10. Synonym: **SET XMIT**.

SET TRANSMIT ECHO { **OFF, ON** }
  Tells C-Kermit whether to echo file characters on your screen during the TRANSMIT command. Normally ON. Chapter 10.

SET TRANSMIT EOF [*text*]
  Tells C-Kermit the character or characters to send after it TRANSMITs the last line of the file or when you type Ctrl-C to interrupt a transmission. Normally, no characters are sent. Chapter 10.

SET TRANSMIT FILL *number*
  Tells C-Kermit the numeric ASCII code of the character to be used to fill blank lines during execution of the TRANSMIT command. Normally, no fill character is transmitted. Chapter 10.

SET TRANSMIT LINEFEED { **OFF, ON** }
  Normally, C-Kermit strips linefeeds from TRANSMITted text files. SET TRANSMIT LINEFEED ON tells C-Kermit to leave them in. Chapter 10.

SET TRANSMIT LOCKING-SHIFT { OFF, ON }
    Tells C-Kermit whether to use locking shifts (Shift-In/Shift-Out) to transmit 8-bit characters on a 7-bit connection; that is, when PARITY is not NONE. Normally OFF. Effective only when FILE TYPE is TEXT. Chapter 10.

SET TRANSMIT PAUSE *number*
    Tells C-Kermit how many milliseconds (thousandths of seconds) to pause after transmitting each line of text. Effective only when FILE TYPE is TEXT. Chapter 10.

SET TRANSMIT PROMPT *number*
    Tells C-Kermit the numeric ASCII code of the character to wait for after TRANSMITting each line of a file. Normally C-Kermit waits for the host to echo a linefeed (ASCII 10) after the carriage return that is sent at the end of each line. A value of zero tells C-Kermit not to wait at all, and to transmit all the characters of the file without pausing. Effective only when FILE TYPE is TEXT. Chapter 10.

SET UNKNOWN-CHAR-SET { DISCARD, KEEP }
    Whether to keep or discard an arriving file whose Attribute packet announces a transfer character-set unknown to C-Kermit. The default is DISCARD. Chapter 9.

SET WILDCARD-EXPANSION { KERMIT, SHELL }
    (UNIX only) Tells whether wildcards in filenames (e.g., in the SEND command) should be expanded by Kermit itself (the default) or by your login shell. Appendix III.

SET WINDOW-SIZE *number*
    Tells C-Kermit the maximum window size to be used in file transfers. This is the number of packets (1 through 31) that C-Kermit can send before acknowledgements are required, or the number of packets it can receive that are later than a missing packet. Chapter 8.

SET X.25 CALL-USER-DATA { OFF, ON *text* **}**
    (X.25 only) ON lets you specify up to 12 characters of call user data required by the X.25 host you are calling. Normally OFF. Chapter 3.

SET X.25 CLOSED-USER-GROUP { OFF, ON *n* **}**
    (X.25 only) OFF = no closed user group, ON *n* specifies the user group number, 0 to 99. OFF by default. Chapter 3.

SET X.25 REVERSE-CHARGE { OFF, ON }
    (X.25 only) OFF = caller pays, ON = callee pays. Default is OFF. Chapter 3.

SET XFER
    Synonym for SET TRANSFER.

SET XMIT
    Synonym for SET TRANSMIT.

SHOW
Lists C-Kermit's most important settings.

SHOW ARGUMENTS
Shows the arguments to the currently active macro, if any. Chapter 11.

SHOW ARRAYS
Lists the names and dimensions of all currently declared arrays. Chapter 12.

SHOW ATTRIBUTES
Lists C-Kermit's file attributes and tells whether each is ON or OFF. Chapter 8.

SHOW CHARACTER-SETS
Lists the current file, transfer, and terminal character-sets. Chapter 9.

SHOW COMMUNICATIONS
Lists the current communication device or network host and the other communication-related items: speed, parity, duplex, DIAL parameters, modem signals, etc. Chapter 3.

SHOW COUNT
Displays the current value of the COUNT (\v(count)) variable.

SHOW DEFAULT
Shows the current directory. Synonym for PWD.

SHOW DIAL
Displays the current SET DIAL and related settings. Chapter 3.

SHOW ESCAPE
Shows current CONNECT-mode escape character. Chapter 4.

SHOW FEATURES
Lists the features that C-Kermit was configured with and the features that were omitted, along with compilation options. Chapter 1.

SHOW FILE
Lists current values of file-related parameters. Chapters 5–10.

SHOW FUNCTIONS
Lists the names of C-Kermit's built-in functions. Chapter 12.

SHOW GLOBALS
Lists the names and values of currently defined global variables, \%a through \%z. Chapter 11.

SHOW KEY
C-Kermit asks you to press a key. In response, C-Kermit tells you the key's key-press code (for use with SET KEY) and its current definition, if any. Chapter 4.

SHOW LABELED-FILE-INFO
   (VMS and OpenVMS only) Displays current SET FILE LABEL settings. Appendix IV.

SHOW LANGUAGES
   Lists the languages supported by the C-Kermit SET LANGUAGE command, along with the current language, file character-set, and transfer character-set. Chapter 9.

SHOW MACROS *[name]*
   Lists the definitions of all macros whose names begin with *name*. If *name* is omitted, all defined macros are listed. To get a list of the names of defined macros without their definitions, type DO ?. Chapter 11.

SHOW MODEM-SIGNALS
   Shows the current modem type and, if the underlying operating system supports it, lists the state of modem signals on the currently selected communication device, if it is a serial device. Chapter 3.

SHOW NETWORK
   Shows network protocols, current settings, and active connections. Chapter 3.

SHOW PAD
   (X.25 only) Lists X.25 PAD-related parameters. Chapter 3.

SHOW PROTOCOL
   Lists the current Kermit file-transfer protocol-related settings. Chapters 5, 6, 8.

SHOW SCRIPTS
   Lists the current SET TAKE, SET MACRO, SET INPUT, and SET SCRIPT values. Chapters 11–13.

SHOW SERVER
   Lists server-related settings, including which server commands are enabled and disabled. Chapter 7.

SHOW STATUS
   Tells whether the previous command succeeded or failed. Chapter 12.

SHOW TERMINAL
   Lists SET TERMINAL settings. Chapters 4, 9, 10.

SHOW TRANSMIT
   Lists the current SET TRANSMIT settings. Chapter 10. Synonym: **SHOW XMIT**.

SHOW VARIABLES
   Lists the names and values of C-Kermit's built-in variables. Chapter 11.

SHOW VERSIONS
   Lists the version numbers and dates of each of the C-Kermit program modules.

SLEEP *[n]*
Sleeps for *n* seconds. Synonym for PAUSE. See PAUSE.

SPACE *[device]*
Displays operating-system-specific information about disk usage in the specified or current device and directory on the computer where C-Kermit is running. Chapter 2.

SPAWN *[command]*
Synonym for RUN, PUSH.

STATISTICS
Displays statistics about the most recent file transfer. Chapter 8.

STOP *[number [message]]*
Returns from the current command file or macro to the topmost command level: the C-Kermit prompt if the program is in interactive mode, or to the host operating system if C-Kermit was invoked with command-line action arguments. If the optional *number* is included, it becomes the status of the top-level TAKE or DO command, 0 for success, nonzero for failure. If a message is given, it is printed on the screen. The text may be enclosed in braces to include leading or trailing spaces. Chapter 12.

SUSPEND
(UNIX only) Halts C-Kermit and returns to the host operating system in such a way that C-Kermit can be continued later, either in the foreground or in the background. Appendix III. Synonym: **Z**.

TAKE *filename*
Executes commands from the named file until the end of the file is reached, an END, STOP, RETURN, EXIT, or QUIT command is encountered, a command error occurs and TAKE ERROR is ON, or a GOTO command is encountered whose target label is outside the file. Chapters 2, 11.

TELNET *[host [service]]*
Establishes a TCP/IP TELNET connection to the given host, which can be an IP host name or dotted numeric address. The service can be a TCP service name or number. The default service is 23, TELNET. If the *host* and *service* are both omitted, resumes the currently active TCP/IP connection, if any. Chapter 3.

TRANSLATE *file1 cs1 cs2 [file2]*
Translates the file *file1* from the character set *cs1* into the character set *cs2* and puts the result in *file2* or, if *file2* is not specified, on the screen. The available character sets are the same as for SET FILE CHARACTER-SET. Chapter 9. Synonym: **XLATE**.

TRANSMIT *filename*
Sends the characters from the file out the currently selected communication device. Use this command for sending files to computers that don't have Kermit programs.

No error checking is done. If the FILE TYPE is TEXT, character-set translation is done and transmission is line-oriented. If FILE TYPE is BINARY, characters are sent in a constant stream with no modification. Chapter 10. Synonym: **XMIT**.

TYPE *filename*
Displays the named local file on the screen. Chapter 2.

VERSION
Displays C-Kermit's main version number. Chapter 2.

WAIT *[number=1 [{ CD, CTS, DSR } ...]]*
Waits up to the given number of seconds for all of the specified modem signals to appear on the currently selected (SET LINE) communication device. Completion status is SUCCESS if all of the given modem signals were sensed before the timeout expired, otherwise FAILURE. Can be interrupted from the keyboard. Chapter 13.

WHILE *condition { command, [command [, ...]] }*
While the condition is true, executes the commands in the command list. The conditions are the same as for the IF command. Chapter 12.

WHO *[{ user, user@host, @host]*
Lists users logged in to the local computer, or lists information about the specified user on the local computer or on the specified remote host computer. (@*host* notation available on UNIX only.) Chapter 2.

WRITE *{ DEBUG-LOG, ERROR, FILE, PACKET-LOG, SESSION-LOG, SCREEN, TRANSACTION-LOG } [{] text [}]*
Writes the text to the indicated file. All backslash codes, variables, and functions are evaluated first. Carriage return and linefeed are *not* supplied automatically at the end of the text, as they are by the ECHO command. Leading and trailing spaces are discarded unless the *text* is surrounded by { braces }, in which case the enclosing braces themselves are discarded. Chapter 12.

XIF *condition { command [, command ...] } [ELSE { command [, command ...] }]*
If the condition is true, executes the command or commands enclosed in the first set of curly braces. If an ELSE-part is provided, and the condition is not true, executes the commands inside the second set of curly braces. The conditions are the same as for the regular IF command. Chapter 12.

XLATE
Synonym for TRANSLATE.

XMIT
Synonym for TRANSMIT.

Z Synonym for SUSPEND.

Appendix II

A Condensed Guide to Serial Data Communications

Communication between two computers requires not only a physical connection, but also an agreement about how the computers will use it. When you establish the connection yourself, for example by dialing up or installing your own cable, you need to understand the elements that must agree. Otherwise a working connection is an unlikely stroke of good fortune.

Character Format and Parity

A byte, or character, is generally made up of 8 bits. Textual data is represented by a specific code, such as ASCII or ISO Latin-1. ASCII and other 7-bit codes leave one of the 8 bits unused, so in many applications this spare bit is dedicated to a rudimentary kind of error detection called *parity*. The extra bit, or *parity bit*, is set to 0 or 1 to make the overall number of 1 bits even (or odd). For reasons lost in antiquity, or perhaps simply for completeness, there also exist "mark parity" (in which the parity bit is always 1), and "space parity" (in which the parity bit is always 0). Thus there are five possibilities for parity: even, odd, mark, space, and none. Parity is commonly used with 7-bit character codes. Figure II-1 on the next page shows a 7-bit character with even parity and an 8-bit character with no parity.

The devices on both ends of a data connection should agree on their parity settings, otherwise data can be misinterpreted. For example, 11000101 is Latin-1 A-ring on an 8-bit connection, uppercase E on a 7-bit connection with even or mark parity, and it's an illegal bit combination on a 7-bit connection with odd or space parity (see Figure II-1).

359

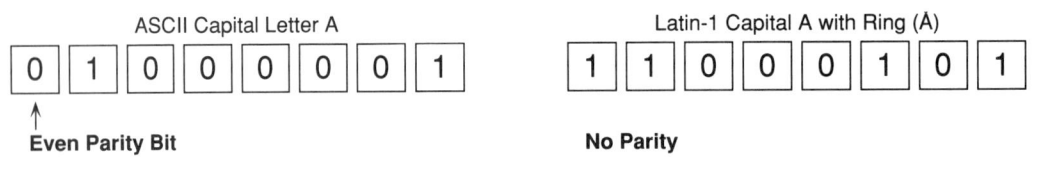

```
         ASCII Capital Letter A                    Latin-1 Capital A with Ring (Å)
       ┌─┬─┬─┬─┬─┬─┬─┬─┐                         ┌─┬─┬─┬─┬─┬─┬─┬─┐
       │0│1│0│0│0│0│0│1│                         │1│1│0│0│0│1│0│1│
       └─┴─┴─┴─┴─┴─┴─┴─┘                         └─┴─┴─┴─┴─┴─┴─┴─┘
        ↑
       Even Parity Bit                             No Parity
```

Figure II-1 Character Formats

Serial Asynchronous Transmission

Characters are transmitted over short distances using digital signals: small discrete voltages representing the binary digits (bits) 0 and 1, such as +12V for 0 and −12V for 1, transmitted through copper wires. The electrical characteristics and distance limitations are spelled out in a venerable industry standard, EIA RS-232 [28] (or CCITT V.24 [8], its international counterpart) followed by practically every computer manufacturer. In the terminology of RS-232 and V.24, a computer or terminal is *data terminal equipment*, DTE for short. The word *terminal* designates a device that is at the end of a connection, which is often, indeed, a terminal; that is, a device with a keyboard, a screen, and a communications interface.

The bits within a character are transmitted in series, one after the other, in a specified order [2] through a wire connecting the two devices. This method of transmission, referred to as *serial* transmission, is preferred for all but very short distances over the more expensive parallel method, which requires one wire for each of the 8 bits in a character.

When a terminal is connected to a computer, the computer cannot predict when the person at the terminal will strike a key; the terminal and the computer are not synchronized. During serial transmission in this environment, characters are delimited using a "start bit" (0) and a "stop bit" (1) so the receiver knows where each character begins and ends [3], as shown in Figure II-2. The stop bit lasts until the next character comes. This mode of serial communication is said to be *asynchronous*.

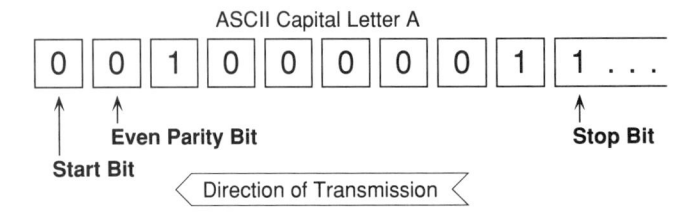

```
                 ASCII Capital Letter A
       ┌─┬─┬─┬─┬─┬─┬─┬─┬─┬─┐
       │0│0│1│0│0│0│0│0│1│1│ . . .
       └─┴─┴─┴─┴─┴─┴─┴─┴─┴─┘
        ↑ ↑                 ↑
        │ Even Parity Bit   Stop Bit
        Start Bit
              ⟨ Direction of Transmission ⟨
```

Figure II-2 Asynchronous Character Transmission Format

360   A Condensed Guide to Serial Data Communications / Appendix II

Transmission Speed

Even in asynchronous communication, however, two DTEs are not entirely unsynchronized. The transmitters and receivers of each computer must be running at the same *speed* for the receiving computer to recognize each bit correctly, based on how long a bit "lasts." The transmission speed is expressed in bits per second (bps), sometimes called *baud*. Speeds commonly used in asynchronous serial data communication are 75, 110, 150, 300, 600, 1200, 2400, 4800, 9600, 14400, 19200, 38400, and 57600 bps.[44] If the speeds of the two devices do not agree, successful communication can not occur.

Ten bits are required to transmit a character: the 8 bits of the character itself plus the start and stop bits. Therefore, 10 bits per second (bps) is the same as one character per second (cps) if characters are transmitted without gaps (long stop bits) between them.

It is possible, and common in some parts of the world, for the receiver and transmitter to run at different speeds. For example, a terminal sends characters at 75 bps and the computer receives them at 75 bps, but the computer sends and the terminal receives at 1200 bps. This is called *split speed* operation.

"Plex"

An asynchronous serial connection between two DTEs can be characterized by how the data flows. If data may go in one direction only, the connection is said to be *simplex*, or *one-way*. If data can go in both directions, the connection is *duplex*, or *two-way*.[45]

A duplex connection can be made using a single data wire or channel if the data goes in one direction at a time; this mode of transmission is called *half duplex* or *two-way alternate*. A special signal, called a *handshake*, is required to turn the direction around. Single-wire connections are rare, but half duplex communication is still common in mainframe computing environments. On a half duplex connection between a terminal and a computer, the terminal must *echo* each character you type. This is called *local echoing*.

Today, most asynchronous serial communication takes place over two data wires, one for each direction. Data can go in both directions at once; this is called *full duplex* or *two-way simultaneous*. A full-duplex connection lets you type characters at the same time received characters are being displayed on your screen, and it allows a computer to control the appearance of your screen by echoing characters selectively.

---

[44]RS-232 is not designed to work at speeds beyond about 20000 bps, but many modern communication boards offer higher speeds. Speeds in excess of 19200 require very short direct connections, perhaps using special shielded and/or low capacitance cables.

[45]Notice the dual terminology. The first term is the one used in American data communications literature, and the second term is the one used by international standards.

Flow Control

Whenever Computer A is sending data to Computer B, there is always the chance that Computer A's data will arrive faster than Computer B can process it. On a full duplex connection, where characters can travel in both directions at once, Computer B can tell Computer A to stop sending data even while the data is arriving. This gives Computer B a chance to "catch up"; when it has finished processing the characters that have accumulated, it tells Computer A to resume sending.

This process is called *flow control*. It is most commonly accomplished using the control characters Ctrl-S (ASCII DC3) to stop the flow of data, and Ctrl-Q (ASCII DC1) to resume it. In the context of flow control, these characters are called XON and XOFF, respectively. Flow control accomplished by mixing special characters with the data itself is called "in-band" or "software" flow control. Xon/Xoff flow control works when the computers have a full-duplex connection, both computers observe this convention, and the connection between them is clean enough not to damage these special characters during transmission.

Hardware flow control is accomplished using separate wires, most commonly the RS-232 RTS and CTS circuits, and is therefore "out of band." It is much more reliable and responsive than software flow control, but can generally be used only over short distances, such as between a computer and the modem it is directly connected to.

Modems

The maximum distance allowed by RS-232 is 50 feet, about 15 meters. To connect two DTEs over longer distances requires special *data communications equipment*, or DCEs. These are usually powered devices that boost the data's signal strength and modulate its form to allow it to travel greater distances. A *modem*[46] is a DCE that translates between the digital representation of computer data and the type of analog signaling that is used by traditional voice telephones. Modems are commonly used to connect distant computers to each other over the switched telephone network by placing telephone calls. Modems let any two computers in the world communicate with each other when a phone call can be placed between them and the modulation techniques of the two modems are compatible.

In a dialup modem connection, the modem actually replaces the telephone. It does what the telephone does, but instead of converting between human voice and analog electronic signals on the phone wire, it converts between the computer's digital signals and the analog phone signals.

---

[46]The word *modem* is derived from the words *modulator* and *demodulator*.

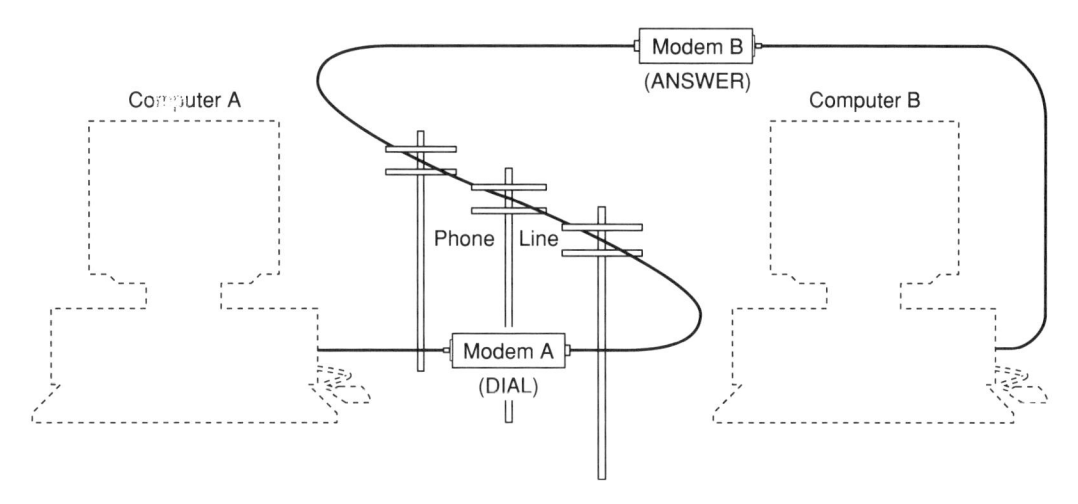

Figure II-3 Computers Connected by Modems

Each computer must have its own modem, as shown in Figure II-3. The computer placing the call tells the modem to dial the number; it picks up the phone, listens for dialtone, and dials the given number by simulating the clicks or beeps of the telephone it is mimicking. When the other modem answers the call, the originating modem sends a constant tone at a certain (originating) frequency. The answering modem recognizes this tone and replies with its own tone at a different (answering) frequency. When the two modems recognize each other's tones, the connection is complete and ready to use. These tones are called the *carrier* signal, and remain active throughout the connection. Transmitted data is impressed upon the carrier signals to alter their frequency, amplitude, or phase.

Modem Signals

Computers communicating through modems must be able to monitor and control them, just as people can monitor and control a phone call. For example, if you hear a click and a dialtone in the middle of a telephone conversation, you have good cause to suspect you've been disconnected and you can hang up your phone. This means you don't have to wait forever for the other party to finish a sentence. This sounds silly, but it's the kind of thing a computer might do if it couldn't tell when a connection is broken.

Modems handle such problems quite nicely, using special circuits defined by RS-232 and V.24 for signaling between the modem and the computer. The 10 circuits used in asynchronous serial communication are listed in Table II-1 on the next page. The *Circuit* column shows the RS-232 name for the circuit; the V.24 column shows the CCITT V.24 circuit number. The DB-25 column shows the pin assignments for a standard RS-232 25-pin connector; the DB-9 column shows the pin assignments for the 9-pin connector used on the IBM PC/AT and PS/2.

Table II-1 RS-232-C Modem Signals and Pins

Circuit	V.24	Name	Direction	DB25	DB9	Comments
FG		Frame Ground		1	–	Electrical safety
TD	103	Transmitted Data	To DCE	2	3	Data from computer
RD	104	Received Data	To DTE	3	2	Data to computer
RTS	105	Request To Send	To DCE	4	7	Hardware Flow Control
CTS	106	Clear To Send	To DTE	5	8	Hardware Flow Control
DSR	107	Data Set Ready	To DTE	6	6	DCE on and in data mode
SG	102	Signal Ground		7	5	Voltage measurement reference
CD	109	Carrier Detect	To DTE	8	1	Modems are communicating
DTR	108	Data Terminal Ready	To DCE	20	4	DTE on and in data mode
RI	125	Ring Indicator	To DTE	22	9	Phone is ringing

A modem call from computer A to computer B progresses something like this, as seen from the point of view of computer A (the originator of the call):

1. Computer A checks to see that Modem A's DSR signal is on. If not, the computer concludes that the modem is not connected or not turned on, and the call fails.

2. Computer A turns on its DTR signal to let the modem know that it wants to begin communicating.

3. Computer A gives Modem A the command to dial a phone number.

4. Modem A takes the phone "off hook" and listens for dialtone; if there is none, the process stops here. Otherwise Modem A dials the number and waits for an answer.

5. If there is no answer within a prescribed amount of time, Modem A reports failure to the computer, and the process stops here.

6. When the other modem answers, Modem A sends its originate-frequency tone to it and waits for an answer-frequency tone. If none appears within a certain time, the process fails and stops here.

7. When the originating modem hears the answering modem's tone, it turns on its CD circuit, so the computer knows it may exchange data with the other computer.

8. If Computer A turns off its DTR signal at any time during the connection, Modem A hangs up the phone. If Modem A stops hearing Modem B's carrier tone at any time during the connection, it turns off its CD signal.

The situation on the answering end (B) is similar. Modem B "hears" the phone ring and turns on its RI signal. Computer B sees RI come on, prepares itself to communicate, and then turns on its DTR signal. Modem B sees DTR and starts sending its carrier tone to the other modem. The two modems attempt to settle on a modulation technique (explained on page 367) and, if they succeed, both modems turns on their CD signals and communication between Computers A and B commences.

Detecting Failures Automatically

During the connection between computers A and B, at least five different components can fail: Computer A, Modem A, Computer B, Modem B, and the dialed connection itself. Using only two modem signals, CD and DTR, all components of the connection can detect a failure anywhere in the communication path and can shut themselves down gracefully in the event of any failure so computer data can be preserved and the telephone connection can be hung up:

- If Computer A dies suddenly, its DTR signal goes off. Modem A notices this and stops sending its carrier tone and hangs up the phone. This makes Modem B turn off its CD signal, which makes Computer B turn off its DTR signal, which makes Modem B hang up its end of the phone connection. The same thing happens in the other direction if Computer B dies.

- If Modem A suddenly stops working (because, for example, you tripped over the power cord and pulled it out of the receptacle), then Computer A no longer receives the CD or DSR signals and knows the connection is broken. Meanwhile, Modem B notices the absence of carrier and turns off CD and hangs up its end of the phone connection. The same thing happens if Modem B dies—just exchange A and B in all the sentences in this paragraph (except this one).

- If the connection itself is broken, both modems notice the loss of carrier and both turn off CD, so both computers know the connection is broken. Of course, the computers also turn off their DTR signals to make the modems hang up the phone, but since the connection is broken already, who cares?

Automatic Dialing

Most modern modems contain a little computer that accepts commands from the terminal or PC in the form of characters and reports the results back, also in character form. Although there is an international standard [9] specifying the repertoire and format of these commands and responses, it is not widely followed. In most parts of the world, modem dialing languages are defined by the modem makers, and there are many such languages. Perhaps the most popular dialing language is the Hayes AT command set, partially listed in Table II-2 on the next page.

Table II-2 Selected Hayes Smartmodem 2400 Commands

Command	Action
AT	No action. Modem responds "OK" if it is in command state.
AT&C1	CD signal tracks carrier (recommended). AT&C0 keeps CD on always.
AT&D2	Modem hangs up and returns to command state if PC turns off DTR (recommended). AT&D0 makes modem ignore DTR signal from PC.
ATE1	Enables echoing of modem commands (recommended). ATE0 disables echoing.
ATM0	Turns off speaker. ATM1 turns on speaker while dialing.
ATQ0V1	Selects verbal result codes (OK, CONNECT) rather than numeric.
ATX0	Enables OK, CONNECT, RING, and NO CARRIER result codes.
ATX1	Enables OK, CONNECT, RING, NO CARRIER, ERROR, CONNECT 1200, and CONNECT 2400 result codes.
ATX4	Enables OK, CONNECT, RING, NO CARRIER, ERROR, CONNECT 1200, NO DIALTONE, BUSY, CONNECT, and CONNECT 2400 result codes (factory setting).
ATDT*nnnnnnn*	Dials the phone number *nnnnnnn* (simulate Touch-Tone dialing). The phone number may contain digits, spaces, parentheses, and hyphens, which are ignored. A comma in the dial string causes the modem to pause (normally 2 seconds, specified in register S8). The letter W means wait up to 30 seconds (limit specified in register S7) for dial tone. An exclamation mark (!) means "hook flash"—hang up the phone for half a second, then reconnect. An at-sign (@) means to wait for the phone to stop ringing.
ATDP*nnnnnnn*	Dials the phone number, like ATDT, but with pulse (rotary) dialing.
ATD*nnnnnnn*	Dials the phone number using the modem's default dialing method (Touch-Tone or Pulse).
ATH0	Hangs up the phone.
+++	Returns to command state without dropping the connection. This is the modem's escape sequence. It is ignored unless a full second of silence precedes and follows it, to prevent consecutive plus signs in your data from interfering with communication.
ATO	(Letter O) Returns to online state from command state.
ATZ	Initialize: Restores normal configuration.
ATS0=0	Enters answer mode (wait for a call).
ATS7=*nnn*	Waits up to *nnn* seconds for carrier. Default depends on modem model.
ATS8=*nnn*	Duration of comma dial modifier. Default is 2 seconds.
ATS10=*nnn*	Delay between carrier loss and hangup, 10ths of seconds.
ATS25=*nnn*	DTR change detect time, 100ths of seconds.

In Hayes language, commands begin with the two letters AT. The command to dial a phone number is ATDT or ATDP (depending on whether Touch-Tone or pulse dialing is required) followed by the phone number and then a carriage return (press the Return or Enter key). The modem dials the number, waits for a response, and then reports the results using either a numeric code or a descriptive English word or phrase like CONNECT, CONNECT 1200, CONNECT 2400, BUSY, NO ANSWER, NO DIALTONE, or NO CARRIER [32]. Some useful Hayes commands are listed in Table II-2; each command must be terminated by a carriage return. Computer programs are easily written to feed commands to an autodial modem and interpret the results.

According to RS-232 and V.24, there is (or should be) no carrier during the dialing process. Carrier appears only after the connection is complete. Therefore, computer software like Kermit that controls modems must be prepared to ignore carrier during the dialing process, but to pay attention to it after the connection is complete.

However, some computer systems (such as Data General AOS/VS) do not allow serial communication to occur at all in the absence of carrier, so the modem (or the cable connecting it to the computer) must be configured to assert CD all the time. This robs the computer of the ability to detect a broken connection. Similarly, some computers do not turn on their DTR signals properly, so the modem must be configured to ignore DTR. In general, a modem should be configured to:

- Pay attention to DTR from the computer. If DTR goes off, hang up the phone.

- Turn on Carrier Detect only when the two modems have carrier.

Modulation, Error Correction, and Compression

Modems communicate with each other using an ever-expanding variety of modulation techniques, such as the ones listed in Table II-3 on the next page. Most modern modems support more than one such technique. In order for two modems to communicate, they must have at least one modulation technique in common and each must have a way to find the common technique.

When you place a call, the modem begins with a particular modulation technique. The technique is chosen according to the interface speed between your computer and the modem or according to the modem's configuration. For example, a V.32 modem might try to connect to the remote modem using V.32 if your interface speed is 9600, V.22*bis* if it is 2400, V.22 if it is 1200, and V.21 or Bell 103 if it is 300.

Suppose your modem tries to connect using V.32. If the other modem responds with a V.32 carrier signal, the modems recognize each other immediately and your modem raises its CD signal and tells you the connection is complete. If, however, the other modem does

Table II-3 Modem Modulation Techniques

Designation	Description
CCITT V.32*bis*	14400 bps; full duplex
CCITT V.32	9600, 4800, 2400; full duplex
CCITT V.29	9600 bps; for leased lines, but used by MNP Class 6
CCITT V.26*ter*	2400 bps; full duplex
CCITT V.26*bis*	2400, 1200 bps; half duplex with 75 bps back channel
CCITT V.22*bis*	2400, full duplex
CCITT V.22	1200 bps, full duplex
Vadic VA3400	1200 bps, full duplex
Bell 212A	1200 bps, half duplex
CCITT V.23	600, 1200 bps, half duplex with 75 bps back channel
CCITT V.21	300 bps, full duplex, incompatible with Bell 103
Bell 103	110, 150, 300 bps, full duplex

not support V.32, your modem will execute its *fallback* procedure. The fallback procedure is what allows modems of differing capabilities to find a common language. In this case your modem might fall back to V.22*bis* and, if that doesn't work, to V.22, and so on.

Modems that implement different fallback strategies might not be able to connect to each other automatically, even if they *do* have a modulation technique in common. In such cases, it is your job to configure your modem to change its initial modulation technique, its fallback scheme, or both.

Error Correction

Error-correcting modems have been available for about ten years. They are designed to overcome transmission errors caused by noisy telephone connections. Error correction, when it is effective, occurs only on the connection between the two modems, and *not* on the connection between each modem and its computer or terminal.

Error correction requires a communications protocol, similar to Kermit's, between the two modems. Data sent by each modem is packaged with framing and checksum information; the other modem receives these structured messages, checks them for damage, and requests retransmission if necessary or else extracts the original data and passes it along to the receiving computer.

Several techniques are commonly used for error correction. Some of them are listed in Table II-4. To achieve an error-free connection, two modems must share at least one error

Table II-4 Modem Error Correction and Compression Techniques

Designation	Description
MNP Class 1	Error Correction: Asynchronous byte-oriented half duplex ARQ
MNP Class 2	Error Correction: Asynchronous byte-oriented full duplex ARQ
MNP Class 3	Error Correction: Synchronous bit-oriented full duplex ARQ
MNP Class 4	Error Correction: MNP Class 3 plus dynamic packet size
MNP Class 5	Data Compression: Used in conjunction with MNP Class 4
MNP Class 6	MNP Class 5 plus Universal Link Negotiation and Statistical Duplexing
MNP Class 7	Enhanced Data Compression: used in conjunction with MNP Class 4
MNP Class 9	MNP Class 7 combined with V.32 modulation
PEP	Telebit Packet Ensemble Protocol, a combination of modulation, error control, and compression
CCITT V.42	Error Correction: Link Access Protocol for Modems (LAPM), the international standard error correction technique for modems
CCITT V.42*bis*	Data Compression: The international standard compression technique for modems

correction technique. The error-correction method is settled after carrier has been established; that is, after the two modems have found a common modulation technique. Now that the modems can communicate with one another, they send messages attempting to negotiate an error-correction protocol.

Suppose, for example, you are dialing with an MNP Class 4 modem. Once carrier is established, your modem sends a message to the other modem requesting to use MNP Class 4 error correction. If the other modem is capable of MNP Class 4 operation, it agrees. If it is capable of a lower MNP class of error control, it notifies your modem and your modem falls back to the lower level. However, if the other modem does not support any level of MNP operation, it passes your modem's negotiation message through to the remote computer or service, which is very likely to result in incorrect speed recognition, a failed login, or a hung-up connection.

Most modern modems can be configured to use or skip error-correction, and to employ various fallback schemes in negotiating the error-correction method with the other modem. If you have trouble establishing a connection from an error-correcting modem, try turning off its error-correction feature, choosing a different error-correction method, or altering the modem's error-correction fallback scheme.

After you have made a successful error-corrected connection between two modems, your troubles are still not over. Suppose, for example, you have told the remote host to display a long file. Suddenly there is a period of severe noise on the telephone connection, causing many retransmissions between the two modems. The remote modem is so busy retransmitting previous data that it is not able to accept new data from the remote computer, yet the remote computer continues to send it. The modem needs a way to tell the computer to stop sending data for a while; that is, an effective flow control method. Without one, data will be lost.

Similarly, you need effective flow control between your own computer and modem, otherwise the modem might deliver data to your computer faster than the computer can handle it, or vice versa.

Data Compression

Above your modem's modulation and error-correction techniques, there can be still another layer of protocol between the two modems: data compression. As with modulation and error-correction, various compression techniques are available, some of which are listed in Table II-4, and the same cautions about negotiation, fallback, and flow control hold true.

Flow control is absolutely essential when compression is operational. In theory, data cannot come out of modem B faster than it went in to modem A. In practice, however, it is common that the interface speeds of the two modems are different, and therefore the data sent to the slower modem by the faster one must be flow-controlled by the slower modem's computer. If you do not have an effective method of flow control—preferably RTS/CTS—you should disable your modem's compression feature.

A glance at Tables II-3 and II-4 gives you an idea of the many possible combinations of modulation, error-correction, and compression techniques offered by modern modems. Each modem manufacturer offers a different selection, different default configurations, different fallback schemes, and different ways to control all of these. New techniques are developed with alarming frequency and hit the marketplace with little delay. When you buy a new, full-featured modem, be prepared to spend long hours studying the manual and experimenting with its configuration and settings.

Cables and Connectors

The cable that connects a computer to a modem—that is, a DTE to a DCE—is called a *modem cable*. It includes at least the circuits listed in Table II-1 on page 364, and illustrated in Figure II-4, which also shows the direction of the signal and the connector pin numbers for standard 25-pin connectors. In a modem cable, the wires go "straight through," connecting DTR on one side to DTR on the other, CD on one side to CD on the other, and so on, for each circuit. The cable terminates in *connectors* on each end.

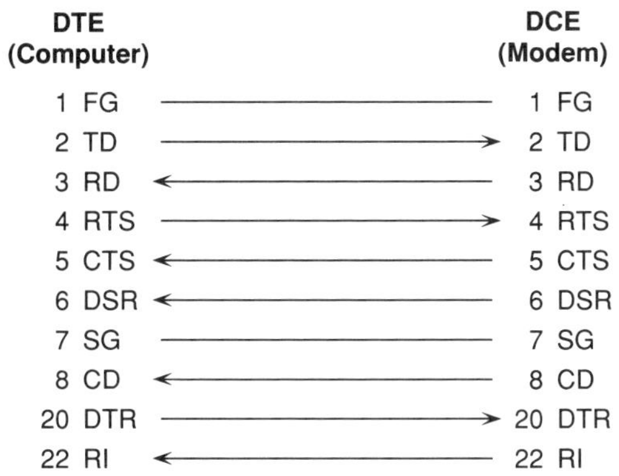

```
    DTE                      DCE
(Computer)                 (Modem)
  1 FG    ───────────────   1 FG
  2 TD    ──────────────→   2 TD
  3 RD    ←──────────────   3 RD
  4 RTS   ──────────────→   4 RTS
  5 CTS   ←──────────────   5 CTS
  6 DSR   ←──────────────   6 DSR
  7 SG    ───────────────   7 SG
  8 CD    ←──────────────   8 CD
 20 DTR   ──────────────→  20 DTR
 22 RI    ←──────────────  22 RI
```

Figure II-4 Asynchronous Modem Cable Schematic

Gender

A connector is either *female* or *male*, like the ones shown in Figure II-5 on the next page. Male connectors have pins sticking out, female connectors have holes to plug the pins into. By convention, DTEs have male connectors, DCEs female.[47]

Number of Pins

The most common type of connector has 25 pins (or holes), one for each of the 25 RS-232 circuits; this is called a DB-25 connector. The assignment of connector pins to RS-232 circuits is specified by the RS-232 standard. 9-pin (DB-9) and 8-pin (Din-8) varieties are becoming increasingly common, but vendors don't follow a particular standard in assigning circuits to pins; each pin is numbered and assigned a circuit arbitrarily.

Case

The pins or holes are joined to the wires and housed inside a compact case, as shown in the figure, for protection and ease of handling. So, like Latin nouns, data connectors have *gender*, *number*, and *case*.

Null Modems

It is possible to connect two DTEs (such as two computers, or a terminal and a computer) directly to each other without any intervening modems. This is done using a *null modem cable*,[48] in which the wires do not go straight through, but are cross-connected in various ways as shown in Figure II-6 on the next page, which also shows the DB-25 pin numbers.

---

[47] But conventions are made to be broken. When a connector is the wrong gender, an inexpensive adapter called a *gender changer* can be employed.

[48] Small null modem adapters, or *modem eliminators*, turn a modem cable into a null modem cable.

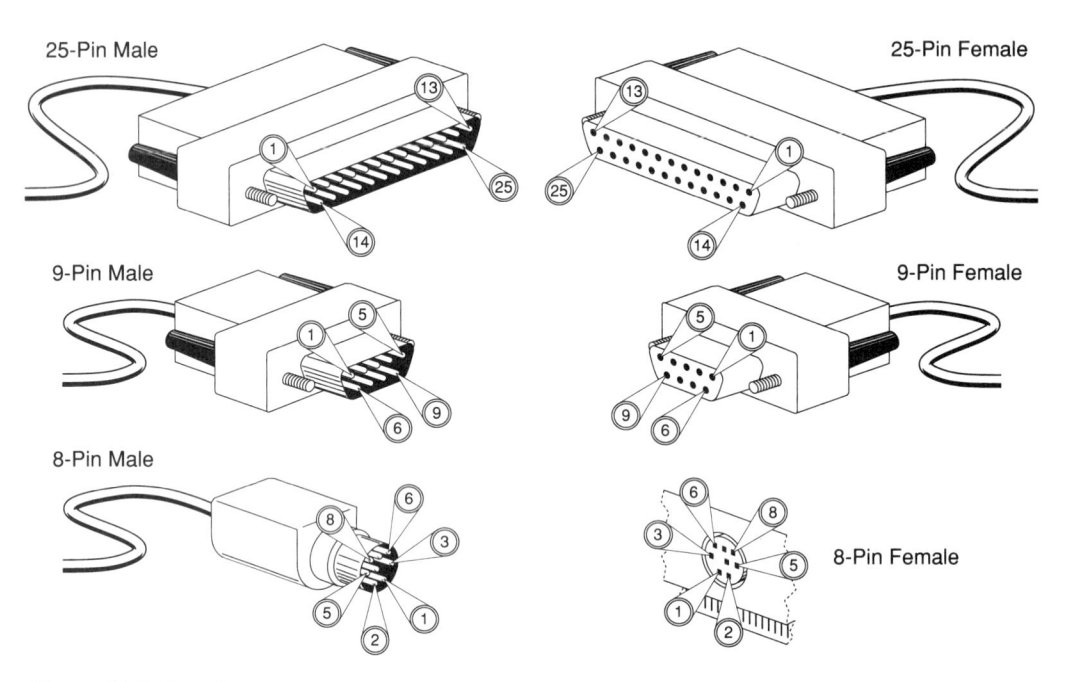

Figure II-5 Data Connectors

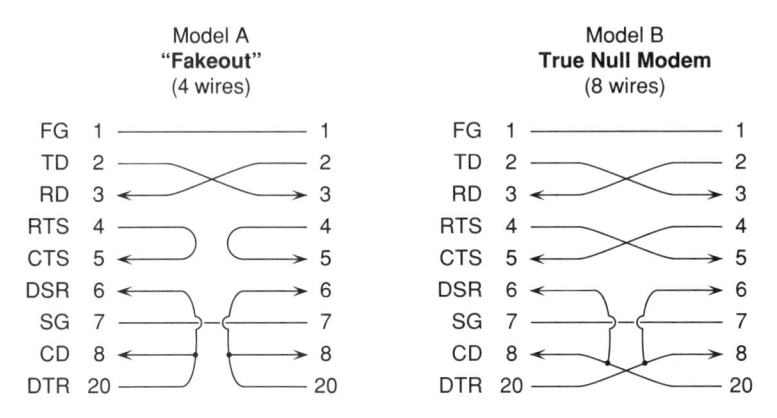

```
           Model A                        Model B
          "Fakeout"                   True Null Modem
          (4 wires)                      (8 wires)

   FG   1 ─────────── 1          FG   1 ─────────── 1
   TD   2 ─────────── 2          TD   2 ─────╲ ╱─── 2
   RD   3 ←────╲ ╱─── 3          RD   3 ←────╳ ──→ 3
   RTS  4 ───╮      ╭─ 4         RTS  4 ─────╲ ╱─── 4
   CTS  5 ──╯      ╰── 5         CTS  5 ←────╳ ──→ 5
   DSR  6 ←──╮    ╭──→ 6         DSR  6 ←──╮   ╭──→ 6
   SG   7 ───┼────┼─── 7         SG   7 ───┼───┼─── 7
   CD   8 ←──╯    ╰──→ 8         CD   8 ←──┤   ├──→ 8
   DTR 20 ───────────20          DTR 20 ───╯   ╰───20
```

Figure II-6 Asynchronous Null Modem Schematics

The computers are tricked into believing they are connected to real modems. With the "fakeout" model (A), the two computers can transmit data but cannot signal each other in any other way. With a true null modem (B), each computer can detect when the other computer crashes or otherwise stops communicating.

In UNIX, VMS, and OpenVMS computer systems, the system administrator may define serial communication devices as either modem-controlled or direct lines. On a modem-controlled line, the operating system insists upon receiving the CD signal, and possibly also DSR and CTS. If carrier drops, the next attempt to read a character from the device will result in a "device error," unless the device is opened in a special mode (such as the CLOCAL mode in UNIX).

On a direct line, modem signals are ignored. A direct line is typically used for a terminal, PC, or printer connected directly to a computer serial communication device with a short RS-232 null modem cable containing as few as three or four wires (sometimes the frame ground wire is omitted, but this is not recommended).

It is impossible to list specific cabling requirements for every kind of computer that C-Kermit runs on. You will probably have to consult the technical documentation for your computer. But a few general tips might smooth the way:

- On PCs and workstations, don't use an internal modem unless it is fully supported by your computer's operating system. Before buying an internal modem, make sure it works with Kermit.

- For modem connections, use whatever modem cable is supplied or recommended by your computer manufacturer.

- For direct connections between two computers, use the supplied or recommended modem cable for each computer and interconnect the two modem cables with a modem eliminator.

- If your connections suffer from electrical interference, *shielded* cables and connectors (which are more expensive) might help.

Detailed debugging of modem signals and null modem cables can be accomplished with a device called an RS-232 breakout box, available in computer supply catalogs. Another handy tool is the loopback connector, which can be used to test cable integrity.

Appendix III

UNIX C-Kermit

This appendix explains how to configure and use C-Kermit on a computer with the UNIX operating system. For an up-to-date list of limitations and restrictions in the UNIX version of C-Kermit, also read the files `ckcker.bwr` and `ckuker.bwr`.

UNIX has become a generic term, referring to a large family of operating systems whose members include AIX, A/UX, BSD, CTIX, DG/UX, DNIX, DYNIX, DRS/NX, ESIX, HP-UX, IRIX, ODT, OSF/1, POSIX, Solaris, SunOS, System V, ULTRIX, UMAX, UMIPS, UNICOS, UNOS, XENIX, and many more. Each of these products differs from the others in numerous ways and each product goes through numerous releases. An important goal in the design of C-Kermit has been portability among the many releases of the many UNIX products on the market (see page 13 for a list) and easy adaptibility to future products and releases; see the files `ckcplm.doc` and `ckccfg.doc` for details.

Installation

○○○○
Detailed instructions for building and installing UNIX C-Kermit are given in the file `ckuins.doc` in the C-Kermit distribution and in the UNIX C-Kermit makefile itself. This section discusses the thorny issues of dialout device access that are of interest not only to the C-Kermit installer but all too often to the C-Kermit user too. Skip ahead to page 382 if you do not need to use C-Kermit for dialing out, or if C-Kermit is already configured correctly for dialing out on your UNIX computer.

Configuring tty Devices for Dialing Out

A device appears to the UNIX user as a file, usually in the /dev area. Here are some samples from a Sun-4 (`ls -l /dev/*`):

```
crw-rw-rw-  1 root   13,  0 Jun 26 11:33 /dev/mouse  (A Mouse)
crw-rw-rw-  1 root    3,  2 Aug  3 13:44 /dev/null   (The null device)
crw-rw-rw-  1 root   30,  0 Aug  3 12:38 /dev/rmt0   (A magnetic tape)
crw-rw-rw-  1 root    2,  0 Aug  3 14:24 /dev/tty    (Controlling tty)
crw-rw-rw-  1 root   44,  0 Jun 26 12:03 /dev/ttyh0  (Specific ttys)
crw--w--w-  1 root   44,  1 Aug  3 15:03 /dev/ttyh1
crw--w----  1 cmg    44,  2 Aug  8 15:00 /dev/ttyh2
crw--w----  1 fdc    44,  3 Jun 11 05:09 /dev/ttyh3
```

The tty devices are what we're interested in. Different UNIX systems have different names for them, but they are generally of the form /dev/tty followed by two characters, such as 00 or h2 (/dev/tty by itself is a special generic device that refers to the user's controlling terminal, or console). Other commonly used forms include /dev/acu, /dev/cua, /dev/cub, etc. (cu stands for "calling unit," acu for "automatic calling unit"). Write permission (w) does not allow users to delete the file, but it does allow them to write to the associated device.

A UNIX terminal device is *inbound*, *outbound*, or both. An inbound terminal is for people to use as the controlling terminal of an interactive UNIX session. Each inbound terminal on the computer is being watched by a process called "getty," which waits for a connection to appear, and then issues the login prompt. Outbound terminals are not watched by getty, and cannot be logged in on. These are used for dialing out to other computers. Some UNIX systems allow terminal devices to be *bidirectional*, meaning they can be used both for logging in and for dialing out.

The system administrator (superuser) configures each terminal device as inbound, outbound, or bidirectional. The method varies from system to system. You must consult your UNIX system administration manual for the relevant method. Traditionally, tty configuration is done by editing a file called /etc/ttys, which contains entries that look like this:

```
12console
02ttya
12ttyb
02ttyh0
12ttyh1
12ttyh2
12ttyh3
```

This file is read by the *init* process at system startup time. Two digits precede the tty name; you are concerned with the first digit: 0 means the line is outbound (no getty), 1 means the line is inbound (has getty).

Some UNIX systems have a more generalized way of defining terminals to the init process. For example, SunOS uses the file /etc/ttytab, which includes information about the terminal speed and type as well as whether getty is on or off:

```
ttyh0    "/usr/etc/getty std.9600"      vt100      off
ttyh1    "/usr/etc/getty std.19200"     vt100      on
ttyh2    "/usr/etc/getty std.9600"      vt100      on
ttyh3    "/usr/etc/getty std.9600"      vt100      on
```

Dialout lines must be configured with getty off, or if your system allows it, as bidirectional lines.

It is normally not necessary to shut down and restart your UNIX system in order to reconfigure a terminal device. Rather, you can edit the appropriate tty configuration file and then restart the init process, which is always process number 1:

```
$ kill -1 1
```

This operation, of course, requires superuser (root) privilege.

Once the tty device is configured to allow dialout, its permissions must also be set to let users access it in read and write mode:

```
$ ls -l /dev/ttyh4
crw--w----   1 root       44,   2 Aug  8 15:00 /dev/ttyh4
$ chmod go+rw /dev/ttyh4
$ ls -l /dev/ttyh4
crw-rw-rw-   1 root       44,   2 Aug  8 15:00 /dev/ttyh4
```

The chmod command adds read and write (rw) permission to ttyh4 for members of its group (g) and all others (o).

Finally, on certain workstations, it might be necessary to configure the terminal driver for dialing out. For example, Sun SPARCstations might come with serial ports that are *not* set up for use with a modem. To configure the serial port for dialout use, follow the directions in your system installation or system and network manager's guide. This might involve changing jumpers on your serial port board, reconfiguring the serial device driver, or both.

Ensuring Exclusive Access

Most operating systems allow serial devices such as terminals and magnetic tapes to be opened by only one job at a time. Any attempt to open the same device by another job results in an error like "exclusive access denied" or "device assigned by another user."

UNIX devices, however, can be shared by all users who have access to them based on their permissions. So if user A has a dialout connection over /dev/ttyh4, UNIX does not prevent user B from using /dev/ttyh4 at the same time, even though there is no conceivable reason to allow this. The result of multiple users reading from the same serial device is that the incoming characters are fanned out to them, as if they were hands of poker—nobody sees the whole deck. And of course, if multiple users write to the same device, then who- or whatever is on the other end will receive only a confused jumble of characters, impossible to sort out.

Before there was Kermit, there was UUCP, the UNIX-to-UNIX Copy Program [55]. UUCP was developed at AT&T Bell Laboratories by Mike Lesk in 1976, and publicly distributed for the first time with Version 7 of UNIX. It soon became the basis of Usenet, a loose voluntary confederation of UNIX computers that call each other up at night and exchange files, news, and electronic mail. It was not long until someone discovered that running two copies of UUCP at the same time on the same dialout line resulted in no useful exchange of data. The solution was, and remains to this day, the UUCP lock file.

UUCP and every other program on the computer that might be using a dialout line, including kermit, cu, tip, umodem, sz, and rz, are expected to observe a special convention: if the program wants to use a particular dialout tty device, first it checks to see if a file with a certain name exists in a certain directory, and if so the program does not attempt to use the tty device. If the file does not exist, the program must create it before starting to use the device and must destroy the file when it is finished. This file is called the UUCP lock file; its name is based on the tty device name.

Within a particular UNIX vendor's software offerings, this convention tends to work—uucp, cu, and tip are produced in the vendor's controlled proprietary environment. Unfortunately, the situation is not so controlled for Kermit, which needs to run on UNIX platforms from many manufacturers:

- The directory that contains the UUCP lock files is different on different systems: `/usr/spool/uucp`, `/usr/spool/locks`, `/var/spool/locks`, many others.

- The directory that contains the lock file may or may not be publicly readable and/or writable.

- The format of the lock file name can vary from system to system: `ttyh4`, `LCK..ttyh4`, and so on.

- Although the lock file name includes the device name, it might be subtly modified; for example, in SCO Xenix, the lock file for `/dev/tty1A` is `LCK..tty1a` (lowercase letter *a*).

- There might be more than one lock file; certain versions of IBM AIX require two lock files, one named (for example) `LCK..tty0`, and the other simply `tty0` (in fact, the second is a link to the first).

- The lock file itself may or may not be publicly readable and/or writable.

- The creation date and time of the lock file may or may not be significant.

- The contents of the lock file may or may not be significant. Some versions of UUCP require that the lock file contain the process ID (pid) of the process that created it.

- The format of the contents of the lock file can vary from system to system: the pid may be a binary integer (or other data type, such as short or long), or an integer in ASCII string format.

- Even on the same computer, lock file conventions can change from one UNIX release to the next, for example from SunOS 4.0 to SunOS 4.1 on Sun computers, or from AT&T System V R3 to R4.

- Recent UNIX standards like POSIX don't even try to address this issue.

Therefore, you must determine what lock file conventions are in use on your system and build Kermit to correspond to them; this is not always an easy task, because this information tends to be missing from vendor documentation. Each C-Kermit "make" option takes a best guess, but for Kermit to fit in properly with uucp, cu, and tip, you should make certain that this guess is correct. Here is one way to check:

1. Get a directory listing (`ls -lg`) from each of the possible lock file directories: `/usr/spool/uucp`, `/usr/spool/locks`, `/var/spool/locks`, `/etc/locks` (this is not necessarily a complete list).

2. Run one of your vendor-supplied UUCP-family communication programs, such as cu, giving the name of your dialout device. Example:

   `$ cu -l /dev/ttya`

   This procedure assumes you are using cu.

3. Escape from cu back to your local shell by typing carriage return, then tilde (~), then exclamation mark (!).

4. At the shell prompt, repeat step 1.

5. Exit from the inferior shell, exit from cu (carriage return, tilde, period).

6. Compare the directory listings to see which files, in what format, with what permissions, in which directories were created by cu.

In recent years, UNIX vendors have been converting to a new and somewhat more standardized version of UUCP called "Honey DanBer" (after its authors, Peter Honeyman, David A. Nowitz, and Brian E. Redman, who rewrote the original UUCP in 1983). If this trend continues, much of the confusion can be eliminated.

Installing Kermit without Privileges

If you are the sole user of a UNIX workstation, you don't have to worry about other users abusing their privileges or interfering with your work, so you need not be concerned with the material in this section.

If you are the manager of a multiuser UNIX system where all the users trust each other, and you trust them, you can make access to your tty devices and lock file directory unrestricted. For example, if your lock file directory is `/usr/spool/uucp` and your dialout device is ttyh4, give the following commands from superuser command level:

```
su% chmod 777 /usr/spool/uucp
su% chmod 666 /dev/ttyh4
```

The risk here is a free-for-all in the lock file directory; users can store any file there at all, and delete any file as well. They can even remove each others' lock files, despite the fact that the lock files are created with 444 (read-only) permission. Deletion is possible because the *directory* has write permission, which is required for people to create their lock files in the first place. And there is also some risk of one user interfering with another's use of the tty device.

To make your tty devices available only to a selected group of users, put those users in the uucp group (or whatever other group is used by uucp, tip, and cu). The method for doing this varies from system to system, but generally involves editing the `/etc/group` file to add these users to the uucp entry in that file. You don't have to make the Kermit program setuid or setgid, or give it any particular owner or group, but you do have to ensure that the uucp lock directory and the appropriate tty devices are members of the uucp group, and have the appropriate permissions in the group field:

```
su% chgrp uucp /usr/spool/uucp
su% chmod 770 /usr/spool/uucp
su% chgrp uucp /dev/ttyh4
su% chmod 660 /dev/ttyh4
```

Installing Kermit with Privileges

On multiuser UNIX systems where access to the uucp directory or to tty devices is a security issue, it is possible to restrict access to the lock file directory and the dialout tty devices, then give the Kermit program privileges to override these restrictions, and some or all users the ability to run the privileged Kermit. This prevents users from circumventing the lock file conventions built into Kermit (and uucp, cu, and tip), and therefore from accessing a tty device that somebody else is already using. It also prevents them from creating, modifying, or destroying files in the lock file directory.

Despite the attractions of this setup, there are also serious risks. Any program that runs in privileged mode poses a tremendous security threat to your system, much greater than the possible inconveniences of open lock directories and tty devices. Although every effort has been made to ensure C-Kermit contains no loopholes, the slightest bug or oversight on the part of the authors or anyone who has modified or customized the source code—not to speak of the damage that could be done intentionally—could open doors for intruders. This warning is not particular to Kermit: it applies to *all* UNIX programs.

If you *really want* to make Kermit a privileged program, first make sure you have built it correctly for your system. There are several important compile-time options that must be considered, and that vary from system to system. The most important of these is whether your version of UNIX supports the "saved original setuid" feature. If it does not, then Kermit will not work right as a privileged program—it should not pose a security risk, but it won't be able to access protected files or tty devices either. For details, read the files `ckuins.doc` (the installation instructions), `ckuker.bwr` (the "beware" file), and `ckcplm.doc` (the program logic manual).

To install Kermit as a privileged program, make the owner of the Kermit program the same as the owner of the lock file directory and the tty device, and set the setuid bit in the Kermit program's permissions, so that while running Kermit, the user has the privileges of user uucp. For example:

```
su% chown uucp kermit              (kermit's owner is uucp)
su% chmod u=srwx,g=rx,o=rx kermit  (Turn setuid bit on)
su% chown uucp /usr/spool/uucp     (Lock directory owned by uucp)
su% chmod 700 /usr/spool/uucp      (Can only be accessed by owner)
su% chown uucp /dev/ttyh4          (Dialout device owned by uucp)
su% chmod 600 /dev/ttyh4           (Can only be accessed by owner)
```

The UNIX version of C-Kermit includes special code to turn off these privileges as soon as it starts up, and to turn them on only when it is manipulating lock files or accessing the tty device, so that files are accessed and subprocesses are run with the user's own identity and access rights, but this code cannot be guaranteed to work correctly for every release of every variation of UNIX.

Caveat Installator!

For the lock file mechanism to achieve its desired purpose—prevention of access to the same tty device by more than one process at a time—*all* programs on a given computer that open, read or write, and close tty devices (kermit, uucp, cu, tip, sz, rz, and so on) must use the *same* lock file conventions.

Be alert to changes in new releases of your UNIX operating system. The installation procedure might change the permissions on your lock file directories and tty devices. What's more, it is quite common these days for new UNIX releases to change their lock file conventions; the new versions of uucp, tip, and cu will follow the new conventions, but Kermit and other communication programs that are not distributed by your UNIX vendor will still be using the old ones until you reconfigure (or reprogram!) them.

Using UNIX C-Kermit

UNIX operating systems are available for computers ranging from small desktop systems to large mainframes and supercomputers. To accommodate smaller computers that have restrictions on physical memory, address space, disk space, or compiler or linker capacity, C-Kermit can be built in reduced configurations. This is required primarily for UNIX versions running on DEC PDP-11s and on 8088, 8086, 80186, or 80286 PCs, and is generally not necessary elsewhere. The three major C-Kermit configurations are:

1. Fully configured, but perhaps without Kanji character set and/or fullscreen display. In most cases, these features can be added by simple changes to the build procedure (see the files ckccfg.doc and ckuins.doc for instructions).

2. Minimum interactive. The C-Kermit prompt appears and a minimum set of commands is available for terminal connection and file transfer. There is no character-set translation, script programming language, or built-in HELP text.

3. Command-line only. This configuration has no prompt, no interactive dialog, and no initialization file. It is controlled exclusively with the command-line options listed in Chapter 14, with the exception of -y, -Y, -c, -s, and any others that imply the availability of interactive commands.

See the file ckccfg.doc for detailed information about C-Kermit configuration options.

If you have an interactive version of C-Kermit, you can use the SHOW FEATURES command to find out exactly which features are included and excluded. If the SHOW FEATURES command itself is missing, you can use the CHECK command, which is included in all interactive configurations, for example:

```
C-Kermit>check kanji
 Not available
C-Kermit>
```

Preparing UNIX for C-Kermit

To make effective use of C-Kermit in the UNIX environment and, for that matter, to use UNIX itself to best advantage, you should ensure that your UNIX session is speaking the same language as the terminal or emulator that you are using to access it.

Establishing Your Terminal Type

Before starting C-Kermit, you should tell the UNIX system what kind of terminal you have so C-Kermit's FULLSCREEN file transfer display (if available) will work correctly.

To identify your terminal to UNIX, try one of the methods from Table III-1, which uses the DEC VT300-series terminal as an example. The actual method used depends not only

Table III-1 Setting Your Terminal Type in UNIX

Shell	Command
Bourne shell (sh)	`TERM=vt300 ; export TERM`
Korn shell (ksh)	`TERM=vt300 ; export TERM`
C-shell (csh)	`setenv TERM vt300`

on your shell, but on the site- or vendor-dependent peculiarities of your UNIX system. For example, some UNIX systems use a program called `term` or `tset`; others might prompt you for a terminal type when you log in.

To test whether your terminal type is set correctly, try a command that changes the appearance of your screen, such as "clear" (Berkeley UNIX) or "tput clear" (AT&T UNIX) to erase the terminal screen, or start a screen-oriented editor like VI or GNU EMACS. If your screen does not respond as expected, try another terminal type. In most cases, lowercase letters are required in the terminal name.

If you use a speaking or Braille device to read the screen to you, tell UNIX that you have a simple hardcopy terminal, such as a Teletype Model 33. Most UNIX systems support this under the name "tty" or "tty33." Also use this terminal type if you are logging in from a real hardcopy terminal, such as a TDD (Telecommunication Device for the Deaf).

Checking and Setting Your Communication Speed

When you use C-Kermit to transfer files in remote mode, it calibrates its packet timeouts based on what UNIX thinks is the communication speed of your login terminal. If your terminal or PC is connected directly or via modem to a serial communication port on your UNIX computer, UNIX knows your communication speed. But if you have dialed in at (say) 2400 bps through a terminal server, UNIX probably thinks your speed is 38400 bps, and file transfers might not work well, or at all.

To be sure UNIX knows your true serial communication speed, give the commands `tty` and `stty`; you'll see something like this (ignore the incomprehensible parts):

```
$ tty                             (Show my terminal's device name)
/dev/ttyh3
$ stty                            (Show its characteristics)
speed 9600 baud; evenp hupcl clocal
$
```

If you have entered the UNIX system through any kind of network connection—a terminal server or a TELNET or rlogin session—you are not logged in on a "real terminal" (`tty`), but rather to a "pseudoterminal" (`pty`), so UNIX does not know the actual communication speed of your terminal:

```
$ tty
/dev/ttyp5                              (Device name has "p" in it)
$ stty
speed 38400 baud; evenp                 (Speed is probably wrong)
$
```

If there is a serial device anywhere along the communication path between your desktop and the UNIX system, tell UNIX the true speed of the device as soon as you log in, before starting C-Kermit, EMACS, or any other software that might be speed-sensitive:

```
$ stty 2400
$ stty
speed 2400 baud; evenp
$
```

UNIX Control Characters

The UNIX operating system and many UNIX applications support the use of control characters (and sometimes also printable characters) for editing or interrupting commands. The repertoire of functions available, and the characters that are assigned to them, can be discovered by using the `stty` command:

% `stty all`

(or `stty -a`, or `stty everything`).

In response, you should see a report that includes the following information (specific appearance may vary):

```
erase  kill  werase  rprnt  flush  lnext  susp    intr  quit  stop    eof
^?     ^U    ^W      ^R     ^O     ^V     ^Z/^Y   ^C    ^\    ^S/^Q   ^D
```

These are the "significant characters" in your UNIX login session. Their meanings are listed in Table III-2. Control characters are shown in circumflex notation; ^U means Control-U, ^\ means Control-Backslash, and ^? means Delete. (For a complete listing of circumflex notation, see Table VIII-2 on page 462.)

You can change the interrupt character or any of the others in the list with the `stty` command. Normally, the method is to give the name of the terminal function you want to change, followed by the character you want to change it to, written in circumflex notation. For example, to change your interrupt character to Ctrl-B, enter:

% `stty intr ^B`

(that's circumflex followed by the letter B, not a real Ctrl-B). To disable a function altogether, use (depending on your UNIX version) `undef` or `^-` (circumflex hyphen):

% `stty quit undef`   or   `stty quit ^-`

For details about the use of the `stty` command on your system, type `man stty`.

Table III-2 UNIX Terminal Control Characters

Notation	Meaning
eof	The character that generates an end of file condition at the terminal
erase	The character that erases the rightmost character from the current line
flush	The character that starts or stops discarding screen output
intr	The character that interrupts the current foreground process
kill	The character that erases the current line
lnext	The character that quotes the next character
quit	The character that terminates a process and creates a "core dump" file
rprnt	The character that reprints the current line to show the effects of any editing
stop	The software flow control stop and start characters
susp	The character that suspends the current foreground process
werase	The character that erases the rightmost word from the current line

Flow Control

In your terminal session with the UNIX system, before you start C-Kermit, you should ensure that your UNIX login terminal device is using the same kind of flow control as your local terminal or emulator. For example, if your local terminal is using Xon/Xoff software flow control, then your UNIX session should be using it too. This can help prevent loss of data and fractured screens during your terminal session. Use the `stty` command to check whether Xon/Xoff flow control is enabled for your UNIX session. The Xon/Xoff characters are shown in the "stop" field of the stty report. If they are missing, you can enable them with a command like:

```
$ stty ixon ixoff
```

Consult `man stty` for details specific to your UNIX system.

If you are entering UNIX through a terminal server, you might find that Xon/Xoff flow control does not work promptly enough to prevent loss of data. In that case, you can enable it at the terminal server rather than at your UNIX session. For example, at the prompt of a Cisco terminal server, use:

```
ts>terminal flowcontrol software in out
```

However, this prevents transmission of Ctrl-S and Ctrl-Q characters as data, as required by certain UNIX applications such as the EMACS editor.

Some UNIX systems also support hardware flow control, most commonly RTS/CTS, but in most cases it won't be used unless you request it. In certain UNIX versions, like Dell

System V Release 4, a login terminal must be permanently configured by the system manager for hardware flow control. In others, you can enable or disable hardware flow control by giving a UNIX command after you have logged in. Consult your system's "man pages" to find out the proper incantation. Here are some examples:

```
$ stty crtscts            (SunOS 4.0 or later)
$ stty rtsxoff ctsxon     (System V R4, some versions)
```

If you are entering UNIX through a terminal server, you might be able to enable hardware flow control there. On a Cisco terminal server, for example, the command is:

```
ts>terminal flowcontrol hardware in out
```

When C-Kermit is active, it attempts to use the type of flow control you have specified in your most recent SET FLOW command (Xon/Xoff by default). Hardware flow control, however, is often available only through the use of tricks that C-Kermit might not know about, for example `stty` commands like the ones just shown, special device names such as `/dev/tty00h` instead of `/dev/tty00`, or `/dev/cufa` instead of `/dev/cua`. Once again, consult your system documentation for details.

It can't be stressed enough that terminal connection and file transfer work best when an effective flow control method is active. Hardware flow control, if available, should be used in preference to software flow control.

Using International Characters in UNIX

Even though C-Kermit has extensive facilities for handling and converting character sets, you can't depend on UNIX itself for any help in this area. Older versions of UNIX do not support 8-bit no-parity terminal connections. They give you 7-bit terminal connections with even parity, restricting you to using only ASCII or a 7-bit national character set during your UNIX terminal session. UNIX terminal drivers make no provision, such as Shift-In/Shift-Out, for use of 8-bit characters in the 7-bit communications environment.

There is, however, a movement afoot to make new versions of UNIX "8-bit clean" so 8-bit character sets such as the ISO Latin alphabets can be used. 8-bit cleanliness is a standard feature of the NeXT workstation and of Dell UNIX SVR4/386 Issue 2.1. It is also available in SunOS 4.1 and ULTRIX 4.0, but it must be enabled by command:

```
$ stty pass8
```

Other UNIX systems might or might not be 8-bit clean. Try `stty pass8`, `stty -parenb cs8`, or `stty -parity`. Check your UNIX system manuals or `man stty` for details. If you are accessing UNIX from a terminal or emulator, make sure that it is also set up for 8 data bits and no parity, as well as for the character set you want to use. If you are coming into UNIX through a terminal server or network connection, make sure that it is set up for 8-bit transparency too; for example, use `rlogin -8` rather than `rlogin`.

Program Control

C-Kermit is a character-mode application designed to be used from a terminal. If you are accessing your UNIX system from a terminal or terminal emulator, you can start the Kermit program in the normal way; that is, by typing its name possibly followed by command line arguments. Then you can have an interactive dialog with it, using your keyboard and screen in the traditional manner.

If you have a desktop UNIX workstation with a mouse-and-window-oriented graphical user interface (GUI) such as Motif, NeXTstep, SunView, DECwindows, AIX Windows, and the like, you might find that clicking on C-Kermit in the File Browser, File Viewer, or whatever else it might be called in your windowing environment, does not work well. Some workstations complain that C-Kermit is not a *(name-of-GUI)* application. Others might automatically create a terminal window for C-Kermit, but one that does not have all the features of a UNIX terminal device, in which case C-Kermit will not work correctly. This happens, for example, on the NeXT.

The best way to start Kermit in a GUI environment is first to open a terminal emulation window that gives you the UNIX shell prompt, then start Kermit in the normal way from the shell prompt. On some systems you can write a shell script to do this, then you can click on the shell script in your GUI environment. See the `ckuker.bwr` file for ideas.

Starting C-Kermit

To start C-Kermit, just type "kermit" at the shell prompt:

```
$ kermit
C-Kermit 5A(188) 23 Nov 92, 4.4 BSD
Type ? or HELP for help
C-Kermit>
```

If you get a message like "not found" rather than C-Kermit's herald and prompt, it means that C-Kermit's directory is not in your PATH (in which case you should change the PATH definition in your login profile to include it), or it is called by some other name (such as "wermit" or "ckermit"), or it isn't there at all. If you get a message like "cannot execute" or "permission denied," C-Kermit is installed incorrectly. Review the installation instructions in the file `ckuins.doc`, or show them to whoever is responsible.

Initialization File

UNIX C-Kermit's initialization file is called `.kermrc`. Because the name begins with a period, it is a hidden file and normally does not show up in directory listings, and it is normally immune from `rm *` operations. The `.kermrc` file must be located in your home (login) directory. We recommend that you use the standard C-Kermit initialization file; create a separate file called `.mykermrc` to make any desired personal customizations. Your dialing directory file, if any, should be called `.kdd` and your services directory file should be `.ksd`, both in your home directory.

Redirection of Input and Output

C-Kermit reads its interactive-mode commands from the standard input device, normally your keyboard, and prints its messages on the standard output device, your screen. To redirect Kermit's standard input to come from a file, use the < operator on the UNIX command line:

```
$ kermit < kermit.tak
```

In this example, the file `kermit.tak` contains Kermit commands. Kermit executes them, one after the other, until it comes to the end of the file (or to a QUIT or EXIT command), and then it exits back to the system prompt.

You can also redirect Kermit's screen output to a file using similar mechanisms:

```
$ kermit > kermit.log
```

Of course, redirecting Kermit's screen output without also redirecting its input doesn't make much sense, because then you'll be typing Kermit commands to a blank screen. To redirect both input and output:

```
$ kermit < kermit.tak > kermit.log
```

You can even feed commands to Kermit from another process, if your mind is agile enough to conceive of a reason to do this:

```
$ grep ^send cmdfile | sort | kermit
```

Background Operation

If you're using Kermit in local mode, you can have it transfer files in the background while you do other work in the foreground. This can be accomplished by redirecting Kermit's standard input and output to command and log files and terminating the shell command that invokes Kermit with an ampersand:

```
$ kermit < cmdfile > logfile &
```

C-Kermit makes various system-dependent tests to see if it is running in the background. If it concludes that it is, prompts and most messages are not issued. If you start Kermit interactively but get no prompt after the greeting is printed, that means your operating system is reporting the symptoms of background operation even though Kermit is in the foreground. In such cases, you can force Kermit to behave as though it were in the foreground by including the -z command-line option:

```
$ kermit -z
C-Kermit 5A(188) 23 Nov 92, MIPS RISC/OS
Type ? or HELP for help
C-Kermit>
```

Don't use the -z option if you really *are* starting C-Kermit in the background.

Interrupting C-Kermit

C-Kermit can be interrupted at its prompt, while typing a command, during execution of any command except CONNECT or remote-mode file transfer, and during local-mode file transfer by typing C-Kermit's interrupt character, which is normally Ctrl-C. The interrupt character should echo as ^C... and it should return you to the C-Kermit prompt immediately if you were running C-Kermit interactively, or back to the system prompt if you started C-Kermit with command-line action options (Chapter 14).

If Ctrl-C does not interrupt C-Kermit, use the UNIX `stty` command as described on page 384 to find out what your UNIX `intr` character is. Use that character instead or change your interrupt character to Ctrl-C.

To interrupt C-Kermit during remote-mode file transfer, type two Ctrl-C characters in a row. Ctrl-C is always used for this purpose, no matter what your interrupt character is. To interrupt C-Kermit during CONNECT mode, use the CONNECT-mode escape character, followed by the letter C to get back to the prompt, or any of the other escape-level commands described in Chapter 4.

Suspending C-Kermit

On UNIX systems with job control (generally those that are based on Berkeley UNIX, AT&T UNIX System V R4, or POSIX), you can suspend Kermit by typing Ctrl-Z or whatever your suspend character is (you can find out by using the `stty` command as described on page 384; your suspend character is listed under `susp`):

```
C-Kermit>^Z
[4] + Stopped (signal) kermit
$
```

You can suspend C-Kermit this way at any time except when it is in CONNECT mode or engaged in remote-mode file transfer. When at C-Kermit prompt level, you can also suspend Kermit by using the SUSPEND command:

SUSPEND

   Suspends C-Kermit. Stops C-Kermit and returns to the system prompt, but does not remove C-Kermit from memory. Synonym: **Z**.

SET SUSPEND { ON, OFF }

   ON, the normal setting, means C-Kermit handles SUSPEND signals if it was built in an environment that supports them. OFF means C-Kermit ignores SUSPEND signals.

After you have suspended C-Kermit, you can get back to it by using the UNIX `fg` (foreground) command with Kermit's job number (as shown when you suspended Kermit, and also shown by the shell's `jobs` command) preceded by a percent sign:

```
$ fg %4
C-Kermit>
```

or its process number (as shown by the UNIX `ps` command). If Kermit was executing a command, it should resume where it left off. If it was at the prompt, you should get a new prompt. If you type "kermit" again, instead of "fg", you will start a new copy of Kermit; the old one will still be sitting in the background.

> **WARNING:** The UNIX version of C-Kermit allows itself to be suspended and continued if the underlying operating system supports this feature. But (and this is a *big But*), you should not attempt to suspend Kermit or any other program if your UNIX shell does not also support this feature (Kermit cannot tell). Most C-Shells and K-Shells do, but most Bourne shells do not.[49] If you suspend C-Kermit in an environment that does not properly support job control, your session might become hopelessly hung. Your login session must be killed from another terminal (use the UNIX `ps` and `kill` commands).

There are three ways to deal with this problem:

1. Use a shell that supports job control. At most sites, you can use the `chsh` command to choose a different shell. For example, to use the C-Shell (csh):

   ```
   $ chsh csh
   ```

   Type `man chsh` for further information.

2. Give C-Kermit the command SET SUSPEND OFF to make C-Kermit ignore the suspend signal:

   ```
   C-Kermit>set suspend off
   ```

3. Disable the suspend signal before starting C-Kermit:

   ```
   % stty susp undef
   ```

Fixing Your UNIX Login Terminal Modes

If C-Kermit exits abnormally, for example because it was halted from another terminal, your login terminal might not function normally. In particular, it might not echo the characters you type and it might not recognize the Return or Enter key as a command terminator. In such cases, you should be able to restore your terminal to normal operation by issuing the `reset` or `stty sane` command (depending on your UNIX version). Type Ctrl-J, then the characters of the command, and terminate with another Ctrl-J (not Return or Enter).

---

[49] An exception is the Bourne shell distributed with AT&T System V Release 4.

UNIX C-Kermit Command Procedures

When creating a shell script program in UNIX, you can specify which shell (such as sh, csh, or ksh) is to execute the program by including a special type of "comment" as the first line, for example:

`#!/bin/ksh`

The # character is the shell comment introducer, and the second character, !, tells the shell that the rest of the line gives the name of the program that should be run to execute the shell script. The example tells your current shell to start `/bin/ksh` and to feed the file into ksh's standard input.

C-Kermit follows the same convention, which is possible because the # character is not only a UNIX shell comment introducer but also, by happy coincidence, a C-Kermit comment introducer. If you put a line like this:

`#!/usr/local/bin/kermit`

at the beginning of a C-Kermit command file and you also give execute permission to the file, you can run the file simply by typing its name at the system prompt, just as you would run a shell script. But in this case, the shell feeds the file to Kermit rather than to a UNIX shell. Of course, you can also use C-Kermit's TAKE command to execute the same file, in which case the #! line is ignored.

On your own UNIX system, substitute the actual pathname of the Kermit program if it is not `/usr/local/bin/kermit`. To give execute permission to the command file, use the `chmod +x` command at the UNIX shell prompt:

`$ chmod +x cmdfile`

The commands in the file are executed *after* your initialization file has been completely processed, but *before* the C-Kermit prompt appears. If you want the command file to exit to the system without issuing the C-Kermit prompt, include an EXIT command at the end.

You can also include C-Kermit command-line options in the command file invocation:

`$ cmdfile -p e -l /dev/ttyh8`

or, to have C-Kermit skip its initialization-file processing:

`$ cmdfile -Y`

When you start Kermit from a command file, the UNIX shell constructs a command of this form:

`kermit-path-name command-file-name options`

so you can also invoke Kermit like this yourself, for example:

`$ kermit cmdfile -p e -l /dev/ttyh8`

Terminal Connection

In the UNIX version of C-Kermit, terminal emulation is provided by your console driver, workstation terminal window, terminal emulator, or terminal. C-Kermit does not, itself, provide any particular type of terminal emulation beyond what is described in Chapter 4.

The CONNECT-Mode Escape Character

UNIX C-Kermit's default CONNECT-mode escape character is Ctrl-\ (Control-Backslash) except on certain workstations (such as the NeXT) that cannot generate this character from the keyboard, in which case Ctrl-] (Control-Rightbracket) is used. Use SHOW ESCAPE to find out what your escape character is, and SET ESCAPE to change it.

Key Mapping

C-Kermit's SET KEY command is effective only with keys that generate single-byte 7-bit or 8-bit codes. 7-bit keycodes are supported by C-Kermit for all UNIX versions, provided C-Kermit was configured with the key-mapping feature. 8-bit codes can be used if you have a keyboard capable of generating them, if C-Kermit has a clean 8-bit path to the keyboard, and if you have told C-Kermit to SET COMMAND BYTESIZE 8.

Suspending C-Kermit While in CONNECT Mode

During terminal connection, you can follow the CONNECT-mode escape character by the letter Z to suspend Kermit. This stops Kermit without breaking the connection and returns you to the same UNIX shell that you started Kermit from. Unlike the ! option, the Z option lets you get at any other jobs (text editors, mail programs, etc.) that you might be running in parallel with Kermit. Use the UNIX fg command to continue Kermit's CONNECT session, as in this example:

```
C-Kermit>connect                          (CONNECT to remote host)
%                                         (Remote system prompt is %)
% ^\z                                     (Suspend Kermit)
[3]  + Stopped (signal)    kermit
$                                         (Back at local system, prompt is $)
$ jobs                                    (List my jobs)

[3]  + Stopped (signal)    kermit
[2]  - Stopped             emacs
[1]    Stopped (signal)    mm

  (Here you can run other programs,
   continue your background jobs, etc.)
$
$ fg %3                                   (Restart C-Kermit)
%                                         (Connect session continues)
%
```

The usual cautions apply here. Don't try to suspend C-Kermit if it was invoked from a shell that does not support job control.

File Transfer

UNIX C-Kermit offers the full range of file transfer features, including text and binary transfers, file groups, attributes, and the FULLSCREEN file transfer display if it has been configured in your version (use the CHECK FULLSCREEN command to find out). For text files, UNIX record format (lines terminated by LF) is automatically converted to Kermit's standard intermediate form (CRLF) during file transfer.

If your version of UNIX C-Kermit was built with the DYNAMIC compilation option (use CHECK DYNAMIC to find out) you have approximately 9000 bytes of packet buffer allowing, for example, a window size of 9 and a packet length of 1000, or a window size of 18 and a packet length of 500. You can use the SET BUFFERS command to increase the buffer size to allow more window slots or longer packets, for example:

```
C-Kermit>set buffers 80000 80000
C-Kermit>set window 20
C-Kermit>set receive packet-length 4000
```

If your C-Kermit was built without the DYNAMIC feature, your packet buffer size is restricted to approximately 3000.

Interruption of Local-Mode File Transfer

In most C-Kermit versions, you can interrupt a local-mode file transfer by typing single letters like X, Z, or E (see Chapter 5). In C-Kermit versions based on AT&T System V UNIX or in POSIX, however, you must type the CONNECT-mode escape character (normally Ctrl-Backslash) before you type the interruption key.[50] C-Kermit's message at the start of file transfer gives you the information you need. Example:

```
C-Kermit>s oofa.txt
SF
Type escape character (^\) followed by:
X to cancel file,  CR to resend current packet
Z to cancel group, A for status report
E to send Error packet, Ctrl-C to quit immediately:
A
Sending: oofa.txt => OOFA.TXT
Size: 20659, Type: text
..........Ctrl-\X
Cancelling File   [interrupted]
ZB
C-Kermit>
```

In this case the escape character was Control-Backslash, so the user typed Ctrl-\ followed by the letter X to interrupt the file transfer.

---

[50]The control-character prefix is required because of limitations in the System V and POSIX terminal drivers. Nevertheless, your version of C-Kermit might include a workaround, so also try entering the interruption characters without the control-character prefix.

Background File Transfer

On UNIX systems with job control, you can type your suspend character (normally Ctrl-Z) to suspend Kermit during local-mode file transfer. This stops Kermit so you can talk to your shell or run other programs. Later (but not too much later) you can bring it back in the foreground (using the UNIX `fg` command); the file transfer resumes where it left off, provided the other Kermit has not timed out.

```
C-Kermit>s order.log
SF
Sending: order.log => ORDER.LOG
Size: 3712745, Type: text
X to cancel file,  CR to resend current packet
Z to cancel group, A for status report
E to send Error packet, Ctrl-C to quit immediately: A
........Ctrl-Z
[3] + Stopped (signal)   kermit
$ fortune                        (Quick, I need a fortune)
The moon is full.  Today is your lucky day.  You are very hungry.

$ fg %3                          (Resume Kermit)
kermit
N%.......................... [OK]
ZB<BEEP>
C-Kermit>exit
```

You can also continue the file transfer in the background, leaving your terminal free for other work in the meantime:

```
.....Ctrl(Z)
[3] + Stopped (signal)   kermit
$ bg %3                          (Continue Kermit in the background)
[3] kermit&
$ jobs
[3] + Running            kermit
[2] - Stopped            emacs
[1]   Stopped (signal)   mm
```

Eventually, your shell will give you a message that the job has stopped because it wants "tty input," which means the transfer has completed. At that point you can put Kermit back in the foreground:

```
[3] + Stopped (tty input) kermit
$ fg %3                          (Back to the foreground)
C-Kermit>                        (Prompt reappears)
```

Sending Files

C-Kermit processes wildcard characters (metacharacters) in the SEND and MSEND commands, and the C-Kermit server also processes them when it receives a GET command.

UNIX C-Kermit offers two options for processing wildcards: its own internal wildcard expander and that of your shell. Select the desired expansion method with this command:

SET WILDCARD-EXPANSION { KERMIT, SHELL }

Unless you say otherwise, Kermit expands wildcards itself. In this case, three special characters are recognized and expanded:

~ (Tilde) (at the beginning of a filename only) is translated into your login directory name (if followed immediately by a slash) or into the login directory of the user whose username immediately follows the tilde:

```
C-Kermit>send ~/.profile          (My own .profile file)
C-Kermit>send ~jrd/mskermit.ini   (JRD's mskermit.ini file)
```

* (asterisk) Matches zero or more characters within a file or directory name. The asterisk does not match the slash (/) character; that is, it does not work across directory separators.

```
C-Kermit>send *           (All files in current directory)
C-Kermit>send ~/*/*.ini   (.ini's in all subdirectories)
C-Kermit>send o*a         (o-anything-a)
```

In UNIX, "hidden" files (whose names begin with a period character), such as .login, are not sent unless the *filespec* also begins with a period:[51]

```
C-Kermit>send *           (All nonhidden files)
C-Kermit>send .*          (All hidden files)
C-Kermit>msend * .*       (All files)
```

? (question mark) Matches any single character except a directory separator (slash) or the leading period of a hidden file. You must quote the question mark with a backslash to override its normal help-giving function:

```
C-Kermit>send ckcker.\?       (ckcker.1-character)
C-Kermit>send ckcker.\?\?\?   (ckcker.3-characters)
C-Kermit>send ~kermit/\?*     (~kermit/-at-least-1-character)
```

If you don't quote the question mark, you get a list of matching filenames, and then you are reprompted with what you have typed so far:

```
C-Kermit>send ckcmai.? File(s) to send, one of the following:
 ckcmai.c           ckcmai.o
C-Kermit>send ckcmai.
```

The UNIX shells csh, ksh, and bash, but not the original Bourne shell, provide additional filename-matching wildcard characters. If you SET WILD SHELL, Kermit uses the shell whose file specification is given in the SHELL environment variable:

```
$ echo $SHELL
/bin/ksh
```

---

[51]This is compatible with the file matching of the UNIX shell and the ls command.

Using UNIX C-Kermit 395

or if that fails, it uses your login shell (as recorded in the `etc/passwd` file). Internally, Kermit uses the specified shell's `echo` command to expand metacharacters. Exactly which metacharacters are available depends on your shell and its `echo` command. The following are generally available in addition to those listed; consult your shell's "man page" for further information.

[abc]
> (csh, ksh, bash) Matches any single character that appears within the brackets:
>
> `C-Kermit>send ck[cuw]*.[cwh]`   *(The UNIX Kermit source files)*

[a-z]
> (csh, ksh, bash) Matches any single character in the range indicated in the brackets, in this case a through z. The characters in the range are determined by the internal numeric codes for the characters (for example their ASCII values):
>
> `C-Kermit>send x[0-9][0-9].log`   *(x00.log thru x99.log)*
> `C-Kermit>send [Ff][Ii][Ll][Ee]`   *("file" in any case)*

{aaa,bbb}
> (csh, bash) Matches any of the comma-separated character strings within the braces:
>
> `C-Kermit>send ckcker.{upd,bwr}`
> `C-Kermit>send {oofa.txt,hex.c}`
> `C-Kermit>send ck[cuw]*.{[cwh],doc,bwr,nr}`

As you can see, shell expansion can be more flexible than Kermit's own, and it is consistent with your own use of your preferred shell. But it also has several possible drawbacks:

- It might be difficult or impossible to refer to files whose names contain shell metacharacters. (Try quoting such characters with a backslash or two, or enclosing the filename in doublequotes, but this might not always work.)

- The same Kermit file transfer command might behave differently depending on what your current shell is. This is a particularly important consideration for command files. Kermit's internal expansion, on the other hand, works consistently.

- The `echo` command of certain shells (notably csh) might print not only filenames, but other words. For example, in the C-Shell:

  `$ echo foo*`
  `echo: no match`

  In this case, if you happen to have files called `echo:`, `no`, or `match`, Kermit might try to transfer them.

- The `echo` command has an option -n. If you try to refer to a file whose name is -n, you must prefix it with a directory specification (for example, `./-n`) to prevent `echo` from interpreting its name as a command option.

When you give the -s option on the C-Kermit command line, the file specification that follows can include any wildcard notation that is understood by your shell, regardless of C-Kermit's WILDCARD-EXPANSION setting. The shell expands wildcards into a list of files that is provided to Kermit via the "argv" mechanism. For example:

$ kermit -s *.txt

The shell, not Kermit, expands *.txt into a list of all the files in your current directory whose names end with ".txt". If any of the files actually contains a wildcard character as part of its name, C-Kermit makes no attempt to expand it further.

Receiving Files

Incoming files are stored in the current directory unless you told the RECEIVE command otherwise or if the incoming file header packet includes a pathname. A file can be created only if you have write access to the directory where the file is to be stored. If a file of the same name already exists in the target directory, and C-Kermit's FILE COLLISION is set to BACKUP or OVERWRITE, you must also have write access to the previously existing file. C-Kermit will not create or delete files for you that you could not otherwise create or delete yourself.

Files are stored with the permissions of the containing directory combined with your "umask" (see the "man page" for your shell for further information). In other words, C-Kermit creates files with exactly the same permissions they would have if you created them any other way, for example with the cat command, or with a text editor.

C-Kermit does not set execute permission on incoming files. If you are using C-Kermit to receive shell scripts, executable binary programs, or other types of files that require execute permission, use chmod +x after the transfer.

If a UNIX file must be renamed because of your FILE COLLISION setting, C-Kermit appends a pseudo-version-number to the end of the file's name:

oofa.~n~

where oofa is the name the two files share and .~n~ is a version number, for example:

resume.mss.~8~

If oofa exists, the new file is called oofa.~1~. If oofa and oofa.~1~ exist, the new file is oofa.~2~, and so on. If the new name would be longer than the maximum length for a filename on your UNIX system, then characters are deleted from the end first. For instance, thelongestname on a system with a limit of 14 characters would become thelongest.~1~. This scheme is compatible with the backup mechanism used by GNU EMACS on UNIX, and in fact the renamed files are recognized as backup files by EMACS, which can be used to clean up excessive numbers of them.

Appendix IV

VMS C-Kermit

○ ○ ○ ○
This appendix explains how to use C-Kermit on a Digital Equipment Corporation VAX or AXP computer with the VMS or OpenVMS operating system. For a current list of limitations and restrictions of VMS C-Kermit, also read the files `CKCKER.BWR` and `CKVKER.BWR` provided with the VMS C-Kermit distribution files.

VMS (Virtual Memory System) is the operating system for Digital Equipment Corporation 32-bit VAX (Virtual Address Extended) computers, a product line ranging from desktop workstations to minicomputers to large mainframes. VMS is a multiuser, multitasking operating system. OpenVMS is the new name for the VMS operating system; OpenVMS runs on both VAX and AXP processors. C-Kermit runs under both VMS and OpenVMS, on both VAX and AXP processors. In this appendix, the word VMS also includes OpenVMS on both VAX and AXP architectures.

Preparing Your VMS Session for C-Kermit

Before starting C-Kermit, make sure that VMS knows what kind of terminal you have so C-Kermit's FULLSCREEN file transfer display will work correctly. VMS C-Kermit (like VMS itself) supports only the VT52 and VT100 and higher terminal types for formatted screen display functions. If you are using C-Kermit on a terminal that is not compatible with these terminals, you should not use Kermit's FULLSCREEN file transfer display.

VMS is designed to be used from DEC terminals. When you log in, most VMS systems send a special "What Are You?" query (the ESC character followed by the letter Z) to the terminal. All DEC terminals respond automatically with a character sequence indicating the terminal model—LA36, VT52, VT100, VT200, VT300, VT400, etc. If you are using a VT or compatible terminal, or a PC with a correctly functioning VT terminal emulator, such as MS-DOS Kermit, your VMS terminal type is set automatically. Otherwise, there is a lengthy pause while VMS waits for a valid reply, doesn't get one, and then sets your terminal type to UNKNOWN.

You can find out what terminal types are supported by your VMS system by issuing the VMS command HELP SET TERMINAL/DEVICE. If your terminal appears on this list, you can give a VMS command to set your terminal type correspondingly, like:

```
$ set terminal /device=vt100
```

You can find out your VMS terminal characteristics with the SHOW TERMINAL command.

If you are using a speaking device or a TDD (Telecommunication Device for the Deaf), you should choose a hardcopy terminal type, such as LA36.

Checking and Setting Your Communication Speed

When you use C-Kermit to transfer files in remote mode, it bases its packet timeouts on the communication speed of your login terminal as reported by VMS. If you have dialed in at (say) 2400 bps but VMS thinks your speed is 19200 bps, file transfers might not work well, or at all.

VMS knows your communication speed if your terminal or PC is connected directly, or through a modem, to a communication port on the VMS system. If you give the SHOW TERMINAL command, you'll see a display like this:

```
$ sho term
Terminal: _TXA3:        Device_Type: VT300_Series   Owner: IVAN

   Input:  2400         LFfill: 0      Width: 80       Parity: None
   Output: 2400         CRfill: 0      Page:  24
```

If you have entered the VMS system through a network connection—a terminal server using TCP/IP TELNET or RLOGIN (but not LAT) protocol, or a TELNET or RLOGIN (but not CTERM) session from another host—you are not attached to a real communication port, so VMS might not know your true communication speed. Check to see:

```
$ sho term
Terminal: _NTY2:        Device_Type: VT300_Series   Owner: IVAN
Remote Port Info: watsun.cc.columbia.edu

   Input:  19200        LFfill: 0      Width: 80       Parity: None
   Output: 19200        CRfill: 0      Page:  24
```

If the speed is wrong, you should let VMS know your true speed as soon as you log in (but don't do this on a LAT connection):

```
$ set term /speed=1200
```

Using International Characters

If the communication channel between you and the VMS system permits transmission of 8-bit data, you can use 8-bit character sets such as ISO Latin-1 and the DEC Multinational Character Set in your VMS session. VMS applications support the use of 8-bit characters, but you might have to tell VMS that your terminal is able to use them. The command is:

```
$ set terminal /noparity /eight
```

If you can't obtain an 8-bit connection, you are restricted to a 7-bit character code during terminal operations. This code may be ASCII or any other 7-bit code supported by your terminal or terminal emulator, such as an ISO 646 national character set.

Using VMS C-Kermit

VMS users might find C-Kermit's command processing to be somewhat unfamiliar. It lacks certain VMS features and has some others that you will soon wish VMS had. C-Kermit's "user interface" is intended to be compatible with other Kermit programs, rather than with a particular operating system. Once you have learned to control one Kermit program, you will also be conversant with most others.

Program Control

C-Kermit is a character-mode application designed to be used from a terminal. If you are accessing your VMS system from a terminal or terminal emulator, you can start the Kermit program in the normal way, that is, by typing its name possibly followed by command line arguments.[52] Then you can have an interactive dialog with C-Kermit, using your keyboard and screen:

```
$ kermit
C-Kermit 5A(188) 23 Nov 92, OpenVMS VAX
Type ? or HELP for help
C-Kermit>
```

If you have a desktop VMS workstation with a mouse-and-window-oriented graphical user interface (GUI) such as DECwindows, you should run C-Kermit in a VT terminal emulation window, also known as a DECterm.

---

[52] Or, if Kermit has not been installed as a system command, use the RUN command. The RUN command, however, does not permit command-line arguments.

Command-line options are converted to lowercase before C-Kermit sees them, which can interfere with important case distinctions, for example between the -y and -Y or -c and -C options. To include an uppercase option on the VMS C-Kermit command line, enclose it in doublequotes:

```
$ kermit "-Y"
```

Interrupting C-Kermit

C-Kermit can be interrupted at its prompt, in the middle of typing a command, during execution of any command except CONNECT or remote-mode file transfer, and during local-mode file transfer by typing either one of the VMS interrupt characters, Ctrl-C or Ctrl-Y. Both should have the same effect.

The interrupt character should echo as ^C... and return you to the C-Kermit prompt immediately (if you were running C-Kermit interactively), or else back to the system prompt if you started C-Kermit with command-line action options (Chapter 14).

To interrupt C-Kermit during remote-mode file transfer, type two consecutive Ctrl-C characters. This should return you to the C-Kermit prompt or, if you started C-Kermit with command-line action options, to the VMS system prompt.

To interrupt C-Kermit during CONNECT mode, use the CONNECT-mode escape character, followed by C to get back to the prompt, or any of the other escape-level commands described in Chapter 4.

Redirection of Input and Output

C-Kermit reads its interactive-mode commands from the standard input device, normally your keyboard, and prints its messages on the standard output device, which is normally your screen. To redirect Kermit's standard input to come from a file, redefine the SYS$INPUT logical name:

```
$ define sys$input kermit.cmd
$ kermit
$ deassign sys$input
```

In these examples, the file KERMIT.CMD contains C-Kermit commands. C-Kermit executes them, one after the other, until it comes to the end of the file (or to an EXIT, STOP, or similar command), and then it exits back to the system prompt.

You can also redirect C-Kermit's screen output to a file by redefining the SYS$OUTPUT logical name before starting C-Kermit:

```
$ define sys$output kermit.log
$ kermit
$ deassign sys$output
```

But if you redirect Kermit's screen output without also redirecting its input, you'll be typing Kermit commands to a blank screen. To redirect both input and output:

```
$ define sys$input kermit.cmd
$ define sys$output kermit.log
$ kermit
$ deassign sys$output
$ deassign sys$input
```

Background operation in VMS can be accomplished with the SPAWN/NOWAIT command:

```
$ spawn /nowait /input=kermit.cmd /output=kermit.log kermit
```

or by running Kermit in a batch job, using the VMS SUBMIT command.

Running C-Kermit in DCL Command Procedures

In a DCL .COM file, lines beginning with dollar sign are commands that you would type at the VMS system prompt; all others are input for a program. The following example shows how to construct a DCL command file that feeds interactive-mode commands to C-Kermit. The first two lines are DCL commands, the next three are C-Kermit commands, and the last line is another DCL command:

```
$ write sys$output "Starting Kermit..."
$ kermit
set file type binary
receive
exit
$ write sys$output "Kermit finished."
```

To make VMS C-Kermit read its commands from your keyboard when invoked from a DCL command procedure, include the following redefinition of the SYS$COMMAND logical name:

```
$ write sys$output "Starting Kermit..."
$ define /user sys$input sys$command
$ kermit
$ write sys$output "Kermit finished."
```

DCL command procedures can pass their command-line arguments along to C-Kermit. For example, the following DCL command file, KSEND.COM, sends up to eight files (or groups of files) from a remote VMS system to the user's local Kermit program:

```
$ kermit -s 'p1' 'p2' 'p3' 'p4' 'p5' 'p6' 'p7' 'p8'
```

The p's in single quotes are DCL variables, similar to Kermit's macro argument variables. They are used here to pass command-line arguments from the DCL command procedure to C-Kermit. To use this command procedure, type (for example):

```
$ @ksend ckvker.mak ck*.h ck*.c
```

This example assumes the KSEND.COM file is in your current directory.

The C-Kermit Initialization File

VMS C-Kermit identifies its initialization file by the following steps:

1. The file `CKERMIT.INI`, if it exists, in the directory designated by the system-wide logical name `CKERMIT_INI:`, if it is defined. You can override the system-wide definition, if any, by redefining this logical name.

2. The file designated by the logical name `CKERMIT_INIT`, if it is defined.

3. The file `CKERMIT.INI` in your login (home) directory.

If the `CKERMIT_INI` logical name does not exist, or does not turn up a `CKERMIT.INI` file, then the search proceeds down the list.

The system manager can install the standard C-Kermit initialization file in a central location and define the system-wide logical name `CKERMIT_INI` to identify the directory where this file is. To institute site-wide customizations, a C-Kermit command file called `CKERMIT.SYS` can be placed in the same directory as the system-wide `CKERMIT.INI` file.

The standard initialization file automatically executes the user's own customization file, `CKERMOD.INI`, if it exists in the user's home directory, so each user can create a personalized C-Kermit environment without having to duplicate the common material from the standard initialization file.

Users can further customize C-Kermit to use different settings when started from different directories. For example, you can put a `CKERMIT.INI` file in your `BINARIES` directory to SET FILE TYPE BINARY, and another one in your `TEXT` directory to SET FILE TYPE TEXT. Then include the following as the last line in your login directory's `CKERMOD.INI` file:

```
if not equal \v(home) \v(dir) -
  if exist []ckermit.ini take []ckermit.ini
```

If you have a dialing directory file, it should be installed in your login directory with the name `CKERMIT.KDD`. If you have a services directory file, it goes in the same place under the name `CKERMIT.KSD`.

Terminal Connection

VMS C-Kermit's default CONNECT-mode escape character is Ctrl-\ (Control-Backslash). Terminal emulation is provided by your console driver, workstation terminal window, terminal emulator, or terminal. VMS C-Kermit recognizes keystrokes as single 7- or 8-bit bytes. 8-bit codes can be used if you have a keyboard capable of generating them, if C-Kermit has a clean 8-bit path to the keyboard, if you have told C-Kermit to SET COMMAND and TERMINAL BYTESIZE 8, *and* if your VMS terminal has the EIGHTBIT characteristic, as shown by the VMS SHOW TERMINAL command.

File Transfer

VMS C-Kermit transfers most common types of files in the correct manner automatically, with no SET FILE TYPE commands required. When sending files, VMS C-Kermit supports the full range of VMS wildcard characters for file group selection.

Wildcards

VMS lets you refer to groups of files in a single file specification by using wildcard characters. VMS wildcard characters are asterisk (*) and percent (%). Asterisk matches all or part of a directory name, file name, or file type. It can also be used to stand for all version numbers, but it cannot be used to match part of a version number. In the directory field, the asterisk does not operate across the periods that separate directory names. Percent sign matches any single character in a directory name, file name, or file type, but it cannot be used in the version number field. The following command:

```
$ directory [kermit.*]a*.%%%;0
```

lists the names of the most recent versions (;0) of all files whose names start with the letter *A* (alphabetic case does not matter in VMS filenames) and that have a three-character filetype, in all subdirectories of the [KERMIT] top-level directory of the current disk.

There are also two special wildcards for use with directory names. The ellipsis (...) means "from here all the way down," and hyphen (-) means "one level up." Two hyphens means two levels up, and so on.

Here are some sample wildcard file specifications:

```
$ dir [*]
```
All files in all top-level directories

```
$ dir [.*]
```
All files in all directories immediately below the current directory (one level down)

```
$ dir [...]
```
All files in the current directory and all directories below it

```
$ dir [OLGA.PROGRAMS...]
```
All files in OLGA.PROGRAMS and all directories below it

```
$ dir [-]
```
All files in the directory immediately above the current directory (one level up)

```
$ dir [--]
```
All files in the directory two levels up

```
$ dir [000000]
```
All files in the root directory of the current disk (if you have access)

Using VMS C-Kermit 405

Sending Files from VMS

When you are sending files from VMS C-Kermit, and its FILE TYPE is set to TEXT or BINARY, it chooses the mode of transfer automatically. The rules are:

1. If the record format is Undefined, BINARY mode is used.

2. If the record format is Fixed, *and* the file has no record attributes (the VMS DIRECTORY/FULL command reports "Record attributes: None"), BINARY mode is used.

3. If the record format is Fixed and the file has any record attributes (for example, Carriage Return Carriage Control), TEXT mode is used.

4. In all other cases, including Stream and Variable record formats, TEXT mode is used.

VMS C-Kermit automatically tells the receiving Kermit the file's type in an Attribute packet. This allows the receiving Kermit to interpret and store the file in the correct mode automatically if it understands Attribute packets (most modern Kermit programs do; see Table 1-1 on page 8). It also lets VMS C-Kermit send a mixture of text and binary files in a single SEND command. For example, you can send the C-language (text) source file OOFA.C and the (binary) executable OOFA.EXE together with one command:

```
C-Kermit>send oofa.*
```

When sending a text file, C-Kermit handles all combinations of record format and carriage control, including Fortran (ANSI) and Print, converting each into Kermit standard ASCII/CRLF stream format. It also translates the file's character set according to any SET FILE CHARACTER-SET and SET TRANSFER CHARACTER-SET commands you have given.

When sending a binary file, VMS C-Kermit does no interpretation, translation, or reformatting of the file's data. Record-length and carriage control fields are discarded, and no characters are inserted at record boundaries or at the end of the file.

VMS C-Kermit also sends the file's size and creation date and time in the Attribute packet. This allows the receiving Kermit program to reject the file if it is too big for available storage and to set the file's creation date to match the original or to take file collision actions based on the date. The reported size of a text file might differ from the actual size due to record format conversions.

VMS C-Kermit also lets you include DECnet node names in filenames:

```
C-Kermit>send netlab::$disk1:[jrd.kermit]msvibm.boo
C-Kermit>send spcvxa"TERRY 32PASSWORD"::kermit:ckvcvt.c
C-Kermit>receive cumin::lpt:
```

The first example sends a publicly readable file from node NETLAB. The second example sends a file that is not publicly readable from node SPCVXA, so a valid user ID and password for that node must be included as part of the node name. These must be given in uppercase and the space that normally separates the user ID and password must be entered as \32 to prevent C-Kermit from thinking that the space introduces the next field of the command. The final example receives a file to a publicly accessible line printer on DECnet node CUMIN and then prints it.

If you invoke VMS C-Kermit with the command-line option to send files (-s, see Chapter 14), wildcard characters are expanded internally by C-Kermit, using underlying VMS operating system services:

```
$ kermit -s a*.* login.com ckermit.ini [.*]*.com
```

This example sends all files in the current directory whose names start with A, plus LOGIN.COM and CKERMIT.INI from the current directory, plus all .COM files from all immediate subdirectories of the current directory.

VMS C-Kermit sends the most recent version of each file unless you include a specific version number:

```
C-Kermit>send [olaf]paper.txt        (Most recent version only)
C-Kermit>sen [olaf]stone.txt;3       (A specific version)
C-Kermit>s [olaf]scissors.txt;*      (All versions)
```

Receiving Files

When receiving files, VMS C-Kermit chooses between text and binary mode as follows:

1. If the Kermit program that is sending the file to C-Kermit includes an Attribute packet specifying the file type (text or binary), C-Kermit uses the given type.

2. If there is no Attribute packet, if the Attribute packet does not mention a file type, or if you have given the command SET ATTRIBUTE TYPE OFF, C-Kermit uses your current FILE TYPE setting.

VMS C-Kermit checks for sufficient free disk space if the remote Kermit supplies file size information. If there isn't enough space on the disk, the file is rejected. User quotas are not checked. If the device for the received file is not a disk (for example, the system lineprinter) the file is assumed to fit. To defeat space checking, give the command SET ATTRIBUTE LENGTH OFF.

Received text files are stored in "Sequential variable, carriage-return carriage control" format, with each line (record) terminated by carriage return and linefeed (CRLF). Lone carriage returns or linefeeds are stored within the record.

Files received in binary mode are stored by C-Kermit in fixed 512-byte records. If the last record does not end on a 512-byte boundary, the exact end of the file is marked using the RMS "first free byte" construct.

If there is valid date and time information in the incoming Attribute packet, C-Kermit sets the new file's creation date and time accordingly. The file is marked as being revised once (initial creation) on the *current* date and time to ensure that the file is backed up on the next BACKUP run.

When the Automatic Methods Don't Work

○ ○ ○ ○
If you can successfully transfer both text and binary files to and from VMS with C-Kermit, feel free to skip the rest of this Appendix, which presents special methods for transferring the kinds of VMS files that C-Kermit does not handle automatically.

VMS supports a wide variety of file formats. Information about each file is recorded in the file's directory entry and, in most cases, also in the file itself. Most other computers have simpler file systems, with no natural way to record or represent VMS's file types and attributes. When a complicated type of file is sent from VMS to, say, UNIX or MS-DOS, much of the VMS-specific information can be lost. When the file is sent back to VMS, it is no longer in its original format and might be unusable. Even when a file is transferred from VMS to VMS the results can be less than satisfactory if the transfer program can't convey all the descriptive information along with its contents.

Each VMS application defines its own data file formats. Everyday text-oriented applications like the CREATE command and the editors EDT and EVE use ordinary text files: stream files with lines terminated by carriage return and line feed, the same as Kermit's default for text files. The VMS operating system requires its executable program images to be in fixed 512-byte record format, the same as Kermit's default for binary files.

But the VMS linker requires its (binary) object files to have variable length records. A BACKUP saveset must have fixed-length records with a record length of at least 2048 bytes. A database file might have indexed or relative organization, rather than sequential. Some applications deliberately coerce their files into unusual formats to make it difficult for other applications to use them. File attributes such as record format and length can't be handled by other operating systems like MS-DOS, OS/2, UNIX, or CP/M, so these files need special handling when you transfer them.

You can find out the particulars of a VMS file with the DIR/FULL command, for example:

```
$ dir /full oofa.obj
```

```
Directory $DISK1:[OLGA]

OOFA.OBJ;2                        File ID:  (3201,349,0)
Size:              37/38          Owner:    [USER,OLGA]
```

```
Created:    14-FEB-1992 14:20:55.17
Revised:    14-FEB-1992 14:21:48.47 (1)
Expires:    <None specified>
Backup:     8-FEB-1992 09:19:47.43
File organization:  Sequential
File attributes:    Allocation:38, Extend:10, Global buffercount:0
                    No version limit
Record format:      Variable length, maximum 512 bytes
Record attributes:  None
RMS attributes:     None
Journaling enabled: None
File protection:    System:RWED, Owner:RWED, Group:RE, World:
Access Cntrl List:  None

Total of 1 file, 37/38 blocks.
```

VMS C-Kermit lets you store incoming binary files with any record length you like in either fixed or undefined format, and it offers you two VMS-specific file types for transferring VMS files that don't fit the normal mold.

Selecting the Record Length for Incoming Files

When VMS C-Kermit receives a text file, it stores it on disk using variable-length records, one record per line, using carriage return and linefeed to delimit the lines. The maximum length for a line is 32,767 characters. If you try to send VMS C-Kermit a line of text longer than this, the file transfer will fail with the message "Error writing data."[53]

Binary files, however, do not have lines and there is no automatic way for C-Kermit to sense record boundaries in arriving binary files. So unless you say otherwise, C-Kermit stores incoming binary files using fixed-length 512-byte records. When an incoming binary file, such as a BACKUP saveset, must be stored using some other record length, you can use the following command:

SET FILE RECORD-LENGTH *number*
    Specifies the record length used by VMS C-Kermit to store an incoming file of type BINARY or IMAGE. The number can be up to 32767.

The record length setting is ignored when sending files; VMS C-Kermit uses the file's record length from its VMS directory entry. The record-length setting is also ignored when receiving text files.

To illustrate, let's create a BACKUP saveset on disk and transfer it to a PC. Remember to take careful note of the file's record length:

---

[53] This is a limitation of the VMS file system. If you *really* have a text file with lines longer than 32K, you can send it in binary mode.

Using VMS C-Kermit   409

```
$ backup oofa.* /interchange testing.bck /save
$ dir /full testing.bck
...
Record format:   Fixed length 32256 byte records
...
$ kermit
C-Kermit>send testing.bck           (Send the file)
Alt-x                               (Escape back to the PC)
MS-Kermit>receive                   (Receive the file)
```

Note that no SET commands were necessary. VMS C-Kermit recognizes the file as binary because it has fixed-length records and automatically tells MS-DOS Kermit that the file is binary.

Now let's send the BACKUP saveset from the PC to a different VMS system and restore the files from it. The connection is already made and VMS C-Kermit is already started. The trick here is to tell VMS C-Kermit what record length to use when storing the file and to tell MS-DOS Kermit to send the file in binary mode, which also causes MS-DOS Kermit to tell C-Kermit that it is a binary file:

```
C-Kermit>set file record-length 32256 (Use the same number!)
C-Kermit>receive                      (Wait for the file)
Alt-x                                 (Escape back to the PC)
MS-Kermit>set file type binary        (Use binary mode)
MS-Kermit>send testing.bck            (Send the file)

   (The file is transferred)

MS-Kermit>connect                     (Go back to VMS)
C-Kermit>exit                         (Quit from C-Kermit)
$ backup testing.bck/save/log *.*     (Restore the files)
%BACKUP-S-CREATED, created OOFA.C;12
%BACKUP-S-CREATED, created OOFA.H;3
%BACKUP-S-CREATED, created OOFA.EXE;8
%BACKUP-S-CREATED, created OOFA.OBJ;11
$
```

If the record length had not been set correctly, BACKUP would have become very upset when you tried to restore the files:

```
%BACKUP-E-READERR, error reading TESTING.BCK
-BACKUP-E-BLOCKCRC, software block CRC error
%BACKUP-E-INVBLKSIZE, invalid block size in save set
%BACKUP-E-INVRECSIZ, invalid record size in save set
%BACKUP-E-INVRECSIZ, invalid record size in save set
%BACKUP-E-READERRS, excessive error rate reading TESTING.BCK
-BACKUP-I-HDRCRC, software header CRC error
%BACKUP-I-OPERSPEC
%BACKUP-I-OPERASSIST, operator assistance has been requested
```

Not only has BACKUP flooded your screen with complaints, it has also reported your misbehavior to the system operator!

Storing Incoming Binary Files in Undefined Format

We have said that VMS C-Kermit detects the transfer mode of an incoming file automatically if the Attribute packet information is given. If an incoming file is announced as binary, C-Kermit normally stores it in Fixed format. But certain applications (such as Concept Omega Thoroughbred BASIC) require their files to be in Undefined format. VMS C-Kermit's SET FILE TYPE BINARY command has an optional trailing field to let you specify whether incoming binary files should be stored in Fixed or Undefined format. Here is a complete description of the SET FILE TYPE BINARY command for VMS:

SET FILE TYPE BINARY *[{ FIXED, UNDEFINED }=FIXED]*

Incoming files are to be processed in binary mode unless they are accompanied by an Attribute packet identifying their type as text. When receiving a binary file, C-Kermit stores it using fixed-length records (no length fields), with the record length specified in the most recent SET FILE RECORD-LENGTH command, 512 by default, and uses the RMS "first free byte" attribute to record the precise end of file. By default, the record format of the incoming file is set to Fixed. If you SET FILE TYPE BINARY UNDEFINED, the record format of the incoming file is set to Undefined instead of Fixed. Only the directory entry is affected by your choice of Fixed or Undefined, not the storage of the data itself.

RMS, the VMS Record Management System, cannot deal with undefined-format files, so only use BINARY UNDEFINED if you have an application that requires it. Here is an example in which a Thoroughbred BASIC file is transferred from a PC to a VAX:

```
$ kermit                              (Start Kermit on the VAX)
C-Kermit 5A(188) 23 Nov 92, VAX/VMS
Type ? or HELP for help
C-Kermit>set file type binary undef
C-Kermit>receive
Alt-x                                 (Escape back to the PC)
MS-Kermit>set file type binary        (PC uses binary mode)
MS-Kermit>send schedule.bas           (Send the file)

   (The file is transferred)

MS-Kermit>connect                     (Let's go back and take a look)
C-Kermit>dir /full schedule.bas
 ...
Record format:       Undefined, maximum 512 bytes
 ...
C-Kermit>
```

When C-Kermit is sending files from VMS, it determines text or binary mode automatically. Undefined-format files are sent correctly in binary mode.

The SET FILE TYPE IMAGE Command

IMAGE mode is a kind of "super-binary" mode, in which raw disk blocks are transmitted. Use it when SET FILE TYPE BINARY doesn't work.

SET FILE TYPE IMAGE

This command might better be called "binary, and this time I mean it!" When receiving a file, this mode is equivalent to SET FILE TYPE BINARY, except that it overrides the incoming Type attribute, if any. When sending a file, C-Kermit declares the file to be of type Binary in the Attribute packet and the blocks of the file are sent exactly as stored on disk, including any imbedded record-length fields and excluding any formatting characters (such as line terminators) that would normally be supplied by RMS based on the file's carriage-control attributes. Use SET FILE TYPE IMAGE to send files that have inappropriate or unusual file characteristics, such as a binary file that is stored in Stream LF format. Synonym: **SET FILE TYPE BLOCK**.

Here's an example. You have Lotus 1-2-3 on your PC and a version of Lotus 1-2-3 running on your VMS system. You can send a PC Lotus spreadsheet file to VMS using SET FILE TYPE BINARY, and VMS Lotus reads it perfectly and without complaint. But when you try to send a VMS Lotus spreadsheet to the PC in the same way, PC Lotus can't read it at all. Why not? Because VMS Lotus creates its spreadsheet files with carriage return carriage control, which makes C-Kermit send carriage return and line feed at the end of each record, resulting in an invalid format for PC Lotus. Use SET FILE TYPE IMAGE to circumvent the problem:

```
C-Kermit>set file type image    (The important command)
C-Kermit>send budget.wks        (Send the file)
Alt-x                           (Escape back to the PC)
MS-Kermit>receive               (Receive the file)
```

Another case where IMAGE mode is required is for files created by the VMS version of UNZIP, a dearchiving program, from VMS-resident ZIP files. Even when these are binary files, the VMS ZIP program creates them with a "Stream_LF" record format, which C-Kermit treats as text unless you tell it otherwise. Use IMAGE for sending. BINARY works for receiving.

VMS Labeled File Transfer

We've seen how to coax VMS C-Kermit into transferring simple types of sequential files whose record size or format might not match C-Kermit's defaults. But there still remain certain types of VMS files that defy all normal means of transfer—databases with indexed or relative organization, binary files with variable length records, and so on. Yes, you can transfer them, but when you bring them back to VMS, they are unusable. You can't even transfer them directly from one VMS system to another.

To illustrate, let's look at VMS object files. These are the files created by language compilers like Macro, Fortran, Pascal, and C, with names that end in `.OBJ`. For example, the command:

$ `macro ckvhex`

runs the Macro assembler on a source file called `CKVHEX.MAR` and produces an object file called `CKVHEX.OBJ`. This object file is composed of variable length records, like a text file, but it is binary. You can't use text mode to transfer it because the format of the record boundaries would be changed (carriage returns and linefeeds would be added), and you can't use binary mode because the record boundaries would be lost altogether. Image mode doesn't work either; the record boundaries are preserved but the record format information is lost from the directory entry.

For situations like this, you need a way of sending not only the contents of the file, but its entire directory entry along with it. To do this, C-Kermit offers a fourth file type, called LABELED. Labeled mode is used to preserve all the characteristics of the file after transfer, including its directory entry, internal record layout, RMS attributes, and so forth. It can be used directly between two VMS systems, in which case the file arrives and is stored with all its proper characteristics.

Labeled mode transfers can also be done between VMS and any other kind of computer. A VMS file sent in labeled form to a non-VMS computer is unusable on the other computer. A labeled file sent *to* a VMS computer is recreated in its original form.

Thus labeled mode is suitable both for VMS-to-VMS transfers and also for archiving VMS files on non-VMS systems. A labeled file can float from one computer to another until it finally finds its way back to a VMS system, where it is reincarnated. The command to select labeled file transfers is:

SET FILE TYPE LABELED

When sending a file, C-Kermit sends an Attribute packet declaring the file to be of type Binary, then transmits all of the file's characteristics in a specially coded heading as part of the file data. The file data itself is transmitted in Image mode.

When C-Kermit's FILE TYPE is LABELED, incoming files (which must be sent in binary mode) are treated as LABELED if the Type Attribute says the file is binary, or if there is no Attribute packet at all. If C-Kermit's file type is LABELED and the incoming attribute says the file is Text, C-Kermit rejects the file. Once having agreed to accept a file in labeled mode, VMS C-Kermit interprets the labeling information and attempts to use it to create the transferred file with all the same characteristics as the original, but with the version number set in the normal way.

Labeled files carry with them certain information that you will want to use in certain circumstances and not in others. C-Kermit always includes this information when sending files in labeled format. Use the SET FILE LABEL command to say what it should do with this information when receiving files:

SET FILE LABEL NAME { OFF, ON }
The labeled file contains the file's full VMS file specification. The default is ON, meaning C-Kermit attempts to store the incoming file with its original name rather than the name that the other Kermit sent it with. Use SET FILE LABEL OFF to have it stored under the name it was sent with or any alternate name you may have given in the RECEIVE command.

SET FILE LABEL PATH { OFF, ON }
The labeled file also includes the file's original disk and directory name. Normally C-Kermit stores an incoming labeled file in the current disk and directory. Use SET FILE LABEL PATH ON to have C-Kermit attempt to store the file in the disk and directory recorded within the labeled file itself. If FILE LABEL PATH is OFF, the path is ignored.

SET FILE LABEL ACL { OFF, ON }
The labeled file includes the file's original ACL (access control list), which contains information that would normally be useful only on the computer where the file originated. For example, VMS records access lists as binary numbers; restoring them on a different computer could wind up granting access to a random collection of users. Normally this data is ignored. SET FILE LABEL ACL ON to use it.

This command also governs the RMS Journaling, RMS Statistics, DDIF, PATHWORKS, and other file ACL entries. Note that you can create ACL entries that you can't see with DIR/FULL unless you have VMS Security privilege (but you should still be able to view—but not modify—them with EDIT/ACL). Unprivileged users can not delete or modify incorrect ACL entries without deleting the file itself. Even when FILE LABEL ACL is ON, RMS Journaling is not enabled for a received file.

SET FILE LABEL BACKUP { OFF, ON }
This tells C-Kermit whether to preserve the file's backup date, if one was included. OFF, which is the default, means that C-Kermit should ignore the backup date in the incoming labeled file and store the new file so it will be backed up. ON means to keep the labeled file's backup date.

SET FILE LABEL OWNER { OFF, ON }
C-Kermit normally makes you the owner of the incoming file. SET FILE LABEL OWNER ON if you want C-Kermit to preserve the file's original owner (privileges required).

SET FILE TYPE LABELED can be used for all VMS-to-VMS transfers, as long as character set translation is not required and C-Kermit is running on both ends. It is the only mode of transmission that works for all kinds of VMS files. The SET FILE TYPE LABELED command must be given to *both* VMS C-Kermit programs.

To send a VMS file to another kind of computer (UNIX or MS-DOS, for example) for archival, just give the SET FILE TYPE LABELED command to VMS C-Kermit before sending the file and make sure the other Kermit receives it in binary mode (it will do so automatically if it understands Attribute packets):

```
C-Kermit>set file type labeled   (Archival format)
C-Kermit>send oofa.x             (Send any kind of file)
Alt-x                            (Escape back to PC)
MS-Kermit>r                      (Receive the file)

  (The file is transferred)
```

The resulting file contains all the necessary information to reconstruct it on a VMS system, no matter where it may travel in the meanwhile, as long as all its travels are in binary mode. When the time eventually comes for it to return to VMS, make sure to send it in binary mode and to tell VMS C-Kermit to SET FILE TYPE LABELED:

```
C-Kermit>set file type labeled   (Archival format)
C-Kermit>r                       (Wait for the file)
Alt-x                            (Escape back to PC)
MS-Kermit>set file type binary   (Use binary mode)
MS-Kermit>send oofa.x            (Send the file)

  (The file is transferred)
```

You can easily identify a labeled file. Its first 20 characters are "KERMIT LABELED FILE:". If one of these files should happen to find its way back to VMS without being decoded by Kermit, you can use a separate program distributed with C-Kermit, called CKVCVT, to decode it into its original form, just as C-Kermit would have done if it had received the file with SET FILE TYPE LABELED in effect:

```
$ ckvcvt oofa.x
Creating OOFA.X...
...done.
$
```

A labeled file stored on your VMS disk can even be mistakenly sent in labeled mode to another computer, and then brought back to VMS in this form: labels within labels! The CKVCVT program can be used to peel away excessive layers of labeling.

VMS C-Kermit Summary

Important filenames:

CKERMIT.INI
> The standard initialization file. It can be in your home (login) directory, or in a central shared location designated by the system-wide logical name CKERMIT_INI.

CKERMIT.SYS
> The system-wide customization file, used to augment or override the definitions made in the standard initialization file on a system-wide basis. VMS C-Kermit executes this file if it can be found in the directory denoted by the CKERMIT_INI logical name.

CKERMOD.INI
> Your personal customization file, used to augment or override the definitions made in the standard initialization file. Must be stored in your home directory.

CKERMIT.KDD
> Your dialing directory, stored in your home directory.

CKERMIT.KSD
> Your services directory, stored in your home directory.

VMS C-Kermit has the unique ability to send a mixture of text and binary files in the same SEND or MSEND command. Any other Kermit program that supports Attribute packets (see Table 1-1 on page 8) can accept such a mixture. Table IV-1 summarizes the interaction of the various file types, the SEND and RECEIVE commands, and Attribute (A) packets in VMS C-Kermit.

Table IV-2 shows the types and record lengths to be used for transferring selected types of files between VMS C-Kermit and MS-DOS Kermit. The same settings should apply for other non-VMS Kermits, such as C-Kermit for UNIX or IBM mainframe Kermit. You can fill in the bottom of the table with any others that you encounter.

Table IV-1 VMS Kermit SET FILE Commands

SET FILE Command	Send	Receive
RECORD-LENGTH	Ignored	Used for Binary and Image, but not Text, transfers
TYPE TEXT	Ignored	Used unless overridden by A-packet
TYPE BINARY	Ignored	Used unless overridden by A-packet
TYPE IMAGE	Used	Used, overrides A-packet
TYPE LABELED	Used	Used if A-packet does not say the file is text and if the file is in legitimate Labeled format.

Table IV-2 MS-DOS – VMS File Transfer

Application	VMS File Type	MS-DOS File Type	VMS Record Length	Comments
VMS EDT, EVE, etc.	TEXT	TEXT	N/A	Files created with text editors
VMS FORTRAN	TEXT	TEXT	N/A	Fortran CC becomes CRLF
DCL-created	TEXT	TEXT	N/A	VFC files become stream
VMS LOTUS	IMAGE	BINARY	512	Can be used on VMS and PC
PC LOTUS	IMAGE	BINARY	512	Can be used on VMS and PC
VMS .EXE	BINARY	BINARY	512	Cannot be executed on PC
VMS .OBJ	LABELED	BINARY	N/A	Object files
VMS .OLB	BINARY	BINARY	512	Object libraries
BACKUP Saveset	BINARY	BINARY	≥ 2048	Use same record length as original
PC .EXE	BINARY	BINARY	512	Cannot be executed on VMS
SPSS Export	TEXT	TEXT	80	Can be used on VMS and PC
Thoroughbred BASIC	BINARY UNDEFINED	BINARY	N/A	A closed, non-RMS application
VMS .ZIP	IMAGE	BINARY	512	Can be used on both VMS and PC
PC .ZIP	BINARY	BINARY	512	Can be used on both VMS and PC
VMS Indexed	LABELED	BINARY	N/A	
VMS Relative	LABELED	BINARY	N/A	

Add others:

Appendix V

OS/2 C-Kermit

○ ○ ○ ○
This appendix supplies particulars about installing and using C-Kermit under OS/2. If you are not familiar with the fundamentals of OS/2, you can get an introduction by double-clicking on the "Start Here" icon on your OS/2 desktop. If C-Kermit is already installed on your OS/2 system, skip ahead to page 423.

OS/2 C-Kermit runs on personal computers with an 80286 or higher processor with OS/2 version 1.0 or higher (80386SX or higher is required by OS/2 2.0). OS/2 C-Kermit runs in character mode, either full-screen or in a window. It supports serial communication through your PC's communication ports, either direct or dialed, as well as selected networking methods.

In addition to all the standard C-Kermit communication, file transfer, character-set translation, and script programming features, OS/2 C-Kermit also includes its own built-in VT102 terminal emulator with extensions for color, key mapping, and screen rollback, fully described in this appendix.

Installation

The following installation procedure ensures that your OS/2 system is configured correctly for C-Kermit and allows you to choose where to put the C-Kermit files on your hard disk, whether C-Kermit is to be a windowed or full screen application, and where its icon should go.

Preparing Your Serial Port

If you will be using C-Kermit to communicate through a serial port, the OS/2 serial port device driver must be installed in your CONFIG.SYS file as follows. For version 1 of OS/2 on a PC with an ISA (PC/AT) or EISA bus, the following line is required:

DEVICE=C:\OS2\COM01.SYS

For version 1 of OS/2 on a PC with a Micro Channel (PS/2) bus, the following line is needed:

DEVICE=C:\OS2\COM02.SYS

If you are running version 2 of OS/2 on a PC with either kind of bus, the following line must be present:[54]

DEVICE=C:\OS2\COM.SYS

If you find that the appropriate line is missing from your CONFIG.SYS file, you can add it with a text editor such as OS/2's E editor. If the driver is not available, unpack it from the distribution diskettes or use OS/2's selective install feature (version 2 of OS/2 only). Then restart your OS/2 system by clicking on "Shut down" in the desktop menu and holding down the Ctrl, Alt, and Del keys simultaneously after receiving the final shutdown message.

You can use the OS/2 MODE command to inquire about the current settings of the serial port device driver:

```
[C:\]mode com1
BAUD = 1200         PARITY = EVEN
DATABITS = 7        STOPBITS = 1
TO = OFF            XON = OFF
IDSR = ON           ODSR = ON
OCTS = ON           DTR = ON
RTS = ON            BUFFER = AUTO
```

These parameters can be changed by using the OS/2 MODE command. When your OS/2 serial port device driver is active, its default configuration requires the RS-232 DSR and CTS signals (see Appendix II) to be asserted by the communication device (modem or other computer). If your communication device does not assert CTS and DSR, a condition that can block successful communication, you can give the following MODE command to change the default behavior:

```
[C:\]mode com1: octs=off,odsr=off,idsr=off
```

---

[54]For IBM PS/2 Models 90 and 95, a special driver, COMDMA.SYS, provides high-speed direct memory access.

You can get information about the MODE parameters by typing HELP MODE at the OS/2 CMD prompt or by clicking on the Information icon. Most settings are handled automatically by C-Kermit itself. Of those that are not, the recommended settings are:

TO=ON
> Output timeout: None.

BUFFER=ON
> To enable hardware character buffering for more efficient communication. This requires 16550 or similar buffered serial port hardware, such as found in IBM PS/2s.

Installing the C-Kermit Files

To install the C-Kermit files on your PC's hard disk, follow these steps:

1. In the Command Prompts window, select OS/2 Full Screen or OS/2 Window to get the CMD prompt, which normally is your current disk and directory enclosed in square brackets:

   [C:\]

2. Create a directory called CKERMIT on your hard disk to hold the OS/2 Kermit files and then CD to it:

   [C:\]mkdir c:\ckermit
   [C:\]cd c:\ckermit
   [C:\CKERMIT]

   If you wish to install C-Kermit on a different disk, substitute its disk letter for C:.

3. Insert the OS/2 C-Kermit diskette into your diskette drive and copy the files from it to the hard disk directory:

   [C:\CKERMIT]copy a:*.* .

   The files include CKERMIT.EXE (the executable OS/2 C-Kermit program), CKERMIT.ICO (the C-Kermit icon), CKERMIT.INI (the standard initialization file), CKERMOD.INI (a sample customization file), and CKERMIT.CMD (a sample REXX file for starting C-Kermit). As distributed, CKERMIT.CMD looks like this:

   ```
   /* C-Kermit Startup File */
   "@echo off"                      /* Don't echo these commands */
   "echo Executing CKERMIT.CMD..."
   "chcp 850"                       /* Use Code Page 850 */
   "mode co80,25"                   /* Screen size 80 by 25 lines */
   "mode com1 buffer=on,to=on"      /* Hardware buffering, no timeout */
   "ckermit.exe %1 %2 %3 %4 %5 %6 %7 %8 %9"  /* Start C-Kermit */
   ```

   The doublequotes are required to distinguish OS/2 commands from REXX commands. The %1..%9 variables pass any C-Kermit command line arguments (up to nine of them) through the command file to C-Kermit itself (see Chapter 14).

4. Use the OS/2 editor, E, to make any desired changes to the CKERMOD.INI and CKERMIT.CMD files:

   ```
   [C:\CKERMIT]e ckermod.ini
   [C:\CKERMIT]e ckermit.cmd
   ```

   For example, if you want to run C-Kermit in a 43-line window, change "mode co80,25" to "mode co80,43" in CKERMIT.CMD.

5. Exit from the OS/2 window back to the desktop:

   ```
   [C:\CKERMIT]exit
   ```

Now create a desktop object that you can double-click on to start C-Kermit. In OS/2 version 1, make an entry in the Desktop Manager Group Window. In OS/2 version 2, make a new Program Reference Object:

1. Double-click on the Templates folder on your desktop.

2. Use the mouse to drag the program template to the desired location on your desktop. The settings notebook of the new object should pop up automatically.

3. Fill in the full pathname of the CKERMIT.CMD file, for example:

   C:\CKERMIT\CKERMIT.CMD

4. Fill in any desired (optional) command-line arguments for C-Kermit, for example:

   -l com2 -b 2400 -p e

   to always start C-Kermit on COM2 at 2400 bps and even parity (see Chapter 14 for a description of C-Kermit's command-line options).

5. Set C-Kermit's working directory to the directory where C-Kermit and its initialization file are stored, so C-Kermit can find its initialization file. If you don't want this directory to be C-Kermit's default directory for file transfer, you can also put a CD command in the CKERMOD.INI file.

6. By default, C-Kermit will be installed as a windowed application, but you can also choose to run it as a fullscreen application:

   - In a window, text is simulated by graphics operations (causing C-Kermit to run more slowly than it would in fullscreen mode), and the window is restricted to 80 characters in width. But when you run C-Kermit in an OS/2 window, you can cut and paste, move around among different windows easily, and you have access to the title-bar pop-up menu for changing fonts, closing C-Kermit in case of disaster, and so on.

- If you choose to make C-Kermit a fullscreen application, the screen is updated more quickly and it can contain as many characters per line as your display adapter permits, such as 132 columns on the XGA. But you will not have access to the pop-up menu and you won't be able to cut and paste.

- In both fullscreen and windowed mode, C-Kermit can use more than 25 lines if you execute a MODE command like MODE CO80,43 before starting C-Kermit.

  To choose fullscreen operation, click on the Session tab of the settings notebook and then click on "OS/2 full screen."

7. By default, double-clicking on the C-Kermit icon when C-Kermit is already active continues the active copy of C-Kermit. If you want to run multiple copies of C-Kermit simultaneously, click on the Window tab of the settings notebook and then select "Create new window."

8. Finally, click on the General tab of the settings notebook. Fill in the title, "C-Kermit," uncheck the Template item (if it is checked), and then close the settings window.

Your installation of C-Kermit is now complete. The C-Kermit icon should be available on the OS/2 desktop or in the folder that you chose in step 2.

Using OS/2 C-Kermit

Once C-Kermit is installed, you can start it by clicking on its icon or you can run it from the OS/2 CMD prompt.

Starting C-Kermit from Its Icon

Double-click on the C-Kermit icon. C-Kermit starts, occupying the full screen or a window, depending on the setting you chose in step 6. The C-Kermit initialization file issues a greeting message, such as:

```
Executing C:\CKERMIT\CKERMIT.INI...
```

If you don't see this message, the CKERMIT.INI file is not in the same directory as CKERMIT.EXE or C-Kermit isn't configured to use the CKERMIT directory as its startup directory.

At this point you should see C-Kermit's herald and prompt:

```
C-Kermit 5A(188), 23 Nov 92, OS/2 2.00
Type ? or HELP for help
C-Kermit>
```

If you have chosen windowed operation, you might notice the first time you start C-Kermit that its window is not full size. This is normal for VGA and lower-resolution video adapters. To bring C-Kermit's window to the desired size, hold down the Shift key and click on the "maximize" (square) box at the right end of C-Kermit's title bar. This grows the C-Kermit window to the size specified in your MODE command and makes it C-Kermit's permanent startup window size.

Starting C-Kermit from the CMD Prompt

You can also start C-Kermit from the OS/2 command prompt by typing its name followed by any desired command line options, for example:

[C:\]ckermit -l com3 -b 19200 -p m

All the settings in the Program Reference Object are bypassed, and C-Kermit fills the current OS/2 window. If you have both a CKERMIT.EXE and CKERMIT.CMD file in the same directory, OS/2 runs the .EXE file if you don't specify a filetype. To start C-Kermit from the OS/2 command file, include the .CMD filetype:

[C:\]ckermit.cmd -l com3 -b 19200 -p m

If C-Kermit is not in your current directory or in any directory in your OS/2 PATH, OS/2 won't find it. You can change your OS/2 PATH by altering the SET PATH command in the CONFIG.SYS file, or you can invoke C-Kermit by its complete pathname:

[C:\]c:\ckermit\ckermit.cmd

OS/2 C-Kermit Command Procedures

C-Kermit command files can be executed directly without having to start C-Kermit first if they include an EXTPROC command as the first line in the file, specifying the full pathname of the C-Kermit program, for example:

extproc c:\ckermit\ckermit.exe

EXTPROC is an OS/2 command for running external procedures. It runs the program whose name is given, and feeds the remaining lines in the file to that program. To C-Kermit, EXTPROC is a synonym for COMMENT.

Create the command file with a text editor like E, using a file type of .CMD, and save it as an OS/2 command procedure. You can run it from the OS/2 command line by typing its name. You can also create a desktop program object for it, just as you did for the CKERMIT.CMD file when you installed it, copying the C-Kermit icon or creating a new icon of your own, and then double-clicking on the icon to run it.

For example, suppose there are two different connections you normally make, one of them a 2400-bps dialed connection on COM1, and the other a 38400-bps direct connection on COM2. Create a separate command procedure for each connection:

```
extproc c:\ckermit\ckermit.exe
set modem hayes                 ; Hayes modem dialing
set line com1                   ; on communication port 1
set speed 2400                  ; at 2400 bps
dial 7654321                    ; Dial the number
if success connect              ; CONNECT if it answered
else exit 1                     ; otherwise quit
```

and:

```
extproc c:\ckermit\ckermit.exe
set line com2                   ; Direct connection through COM2
set speed 38400                 ; at 38400 bits per seconds
set flow rts/cts                ; using hardware flow control
connect                         ; Begin terminal emulation
```

Call these files, say, DIALUP.CMD and DIRECT.CMD, and run the appropriate one whenever you want to make a connection. You can even run them both at the same time.

Serial Communications

OS/2 version 1 supports the COM1 and COM2 serial devices on all PC models, plus COM3 on Micro Channel PS/2 systems. OS/2 version 2 supports COM1 through COM4. C-Kermit can use any communication speed supported by the communication port driver, up to 57600 bps on most systems, and possibly 76800 and 115200 bps. But the fact that the communication driver allows high speeds does not necessarily mean that C-Kermit, or any other application, or the driver itself, can keep up with high-speed input.

Communication Port, Speed, and Modem Signals

When C-Kermit starts, its communication device is set to COM1, serial port number 1, and the communication speed is set to the current speed of that device. You can select different serial ports with the SET LINE command and change their speeds with SET SPEED.

The port's DTR and RTS signals both go ON when C-Kermit opens it and they go OFF when the port is closed or when C-Kermit terminates. OS/2 C-Kermit treats the carrier signal according to your most recent SET CARRIER command, AUTO by default. Unless you SET CARRIER OFF, loss of carrier during CONNECT mode causes C-Kermit to return to its prompt automatically.

Parity, Data Bits, and Stop Bits

C-Kermit always sets the port driver to 8 data bits and no parity, then handles parity internally according to your SET PARITY setting. When C-Kermit's parity is NONE, 8 data bits are used. When it is EVEN, ODD, MARK, or SPACE, C-Kermit uses 7 data bits and handles the parity bit itself. These operations are internal to C-Kermit; the port driver's parity handling is not used. You can change the number of stop bits with the OS/2 MODE command before starting Kermit if necessary.

Flow Control

OS/2 C-Kermit supports both Xon/Xoff and RTS/CTS flow control. The flow-control method is specified by C-Kermit's SET FLOW command. The default is KEEP, meaning the serial port device driver is to use whatever flow-control method it was already configured with, for example by the OS/2 MODE command.

Use the C-Kermit command SET FLOW XON/XOFF to select software flow control, or SET FLOW RTS/CTS if you want to use RTS/CTS hardware flow control. SET FLOW NONE turns off flow control altogether. Xon/Xoff (software) flow control is available on both serial and network connections. When you have selected this type of flow control, the OS/2 serial communication driver does not allow the transmission of Ctrl-Q and Ctrl-S as data characters. RTS/CTS (hardware) flow control works only on serial connections, and then only when the device to which your serial port is immediately connected supports it and is configured to use it.

You should use RTS/CTS hardware flow control whenever your connection permits. Hardware flow control is far more reliable and responsive than software flow control, and it also permits the transmission of Ctrl-S and Ctrl-Q characters as ordinary data.

Network Connections

OS/2 C-Kermit supports DECnet LAT connections if you have installed DEC PATHWORKS on your PC. Use C-Kermit's SHOW NETWORK command to check whether any other networks are supported, such as IBM TCP/IP or Microsoft LAN Manager. Use SET NETWORK to select any of the available network types, and SET HOST to select a host on the given network, as described in Chapter 3.

Terminal Emulation

When you first issue the CONNECT command, you get a blank screen with a blinking cursor in the top left corner and a status line on the bottom. This indicates that C-Kermit is ready to communicate. The CONNECT command fails if the communication device is not properly conditioned, for example if you CONNECT to a modem before dialing without having first issued the SET CARRIER OFF command.

The screen dimensions are determined by your display adapter and your most recent MODE command in the current window (see the Installation section of this appendix). The cursor shape, as well as the foreground, background, and status-line colors are chosen by default, but special SET TERMINAL commands (listed on p. 432 in this appendix) allow you to change them.

In CONNECT mode, OS/2 C-Kermit emulates the Digital Equipment Corporation VT102 and VT52 terminals with extensions for color, key redefinition, and screen rollback. The control codes and escape sequences recognized by the terminal emulator are listed in Tables V-4 through V-10, beginning on page 435 at the end of this appendix.

Keyboard input is obtained through the OS/2 KBD subsystem, and screen output is through the VIO subsystem. It is therefore not possible to redirect terminal I/O.

Terminal Character Sets

The VT102 terminal, and therefore OS/2 C-Kermit's CONNECT command, does not support host-controlled ISO 2022 character-set designation and invocation except for switching between ASCII and the DEC Special Graphics character set. Use the SET TERMINAL CHARACTER-SET command to select your terminal emulation character set, and SET TERMINAL LOCKING-SHIFT to enable the use of 8-bit character sets in a 7-bit communication environment where the Shift-In/Shift-Out mechanism is supported. Both of these commands are explained in Chapter 9.

Your file character-set, and therefore also the local end of your terminal character-set, is automatically set to be your current PC code page, for example, CP437 or CP850. Thus you only need to specify the remote character set in your SET TERMINAL CHARACTER-SET command.

The Status Line and Alt-Key Commands

The bottom (normally 25th) line on the screen is used as a status line, giving the name of the communication port, the current speed, how to return to the prompt, and how to get help. The default CONNECT-mode escape character is Ctrl-] (Control-Rightbracket), but you can change it with the SET ESCAPE command. You can also use Alt-key combinations to accomplish many of the CONNECT-mode escape functions, for example Alt-X to escape back to the C-Kermit prompt. Typing Alt-? or the escape character followed by a question mark displays a pop-up help window showing the available options. These are also listed in Table V-1 on the next page.

When you escape back to the prompt, the screen is restored to its state when the CONNECT command was issued. A subsequent CONNECT command redisplays the previous terminal emulation screen.

Cutting and Pasting

Cut-and-paste (mouse editing) is available when C-Kermit is running in a window. You can copy text from any text window (including C-Kermit's own window) and paste it into the C-Kermit window at the current cursor location. If C-Kermit is at its command prompt, the text is interpreted as a command. If C-Kermit is in CONNECT mode, the pasted text is transmitted out the communication port just as if you had typed the text on the keyboard. You can also copy text from the C-Kermit command or terminal window and paste it into any other text window, or even into the same window, for example to reissue an earlier command.

The Keyboard

C-Kermit's normal CONNECT-mode escape commands (Chapter 4) are available in CONNECT mode. In addition, OS/2 C-Kermit's terminal emulator supports several categories of special keys including Alt-key equivalents for CONNECT-mode escapes, screen rollback keys, a no-scroll key, keys for screen printing, as well as VT-terminal function key equivalents. These are listed in Table V-1 and described in detail on the following pages.

Table V-1 Special PC Keys in CONNECT Mode

IBM Key	Key Code	Action
Alt =	\387	Clears screen and resets terminal emulator
Alt ? (or Alt-/)	\309	Displays help message
Alt X (or Alt-x)	\301	Returns to the C-Kermit prompt
Alt H (or Alt-h)	\291	Hangs up and returns to the prompt
Alt Q (or Alt-q)	\272	Exits CONNECT mode, hangs up, and exits C-Kermit
Alt B (or Alt-b)	\304	Sends a BREAK signal
Alt L (or Alt-l)	\294	Sends a Long BREAK signal
Home	\327	Rolls screen up (text down) to beginning of rollback buffer
Gray Home	\583	Same as Home
End	\335	Rolls screen down (text up) to current screen
Gray End	\591	Same as End
PgUp	\329	Rolls screen up (back, earlier) one screen
Gray Page Up	\585	Same as PgUp
PgDn	\337	Rolls screen down (forward, later) one screen
Gray Page Down	\593	Same as PgDn
Ctrl-PgUp	\388	Rolls screen up one line
Ctrl-Gray-Page-Up	\644	Same as Ctrl-PgUp
Ctrl-PgDn	\374	Rolls screen down one line
Ctrl-Gray-Page-Down	\630	Same as Ctrl-PgDn
Scroll Lock	\767	No Scroll (freezes screen)
Print Screen		Prints current screen (handled by OS/2)

The Scroll Lock Key

The PC's Scroll Lock key (equivalent to the VT102 No Scroll key) freezes the screen during CONNECT mode. It is typically used when displaying a long file to prevent information from scrolling off the top of the screen. The Control-S and Control-Q (Xon/Xoff) keys should not be used for this purpose if FLOW-CONTROL is set to XON/XOFF, because they interfere with the operation of the communication device driver's flow control.

When the Scroll Lock key is pressed, the current flow-control mechanism (Xon/Xoff or RTS/CTS) is used to stop the flow of characters from the other computer, for example by sending an XOFF character (Ctrl-S) or by turning off the RTS signal. Obviously, the other computer or communication device must be configured to cooperate. When Scroll Lock is pressed again, the flow of characters resumes. All other keys are ignored when the screen is frozen. The status line indicates when Scroll Lock is in effect.

The Arrow Keys and the Numeric Keypad

Table V-2 shows the PC arrow keys, their key codes, and the escape sequences they send. These sequences depend on whether the arrow keys are in application mode or cursor mode. The mode is set by control sequences from the host (SM parameter DECCKM, see Table V-8 on page 439), or by you with the SET TERMINAL ARROW-KEYS command. Table V-2 applies to the arrow keys on the numeric keypad if Num Lock is Off, and also (on enhanced PC keyboards) to the gray cursor (arrow) keypad.

Table V-3 on the next page shows the DEC VT102 and VT52 keyboard numeric keypad keys, the corresponding PC keyboard assignments (which are *not* on the PC's numeric keypad), the SET KEY codes for the PC keys, and the characters or escape sequences sent by these keys.

The DEC keypad can be in either numeric mode or application mode. The keypad mode is set by control sequences from the host (SM parameter DECNKM, see Table V-8), or with C-Kermit's SET TERMINAL KEYPAD-MODE command. Kermit's initial keypad mode is numeric. The Alt-key combinations use the number keys along the top row of the keyboard, not the ones on the numeric keypad.

Table V-2 The Arrow Keys

Key	Keypad Code	Gray Key Code	VT102 Cursor Mode	VT102 Application Mode	VT52 All Modes
Up-Arrow	\328	\584	ESC [A	ESC O A	ESC A
Down-Arrow	\336	\592	ESC [B	ESC O B	ESC B
Right-Arrow	\333	\589	ESC [C	ESC O C	ESC C
Left-Arrow	\331	\587	ESC [D	ESC O D	ESC D

Table V-3 The Numeric Keypad

DEC Key	IBM Key	Code	VT102 Numeric Mode	VT102 Application Mode	VT52 Numeric Mode	VT52 Application Mode
PF1/Blue	F1	\315	ESC O P	ESC O P	ESC P	ESC P
PF2/Red	F2	\316	ESC O Q	ESC O Q	ESC Q	ESC Q
PF3/Gray	F3	\317	ESC O R	ESC O R	ESC R	ESC R
PF4	F4	\318	ESC O S	ESC O S	ESC S	ESC S
0	Alt-0	\385	0	ESC O p	0	ESC ? p
1	Alt-1	\376	1	ESC O q	1	ESC ? q
2	Alt-2	\377	2	ESC O r	2	ESC ? r
3	Alt-3	\378	3	ESC O s	3	ESC ? s
4	Alt-4	\379	4	ESC O t	4	ESC ? t
5	Alt-5	\380	5	ESC O u	5	ESC ? u
6	Alt-6	\381	6	ESC O v	6	ESC ? v
7	Alt-7	\382	7	ESC O w	7	ESC ? w
8	Alt-8	\383	8	ESC O x	8	ESC ? x
9	Alt-9	\384	9	ESC O y	9	ESC ? y
comma (,)	F7 or F8	\321 or \322	,	ESC O l	,	ESC ? l
minus (-)	F5 or F6	\319 or \320	-	ESC O m	-	ESC ? m
period (.)	F9	\323	.	ESC O n	.	ESC ? n
Enter	F10	\324	CR,CRLF	ESC O M	CR,CRLF	ESC ? M

Screen Rollback

Information that scrolls off the top of the screen is kept in a rollback buffer that can be viewed by pressing the numeric keypad PgUp key or the gray keypad Page Up key. The rollback buffer holds 10 24-line screens of data, and you can use the PgUp, Page Up, PgDn, and Page Down keys to range freely through it. PgUp goes to a previous screen, and Ctrl-PgUp scrolls the screen back one line. Similarly, PgDn goes to a newer screen, and Ctrl-PgDn scrolls the screen forward one line.

The End key returns immediately to the current (bottom, latest) screen, and the Home key goes immediately to the top of the rollback buffer. If any other key is pressed while the rollback buffer is visible, the current screen contents are redisplayed and the keystroke is sent out the communication device.

Key Redefinition

OS/2 C-Kermit's SET KEY command provides the normal keyboard mapping for keys that are associated with 7- or 8-bit characters; that is, the keys that have codes ranging from 0 to 255 as shown by the SHOW KEY command. A particular key can be mapped to itself, to another key (a single key stroke), or to a sequence of key strokes (a character string).

OS/2 C-Kermit also supports the special PC keys, such as cursor and function keys, in various combinations with Shift, Control and Alt. These have codes ranging from 256 to 767 and can also be displayed with SHOW KEY.

The PC keys listed in Tables V-1 through V-3 have special functions associated with them. These include the arrow (cursor) keys, F1 through F4, Alt-0 through Alt-9, Scroll Lock, as well as keypad comma, minus, period, and Enter. In addition, the PgUp (Page Up), PgDn (Page Down), and End keys are used to control screen rollback; Print Screen is used by OS/2 for printing, and various Alt-key combinations are used as CONNECT-mode escape equivalents.

If you use SET KEY to assign anything other than "Self, no translation" to these special keys, their special function is lost. For example:

```
C-Kermit>set key \787 hello
```

assigns the string "hello" to the Scroll Lock key and, since the no-scroll function is associated with only one key, this disables the no-scroll feature entirely.

If you assign the code of a special key to another key, it is the same as copying the function of the special key to the second key. For example:

```
C-Kermit>set key \315 \787
```

assigns the no-scroll function to the F1 key as well as to the Scroll Lock key. Note: you can't actually *move* a function, only copy it or disable it.

Printing

If you have a printer driver installed, you can use the Print Screen key to copy the current C-Kermit screen (command or terminal) to your printer.

C-Kermit also supports host-controlled "transparent printing." If the host sends the Enter Transparent Print (see Table V-6 on page 437) sequence to Kermit, subsequent text is sent transparently (that is, without interpretation of escape sequences or translation of characters) to your printer instead of the screen, until C-Kermit receives the Exit Transparent Print sequence.

You may also have your CONNECT session copied to the printer by specifying the generic OS/2 printer device, PRN, as the destination of a LOG SESSION command.

Terminal Emulation Settings

OS/2 C-Kermit includes several special SET TERMINAL commands to control its built-in terminal emulator during CONNECT mode:

SET TERMINAL ARROW-KEYS { APPLICATION, CURSOR }

Explicitly sets the arrow key mode. The default mode is CURSOR. Use this command to change the arrow key mode if you are having trouble making the arrow keys work with a host application.

SET TERMINAL CHARACTER-SET *remote-cset [local-cset]*

Use this command to specify the remote character set for terminal emulation. The local character set is, by default, your current PC code page, which OS/2 C-Kermit senses automatically. So, for example, to prepare OS/2 C-Kermit for a terminal session with a computer that uses the Latin-1 character set:

```
[C:\]chcp 850                      (Use Code Page 850)
[C:\]ckermit                       (Start C-Kermit)
C-Kermit>set term character-set latin1
```

SET TERMINAL COLOR *text-type foreground-color background-color*

This command lets you set the foreground and background colors for various types of text during CONNECT mode. The color choices include: BLACK, BLUE, BROWN, CYAN, DGRAY (dark gray), GREEN, LBLUE (light blue), LCYAN (light cyan), LGREEN (light green), LRED (light red), MAGENTA, RED, WHITE, and YELLOW. The text types are: HELP (the pop-up CONNECT-mode help screens), NORMAL (the normal terminal screen), REVERSE (the reverse video terminal screen), STATUS (the status line), and UNDERLINED (underlined text on the terminal screen is simulated by color due to restrictions in the PC video adapter design).

SET TERMINAL CURSOR { FULL, HALF, UNDERLINE }

Selects the cursor shape for terminal emulation. FULL is a large block cursor, HALF is a half-height block cursor, and UNDERLINE is an underline-shaped cursor.

SET TERMINAL KEYPAD-MODE { APPLICATION, NUMERIC }

Explicitly sets the keypad mode; the default is NUMERIC. Use this command if you are having trouble making the keypad keys work with host applications.

SET TERMINAL TYPE { VT102, VT52 }

Chooses the desired terminal emulation. Unless you say otherwise, C-Kermit emulates the VT102 terminal.

SET TERMINAL WRAP { ON, OFF }

Turns line wrap on and off. Normally ON: the emulator automatically wraps long lines onto new lines. OFF means long lines are cut off at the screen edge.

File Names and Formats

The OS/2 directory separator is the backslash (\) character, the same as in MS-DOS. But backslash is also used by C-Kermit's command interpreter to quote special characters, introduce variables, and so on. Therefore, when including OS/2 (or MS-DOS) file specifications in a C-Kermit command, you have to type two copies of each backslash, for example:

```
C-Kermit>send c:\\files\\ckermit.ini
C-Kermit>cd a:\\binaries
```

For convenience, C-Kermit also accepts forward slash (/) as a directory separator in OS/2 file and directory specifications. When you use forward slash rather than backslash, you don't have to double the directory separators:

```
C-Kermit>send c:/ckermit/ckermit.ini
C-Kermit>cd a:/binaries
```

Wildcards

OS/2 allows a group of files to be specified in a single file specification by including the wildcard characters, asterisk (*) and question mark (?). Asterisk matches any string of characters from the current position to the end of the field, including no characters at all; question mark matches any single character.

The question mark must be quoted by backslash in C-Kermit commands to override its normal use for requesting a file menu. Example:

```
C-Kermit>send *.txt   (All ".txt" files)
C-Kermit>send x*.? Filename, one of the following:
 xray.1      xray.2      xray.3      xray.4
 xray.5      xray.6      xray.7      xray.10
 xray.31     xray.111    xray.112
C-Kermit>send x*.\?  ("xray" files, 1 thru 7)
```

File Formats

OS/2 systems store files as streams of 8-bit bytes, with no particular distinction among text, program code, and binary files. Plain text files consist of lines of text separated by carriage-return-linefeed sequences, with no font or rendition information (boldface, italic, point size) imbedded among the text characters. Most other types of files (word processor documents, spreadsheets, databases, application-specific data, and so on) should be considered binary.

By longstanding convention, observed by most OS/2 and MS-DOS (and CP/M) application software, the end of a text file is marked by the first Ctrl-Z character it contains, even if the Ctrl-Z occurs before the true end of the file. The end of a binary file is the final byte in the file, determined by the size recorded in the file's directory entry.

File Transfer

OS/2 C-Kermit supports all of C-Kermit's file transfer features, including text character-set translation for many character sets, and the full complement of file-transfer display styles, including fullscreen, which is handled by OS/2's built-in ANSI console driver. If your connection supports it, RTS/CTS (hardware) flow control is recommended for file transfer through a high-speed serial communication device.

Sending Files

In the SEND and MSEND commands, OS/2 C-Kermit understands both FAT (short MS-DOS style) file names as well as HPFS (long OS/2) file names, and can work with any mixture of FAT and HPFS disk volumes. The same is true of OS/2 C-Kermit in server mode when it receives a GET command.

When sending files in text mode, OS/2 C-Kermit treats the first Control-Z in the file as the end of the file, in accordance with MS-DOS and OS/2 convention. Neither the Ctrl-Z nor any characters that follow it are transmitted to the other computer.

When sending files in binary mode, no conversions or translations are performed, Ctrl-Z characters are treated as ordinary data, and the end of the file is determined by its length as shown by the DIRECTORY command.

Receiving Files

When receiving files, C-Kermit takes advantage of long HPFS and NFS file names if these files are received onto an HPFS or NFS disk. When receiving onto a FAT file system, the name is automatically truncated if it is too long. Received files are always stored in their entirety, regardless of the transfer mode and the presence of Ctrl-Z characters in the data.

If a file arrives that has the same name as an existing file, OS/2 C-Kermit might rename the incoming file or the existing file, depending on your FILE COLLISION setting. When renaming files, a number is appended to the end of the name before the period. For example, OOFA.TXT would be renamed to OOFA0001.TXT. If another OOFA.TXT arrives, an OOFA0002.TXT is created, and so forth. With HPFS, a suffix is added after the filetype: OOFA.TXT.~1~, OOFA.TXT.~2~, and so on.

File Transfer Character Sets

OS/2 C-Kermit's default file character-set is your current PC code page, normally CP437 or CP850. So when transferring international text, you normally need only give the SET TRANSFER CHARACTER-SET command, for example:

C-Kermit>set transfer character-set latin1

Or you can put this command in your CKERMOD.INI file.

VT102 Escape Sequences

The tables in this section list the control characters and escape sequences recognized by OS/2 C-Kermit's VT102 terminal emulator. See the DEC VT102 manual [25] for further details. Control characters and escape sequences are recognized only in their 7-bit forms. Host-controlled character-set designation and invocation is not supported, except for the DEC Special and Line Drawing character set, but you can choose character sets yourself with C-Kermit's SET TERMINAL CHARACTER-SET command. The VT102 emulator also includes a VT52 submode, whose escape sequences are shown in Table V-10 on page 440.

Table V-4 shows the terminal emulator's response to control characters received from the communication device; control codes not shown are ignored.

Table V-4 Control Characters

Name	Dec	Hex	Keyboard	Description
NUL	000	00h	^@	Ignored except during transparent printing
ENQ	005	05h	^E	Sends answerback sequence "OS/2 C-Kermit"
BEL	007	07h	^G	Sounds DEC-style beep or flashes screen
BS	008	08h	^H	Backspace, moves cursor left one character
HT	009	09h	^I, Tab	Horizontal tab, moves cursor to next tabstop
LF	010	0ah	^J	Linefeed, moves cursor down one line
VT	011	0bh	^K	Vertical Tab, treated as a linefeed
FF	012	0ch	^L	Formfeed, treated as a linefeed
CR	013	0dh	^M, Enter	Carriage return, moves cursor to column 1
SO / LS1	014	0eh	^N	Locking shift 1, selects G1 character set
SI / LS0	015	0fh	^O	Locking shift 0, selects G0 character set
DC1	017	11h	^Q	XON flow control, resumes communication
DC3	019	13h	^S	XOFF flow control, suspends communication
CAN	024	18h	^X	Cancels escape or control sequence in progress
SUB	026	1ah	^Z	Treated the same as CAN
ESC	027	1bh	^[, Esc	Starts an escape sequence, cancels any others
DEL	127	7fh	Del	Ignored except during transparent printing

Table V-5 lists the escape sequences recognized by the VT102 terminal emulator when received from the communication device, or when typed at the keyboard when TERMINAL ECHO is ON. The mnemonic is the DEC name for the escape sequence.

Table V-5 VT102 Escape Sequences

Escape Sequence	Mnemonic	Description of Action
ESC 7	DECSC	Saves cursor position, attributes, GL and GR character sets, wrap flag, origin mode (DECOM)
ESC 8	DECRC	Restores cursor and other information from DECSC
ESC # 3	DECDHL	Double-height and -width line, top half (simulated)
ESC # 4	DECDHL	Double-height and -width line, bottom half (simulated)
ESC # 5	DECSWL	Single-height and -width line
ESC # 6	DECDWL	Double-width single-height line (simulated)
ESC # 8	DECALN	Screen alignment test, fills screen with E's
ESC (B	SCS	Designates ASCII to G0
ESC (0	SCS	Designates line-drawing characters to G0
ESC <		Exits VT52 mode to ANSI (VT102) mode
ESC =	DECKPAM	Enters numeric keypad application mode
ESC >	DECKNPNM	Enters numeric keypad numeric mode
ESC D	IND	Index; cursor down one line, can scroll
ESC E	NEL	New Line; cursor to start of line below, can scroll
ESC H	HTS	Sets horizontal tab stop at current position
ESC M	RI	Reverse Index; cursor up one line, can scroll
ESC Z	DECID	Identifies terminal. Response is ESC [? 6 c in VT102 mode, ESC / z in VT52 mode.
ESC [	CSI	Control Sequence Introducer; see Table V-6
ESC c	RIS	Hard reset; resets terminal to initial state

Table V-6 shows the control sequences recognized by VT102 emulator.

Table V-6 VT102 Control Sequences

Control Sequence	Mnemonic	Description of Action
ESC [*Pn* A	CUU	Cursor up *Pn* lines, does not scroll
ESC [*Pn* B	CUD	Cursor down *Pn* lines, does not scroll
ESC [*Pn* C	CUF	Cursor forward, stays on same line
ESC [*Pn* D	CUB	Cursor backward, stays on same line
ESC [*Pr*; *Pc* H	CUP	Sets cursor to row *Pr*, column *Pc* (same as HVP)
ESC [*Ps* J	ED	Erase-in-display, *Ps* = 0, 1, or 2:
ESC [0 J	ED	Erases from cursor to end of screen, inclusive
ESC [1 J	ED	Erases from start of screen to cursor, inclusive
ESC [2 J	ED	Erases entire screen, resets lines to single width, cursor does not move
ESC [*Ps* K	EL	Erase-in-line:
ESC [0 K	EL	Erases from cursor to end of line, inclusive
ESC [1 K	EL	Erases from start of line to cursor, inclusive
ESC [2 K	EL	Erases entire line, cursor does not move
ESC [*Pn* L	IL	Inserts *Pn* lines preceding current line
ESC [*Pn* M	DL	Deletes *Pn* lines from current downward
ESC [*Pn* P	DCH	Deletes *Pn* chars from cursor to left
ESC [c	DA	Primary device attributes request. Terminal type and features. Responses are the same as to the DECID query.
ESC [*Pr*; *Pc* f	HVP	Sets cursor to row *Pr*, column *Pc* (same as CUP)
ESC [*Ps* g	TBC	Clears tabs, *Ps*: 0 = at this position, 3 = all
ESC [4 i	MC	Media Copy, exits transparent print

Table V-6   VT102 Control Sequences (continued)

Control Sequence	Mnemonic	Description of Action
ESC [5 i	MC	Media Copy. Enters transparent print. Sends all characters, except the ESC [4 i termination string, to the printer and not the screen. All translation and character set selections are bypassed.
ESC [Pa;...Pa h	SM	Sets ANSI mode, see Table V-7
ESC [Pa;...Pa l	RM	Resets ANSI mode, see Table V-7
ESC [? Ps;...;Ps h	SM	Sets DEC mode, see Table V-8
ESC [? Ps;...;Ps l	RM	Resets DEC mode, see Table V-8
ESC [Ps;...Ps m	SGR	Selects graphic rendition (see Table V-9)
ESC [5 n	DSR	Device Operating Status request
ESC [6 n	DSR	Cursor Position Report request. Response is ESC [Pr; Pc R, where Pr is the row and Pc is the column. The origin (home) is 1,1.
ESC [Pt; Pb r	DECSTBM	Sets top and bottom scrolling margins, respectively. ESC [r resets margin to full screen.
ESC [1 x	DECREQTPARM	Requests Terminal Parameters

Kermit's response to DECREQTPARM is:

ESC [sol;par;nbits;xspeed;rspeed;clkmul;flags x

where *sol* is 1 (terminal reports sent on request), or 2 (this is a report). *par* tells the parity setting: 1 (none), 2 (space), 3 (mark), 4 (odd), 5 (even). The transmit and receive speeds xspeed and rspeed are given by a code: 0, 8, 16, 24, 32, 40, 48, 56, 64, 72, 80, 88, 96, 104, 112, 120, and 128 corresponding to speeds of 50, 75, 110, 134.5, 150, 200, 300, 600, 1200, 1800, 2000, 2400, 3600, 4800, 9600, 19200, and 38400 baud or above. *clkmul* is always 1. *flags* are always reported as 0.

Table V-7 lists the parameters for Set and Reset ANSI Mode.

Table V-7 Set / Reset ANSI Mode Parameters

Parameter	Mnemonic	Mode	Set (h)	Reset (l)
2	KAM	Keyboard mode	Locked	Unlocked
4	IRM	Insert / Replace Mode	Insert	Replace
20	LNM	New line mode	Display CR as CRLF	Display CR as CR

Table V-8 lists the parameters for Set and Reset DEC Mode.

Table V-8 Set / Reset DEC Mode Parameters

Parameter	Mnemonic	Mode	Set (h)	Reset (l)
1	DECCKM	Cursor keys	Application	Cursor / Numeric
2	DECANM	ANSI mode	VT102	VT52
5	DECSCNM	Screen, whole	Reverse video	Normal
6	DECOM	Origin	Relative	Absolute
7	DECAWM	Autowrap	On	Off

Table V-9 lists the parameters for Set Graphic Rendition (ESC [Ps;...Ps m). Colors are 1 (red), 2 (green), 4 (blue), or any sum of these, with the result added to 30 for a foreground color or to 40 for a background color, compatible with ANSI.SYS and MS-DOS Kermit.

Table V-9 Set Graphic Rendition Parameters

Parameter	Description
0	Attributes 1, 4, 5, 7, and 8 off and restore original colors
1	Bold (intensify foreground)
4	Underline
5	Blink
7	Reverse video, per character
8	Invisible (Kermit extension)
30–37	Foreground color = 30 + colors (Kermit extension)
40–47	Background color = 40 + colors (Kermit extension)

DEC VT52 Emulator Escape Sequences

Table V-10 shows the valid escape sequences for VT52 mode, which is entered with the command SET TERMINAL TYPE VT52, or upon receipt of ESC [? 2 l (l is lowercase L) when the terminal emulator is in VT102 mode.

Table V-10   VT52 Escape Sequences

Escape Sequence	Description of Action
ESC 7	Saves cursor position
ESC 8	Restores cursor position
ESC A	Cursor up
ESC B	Cursor down
ESC C	Cursor right
ESC D	Cursor left
ESC F	Enters graphics mode
ESC G	Exits graphics mode
ESC H	Cursor home
ESC I	Reverse linefeed
ESC J	Erases to end of screen
ESC K	Erases to end of line
ESC V	Prints cursor line
ESC X	Exits printer controller (transparent print)
ESC Y *row column*	Direct cursor addressing, offset from Space
ESC W	Enters printer controller (transparent print)
ESC Z	Identifies terminal (response is ESC / Z)
ESC ^	Enters autoprint mode (printer echoes screen)
ESC _	Exits autoprint mode
ESC]	Prints screen
ESC =	Enters alternate keypad mode
ESC >	Exits alternate keypad mode
ESC <	Returns to ANSI mode

Appendix VI

AOS/VS C-Kermit

○ ○ ○ ○
This appendix lists the particulars of using C-Kermit on Data General MV-series computers with the AOS/VS and AOS/VS-II operating systems. For a current list of limitations and restrictions of C-Kermit for AOS/VS, also read the files CKCKER.BWR and CKDKER.BWR that were provided with the C-Kermit distribution.

AOS/VS (Advanced Operating System/Virtual System) is the operating system for the Data General Eclipse MV family of minicomputers. It is a multiuser, multitasking operating system that comes in two basic varieties: AOS/VS itself and an enhanced version called AOS/VS II. Outgoing TCP/IP TELNET connections can only be established on AOS/VS II systems configured with TCP/IP II.

C-Kermit runs on both AOS/VS and AOS/VS II. As of this writing, the current revisions are $7.6x$ for AOS/VS and $2.2x$ for AOS/VS II, where the x in the revision number signifies a minor update, and appears as a single digit, 0–9. In this book, the term AOS/VS (or simply VS) refers to both operating systems, unless explicitly noted otherwise.

See reference [21] for a general introduction to AOS/VS. Reference [24] is the Command Language Interface (CLI) manual. Reference [22] describes the structure and functions of the AOS/VS operating system. For information about using AOS/VS CLI commands, you can also give the HELP command.

C-Kermit must be installed by the AOS/VS system manager. Refer to the file
CKDINS.DOC for detailed instructions for installing C-Kermit under AOS/VS and configuring MV system communication devices (particularly serial ports and modems) appropriately.

Using C-Kermit in AOS/VS

C-Kermit for AOS/VS includes support for serial connections, both direct and dialed, as well as for TCP/IP TELNET connections.

Preparing Your AOS/VS Session for Kermit

AOS/VS systems are normally accessed via Data General DASHER terminals or emulators. When you log in to AOS/VS, it automatically sends a DASHER-specific "Read Model ID" escape sequence to your terminal. If you have a DASHER terminal or emulator, it responds appropriately and your terminal type is set automatically.

AOS/VS also supports DEC VT-100, 200, and 300 series terminals to a limited extent. To identify this type of terminal to AOS/VS, you must issue the following command:

```
) characteristics/on/nas/xlt
```

where NAS and XLT are defined as follows:

NAS

When ON, NAS specifies a non-ANSI standard terminal. On input, this causes a carriage return to be converted to a carriage return and a line feed, and a line feed to be converted to a carriage return. On output, it causes a line feed to be converted to a carriage return and a line feed.

XLT

When ON, XLT enables support for the VT100-compatible family of terminals. Support for VT100-compatible terminals must have been specified by the system manager in advance during system generation. If you turn on XLT, but still have problems with the backspace key, check with the system manager.

If you are using a speaking device or hardcopy terminal, you can inform AOS/VS with the following command:

```
) characteristics/hardcopy
```

You should also be sure that your terminal has the BMOB characteristic:

```
) characteristics/break=bmob
```

This ensures that if C-Kermit ever gets stuck, you can interrupt it by typing CMD-BRK[55] followed by Ctrl-C and Ctrl-B, which is the normal AOS/VS method for interrupting a process.

To enable Xon/Xoff software flow control on your login terminal, give this command:

) `characteristics/on/ifc/ofc`

and you can enable RTS/CTS hardware flow control as follows:

) `characteristics/on/hifc/hofc`

To use international character sets, you must issue the following command:

) `char/on/8bt`

which causes all 8 bits of each character to be treated as data. You can also use /16BT (and, for VT terminals, /XLT/KVT) to enable 16-bit character sets, such as for Japanese Kanji. The 8-bit text character set most commonly used in the AOS/VS environment is Data General International (DGI, see Table VIII-4 on page 464).

The changes you make to your console's characteristics via the CHARACTERISTICS command are in effect only for the current session. To have them take effect in all of your terminal sessions, you can include the CHARACTERISTICS command that sets them to the desired values in your login macro, normally called `LOGON.CLI`. Check with your system manager for more information.

Starting C-Kermit in AOS/VS

The name of the C-Kermit executable image is `KERMIT.PR`. To see if it exists on your system, issue the following command:

) `pathname kermit.pr`

If the system returns an indication that it found `KERMIT.PR`, then you should check its revision number by issuing a REVISION command:

) `rev/v kermit.pr`

The revision should be 00.05.188.00, or greater. If it is not, it might lack some of the capabilities described in this book; consult your system manager. Otherwise, check to see if the `KERMIT.CLI` macro exists:

) `pathname kermit.cli`

---

[55]This is the DASHER key combination to send a BREAK signal; hold down CMD and press BRK/ESC. On other terminals or emulators, use the normal method for sending a BREAK, such as Alt-B in MS-DOS Kermit.

You can use this macro to start C-Kermit:

) <u>kermit</u>

Otherwise, you can start KERMIT.PR directly by typing:

) <u>x kermit</u>

C-Kermit can also be run with redirected input and output. Suppose you have a file called INPUT.TEST containing C-Kermit commands:

```
echo Hello from Kermit.
exit
```

and you also have a file called OUTPUT.TEST, which is empty, but it has to exist. If you start C-Kermit like this:

) <u>process/block/default/input=input.test/output=output.test kermit</u>

then, after C-Kermit exits, OUTPUT.TEST has the following contents:

```
C-Kermit 5A(188), 23 Nov 92, Data General AOS/VS
Type ? or HELP for help
C-Kermit>Hello from Kermit.
C-Kermit>
```

Initialization File

AOS/VS C-Kermit uses the standard initialization file, CKERMIT.INI. If a file with this name exists in your home directory, it is used. Otherwise, if a file of this name exists in the UTIL: directory, it is used. The file CKERMOD.INI, if it exists in your home directory, is executed after CKERMIT.INI. You can use SED or another text editor to create or modify your CKERMOD.INI file (type X SED *filename* to start the SED editor, then issue the HELP command for instructions on how to use it).

Interrupting C-Kermit

Most C-Kermit commands can be interrupted by typing Ctrl-C. C-Kermit commands, such as DIRECTORY or WHO, that work by running the AOS/VS command processor (CLI) as an inferior process, must be interrupted with the CLI interrupt sequence, BREAK followed by Ctrl-C and then Ctrl-A.

To interrupt C-Kermit during remote-mode file transfer, type two Ctrl-C characters in a row. Ctrl-C is always used for this purpose, no matter what your interrupt character is:

```
C-Kermit>send oofa.txt          (Send a file)
...
^A0 Sz* @-#Y1~*  yE             (A packet appears)
^C^C                            (Type two Ctrl-C's)
^C...                           (Ctrl-C is echoed by C-Kermit)
C-Kermit>                       (The prompt returns)
```

To interrupt C-Kermit during CONNECT mode, use the CONNECT-mode escape character, followed by the letter C to get back to the prompt, or any of the other escape-level commands described in Chapter 4.

In an emergency, the C-Kermit process itself can be interrupted by sending a BREAK signal and then typing Ctrl-C and Ctrl-B.

Terminal Emulation

C-Kermit's CONNECT command and associated features work in AOS/VS as described in Chapter 4. The default CONNECT-mode escape character is Ctrl-Backslash, which is entered on DASHER terminals by holding down the CTRL key and pressing the backslash (\) key.

The default local terminal character-set is DG-International. If this agrees with your terminal or emulator, you need only specify the remote set when selecting your terminal character-set, for example:

`C-Kermit>set term char latin1`

Otherwise you must specify the appropriate local set too, for example:

`C-Kermit>set term char latin1 spanish`

File Transfer

C-Kermit for AOS/VS offers the full range of file transfer features. For text files, AOS/VS record format (lines terminated by the single character, linefeed) is automatically converted to Kermit's standard intermediate form during file transfer.

As in other C-Kermit versions, character-set translation is available. The default file character-set is DG-International, so to enable translation the only command you need to give is:

`set transfer character-set latin1`

If you are using some other file character-set on your AOS/VS system, you should also specify it:

```
set file character-set french
set transfer character-set latin1
```

If you always use the same character sets for file transfer, add these commands to your CKERMOD.INI file.

Table VI-1 AOS/VS Template Characters

Character	Meaning
+	(plus sign) Matches any character string.
*	(asterisk) Matches any single filename character except a period (.). Example: `FIG*` matches `FIG1` and `FIG2`, but not `FIG.` or `FIGURE`.
-	(dash) Matches any series of filename characters that does not contain a period. Example: `TEST-` matches `TEST1` and `TESTING`, but not `TEST.1`.
\	(backslash) Omits the specified series of characters from the search. Example: `+.DOC\KERMIT+` matches all files ending in `.DOC` except for files that start with the string `KERMIT`. Because backslash is also C-Kermit's command-quote character, you must enter two copies of it.
^	(circumflex) Causes the action to be applied to the parent directory instead of the current one. Example: `^+.DOC` matches all files in the parent directory whose names end in `.DOC`.
#	(number sign) Causes the action to be applied to all directories beneath the current one. Example: `#+.DOC` matches all files in all inferior directories with names ending in `.DOC`.

Sending Files

In outbound AOS/VS filenames, dollar sign ($) and question mark (?) are converted to the letter X unless you have SET FILE NAMES LITERAL.

You can use AOS/VS templates to specify a group of files in any of C-Kermit's commands that accept wildcard file specifications, as well as in GET commands sent to an AOS/VS C-Kermit server. AOS/VS template characters are listed in Table VI-1.

Receiving Files

Incoming files are stored in the current directory unless you specified a filename in the RECEIVE command, or the incoming file header packet includes a pathname, in which case C-Kermit attempts to store the file in the specified directory (and fails if the directory does not exist or is not writable).

A file can be created only if you have write access to the directory where the file is to be stored. The file is created using your default access control list (ACL), which, unless you have changed it with the AOS/VS DEFACL command, grants the site-dependent default access control list.

If a file of the same name already exists in the target directory and C-Kermit's FILE COLLISION is set to BACKUP or OVERWRITE, you must also have write access to the previously existing file. C-Kermit will not create, rename, or delete files for you that you could not otherwise create, rename, or delete yourself.

When AOS/VS C-Kermit receives a file that has the same name as an existing file, it might rename the existing file or the incoming file, according to your FILE COLLISION setting. The new name is the old name with a period and a version number appended. For example, OOFA.TXT would become OOFA.TXT.1. If both OOFA.TXT and OOFA.TXT.1 existed, an OOFA.TXT.2 would be created, and so on.

Dash (-) characters in incoming filenames are converted to underscores (_) unless you have SET FILENAMES LITERAL.

Appendix VII

Other C-Kermit Versions

C-Kermit is also available for several other computers and operating systems, including the Commodore Amiga, the Atari ST, Microware OS-9, and perhaps others by the time you read this. Consult the file CKCKER.UPD for news.

Amiga C-Kermit

○ ○ ○ ○

This section describes the Commodore Amiga version of C-Kermit. For further information, refer to the files CKCKER.BWR and CKIKER.BWR.

The Commodore Amiga is a desktop workstation with a graphical user interface called Intuition. Its multiprocessing operating system, AmigaDOS, gives you multiple windows selectable by mouse. You may create one or more character-oriented Command Line Interpreter (CLI) or Shell windows in which to type AmigaDOS commands. Commonly-used commands include LIST to display a list of files, DELETE to delete a file or files, TYPE to display the contents of a file, CD to change directory, INFO to display information about system usage, and STATUS to display process status. CLI and Shell are not case-sensitive; commands may be entered in uppercase, lowercase, or any mixture.

AmigaDOS has a hierarchical file system similar to OS/2. File specifications can optionally begin with a device name terminated by a colon (:). The directory specification shows the path through the directory tree from its root on the given device; the directory separator is slash (/), as in UNIX. Upper- and lowercase letters are not distinguished in

Amiga file specifications. File specifications that do not begin with a device name are on the current device. File specifications that do not have a slash at the beginning (or immediately after the device name) are relative to the current directory.

Install the KERMIT program in your `C:` directory or another directory along your PATH, and place your initialization file `CKERMIT.INI`, your customization file `CKERMOD.INI`, and your services directory `CKERMIT.KSD` in the `S:` directory. If desired, you can create an icon for C-Kermit by using the Icon Editor; create a script file containing the two commands:

```
stack 10000
Kermit
```

and save it. Then use the Icon Editor to create a Project icon whose "default tool" is `C:IconX` for this file.

You can start C-Kermit from the desktop by clicking on its icon (if you made one) or from a CLI or Shell window by typing KERMIT or RUN KERMIT. In both cases, C-Kermit creates a new window for itself. Before starting C-Kermit in a CLI or Shell window, allocate a stack size of at least 10000 with the AmigaDOS STACK command as shown above.

When starting C-Kermit in a CLI or Shell window, you can include command-line options (see Chapter 14). If any of these are action options, C-Kermit exits automatically when they are complete. If you want to run C-Kermit in this manner without having it create a new window, include the -q (quiet) command-line option.

During interactive operation, Amiga C-Kermit can be interrupted by typing Ctrl-C (hold down the Ctrl key and press the C key). A requestor window pops up to let you choose whether to quit C-Kermit or continue it.

Communications and Terminal Emulation

The default communication device is `serial.device/0`. Other devices can be specified using the same form: `type.device/unit-number`. You can configure the communication device in the Preferences window, including (for a serial device) its speed and flow control. Both software (Xon/Xoff) and hardware (RTS/CTS) flow control options are available.

Network connections, including TCP/IP and DECnet, can be accomplished by running a `serial.device` emulator over the network link, provided you have the underlying network hardware, software, and connection, and a suitable `serial.device` emulator.

The CONNECT command creates an AmigaDOS console device window. Using the default Preferences setting, this gives a 23-row by 77-column screen. In AmigaDOS 2.0 and later, you can increase the screen size in Preferences. In AmigaDOS releases prior to 2.0, the MoreRows program allows you to increase the size of the Workbench window beyond the 640 by 200 default size; increasing the number of rows by 8 and the number of columns by 16 will allow a 24-row by 80-column Kermit window.

The Amiga console driver provides ANSI [3] (similar to VT100) terminal emulation; C-Kermit CONNECT mode uses the console driver, and does not provide any particular terminal emulation of its own.

The default CONNECT-mode escape character is Control-Backslash (`Ctrl-\`). You can use `Ctrl-\H` to close the serial device and exit CONNECT mode; this turns the DTR signal off, causing most modems to hang up the phone line. In addition to the normal CONNECT-mode commands, extra session-logging control is available. If a session log file is open, the `Ctrl-\Q` sequence lets you temporarily suspend logging and the `Ctrl-\R` sequence resumes logging if it has been suspended.

Character-set translation is not available during CONNECT mode. The Amiga's native character set is ISO 8859 Latin Alphabet 1, and it is used during CONNECT mode if PARITY is NONE and you SET COMMAND BYTESIZE 8. Special characters are entered according to your keymap, configurable in Preferences, normally using "dead keys."

File Transfer

Amiga C-Kermit supports most of the file transfer features described in this book, including character-set translation (Latin-1 is the normal file character-set), the FULLSCREEN file transfer display, and the full range of file collision options.

When sending files, Amiga C-Kermit internally expands wildcards in SEND and MSEND commands, as well as in GET commands sent to an Amiga C-Kermit server. Asterisk (*) stands for any sequence of characters and question mark (?) matches any single character. When you use ? in a command, it must be preceded by backslash (\) to suppress its normal function of displaying a file menu:

`C-Kermit>send cki*.\?`

If the use of Attribute (A) packets has been successfully negotiated, Amiga C-Kermit includes an A-packet with each file it sends, containing the file's length, creation date, and transfer mode (text or binary).

When receiving files, Amiga C-Kermit reads the incoming A-packet (if any), sets the transfer mode (text or binary) accordingly, and sets the incoming file's creation date from the A-packet if a date is given and ATTRIBUTE DATE is ON. If an incoming file has the same name as an existing file, the selected FILE COLLISION action is taken. Files that must be renamed because of collision have a tilde (~) and a number appended; for example, `oofa.txt` becomes `oofa.txt~1`; `oofa.txt~1` becomes `oofa.txt~2`, and so on.

Atari ST C-Kermit

○ ○ ○ ○
This section describes the Atari ST version of C-Kermit. For further information, refer to the files `CKCKER.BWR` and `CKSKER.BWR`.

The Atari ST is a desktop workstation with a graphical user interface. Its operating system, GEMDOS, is normally incapable of running multiple programs concurrently.

A character-oriented command processor is not furnished with the system, but MSH, a product of Mark Williams Company, and Gulam and bash, public-domain offerings, are among the command processors that are commonly used. Each of these "shells" is case-sensitive; that is, each treats uppercase and lowercase letters as distinct characters in commands and filenames.

The Atari ST file system is almost identical to the MS-DOS file system. Device names and directory structure are the same as in DOS. Device names are a single letter followed by a colon (:), and directories are arranged hierarchically, with levels separated by the backslash character (\). Filenames may be up to 11 characters long: up to eight characters before the period and three after. Even though your shell might care about alphabetic case in filenames, GEMDOS itself does not. Besides handling its own native file system and disk formats, the Atari ST can also read and write 3.5-inch MS-DOS-format diskettes.

Installing and Running C-Kermit

Atari ST C-Kermit supports most, but not all, of C-Kermit's features. Type SHOW FEATURES at the C-Kermit prompt for a full accounting of which C-Kermit features are available and which are not, or read the `CKSKER.BWR` file.

The C-Kermit program should be installed on a device and in a directory that is in your PATH. The initialization files, `CKERMIT.INI` and `CKERMOD.INI`, should be stored in your home directory, as defined by the environment variable, HOME.

C-Kermit can be run from the desktop or started from within a command processor. In all cases, C-Kermit takes over the full screen. If C-Kermit is run from the desktop, a dialog box pops up and asks you for command-line options. It is quite likely that no environment variables will be accessible.

When run from a shell, C-Kermit has access to environment variables if the shell uses the Mark Williams C language conventions. Environment variables specific to the Atari ST include the following:

HOME   Used by C-Kermit to find its initialization and other files, and to expand ~ notation in file specifications.

PATH   Used by most shells to find their programs.

SPEED   The serial communication speed for the AUX device.

BAUD   Same as SPEED.

Assuming C-Kermit is installed as `KERMIT.TTP` somewhere in your PATH, you can run it by typing the word *kermit* at your command processor prompt. Command-line options are accepted; the shell expands any unquoted wildcards, for example in the -s option. The available wildcard characters depend on the shell, but usually * matches any sequence of characters not containing a period or backslash and ? matches any single character except period.

If you start C-Kermit with command-line action options (see Chapter 14), C-Kermit executes the given commands and exits. In this mode of operation, C-Kermit's standard input and output can be redirected and C-Kermit can be used in a pipeline with msh or bash, but not with Gulam, which does not support pipes. In msh, pipes are text-only.

If you start C-Kermit without command-line action options, it issues its prompt and runs interactively. The interruption character is Control-C, which can be taken over by the runtime library at various times; sometimes you must type it several times.

Communications and Terminal Emulation

Atari ST C-Kermit supports serial connections only. The only serial communication device is AUX, and this is C-Kermit's default communication device. Available speeds range from 50 to 19200 bps, but flow control is problematic due to limitations of the underlying serial device driver.

The communication speed cannot be read from the device. You have to set it with the SET SPEED command or use the SPEED environment variable, which C-Kermit will read automatically if it is defined.

The terminal emulation is performed by the GEMDOS console driver. The terminal is a superset of the DEC VT-52 (see Table V-10 on page 440). VT52 emulation is effective during command mode, CONNECT mode, and file transfer.

The CONNECT-mode escape character is Control-Rightbracket (`Ctrl-]`). There is no special provision for entering or displaying accented characters, but you can use them transparently to C-Kermit if your keyboard and display support them and if they are configured to use them, and if you have told C-Kermit to SET COMMAND BYTESIZE 8, and, for CONNECT-mode, SET TERMINAL BYTESIZE 8.

File Transfer

Atari ST C-Kermit expands wildcards internally in the SEND and MSEND commands, recognizing * and ? as wildcard characters, and it expands a leading tilde (~) character in file specifications according to the definition of your HOME environment variable. Backslash characters within filenames must be doubled, for example:

```
C-Kermit>send c:\\mydir\\oofa.txt
```

File attributes are sent along with each file, if successfully negotiated with the other Kermit program. These include transfer mode (text or binary, according to your most recent SET FILE TYPE command; text by default), creation date, and size.

When receiving files, Atari ST C-Kermit obtains the transfer mode (text or binary) from the incoming Attribute packet, if any, and this overrides the current FILE TYPE setting. The file size is also read from the Attribute packet and the file is rejected if it is bigger than available disk space (as shown by the SPACE command) unless you have SET ATTRIBUTE LENGTH OFF. Incoming files are stored with the creation date from the Attribute packet or, if there is no Attribute packet or if you have SET ATTRIBUTE DATE OFF, they are created with the current date and time.

If a file arrives that has the same name as an existing file, it is handled according to your FILE COLLISION setting. Renaming of files is done by inserting digits between the filename and filetype, for example oofa.txt becomes oofa0000.txt; oofa0000.txt becomes oofa0001.txt, and so on. As with other C-Kermit versions, the default file collision action is BACKUP.

OS-9 C-Kermit

○ ○ ○ ○
This section describes the OS-9 version of C-Kermit. For further information, refer to the files CKCKER.BWR and CK9KER.BWR.

OS-9/68000 is a multiuser, multitasking operating system designed to run on all Motorola 68000-family processors. A related operating system, OS-9000, is more portable; for example, to Intel as well as to various RISC processors. However, OS-9 C-Kermit has not, as of this writing, been tested under OS-9000. For news about this, as well as further information about C-Kermit under OS-9, please read the file CK9KER.BWR.

OS-9's 100% ROM-able, fast, compact code in conjunction with its real-time capabilities make OS-9/68000 ideal for ROM-based systems used in measuring and control systems in scientific and industrial spheres. Yet, a full disk-based OS-9 system offers a program development environment similar to UNIX, including limited UNIX software compatibility at the C source-code level and conformance to the UNIX input/output and task models as well as a UNIX-like shell and networking environment.

The basic commands of OS-9 are somewhat different from their UNIX counterparts:

DEL Deletes a file

DELDIR Deletes a directory

MAKDIR Creates a directory

DIR Displays a directory listing

PROCS Shows processes currently running

LIST Displays the contents of a text file

CWD Changes working directory

PD Prints working directory

Command references (like all references to names on OS-9/68000) are case-independent. All commands can be given a -? switch, which displays a brief (usually sufficient) help message.

OS-9 allows redirection of standard input, standard output, and standard error, just like UNIX, and supports command pipelines as well as background execution of programs and commands.

The OS-9 File System

All devices (terminal lines, networks, disks) can have arbitrary names but the usual conventions are:

Terminal devices:
- term The console terminal
- t1 Terminal line number 1
- tn Terminal line number n

Hard disks:
- h0 Hard disk number 0
- h1 Hard disk number 1
- hn Hard disk number n

Diskettes:
- d0 Diskette drive number 0
- d1 Diskette drive number 1
- dn Diskette drive number n

Directories are hierarchical, as in UNIX, MS-DOS, and OS/2. The directory separator is slash (/). A pathname (file specification) starting with a slash must always include a device name as the first field. Pathnames that do not start with a slash are relative to the current device and directory.

OS-9/68000 files are sequential streams of 8-bit bytes, just like in UNIX, except that carriage return (CR, ASCII 13) is the line terminator, rather than linefeed (LF, ASCII 10). Binary files are simply streams of arbitrary 8-bit bytes. The OS-9 operating system and utilities are "8-bit clean," so text files can use any character set that is compatible with your display and data entry devices, for example ISO 8859-1 Latin Alphabet 1.

The OS-9 Console

The console terminal is either a real terminal, or the screen and keyboard of a workstation such as a Macintosh, Amiga, or Atari ST that is running OS-9. Terminal emulation is not done by OS-9 C-Kermit, but rather by the real terminal or the workstation console driver. This includes the capability to display national and international characters. As with other C-Kermit versions, you must SET COMMAND BYTESIZE 8 in order to enter and view 8-bit characters.

Using OS-9 C-Kermit

The C-Kermit program should be installed somewhere in your OS-9 PATH. Start it simply by typing its name, *kermit*. It reads its initialization, dialing directory, and services directory files from your home directory.

The OS-9 version of C-Kermit is very similar to the UNIX version. The primary differences between OS-9 and UNIX are the names of the common system commands and the line terminator used in text files.

If you start OS-9 C-Kermit with command-line action options (see Chapter 14), C-Kermit executes the given commands and exits. The shell expands any unquoted wildcards on the command line, for example in the -s option. The available wildcard characters are *, which matches any sequence of characters of any length, and ?, which matches any single character.

If you start C-Kermit without command-line action options, it issues its prompt and runs interactively. C-Kermit's interruption character is Control-C. C-Kermit also expands wildcards itself, using the same notation as the OS-9 shell, for example:

```
C-Kermit>send ck*.\?
```

Note that the question mark must be prefixed by backslash to override its normal function of giving a help message.

When receiving files, OS-9 C-Kermit handles the full range of file collision options. When C-Kermit renames a file because of a collision, it appends an underscore and a digit to the file name:

oofa.txt

becomes:

oofa.txt_1

oofa.txt_1 becomes oofa.txt_2, and so on.

The commands and operation of OS-9 C-Kermit should be identical to those of UNIX C-Kermit, with the exceptions noted above and in the "beware file," CK9KER.BWR.

Appendix VIII

Character Set Tables

The standard structure for character sets is specified in ISO Standard 4873 [38] and illustrated in Figure VIII-1 on the next page.

A standard 7-bit character set consists of 32 control characters (C0), 94 graphic (printing) characters (GL = Graphics Left), plus the characters Space (SP) and Delete (DEL), for a total of 128 characters, as shown in the left half of the figure.

The left half of a standard 8-bit character set is the 7-bit 128-character set known as the International Reference Version of ISO 646 [36], which happens to be identical to ASCII [1] and which is listed in greater detail in Tables VIII-1 and VIII-2 on pages 461–462. Many nonstandard 8-bit character sets, such as PC code pages, also use ASCII as their left halves.

The right half of a standard 8-bit character set has a similar structure to the left half. There is a second control region (C1) with 32 additional control characters and a second graphic region (GR = Graphics Right) with 94 or 96 additional graphic characters. The best-known standard 8-bit character sets are those specified by ISO Standard 8859 [39]: the Latin Alphabets. The blank GR area in the figure can have any of the various Latin Alphabets plugged into it: Latin-1, Latin-2, Latin/Greek, Latin/Arabic, Latin/Hebrew, Latin/Cyrillic, and so on. The blank C1 area is most commonly used for the control characters specified by ISO Standard 6429 [41]. A 94-character graphics set does not use the 10/0 and 15/15 positions, shown gray in the figure. A 96-character set does use them.

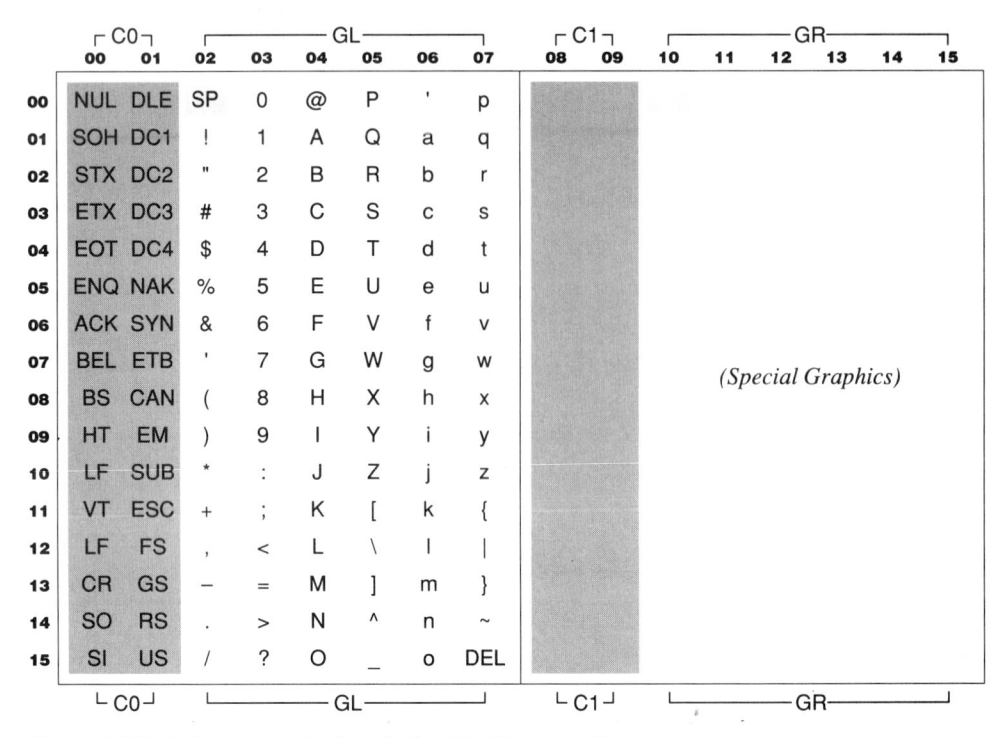

	00	01	02	03	04	05	06	07	08	09	10	11	12	13	14	15
00	NUL	DLE	SP	0	@	P	`	p								
01	SOH	DC1	!	1	A	Q	a	q								
02	STX	DC2	"	2	B	R	b	r								
03	ETX	DC3	#	3	C	S	c	s								
04	EOT	DC4	$	4	D	T	d	t								
05	ENQ	NAK	%	5	E	U	e	u								
06	ACK	SYN	&	6	F	V	f	v								
07	BEL	ETB	'	7	G	W	g	w								
08	BS	CAN	(	8	H	X	h	x						*(Special Graphics)*			
09	HT	EM	)	9	I	Y	i	y								
10	LF	SUB	*	:	J	Z	j	z								
11	VT	ESC	+	;	K	[	k	{								
12	LF	FS	,	<	L	\	l	|								
13	CR	GS	–	=	M	]	m	}								
14	SO	RS	.	>	N	^	n	~								
15	SI	US	/	?	O	_	o	DEL								

Figure VIII-1 Structure of a Standard 8-Bit Character Set

Nonstandard 8-bit character sets, such as PC code pages or the Macintosh and NeXT character sets, use C1 and sometimes even C0 for graphic characters.

Each character in an 8-bit character set is represented internally by a number in the range 0–255. This can be a simple decimal number, like 65 for uppercase letter A, the hexadecimal (base 16) or octal (base 8) equivalent, or the column and row position from the table, for example 04/01 for uppercase letter A, where the value (code) of a character is 16 times the column number plus the row number ($16 \times 4 + 1 = 65$).

Rules for designation and invocation of character sets during data transmission are specified in ISO Standard 2022 [37]. In the 8-bit communications environment, a character with its 8th (high order) bit set to 0 denotes a character from the left half and a character with its 8th bit set to 1 denotes a right-half character. The rules for transmission of 8-bit characters in the 7-bit communication environment are, predictably, somewhat more complicated.

The ASCII and ISO 646 IRV Character Set

Key: *Dec* = decimal value, *Hex* = hexadecimal value, ^X = Ctrl-X.

Table VIII-1 Character Codes of ASCII and ISO 646 IRV

Dec	Hex	Name	Char	Dec	Hex	Char	Dec	Hex	Char	Dec	Hex	Char
000	00	NUL	^@	032	20	SP	064	40	@	096	60	`
001	01	SOH	^A	033	21	!	065	41	A	097	61	a
002	02	STX	^B	034	22	"	066	42	B	098	62	b
003	03	ETX	^C	035	23	#	067	43	C	099	63	c
004	04	EOT	^D	036	24	$	068	44	D	100	64	d
005	05	ENQ	^E	037	25	%	069	45	E	101	65	e
006	06	ACK	^F	038	26	&	070	46	F	102	66	f
007	07	BEL	^G	039	27	'	071	47	G	103	67	g
008	08	BS	^H	040	28	(	072	48	H	104	68	h
009	09	HT	^I	041	29	)	073	49	I	105	69	i
010	0A	LF	^J	042	2A	*	074	4A	J	106	6A	j
011	0B	VT	^K	043	2B	+	075	4B	K	107	6B	k
012	0C	FF	^L	044	2C	,	076	4C	L	108	6C	l
013	0D	CR	^M	045	2D	-	077	4D	M	109	6D	m
014	0E	SO	^N	046	2E	.	078	4E	N	110	6E	n
015	0F	SI	^O	047	2F	/	079	4F	O	111	6F	o
016	10	DLE	^P	048	30	0	080	50	P	112	70	p
017	11	CD1	^Q	049	31	1	081	51	Q	113	71	q
018	12	DC2	^R	050	32	2	082	52	R	114	72	r
019	13	DC3	^S	051	33	3	083	53	S	115	73	s
020	14	DC4	^T	052	34	4	084	54	T	116	74	t
021	15	NAK	^U	053	35	5	085	55	U	117	75	u
022	16	SYN	^V	054	36	6	086	56	V	118	76	v
023	17	ETB	^W	055	37	7	087	57	W	119	77	w
024	18	CAN	^X	056	38	8	088	58	X	120	78	x
025	19	EM	^Y	057	39	9	089	59	Y	121	79	y
026	1A	SUB	^Z	058	3A	:	090	5A	Z	122	7A	z
027	1B	ESC	^[	059	3B	;	091	5B	[	123	7B	{
028	1C	FS	^\	060	3C	<	092	5C	\	124	7C	|
029	1D	GS	^]	061	3D	=	093	5D	]	125	7D	}
030	1E	RS	^^	062	3E	>	094	5E	^	126	7E	~
031	1F	US	^_	063	3F	?	095	5F	_	127	7F	DEL

7-Bit Control Characters

Table VIII-2 lists the 7-bit control characters used in the ASCII ISO 646 IRV character sets and in character sets based upon them, including the ISO 646 national sets and the ISO 8858 international sets as well as IBM code pages and other private sets. The official abbreviation and full name of each character is shown, along with the control-key combination normally used to produce each character on a US keyboard.

Table VIII-2 7-Bit C0 Control Characters

	00				01				07		
00	NUL	^@	Null	DLE	^P	Data Link Escape					
01	SOH	^A	Start of Heading	DC1	^Q	Device Control 1					
02	STX	^B	Start of Text	DC2	^R	Device Control 2					
03	ETX	^C	End of Text	DC3	^S	Device Control 3					
04	EOT	^D	End of Transmission	DC4	^T	Device Control 4					
05	ENQ	^E	Enquiry	NAK	^U	Negative Acknowledge					
06	ACK	^F	Acknowledge	SYN	^V	Synchronous Idle					
07	BEL	^G	Bell	ETB	^W	End of Transmission Block					
08	BS	^H	Backspace	CAN	^X	Cancel					
09	HT	^I	Horizontal Tab	EM	^Y	End of Medium					
10	LF	^J	Line Feed	SUB	^Z	Substitute					
11	VT	^K	Vertical Tab	ESC	^[	Escape					
12	FF	^L	Form Feed	FS	^\	File Separator					
13	CR	^M	Carriage Return	GS	^]	Group Separator					
14	SO	^N	Shift Out	RS	^^	Record Separator					
15	SI	^O	Shift In	US	^_	Unit Separator	DEL	^?	Delete		

7-Bit Roman Character Sets

Table VIII-3 shows the 7-bit character sets used by C-Kermit. These sets are identical to ASCII (Table VIII-1) except in the positions shown in this table. ASCII is United States ANSI X3.4-1986, which is the same as the ISO 646 International Reference Version. British, French, German, Hungarian, Italian, Japanese Roman, Norwegian, Portuguese, Spanish, and Swedish are ISO 646 national versions registered in the ISO International Register of Coded Character Sets. The others are taken from DEC VT terminal manuals and other sources. The Icelandic 7-bit set, rarely used any more, also includes two-character sequences to represent vowels with acute accents, not shown in the table.

Table VIII-3 7-Bit National Character Sets, Differences from ASCII

Row/Column	2/03	4/00	5/11	5/12	5/13	5/14	5/15	6/00	7/11	7/12	7/13	7/14
Decimal	35	64	91	92	93	94	95	96	123	124	125	126
Hexadecimal	23	40	5B	5C	5D	5E	5F	60	7B	7C	7D	7E
ASCII	#	@	[	\	]	^	_	`	{	|	}	~
British	£	@	[	\	]	^	_	'	{	|	}	~
Chinese Roman	#	@	[	¥	]	^	_	'	{	|	}	‾
Danish	#	@	Æ	Ø	Å	^	_	'	æ	ø	å	~
Dutch	£	¾	ÿ	½	|	^	_	'	¨	f	¼	´
Finnish	#	@	Ä	Ö	Å	Ü	_	é	ä	ö	å	ü
French	£	à	°	ç	§	^	_	µ	é	ù	è	¨
Fr-Canadian	#	à	â	ç	ê	î	_	ô	é	ù	è	û
German	#	§	Ä	Ö	Ü	^	_	'	ä	ö	ü	ß
Hungarian	#	Á	É	Ö	Ü	^	_	ú	é	ö	ü	˝
Icelandic	#	Þ	Ð	\	Æ	Ö	_	þ	ð	|	æ	ö
Italian	£	§	°	ç	é	^	_	ù	à	ò	è	ì
Japanese Roman	#	@	[	¥	]	^	_	'	{	|	}	‾
Norwegian	§	@	Æ	Ø	Å	^	_	'	æ	ø	å	|
Portuguese	#	'	Ã	Ç	Õ	^	_	'	ã	ç	õ	~
Spanish	£	§	¡	Ñ	¿	^	_	'	°	ñ	ç	~
Swedish	#	É	Ä	Ö	Å	Ü	_	é	ä	ö	å	ü
Swiss	ù	à	é	ç	ê	î	è	ô	ä	ö	ü	û

West European Character Sets

Table VIII-4 shows the graphic characters of the right half of ISO 8859-1 Latin Alphabet 1, which is supported as both a transfer character-set and a file character-set by C-Kermit, along with the code values in Latin-1, the DEC Multinational Character Set (MCS), the Data General International Character Set (DGI), Kermit's Macintosh Extended Latin character set (MAC), the NeXT workstation character set, and PC code pages 437 and 850. Characters shown in italics in the MAC column differ from the US version of the Apple Quickdraw character set. Characters that are not present in Latin-1 cannot be translated by Kermit.

Table VIII-4 West European Character Sets

	Character Name	Latin-1 dec hex	MCS dec hex	DGI dec hex	MAC dec hex	NeXT dec hex	CP437 dec hex	CP850 dec hex
	No-break space	160 A0	160 A0	160 A0	202 CA	128 80	255 FF	255 FF
¡	Inverted exclamation	161 A1	161 A1	171 AB	193 C1	161 A1	173 AD	173 AD
¢	Cent sign	162 A2	162 A2	167 A7	162 A2	162 A2	155 9B	189 8B
£	Pound sign	163 A3	163 A3	168 A8	163 A3	163 A3	156 9C	156 9C
¤	Currency sign	164 A4	168 A8	166 A6	219 DB	168 A8		207 CF
¥	Yen sign	165 A5	165 A5	181 B5	180 B4	165 A5	157 9D	190 BE
¦	Broken bar	166 A6			201 C9	181 B5		221 DD
§	Paragraph sign	167 A7	167 A7	187 BB	164 A4	167 A7	021 15	021 15
¨	Diaeresis	168 A8		189 BD	172 AC	200 C8		249 F9
©	Copyright sign	169 A9	169 A9	173 AD	169 A9	160 A0		184 B8
ª	Feminine ordinal	170 AA	170 AA	170 AA	187 BB	227 E3	166 A6	166 A6
«	Left angle quotation	171 AB	171 AB	176 B0	199 C7	171 AB	174 AE	174 AE
¬	Not sign	172 AC		161 A1	194 C2	190 BE	170 AA	170 AA
-	Soft hyphen	173 AD	173 AD		*208 D0*			240 F0
®	Registered trade mark	174 AE		174 AE	168 A8	176 B0		169 A9
¯	Macron	175 AF			248 F8	197 C5		238 EE
°	Degree sign, ring	176 B0	176 B0	188 BC	161 A1	248 F8		248 F8
±	Plus-minus sign	177 B1	177 B1	182 B6	177 B1	209 D1	241 F1	241 F1
²	Superscript two	178 B2	178 B2	164 A4	*170 AA*	201 C9	253 FD	253 FD

Table VIII-4 West European Character Sets (continued)

	Character Name	Latin-1 dec hex	MCS dec hex	DGI dec hex	MAC dec hex	NeXT dec hex	CP437 dec hex	CP850 dec hex
³	Superscript three	179 B3	179 B3	165 A5	*173 AD*	204 CC		252 FC
´	Acute accent	180 B4	180 B4	190 BE	171 AB	194 C2		239 EF
µ	Micro sign	181 B5	181 B5	163 A3	181 B5	157 9D	230 E6	230 E6
¶	Pilcrow sign	182 B6	182 B6	178 B2	166 A6	182 B6	020 14	244 F4
•	Middle dot	183 B7	183 B7	185 B9	165 A5	180 B4	250 FA	250 FA
¸	Cedilla	184 B8	184 B8		252 FC	184 B8		247 F7
¹	Superscript one	185 B9	185 B9		*176 B0*	192 C0		251 FB
º	Masculine ordinal	186 BA	186 BA	169 A9	188 BC	235 EB	167 A7	167 A7
»	Right angle quotation	187 BB	187 BB	177 B1	200 C8	187 BB	175 AF	175 AF
¼	One quarter	188 BC	188 BC		*178 B2*	210 D2	172 AC	172 AC
½	One half	189 BD	189 BD	162 A2	*179 B3*	211 D3	171 AB	171 AB
¾	Three quarters	190 BE			*186 BA*	212 D4		243 F3
¿	Inverted question mark	191 BF	191 BF	172 AC	192 C0	191 BF	168 A8	168 A8
À	A grave	192 C0	192 C0	193 C1	203 CB	129 81		183 B7
Á	A acute	193 C1	193 C1	192 C0	231 E7	130 82		181 B5
Â	A circumflex	194 C2	194 C2	194 C2	229 E5	131 83		182 B6
Ã	A tilde	195 C3	195 C3	196 C4	204 CC	132 84		199 C7
Ä	A diaeresis	196 C4	196 C4	195 C3	128 80	133 85	142 8E	142 8E
Å	A ring above	197 C5	197 C5	197 C5	129 81	134 86	143 8F	143 8F
Æ	A with E digraph	198 C6	198 C6	198 C6	174 AE	225 E1	146 92	146 92
Ç	C Cedilla	199 C7	199 C7	199 C7	130 82	135 87	128 80	128 80
È	E grave	200 C8	200 C8	201 C9	233 E9	136 88		212 D4
É	E acute	201 C9	201 C9	200 C8	131 83	137 89	144 90	144 90
Ê	E circumflex	202 CA	202 CA	202 CA	230 E6	138 8A		210 D2
Ë	E diaeresis	203 CB	203 CB	203 CB	232 E8	139 8B		211 D3
Ì	I grave	204 CC	204 CC	205 CD	237 ED	140 8C		222 DE
Í	I acute	205 CD	205 CD	204 CC	234 EA	141 8D		214 D6
Î	I circumflex	206 CE	206 CE	206 CE	235 EB	142 8E		215 D7
Ï	I diaeresis	207 CF	207 CF	207 CF	236 EC	143 8F		216 D8

Table VIII-4   West European Character Sets (continued)

Character	Name	**Latin-1** dec hex	**MCS** dec hex	**DGI** dec hex	**MAC** dec hex	**NeXT** dec hex	**CP437** dec hex	**CP850** dec hex
Ð	Icelandic Eth	208 D0			*220 DC*	144 90		209 D1
Ñ	N tilde	209 D1	209 D1	208 D0	132 84	145 91	165 A5	165 A5
Ò	O grave	210 D2	210 D2	210 D2	241 F1	146 92		277 E3
Ó	O acute	211 D3	211 D3	209 D1	238 EE	147 93		224 E0
Ô	O circumflex	212 D4	212 D4	211 D3	239 EF	148 94		226 E2
Õ	O tilde	213 D5	213 D5	213 D5	205 CD	149 95		229 E5
Ö	O diaeresis	214 D6	214 D6	212 D4	133 85	150 96	153 99	153 99
×	Multiplication sign	215 D7			*165 A5*	158 9E		158 9E
Ø	O oblique stroke	216 D8	216 D8	214 D6	175 AF	233 E9		157 9D
Ù	U grave	217 D9	217 D9	217 D9	244 F4	151 97		235 EB
Ú	U acute	218 DA	218 DA	216 D8	242 F2	152 98		233 E9
Û	U circumflex	219 DB	219 DB	218 DA	243 F3	153 99		234 EA
Ü	U diaeresis	220 DC	220 DC	219 DB	134 86	154 9A	154 9A	154 9A
Ý	Y acute	221 DD	221 DD		*160 A0*	155 9B		237 ED
Þ	Icelandic Thorn	222 DE			*222 DE*	156 9C		231 E7
ß	German sharp s	223 DF	223 DF	252 FC	167 A7	251 FB	225 E1	225 E1
à	a grave	224 E0	224 E0	225 E1	136 88	213 D5	133 85	133 85
á	a acute	225 E1	225 E1	224 E0	135 87	214 D6	160 A0	160 A0
â	a circumflex	226 E2	226 E2	226 E2	137 89	215 D7	131 83	131 83
ã	a tilde	227 E3	227 E3	228 E4	139 8B	216 D8		198 C6
ä	a diaeresis	228 E4	228 E4	227 E3	138 8A	217 D9	132 84	132 84
å	a ring above	229 E5	229 E5	229 E5	140 8C	218 DA	134 86	134 86
æ	a with e digraph	230 E6	230 E6	230 E6	190 BE	241 F1	145 91	145 91
ç	c cedilla	231 E7	231 E7	231 E7	141 8D	219 DB	135 87	135 87
è	e grave	232 E8	232 E8	233 E9	143 8F	220 DC	138 8A	138 8A
é	e acute	233 E9	233 E9	232 E8	142 8E	221 DD	130 82	130 82
ê	e circumflex	234 EA	234 EA	234 EA	144 90	222 DE	136 88	136 88
ë	e diaeresis	235 EB	235 EB	235 EB	145 91	223 DF	137 89	137 89
ì	i grave	236 EC	236 EC	237 ED	147 93	224 E0	141 8D	141 8D

Table VIII-4 West European Character Sets (continued)

Character	Name	Latin-1 dec hex	MCS dec hex	DGI dec hex	MAC dec hex	NeXT dec hex	CP437 dec hex	CP850 dec hex
í	i acute	237 ED	237 ED	236 EC	146 92	226 E2	161 A1	161 A1
î	i circumflex	238 EE	238 EE	238 EE	148 94	228 E4	140 8C	140 8C
ï	i diaeresis	239 EF	239 EF	239 EF	149 95	229 E5	139 8B	139 8B
ð	Icelandic eth	240 F0			*221 DD*	230 E6		208 D0
ñ	n tilde	241 F1	241 F1	240 F0	150 96	231 E7	164 A4	164 A4
ò	o grave	242 F2	242 F2	242 F2	152 98	236 EC	149 95	149 95
ó	o acute	243 F3	243 F3	241 F1	151 97	237 ED	162 A2	162 A2
ô	o circumflex	244 F4	244 F4	243 F3	153 99	238 EE	147 93	147 93
õ	o tilde	245 F5	245 F5	245 F5	155 9B	239 EF		228 E4
ö	o diaeresis	246 F6	246 F6	244 F4	154 9A	240 F0	148 94	148 94
÷	Division sign	247 F7			*214 D6*	159 9F	246 F6	246 F6
ø	o oblique stroke	248 F8	248 F8	246 F6	191 BF	249 F9		155 9B
ù	u grave	249 F9	249 F9	249 F9	157 9D	242 F2	151 97	151 97
ú	u acute	250 FA	250 FA	248 F8	156 9C	243 F3	163 A3	163 A3
û	u circumflex	251 FB	251 FB	250 FA	158 9E	244 F4	150 96	150 96
ü	u diaeresis	252 FC	252 FC	251 FB	159 9F	246 F6	129 81	129 81
ý	y acute	253 FD			224 E0	247 F7		236 EC
þ	Icelandic thorn	254 FE			*223 DF*	252 FC		231 E7
ÿ	y diaeresis	255 FF	255 FF	253 FD	216 D8	253 F3	152 98	152 98
ı	Dotless i				245 F5	245 F5		213 D5
Ł	L with stroke		195 C3		*195 C3*	232 E8		
ł	l with stroke		212 D4		*212 D4*	248 F8		
Œ	O with E digraph		215 D7	215 D7	206 CE	234 EA		
œ	o with e digraph		247 F7	247 F7	207 CF	250 FA		
Ÿ	Y diaeresis		221 DD	221 DD	216 D8			
ƒ	Florin sign			180 B4	196 D4	166 A6	159 9F	159 9F

East European Character Sets

Table VIII-5 shows the graphic characters of the right half of ISO 8859 Latin Alphabet 2 for East European languages, which is supported as both a transfer character-set and a file character-set by C-Kermit, along with the code values in Latin-2 and PC code page 852.

Table VIII-5
East European Character Sets

Character	Name	Latin-2 dec hex	CP852 dec hex
	No-break space	160 A0	255 FF
Ą	A ogonek	161 A1	164 A4
˘	Breve	162 A2	244 F4
Ł	L with stroke	163 A3	157 9D
¤	Currency sign	164 A4	207 CF
Ľ	L caron	165 A5	149 95
Ś	S acute	166 A6	151 97
§	Paragraph sign	167 A7	245 F5
¨	Diaeresis	168 A8	249 F9
Š	S caron	169 A9	230 E6
Ş	S cedilla	170 AA	184 B8
Ť	T caron	171 AB	155 9B
Ź	Z acute	172 AC	141 8D
	Soft hyphen	173 AD	170 AA
Ž	Z caron	174 AE	166 A6
Ż	Z dot above	175 AF	189 BD
°	Degree sign, ring	176 B0	248 F8
ą	a ogonek	177 B1	165 A5
˛	Ogonek	178 B2	242 F2
ł	l with stroke	179 B3	136 88
´	Acute accent	180 B4	239 EF
ľ	l caron	181 B5	150 96

Table VIII-5
East European Sets (continued)

Character	Name	Latin-2 dec hex	CP852 dec hex
ś	s acute	182 B6	152 98
ˇ	Caron	183 B7	243 F3
¸	Cedilla	184 B8	247 F7
š	s caron	185 B9	231 E7
ş	s cedilla	186 BA	173 AD
ť	t caron	187 BB	156 9C
ź	z acute	188 BC	171 AB
˝	Double acute	189 BD	241 F1
ž	z caron	190 BE	167 A7
ż	z dot above	191 BF	190 BE
Ŕ	R acute	192 C0	232 E8
Á	A acute	193 C1	181 B5
Â	A circumflex	194 C2	182 B6
Ă	A breve	195 C3	198 C6
Ä	A diaeresis	196 C4	142 8E
Ĺ	L acute	197 C5	145 91
Ć	C acute	198 C6	143 8F
Ç	C cedilla	199 C7	128 80
Č	C caron	200 C8	172 AC
É	E acute	201 C9	144 90
Ę	E ogonek	202 CA	168 A8
Ë	E diaeresis	203 CB	211 D3

468 Character Set Tables / Appendix VIII

Table VIII-5
East European Sets (continued)

Character	Name	Latin-2 dec hex	CP852 dec hex
Ě	E caron	204 CC	183 B7
Í	I acute	205 CD	214 D6
Î	I circumflex	206 CE	215 D7
Ď	D caron	207 CF	210 D2
Đ	D stroke	208 D0	209 D1
Ń	N acute	209 D1	227 E3
Ň	N caron	210 D2	213 D5
Ó	O acute	211 D3	224 E0
Ô	O circumflex	212 D4	226 E2
Ő	O double acute	213 D5	138 8A
Ö	O diaeresis	214 D6	153 99
×	Multiplication sign	215 D7	158 9E
Ř	R caron	216 D8	252 FC
Ů	U ring	217 D9	222 DE
Ú	U acute	218 DA	233 E9
Ű	U double acute	219 DB	235 EB
Ü	U diaeresis	220 DC	154 9A
Ý	Y acute	221 DD	237 ED
Ţ	T cedilla	222 DE	221 DD
ß	German sharp s	223 DF	225 E1
ŕ	r acute	224 E0	234 EA
á	a acute	225 E1	160 A0
â	a circumflex	226 E2	131 83
ă	a breve	227 E3	199 C7
ä	a diaeresis	228 E4	132 84
ĺ	l acute	229 E5	146 92
ć	c acute	230 E6	134 86
ç	c cedilla	231 E7	135 87

Table VIII-5
East European Sets (continued)

Character	Name	Latin-2 dec hex	CP852 dec hex
č	c caron	232 E8	159 9F
é	e acute	233 E9	130 82
ę	e ogonek	234 EA	169 A9
ë	e diaeresis	235 EB	137 89
ě	e caron	236 EC	216 D8
í	i acute	237 ED	161 A1
î	i circumflex	238 EE	140 8C
ď	d caron	239 EF	212 D4
đ	d stroke	240 F0	208 D0
ń	n acute	241 F1	228 E4
ň	n caron	242 F2	229 E5
ó	o acute	243 F3	162 A2
ô	o circumflex	244 F4	147 93
ő	o double acute	245 F5	139 8B
ö	o diaeresis	246 F6	148 94
÷	Division sign	247 F7	246 F6
ř	r caron	248 F8	253 FD
ů	u ring	249 F9	133 85
ú	u acute	250 FA	163 A3
ű	u double acute	251 FB	251 FB
ü	u diaeresis	252 FC	129 81
ý	y acute	253 FD	236 EC
ţ	t cedilla	254 FE	238 EE
˙	Dot above	255 FF	250 FA

Cyrillic Character Sets

Table VIII-6 shows the characters of the ISO 8859-5 Latin/Cyrillic Alphabet (also known as ECMA-113), Microsoft Code Page 866, Old KOI-8, and the Short KOI equivalents that are used for displaying Russian words on ASCII devices by showing Cyrillic letters as lowercase ASCII and Roman letters as uppercase ASCII; for example, Протокол Передачи Файлов **Kermit** is written `protokol pereda~i fajlow KERMIT`.

The character names are taken from ISO Standard 8859-5, modified to show upper- or lowercase typographically rather than spelling out UPPERCASE and LOWERCASE for each letter. Unfortunately, the same name is used by ISO for two different characters: Cyrillic I (1) is the one that looks like a backwards Roman letter *N*, and Cyrillic I (2) looks like a Roman letter *I*.

CP866 and the KOI character sets lack the Macedonian and Serbocroatian letters, as well as the old Cyrillic letters and one of the Ukrainian letters, that are found in ISO 8859-5. The CP866 characters B0 through DF (hex) are identical to the line- and box-drawing characters of IBM CP437. The 8-bit ISO, KOI-8, and CP866 sets all include ASCII (ISO 646 IRV) as their first 128 characters (except $ is replaced by ¤ in KOI-8).

Table VIII-6   Cyrillic Character Sets

Character	Name	ISO Dec Hex	CP866 Dec Hex	KOI-8 Dec Hex	Short KOI
А	Cyrillic A	176 B0	128 80	225 E1	a
а	Cyrillic a	208 D0	160 A0	193 C1	a
Б	Cyrillic Be	177 B1	129 81	226 E2	b
б	Cyrillic be	209 D1	161 A1	194 C2	b
В	Cyrillic Ve	178 B2	130 82	247 F7	w
в	Cyrillic ve	210 D2	162 A2	215 D7	w
Г	Cyrillic Ghe	179 B3	131 83	231 E7	g
г	Cyrillic ghe	211 D3	163 A3	199 C7	g
Д	Cyrillic De	180 B4	132 84	228 E4	d
д	Cyrillic de	212 D4	164 A4	196 C4	d
Е	Cyrillic Ie	181 B5	133 85	229 E5	e
е	Cyrillic ie	213 D5	165 A5	197 C5	e

Table VIII-6 Cyrillic Character Sets (continued)

Character	Name	ISO Dec Hex	CP866 Dec Hex	KOI-8 Dec Hex	Short KOI
Ё	Cyrillic Io	161 A1	240 F0		e
ё	Cyrillic io	241 F1	241 F1		e
Ж	Cyrillic Zhe	182 B6	134 86	246 F6	v
ж	Cyrillic zhe	214 D6	166 A6	214 D6	v
З	Cyrillic Ze	183 B7	135 87	250 FA	z
з	Cyrillic ze	215 D7	167 A7	218 DA	z
И	Cyrillic I (1)	184 B8	136 88	233 E9	i
и	Cyrillic i (1)	216 D8	168 A8	201 C9	i
Й	Cyrillic Short I	185 B9	137 89	234 EA	j
й	Cyrillic Short i	217 D9	169 A9	202 CA	j
К	Cyrillic Ka	186 BA	138 8A	235 EB	k
к	Cyrillic ka	218 DA	170 AA	203 CB	k
Л	Cyrillic El	187 BB	139 8B	236 EC	l
л	Cyrillic el	219 DB	171 AB	204 CC	l
М	Cyrillic Em	188 BC	140 8C	237 ED	m
м	Cyrillic em	220 DC	172 AC	205 CD	m
Н	Cyrillic En	189 BD	141 8D	238 EE	n
н	Cyrillic en	221 DD	173 AD	206 CE	n
О	Cyrillic O	190 BE	142 8E	239 EF	o
о	Cyrillic o	222 DE	174 AE	207 CF	o
П	Cyrillic Pe	191 BF	143 8F	240 F0	p
п	Cyrillic pe	223 DF	175 AF	208 D0	p
Р	Cyrillic Er	192 C0	144 90	242 F2	r
р	Cyrillic er	224 E0	224 E0	210 D2	r
С	Cyrillic Es	193 C1	145 91	243 F3	s
с	Cyrillic es	225 E1	225 E1	211 D3	s
Т	Cyrillic Te	194 C2	146 92	244 F4	t
т	Cyrillic te	226 E2	226 E2	212 D4	t
У	Cyrillic U	195 C3	147 93	245 F5	u

Table VIII-6 Cyrillic Character Sets (continued)

Character	Name	ISO Dec Hex	CP866 Dec Hex	KOI-8 Dec Hex	Short KOI
у	Cyrillic u	227 E3	227 E3	213 D5	y
Ф	Cyrillic Ef	196 C4	148 94	230 E6	f
ф	Cyrillic ef	228 E4	228 E4	198 C6	f
Х	Cyrillic Ha	197 C5	149 95	232 E8	h
х	Cyrillic ha	229 E5	229 E5	200 C8	h
Ц	Cyrillic Tse	198 C6	150 96	227 E3	c
ц	Cyrillic tse	230 E6	230 E6	195 C3	c
Ч	Cyrillic Che	199 C7	151 97	254 FE	~
ч	Cyrillic che	231 E7	231 E7	222 DE	~
Ш	Cyrillic Sha	200 C8	152 98	251 FB	{
ш	Cyrillic sha	232 E8	232 E8	219 DB	{
Щ	Cyrillic Shcha	201 C9	153 99	253 FD	}
щ	Cyrillic shcha	233 E9	233 E9	221 DD	}
Ъ	Cyrillic Hard Sign	202 CA	154 9A		
ъ	Cyrillic hard sign	234 EA	234 EA	207 CF	
Ы	Cyrillic Yeri	203 CB	155 9B	249 F9	y
ы	Cyrillic yeri	235 EB	235 EB	217 D9	y
Ь	Cyrillic Soft Sign	204 CC	156 9C	248 F8	x
ь	Cyrillic soft sign	236 EC	236 EC	216 D8	x
Э	Cyrillic E	205 CD	157 9D	252 FC	|
э	Cyrillic e	237 ED	237 ED	220 DC	|
Ю	Cyrillic Yu	206 CE	158 9E	224 E0	@
ю	Cyrillic yu	238 EE	238 EE	192 C0	@
Я	Cyrillic Ya	207 CF	159 9F	241 F1	q
я	Cyrillic ya	239 EF	239 EF	209 D1	q
Ц	Cyrillic Dze	175 AF			
џ	Cyrillic dze	255 FF			
I	Cyrillic I (2)	166 A6			
i	Cyrillic i (2)	246 F6			

472   Character Set Tables / Appendix VIII

Table VIII-6 Cyrillic Character Sets (continued)

Character	Name	ISO Dec Hex	CP866 Dec Hex	KOI-8 Dec Hex	Short KOI
Ј	Cyrillic Je	168 A8	244 F4		
ј	Cyrillic je	248 F8	245 F5		
Љ	Cyrillic Lje	169 A9			
љ	Cyrillic lje	249 F9			
Њ	Cyrillic Nje	170 AA			
њ	Cyrillic nje	250 FA			
Ў	Bielorussian Short U	174 AE	246 F6		
ў	Bielorussian short u	254 FE	247 F7		
Ѕ	Macedonian Dze	165 A5			
ѕ	Macedonian dze	245 F5			
Ѓ	Macedonian Gje	163 A3			
ѓ	Macedonian gje	243 F3			
Ќ	Macedonian Kje	172 AC			
ќ	Macedonian kje	252 FC			
Ђ	Serbocroatian Dje	162 A2			
ђ	Serbocroatian dje	242 F2			
Ћ	Serbocroatian Chje	171 AB			
ћ	Serbocroatian chje	251 FB			
Є	Ukrainian Ie	164 A4	242 F2		
є	Ukrainian ie	244 F4	243 F3		
І	Ukrainian Yi	167 A7			
і	Ukrainian yi	247 F7			
	No-break space	160 A0	255 FF		
№	Number Acronym	240 F0	252 FC		
§	Paragraph sign	253 FD			
	Soft hyphen	173 AD			

Appendix IX

DOS/UNIX File Conversion Script

This is a UNIX Bourne shell script to convert MS-DOS-format files and filenames to UNIX format. It assumes that the DOS-format files are in one directory and that another, empty, directory has been created for the converted files. Type this script in to a UNIX editor, save it as `convert.sh`, then make it executable using the command:

$ `chmod +x convert.sh`

Then run it, specifying the source and target directory names on the command line (without any terminating slash), for example:

$ `./convert.sh /usr/me/doskermit /usr/me/kermit`

The convert procedure will keep you informed of its progress and will print the message `Done.` when it is finished.

```sh
#!/bin/sh
if [ $# -lt 2 ]; then
  echo "usage: $0 source-directory target-directory"
  exit 1
fi
cd $1
echo "Converting files from $1 to $2"
for i in *; do
  j=`echo $i | tr 'A-Z' 'a-z'`
  echo $1/$i =\> $2/$j
  tr -d '\015\032' < $i > $2/$j
done
echo Done.
```

Appendix X

Hexification Programs

The C programs `hex.c` and `unhex.c` translate between 8-bit binary files and straight hex files, in which every pair of hexadecimal digits corresponds to a single 8-bit byte.

The `hex.c` program translates the standard input into hexadecimal notation and sends the result to standard output. Usage on UNIX or MS-DOS:

```
hex < binaryfile > hexfile

#include <stdio.h>              /* For EOF symbol */
#ifdef MSDOS
#include <fcntl.h>              /* For MS-DOS O_BINARY symbol */
#endif
unsigned int c; int count = 0; char a, b;
char h[16] = {
 '0','1','2','3','4','5','6','7','8','9','A','B','C','D','E','F'};
main() {
#ifdef MSDOS
    setmode(fileno(stdin),O_BINARY);   /* Avoid DOS conversions */
#endif
    while ((c = getchar()) != EOF) {   /* For each file char */
        b = c & 0xF;                   /* Get low 4 bits */
        a = (c >> 4) & 0xF;            /* and high 4 bits */
        putchar(h[a]);                 /* Hexify & output them */
        putchar(h[b]);
        if (++count == 36) {           /* 72 chars per line */
            putchar('\n'); count = 0;
        }
    }
    putchar('\n');                     /* Terminate final line */
}
```

The unhex program converts a hex file back into its original binary format. Usage on UNIX or MS-DOS:

unhex < hexfile > binaryfile

```
#include <stdio.h>                    /* Include this for EOF symbol */
#ifdef MSDOS
#include <fcntl.h>                    /* For MS-DOS setmode() symbol */
#endif
unsigned char a, b;                   /* High and low parts of byte */
unsigned int c;                       /* Char to translate them into */
unsigned char decode();               /* Function to decode them    */
main() {
#ifdef MSDOS
    setmode(fileno(stdout),O_BINARY);  /* Avoid DOS conversions */
#endif
    while ((c = getchar()) != EOF) {  /* Read first hex digit */
        a = c;                        /* Convert to character */
        if (a == '\n' || a == '\r') { /* Ignore line ends */
            continue;
        }
        if ((c = getchar()) == EOF) { /* Read second hex digit */
            fprintf(stderr,"File ends prematurely\n");
            exit(1);
        }
        b = c;                        /* Convert to character */
        putchar( ((decode(a) * 16) & 0xF0) + (decode(b) & 0xF) );
    }
    exit(0);                          /* Done */
}
/* Function to decode a hex char */
unsigned char
decode(x) char x; {
    if (x >= '0' && x <= '9')         /* 0-9 offset by hex 30 */
        return (x - 0x30);
    else if (x >= 'A' && x <= 'F')    /* A-F offset by hex 37 */
        return(x - 0x37);
    else {                            /* All others illegal */
        fprintf(stderr,"\nInput is not in legal hex format\n");
        exit(1);
    }
}
```

Appendix XI

Shift-In/Shift Out Filter

Use this program, so.c, to display 8-bit text on your screen when your connection to the host is 7 bits. Usage examples:

```
$ so < german.txt
$ kermit -z | so
```

```c
#include <stdio.h>                          /* Standard i/o library */
main() {                                    /* Main routine */
    int x = 0, shift = 0;                   /* Declarations */
    unsigned char c;
    while ((x = getchar()) != EOF) {        /* Read a character */
        c = x;                              /* Convert int to char */
        if (c > 127) {                      /* 8-bit character */
            if (shift == 0) {               /* Shifted already? */
                putchar('\16');             /* No, output SO (^N) */
                shift = 1;                  /* Remember shift */
            }
        } else {                            /* 7-bit character */
            if (shift == 1) {               /* Shifted? */
                putchar('\17');             /* Yes, output SI (^O) */
                shift = 0;                  /* Remember */
            }
        }
        putchar(c & 0x7F);                  /* Output the character */
    }
    putchar('\17');                         /* Return to normal */
}
```

Acronyms and Abbreviations

3270
A type of block-mode terminal used with IBM 370-series mainframes.

ACK
Acknowledgement.

ACL
Access Control List, a property of the VMS, OpenVMS, and AOS/VS file systems.

ACS
Asynchronous Communication Server. A device on a PC network that houses one or more serial ports that can be shared by all the PCs on the network.

ACU
Automatic Calling Unit. A modem that includes a dialer.

Alt
The key that you hold down while pressing another key in order to produce an Alt character, on keyboards that have an Alt (or Alternate) key. For example, `Alt-X` is produced by holding down Alt and pressing X.

ANSI
The American National Standards Institute, which issues standards such as ASCII.

AOS/VS
Advanced Operating System / Virtual System, the operating system for Data General Eclipse MV-series computers.

ARQ
Automatic Repeat (or Retransmission) Request. Applies to a communications protocol in which retransmission of damaged messages can be requested.

ASCII
American Standard Code for Information Interchange, ANSI X3.4-1986. A 128-character code widely used by computers for representing and transmitting character data, in which each character corresponds to a number between 0 and 127. See Table VIII-1.

AXP
The Digital Equipment Corporation 64-bit computer architecture, also called Alpha.

BBS
Bulletin board system. A dialup computer service that lets you exchange messages with other users of the same BBS, read news on various topics, and upload and download software and files.

bps
Bits per second (transmission speed).

C
The programming language used predominantly on UNIX systems, and in which C-Kermit is written.

C0
(C Zero) A set of 32 7-bit control characters.

C1
(C One) A set of 32 8-bit control characters.

CB
Citizens Band.

CCITT
The International Telegraph and Telephone Consultative Committee of the International Telecommunications Union, which issues standards called Recommendations, such as CCITT Recommendations V.24, X.25 (*q.v.*).

CD
Carrier Detect. The signal from a modem that indicates it is connected to another modem. Also called Data Carrier Detect (DCD) and Receive Line Signal Indicator (RLSI).

cd
Change Directory. The command used in UNIX, MS-DOS, OS/2, and several other operating systems to change your current (default) directory.

CECP
Country Extended Code Page. An EBCDIC-based national or international character set used on IBM mainframes.

CK
Filename prefix for C-Kermit files.

CLI
Command Line Interpreter (AOS/VS and Commodore Amiga).

CP
Code page, a character set used on PCs or IBM mainframes.

CPS
Characters per second, usually equivalent to 10 bits per second.

CPU
Central processing unit. The "brain" of a computer.

CR
Carriage return (ASCII 13, Control-M).

CRC
Cyclic redundancy check, an error-checking technique.

CRLF
Carriage return and linefeed, the sequence of ASCII characters (numbers 13 and 10) used by MS-DOS, OS/2, and other file systems to delimit lines in a text file.

CRT
Cathode ray tube. Commonly used to mean a video terminal.

csh
The C-Shell, the command interpreter supplied with Berkeley UNIX.

CTERM
The DECnet virtual terminal protocol used by the DECnet SET HOST command.

Ctrl
Control. The key that you hold down while pressing another key (a letter or certain others) in order to produce a control character. For example, *Ctrl-C* is produced by holding down Ctrl and pressing C.

CTS
Clear To Send. The RS-232 signal that indicates the DCE's readiness to accept data from the DTE.

DCC
Data Country Code (part of an X.121 address).

DCE
Data Communications Equipment, such as a modem.

DCL
DIGITAL Command Language. A command interpreter as well as a language for writing command procedures on Digital Equipment Corporation computers.

DG
Data General Corporation.

DEC
Digital Equipment Corporation.

DMA
Direct Memory Access.

DNIC
Data Network Identification Code (part of an X.121 address).

DOS
Disk Operating System. A computer operating system that uses a magnetic disk as its principal medium of permanent storage. Also, short for MS-DOS and PC-DOS.

DSR
Data Set Ready. A signal from a DCE to a DTE that says the DCE is turned on and in data mode.

DTE
Data Terminal Equipment, such as a computer or a terminal.

DTR
Data Terminal Ready. A signal from a DTE to a DCE that says the DTE is turned on and ready to communicate.

EBCDIC
Extended Binary Coded Decimal Interchange Code. The 8-bit character code used on IBM mainframes. Many variations exist, described in reference [35].

EIA
The Electronic Industries Association, sponsor of RS-232.

EISA

Extended Industry Standard Architecture, a 32-bit extension to the 16-bit ISA bus architecture used by the IBM PC/AT and compatibles.

ESC

Escape, ASCII character 27, Control-[.

FAT

File Allocation Table. The MS-DOS file system that is also supported by OS/2, in which file names are limited to 8.3 format (eight characters before the dot, three after).

G0

(G Zero) A set of 94 graphic characters, normally the graphic characters of ASCII (ISO 646 International Reference Version).

G1

(G One) A set of 94 or 96 graphic characters.

G2

(G Two) A set of 94 or 96 graphic characters.

G3

(G Three) A set of 94 or 96 graphic characters.

GL

Graphics Left. The set of graphic characters selected by a 7-bit character whose encoding is in the range 33–126.

GNU

GNU is Not UNIX. An effort to develop, collect, and distribute free software, mostly for UNIX, by the Free Software Foundation.

GOST

The (former) USSR State Committee on Standards.

GR

Graphics Right. The set of graphic characters selected by an 8-bit character whose encoding is in the range 160–255 (96-character sets) or 161–254 (94-character sets).

GUI

Graphical User Interface.

HD

High Density, such as the recording format of a diskette.

HPFS

The OS/2 High Performance File System, which supports long filenames.

IBM
International Business Machines Corporation.

I/O
Input/Output.

IP
Internet Protocol. The routing protocol and addressing conventions used in the Internet.

IRV
International Reference Version (of ISO 646).

ISA
Industry Standard Architecture, referring to the 16-bit bus used by the IBM PC/AT and compatibles.

ISO
International Organization for Standardization. A voluntary international group of national standards organizations that issues standards in a number of areas, including computers, information processing, and character sets.

ISO 646
The ISO standard for country-specific 7-bit character sets.

ISO 8859
The ISO standard for international 8-bit character sets.

JIS
Japan Industrial Standard.

JIS X 0201
The Japanese standard single-byte code for Roman and Katakana characters.

JIS X 0208
The Japanese standard two-byte code for Kanji characters, including also Katakana, Roman, Cyrillic, Greek, and others.

K
Kilo, meaning either 1,000 or 1,024.

KDD
Kermit Dialing Directory.

KOI
(КОИ) Russian abbreviation for Код для Обмена Информатсией —Kod dlia Obmiena Informatsiyey (Code for Information Interchange).

KSD
Kermit Services Directory.

ksh
The K-Shell, or Korn shell [5]. An alternative command interpreter supplied with some versions of UNIX.

LAN
Local area network.

LAPM
Link Access Procedure for Modems, specified in CCITT V.42.

LAT
Local Area Transport protocol, used by DEC Ethernet terminal servers.

LDM
Limited Distance Modem.

LZW
Lempel, Ziv, Welch data compression.

M
Mega, meaning either one million or 1,048,576.

MNP
Microcom Networking Protocol, used by modems for error correction and data compression. Levels 1 through 4 provide error correction. Levels 5 and above also provide compression.

MS-DOS
Microsoft's Disk Operating System for microcomputers based on the Intel 8086 CPU family.

NAK
Negative Acknowledgement.

NFS
Network File System.

NRC
National Replacement Character set. A 7-bit character set, usually, but not always, an ISO 646 national version.

NTN
Network Terminal Number (part of an X.121 address).

NUL
ASCII character number 0, as distinct from the number zero or the ASCII character digit 0 (ASCII 48). Also, the OS/2 and MS-DOS null device.

OS
Operating system.

PAD
Packet Assembler and Disassembler, the terminal interface to an X.25 network, specified in CCITT X.3.

PBX
Private Branch Exchange. A telephone system that serves the internal needs of an organization and that provides connections to the external telephone network. Some PBX's can be used for data as well as voice transmission within the organization.

PC
Personal computer.

PDN
Public data network, usually using X.25 protocols.

PEP
Telebit's Packet Ensemble Protocol, used between Telebit modems.

PM
Presentation Manager. The OS/2 graphical user interface.

PSN
Packet switched network.

REXX
Procedures Language/2 for OS/2 and other operating systems. A batch-oriented language for writing system command procedures.

RMS
Record Management System. The file system interface for VMS, OpenVMS, and other DEC operating systems.

ROM
Read-Only Memory.

RS-232
An Electronic Industries Association (EIA) standard that gives the electrical and functional specification for serial binary digital data transmission. The most commonly used interface between DTEs and DCEs. The American equivalent of CCITT Recommendation V.24.

RTS
Request To Send. A signal used by a DTE to regulate the flow of data from a DCE. When the DTE turns RTS on, the DCE is not supposed to send data. When the DTE turns RTS off, the DCE is allowed to send data.

RTS/CTS
A form of full-duplex flow control or half-duplex line access control that uses the RTS and CTS signals. Unlike Xon/Xoff, this is generally not an end-to-end mechanism; rather, it works between the PC and the device it is directly connected to, such as a high-speed modem. *Also see* RTS and CTS.

sh
The standard UNIX shell, also known as the Bourne shell.

TCP
Transmission Control Protocol. The transport layer of the TCP/IP protocol.

TCP/IP
A network protocol in widespread use for both local and wide area networking. The protocol of the worldwide Internet.

TDD
Telecommunication Devices for the Deaf. Usually a Teletype or other hardcopy terminal with a built-in modem, communicating at a very slow speed using a special modulation technique and a limited 5-bit character code called Baudot.

TTY
Teletype, an abbreviation commonly used to designate a terminal or a computer terminal port.

UART
Universal Asynchronous Receiver/Transmitter. An asynchronous communication port.

UNIX
A popular operating system originally developed at AT&T Bell Laboratories and noted for its portability.

UUCP
UNIX-to-UNIX Copy Program.

V.22
CCITT standard for 1200 bps full-duplex modems.

V.22*bis*
CCITT standard for 2400 bps full-duplex modems.

V.23
CCITT standard for 600 and 1200 bps half-duplex modems with 75 bps back channel (split-speed modems).

V.24
CCITT standard that gives the electrical and functional specification for serial binary digital data transmission; the European equivalent of RS-232.

V.25*bis*
CCITT standard modem dialing language.

V.32
CCITT standard for 9600 bps modem connection.

V.32*bis*
CCITT standard for 14400 bps modem connection.

V.42
CCITT standard error correction for modems, also called LAPM.

V.42*bis*
The CCITT data compression standard.

VAX
Virtual Address Extended. The Digital Equipment Corporation 32-bit computer architecture.

VMS
Virtual Memory System, the operating system for DEC VAX computers. Renamed to OpenVMS in later releases for both VAX and AXP architectures.

X.3
The protocol specifying the interface between a terminal and an X.25 network, specified by CCITT Recommendation X.3, used on public data networks.

X.25
A networking method, specified by CCITT Recommendation X.25, used on public data networks.

X.121
An addressing method used on X.25 networks.

Xon/Xoff
The most common full-duplex flow control method, in which the receiver sends an Xoff character when its input buffer is close to filling up and an Xon when it has made room for more data to arrive. Also called software flow control, to distinguish it from hardware flow control methods such as RTS/CTS.

Bibliography

[1] *ANSI X3.4-1986, Code for Information Interchange*
American National Standards Institute, 1986.
The ASCII specification; the US version of ISO 646.

[2] *ANSI X3.15-1976, Bit Sequencing of ASCII in Serial-By-Bit Data Transmission*
American National Standards Institute, 1976.
The standard that specifies how characters are transmitted on a serial connection.

[3] *ANSI 3.16-1976, Character Structure and Character Parity Sense for Serial-By-Bit Data Communication in ASCII*
American National Standards Institute, 1976.
The standard that specifies the transmission format for ASCII characters.

[4] *ANSI X3.64-1979, Additional Controls for Use with the American National Standard Code for Information Interchange*
American National Standards Institute, 1979.
Control sequences for video terminals and peripherals.

[5] Bolsky, Morris I., and David G. Korn.
The Kornshell.
Prentice-Hall, Englewood Cliffs, NJ, 1989.

[6] Bryabin, V.M., et al.
О Системе Кодиробания для Персональных ЭВМ.
Микропроцессорные Средства и Системы (4), 1986.
The article in which the "Alternative Cyrillic" character set for PCs was first proposed.

[7] *British Standard BS 4730, The Set of Graphic Characters of the United Kingdom 7-Bit Data Code*
British Standards Institution, 1975.

[8] *CCITT V.24, List of Definitions for Interchange Circuits between Data Terminal Equipment and Data Circuit-Terminating Equipment*
CCITT, Geneva, 1984.
The European equivalent of RS-232.

[9] *CCITT V.25bis, Automatic Calling and/or Answering Equipment on the General Switched Telephone Network (GSTN) Using the 100-Series Interchange Circuits*
CCITT, Geneva, 1984, 1988.

[10] *CCITT Recommendation X.3, Packet Assembly Disassembly Facility (PAD) in a Public Data Network*
CCITT, Geneva, 1988.

[11] *CCITT Recommendation X.25, Interface between Data Terminal Equipment (DTE) and Data Circuit-Terminating Equipment (DCE) for Terminals Operating in the Packet Mode and Connected to Public Data Networks by Dedicated Circuit*
CCITT, Geneva, 1989.

[12] *CCITT X.28, DTE/DCE Interface for a Start-Stop Mode Data Terminal Equipment Accessing the Packet Assembly/Disassembly Facility (PAD) in a Public Data Network Situated in the Same Country*
CCITT, Geneva, 1977.

[13] *CCITT X.29, Procedures for the Exchange of Control Information and User Data Between a Packet Mode DTE and a Packet Assembly/Disassembly Facility (PAD)*
CCITT, Geneva, 1977.

[14] *CCITT Recommendation X.121, International Numbering Plan for Public Data Networks*
CCITT, Geneva, 1988.

[15] Chandler, John.
Dynamic Packet Size Control.
Kermit News 3(1), June, 1988.

[16] Chandler, John.
IBM System/370 Kermit User's Guide
Columbia University Center for Computing Activities, 1991.
Available in separate versions for VM/CMS, MVS/TSO, and CICS.

[17] Comer, Douglas and David L. Stevens.
Internetworking with TCP/IP.
Prentice-Hall, Englewood Cliffs, NJ, 1991.

[18] da Cruz, Frank.
Kermit, A File Transfer Protocol.
Digital Press, Bedford, MA, 1987.

[19] da Cruz, Frank, and Christine Gianone.
How Efficient Is Kermit?
Kermit News (4), June, 1990.

[20] da Cruz, Frank.
Kermit in Antarctica.
Kermit News 2(1), November, 1987.

[21] Data General.
Learning to Use Your AOS/VS System
Data General, Westboro, MA, 1986.
093-000031-02.

[22] Data General.
AOS/VS System Concepts
Data General, Westboro, MA, 1986.
093-000335-01.

[23] Data General.
Programming the Display Terminal: Models D217, D413, and D463
Data General, Westboro, MA, 1991.
014-002111-00.

[24] Data General.
Using the CLI (AOS/VS and AOS/VS II)
Data General, Westboro, MA, 1991.
093-000646-01.

[25] Digital Equipment Corporation.
VT102 Video Terminal User Guide
Digital Equipment Corporation, Maynard, MA, 1982.
EK-VT102-UG-003.

[26] Digital Equipment Corporation.
VT330/340 Programmer Reference Manual, Volume 1: Text Programming
Digital Equipment Corporation, Maynard, MA, 1987.
EK-VT3XX-GP-001.

[27] ECMA.
Standard ECMA-113, 8-Bit Single-Byte Coded Graphic Character Sets, Latin/Cyrillic Alphabet
2nd edition, European Computer Manufacturers Association, 1988.
Equivalent to ISO 8859-5 Latin/Cyrillic and GOST 19768-1987.

[28] *EIA Standard RS-232-C, Interface Between Data Terminal Equipment and Data Communication Equipment Employing Serial Binary Data Interchange*
Electronic Industries Association, 2001 Eye Street N.W., Washington, DC 20006, 1969 (Reaffirmed 1981).
Recently supplanted by RS-232-D, which defined several of RS-232-C's unused circuits, and changed some terminology.

[29] Gianone, Christine M.
Using MS-DOS Kermit.
Digital Press, Burlington, MA, 1991.
EY-H893E-DP.

[30] Gianone, Christine M., and Frank da Cruz.
A Kermit Protocol Extension for International Character Sets.
Technical Report, Columbia University, 1990.

[31] Gianone, Christine M. and Frank da Cruz.
A Locking Shift Mechanism for the Kermit File Transfer Protocol.
Technical Report, Columbia University, 1991.

[32] *Hayes Smartmodem 2400 User's Guide*
Hayes Microcomputer Products, Inc., 1986.

[33] Hemenway, Kathy, and Helene Armitage.
Proposed Syntax Standards for UNIX System Commands.
UNIX/WORLD 1(3), 1984.

[34] *IBM National Language Support Reference Manual*
IBM Canada Ltd., National Language Technical Centre, Ontario, 1990.
SE09-8002-01.

[35] *IBM Character Data Representation Architecture, Level 1 Registry*
IBM Canada Ltd., National Language Technical Centre, Ontario, 1990.
SC09-1391-00.

[36] *ISO Standard 646, 7-Bit Coded Character Set for Information Processing Interchange*
Second edition, International Organization for Standardization, 1983.
Also available as ECMA-6, and similar to CCITT T.50.

[37] *ISO International Standard 2022, Information processing — ISO 7-bit and 8-bit coded character sets — Code extension techniques*
Third edition, International Organization for Standardization, 1986.
Also available as ECMA-35.

[38] *ISO International Standard 4873, Information processing — ISO 8-bit code for information interchange — Structure and rules for implementation*
Second edition, International Organization for Standardization, 1986.
Also available as ECMA-43.

[39] *ISO International Standard 8859 Parts 1 through 9, Information Processing—8-Bit Single-Byte Coded Graphic Character Sets*
International Organization for Standardization, 1987–.
ISO 8859-1 through -4 are the Latin Alphabets 1 through 4, also available as ECMA-94. ISO 8859-5 is the Latin/Cyrillic Alphabet (ECMA 113).

[40] *ISO/IEC DIS 10646-1.2, 2nd Draft International Standard 10646, Information Processing—Multiple-Octet Coded Character Set*
ISO/IEC JTC1, 1992.

[41] *ISO International Standard 6429, Information processing — C1 Control Character Set of ISO 6429*
International Organization for Standardization, 1983.

[42] *ISO International Register of Coded Characters to Be Used with Escape Sequences*
European Computer Manufacturers Association (ECMA), 1990, updated periodically.

[43] *JIS X 0201, The Japanese Katakana and Roman Set of Characters*
Japan Industrial Standards Committee, 1969.

[44] *JIS X 0208, The Japanese Graphic Character Set for Information Interchange*
Japan Industrial Standards Committee, 1983.

[45] *JIS X 0212, Supplementary Japanese Graphic Character Set for Information Interchange*
Japan National Committee on ISO/IEC JTC1/SC2, 1991.

[46] Kernighan, Brian W., and Dennis M. Ritchie.
Prentice-Hall Software Series: The C Programming Language.
Prentice-Hall, Englewood Cliffs, NJ, 1988.

[47] McNamara, John E.
Technical Aspects of Data Communication.
Digital Press, Burlington, MA, 1988.
EY8262E-DP.

[48] *Microsoft MS-DOS Version 4.01 in Russian, Product Description*
Microsoft Corporation, Unterschießheim, Germany, 1989–1990.

[49] O'Reilly, Tim, Valerie Quercia, and Linda Lamb.
X Window System User's Guide for Version 11.
O'Reilly & Associates, Inc., Newton, MA, 1988.

[50] Пакеты Прекладныч Программ Телеобработки Данных на МикроЭВМ
International Center for Scientific and Technical Information (ICSTI), Moscow, 1987.
A Russian Kermit User Guide, including character tables for several Cyrillic character sets.

[51] Postel, J., and Reynolds, J.
RFC 854: TELNET Protocol Specification.
Technical Report, Network Working Group, May, 1983.

[52] Rasmussen, Bob.
Who Is Kermit and Why Is He in My Computer?
NCR Monthly, March, 1990.

[53] Siegel, Mark L.
Toward Standardized Video Terminals: ANSI X3.64 Device Control.
BYTE :365–372, April, 1984.

[54] Snedecor, George W. and William G. Cochran.
Statistical Methods.
Iowa State University Press, Ames, 1989.

[55] Todino, Grace, and Dale Dougherty.
Nutshell Handbook: *Using UUCP and Usenet*.
O'Reilly & Associates, Inc., Newton, MA, 1987.

Trademarks

Adobe Systems Incorporated, Mountain View, CA: PostScript
Alliant: Alliant, Concentrix
Altos Computer Systems: Altos
Amdahl: UTS
Apollo: Aegis, Domain, SR10
Apple Computer, Cupertino, CA: Apple, Apple II, Macintosh, Lisa, LaserWriter, A/UX
AT&T, New York, NY: Touch-Tone
AT&T Information Systems, Morristown, NJ: StarLAN, StarGROUP, AT&T 6300, AT&T 6300 PLUS, UNIX PC, 3B2, 3B20
Atari, Sunnyvale, CA: Atari, ST, GEM, GEMDOS
Berkeley Software Design, Inc., Falls Church, VA: BSDI/386
Charles River Data Systems, Inc., Framingham, MA: UNOS
Cisco Systems, Inc., Menlo Park, CA: cisco, Cisco, AGS, AGS+
Commodore Business Machines, West Chester, PA: Amiga, AmigaDOS, Amiga Workbench, Amiga 2000, Amiga 3000, Amiga 3000UX, Commodore 64, Commodore 128, Intuition
CompuServe, Inc. (an H&R Block Company), Columbus, OH: CompuServe
Concept Omega Corporation, Somerset, NJ: Thoroughbred BASIC
Concurrent, Oceanport, NJ: Concurrent, MASSCOMP, RTU, Xelos
Consensys Corporation, Universal City, TX: Consensys
Control Data Corporation: CDC, Cyber
Convergent Technologies, Inc., Santa Clara, CA: Convergent Technologies, Convergent, MegaFrame Computer System, MiniFrame Computer System, CTIX, CTOS
Convex: Convex, ConvexOS
Cray Research, Eagen, MN: Cray X/MP, Y/MP, C90, UNICOS
Data General Corporation, Westboro, MA: AOS/VS, Aviion, CEO, DASHER, DG/UX, ECLIPSE MV, MV/UX, RDOS, DESKTOP GENERATION

Dell Computer Corporation: Dell, Dell System

Diab Data AB, a Bull company, Tdby, Sweden: DIAB, DNIX

Dialog Information Services, Inc., Palo Alto, CA: DIALOG

Digital Equipment Corporation, Maynard, MA: The Digital logo, DEC, PDP-8, OS/8, OS/278, PDP-11, RSTS/E, RSX-11, RT-11, IAX, PDP-12, OS/12, VAX, AXP, Alpha AXP, VMS, OpenVMS, VT52, VT100, VT102, VT220, VT320, Rainbow, VAXmate, DECmate, DECserver, DECstation, DEC-SYSTEM, DECsystem, TOPS-10, TOPS-20, VAXstation, MicroVAX, PATHWORKS, ULTRIX

Digital Equipment Corporation, Intel Corporation, Xerox Corporation: Ethernet

Digitel S/A Indústria Eletrônica, Porto Alegre, Brazil: Digitel DT-22

Dow Jones and Company, Princeton, NJ: Dow-Jones News/Retrieval Service

Encore Computer: Multimax, Umax

ESIX Computer, Inc., Santa Ana, CA: ESIX

EXABYTE Corporation, Boulder, CO: EXABYTE, EXATAPE

Fortune Systems, Redwood City, CA: For:Pro

Fujitsu, Japan: Fujitsu

Groupe Bull, France: Honeywell, VIP

Harris Corporation, Fort Lauderdale, FL: Night Hawk, CX/UX

Hayes Microcomputer Products, Inc., Atlanta, GA: Hayes Smartmodem 1200 and 2400

Heath Company, Benton Harbor, MI: Heath-19

Henson Associates, Inc., New York, NY: Kermit. The Kermit protocol was named after Kermit the Frog, star of THE MUPPET SHOW television series. The name "Kermit" is used by permission of Henson Associates, Inc., New York.

Hewlett-Packard Co., Palo Alto, CA: HP-9000, HP-UX

Insignia Solutions, Inc., Mountain View, CA: SoftPC

Integrated Computer Solutions, Cambridge, MA: ICS, ISI, VS8

Intel Corp., Santa Clara, CA: Intel 8080, 8086, 8088, 80286, 80386, 80486, i286, i386, i486, OpenNET

INTERACTIVE Systems Corporation, Division of SunSoft, Santa Monica, CA: INTERACTIVE UNIX

International Business Machines Corp., Armonk, NY: IBM, Series/1, VM/CMS, MVS/TSO, PC-DOS, Operating System/2, OS/2, Presentation Manager, 3270, 3705, 3725, System/370, IBM PC, IBM PC/XT, IBM PC/AT, IBM PC*jr*, IBM RT PC, PS/1, PS/2, IBM 7171, Token Ring, NETBIOS, CGA, MCGA, EGA, VGA, XGA, RS/6000, RISC System/6000, AIX, AIX Windows, ACIS, Micro Channel, REXX, Procedures Language/2

Linotype AG: Times

Lotus Development Corporation, Cambridge, MA: Lotus 1-2-3

Mark Williams Company, Chicago, IL: COHERENT

Massachusetts General Hospital: MUMPS

Massachusetts Institute of Technology: X-Window System

Masscomp, Framingham, MA: RTU

MCI Communication Corporation, Piscataway, NJ: MCI Mail

Microcom, Inc., Norwood, MA: Microcom Networking Protocol, MNP, Universal Link Negotiation, Statistical Duplexing

Microport: Microport

Microsoft Corporation, Redmond, WA: Microsoft, MS-DOS, LAN Manager, Windows

Microware Systems Corporation, Des Moines, IA: OS-9, OS-9000, OS-9/68000

MIPS Computer Systems, Inc., Sunnyvale, CA: MIPS, RISC/OS, UMIPS

Modular Computer Systems, Inc., Fort Lauderdale, FL: Modcomp: REAL/IX

Motorola Computer Group, Tempe, AZ: System V/68, System V/88, Motorola Delta Series

Motorola Semiconductors, Inc., Austin, TX: Motorola, 68000, 68010, 68020, 68030, 68040

MT XINU, Inc., Berkeley, CA: Mach386
NCR Corporation, Dayton, OH: NCR, Tower
NeXT Computer, Inc, Redwood City, CA: NeXT, NeXTstep, NeXTcube, NeXTstation
Nippon Electric Corporation, Japan: NEC, NEC PC9801
Novell, Inc., Provo, UT: Novell, NetWare, NetWare 286, NetWare 386, LAN Workplace for DOS, Excelan
Ing. C. Olivetti & C., S.p.A., Ivrea, Italy: Olivetti, LSX, X/OS
Open Software Foundation, Cambridge, MA: Motif, OSF, OSF/1
Penril DataComm, Ltd, Hampshire, UK: Penril, Alliance
Plexus, San Jose, CA: Plexus
Prime Computer, Natick, MA: PRIME, PRIMOS, PRIMIX
Pyramid Technology Corp., Mountain View, CA: Pyramid
Racal-Vadic, Milpitas, CA: Vadic, VA3400
Regents of the University of California: Berkeley Software Distribution, BSD
Ridge Computers: Ridge 32
Santa Cruz Operation, Santa Cruz, CA: SCO Xenix, SCO UNIX, Open Desktop, ODT
Sequent Computer Systems, Inc., Beaverton, OR: Sequent, Balance, Symmetry, DYNIX, ptx, DYNIX/ptx
Silicon Graphics, Inc., Mountain View, CA: Silicon Graphics, IRIS, IRIS Indigo, IRIX
Solbourne Computer, Longmont, CO: Solbourne, OS/MP
Sony, Japan: Sony NEWS
SPARC International, Inc.: SPARC, SPARCstation
Sun Microsystems, Inc., Mountain View, CA: Sun Microsystems, Sun Workstation, Sun, Sun-3, Sun-4, SunOS, NFS, SunLink, SunSoft, SunView, Solaris
Tandy Corporation, Fort Worth, TX: Radio Shack, Tandy 16/6000
Andrew S. Tanenbaum: MINIX
Tektronix, Inc., Wilsonville, OR: Tektronix, UTek
Telebit Corporation, Sunnyvale, CA: Telebit, TrailBlazer, QBlazer, WorldBlazer, PEP
Telecom Canada, Ottawa, ON, Canada: Datapac
Teletype Corporation, Skokie, IL: Teletype
TGV, Inc., Santa Cruz, CA: MultiNet
3Com Corporation, Santa Clara, CA: 3Com, Bridge Applications Programmer Interface (BAPI)
Tri Star: Flash Cache
TYMNET, Inc., San Jose, CA: TYMNET
UNISYS Corporation, Blue Bell, PA: Unisys, PW2, PC/IT, Uniservo, CustomCare, Sperry, Burroughs, U6000/65, MightyFrame, S/Series, CTIX, BTOS
UNIX System Laboratories, Inc., Summit, NJ: UNIX, System III, System V, OPEN LOOK
US Robotics: Courier10PitchBT-Roman
US Sprint Communications Company Limited Partnership, Shawnee Mission, KS: US Sprint, SprintNet, Telenet
The Wollongong Group, Inc., Palo Alto, CA: WIN/TCP, WIN/ROUTE
WordPerfect Corporation, Orem, UT: WordPerfect
Xerox Corporation, Stamford, CT: Ethernet
Zenith Data Systems, Glenview, IL: Zenith-19 Terminal
Zilog, Campbell, CA: Zilog, ZEUS

Other brands or product names are trademarks or registered trademarks of their respective holders.

Colophon

The text of this book was entered using MS-DOS Kermit on IBM PC/ATs and PS/2s and C-Kermit 5A on NeXTstations into GNU EMACS on a Sun-4 UNIX system. The text was formatted for PostScript using the Scribe document preparation system on the Sun and set in Times Roman augmented by the Cyrillic Gothic font designed by Jay Sekora of Princeton University, with much time-saving assistance from Trey Matteson's PostScript File Previewer on the NeXT.

MS-DOS Kermit and C-Kermit are products of Kermit Development and Distribution, Columbia University Academic Information Systems, 612 West 115th Street, New York, NY 10025, USA. GNU EMACS is a product of the Free Software Foundation, 675 Massachusetts Avenue, Cambridge, MA 02139, USA. Scribe is a commercial product of Unus, Inc., distributed exclusively by Cygnet Publishing Technologies, Inc., 4111 Seventh Avenue, Suite 1175, Pittsburgh, PA 15219, USA.

Index

! command 34
as comment introducer 23
* as wildcard character 395
- as command continuation character 25
; as comment introducer 23
< comparison operator 236
= comparison operator 236
> comparison operator 237
? as command help request 18
? as wildcard character 22, 395
@ command 34
\ as command quote character 21
\ as command continuation character 25
: label introducer 246
~ notation for home directory 395

\$() environment variables 233
\%0-9 macro arguments 219
\%a-z global variables 224
\&@[] program argument array 228
\&a-z[] arrays 227
\F() built-in functions 253–260
\Fcharacter() function 254
\Fcode() function 254
\Fcontents() function 255
\Fdefinition() function 256
\Feval() function 257
\Fexecute() function 255
\Ffiles() function 260
\Findex() function 256
\Flength() function 256
\Fliteral() function 253
\Flower() function 254
\Flpad() function 255
\Fmax() function 257
\Fmin() function 257
\Fnextfile() function 260
\Frepeat() function 255
\Freverse() function 255
\Fright() function 254
\Frpad() function 255
\Fsubstring() function 254
\Fupper() function 255
\m() macro definition value 226, 256
\v() built-in variables 228–232
\v(argc) variable 228, 242
\v(args) variable 228
\v(cmdfile) variable 229
\v(cmdlevel) variable 228
\v(cmdsource) variable 229
\v(count) variable 241, 248
\v(cpu) variable 229
\v(directory) variable 229
\v(exitstatus) variable 229
\v(filespec) variable 230
\v(fsize) variable 230

\v(home) variable 56, 230
\v(host) variable 230
\v(inchar) variable 279
\v(incount) variable 279
\v(input) variable 280
\v(line) variable 230
\v(local) variable 230
\v(ndate) variable 230
\v(nday) variable 231
\v(ntime) variable 231
\v(platform) variable 231
\v(program) variable 231
\v(return) variable 231
\v(speed) variable 231
\v(status) variable 231
\v(system) variable 231
\v(tfsize) variable 231
\v(time) variable 231
\v(ttyfd) variable 232
\v(version) variable 232, 242

3270 protocol converter 135, 292
   nontransparent 136
   transparent 135
386BSD UNIX 14

8th-bit prefixing 123, 154, 162

ACK (acknowledgement) packet 151
AIX 14, 41, 88
   Also see IBM 1
Alliant computers 14
Alpha. *See* UNIX, VMS
Alt-key in OS/2 C-Kermit 427
Alternative Cyrillic character set 187, 470
Altos computers 13, 14
Amdahl mainframes 13
Amiga C-Kermit 1, 13, 449
   and terminal emulation 88
Answer mode 365
AOS/VS 441–447
   and C-Kermit 442
   and international characters 443
   and TCP/IP TELNET 441
   and VT100 terminals 442
   templates (wildcards) 446
Apollo computers 13
APPEND, file collision option 116
Apple II Kermit capabilities 8
Apple Macintosh. *See* Macintosh
Apple Quickdraw character set 464
Argument vector 228
Arguments
   macro, count of 228
   to macros 219
Arithmetic functions 257
Arrays 227, 260, 272, 298

Arrow keys
   codes sent by 429
   setting mode of 432
   setting mode of, host controlled 439
ASCII
   and C-Kermit commands 169
   and language-specific rules 191
   table of 461
   text file format 112
   transfer character-set 112, 183
ASG command 226
ASK command 261
ASKQ command 261
ASSIGN command 226, 234
Asynchronous serial communication 359–373
AT commands, Hayes. *See* Hayes modem
AT&T computers 13
AT&T modems 52
Atari ST C-Kermit 1, 14, 452
   and terminal emulation 88
Attribute packets 8, 116, 165
   and Amiga C-Kermit 451
   and Atari ST C-Kermit 454
   and character sets 197
   and VMS C-Kermit 406, 407, 412, 416
Autodial modem 365
Aviion 14
AXP. *See* UNIX, VMS

Background file transfer 394
BACKGROUND, IF condition 241
Backslash
   as C-Kermit command quote character 21, 25
   as command continuation character 23
   as function introducer 252
   as variable-name introducer 219, 227, 228
   codes in CONNECT mode 86
   codes, table of 324
   notation for numbers 27
BACKUP, file collision option 116
BACKUP saveset, VMS 409
Bidirectional terminal devices 376
Binary files 143, 321
   and the TRANSMIT command 203
   automatic recognition of in VMS 406
   definition of 113
   transfer of 113
BITNET network 9
Blank-Free-2 block check 136
Block check 128, 136
Boilerplate e-mail example 271
Braille 2, 107, 383
BREAK command 251
BREAK signal 85
   using to change communication speed 289
Breakout box 373
British character set 180, 463

BSD 13
BSDI/386 14
Bubble sort 251
Buffers, packet 161
Built-in variables 228–232
BYE command 141

C-Kermit
   and AOS/VS 441
   and ASCII 169
   and OS-9 454
   and OS/2 419
   and the Atari ST 452
   and the Commodore Amiga 449
   and UNIX 382
   and VMS 399
   argument vector 228
   capabilities of 7
   command files for 23, 210
   description xv
   exit status codes 323
   how to start 15, 423
   initialization file 35, 56
   interactive commands, how to enter 17
   running in a GUI environment 387
   starting in AOS/VS 443
Cables 370
CALL macro 275
Calling card 62
Capturing remote files 200
Carrier signal 45
Case of letters
   and the INPUT command 279
   changing 254
   in C-Kermit commands 17
   in directory names 29
   in environment variable names 233
   in filenames 27
   in macro names 214
   in string comparisons 239
   in system commands 29
   in transferred filenames 96
   in variable names 224
CCITT modems 52
CD (carrier detect). See Carrier signal
CD command 31, 327
Cermetek modems 52
Character, asynchronous transmission format 359
Character set tables
   ASCII 461
   Cyrillic 470
   East European Languages 468
   ISO 646 461, 463
   West European Languages 464
Character sets 169–197
   and ANSI escape sequences 176
   and AOS/VS 443

   and Attribute packets 197
   and C-Kermit commands 174
   and file transfer 180
   and initialization file 197
   and languages 191
   and OS-9 456
   and OS/2 434
   and script programs 282
   and string comparisons 239
   and terminal connection 175
   and the Amiga 451
   and the TRANSMIT command 196, 203
   and UNIX 386
   and VMS 401
   combinations of 170
   Cyrillic 187
   Cyrillic, file transfer examples 188, 193
   Cyrillic, table of 470
   European, file transfer examples 185, 192
   file conversion 194
   Japanese 189
   Japanese, file transfer examples 190
   Kermit designator for 166
   proprietary 170, 459
   Roman alphabet, tables of 464, 468
   standard 171, 459
   terminal 176
   unknown 185
Character-set
   file 180
   terminal 175
   transfer 180, 183
Character-string functions 253
Charles River Data Systems computers 14
CHECK command 382
Checkpoint/Restart. See SET FILE COLLISION
Chinese Roman character set 463
CKVCVT program 415
CLEAR command 281
Clearing the screen
   escape sequences for 437, 440
CLOSE command 271
CLOSE DEBUG command 138
CLOSE PACKETS command 138
CLOSE SESSION command 93
CLOSE TRANSACTIONS command 117
Closing
   a CONNECT session 82
   a network connection 69
   a serial connection 45
Code page 437 180, 464
Code page 850 180, 464
Code page 852 180, 468
Code page 866 180, 187, 470
COHERENT OS 14
Collision of filenames 116
Colophon 500

Index 503

Colors, screen
    escape sequences for 439
    selecting in OS/2 432
Columbia University xv, 9
Command files 23–25, 209–212, 150
    as programs 314, 391, 424
    creation of 23, 210
    getting names of 228
    interruption of 23
    nested 212, 244
    versus macros 218
Command level 228
Command summary, C-Kermit 323–358
Command-line options 311–322
Commands
    AOS/VS 30
    CONNECT-mode escape 82
    OS-9 455
    UNIX 30
    VMS 30
Commands, C-Kermit
    abbreviating 19
    comments in 23, 215
    completion feature 20
    continuation of 25
    correcting mistakes in 20
    default values in 21
    executing from files 23, 209
    for arithmetic 257
    for local file management 31
    for programming 235
    for server mode 141
    getting help in 18
    how to enter 17
    interrupting 22
    keywords in 17
    mistakes in 19
    numbers in 27
    order of execution 323
    quoting special characters in 21
    redisplay of 20
    source of 229
    special characters, table of 23
    success and failure of 240
    syntax of descriptions 26
    termination characters 18
COMMENT command 23
Comments
    in C-Kermit commands 23, 215
    UNIX shell 391
Commodore Amiga. See Amiga
Communication device
    hanging up 45, 69
    network, selecting 69
    serial, selecting 43, 316
    speed of 44, 60, 361
    table of typical names 41

Comparison
    of character strings 238
    of numbers 236
Completion, automatic
    of filenames 20
    of keywords 20
Compression of data
    by Kermit 164
    by modem 59, 62, 66, 370
CompuServe login script 294
Concord modems 52
Concurrent computers 13
CONNECT command 79–93
    and character sets 175
    and key mapping 91
    and locking shifts 90, 178
    and OS/2 C-Kermit 426
    and UNIX C-Kermit 392
    closing the connection 82
    debugging 93
    escape character 80
    escape commands 82
    hanging up from 87
    logging 92
    network functions 86
    quitting Kermit from 87
    returning from 81, 84
    sending BREAK signals 85
    sending special characters 86
    settings for 88
    shell escape 85
    status inquiry 84
Connection establishment 37–77
    all serial connections 42
    automated 274
    dialed serial connections 50
    direct serial connections 48
    in OS/2 425
    network connections 67
Connection release
    in CONNECT mode 82
    network connections 69
    serial connections 45
Connectors 370
Consensys UNIX 14
Console driver 88, 392
Continuation of C-Kermit commands 25
CONTINUE command 251
Control characters
    and file transfer 132
    how to type them 20
    in UNIX 384
    in VT102 emulation 435
    table of 462
Convergent computers 13
Convex computers 13
COPY macro 245

504 *Index*

COUNT variable 248
Counted loops 248, 249
CP/M Kermit 8, 101
CPS (characters per second) 361
Cray computers 13, 133
CRC error detection 129
CREN network 9
CRT file transfer display 108
Cursor, terminal 432
Cut and paste. *See* Mouse
CWD command 31
Cyrillic 171, 470
    file character-sets 180
    text 187, 193
    transfer character-set 183

Danish
    character set 180, 463
    transliteration rules 192
Data bits versus parity 88, 122, 359
Data communications 359–373
Data compression 164, 370
Data General AOS/VS. *See* AOS/VS
Data General Aviion 14
Data General International character set 180, 464
Date variable, \v(date) 229
Date variable, \v(ndate) 230
Day-of-week variable, \v(day) 229
Day-of-week variable, \v(nday) 231
DCL command 227
Deaf, hints for 21, 383
Debug log 138, 270
Debugging a terminal session 93
DEC Alpha AXP. *See* UNIX, VMS
DEC modems 52
DEC Multinational Character Set 180
    tables of 174, 464
DEC PDP-11. *See* PDP-11
DECLARE command 227
DECnet
    and OS/2 C-Kermit 426
    and VMS C-Kermit 406
DECREMENT command 259
Default directory 31
Default values for command fields 21
DEFINE command 214, 224, 234
DEFINED, IF condition 240
DELETE command 31
Dell UNIX 14
Device, communication. *See* Communication device
DIAB DS90 computers 14
DIAL command 54–67
Dialing 50–67, 362
    automated 275, 280
    by modem 365
    directory 55
    directory, UNIX 387

directory, VMS 404
examples 55, 63
macros for 222
manually 65
multistage 62
solving problems 57, 65
tone versus pulse 54
via network modem server 74
with calling-card numbers 62
Digital Equipment Corporation. *See* DEC, VMS
Digitel modems 52
Direct serial connections 48
Directory, default 31
Directory, dialing. *See* Dialing
DIRECTORY, VMS command 408
DIRECTORY command 32
Directory of services 297
DISABLE command 148
DISCARD, file collision option 116
Diskettes, C-Kermit
    and OS/2 421
Display, file transfer
    and efficiency 156
    selecting 106
DNIX 14
DO command 216, 219
Dolphin Server Technology servers 14
Dow Jones News/Retrieval login script 294
Downloading files 98, 101
    without the Kermit protocol 200
DTR/CD, DTR/CTS. *See* Flow control, hardware
Duplex 361
    full 124, 361
    half 127, 361
Dutch
    character set 180, 463
    transliteration rules 192
Dynamic packet length 157
DYNIX 14

E-PACKET command 111
EARN network 9
Echo
    and TELNET connections 72
    terminal 89
ECHO command 32
EDIT macro 242
Editor, text
    macro for using 242
    using to create command files 23, 210
Efficiency of file transfer 151–168, 123
Electronic mail
    and MAIL command 147
    script programming example 271
Eliminator, modem 371
ELSE command 237
EMACS display editor 383, 385, 397

Index 505

Emulation, terminal
    and Amiga C-Kermit 450
    and AOS/VS C-Kermit 445
    and Atari ST C-Kermit 453
    and OS-9 C-Kermit 456
    and OS/2 C-Kermit 426
    and UNIX C-Kermit 392
    and VMS C-Kermit 404
ENABLE command 148
Encore computers 14
END command 243
End-of-file condition 203, 271, 411, 433
End-of-packet character 132
Environment variables 233, 395, 452
EQUAL comparison operator 238
Error correction
    by Kermit 128
    by modem 59, 62, 66, 368
Escape character, CONNECT mode 80
    how to avoid using 266
    how to change 80
    in NeXT C-Kermit 80
    in OS/2 C-Kermit 427
Escape sequences
    and C-Kermit macros 263
    and ISO 646 terminal character sets 176
    for transparent printing 266
    to initiate file transfer 266
    VT100, table of 264
    VT102, tables of 429, 435
    VT52, tables of 429, 440
ESIX 14
EUC (Extended UNIX Code). *See* Japanese
EXIST, IF condition 241
EXIT command 17
Exit status
    codes 323
    variable 229
EXTPROC command 424

FAILURE, command status 240
File character-sets 180
    choosing 185
    table of 180
File names
    and version numbers 116, 407
    collision of 116, 397, 434, 447, 451, 454, 457
    treatment of by C-Kermit 96, 114, 393
File size
    as basis of rejection 166, 454
    variables for 230, 231
File transfer 95–208
    and 8-bit text 162
    and 8th-bit prefixing 123, 162
    and AOS/VS 445
    and attribute packets 165
    and character sets 180

and communication speed 124
and control characters 132
and data compression 164
and file names 97, 114
and filename collisions 116
and half duplex connections 127
and handshake 127
and IBM mainframes 133
and locking shifts 162, 194
and noise interference 128, 134
and OS/2 434
and packet length 156
and parity 122
and server mode 142
and sliding windows 158
and TCP/IP networks 103, 105, 123
and terminal servers 103
and the Amiga 451
and the Atari ST 454
and timeouts 130
and transparency problems 132
and UNIX 393
and VMS 405
and X.25 networks 137
background 394
basic commands for 95
binary files 113
commands 97, 98, 142
display of progress 106, 144
downloading with Kermit protocol 101
downloading without Kermit protocol 200
efficiency, improving 155
examples 98, 133
examples, Cyrillic 188, 193
examples, European 185
examples, Japanese 190
examples, language-specific 192
examples, network 103
features, table of 168
in local mode 104
in remote mode 98
incomplete 117
initiating via escape sequence 266
interruption of 109, 147, 444
interruption of, in UNIX 393
macros for 223
network 103, 105
of binary files 113
of text files 112
recording information about 117
resuming after interruption 116
SEND command 96
summaries of basic steps 5, 118
uploading with Kermit protocol 100
uploading without Kermit protocol 202
VMS labeled mode 412
Filename, defined 27

Files
    binary versus text 112, 113
    checking existence of 241
    menus of 19
    opening and closing 269
    reading and writing 270
    textual encoding of 207, 477
    transferring 95, 121, 139, 151
    translating 194
Files, command. *See* Command files
Filespec, defined 28
FINISH command 141
Finnish
    character set 180, 463
    transliteration rules 192
Flow control 46–48, 124–126, 362
    and Amiga C-Kermit 450
    and Atari ST C-Kermit 453
    and file transfer 124
    and half duplex connections 127
    and network connections 47, 126
    and NeXT computers 40
    and OS/2 426, 429
    and serial connections 46
    and UNIX 385
    hardware 40, 47, 48, 125, 386
    software 47, 124, 126, 385
FOR command 249
FOREGROUND, IF condition 241
Fortune computers 14
FPS computers 14
FPU computers 14
French
    character set 180, 184, 463
    transliteration rules 192
French-Canadian character set 463
Full duplex 124, 361
Fullscreen file transfer display 106
Functions
    built-in 252
    for arithmetic 257, 260
    for character string processing 253
    that call themselves 268
    user-defined 267

GEMDOS 452
Gender of connectors 371
General Datacomm modems 52
German
    character set 180, 463
    text 185, 192
    transliteration rules 192
GET command 142
Global variables 224
GOTO command 246
Groups of files. *See* Wildcard
GUI 387, 401

Half duplex 127, 361
Handshake 127
HANGUP command 45, 69
Hardware flow control. *See* Flow control, hardware
Harris computers 14
Hayes modem 52, 54, 365
    commands, table of 365
Help
    about a command 33
    within a command 18
HELP command 33
Hewlett Packard computers 14, 41
HEX.C program 477
Hexadecimal encoding of files 207, 477
Hidden files, UNIX 395
Hiragana 189
Home directory
    \v(home) variable for 56, 230
    tilde notation for 395, 454
Honey DanBer UUCP 379
Host names and addresses 69
HST modems 52
Hungarian character set 180, 463

IBM code page. *See* Code page
IBM mainframes 14
    and file transfer 133
    fullscreen communication 135
    Kermit-370 capabilities 8
    linemode communication 133
    login scripts for 291
IBM PS/2 AIX 14
IBM PS/2 OS/2 420
IBM RS/6000 14, 41, 88, 184
IBM RT PC 14
Icelandic
    character set 463
    text 196
    transliteration rules 192
ICL computers 14
IF command 235–243
IF COUNT command 248
IF DEFINED command 228
Incomplete file transfers 117
INCREMENT command 259
Initialization file, C-Kermit 35
    Amiga 35
    and character sets 197
    and dialing directory 56
    AOS/VS 35, 444
    Atari ST 35, 452
    customizing 36
    OS-9 35, 456
    OS/2 35, 421
    standard 36, 301
    UNIX 35, 387
    VMS 35, 404

INPUT buffer 280
INPUT command 279
Installation, C-Kermit
    Amiga 450
    AOS/VS 441
    OS/2 419
    UNIX 375
Integrated Solutions computers 14
Intel computers 14
Interactive Systems Corporation UNIX 14
International character sets. *See* Character sets
Internet 9, 69
Interruption
    of C-Kermit commands 22, 23, 389, 402
    of file transfer 109, 147, 393, 444
    of file transfer, table of keys 328
IP address 69
IRV (International Reference Version). *See* ISO 646
ISO 646 character sets
    and escape sequences 176
    tables of 171, 461, 463
ISO 8859-1 464
ISO 8859-2 468
ISO 8859-5 470
ISO Latin Alphabet. *See* Latin
Italian character set 180, 463

Japanese
    character sets 189
    Roman character set 463
    transfer character-set 183, 190
    writing systems 189
JIS (Japan Industrial Standard) 189
Job control 389, 392, 394
Jolix 14

Kanji 189
    and AOS/VS 443
Katakana 189
Kermit
    overview xv, 1, 3
Kermit News
    journal subscription 9
Kermit protocol 95
    and 8-bit data 123
    and character sets 180
    and control characters 132
    negotiation of features 152
    packet types 107
    summary of 151
Kermit software
    features, table of 8
    how to get it 9
    version list 10
Key mapping 91
    and international characters 179
    and OS/2 C-Kermit 431

and UNIX C-Kermit 392
and VMS C-Kermit 404
Keyboard
    OS/2 C-Kermit special keys 428
Keypad mode
    escape sequences to change 440
Keypad, numeric
    codes sent by 429
    controlling mode of via escape sequence 436
    setting mode of 432
KOI-8 character set 180, 187, 470

Label, GOTO 246
Labeled file transfer, VMS 412–415
Language-specific character-set translation 191
Latin alphabet
    as file character-set 180, 451
    as transfer character-set 183
    number 1, tables of 174, 464
    number 2, table of 468
    structure of 172, 459
    supported languages, table of 172
Latin/Cyrillic Alphabet 470
LGT comparison operator 239
Linux/386 14
LLT comparison operator 239
Local computer 3, 37
Local mode
    and server operation 150
    automation of 274
    file transfer 104
Lock file, UUCP 378
Locking shifts
    and file transfer 162, 194
    and terminal connection 90, 178
    and the TRANSMIT command 204
LOG DEBUG command 138
Log files
    closing 138
    debug 138
    packets 138
    session, terminal 92
    transactions, file transfer 117
LOG PACKETS command 138
LOG SESSION command 92
    for capturing files 200
LOG TRANSACTIONS command 117
Logical names, VMS
    as environment variables 233
Login scripts 276–296
    for commercial data services 294
    for IBM mainframes 291
    for UNIX 289
    for VMS 283
    how to write 276
Long BREAK signal 85, 86
Long packets 156

Long variable names 226
Loopback connector 373
Loops
    counted 248, 249
    FOR 249
    WHILE 250
Lotus 1-2-3 412
LS command 32
Luxor computers 14

Macintosh A/UX 13
Macintosh Kermit 8
Macintosh Latin character set 464
Macros 214–223
    arguments of 219
    as user-defined functions 267
    as variables with long names 226
    defining 214
    for dialing 275, 280
    for network connection 274
    invocation of 216
    sampler of 222
    using 216
    versus command files 218
Mail, electronic. *See* Electronic mail
MAIL command 147
MAN command 33
Masscomp computers 13
Maximum function 257
Menu. *See* Help
Microcom modems 52, 62
Microport UNIX 14
MINIX/386 14
MIPS Computer Systems 14
MNP 62, 66, 368, 369
Modcomp computers 14
MODE, OS/2 command 420
Modem eliminator 371
Modem server 74
Modem signals 363
    and dialing 45, 50
    and direct connections 49
    and OS/2 420
    and the SET CARRIER command 45
    debugging 373
    table of 364
    waiting for 283
Modems 50–67, 362–370
    and data compression 59, 62, 66, 370
    and error correction 59, 62, 66, 368
    and hardware flow control 125
    and speed matching 60, 125
    and the DIAL command 54
    autodial 365
    Hayes, table of commands 365
    null 371
    selecting type of 51, 317

table of error-correction techniques 369
table of modulation techniques 368
table of types known to C-Kermit 52
tone and pulse dialing 54
with built-in Kermit protocol 62
Modulation 362, 367
Motorola Delta Series computers 14
Mouse
    and file transfer interruption 109
    and OS/2 C-Kermit 427
MS-DOS Kermit
    and printing 266
    escape sequences 265
    TERMINALR and TERMINALS macros 266
MSEND command 98, 142
MSKERMIT.INI file 266
MSLEEP command 283
Mt Xinu Mach^{386} UNIX 14
MV command 34

NAK (negative acknowledgement) packet 151
National character sets. *See* ISO 646
NCR Tower computers 14
Negotiation of Kermit features 152
NET macro 274
Network connections 67, 68
    and Amiga C-Kermit 450
    and file transfer 103
    and flow control 126
    and OS/2 C-Kermit 426
    automated 274
    CONNECT-mode escapes 86
    establishing 67
    macros for 223
NeXT computer 14
    and hardware flow control 40
    and key mapping 91
    and terminal emulation 88
    character set 180, 184, 464
    Kermit escape character 80
Noise interference
    and file transfer 128, 134
Norsk Data computers 14
Norwegian
    character set 180, 463
    transliteration rules 192
NOT, IF command modifier 235
Null modem 48, 371
Numbers, comparing 236
NUMERIC, IF condition 240

Okistation computers 14
Olivetti computers 14
ON_EXIT macro 218
OPEN command 269
OpenVMS. *See* VMS
OS-9 C-Kermit 1, 454

Index 509

OS/2 C-Kermit 1, 419–440
   and serial communications 425
   and the mouse 427
   command procedures 424
   how to start 423
   installation 419
   terminal emulator escape sequences 435
OSF/1 13
OUTPUT command 278
OVERWITE, file collision option 116

Packet
   acknowledgement 151
   attribute 116, 165
   block check 128, 136
   buffers 161
   format of 151
   handshake 127
   length 156
   log file 138
   padding characters 133
   retransmission 110, 129
   start and end characters 132, 136
   types, table of 108
Packet log 270
PAD. *See* X.25
PAD command 75
Padding characters 133
Parity
   and 8th-bit-prefixing 123
   and file transfer 101, 122
   and OS/2 425
   and TELNET connections 123
   and terminal connection 88
   and X.25 connections 74
   automatic detection of 124
   explained 359
   how to change 123
   setting from dial directory 55
PATH
   Amiga 450
   OS/2 424
PAUSE command 33, 282
PDP-11 13, 137
   Kermit-11 capabilities 8
Penril modems 52
PEP (Telebit Packet Ensemble Protocol) 369
Performance. *See* Efficiency
Perkin-Elmer computers 13
PING command 73
Pins, connector 371
Portuguese character set 180, 463
POSIX 13
Prefix
   8th-bit 123, 162
   control-character 132
PRINT command 33

Printing
   and OS/2 C-Kermit 431, 437
   and server mode 146
   host controlled 437
   PC, transparent 266
   with C-Kermit's PRINT command 33
Problem solving
   dialing 57
   file transfer 121
Program variable 231
Programming commands 235–272
   structured 249
Protection of files 97
   in UNIX 397
Pseudoterminals 383
PWD command 34
Pyramid computers 14

Question mark
   as command help request 18
   as wildcard character 96, 395, 433
QUIT command 17
Quoting
   8-bit characters in Kermit packets 123
   control character in Kermit packets 132
   special characters in C-Kermit commands 21

Racal Vadic modems 52
READ command 270
RECEIVE command 97
Recording a terminal session 92
Recursion 268
Redirection of input and output 319
   in OS/2 C-Kermit 427
   in UNIX C-Kermit 388
   in VMS C-Kermit 402
REINPUT command 280
REMOTE CD command 144
Remote computer 3, 37
REMOTE DELETE command 144
REMOTE DIRECTORY command 145
REMOTE HELP command 141
REMOTE HOST command 146
REMOTE KERMIT command 146
REMOTE LOGIN command 146
REMOTE LOGOUT command 146
REMOTE PRINT command 146
REMOTE SET command 147
REMOTE SPACE command 145
REMOTE TYPE command 145
REMOTE WHO command 146
RENAME, file collision option 116
RENAME command 34
Resuming an interrupted file transfer 116
Retransmission of packets 129
Return code. *See* Exit status
RETURN command 267

Reverse slash. *See* Backslash
Reverse video 439
Ridge computers 14
RM command 32
Rollback. *See* Screen rollback
Rolm 244PC 52, 54
Rolm CBX 52, 64
RS-232, EIA Recommended Standard 360
   explained 363
   table of signals and pins 364
RS/6000. *See* IBM
RTS/CTS. *See* Flow control, hardware
RUN command 33, 34
Russian text 187, 193

Samsung computers 14
SCO UNIX, Xenix, ODT 14, 184, 378
Screen
   clearing, escape sequences 437, 440
   rollback in OS/2 C-Kermit 430
   special effects for 263
SCRIPT command 307
Script programming 273-309
Scroll Lock key 429
Security
   and UNIX C-Kermit 380
   of calling-card numbers 62
   of Kermit server 146
   of server mode 148
SEND command 96, 98, 142
Sequent computers 14
Serial communication explained 359-373
Serial connections 42
   macros for 222
Serial file transfer display 107
SERIAL macro 274
SERVER command 140
Server mode 139-150
   access to host services 146
   and electronic mail 147
   and file transfer 142
   and local operation 150
   and printing 146
   and settings 147
   commands for 141
   entering 140
   file management services 144
   interruption of 147
   security of 148
   terminating 141
Services directory file 297
   UNIX 387
   VMS 404
Session log 92, 270
SET BLOCK-CHECK command 128, 136
SET BUFFERS command 161
SET CARRIER command 46

SET CASE command 239, 341
SET COMMAND BYTESIZE command 88, 174, 178
SET COUNT command 248
SET DEBUG SESSION command 93
   and login scripts 285
SET DEFAULT command 31
SET DIAL DIAL-COMMAND command 61
SET DIAL DIRECTORY command 55
SET DIAL DISPLAY command 57
SET DIAL HANGUP command 59
SET DIAL INIT-STRING command 59
SET DIAL KERMIT-SPOOF command 62
SET DIAL MNP-ENABLE command 62
SET DIAL MODEM-HANGUP command 59
SET DIAL PREFIX command 61
SET DIAL SPEED-MATCHING command 61
SET DIAL TIMEOUT command 58, 62
SET DUPLEX command 127
SET ESCAPE command 80
SET FILE CHARACTER-SET command 182
   and OS/2 434
   for Cyrillic character sets 188
   for Japanese character sets 190
SET FILE COLLISION command 116
SET FILE command, summaries 118, 168
SET FILE DISPLAY command 106
SET FILE INCOMPLETE command 117
SET FILE LABEL command 414
SET FILE NAMES command 114
SET FILE RECORD-LENGTH command 409
SET FILE TYPE command 113
   and the TRANSMIT command 202
   in VMS 411, 412, 413
SET FLOW command 126
SET HANDSHAKE command 127
SET HOST command 69
SET INCOMPLETE command 117
SET INPUT command 281, 293
SET INPUT ECHO command 281
   and escape sequences 289
SET KEY command 91
   and international characters 179
   and OS/2 431
   and UNIX 392
SET LANGUAGE command 191, 195
   and the TRANSMIT command 196
SET LINE command 43
SET LOCAL-ECHO command 127
SET MACRO command 216, 347
SET MODEM command 51
SET NETWORK command 68
SET PAD command 75, 137
SET PARITY command
   and file transfer 162
   and locking shifts 162, 178
   and terminal connection 88
SET PROMPT command 17, 105, 229, 349

SET RECEIVE END-OF-PACKET command 132
SET RECEIVE PACKET-LENGTH command 156
SET RECEIVE PAD commands 133
SET RECEIVE START-OF-PACKET command 132
SET RECEIVE TIMEOUT command 130
SET RETRY command 129
SET SCRIPT ECHO command 308
SET SEND END-OF-PACKET command 132
SET SEND PACKET-LENGTH command 157
SET SEND PAD commands 133
SET SEND START-OF-PACKET command 132
SET SEND TIMEOUT command 130
SET SERVER command 144
SET SESSION-LOG command 93
   and capturing files 200
SET SPEED command 44
SET SUSPEND command 389
SET TAKE ECHO command 211
SET TAKE ERROR command 211, 351
SET TELNET command 72
SET TERMINAL command 88–90
   ARROW-KEY mode 432
   BYTESIZE 88, 178
   CHARACTER-SET 89, 175
   CHARACTER-SET, and OS/2 427, 432
   CHARACTER-SET, and the TRANSMIT command 203
   COLOR 432
   CR-DISPLAY 90
   CURSOR shape 432
   ECHO 90
   ECHO, and the TRANSMIT command 202
   KEYPAD mode 432
   LOCKING-SHIFT 90, 179, 427
   NEWLINE-MODE 90
   TYPE of terminal 432
   WRAP at screen margin 432
SET TRANSFER CHARACTER-SET command 182
   and OS/2 434
   for Cyrillic text 187
   for Japanese text 190
SET TRANSMIT command 203
SET UNKNOWN-CHAR-SET command 185
SET WILDCARD-EXPANSION command 394
SET WINDOW command 159
SET X.25 command 75
SET XMIT command 203
Setuid/setgid installation of UNIX C-Kermit 380
Shift-in/shift-out. *See* Locking shifts
Shift-JIS. *See* Japanese
Short KOI character set 187, 194, 470
SHOW ARGUMENTS command 221
SHOW ARRAYS command 227
SHOW ATTRIBUTES command 167
SHOW CHARACTER-SETS command 192
SHOW COUNT command 355
SHOW DEFAULT command 34

SHOW DIAL command 57
SHOW ESCAPE command 81
SHOW FEATURES command 15, 382
SHOW FILE command 119
SHOW FUNCTIONS command 253
SHOW GLOBALS command 224
SHOW KEY command 91
   and OS/2 431
SHOW LANGUAGE command 192
SHOW MACRO command 215
SHOW MODEM command 356
SHOW NETWORK command 68
SHOW PAD command 356
SHOW PROTOCOL command 168
SHOW SERVER command 149
SHOW STATUS command 240
SHOW TERMINAL command 90
SHOW TRANSMIT command 204
SHOW VARIABLES command 232
SHOW VERSION command 356
Silicon Graphics computers 14
Simplex 361
Single shift 162
Sliding windows 158
Software flow control. *See* Flow control, software
Solaris 13, 14
Solbourne computers 14
Sony computers 14
Sorting 251
SPACE command 34
Spanish character set 180, 463
Speaking devices 383
Special screen effects 263
Speed, communication 361
   and file transfer 103, 124, 131
   and modem speed matching feature 60
   and UNIX 383
   and VMS 400
   of SET LINE device 44
   setting from dial directory 55
   split 75/1200 44
Speed-matching modems 60
   and file transfer 125
Spoof, Kermit 62
SprintNet 137, 294
Stardent computers 14
Start and stop bits 360, 361
Start-of-packet character 132, 136
Starting C-Kermit 15
   in AOS/VS 443
   in OS-9 456
   in OS/2 423
   in UNIX 387
   in VMS 401
   on the Amiga 450
   on the Atari ST 453
STATISTICS command 153

Stop bits   425
STOP command   243
String comparison   238
   case of letters in   239, 279
String functions   253
SUCCESS, command status   240
Sun computers   14, 41, 68, 88
SUSPEND command   389
Suspending C-Kermit   389, 392, 394
Swedish   195
   character set   180, 463
   text   195
   transliteration rules   192
Swiss character set   180, 463

Tab character
   in command files   23
   in dialing directory   55
   in SCRIPT command   308
   in services directory   297
   used for command completion   20
Tabs, terminal   437
   escape sequence to set   436
   using   435
TAKE command   23, 210
Tandy computers   14
TCP/IP networks   67–74, 317
   and TELNET command   72
   ports and services   70
TDD (Telecommunication Device for the Deaf)   383, 400
Tektronix computers   14
Telebit modems   52, 58
   and Kermit spoof   62
TELNET command   72
   and echoing   72
   and SET TELNET command   72
   and terminal type   72
   CONNECT-mode escapes   86
TELNET protocol   86, 89, 93
Terminal
   and FULLSCREEN file transfer display   107
   device, UNIX   376
   modes, UNIX   390
Terminal connection   79–93
   and character sets   175
   and key mapping   91
   and locking shifts   178
   debugging   93
   establishing   79
   hanging up   87
   logging   92
   returning from   80
   settings   88
   shell escape from   85
   status of   84
   TCP/IP TELNET   72, 86

Terminal emulation   88
   and Amiga C-Kermit   88
   and AOS/VS C-Kermit   445
   and Atari ST C-Kermit   88
   and OS/2 C-Kermit   426
   and UNIX C-Kermit   392
   and VMS C-Kermit   404
   and workstation console drivers   88
Terminal servers   103, 131
   and connection speed   383
   and flow control   385
   and VMS   400
   reverse   74
Terminal type
   and Amiga C-Kermit   451
   and AOS/VS   442
   and Atari ST C-Kermit   453
   and OS-9 C-Kermit   456
   and OS/2 C-Kermit   432
   and speaking devices   383
   and TELNET connections   72
   and UNIX   382
   and VMS   399
TERMINALR and TERMINALS macros   266
Text files   143
   and OS/2 C-Kermit   434
   and the TRANSMIT command   203
   and word processors   112
   automatic recognition of in VMS   406
   definition of   112
   transfer of   112
Thoroughbred BASIC   411
Time-of-day variable, \v(ntime)   231
Time-of-day variable, \v(time)   231
Timeouts
   and DIAL command   58
   and file transfer   130
   and server command wait   144
   and SET LINE command   46
   and the INPUT command   279
Tone dialing   54
Trademarks, list of   497
Trailing comments   23, 215
Transaction log   117, 270
Transfer character-set   183
   for Cyrillic text   187
   for Japanese text   190
TRANSLATE command   194
TRANSMIT command   202–207
   and character sets   196
TRANSPARENT
   terminal character-set   175
   transfer character-set   183
Transparent printing   266, 437
Tri Star computers   14
Tty. *See* Terminal
TYPE command   35

ULTRIX 13
Undefined record format, VMS 411
UNHEX.C program 478
UNISYS computers 14
UNIX 375–397
    and character sets 386
    and flow control 385
    and terminal speed 383
    control characters 384
    login script for 289
    terminal type 382
    versions supported by C-Kermit 13
UNIX C-Kermit 375–397
    and UUCP lock files 43, 377
    background operation of 388, 394
    file transfer 393
    initialization file 387
    installation of 375
    interruption of 389, 393
    starting 387
    suspending 389, 392
    terminal connection 392
    wildcard options 394
Unknown character-set 185
UPDATE, file collision option 116
Uploading files 98
US Robotics modems 52
User-defined functions 267
UUCP lock file 378

V.22, CCITT Recommendation 66, 367
V.22*bis*, CCITT Recommendation 66, 367
V.23, CCITT Recommendation 368
V.24, CCITT Recommendation 360
V.32, CCITT Recommendation 66, 367
V.32*bis*, CCITT Recommendation 66, 367
V.42, CCITT Recommendation 369
V.42*bis*, CCITT Recommendation 369
Vadic modems 52
Variables
    array 227
    built-in 228
    defining 224, 226, 261
    displaying values of 224, 227, 232
    environment 233
    global 224
    macro arguments 219
    macros used as 226
    with long names 226
VAX. *See* UNIX, VMS
Ventel modems 52
VERSION, IF condition 241
VMS 399–417
    and character sets 401
    and terminal servers 400
    login script for 283
    wildcard characters 405

VMS C-Kermit 399–417
    and DCL command procedures 403
    and file transfer 405
    and filename collisions 116
    and terminal connection 404
    and terminal speed 103
    and terminal type 399
    starting 401
VT100 escape sequences. *See* Escape sequences
VT52 escape sequences. *See* Escape sequences

WAIT command 33, 283
WHILE command 250
Wildcard characters
    and MSEND command 98
    and SEND command 96
    C-Kermit functions for 260
    in AOS/VS C-Kermit 446
    in OS/2 C-Kermit 433
    in UNIX C-Kermit 394
    in VMS C-Kermit 405
    quoting in C-Kermit 22, 395, 433
Windows, sliding. *See* Sliding windows
Word processor
    and text files 112
    macro for using 242
    using to create command files 23, 210
Wrap. *See* SET TERMINAL WRAP
WRITE command 270
WRITE SCREEN command 32
WRITE SYS$OUTPUT command 32

X.25 networks 68, 74, 318
    and file transfer 137
Xenix 378
XFER. *See* Transfer
XIF command 249
XLATE. *See* Translate
XMIT. *See* TRANSMIT
XON/XOFF. *See* Flow control, software

ZIP files, VMS 412

C-KERMIT SOFTWARE ORDER FORM   *May 1995*

TWO PRICES are shown for each item. The first price applies to the USA, Canada, and Mexico. The second price applies to all other countries. All prices are in US dollars.

COMPLETE C-KERMIT DISTRIBUTION ON MAGNETIC TAPE

Each tape includes all C-Kermit files: sources, installation files and instructions, help files, beware files, initialization files, plus selected binaries in UUENCODE, BOO, or HEX format:

- ❏ 9-track 1600 BPI magnetic tape, ANSI format: $100 / $135
- ❏ 9-track 1600 BPI magnetic tape, UNIX tar format: $100 / $135
- ❏ 9-track 1600 BPI magnetic tape, DG DUMPFILE format: $150 / $185
- ❏ Quarter-inch tape cartridge (QIC), UNIX tar format: $150 / $185
- ❏ 4mm DAT cartridge, UNIX tar format: $150 / $185
- ❏ 8mm EXABYTE tape cartridge, UNIX tar format: $150 / $185
- ❏ TK50 cartridge, VMS / OpenVMS BACKUP format: $150 / $185

Subtotal: $_____

SOURCE CODE ON DOS-FORMAT DISKETTES

Source code, installation files, help and beware files for all C-Kermit versions:

3.5"   5.25"
720K   360K
- ❏   ❏   Source Code on DOS-Format Diskettes: $65 / $80

Subtotal: $_____

BINARIES ON DOS-FORMAT DISKETTES

Includes the binary executable C-Kermit program for the system indicated, plus all relevant installation, initialization, demo, help, and beware files:

3.5"   5.25"
720K   360K
- ❏   ❏   C-Kermit for UNIX, specify version_____: $10 / $15
- ❏   ❏   C-Kermit for OS/2 2.00, 32-bit: $10 / $15
- ❏   ❏   C-Kermit for OS-9/68000: $10 / $15
- ❏   ❏   C-Kermit for the Commodore Amiga: $10 / $15

Subtotal: $_____

ADDITIONAL KERMIT BOOKS

- ❏ *Using C-Kermit:* $36.95 / $47
- ❏ *Using MS-DOS Kermit* (includes Kermit diskette): $36.95 / $47
- ❏ *Kermit MS-DOS Mode d'Emploi* (in French): $36.95 / $47
- ❏ *Kermit, A File Transfer Protocol:* $32.95 / $43
- ❏ Any three of these books: $85 / $115

Subtotal: $_____

TOTAL SOFTWARE AND BOOKS: $_____

(Please turn over . . .)

C-Kermit Order Form **PAYMENT** *May 1995*

Prepayment is required. Shipping by UPS or post is included in the price. Please do not add sales tax. You may pay by CREDIT CARD or by CHECK. Please complete ONE of the following three sections and mail this form, NOT A COPY, to the address shown on the bottom of the page.

1. PAYMENT BY CREDIT CARD, ALL COUNTRIES

❏ MasterCard   ❏ Visa   AMOUNT OF PAYMENT: $_____

Card Number _____   Expires _____

Signature _____   Date _____

2. PAYMENT BY CHECK, USA ONLY   Please enclose a check payable to:

Columbia University Kermit Distribution

TOTAL AMOUNT OF YOUR CHECK: $_____

3. PAYMENT BY CHECK, ALL OTHER COUNTRIES

Please enclose a check for the total amount payable in US dollars. PLEASE DO NOT USE ELECTRONIC BANK TRANSFERS OR INTERNATIONAL POSTAL COUPONS. Make your check payable to:

Columbia University Kermit Distribution

If your check is *not* drawn on a US bank, please add a $35 check-cashing fee:

❏ Check-cashing fee: _____   TOTAL AMOUNT OF YOUR CHECK: $_____

SHIP TO:

Name: _____   Phone: _____

Organization: _____

Address: _____

City: _____   State or Province: _____

Country: _____   Zip or Postal Code: _____

MAIL YOUR COMPLETED ORDER FORM WITH PAYMENT TO

Kermit Distribution, Department CKB
Columbia University Academic Information Systems
612 West 115th Street
New York, NY 10025-7721 USA

Thank you!